D1274545

Precious Volumes

An Introduction to Chinese

Sectarian Scriptures from the

Sixteenth and Seventeenth Centuries

Harvard-Yenching Institute Monograph Series, 49

Precious Volumes

An Introduction to Chinese

Sectarian Scriptures from the

Sixteenth and Seventeenth Centuries

Daniel L. Overmyer

Published by the Harvard University Asia Center
and distributed by Harvard University Press
Cambridge (Massachusetts) and London, 1999

Printed in the United States of America

The Harvard-Yenching Institute, founded in 1928 and headquartered at Harvard University, is a foundation dedicated to the advancement of higher education in the humanities and social sciences in East and Southeast Asia. The Institute supports advanced research at Harvard by faculty members of certain Asian universities and doctoral studies at Harvard and other universities by junior faculty at the same universities. It also supports East Asian studies at Harvard through contributions to the Harvard-Yenching Library and publication of the *Harvard Journal of Asiatic Studies* and books on premodern East Asian history and literature.

Library of Congress Cataloging-in-Publication Data
Overmyer, Daniel L., 1935–
     Precious volumes : an introduction to Chinese sectarian scriptures
from the sixteenth and seventeenth centuries / Daniel L. Overmyer.
       p.   cm. -- (Harvard-Yenching Institute monograph series ; 49)
     Includes bibliographical references.
     ISBN 0-674-69838-X (alk. paper)
     1. Religious literature, Chinese--History and criticism.
2. Chinese literature--Ming dynasty, 1368–1644--History and
criticism.   3. Chinese literature--Ch'ing dynasty, 1644–1912-
-History and criticism.   I. Title. II. Title: Introduction to
Chinese sectarian scriptures from the sixteenth and seventeenth
centuries.   III. Series.
BL1802.O93 1999
299'.51 — DC21
                                          99-19188
                                             CIP
                                           REV

Index by the author

♾ Printed on acid-free paper

Last number below indicates year of this printing
08 07 06 05 04 03 02 01 00 99

In memory of my father,

Elmer Earl Overmyer,

who took us to China in the first place

Contents

Reference Matter

Preface

This study is an introduction to books produced by Chinese popular religious sects in the Ming dynasty (1368–1644) and the first decades of the Ch'ing period (1644–1911). These books are called *pao-chüan* (pron. *bao-juan*, "precious volumes"). The sixteenth and seventeenth centuries were the formative period for these texts, which contain teachings and ritual instructions believed to have been divinely revealed to sect patriarchs, and which were thus considered scriptures.

Since 1976, I have collected, photographed, or read library copies of 131 *pao-chüan* of all types and periods, including a few duplicates in different editions. Although many hundreds more of these books have been lost or destroyed over the centuries, I believe that my collection is a good representation of those that remain. These materials were obtained during two trips to China, in 1981 and 1991; from libraries in the United States, Taiwan, and the Soviet Union; and from scholars in Japan, the United States, and Europe who kindly sent copies to me. I also benefited from a 1994 reprinting of 148 *pao-chüan* by the Shansi People's Publishing House (see Chang et al., eds., *Pao-chüan ch'u-chi*).

This study is based primarily on thirty-four sectarian scripture texts that can reasonably be dated to the sixteenth and seventeenth centuries, some in more than one edition, with references to a number of other books that preceded and followed them. Although several bibliographic surveys of *pao-chüan* have been published, as well as a few studies of individual texts, the present volume is the first book-length study in a Western language focused on the contents of these books as a genre developed over time.

In my own writing, this study has been prepared for by a 1976 book introducing what I then called "folk Buddhist sects," by several articles on *pao-chüan* and their themes, and by a 1986 volume co-authored with David K. Jordan on popular religious sects in Taiwan. (These publications are listed in the Bibliography.) Nonetheless, this book must be considered a preliminary survey that I hope will lead to further research by others.

I am grateful to the following persons who have contributed to this project during its long preparation: Mr. Li Shih-yü, Tianjin Academy of Social Sciences; Dr. Victor Mair, University of Pennsylvania; Dr. Randall Nadeau, Trinity University; Dr. Susan Naquin, Princeton University; Dr. Noguchi Tetsurō, Tsukuba University; Dr. Sakai Tadao, Risshō University; Dr. Richard Shek, California State University, Sacramento; Mr. Wang Chien-ch'uan of Chung-cheng University in Taiwan; and Mr. Wu Hsiao-ling of the Institute for the Study of Literature, Chinese Academy of Social Sciences. I am particularly grateful to Li Shih-yü, the pioneering Chinese scholar of sectarian scriptures, who helped me find and study some of these texts in 1981 and 1991.

I am also grateful to Mr. Neil Parker of the University of British Columbia for preparing the manuscript; to the staff of the Asian Library at U.B.C., particularly S. Y. Tse and T. Gonnami; to my graduate students Philip Clart and Soo Khin-wah; and to John R. Ziemer of the Harvard University Asia Center and Victoria R. M. Scott for their careful editorial work.

Thanks are due as well to the following organizations that provided time and money for my research: the Committee on Scholarly Communication with the People's Republic of China; the National Endowment for the Humanities; the Social Sciences and Humanities Research Council (Canada); the Wang Institute of Graduate Studies; the University of British Columbia; and the Chinese University of Hong Kong.

The love and support of my wife, Estella Overmyer (née Velázquez), have also been of great help in completing this task.

Thanks as well to our dear cat Singa, who kept me company on this project by sitting on the manuscript, biting pages, and batting pens and rubber bands to the floor, thus reminding me that there is more to life than books.

D. L. Overmyer
Hong Kong, August 1998

Precious Volumes

An Introduction to Chinese

Sectarian Scriptures from the

Sixteenth and Seventeenth Centuries

Introduction

Popular religious sects with lay leaders were active in China from the Yuan dynasty (1264–1368) on, characterized by their own forms of organization, ritual, and belief. Although there are occasional references in fourteenth- and fifteenth-century sources to such groups having scripture texts of their own, the earliest such book I have found and read thus far is dated 1430. It is called a *pao-chüan* ("precious volume") and expounds a mythology of three stages of cosmic time presided over by successive buddhas, culminating in Maitreya, the Buddha of the Future, a theme common in these books in the sixteenth century. From historical sources, we know that groups claiming to represent Maitreya had been active for centuries, particularly since the period of civil war in the mid-fourteenth century, during the fall of Mongol (Yuan) rule. In the sectarian scriptures of the Ming, this long-established popular belief took written form.

After 1430, the next sectarian *pao-chüan* known to scholarship are those written by a lay Buddhist named Lo Ch'ing (1442–1527) and published in 1509. They are strongly influenced by the Ch'an Buddhist tradition and do not contain the three-stage mythology, which is resumed and further developed in a 1523 book based to a large extent on the "precious volume" of 1430. Thus by the first quarter of the sixteenth century, there were two streams of *pao-chüan* teaching, with that begun by Lo Ch'ing being the more internally and individually oriented. Lo's "Five Books in Six Volumes" (*Wu-pu liu-ts'e*) became the foundation of a sectarian tradition, the Wu-wei chiao (the religion or sect of noninterference), which looked back to Lo as its original patriarch. This tradition produced several later *pao-chüan*, some of which were influenced by the three-stage / Maitreya mythology. It was this mythology that became constitutive of most *pao-chüan* from the mid-sixteenth century on.

Beginning by at least 1430, the Maitreya-oriented mythology became associated with female deities variously called Mu (Mother), Tsu-mu (Matriarch), or Lao-mu (Venerable Mother), who are not noted in historical records of sectarian activity before that time. There are thirty references to such deities in the 1430 text, all of them functioning as divine officials in a celestial bureaucracy. However, in that text the chief deity is the "Ancient Buddha" Amitābha, who reveals the book out of his love for suffering humanity. This same pattern of mother-deities being present but subordinate to a buddha is continued in the 1523 *pao-chüan* discussed in Chapter Four below.

Lo Ch'ing takes a more abstract and mystical approach; for him, ultimate reality is the realization of "true emptiness" (*chen-k'ung*) that brings spiritual freedom. This emptiness is the source of all things, and in some passages Lo equates it with the "Mother." For him, this was still a mystical symbol, not a mythological deity, but it was charged with a desperate longing for religious security, as graphically described in his spiritual autobiography, the *K'u-kung wu-tao chüan* (Book on awakening to the Way through bitter toil). The effect of Lo Ch'ing's reinterpretation was to elevate the Mother concept to the source of the cosmos. In his own writings this concept does not displace the role of emptiness, variously termed and personified, but in later sectarian writings the Mother became the chief deity, mistress of all the gods and buddhas, cosmic parent of humankind.

Because Lo Ch'ing's texts were well known in sectarian circles, it appears that his teachings were a catalyst in transforming many Mothers into one primordial Mother; in any case, by the late sixteenth century, that is what happened. The Mother became the source who sends the buddhas down to the human realm; thus the two mythological themes became intertwined. From then on, this was the framework of the teachings of most sectarian *pao-chüan*, and it can still be found today in texts produced by spirit-writing—a long-established form of direct revelation from the gods that continues to be revered by religious groups in Taiwan, Hong Kong, and elsewhere in the Chinese-speaking world. Hence the early Ming sectarian mythological tradition has continued down to the present.

All the *pao-chüan* published during the Ming that I have seen are printed in large characters and bound between cardboard rectangles in accordion style, in what is called "the sūtra folded form" (*ching che chuang*), with pages about 14 inches (36 cm) high and 5 inches (13 cm) wide. They are in one or two volumes (*chüan*), divided into varying numbers of chapters (*p'in*) or divisions (*fen*). The title is printed on a strip of paper pasted to the cover. Many of these books open with engravings of buddhas and deities, followed by invocations of long life for the emperor, blessings for the nation and people, and hope for the salvation of all. Next comes an inside title, which may not be the same as that on the cover, followed by verses calling on the buddhas and deities to descend when the book is recited. This opens an introductory section that discusses the book and its message in general terms. This section is in a combination of verse and prose and may include a table of contents listing all the chapter titles.

After several pages of this material, the title and number of the first chapter appear on a separate line, followed by a prose exposition, which in turn is summarized in verse. This alternation continues through the chapter with varying verse styles. In many *pao-chüan*, near the end of each chapter there is the name of an opera tune introducing a rhymed hymn to be sung. This hymn and a few lines of concluding pious verse end the chapter. Each chapter introduces some new theme, but there is much repetition; these books were clearly intended primarily for ritual recitation, not for doctrinal instruction, though that is also present. The end and beginning of each volume are clearly indicated. At the end of some of these texts there are notes on reprinting and lists of donors, with the amounts contributed by each.

There are variations on all these patterns, but enough constants remain to distinguish these books from other types of writing. Although the conventional translation of *pao-chüan* is "precious scrolls," I use the term "volumes" both because these books never had the form of scrolls and because *chüan* can indeed mean "book" or "volume."

In content, sectarian *pao-chüan* are characterized by their use of simple classical language interspersed with vernacular constructions; the alternation of prose sections with seven- or ten-character lines of verse, usually in rhyme; and direct expositions of mythology, doctrinal teaching, and moral exhortation.

As David Johnson has demonstrated,[1] *pao-chüan* were meant to be performed—in the sectarian case, as a part of group worship, by singing and chanting the text in unison after presenting incense and offerings, in a style similar to the recitation of scriptures by monks and nuns in Buddhist monasteries. In other contexts, a text might be recited by a principal performer or a small group of performers for an audience. Passages in some of the "precious volumes" discussed in this book indicate exposition or preaching by a patriarch or buddha followed by dialogue with disciples, but it is not clear to me whether this reflects actual practice or is a literary device.

Pao-chüan teaching is proclaimed to be a new revelation of primordial truth, long concealed but now available to all who believe, particularly those with the proper karmic affinity or destiny (*yu-yuan jen*). This revelation appears just before the chaos and destruction at the end of the *kalpa*, or eon; the Buddha or the Mother has taken pity on wayward, suffering humans, and in the text has provided one last chance for deliverance. Those with the proper belief and practice will survive to enjoy a transformed life in a new realm, free of all suffering. Those who miss the good news (*hsiao-hsi*) will be lost. From this perspective, other religious traditions, including other sectarian groups, may be criticized or ridiculed. This sectarian self-identification is reinforced by references to special protective deities, patriarchs, members, and congregational assemblies.

Another type of book, also called *pao-chüan*, is based on moralistic stories, often taken from other forms of Chinese literature. These books share some of the stylistic characteristics already discussed, but they are not direct expositions of doctrine and do not refer to patriarchs and congregations. Most of these stories recount the lives of pious young men or women, usually of miraculous birth, who overcome many obstacles to become high officials or Buddhist nuns. Although they may rebel against convention along the way, in the end these young protagonists are justified by the status they attain and the blessings or salvation they bring to their parents.

These literary or narrative *pao-chüan* are vehicles of a generalized morality and piety, and they circulated on their own, without the support and constraint of a sectarian context. Lists of texts confiscated from the homes of sectarian leaders do not include books of this literary type. Although some sectarian *pao-chüan* do include brief stories, and some typical terms from sectarian mythology occur in the literary texts, the two are different phases in the development of the genre. It is important to draw attention to their differences as well as their similarities because the best-known theories of the origins of *pao-chüan* have been put forth by historians of Chinese literature, who see *pao-chüan* as descendants of T'ang dynasty *pien-wen* ("transformation texts").

Of course, on a purely stylistic level, all later forms of Chinese vernacular literature were influenced by the prosimetric style of *pien-wen*, as Victor Mair has recently demonstrated anew. Sectarian *pao-chüan*, too, are written in alternating verse and prose, but their contents are very different from *pien-wen*.[2] They are not stories but direct vehicles of teaching and moral exhortation that were revered as ritually chanted scriptures. Indeed, the ritual orientation of these *pao-chüan* should be emphasized. Their structure is repetitive rather than logically connected. Prose expositions are repeated in verse; key phrases appear over and over again in long series, and readers and listeners are assured that reciting the book brings much merit.

With the exception of prose/verse alternation, these and other characteristics described above are usually not present in narrative *pao-chüan*. Neither is the Venerable Mother / Maitreya mythology central to any of the narrative texts I have read; none of their stories is based on it. The focus of this book is on sectarian "precious volumes" because in general they appeared earlier and are related to a specific form of religious organization, within which they were considered to be divinely revealed. There are more than enough of this type of text to form the basis of a book; narrative *pao-chüan* deserve their own study.[3]

Closely related to the typology of *pao-chüan* is the question of their origins, which several earlier scholars have suggested began with the T'ang *pien-wen* already mentioned. From that perspective, *pao-chüan* have been classified with *t'an-tz'u* ("strum lyric") and *chu-kung-tiao* ("medley") as a type of later prosimetric vernacular literature. The problem with this approach is that it does not recognize the specific characteristics of sectarian *pao-chüan*, which are separated from *pien-wen* by a gap of several hundred years. The 1430 book noted above, discussed at length in Chapter Two below, already includes most of the distinguishing characteristics of the genre, but no sources are quoted in it. Eighty years later, Lo Ch'ing quoted a large number of earlier books and tracts, most of them well-known Buddhist texts. Later sectarian authors do not quote other sources, except for a few who imitate Lo Ch'ing by citing him or the materials he quotes. Thus for Lo himself his sources were important, but their impact on other writers was indirect at best.

The question is where to go for origins. I attempt to deal with this in Chapter One by looking at some of the texts Lo Ch'ing cites and going behind them to an earlier fluorescence of indigenous Chinese scriptures written between the fourth and the eighth centuries C.E. Despite their wide separation in time, there are many interesting similarities between the contents of these texts and those of *pao-chüan*—enough to make me wonder whether there wasn't some kind of fragmented oral tradition between the two. Chapter One also discusses other possible antecedents of "precious volumes" in the history of Chinese sacred texts.

Chapters Two, Three, and Four discuss the oldest known texts in each of the two streams of early *pao-chüan* teaching—that of the Maitreya-oriented mythology, and that of Lo Ch'ing. The contents of Chapters One and Two have already been mentioned. Chapter Three is devoted to the books written by Lo Ch'ing and to the sectarian tradition that preserved and reprinted them. Chapter Four discusses the further development of the older stream of *pao-chüan* teaching in a 1523 text in which Maitreya is the chief actor. As much as possible, this study follows the chronological order of appearance of the texts it discusses, in the hope of discerning development over time.

Chapters Five and Six move to a thematic treatment of a number of texts from the sixteenth and seventeenth centuries, again in rough chronological order. The themes discussed include autobiographical statements attributed to patriarchs who transmit the texts; the self-understanding of these books as divine revelation; references to sect names and congregations; mythologies of creation, salvation, and the end of the age; meditation; rituals; ethical teachings; descriptions of purgatory; and social perspectives. This last theme includes explicit criticisms of those in a variety of occupations and economic levels, as well as an interesting affirmation of Confucianism because of its validation of religious practice within ordinary households.

Chapter Seven deals with the *Dragon-Flower Scripture* (*Lung-hua ching*), a lengthy text in four volumes that sets forth the Venerable Mother / Maitreya mythology in the greatest detail and is the culmination of the formative period of books of this type. Such texts continued to be produced, but as variations on what had already appeared.

The book ends with concluding observations and suggestions for further research. Issues of authorship, date, and publication are addressed in appendixes that supplement Chapters Three, Five, and Six, all of which discuss several texts. In Chapters Two, Four, and Seven, each of which discusses a single book, such issues are considered at the beginning of the chapter.

This book is an attempt to understand the origins and development of a textual tradition. It assumes that popular religious texts are just as deserving of such study as any other form of religious literature. Though the focus is on the content and structure of *pao-chüan*, wherever possible their organizational and social contexts are discussed, as well as information about their transmission, recitation, and ritual use. Since I and others have already written extensively about the sects that produced these books, that research is referred to but is not recapitulated here.[4]

Because little of this material has been translated before, I have tried as much as possible to follow the Chinese word order and the literal meaning of verbs in an attempt to understand the dynamics of the texts in their own world of meaning. I have also tried to translate special terms as much as possible in their sectarian contexts, for which some conventional interpretations don't work. The authors of these books were not highly educated; so there are problems of style and of incorrect characters. To make these books more coherent than they really are would be a disservice. My task here is to establish the phenomenon, to clarify the nature and content of these materials so that others can be guided toward further research. With this in mind, I have tried to provide sufficient translations to permit readers to come to their own conclusions about the material, and perhaps to serve as a sourcebook. The combination of this and other recent studies with the publication of a forty-volume reprint of the primary texts should encourage others to continue the task.[5]

Of course, the types, themes, and historical development of the "precious volumes" discussed here are in part an artifact of which *pao-chüan* have been preserved—and of which of those I have been able to find and read. Although old *pao-chüan* may continue to be discovered, I believe that the sources on which this book is based are sufficiently representative to justify the task. Yet despite the fact that I have invested years of work in this book and have done my best to make it as accurate as possible, its topic is so large and complex that mistakes and missed allusions no doubt remain.

Sectarian *pao-chüan* represent a fifth type of scripture text in the history of Chinese religions, along with the Confucian, Taoist, and Buddhist classics and scriptures that preceded them and the popular spirit-writing books that have largely taken their place since the late nineteenth century. They are the literary expression of a lively and widespread alternative religious tradition that was always technically illegal but that nevertheless managed to flourish in many areas over long periods of time. *Pao-chüan* are testimony to the imagination and devotion of religious leaders with a middle level of literacy, most of them obscure but a few of whom became known beyond the circles of their congregations. As such, these books are worthy of study in their own right, both as an aspect of the history of Chinese religions and as documents in Chinese social history.

CHAPTER ONE

Antecedents in the History of Chinese Sacred Texts

Many different kinds of texts have appeared in the history of Chinese religions, beginning with Shang dynasty inscriptions on bones and shells. By Han times, the Confucian school had canonized the *Book of Poetry, Book of History, Book of Changes, Record of Rites,* and *Spring and Autumn Annals.* These books were considered the source of all the essential wisdom necessary for the moral order of the self and society. By the second century C.E., the Celestial Master sect revered the *Tao-te ching* as revelation from a deified Lao-tzu, while at about the same time the *T'ai-p'ing ching* (Scripture of great peace) appeared, the first book we know of in Chinese history that functioned from its outset as revealed scripture. In the second century, too, the first Buddhist books were translated, the beginning of a long and rich tradition of scriptures in China believed to have been first expounded by the Buddha.

By the fourth and fifth centuries, several Taoist groups began producing books that they claimed had been revealed by celestial deities. Along with the *Tao-te ching* and the *Scripture of Great Peace,* these books were the first of many hundreds of volumes in what became known as the *Taoist Canon (Tao-tsang).* Except for some of the earliest Buddhist translations, all these books were written in classical Chinese. By the fifth century, then, all the major and classical types of Chinese scriptures had appeared—Confucian, Taoist, and Buddhist—though others were, of course, produced later. The writers of sectarian *pao-chüan* drew at least indirectly on all of these traditions.

In the fifth century, a new subtype of Buddhist scriptures appeared that is of particular relevance to our understanding of the background of *pao-chüan*, for these books were written by Chinese Buddhists themselves to communicate their teachings in more understandable terms. Because they take the form of translated sūtras yet contain references to Chinese terms and places, these books have long been considered apocryphal or false, but from our perspective they can be accepted as indigenous scriptures that tell us much about Chinese understanding of Buddhism at the time. Although these texts were written by monks, and are much closer in style and language to translated sūtras than to *pao-chüan*, they share many points of similarity with *pao-chüan*.

By the ninth century, another type of indigenous Buddhist text appeared, the "recorded sayings" (*yü-lu*) of Ch'an masters, usually in dialogue form, often including short discourses and written with some vernacular constructions. Although these books were not attributed directly to the Buddha, they came to be revered in the Ch'an school as manifestations of the buddha-mind of enlightened patriarchs; so here again there is the possibility of at least indirect influence on *pao-chüan*, in which patriarchs are also venerated. The Ch'üan-chen (Complete Perfection) Taoist school, which was active in North China when and where the first *pao-chüan* were being composed, had its own version of recorded sayings. Ch'üan-chen writings influenced the terminology of some "precious volumes."[1]

There were other antecedents of possible relevance to our texts as well. The "transformation texts" (*pien-wen*) of the T'ang dynasty (618–907) have already been noted in the Introduction. There was also a variety of Buddhist ritual and penance texts produced from the T'ang through the Ming—texts that Sawada Mizuho has suggested formed the immediate background of *pao-chüan*.[2] Even closer than these materials are two books (later called *pao-chüan*) cited by Lo Ch'ing, the *Hsiang-shan pao-chüan* (Incense Mountain precious volume) and the *Chin-kang k'e-i* (Ritual amplification of the Diamond Sūtra).

The materials discussed in this chapter are all indigenous Chinese products influenced to a greater or lesser degree by translated Buddhist sūtras. All were intended in various ways to make their teachings available to a wide audience, including both laity and clergy.

I have looked at all these types of materials, and in what follows attempt to evaluate their relevance to *pao-chüan*, beginning with the indigenous Buddhist scriptures noted above. Although there are points of similarity and influence, none of these earlier forms of sacred texts was closely emulated by the writers of sectarian "precious volumes," which have a form and intentionality of their own.

INDIGENOUS BUDDHIST SCRIPTURES

Most of the extant indigenous Buddhist scriptures were found at Tun-huang near the beginning of the twentieth century. Though they appeared as much as nine hundred years before *pao-chüan* and are quite different in language, style, and content, there are some interesting points of similarity between the two types of texts. A comparison of them highlights the distinctive orientation of sectarian "precious volumes."

Indigenous scriptures composed during the fifth to eighth centuries appear to have been written by Buddhist monks in a variety of circumstances to communicate what they thought was urgent for other monks and lay adherents to know. These texts are written in classical Chinese, with many Buddhist titles, technical terms, transcriptions from Sanskrit, and non-Chinese place names. Although they include verse sections with lines of varying length, most of these verses do not rhyme, as they usually do in *pao-chüan*. In general, the older texts are composed much more in prose than are the *pao-chüan*, for which short sections of prose and verse always alternate. In every way the earlier indigenous scriptures are much closer to the sūtras translated from the Sanskrit, which they emulate, than they are to "precious volumes," which make no pretense of being Buddhist texts of the classical sort.[3]

There are other differences as well between these two types of texts. In keeping with their more Buddhist orientation, there is evidence in the indigenous scriptures that some of them were written by those concerned with the reform and preservation of the monastic order. There is one whole text devoted to this theme, the *Tsan-seng kung-te ching* (Sūtra on the merit [that comes from] praising the Sangha; T. 2911, 85:1456c–1458a). This scripture emphasizes that laypeople (*pai-i*) who revile monks fall into evil paths of rebirth (p. 1457b), and that

when one sees monks breaking the precepts, one should be lenient and not criticize them, just as, when one enters a fragrant grove to pick beautiful flowers, one should not select withered leaves. In the vast and pure sea of the Buddhadharma, there are many who are diligent in maintaining the precepts. Even if, among them, there are those who violate proper decorum, laypeople should not slander them. . . . One should not listen to slanderers of monks, but should only esteem and revere them.

The last line of this text assures those who practice such piety that "in the future they will meet Maitreya" (pp. 1457c–1458a).

The *Fo-shuo Shan-hai-hui P'u-sa ching* (Sūtra preached by the Buddha on the Bodhisattva Shan-hai-hui; T. 2891, 85:1405c–1409c) emphasizes that support for monks and monasteries leads to rebirth in Amitābha's paradise. In a list of ten pious acts that result in such rebirth, three involve providing food, clothing, and medicine to monks and visiting monasteries to ask about the Dharma. Even the exhortations that don't mention monks specifically urge laypeople to "follow the precepts received from their masters," maintain eight precepts instead of the usual five, meditate, protect the Dharma, and teach the ignorant—all activities that apply to monks as well. Here laypeople are urged both to support monks and to emulate them (p. 1407b). There is nothing like this in the *pao-chüan*, some of which criticize the behavior of monks.

Other indigenous texts found at Tun-huang promise punishments in purgatory for those who rob and oppress monks and who take their food. In contrast, "when good people go into a monastery, when they see monks they show reverence to them, and when they see buddha[-images] they bow. They receive the precepts, repent, and give up their wealth and goods to provide for the Three Jewels, not begrudging their own lives; so they protect the great Dharma." Such people are rewarded in heaven (*t'ien-t'ang*).[4]

These passages reveal the fact that a whole monastic structure is assumed by some of the earlier indigenous scriptures—a monastic structure that is simply not present in *pao-chüan*. Even the *Fo-shuo hsiang-fa chueh-i ching* (Sūtra expounded by the Buddha on resolving doubts during the period of the semblance of the Dharma; T. 2870, 85:1335c–1338c), which is sharply critical of corrupt monks, assumes a monastic structure and urges officials not to tax the clergy (p. 1337b). Sectarian *pao-chüan* are from a different social world.

Another difference is that in the older indigenous scriptures there are more detailed instructions for rituals and confession. In these materials there are whole texts devoted to confession of sins, such as the *Ta-t'ung fang-kuang ch'an-hui mieh-tsui chuang-yen ch'eng fo ching*

(All-pervasive universal scripture of the attainment of buddhahood adorned by the annihilation of sin through penance; T. 2871, 85:1338c–1355b).[5] There are long lists of sins here, summed up in the categories of the "ten evil deeds" (*shih-e*), "five rebellious acts" (*wu-ni*), and "four grave prohibitions" (*ssu-chung*).[6] The named sins include violating the precepts and prohibitions, slandering the true Dharma, and not revering sūtras. These lists are followed by such statements as:

[Since we] have incessantly committed such serious sins as the ten evil deeds and the five rebellious acts, therefore today, with measureless fear and shame, [we] take refuge in the Three Jewels. The compassion of the Buddha is universal, and bodhisattvas know us as parents; may they accept [our] open confession, [by which] we vow to get rid of the weighty sins [accumulated] in rebirths through measureless eons [or kalpas], and [we] vow further not to commit them again. (p. 1350c)

As the text says, "If such sins are not confessed, one will certainly fall into purgatory, and the buddhas, bodhisattvas, śrāvakas, and pratyekabuddhas will be unable to help and protect. Masters, monks, parents, devas, and people will also be unable to save you. So today, with measureless fear and shame, take refuge in the Three Jewels." This penance book continues by listing such sins as associating with evil friends and succumbing to desire, anger, jealousy, and lust: "This multitude of sins [I] now entirely confess." Those who, in fear and trembling, so confess their own sins, and who confess on behalf of others as well, are assured by the Buddha that they are "true great beings" (*chen ta-shih*; pp. 1351a–1351b).

In addition to exhortations to confession, this book provides instructions for its ritual recitation. Those who hear it rejoice and are moved to

believe and reverence it, write copies of it, accept and retain its teachings, and recite it. With their penetrating understanding, [they arrange] a clean and well-ordered room in an empty and pure place. They daub the floor with fragrant mud, and with good banners cover and adorn its interior. First burn good incense, and then invite the buddhas. Bathe with as much fragrant water as one needs, and put on clean clothing. Wash each time you go to the toilet. Arrange a comfortable [lit. "jeweled"] seat and long cultivate [the teachings of] this sūtra.

One is to maintain this recitation ritual for seven days and seven nights without sleeping, reciting the text three times each day. Six times each day, one is to burn incense, make offerings, bow before a buddha-image, and confess, calling out the names of the buddhas and bodhisattvas in this book. From the first until the sixth day, one is again to daub the floor with fragrant mud, bathe in scented water, and burn many different kinds of fine incense, making offerings with deep concentration. The text continues: "Because of this concentration and devotion, the confession of such a person shakes [all within] the ten directions, and I [the Buddha] at that time, with an infinite number of buddhas and bodhisattvas, will follow the sound of the recitation and enter this room, so as to provide verification [of the efficaciousness of the ritual]. Doing this for seven days will certainly wipe out [one's sins]" (p. 1353a).

The *Fo-shuo chueh tsui fu ching* (Sūtra expounded by the Buddha on determining sin and merit; T. 2868, 85:1328b–1333c) contains similar instructions for confession. Here we are told that one is to maintain a vegetarian diet for seven days, each day criticizing oneself three times for past acts, words, and thoughts. "One should take refuge in the Three Honored Ones [i.e., Three Jewels] and uphold the names of the eight buddhas [of the eastern quarter]. One should receive and burn incense, scatter flowers, light lamps, and make offerings." When this has been done for seven days, accompanied by acts of charity and in the company of a pure practitioner of the Way, "then one will obtain long life and wipe out past karma" (p. 1328c).

Elsewhere in this text we find a description of ritual offerings to wipe out past karma that is causing illness, including detailed instructions for incense, banners, and decorations (p. 1330a). Other exhortations to confession can be found in T. 1869, 85:1334c.

The *Fo-shuo chiu-chi ching* (Sūtra expounded by the Buddha on healing illness; T. 2878, 85:1361b–1362c) offers ritual instructions for healing illness that include reciting the names of buddhas and making copies of the text (p. 1362c). The *Contemplation Sūtra* (*Fo-shuo kuan ching*; T. 2914, 85:1459c–1461c) is entirely devoted to methods of visualizing the buddhas in the process of meditation, all of which arise from mental discipline.

Some "precious volumes" of the sixteenth and seventeenth centuries also criticize moral sins and the lack of ritual devotion, but there is less emphasis in them on the need for confession. Buddha visualization also demands a dimension of inner mental awareness and discipline that is not present in this later tradition. The closest the *pao-chüan* come to this interiority is in Lo Ch'ing's discussions of his own anxiety for salvation in his *K'u-kung wu-tao chüan* (On awakening to the Way through bitter toil). Here again, the older indigenous scriptures reveal their relative closeness to monastic Buddhist traditions.

A more problematic difference between the older indigenous scriptures and *pao-chüan* is that whereas some of the earlier texts refer to the need for allegiance to enlightened masters, they do not mention sect patriarchs and assemblies. They tend to draw more attention to their own saving efficacy; it is their faithful recitation that enables the pious to escape disaster, not adherence to a sect. Although there are similar claims in some *pao-chüan*, they are not so strong or pervasive.

The nature of the Taoist influence on these two types of text is also different. Both are influenced by originally Taoist eschatological mythology, as E. Zürcher has demonstrated in detail in the case of the older indigenous scriptures. However, sectarian *pao-chüan* also refer to terms from Taoist "interior alchemy," which had developed in the intervening centuries.

Of course, there is no trace of the Eternal Mother mythology in the earlier books, which in itself is a fundamental difference of content and orientation. All these differences mean that though many of the indigenous scriptures found at Tun-huang are expressions of Buddhist outreach, the same cannot be said for *pao-chüan*, which use Buddhist terms but in a different intentional context. *Pao-chüan* are not Buddhist by traditional definitions of the term; they set forth an alternative religious orientation. The most Buddhist-influenced of the Ming and Ch'ing sectarian authors was Lo Ch'ing, but his understanding of Buddhism is fragmented and based on an understanding of emptiness that has a strong philosophical Taoist flavor. After Lo Ch'ing, the issue of Buddhist orientation is not worth discussing. *Pao-chüan* are an expression of sectarian popular religion, not of Buddhism.

Although there are thus many basic differences between these two forms of literature, there are also similarities, which are best discussed as parallels that developed independently out of a common concern to communicate religious teaching in a more direct and simple way. Because most of the earlier texts were lost nearly a millennium ago and rediscovered only recently, there is little possibility of their textual influence on *pao-chüan*. The most significant parallel is a similar conviction in some books of both types that the end of the age will soon arrive, accompanied by terrible destruction that only the faithful will survive. This time of transition coincides with the coming of a divine savior, usually the Buddha Maitreya, who will establish the elect in a new age of peace, prosperity, and long life. Because the most important indigenous sūtras based on this eschatology have already been discussed by Zürcher, I cite here only a few passages that most closely parallel passages in the *pao-chüan* discussed below. Some of the terms used are similar or even identical.

Although a sense of urgency about the coming end of the kalpa is present in a number of indigenous texts, in nine of the Tun-huang scriptures (reprinted in volume 85 of the *Taishō Tripitaka*) this concern is discussed more explicitly. The values of all these books are those of conventional lay Buddhism: For them, salvation is to be found by practicing the precepts, avoiding sins, copying and reciting these scriptures, and believing their respective messages. In the dramatic eschatological language of these books there is clear Taoist influence—particularly in the emphasis that a savior deity is soon to come or already present—but this language should not be allowed to obscure the fundamentally Buddhist ethical orientation of most of them. Indeed, from an outsider's perspective, the terrifying descriptions of destruction at the end of the age look like attempts to frighten the audience into more devout piety.[7]

The most detailed discussions of what will happen at the end of the eon are found in three of these indigenous scriptures, one from the fifth century, the other two from the sixth. The first is the *Fo-shuo fa mieh-chin ching* (Sūtra expounded by the Buddha on the complete extinction of the Dharma; T. 396, 12:1118c–1119b), which is first cited in a Buddhist catalogue of 515 C.E., and which is discussed by Zürcher as "probably fifth century."[8] Most of this book is devoted to criticisms of the immoral and irreverent behavior of monks when the power of the Buddha's teaching declines. Its closest parallels to *pao-chüan* are passages describing the end of the kalpa and the eventual salvation of the pious:

Because the kalpa is nearly at its end, the days and months will become shorter and shorter, and men's lives will pass more and more hastily; their heads will be white at forty. Men will be filthy and depraved; they will exhaust their semen and shorten their lives, living at most to the age of sixty. The lives of men will become shorter, but the lives of women will become longer, to seventy or eighty or ninety; some will reach a hundred years.

Great floods will suddenly occur; they will strike by surprise, unlooked for. The people of the world will have no faith, and hence they will take the world to be permanent. Living creatures of every variety, with no distinction between gentry and the base, will be drowned and float away, dashed about, to be eaten by fish or turtles.

At that time, there will be bodhisattvas, pratyekabuddhas, and arhats; the gang of maras [demons] will drive them away, and they will not participate in the religious community. These three types of disciples will enter into the mountains, to a land of merit. Tranquil and self-controlled, they will rest content in this. Their lives will grow longer, the various devas will protect and watch over them, and Candraprabha will appear in the world. They will be able to meet him, and together they will make my Way flourish.

After fifty-two years, all the Mahāyāna scriptures will disappear and "the robes of the monks will spontaneously turn white"—that is, monks will become laymen. But there is still hope:

> What will happen then is not possible to describe in detail. But several thousand myriad years after this happens, Maitreya will descend to be Buddha in the world. All under heaven will enjoy peace, prosperity, and equality; the pestilential vapors will be dispersed and expelled. The rain will be just suitable to growth, and the five grains will grow and flourish. Trees will grow large, and people will be eighty feet tall. All of them will live eighty-four thousand years. It is impossible to count how many living things will be able to be saved.[9]

There are no Taoist elements in this text, and Maitreya's advent is still far in the future, but this fundamental structure of destruction and renewal was continued in Ming and Ch'ing texts. There are distant antecedents here as well for sectarian claims to represent an elect lay community that has superseded a decadent monastic tradition.

Two sixth-century texts provide a more dramatic and violent picture of this mythology. The first is the *P'u-hsien P'u-sa shuo cheng ming ching* (T. 2879, 85:1362c–1368b), translated by Zürcher as the *Scripture of the Realization of Understanding Preached by the Bodhisattva Samantabhadra*.[10] In this book the Buddha predicts the descent of Maitreya after the nirvāṇa of Śākyamuni, following thirty years of rule by a "king of the Dharma." There follows a long list of the types of piety that will enable both clergy and laity to see Maitreya, including leaving the household life to meditate, study, and preach to others, building pagodas, temples, and lecture halls, copying scriptures, and making images: "All such people will see Maitreya." The same is true for those who repair roads, dig wells, and make bridges, for those who aid the poor, and for those who simply maintain the five precepts, practice the ten virtues, and fast six times a month.[11]

That is, the response to eschatological opportunity is intensified conventional piety for those at all levels of wealth and education (p. 1363a). A bit later in the text, we are told that those who meditate on Samantabhadra and recite this scripture will be able to get rid of illness, cause officials to have compassion, ease childbirth, and drive away demons, some of which are identified with popular deities of certain localities, households, mountains, and constellations (pp. 1636b, 1364a).

Then comes a list of those who will not be able to see Maitreya, including impious and immoral monks and those who revile the true Dharma, believe in the depraved (*hsin-hsieh*), and are unwilling to practice and recite this scripture. We will see later that this earnest self-righteousness is also found in *pao-chüan*. There, as here, the pious are promised that they will not meet with disasters and difficulties (p. 1364b–c). This sectarian spirit is expressed more forcefully as the *Cheng-ming ching* proceeds, as in a passage where Samantabhadra says to Maitreya:

When the World-Honored One [i.e., the Buddha] appears in the world, he will seize and drive away all forms of pollution and evil and will distinguish five kinds of persons. Those with karmic affinity (*yu-yuan jen*) will be east of the river, and those without such karmic destiny will be on the west. Those on the east will meet the Sage and be able to see the King Who Illuminates the Dharma (Ming fa wang). (p. 1365c)[12]

Samantabhadra then asks Maitreya to construct a Magic City (*hua-ch'eng*) for him, and is told that this city is where Śākyamuni attained the Way (p. 1365c). In subsequent pages this city is described as a glittering paradise which all disciples of the Dharma are summoned to enter (p. 1366a). Then we are told that

Seven hundred years after Śākyamuni's nirvāṇa, Heaven and Earth will shake violently and the sky and earth will cry out. In one month, three apparitions (*san-kuai*) will cause suffering and difficulty for the common people. Evil and pollution will be driven away, distinguishing five kinds [of evildoers?]. [Demon emissaries?] will devote themselves to spreading epidemics and suppressing and ordering sinners. Those who have the Dharma will all live; those who do not have it will all die. After that, when 99 years and 700 years [*sic*] have passed, the myriad worlds will endure six kinds of earthquakes and the sun will be dark for seven days. Several days after that, Heaven will produce a King of Light and Earth will produce a Sage Lord. These two saints will rule together in the Divine Realm (*shen-chou*) [i.e., China].

These two rulers in the Magic City seek to lead all the pious to their paradise. (p. 1366a–b)

The remainder of this text alternates between threats of destruction for sinners and promises of hope for the devout. Its goal is an ideal world where there are no sinners and

states become buddha-states, regions become buddha-regions; commanderies become buddha-commanderies, districts become buddha-districts, villages become buddha-villages, and neighborhoods become buddha-neighborhoods, where all friends within the four seas are like brothers and assemble together in the Magic City. . . . Those who are able there to see the King of Light will with their whole minds willingly receive and maintain [the precepts and teachings]. Those who have doubts will not be able to see this Dharma, and those who backslide will not be able to see this joy. Nor will those who revile [the teaching]. Those of many desires who drink wine and eat meat, who are false and deceptive, with depraved views (*hsieh-chien*), and all like this who do what is not good, will not see this joy. (p. 1366b)

However, those who repent and get rid of their evil ways, and who criticize their own sins, will be able to "enter this Dharma [teaching]" and see the joys of paradise. Here, as in the *pao-chüan*, the boundaries between paradise and a transformed world are not clear. In what follows, the coming destruction of the world and punishment of sinners by demon hordes are described in even more detail: those with karmic affinity are thrice summoned to rebirth in heaven, while those without the Dharma enter purgatory. The Buddha will send an asura king holding seven suns to burn up everything:

All plants will be scorched, mountains and rocks will split, and mountain valleys and dikes will be leveled, with everything fused together. At that time I [the Buddha] will send from heaven a golden-winged bird to go down and summon together those with karmic affinity. This bird is 20 *li* [Chinese miles] long and 30 *li* across; in its mouth it [can] hold seven thousand people, with eighty thousand on its back, and it is able to ascend to [Maitreya's] Tushita Heaven. When Maitreya descends, there will still remain some sinners to be punished, who drink wine and eat meat and do not believe that a buddha has appeared in the world or that Maitreya has descended. As for such people, their nine orifices will leak and blood will come out of their ears, noses, eyes, and mouths. Such people at the end of the kalpa will all be finished [i.e., die] and will all enter purgatory, with no hope of escape. (pp. 1366b–c)

Then hope comes, in the form of a wind of sandalwood incense blowing away evil miasmas, followed by another description of paradise. When Maitreya descends, vast multitudes of bodhisattvas gather for a cosmic battle, at the end of which all the demons submit. Zürcher summarizes what happens next:

Then the earth is reconstructed in successive layers of precious and magical substances—a theme of Buddhist origin, that has been taken over, with many variations, by Taoist cosmography. There are seven layers, that from bottom to top are made of bronze, mercury, rock-crystal, beryl, silver,(?) saffron, and gold. The mountains . . . consist of silver and gold, and the trees are made of silver. This reborn country of Jambudvipa is full of palaces, pavilions and many-storied buildings, and even the city-wards are adorned with luminous jewels, so that there is no more difference between day and night. Under the transforming rule (chih-hua) of Maitreya, all evil powers will have disappeared, for even the demons will have been reborn as human beings. Man's life-span will be 87,000 years, after which they will be reborn in the even more blissful world of Amitābha, or be transported by Samantabhadra himself to Akṣobhya's Eastern Paradise.[13]

We will see that this apocalyptic vision is echoed in detail in the *Chiu-lien pao-chüan* of 1523 discussed in Chapter Four, and other texts that followed it. Terms such as "Magic City" and "those with karmic affinity" are repeated in similar dramatic contexts. The *Cheng-ming* scripture also condemns "depraved and heretical teachers with inverted views" (*yao-hsieh tao-chien chih shih*) who divine to seek out disasters, and who "kill pigs, dogs, cattle, and sheep to make offerings to ghosts and spirits," all of which is without benefit (p. 1368b). This language anticipates similar statements in some "precious volumes" that condemn sectarian rivals and popular religious practices.

The other text most relevant to our topic is the *Shou-lo pi-ch'iu ching* (Scripture of the Monk Shou-lo; T. 2873, 85:1356a–1358c), which Zürcher says probably dates from the sixth century. It is first mentioned in a Buddhist bibliography of 594.[14] The chief savior in this text is the "Moonlight Bodhisattva" (Candraprabha) mentioned above, who is also referred to as the "King of Light" (Ming-wang) and "Lord of Light" (Ming-chün). Its mythological structure is similar to that of the *Cheng-ming* scripture, with its predictions of cosmic destruction and warfare followed by a paradisal state for the elect in the Magic City. Because Zürcher has already provided a detailed summary of this text, I will simply note points of interest for our understanding of textual antecedents of *pao-chüan*.[15] Beyond the promise of a messiah following the destruction at the end of the age, the following terms and concepts are worthy of note:

1. Exhortations not to believe in the "demonic and depraved" (*yao-hsieh*), translated by Zürcher as "evil powers" (p. 1356a).

2. Repeated statements that "great calamities are about to arrive" (*ta tsai chiang chih*) coupled with assurances that "those with karmic affinity will meet me" (*yu-yuan chih wo*; pp. 1358c, 1357a), all of this in a most dramatic context, since "the world is about to end" (*shih chiang yü mo*; p. 1357c).

3. Specific political and geographic references in the vast panorama of eschatological change. We are told the precise cities where the pious can escape disaster, including Yang-chou, in what is now Kiangsu province (p. 1356c). The messiah Yueh-kuang (Moonlight), also called the King of Light, is, we are told, "now in the Han realm" (p. 1356c). He says, "I am about to appear in the world, north of the Yellow River and south of the Weak River (Jo-shui). Between them I will be king in the Han realm" (p. 1357c). Other passages indicate that an unnamed king and his officials are expected to aid the messiah by exhorting all to be good Buddhists, a theme present in Buddhist teachings from their beginning (p. 1357c). We have seen above a reference in the *Cheng-ming* scripture to the King of Light and the Sage Lord ruling China, and the ideal of the whole earthly realm becoming a buddha-land. In the *Shou-lo* text, this geographic specificity is reinforced by locating the end of the age precisely in time, in the *shen* and *yu* cyclical years (p. 1358b), and on a particular day of the month: "Those who think on the words of this scripture will be able to see my body. On the fourteenth day of the seventh month, there will be an apparition; on the fifteenth day, you will see the Buddha and the earth will shake, but do not be afraid" (p. 1358b). All this anticipates similar specificity in *pao-chüan* teachings and in the proclamations of sect leaders.

4. The naming of Chinese saints or patriarchs who assist the messiah's work, some of them present now in disguise. Seventeen "worthies and sages" (*hsien sheng*) are provided with full three-character Chinese names in the *Shou-lo* text, with common surnames such as Liu, Wang, Cheng, and Chao. The first eight listed share a common first character in their given names, *hsien* ("worthy"), which

appears to be a generation name indicating common discipleship. Here the Buddha tells Shou-lo, "You should now go to them; they are really your guiding masters (*tao-shih*) who are able to turn the cycle of birth-and-death. . . . They are now about to appear in the world. Why ask about them further? Only those with reverential minds when the time arrives will be able to see them." After providing a second list of nine names, the Buddha adds, "These worthies are all roaming about and patrolling the world, but with your fleshly eyes you are not able to distinguish them. . . . They are not recognized because some appear insane, some stupid, some ignorant and foolish, poor and of humble position; some drink wine and eat meat, and some break their fasts by eating at night. Since they appear in these ways, how can they be recognized?" (pp. 1356c–1357a).

In later sectarian writings, such lay masters and patriarchs are commonly named, in some cases with shared generational or religious names.

There are other points of interest here, such as references to a Willow City (Liu-ch'eng, p. 1356c) and to a "dragon-flower tree" (p. 1358a)—both terms used in "precious volumes." I note below a reference to women attaining the Way, which is also consonant with the later texts.

There are antecedents in other early indigenous scriptures listed above of *pao-chüan* terms and themes related to the end of the age, such as a common conviction that the end is near; predictions of droughts and epidemics, floods, and the burning of the world by seven suns; and promises of deliverance for the pious and destruction for unbelievers. Most of this material is parallel to that in the *Cheng-ming* and *Shou-lo* texts and so need not be repeated here. One lively little book, the *Sūtra of the Monk Seng-chia Who, Wishing to Enter Nirvāṇa, Expounded on the Six Kinds [of Persons] Who Would Be Saved* (*Seng-chia ho-shang yü ju nieh-p'an shuo liu-tu ching*; T. 2920, 85:1463b–1464a), speaks of its narrator and Maitreya descending together to sit in the Magic City, where all those with good karma—here called the "buddha-nature seeds" (*Fo-hsing chung-tzu*)—would be saved (p. 1463c). This phrase is similar to the term *chung-min* ("seed people"), which is used of the elect in some *pao-chüan*.[16]

In sum, these parallels in eschatological terminology are the closest antecedents of *pao-chüan* teaching that I have found, despite their great separation in time. For me, this is the most puzzling issue in the background of Ming and Ch'ing sectarian scriptures. These similarities are too specific to be due simply to unrelated parallel development, yet I know of no specific connections between the two bodies of texts.

The other similarities I have found between the older indigenous scriptures and *pao-chüan* are no more than indications that similar ideas and themes were available long before they were incorporated in the later texts. Of course, as I have discussed before, much of the content of the indigenous scriptures found at Tun-huang is based on that of canonical sūtras, some of which were widely available. Hence the themes discussed here are part of a larger tradition.

As we have seen in our discussion of eschatologically oriented texts, the fundamental criterion for attaining rebirth in the new world of the elect is lay piety based on observance of the five precepts and recitation of scripture. Monks can also be saved, but most discussions of them criticize their lack of piety and their involvement in secular affairs. Some passages urge respect for monks and their belongings, but that is also an aspect of proper lay devotion. There is an interesting juxtaposition in these texts of dramatic threats with very ordinary means of responding to them, which in turn lead to equally dramatic promises of paradise—all for doing what good lay Buddhists were supposed to do anyway. The eschatology, like purgatory in other contexts, looks like a vast exercise in *upāya* ("skillful means").

The lay orientation of the eschatological texts is more specifically stated in passages from other indigenous scriptures. For example, in the penance text noted above, the *Ta-t'ung fang-kuang ch'an-hui mieh-tsui chuang-yen ch'eng fo ching* (T. 2871), we are told that "even those who are ordinary people who recite and uphold this scripture will [attain] wisdom equal to that of the saints. Even if their [own minds] are confused and attached, if they recite and uphold this scripture, they will attain nirvāṇa the same as all the buddhas." This promise is twice repeated in the lines that follow, even for those who have "broken the precepts, committed five deadly sins, and reviled the true teachings" (T. 2871, 85:1346a). Elsewhere in this text we are told that the Buddha has compassion for all sentient beings, protects and receives them, and looks on them all equally, as if they were one child. He causes all to see the buddha-nature within and to attain peace of mind and enlightenment: "Those who have not yet attained nirvāṇa he makes attain nirvāṇa" (p. 1339b). In the *Shou-lo pi-ch'iu ching* referred to above, we are also told that "girls and married women can all attain the Tao and with diligent progress can avoid these calamities [of the end of the age]" (T. 2874, 85:1358c).

In this context, a most interesting anticipation of an important theme in the later sectarian texts is that of the Buddha as a compassionate parent—either father or mother or both together. For example, in the *Fo-hsing hai-ts'ang chih-hui chieh-t'o p'o hsin-hsiang ching* (Scripture of the mark of thought, thoroughly delivered [i.e., liberated] by the wisdom stored in the sea of buddhahood; T. 2885, 85:1391a–1401c), the Buddha is referred to as the "Supreme Compassionate Father" (Wu-shang tz'u-fu) who says, "I am the father of all sentient beings, and all sentient beings are my children." He loves them as parents love an only child, concerned about it day and night. His disciples plead with him not to enter nirvāṇa, saying that, if he does, "we disciples will have nothing to look up to, we will be like babies who have lost their mother (*ying-erh shih mu*), like fish with no water" (T. 2885, 85:1391a, 1395b, 1401a). The phrase *ying erh shih mu* is found in *pao-chüan* as well.

This theme is repeated in the sixth-century *Fo-shuo Shan-hai-hui P'u-sa ching* (T. 2891) referred to above, where we read, "The Buddha . . . is like compassionate parents (*tz'u fu-mu*) who, seeing their child seriously ill, are concerned about it day and night." Here we are told that those who obtain deliverance through pious worship are like exiles "who are able to return to their native country and see their parents with unbounded joy" (T. 2891, 85:1406a, 1407a). For the older indigenous scriptures, this theme of the Buddha as loving parent is simply one metaphor among many that are scattered throughout the texts, but for sectarian writers of the sixteenth century, this metaphor of a divine parent is taken literally and made a central focus of their books.

In the sixteenth century, Lo Ch'ing emphasized that deliverance is possible for all because all possess the buddha-nature within. On this basis he affirmed that there is no distinction between clergy and laity. This theme, too, is anticipated in the texts found at Tun-huang. As we read in the *Fo-shuo Fa-wang ching* (Scripture of the King of the Dharma, preached by the Buddha; T. 2883, 85:1384c–1390a),

In the buddha-nature is the nature of the mind. Outside of this mind there is nowhere to seek. To seek elsewhere is to be confused. . . . Buddhahood is obtained within the mind. In all minds there is the buddha-nature, and all sentient beings possess the buddha-nature. All those who are able to settle their minds and bodies will attain buddhahood. Outside of this [mind], there is no place to seek the Buddha.

Those who have a correct view of this matter are buddhas. True disciples are produced from the teaching of the correct Dharma; they are produced by the preaching of the Buddha:

Those who attain the four forms of truth and wisdom on which the buddhas rely are bodhisattvas of these Four Truths[17] even if they are ordinary persons. Good men, five hundred or a thousand or fifteen hundred years after my nirvāṇa — those who are able to receive, maintain, and recite this scripture, who take constant pleasure in my pure place with believing minds and correct views, and who further teach this Dharma to sentient beings — [they] will be called bodhisattvas. Even if they are ordinary persons, they will receive reverent worship. They will be [the same as] those who have left the household life. . . . Even ordinary persons who are able to subdue their bodies and minds, who do not give rise to arrogant thoughts of self, who are not stained by the vulgar world of dust, who have long departed from vulgar thoughts, who have an adamantine, indestructible, disciplined nature even though they are ordinary people — they are true monks. (T. 2883, 85:1385c, 1386b–c)

The language here is more precise and rigorous than that of Lo Ch'ing, but the affirmation of the ultimate identity of clergy and laity is the same. Of course, as is discussed in Chapter Three below, Lo Ch'ing learned such ideas from Ch'an-influenced sources that appeared much later than the indigenous scriptures considered here.

At another level, a partial parallel to the role of sect patriarchs in *pao-chüan* can be seen in an emphasis in some of the Tun-huang texts on the importance of giving allegiance to enlightened teachers. For example, in the *Fo-shuo chueh tsui fu ching* (T. 2868) noted above, we read that

one should follow the master's instructions, and should not doubt him. A master has entered deeply into the sūtra storehouse and cannot be measured by the ordinary ideas of the samsaric world. It is very difficult to be a teacher of the Dharma for others. A teacher has a heavy responsibility for them, and serves as their protector and guarantor. . . . A teacher instructs his disciples. Those disciples who do not follow their teacher's instructions, and who do not believe and accept them, later, when they die, will enter purgatory. . . . One should quickly seek out an enlightened teacher and receive the five precepts from him. One should obey and serve him with compassion and filial reverence, and give him clothing and food. When he is ill, give him medicine, and don't let him want for incense, flowers, and lamps. If at the

six [monthly] fasts one can obey his commands, then one will obtain blessings, obtain the Way, and obtain the fruits [of good karma]. . . . An enlightened teacher is skillfully able to communicate the Buddha's teachings. Why
is this? Because a teacher is like a father. (T. 2868, 85:1328c, 1329b)

The word translated as "teacher" here is *shih.*

It seems clear that in this text the teachers are monks, but as we
have seen in the *Shou-lo* scripture, this role can be taken by "worthies" with lay names. Later sectarian leaders were understood to be
a combination of teachers and saints. In the earlier indigenous texts,
loyalty to human leaders is not a strong theme and is subordinate to
loyalty to the scriptures themselves.

From this discussion it can be seen that there are many similarities between indigenous scriptures found at Tun-huang and *pao-
chüan.* Nonetheless, these similarities are outweighed by larger differences of language, structure, and content. With the possible
exception of similar eschatological motifs, there is no question of direct antecedents, only partial parallels. Our quest for sources of *pao-
chüan* must explore other materials.

TRANSFORMATION TEXTS AND SŪTRA-LECTURES

Two other types of texts found at Tun-huang might be considered
antecedents of *pao-chüan:* "transformation texts" (*pien-wen*) and "sūtra-lectures" (*chiang-ching-wen*). *Pien-wen* in particular have been
linked to *pao-chüan* by Chinese scholars since Cheng Chen-to's pioneering work in the 1930s. In his *Chung-kuo su wen-hsueh shih* (History of Chinese vernacular literature), first published in 1938, Cheng
wrote, "*Pao-chüan* are really the direct descendants of *pien-wen.* . . .
[Their] structure is no different from *pien-wen.*" This view was echoed by other scholars in the following decades.[18] The study of *pien-
wen* is a large and complex field with scholarly contributions in
many languages, but the most precise and recent major investiga-
tions have been by Victor Mair, whose work I follow here.[19]

Mair defines *pien-wen* as "narratives written in prosimetric style,
the verse portions chiefly heptasyllabic. They deal with both secular
and religious themes but are all written in semicolloquial language.
. . . [They also] have an intimate relationship to pictures. . . . The antecedent of *pien-wen* was actually a type of picture storytelling
transmitted to China through Central Asia from India." Mair's definition also includes "a unique verse-introductory (or pre-verse) formula, an episodic narrative progression, [and] homogeneity of lan-

guage." He indicates that these texts appeared in the seventh and eighth centuries.

Mair's definition makes it possible to distinguish *pien-wen* from other types of texts found at Tun-huang; by employing it, he maintains that there are about eighteen to twenty-one extant *pien-wen*, based on a total of seven stories.[20] He provides complete translations of three of these seven stories, summaries of them all, and a translation of a closely related text that does not fit his strict definition. Four of these seven basic stories are about military heroes, and one is about the sorrows of a Chinese woman married to a non-Chinese chieftain. Only two deal with religious themes, one about Mu-lien rescuing his mother from purgatory, and the other about a contest of magical powers between the Buddha's disciple Śāriputra and a "heretical" master in an Indian kingdom called Śrāvasti.

On the basis of Mair's discussion and translations, and the corresponding Chinese texts, it is clear that there is very little similarity between *pien-wen* and sectarian *pao-chüan*, although *pien-wen* stories such as that of Mu-lien did appear later in narrative "precious volumes." The one characteristic that *pien-wen* share with *pao-chüan* is composition in alternating sections of prose and pairs of seven-character (heptasyllabic) verse; beyond that, all is different. Sectarian "precious volumes" are not based on stories, do not have secular themes, and (as is discussed in the following chapters) have a more complex structure. The use of vernacular constructions is less obvious in *pien-wen*; the two are simply different kinds of literature that should never have been confused.[21]

Another form of text found at Tun-huang of possible relevance for our understanding of *pao-chüan* is *chiang-ching-wen* ("texts that expound sūtras"), which Victor Mair translates as "sūtra lectures." His comments about them are most instructive:

It is particularly important to differentiate sūtra lectures from transformation texts. Sūtra lectures are line-by-line (occasionally word-by-word) explications of canonical scripture; transformation texts are prosimetric narratives whose sources are more often folk tales and legends than scripture. Depending on the circumstances (whether a cantor or other assistant is present), sūtra lectures are distinguished by formulaic expressions such as "Please sing/intone/chant" or "Let us sing" or "I shall begin to sing" before the quoted scripture passage; transformation texts generally possess the verse-introductory formula described above and in the appendix. Sūtra lectures were part of religious services known as "popular lectures" or "lectures for the laity" (*su-chiang*) that have a history stretching back to the Six

Dynasties period; transformation texts are written versions of folk entertainments that were current during the eighth, ninth, and tenth centuries. And so on. T'ang usage is consistent; *chiang-ching-wen* were not thought by people of the ninth and tenth centuries to be a type of *pien-wen* nor vice versa.[22]

In 1983, Stephan Salzberg completed an M.A. thesis at the University of British Columbia on the *Vimalakīrti* sūtra-lecture text, for which he suggests the date of 944–947. Based on the best available scholarship and the texts themselves, his discussion of these books is in accord with that of Victor Mair; they are lectures on sūtras intended for mixed audiences, during which one monk would chant a passage from a sūtra, which would be expounded in detail by another, called a *fa-shih* ("Dharma master").

Salzberg describes *chiang-ching-wen* as "notes and prompt books for lectures, religious performances really based upon and interpreting abstruse Buddhist canonical books, sūtras, for a congregation of mostly lay people, involving chanting, spoken exposition and sung poetry." The structure of these texts follows that of the preaching assemblies, with a short quote from a sūtra followed by a prose restatement and embellishment of it:

Next comes a long verse section which was sung. This consists of rhymed stanzas generally composed of eight lines of uniform length, for the most part of seven syllables, although examples of five syllable lines are not infrequent and . . . six syllable [stanzas] also occur. . . . The content of the sung section generally parallels and reinforces that of the preceding prose section. . . . The final couplet of each section presages the subject of the next section and ends with a request that [the assistant monk] or . . . the preacher . . . chant out the next passage of the sūtra.

On the *Vimalakīrti* text, Salzberg comments, "A reader is first struck by the sheer volume of exposition relative to text. The actual sūtra text taken up in the manuscript occupies less than two columns of one page in the *Taishō* edition of the *Tripitaka*. [The] manuscript runs to forty-three pages [in the edition used]. . . . All of this is borne out by this text and others of the genre."[23]

The "sūtra-lecture" texts are thus another means composed by evangelistic monks to communicate Buddhist teaching to ordinary folk, parallel in that general sense to the earlier indigenous scriptures, but not presented as preached by the Buddha himself. Nonetheless, the sheer volume and variety of language in these expositions "indicates a nascent independence from the sūtra text itself."[24]

Here again, the closest parallel to *pao-chüan* is the use of alternating sections in prose and verse, but *pao-chüan* make no pretense of expounding sūtras, and indeed, except for those written by Lo Ch'ing, rarely quote any sources at all. The vocabulary and grammar of the sūtra-lecture texts are much less colloquial than those of the *pao-chüan*, with which their content as well has little in common.

Mair notes that "portions of sūtra lecture services were sung,"[25] and we have noted Salzberg's comments on sung verse sections of sūtra-lecture texts. Such sections are parallel to the hymns in *pao-chüan* for which tune names are provided, though of course the content is different and opera tunes were not included in Buddhist preaching services. Here again, the antecedents are weak, indirect, and far removed in time.[26]

CH'AN WRITINGS

Besides the *Platform Sūtra of the Sixth Patriarch*, the most important written materials produced by the Ch'an school were those devoted to the "transmission of the lamp" of the teaching (*ch'uan-teng*) from patriarch to patriarch, collections of the "recorded sayings" (*yü-lu*) of patriarchs and masters, and anthologies of "public cases" (*kung-an*, Japn. *kōan*), records of encounters between masters and disciples intended as subjects for meditation.[27] Those with the most relevance for understanding the background of *pao-chüan* are the *Platform Sūtra* and the "recorded sayings."

The *Platform Sūtra* is attributed to the teachings of a monk named Hui-neng (638–713), but in fact was written by others in about 780. Hui-neng came to be considered the Sixth Patriarch of the Ch'an tradition. The complex textual history of this book has long been studied by Japanese scholars, whose work is summarized in detail by Philip B. Yampolsky in the introduction to his complete translation, which also includes a critical edition of the Chinese text.[28] This book is narrated in the first person as the discourses and dialogues of "Master Hui-neng," who begins with an account of his early life and enlightenment, and then expounds in various ways and contexts his basic message that enlightenment comes through awakening the buddha-nature within. In the sixteenth and seventeenth centuries, Hui-neng and his book were taken as a model by some sectarian authors, particularly Lo Ch'ing. What appealed to them was material such as the following.

Hui-neng describes himself as an impoverished and illiterate firewood-seller who was at first ridiculed by the Fifth Patriarch, Hung-jen, when he came to his monastery, but later recognized by Hung-jen as a more worthy successor than the head monk, Shen-hsiu (pp. 126–133). Though Hui-neng became a revered monk in a thoroughly monastic context, for the sectarians he was a symbol of the validity of lay wisdom and spiritual authority, and hence a figure who marked a fundamental shift in the transmission of saving truth. They maintained that, from Hui-neng on, the old monastic tradition was superseded by one based in lay life; for them, Hui-neng was the first patriarch of a new dispensation. For sectarian leaders, Hui-neng was an exemplar of a lay leader who established himself and a tradition by writing a book of scripture, just as they aspired to do. This understanding was supported by Hui-neng's teaching that all sentient beings possess the potential for buddhahood and hence need only to look within themselves. As the *Platform Sūtra* says:

Therefore we know that, unawakened, even a buddha is a sentient being, and that even a sentient being, if he is awakened in an instant of thought, is a buddha. And thus we know that the ten thousand dharmas are all within our own minds. Why not from your own natures make the original nature of True Reality suddenly appear? If we perceive the mind and see our own natures, then of ourselves we have achieved the Buddha Way. At once, suddenly, we regain our original mind. (p. 151)

This oft-repeated message means that meditation is awareness of one's original nature carried out in the midst of all activities, and hence does not depend on a monastic structure (pp. 136, 141). One may need a "good teacher" to help point the way, but salvation is to be found within one's own body, and true religious practice is to be carried out by oneself:

Good friends, listen! I shall make you see that there is a threefold buddha-body of our own self-natures in your own physical bodies. . . . See for yourselves the purity of your own natures, practice and accomplish for yourselves. Your own nature is the *Dharmakāya* [the highest level of reality], and self-practice is the practice of Buddha; by self-accomplishment you may achieve the Buddha Way for yourselves. (p. 141)

The sociological implications of this resounding affirmation are explicitly stated: "The Master said: 'Good friends, if you wish to practice, it is all right to do so as laymen; you don't have to be in a temple'" (p. 159). This "emancipation proclamation" was taken to heart by later sectarian leaders, who applied it to their own lives and practice. As we shall see in Chapter Three, Lo Ch'ing even took Hui-neng's life as a model for his own spiritual autobiography, complete with an enlightenment inspired by hearing the *Diamond Sūtra*.[29]

On Ch'an "recorded sayings," John McRae comments:

The "recorded sayings" are straightforwardly devoted to the spoken and literary output of individual Ch'an masters. Although they often contain poetry, short essays and details about the lives of their subjects, recorded saying texts are primarily devoted to the transcription of oral exchanges between masters and disciples. These exchanges include both verbal and non-verbal forms of communication—question and answer, silence, shouting, oral vilification, physical abuse, laughter, gesturing and so on. . . . [The dialogue in these texts] was clearly a unique and spirited form of communication aimed at the ultimate achievement of the religious quest, the realization of enlightenment.[30]

These compilations first appeared in the eighth and ninth centuries. According to Yanagida Seizan, the "recorded sayings" were a new form of writing that first developed in the school of Ma-tsu Tao-i (709–788), who emphasized that

all human mental and physical activity . . . [is a function] of the Buddha-nature, that aspect of all living beings which is inherently enlightened. . . . Ma-tsu's position is that the ordinary mind is the Tao. . . . The student must understand that the day-in and day-out activities of the ordinary mind are the activities of a Buddha. In this quest he is guided by a Ch'an Master, whose behavior exemplifies the functioning of mind as Buddha. . . . This attention to the Master's actions as models of enlightened behavior led directly to the development of the "recorded sayings" genre. . . . As a result, the records of those words and actions assumed the status of scripture.[31]

A well-known example is the following dialogue between Lin-chi I-hsüan (d. 866) and his master, Huang-po Hsi-yün (d. 850), both of whom were in the line established by Ma-tsu:

Once, during the group work, Lin-chi was hoeing the ground. Seeing Huang-po coming, he stopped and stood leaning on his mattock.

"Is this guy tired already?" said Huang-po.

"I haven't even lifted my mattock yet. How could I be tired?" answered Lin-chi. Huang-po hit at him. Lin-chi seized Huang-po's stick, jabbed him with it, and knocked him down.

Huang-po called to the *wei-na* [supervisor]: "*Wei-na*, help me up!" The *wei-na* came running and helped him up. "*Ho-shang* ["Monk," = Huang-po], how can you let this lunatic get away with such rudeness!" he said.

Huang-po no sooner got to his feet than he hit the *wei-na.*

Hoeing the ground, Lin-chi said: "Everywhere else, the dead are cremated, but here I bury them alive at once."[32]

The characters translated "this guy" here are *chei-han,* which has this informal meaning. The phrase "How could I be tired?" translates the vernacular line *"Kun ke she-ma."* Both terms illustrate the vernacular usages common in "recorded sayings" literature, in which "this" is often *chei,* "you" is *ni,* the verb "to be" is *shih,* and so on. This use of vernacular terms and constructs in a religious text is perhaps the most important antecedent to *pao-chüan* provided by the Ch'an "recorded sayings."[33] In addition, in *pao-chüan,* a patriarch and his lineage of teachers are sometimes the sources of revelation and authority whose teachings are often presented in dialogues between masters and their disciples or other questioners. In some texts, even the term "transmitting the lamp" is used.

However, for the most part Ch'an patriarchs did not write their "recorded sayings" themselves, whereas sectarian teachers often did compose *pao-chüan.* Lo Ch'ing and one or two other sectarian authors were influenced by the content of Ch'an materials like these, but Ch'an "recorded sayings" are nevertheless very different from *pao-chüan,* which imitate the form and ritual usages of Buddhist sūtras. In *pao-chüan,* the characteristic revealer is the Buddha himself, as befits this more traditional model. Here again, an indigenous antecedent provides only partial precedents.

OTHER POSSIBLE SOURCES OF INFLUENCE

Another obvious influence on *pao-chüan* is the Pure Land Buddhist tradition focused on the compassionate Buddha Amitābha. In this case the influence is structural, built into the history of Chinese popular religious movements since the Sung dynasty (960–1279). I have already discussed this issue at some length in two previous publications and so will not pursue it in detail here.[34]

Amitābha is a buddha residing in a paradise in the West whose saving grace is available to those who think on him and recite his name in faith. By this means, they can be reborn in his Pure Land at death. This direct and simple path to deliverance appealed to both monks and laypeople, and during the Sung period, societies of those devoted to reciting Amitābha's name developed in association with monasteries and were led by monks. By the twelfth century, Pure

Land groups independent of monasteries appeared and became the forerunners of later popular religious sects, which from then on retained a strong orientation toward Amitābha, whatever additional teachings they espoused. This orientation came not only from the sectarian tradition but from orthodox Buddhism as well, in which devotion to Amitābha was a powerful force from the Sung on.[35]

The textual foundation of Pure Land piety was translated sūtras, particularly the *Fo-shuo A-mi-t'o ching* (Amitābha sūtra, expounded by the Buddha; T. 366, 12:346b–348b), translated by Kumārajīva (c. 344–413), which is also available in an English translation.[36] In addition, a large number of devotional tracts were composed by Pure Land monks and lay scholars from the Sung period on, many of which have been reprinted in volume 47 of the *Taishō Tripitaka* and in volumes 107 and 108 of its supplement, the *Dai Nihon Zokuzōkyō* (Chin. *Hsu Tsang-ching*). Lo Ch'ing knew of some of these books, particularly the *Lung-shu ching-t'u wen* (Pure Land text of Lung-shu; T. 1970, 47:251a–289c) by the Sung lay devotee Wang Jih-hsiu (d. 1173).[37]

The most important influences of Pure Land literature on *pao-chüan* are Amitābha as a symbol of divine compassion and descriptions of his paradise. Amitābha's love was incorporated into the figure of the Venerable Mother, and his Pure Land became a model for sectarian visions of paradise, down to detailed terms for its palaces and pools.

Sawada Mizuho has suggested another type of Buddhist writings that may have influenced *pao-chüan*: ritual and penance texts from the T'ang to the Ming periods. Twenty-four such texts have been conveniently reprinted in the *Zokuzōkyō*, volumes 128–129, together with fourteen more from the Ch'ing period. With Lo Ch'ing's books primarily in mind, Sawada comments that "the common features between these books and Ming *pao-chüan* are clear." These include invitations to all the Buddhas of the Ten Directions to approach, accompanied by the burning of incense, recitations of the names of buddhas, and the use of five- and seven-character lines of verse—all basic characteristics of penance texts that were patterns in old *pao-chüan*. Other penance text terms found in "precious volumes" include *t'i-kang* ("raising the main points"), *kai-wen* ("I have heard that"), and *ching-yun* ("the scripture says"). Sawada goes on to say that the penance texts do not include tune names, though such names are not present in all the older *pao-chüan*, either. He concludes that "precious volumes" continued the style and methods of presentation of the Buddhist ritual and penance texts.[38]

The points that Professor Sawada makes are correct as far as they go, but after examining all the texts he cites, I find little basic similarity with *pao-chüan*. The penance texts are all orthodox Buddhist books written in classical Chinese. Unlike "precious volumes," they contain detailed instructions for rituals and the confession of sins. Most are not written in the alternating prose and verse style of *pao-chüan*, nor do they expound teachings or myths. With one or two exceptions, they do not have chapter titles or tune names, as do many of the sectarian texts. Perhaps most important, these books do not present themselves as scriptures, as holy books newly revealed, as is the case with *pao-chüan*; rather, they are intended as ritual adjuncts to sūtra literature. Most of them focus on Amitābha and his Pure Land, which is further evidence of the prevalence of that tradition. It is interesting to note that in one such book Amitābha is called the "Great Merciful Father" (Ta tz'u-en fu), which we have noted is the characteristic of this buddha that had the most influence on sectarian mythology.[39]

The chief exceptions to this general lack of similarity are aspects of the ritual texts (*k'e-i*) found in *Zokuzōkyō* volume 129, particularly the *Ritual Amplification of the Diamond Sūtra* (*Chin-kang ching k'e-i*), which had a profound influence on Lo Ch'ing, as is discussed in Chapter Three below.[40]

THREE PRE-SECTARIAN "PRECIOUS VOLUMES"

Two of the sources cited most frequently by Lo Ch'ing in the early sixteenth century are the *Ritual Amplification of the Diamond Sūtra* (*Chin-kang ching k'e-i*) and the *Sūtra of the Deeds of the Bodhisattva Kuan-yin*, otherwise known as the *Hsiang-shan* (Fragrant Mountain) *pao-chüan*. Of the books of this type cited by Lo, these are the two still extant that are believed to be substantially the same as the editions he knew. Both books are fundamentally expositions of orthodox Buddhist teaching apparently composed by monks and intended for a wide audience. Though they were not written by lay sectarian authors to put forth their own teachings, aspects of each influenced "precious volume" literature.

The teaching of the *Ritual Amplification of the Diamond Sūtra* concerning inborn potential for enlightenment led to Lo's conversion and evangelistic mission, and through his writings influenced many others. The *Hsiang-shan pao-chüan* story of a heroic princess who, against all odds, persists in her faith and is revealed to be a manifestation of the Bodhisattva Kuan-yin became a model for similar themes in several narrative "precious volumes" later on. A third such book is the *Precious Volume on Mu-lien Rescuing His Mother from Purgatory*, a popular Buddhist story also well known to Lo Ch'ing.

The edition of the *Chin-kang ching k'e-i* available to me (*Zokuzōkyō* volume 129, pp. 129b–144b) was transcribed by a monk named Chien-chi in 1835. It is provided with two titles on its opening page: *Chin-kang ching k'e-i pao-chüan* (Precious volume of the ritual amplification of the *Diamond Sūtra*) and *Hsiao-shih Chin-kang k'e-i* (Ritual amplification explaining the *Diamond* [*Sūtra*]). There are two references in this book to a Tsung-ching (pp. 131b, 143b), the second clearly in the first person, and indeed, it is a Northern Sung (960–1127) monk of that name to whom the original version of this book has traditionally been attributed. Sawada Mizuho discusses its authorship in some detail, first demonstrating that the extant versions are not from the Northern Sung, then agreeing with the view that the book was composed in 1242 by a Southern Sung Ch'an monk named Tsung-ching. He says that it is Kumārajīva's translation of the *Diamond Sūtra* formulated for use in penance rituals.[41]

The *Chin-kang k'e-i* is divided into thirty-two sections (*fen*), each with a title. There are several pages of introductory and closing material before and after the first and last sections. Each section begins with a passage from the sūtra, followed by a prose comment (*pai*), a question (*wen*), and then an answer (*ta*) in couplets of seven-character verse. The title and number for the first section are missing, but the first line of sūtra text is on p. 132a, almost six pages from the beginning of the book. There are some vernacular constructions in the commentarial material, particularly *she-ma* ("what?") and *chei* ("this"), as we have seen is the case with Ch'an "recorded sayings." The *Chin-kang k'e-i* is thus, in effect, a combination of a modified sūtra-lecture text with the form of Ch'an "recorded sayings."

The *Diamond Sūtra* is devoted to the Mahāyāna concepts of emptiness and nonduality, and these concepts are amplified in Tsung-ching's commentary, which is itself influenced by both the Ch'an and Pure Land traditions. Its emphasis is on attaining enlightenment through realizing the buddha-nature within. This nature is in turn equated with Amitābha and the Pure Land of the West, although in some passages a more literal spatial imagery seems still to be

present. The key to transcending the insubstantiality and fleetingness of life is to attain a nondual perspective, based on the inner potential for attaining buddha-cognition that is shared by all beings.
Thus, all are promised deliverance.

The basic teaching of the *Chin-kang k'e-i* is indicated by the following passages:

The illusory body does not last long; the floating world is not firm. (p. 130a)

Some follow the wrong path of spiritual discipline and do not examine the
meaning [of this text]; they do not recognize that the enlightened *bodhi* nature is complete in each [being]; everyone is able to understand the good
roots of wisdom. Do not ask about degrees of enlightenment; stop differen-
tiating between those who remain in the household life and those who leave
it, do not adhere to [the difference between] clergy and laity. One needs only
to understand that in the mind there is fundamentally neither male nor female; why must one cling to outer forms? (p. 130b)

Do not seek far off for the Buddha on Spirit Vulture Peak (Ling-shan), for
this peak is in your own mind. Everyone possesses a Ling-shan pagoda. (p.
131a)

Question: Where does the Tao mind manifest itself?
Answer: . . . Everyone possesses the Pure Land of the West;
Do not in error devote yourself to what has already appeared [in the outer
    realm].
If superior beings and good people see into their natures,
they stand side by side with Amitābha Buddha. (p. 132a)

Every step and everything is the Way.
Amitābha never lived in the West.
The Dharma body fills all the three thousand worlds. (p. 133a)

Poverty, wealth, nobility, and humble position are all like a dream.
When one awakens from this dream,
one returns [to true understanding]. (p. 133b)

In the Dharma there is neither high nor low. Therefore, sentient beings in the
minds of the buddhas constantly attain the Way, apart from "self" and
"other." And the buddhas in the minds of sentient beings with every
thought realize the true. Thus to recite the Buddha's name does not block
meditating, and meditating is no obstacle to reciting the Buddha's name, to
the point that one recites without reciting and meditates without meditating
. . . [and] thoroughly understands the Pure Land of mind only (*wei-hsin
Ching-t'u*). (p. 140a)

For every household there is a road to Ch'ang-an. (p. 140a)

Here it is made clear that all can attain deliverance directly and easily, because such deliverance is simply a matter of insight into the true nature of one's own mind. Buddhahood consists essentially of a detached attitude, an attitude that brings acceptance and peace. This being the case, conventional buddhas depicted in images and mythology are simply symbols of what we have the potential to become. This perspective is egalitarian; there is no justification for distinctions based on social or religious status, wealth, or gender. There is no need to adopt a celibate lifestyle in a monastery, to worship buddhas imagined to be in some other realm, or to spend years in arduous meditation.[42]

As we will see in Chapter Three, Lo Ch'ing seized upon these teachings with great enthusiasm and much repetition. It is instructive to realize that this influential figure in the development of the sectarian scriptural tradition was himself deeply influenced by a text with such an egalitarian point of view, made to order for a lay leader speaking to ordinary people.[43]

Beyond its basic teachings, the *Chin-kang k'e-i* anticipates a few other terms and themes found in "precious volumes." In its introductory material it is referred to again as a *pao-chüan* (p. 130a), which may be the earliest known use of this term. In this same material homage is paid to several non-Buddhist holy personages, including the deity of the north Chen-wu, the Taoist immortal Lord Lü (Lü kung, = Lü Tung-pin), the T'ang Confucian scholar Han Wen-kung (Han Yü), "Scholar Su" (Su *hsueh-shih*), the Sung poet and essayist Su Tung-p'o, the God of the (Eastern) Peak, and such Buddhist stalwarts as Śākyamuni, Bodhidharma, the Sixth Patriarch, Layman P'ang, and Miao-shan, the heroine of the *Hsiang-shan pao-chüan* and earlier texts (p. 130b). Such homage to figures from various traditions is found in sectarian *pao-chüan* as well. However, as in later *pao-chüan*, readers of the *Chin-kang k'e-i* are told that if they "want to transcend the revolving flow of the six paths of samsaric existence, there is only the straight path of the one vehicle. One must seek for correct views and must not believe in heretical masters" (*mo hsin hsieh-shih*; p. 130b).

The term "Ling-shan" in one of the passages just translated became a name for the Eternal Mother's paradise; the phrase "the last act" (*mo-hou i cho*) occurs here as well (p. 130b) but does not yet have its sectarian eschatological reference. At one point Tsung-ching writes, "I think of Amitābha as a parent, and Amitābha looks on me as a child" (p. 140a), thus bringing a long-established theme to the threshold of sectarian consciousness. There is even the Taoist-style phrase *fan-pen huan-yuan* ("return to the origin and source"), here referring to Buddhist enlightenment but later a summons to paradise. Finally, near the end, in a passage quoted from "The Hymn of the Venerable One from Szechuan(?)" (Ch'uan lao sung), there is the phrase "little children see their mother" (*ying-erh chien-niang*; p. 144a), here made available for its later sectarian context. I have not been able to identify this hymn, which is also quoted in one of the first known sectarian *pao-chüan*, the *Huang-chi* book of 1430, discussed in Chapter Two below.

These fragmentary references in the *Chin-kang k'e-i* further indicate how close it was to the boundary between Buddhist and sectarian expositions. In it, the old Buddhist evangelistic tradition hovers on the brink of transformation into something new.

The oldest extant edition of the *Hsiang-shan pao-chüan* was reprinted in Ch'ing Ch'ien-lung 38 (1773). The original is owned by Yoshioka Yoshitoyo, who published it in 1971. The title given is *Kuan-shih-yin P'u-sa pen-hsing ching* (Sūtra of the deeds of the Bodhisattva Kuan-yin [Avalokiteśvara]); in the Ch'ing colophon it is called *Hsiang-shan pao-chüan*. This is one of the best-known "precious volumes." Yoshioka lists eight editions printed in the Ch'ing and early Republican periods, while Li Shih-yü in his *Pao-chüan tsung-lu* also lists eight, in nineteen reproductions including five manuscripts, all dating from 1850 to 1934. The titles given by Yoshioka are all called *ching* ("scriptures") and begin with *Kuan-yin* or *Kuan-shih-yin*, but also give *Hsiang-shan pao-chüan* as an alternate title. In the *Pao-chüan tsung-lu*, all but two of the texts listed have the name *Hsiang-shan* in their titles, with the most frequently reprinted title being the *Ta-sheng fa-pao Hsiang-shan pao-chüan* (The Fragrant Mountain precious volume, Dharma Jewel of the Great Vehicle).[44]

The 1773 edition, in one *chüan* with 130 folio pages, begins with a picture of Kuan-yin robed in white, seated, and attended by two acolytes. Then follow a homage to the emperor ("Ten thousand years to the present emperor, ten thousand times ten thousand years!") and a preface that praises the breadth and unfathomable wonder of the Buddhist Way, which brings benefit, protection, and blessings for unending kalpas.

The text itself begins by listing its editor and compiler, distributor, reviser, and transcriber, all described as Buddhist monks. The editor is given as the Ch'an Master P'u-ming of Hang-chou (in modern Chekiang). The introduction gives the date of P'u-ming's work as Sung Ch'ung-ning 2 (1103).

The *pao-chüan* opens with an introduction to its origin and purpose, and then proceeds to the story of a young princess in a land far away, who, after a long struggle, becomes enlightened and discovers that in fact she is Kuan-yin. This story in effect provides mythic background for the cult of Kuan-yin of a thousand eyes and arms, who sees and aids all. This edition ends with a colophon dated 1773.

The language of the text is mixed, in some sections in a late classical form, in others, in old *pai-hua* (vernacular). Though the story flows freely enough, the differences in language may indicate different sources or compilers in the history of the text.[45]

The *Hsiang-shan pao-chüan* alternates between prose and rhyming lines of seven-character verse. The verse sections both sum up the preceding prose and anticipate what happens next. The whole is basically narrative in form, with very little of the first- and second-person dialogue found in some sectarian *pao-chüan*.

Both the introductory section and the colophon indicate the nature and role of this book as its editors understood them. The introductory section (which is an integral part of the text) begins as follows:

At present, when people look at the old teaching, they cannot avoid being troubled in their minds. If one wishes to escape being so troubled, one must look at how the old teaching and the patriarchs of the Way expound to the multitudes according to the opportunity at hand.

In the past, the Ch'an Master Pao-feng [listed as the distributor of this text] long dwelt in seclusion at Lu-shan in Kiangsi, [where] he once saw a female noble being (mahāsattva) named Miao-k'ai, who took from her sleeve this section [i.e., story] about karma and brought it to where he was sitting. [She] said, "This was compiled by P'u-ming and should be circulated throughout the world."

Pao-feng responds with several illustrations of monks in the past who obtained enlightenment alone, by nonverbal means, concluding, "In both past and present, the Way has been realized from the mind; why be troubled about words?" The noble being replies,

Though such is the case, nevertheless one should also save all living beings, as did the Buddha. If you don't bring about universal salvation in the world, you are still in the place of [one who attains] solitary enlightenment, unable to receive others and bring benefit to them. [The situation] may be compared with small children crossing a river; the deep places they are unable [to cross], [but] when they come to a shallow place, they can. The meaning of the sūtra teachings is deep, but the meaning of karma is shallow, which permits people to practice it with ease.

After being assured that the person who devotes himself to saving others "will in the future certainly attain buddhahood," Master Pao-feng vows to circulate the text and proceeds to make ten copies, bowing three times for each character. He then distributes the book everywhere.

A similar account is given of Master P'u-ming, who is described as engaged in a three-month period of solitary meditation. He is approached by an old monk who says, "You practice alone the Supreme Vehicle, the correct and true Way; if you thus act alone, how will you be able to bring about universal salvation? You should carry out transformation on behalf of the Buddha (ju tang tai Fo hsing-hua), expound the three vehicles, and practice both the sudden and gradual [methods of attainment]. Then you can save all sentient beings of the middle and lower levels. Only thus will you repay the Buddha's grace." P'u-ming then asks, "With what method can I save others?"

At this, recognizing that P'u-ming has karmic affinity with Kuan-yin, the old monk tells him the story of the bodhisattva's activities from beginning to end, that it might be distributed throughout the world. After describing and explaining all, the old monk disappears, but P'u-ming, "with only one glance, edits this sūtra." At this, Kuan-yin manifests herself in all her glory, and from then on the text is known throughout the world, as a result of which numberless people attain the Way.

This introductory material thus clarifies the basic religious concern of the text, which is to make a simple and direct presentation of saving knowledge in story form.

The story itself is too long and complex to summarize adequately here. Unlike the other pao-chüan I have read, it is set outside China in a land called Hsing-lin, west of Mount Sumeru, in the time of the Buddha Kāśyapa. Hsing-lin is a mythic land, a paradise on earth, described in terms rich with Buddhist symbolism yet with a Chinese flavor. It is ruled by a great and wise emperor, Miao-chuang, who enjoys all the pleasures of life except that he has no son. In time, his wife gives birth to two daughters named Miao-shu and Miao-yin.

The queen continues to pray for a son, and four years after the birth of her second daughter, she has a dream in which two devas tell her that the Jade Emperor has invited her to the Thirty-third Heaven, there to see the Buddha and learn of the Dharma. She ascends in a carriage sent for her and sees a brilliant "theophany," the glittering paradise of Maitreya, whose name she is told to recite.

Upon her return, she wakes up in her bed and subsequently reports all to her husband. He summons all his dream interpreters, among whom is a venerable white-haired gentleman leaning on a cane. The emperor, rejoicing, asks, "Sir, where do you live?" to which the old man replies, "Your servant's home is at Le-pang [Joyous Land]: My surname is Mi [the first syllable in Maitreya's name, Mi-le Fo]." The seer tells the emperor that his wife will give birth to a bodhisattva who will bring salvation to many.

In due course a third daughter, Miao-shan, is born in a great epiphany of light, music, and divine fragrance. The rest of the story is about this girl and her struggle for enlightenment despite her father's opposition. At an early age she shows marked intelligence and a propensity for Buddhism, and at nineteen she resolves to leave the household to become a nun. The emperor, however, forbids her to do so; he has ordered all his daughters to marry, that he might at least have a son-in-law to succeed him. The older daughters agree, but Miao-shan refuses, confounding all threats and attempts to persuade her with brilliant homilies on the suffering and impermanence of saṃsāra, which cannot compare with the joyous freedom of enlightenment. She rejects all the luxuries of palace life as an empty, destructive snare and drives her father mad with rage. He accuses her of disobedience, lack of filial devotion, heresy, and witchcraft, and has her whipped and imprisoned in a palace garden, all to no avail. For her, true filial piety is to bring about the eternal salvation of one's parents, not simply to provide them with physical comfort and security.

Finally, the emperor releases her, and she goes to the White Sparrow Ch'an nunnery, where five hundred nuns are skilled at making progress in the Way. But when she arrives, the abbess accuses her of disobedience to the emperor and thus of bringing potential trouble to the nunnery. Miao-shan replies that the abbess does not understand Buddhism. To test her resolve, she alone is made responsible for meeting the physical needs of all five hundred nuns: cooking, cleaning, drawing water, ringing bells, and sounding drums. This she does cheerfully, her dedication firmer than ever, though she is soon exhausted. The Stove God, moved by her devotion, reports the situation to Shang-ti, who orders all the gods to assist her. Whereas before she had to carry water from 3 *li* away, now the Venerable Dragon of the Eastern Sea opens a well right in the kitchen. Wild animals bring firewood and birds bring vegetables, the bells and drums sound by themselves, and all the while Miao-shan meditates in the kitchen.

The nuns report the whole situation to the emperor, who, enraged, orders troops to annihilate his daughter and the nuns and to burn the buildings so that not a trace remains. When the fire begins, Miao-shan prays to all the buddhas for aid, pricks her mouth, and spits blood into the sky. At this a great rain falls, the fire is put out, and all are saved. The troops return to the palace to report that the girl is a witch.

As a result Miao-shan is arrested and sent to be executed, despite several opportunities to repent and take a husband. Her father himself pleads with her, saying that all her Buddhist beliefs are empty and false, to which she replies, "What is empty is real, and reality is empty: Those who are enlightened know this" (p. 66b). When he asks her how she can withstand the torment of punishment, she answers that "the true nature is not destroyed" (*chen-hsing pu-huai*; p. 66b).

Finally, Miao-shan is strangled with a bowstring, at which the heavens shake and all turns black. The officers report that suddenly it grew dark and a tiger came to take away her body. When she awakes, she finds to her consternation that she is in purgatory, but is told not to worry: She is there because of her filial disobedience but will not suffer. The Ten Kings of purgatory, having heard of her piety, want simply to meet her.

In purgatory, she encounters the five hundred nuns who had been killed on the emperor's orders; she vows to save them, at which the Bodhisattva Ti-tsang manifests himself in glory and leads them all directly to the Pure Land. Wherever Miao-shan goes, she delivers the inhabitants of purgatory, and she is invited by the Ten Kings to stay and preach the Dharma. Her message is so effective that orders are given to release all the spirits of the dead, but at the last minute a delegation of officials comes in to protest: If purgatory is emptied, what incentive will there be for the living to do good? If all the souls leave, what will there be left for us officials to do?

Hence Miao-shan is sent back to life, her soul rejoining her body, which has been preserved whole by a Locality God. She sees her father's city in the distance and weeps because she cannot return. As she wanders along, she meets an old man who tells her about a marvelous place called Fragrant Mountain. There she can go to meditate and attain enlightenment, surrounded by immortals and bodhisattvas. The old man is Shang-ti in disguise; he gives her a magic peach to sustain her and orders a Locality God to manifest himself as a tiger to protect and carry her. Riding on the tiger's back, she comes to Hsiang-shan, there to meditate in a grotto. One day, upon hearing the call of an ape in the valley, she is suddenly enlightened and, casting off all worldly perceptions, for the first time understands that her name is Kuan-shih-yin.

In the meantime, at Shang-ti's request, all the gods have met together to discuss the case of Emperor Miao-chuang, who has repeatedly reviled the Dharma and attacked Buddhism. As a result, disease-bearing envoys from the Board of Plagues are sent to afflict him. He falls ill with a loathsome disease that rots his body and causes a horrible stench. None of his officials or concubines will come near him; his prized sons-in-law both flee, holding their noses. Only his faithful wife tries to care for him, but nothing helps. Physicians and drugs are of no use. All his wealth and comforts turn, as it were, to ashes, his palace is like a prison, his wine and meat like excrement, his music like wailing and weeping, his bed like swords.

In desperation, he sends out a decree summoning all the physicians in the land to come and cure him, and just at this point, the "Lord Buddha of Hsiang-shan" is looking over the world, ready to give aid to those who call out in distress. When she hears the summons, she transforms herself into a ragged old monk covered with sores and goes to the palace gates carrying a medicine bag on a stick. After examining the emperor, the old monk says that his illness is so severe that only the most drastic means will cure it: a potion made of human eyes and arms. The ruler replies that no one will willingly cut off eyes and arms, no matter how much money might be offered, but the monk says that he knows an immortal on Fragrant Mountain who he believes would be willing to make such a sacrifice.

An official is sent to the mountain, where he finds a female immortal meditating in a cave. When he explains his mission, she willingly permits him to cut off her left arm and pluck out her left eye. These the official takes back to the palace, where they are used to make a healing drug. After another trip for the right arm and eye, the emperor is completely cured and, rejoicing, begins to fulfill his vow to become a Buddhist if he were made well. The old monk refuses the exalted title of "Imperial Preceptor" and suggests that the proper thing to do is to go and thank the immortal.

The whole court travels to Hsiang-shan, there to find the girl—blind, covered with blood and dust—meditating. The queen had begun to suspect the truth when she saw the marks of a buddha on the right arm when it was brought to the palace. Now she tenderly washes the girl and tends her wounds, asking insistently who she is. The immortal finally tells her that she is indeed her daughter, at which all rejoice and pray to the buddhas that she might be restored. At once her eyes and arms reappear, and all bow to worship her. Then Amitābha himself descends to recount the karmic history and destiny of Miao-shan, now the Bodhisattva Kuan-yin. Because she has given up two eyes and arms, she is repaid with a thousand arms and eyes and is henceforth to be called "World-Honored One, Teacher of Gods and Men, Supreme Lord of a Thousand Arms and Eyes, Who with Great Compassion and Pity Rescues from Suffering and Difficulty" (p. 119a).

At this the emperor and queen, together with the whole court, leave the household life and devote themselves to meditation, all to be saved. At death, all go to Amitābha's Pure Land.

The text ends with a sermon by the bodhisattva on seeing into one's true nature and realizing that the Pure Land is in one's own mind. Buddhism is triumphant, karma is justified and demonstrated, and filial devotion is fulfilled in the highest possible way. A closing exhortation speaks repeatedly of "attaining buddhahood upon seeing [one's true] nature" (*chien-hsing ch'eng fo*), warns against "seeking [the truth] on the outside," and continues:

Let all understand this story of the manifestation of the Bodhisattva Kuan-yin, realize the great Tao, and experience the joy which follows. Good men and believing women, once you have heard [this story], you will no longer be called common and lost but will forever be children of the Most Precious Dharma King, moving all the Buddhas of the Ten Directions to rejoice. The celestial gods of the three realms will all bear you up, and you will attain much merit, never going to purgatory but always being reborn in heaven above. There, experiencing the highest joy, you will not taste karma but go directly to buddhahood. (p. 130a)[46]

Though reciting Kuan-yin's name is mentioned, it is not stressed either here or in the text, nor is any sectarian flavor present.

For Yoshioka, the background of the *Hsiang-shan pao-chüan* is the theory that Maitreya and Kuan-yin are of the same substance, because Miao-shan, who becomes Kuan-yin, is a manifestation of Maitreya. He points out that a connection between these two figures can be traced back several centuries, then goes on to present evidence for the first formulation of the Miao-shan story in the twelfth century, at about the time claimed by the *pao-chüan* itself. He also discusses other versions of this story from the Yuan period and notes instances of Yuan usage in the vocabulary of the *pao-chüan*.[47]

In his 1978 *The Legend of Miao-shan*, Glen Dudbridge demonstrates that the story was known by 1100. Though the date of the original *pao-chüan* version is unknown, after a careful discussion Dudbridge places it in his "pre-1500" category, "primarily because of its remarkable internal pedigree." What emerges from its study is "a sense of internal preservation through a tradition."[48]

In its basic thought, the *Hsiang-shan pao-chüan* is a popularization of a blend of Pure Land and Ch'an teaching. It is this blend that had some influence on Lo Ch'ing, with Ch'an predominating. The other major influence of the *Hsiang-shan* text on later *pao-chüan* is its story of an intelligent, determined, and heroic woman who refuses marriage and triumphs over all opposition. This story became the prototype for many others involving both young women and young men whose lives demonstrate that morality and piety win in the end. The *Hsiang-shan* book is thus a source for both sectarian and narrative "precious volumes."

Other aspects of this book can also be seen as antecedents of later *pao-chüan*, although, as Dudbridge points out, there are "some unambiguous signs that the text of the 'Yoshioka' edition must have at least undergone revision in the Ming or Ch'ing periods."[49] As we have seen, Maitreya has a role in this text, as do such non-Buddhist deities as the Jade Emperor, Shang-ti (the Lord on High), the Ten Kings of purgatory, and the Stove God. The involvement of a variety of deities is characteristic of "precious volume" teaching. We also find other phrases or themes that are common later, such as *yu-yuan jen* ("those with karmic affinity," p. 93a), *fan-pen huan-yuan* ("return to the origin and source," p. 98b), *shih-ti kung-fu* ("religious practice in ten stages," p. 125a), and such statements as, "If, during life, one does not enter the Dragon-Flower Assembly [of Maitreya] (Lung-hua hui), after death how can one avoid saṃsāra?" (p. 113a). These themes are part of the body of the text here, but are scattered about without the mythological context that developed later. They are reminiscent of similar usages in the *Chin-kang k'e-i*.

There are other less specific antecedents here as well. Salvation in the *Hsiang-shan* book is firmly egalitarian, and Princess Miao-shan rejects class distinctions in her refusal of special treatment when she enters the nunnery (p. 42a). The abbess and supervisor of the nunnery are portrayed as unenlightened, cowardly, and cruel (pp. 42–44). In her sermon in purgatory, Miao-shan emphasizes the importance of maintaining a vegetarian diet, reciting the Buddha's name, establishing one's nature, and "contemplating emptiness" (p. 76a). All these themes are continued in later *pao-chüan*, though only Lo Ch'ing had some understanding of what "contemplating emptiness" meant. In general terms, the alternating prose and verse style of the *Hsiang-shan* book is also similar to that of the later texts, though it does not have chapter divisions or tune names.

A third early "precious volume" concerned with making Buddhist teaching understandable and acceptable to a Chinese audience is the *Mu-lien chiu mu ch'u-li ti-yü sheng t'ien pao-chüan* (Precious volume of Mu-lien rescuing his mother to escape from purgatory and ascend to heaven), which is dated to the third year of the Hsuan-kuang reign period of the Northern Yuan dynasty, or 1372. This book was collected and discussed by Cheng Chen-to in his 1938 *Chung-kuo su wen-hsueh shih* (History of Chinese vernacular literature). This version of the *Mu-lien pao-chüan* is now in the rare book room of the Beijing Library. It is an extended narration of the well-known story of the pious Mu-lien's efforts to rescue his sinful mother from purgatory. The combination of Buddhist faith with filial piety ensured the widespread popularity of this story.[50]

The first half of Cheng Chen-to's copy is missing, but the latter part is written in the combination of prose and verse, interspersed with tune names, that became the standard style of early "precious volumes." Its moral is that "all should imitate the Honored Mu-lien in being filial to their parents and seek out enlightened teachers, recite the Buddha's name, and maintain a vegetarian diet so that [for them] birth-and-death will forever stop. [All should] cultivate the Way with determination, so as to repay the profound kindness of their parents in raising and nourishing them."

In the midst of this popularized Buddhist language, there are a few phrases that seem to anticipate later sectarian teachings. The first is "raise up discussions of the Unborn (*t'i-ch'i wu-sheng yü*) and yearn to soon return to the Native Place. Those who understand perfect wisdom do not fear evil Lord Yama." The second occurs in the immediately following lines, urging filiality, recitation of the Buddha's name, burning incense, providing vegetarian food to monks, bestowing alms, and listening to the Dharma so that "little children will see their mother" (*ying-erh chien-niang*). These are the only such references in the extant half of this *Mu-lien pao-chüan*, and they can be understood, in their fundamentally orthodox Buddhist context, as expressions of the hope for salvation, augmented in the latter case by analogy to Mu-lien's search for his own mother. Here again, we find language in a pre-sectarian text that helped provide material for later mythology.[51]

CH'ÜAN-CHEN (COMPLETE PERFECTION) TAOISM

Early Taoism was the first sectarian religious tradition in China with its own organization, leaders, rituals, and teachings, and hence with a clear sense of the difference between those who gave allegiance to the Tao and those who did not. From the beginning, it emphasized the salvation of an elect in a time of chaos and decline. These Taoist themes provided antecedents for all similar emphases in later Chinese religious traditions, including the popular religious sects that produced *pao-chüan*. Richard Shek has discussed such themes in his "Daoist Elements in Late Imperial Chinese Sectarianism," which emphasizes "the perception of immortality as salvation," "eschatological vision and messianism," "the idea of election and chosenness," "the union of Mother-Child," and "techniques of salvation: alchemy, sexual union, meditation [and] breath control." In each case he cites both passages in *pao-chüan* and their Taoist background.[52] In a representative collection of Taoist texts such as the *Yun-chi ch'i-ch'ien* (Seven lots from the bookbag of the clouds), an encyclopedic compilation presented to the Sung court in 1028 or 1029, we see a number of terms and concepts that appear later in "precious volumes." These include *hun-yuan* ("chaotic prime"); cycles of cosmic time, including the three stages of past, present, and future; colored *ch'i* related to such cycles, with the color white for the third; and an emphasis on the idea that our earthly parents are not our true parents, who are described as the Tao, or "emptiness and karma." Of course, at a deeper level Taoist influence is present in *pao-chüan* mythology in its emphasis on returning to a primal source, in Lo Ch'ing's nonactivism (*wu-wei*), and in the understanding that the cosmic Tao can be personified as a mother. All this can be understood as deep or indirect Taoist influence.[53]

At a more proximate level, however, it was the Ch'üan-chen (Complete Perfection) Taoist school that had the most direct influence on *pao-chüan*. This tradition was founded by Wang Che (1112–1170), whose religious title was Ch'ung-yang. Wang, from Shensi, traveled to Shantung province on the eastern seaboard, where he gathered disciples and founded a new religious movement. At about the same time, a similar tradition took form in the south, led by Chang Po-tuan (d. 1082) of Chekiang province, who also was said to have had a close group of associates and successors who were considered patriarchs of his tradition, called the school of the "Golden Elixir" (Chin-tan). By the fourteenth century, the teachings and patriarchal traditions of these schools merged under the common name "Ch'üan-chen," a tradition that continues to exist today, with its own temples, priests, and texts.

According to the research of Stephen Eskildsen at the University of British Columbia, early Ch'üan-chen practice involved a rigorous ascetic quest for enlightenment based on long-established Taoist traditions of nurturing the vital force within the body. Those who so perfected themselves were believed to attain mystical powers that they used for healing and the relief of other forms of suffering. Ch'üan-chen was a combination of self-perfection with compassionate outreach toward others. This outreach took the form of rituals of community renewal and exorcism, much as was the case with other Taoist schools.[54]

The Golden Elixir school was best known for its inner or physiological alchemy, in which bodily organs, processes, and fluids were identified with those of the alchemical furnace. This quest for nurturing the "inner elixir" (*nei-tan*) was expressed in symbolic terminology based on ancient systems of classification, such as the sixty-term cycle of the "celestial stems and earthly branches," the sixty-four hexagrams of the *Book of Changes*, and the interaction of the Five Phases (wood, fire, earth, metal, and water). This symbolism also involved that of metals, such as mercury and lead, which were associated with psycho-physiological processes. This symbolic terminology was also used by Ch'üan-chen writers.

Mention of this tradition is necessary here because, beginning in the fifteenth century, some *pao-chüan* refer to terms from it, and to the names of the earlier schools themselves, Ch'üan-chen and Chin-tan. Almost all such references I have found are fragmentary and superficial; Taoist terms seem to be evoked for their residual numinous power rather than out of real understanding, but this can be true of *pao-chüan* use of Buddhist terms as well. There is no indication in *pao-chüan* of the sustained, rigorous self-perfecting practice of the early Ch'üan-chen tradition, which sectarian writers adopted in a depleted form at best. Nonetheless, as is discussed in more detail in Chapters Five and Six below, Taoist terms were known to some of these writers, though how the connection was made is not yet clear. Ch'üan-chen and Chin-tan texts are in classical language, full of abstruse symbolism; they are an entirely different kind of literature from *pao-chüan*. Perhaps it was later Ch'üan-chen preachers and healers who got the message out in terms that could be understood and used by literate lay sectarians for their own purposes. The matter deserves further research.

In geographical terms, such contact was possible because the earliest sectarian *pao-chüan* appeared in North China, in the general area where Ch'üan-chen was active. Although most of the early Ch'üan-chen masters were from Shantung, several of them spent time in the capital at Yenching (present Beijing), where an important Ch'üan-chen temple was founded. In the twelfth and thirteenth centuries, some Ch'üan-chen leaders received recognition and support from Chin and Mongol emperors, which would have facilitated proselytization. That Ch'üan-chen evangelists were effective is indicated by Judith Boltz, who notes that the teachings of one of them "were so much a part of local culture that many people were known to recite them verbatim. His quotability was no doubt due in part to an effective use of rhythmic repetitions in both prose and prosodic compositions." Of another preacher and leader we are told that "wherever he went he was said to have drawn large crowds and inspired the construction of many new temples." Of yet a third we read that, in 1227, he "began leading large congregations southward in a massive evangelistic mission. Countless new temples were built to accommodate the thousands of converts, and one of the [master's] disciples was put in charge of each parish." Such large-scale missionary efforts would have made it easy for outsiders to learn something of this tradition.[55]

Ted Tao-chung Yao discusses several Yuan dynasty dramas based on Ch'üan-chen themes and characters, and notes that one dramatist in particular had "a rather thorough knowledge of Ch'üan-chen Taoism." He also mentions Ch'üan-chen material in Ming novels and two nineteenth-century popular biographies devoted to stories about Wang Che and his disciples. Here again, we see that there was ample opportunity for sectarian authors to learn of this tradition.[56]

In sum, though sectarian *pao-chüan* were influenced by a number of earlier types of texts, there was nothing quite like them before they appeared. Their closest antecedents in time were the *Chin-kang k'e-i*, the *Hsiang-shan pao-chüan*, and the *Mu-lien pao-chüan*, but sectarian authors neither wrote ritual amplifications of sūtras nor based their teachings entirely on stories, so even here there are important differences. The existence of one other pre-sectarian "precious volume" has been proposed, but the case for it is not convincing (see Appendix A). *Pao-chüan* teachings about the end of the age were anticipated by several hundred years in earlier forms of indigenous scriptures, but what connections there may have been are unknown. We will see that Lo Ch'ing cited a number of sources, and that his own writings influenced those of other sectarian leaders, but with this exception direct quotations are rare in this genre.

In retrospect we can see antecedents, but in most cases it is not clear how they were known to the authors of *pao-chüan*, who had their own ways of putting things together. The result was a new form of religious literature with its own distinctive content and style. As with other forms of human creativity, it was fresh imagination working on fragments of old material that led to a new creation. The results may not always be aesthetically or intellectually satisfying to us, but they have worked well for their intended audiences over a period of several hundred years.[57]

An Early Model: The Bureaucracy of Salvation in a Fifteenth-Century Text, the 'Huang-chi pao-chüan'

On March 16, 1991, Thomas S. Y. Li (Li Shih-yü) visited the apartment of a retired Chinese scholar named Lu Kung, a researcher with the Beijing University Library and an officer of the Chinese Vernacular Literature Study Association. Among the antiquities in Lu Kung's collection, Mr. Li found a sectarian *pao-chüan* ("precious volume") dated (Ming) Hsuan-te 5 (1430 C.E.)—about eighty years earlier than what had been believed to be the oldest such texts, and the oldest I have read. Due to other appointments, Mr. Li was unable to examine the book at that time.[1] On October 7 and 8, 1991, Mr. Li and I returned to Lu Kung's apartment to photograph the book, entitled the *Fo-shuo Huang-chi chieh-kuo pao-chüan* (The precious volume, expounded by the Buddha, on the [karmic] results of [the teaching of] the Imperial Ultimate [period]; hereafter "the *Huang-chi* book"). It was very old and fragile but appeared to be complete. In it, the path to deliverance is discussed in an intensely bureaucratic way.

This book, bound in the accordion style[2] common to Chinese Buddhist scriptures, is in two volumes (*chüan*) and fifteen chapters (*p'in*). There is no information about the place of publication, but the following line appears at the end of volume 1: "Printed on the first day of the first month of spring in the fifth year of the [Ming] Hsuan-te [reign period]." The dates of this reign period are 1426–1435 by the Western calendar; the first day of the first lunar month of the fifth year corresponds to January 24, 1430. On the back cover of volume 2 is the following inscription:

The Buddha is on Mount Ling; do not look for him afar. Mount Ling is in your own mind. Everyone has a Mount Ling monastery [in his or her mind], so go to your Mount Ling pagoda to carry out religious practice.

Poorly transcribed by the Patriarch of Gathering in the Primal Ones (Shou-yuan tsu), the Principal Altar Master of the Dragon-Flower Assembly (Lung-hua hui cheng t'an-chu).[3]

The *Huang-chi* book is written in relatively simple classical Chinese in alternating sections of prose and verse, with many vernacular terms and constructions (for a list of vernacular terms used, see Appendix B). On the inside cover are pictures of three figures seated on platforms with their legs crossed, surrounded by acolytes. The central figure is a buddha, with mustached male Chinese figures on either side, whom I have not yet been able to identify.[4]

On the next opening panel there are four lines of four-character verse:

May the imperial realm be forever secure,
May the emperor's Way long prosper,
May the sun of the Buddha increase its brilliance,
May the Wheel of the Dharma always turn.

This is followed by the line "Ten thousand years to the emperor, ten thousand times ten thousand years!"

Then comes a general invocation of blessings in eighteen lines of four-character verse, preceded by the words *yü-chih* ("produced by imperial authorization"):[5]

May [all] in the six directions be pure and at peace, [and] the seven regulators [sun, moon, and planets] follow their proper sequences.
May rain and sunshine be timely, [and] all the myriad creatures be abundant.
May all the myriads of people be in health and harmony, [and] the nine dark [courts of purgatory] be brightened.
May all equally live to a happy old age [and] widely sow fields of good karma.
May the goodness of superiors reach into the distance [and] their obstacles be removed.
May families honor loyalty and filial piety, [and] people enjoy kindness and goodness.

May officials be pure and their administration fair, [with] lawsuits few and punishments put aside.

May conduct be transformed and customs beautified, with the Way of prosperity successful for all.

May all that lives attain the fruit of buddhahood.

This preliminary material is repeated verbatim in many sectarian scriptures for the next four hundred years. After a long introductory section, the first chapter begins with its title, followed by an extended prose dialogue between the Buddha and one or more named questioners. In each chapter this discussion begins with the words, "At that time the Buddha was seated upright on Mount Ling, when suddenly [so and so] came forward, bowed, and asked, 'Our Buddha, Tathāgata, suppose your disciple(s) had . . . .'" From this point on the discussion alternates between *Fo yen* ("the Buddha said") and [so and so] *yen* ("so and so said"), which I translate "replied" and "asked," respectively.

In each chapter there are usually thirty to thirty-five lines of this prose dialogue, with fifteen characters per line. This is followed by two parallel lines of seven-character verse, centered on the page, which introduce eighteen more lines of seven-character verse, each in two stanzas. This verse, which does not rhyme, recapitulates the Buddha's teaching in the preceding prose section, adding a bit more detail. The 7/7 verse is followed by two or three lines of prose, which moves directly to two lines of rhyming five-character verse, each in two stanzas. This is succeeded by about ten lines of blank verse, arranged 3/3/4 characters per line. After this comes the name of a tune from Chinese opera, in three characters, which introduces a section printed in prose form but in fact consisting of rhyming seven-character stanzas. After about twenty-three such stanzas, the chapter ends. These hymns are pious repetition, adding little or no new content (for a list of the tune names in the *Huang-chi* book, see Appendix C).

Unfortunately, not all the chapters follow this pattern as neatly as one might wish because some of the pages in the early chapters of each volume are out of order. After they fell apart at some time in the past, someone carelessly pasted them together from the back without noting their proper order. In volume 2, part of chapter 12 precedes chapters 10 and 11. However, with care, most of the correct order can be reconstructed.

The basic message of this book is that it is a new revelation of a path to heaven for those with the right karma who believe and practice its rituals. Its orientation is external and bureaucratic; the path to heaven is blocked by many passes (*kuan*), each guarded by deities and spirits, and only those with the proper documents will be admitted. Of these documents, the most important are memorials (*piao*) that are sent ahead and tablets (*p'ai*) that accompany one on the journey; in each case, the vital information included is the person's title (*hao*). At each pass, these titles are investigated and compared with those already received; every item and character must be correct; if not, the soul is sent back to earth to be reborn in saṃsāra. Those who are accepted are eventually admitted to a special heaven described as hitherto not revealed, the "Red Canopy Heaven" (Hung-lo t'ien), where they are appointed to office. All this is described as sharing the same principle as government administration in the human realm.

The temporal setting of this revelation is the near future (*tang-lai*), to be ruled by the Buddha Maitreya, who replaces the Buddha Śākyamuni. Eons ago, Śākyamuni in turn replaced the Buddha Janteng (Dīpaṃkara). In each case the Dharma, or teaching, of the Buddha eventually ran its course and the human condition decayed until a new messenger appeared. In the *Huang-chi* book, the reigns of these buddhas are correlated with temporal periods called "apexes" (*chi*), for which I sometimes provide the conventional translation of "ultimate" — the Ultimate of Nonbeing (Wu-chi) for Dīpaṃkara, the Great Ultimate (T'ai-chi) for Śākyamuni, and the Imperial Ultimate (Huang-chi) for Maitreya.

The revelation of this book is provided at the very end of Śākyamuni's Dharma (*mo-fa*), just before the new dispensation by Maitreya; hence its title, *The Precious Volume, Expounded by the Buddha, on the [Karmic] Results of [the Teaching of] the Imperial Ultimate [Period]*. It is thus an eschatological message, promising hope to the pious that they will survive the disasters at the end of the age and attain rebirth in paradise. There is no hint in this book that the world itself will be transformed, only that an elect will be delivered from it (*ch'u-shih*). This message of hope is reinforced by the alternative title of the book, *Shou-yuan pao-chüan* (The precious volume of gathering in to completion), which refers to the reunion and deliverance of all the pious in the last age. With *yuan* as "primal," this term also refers to the revealing patriarch of that same name.

The other side of this message is repeated condemnation of "heretical traditions and nonbelievers" (hsieh-tsung wai-tao),[6] whose chief defect is their ignorance of the proper rituals and documents. Without correct belief and rituals, they are condemned to eternal rebirth in the sufferings of birth-and-death. This distinction is reinforced by that between those with the "proper karmic affinity" (yu-yuan jen) and those who "lack the proper karmic destiny" (wu-fen jen). In theory, only the former can respond to this new message, but the book includes a few statements to the effect that even heretics can be saved if they repent and adopt correct belief and practice. Hence the resounding last sentence of volume 2: "May all the ordinary and holy from antiquity to the present, [those in] purgatory and heaven, of all the myriad realms and all classes of people, all enter the great ritual arena of the Imperial Ultimate."

The intention and self-understanding of the Huang-chi book are clearly set forth in its introductory and concluding sections. The introductory material at the beginning of volume 1 opens with an invocation to all the buddhas and bodhisattvas to descend to the altar, there

to gather in all types of beings, that they may soon ascend on the journey to the clouds (yun-ch'eng). The supreme, profound, subtle, and wonderful Dharma is difficult to encounter in a myriad of kalpas. I now, having seen and heard it, have been able to receive and maintain it, and I wish to explain the true message of the Tathāgata's [teaching]. I have heard that the three buddhas putting the world in order (chih-shih) is the root of the single vital force of the origin in primal chaos. The five patriarchs matching [i.e., corresponding to] the apexes is really a continuation of the vast mist of the Prior Realm (Hsien-t'ien). Establishing Heaven and Earth depends only on the holy; becoming patriarchs and attaining buddhahood resides in religious self-cultivation. Each lamp continues the last, to be transmitted for a thousand years. From patriarch to patriarch, [the message] has been transmitted for myriad ages down to the present. I, [so and so,] reverence the saints and sages of the ten directions who, manifesting themselves, sit in the ritual arena.

Homage to the Literary Buddha Śākyamuni and to the two great bodhisattvas Mañjuśrī (Wen-shu) and Samantabhadra (P'u-hsien), and to all the multitudes of sages and gods filling the sky.

Take refuge in all the Buddhas of the Ten Directions, the Dharma, and the Sangha; may the Wheel of the Dharma constantly turn to save all living beings.

Now, by using [this] Shou-yuan pao-chüan, one is able to summon the six types of persons to be saved (*liu-tu*),[7] so that they raise their heads and re-turn to the origin and the true tradition. It skillfully distinguishes heretical traditions and explains inner and outer beliefs. Those who bestow and maintain it see the light and see and hear about [their] true natures. Those who joyfully accord with it are all awakened to *bodhi* [enlightenment]. [Its truth] flows and penetrates everywhere, in heaven and among humans, in all the continents and islands. The *Shou-yuan pao-chüan* has fifteen chapters; each chapter distinguishes true from false; it is the true tradition of returning to the origin.

[Those who accept the teachings of this book] avoid the eight difficulties (*pa-nan*)[8] and do not suffer from evil rebirths. For those who hear the *Shou-yuan* [book], the passes to the twelve [celestial] palaces are not blocked. For those who return to the origin, there are seventy-two roads to the clouds; all the gods reverence and uphold them, they realize the Imperial Ultimate and do not fall into the four forms of rebirth as animals; they enter the nine-[petaled] lotus and do not suffer in the six paths of sentient existence.[9]

The scriptures of the world are many and vast, but this whole scripture is [composed of] wonderful verses. Each verse distinguishes guest and host [the Buddha and his interlocutors]; it is [teaches] the root source of the three buddhas establishing the world. It is really [that by which] the five patri-archs arranged Heaven and established Earth; it explains [the time] before the single vital force of the origin in primal chaos of the Prior Realm, and discusses the sequence of the Five Phases [that emerged from] the vast mist of creative chaos. The Ancient Buddha established [its] teaching, and the myriad sages bestowed the truth. He sent the *Shou-yuan* [book] to save all the patriarchs, to return to emptiness (*kuei-k'ung*; here "go to heaven"), to establish the Great Vehicle [of deliverance], and to transform the myriad classes of beings, so that all return to the lotus. [This book] is able to open up the confused minds of heretics and nonbelievers. It skillfully explains the profound meaning of "the head leader and the boat captain."[10] When one intones its mantras, the myriad sages descend to the [ritual] arena. When one recites its wonderful teaching, all the gods come to protect. It is really a good prescription for leaving the world behind.

The *pao-chüan* of the world are limitless, [but when one] uses this book, the whole book is a sharp blade for splitting open heretical traditions, a steel sword for chopping nonbelievers. When deviant schools (*p'ang-men*) see it, they are terrified. . . but if the primal ones (*yuan-jen*) are willing to have faith in it, they will soon attain buddhahood.

This pious hyperbole is repeated in varying forms throughout the introductory section of volume 1. Some of the more detailed discus-sions in this material are analyzed later in this chapter; it remains to mention a few other points that illustrate the basic orientation of the book. These include a reference to Maitreya at the Imperial Ultimate

Assembly, where he will be in charge of the "White Yang teaching" (Pai-yang chiao). The narrator of the book adds, "I first sent thirty-six patriarchs to descend to the ordinary [world]; I handed them over to blend in and descend to humankind, where they are to devote themselves solely to creating the world of the future (*chuan tsao tang-lai shih-chieh*)." The interlocutor in this section is the First Emperor of the Ch'in dynasty, who, after a description of the calamities and destruction of the world that accompany the last age, asks the Buddha how he knows all this. The Buddha replies:

You don't know about the "three apexes" of our sect (*tsa-p'ai*). . . . You don't understand the teaching established by our sect of the three buddhas in turn being in charge of the teaching (*chang-chiao*). The five patriarchs have come and gone in response to the apexes; after going around, it begins again. The people of the great earth are lost and confused. Now the years of the end kalpa (*mo-chieh*) are coming.

All this is described in more detail in a section of 7/7 verse, where we are told that in the time of the Lamplighter Buddha (Jan-teng), the celestial golden lotus had three leaves. This was the time of the Green Yang Assembly, which lasted for nine kalpas. Then the calamities of water, fire, and wind were released. Those with good karma were able to ascend the road to the clouds; those without it were "drowned in stupidity and lust" (*ch'en-ch'ih*). Then Śākyamuni

With the light of his body refined the world, [and]
For eighteen kalpas manifested himself and corresponded to the apex.
He controlled and fixed the wind, clouds, thunder, and rain;
The myriad phenomena and all the gods were in his charge.
Then, seeing that the celestial primordial kalpas were complete,
It was Maitreya who was in charge of the stars and constellations.
He personally inquired about our school and sent down commands,
Wanting to put in order the nine-leafed lotus that is about to come.
The time of the nine-leafed lotus is that of the White Yang Assembly, which "is in charge of the Imperial Ultimate."
Then the Ancestral Mother [Matriarch] of the passes (Kuan-k'ou tsu-mu) examines the tablets and titles [of devotees].
If anything at all is missing, [they] are deficient [and so] are returned to the Eastern Land to continue their religious practices.
[I] fear only that people will die and this book be scattered.
When the ten steps of religious practices are complete, buddhahood is attained.
[Those of the] same names and titles are put in charge of stars and constellations;

They escape the three calamities and eight difficulties, [and] forever [enjoy]
    the blessings and long life of the primal body (*yuan-shen*).
Those who have tablets and titles are children of the Imperial Apex;
Those who do not have them are heretical branches [i.e., sects] (*hsieh-chih*).
Those who have memorials and prayer texts are first to send them forward;
Those who do not have them are unable to understand.[11]

The introductory section ends with a discussion of Amitābha in a
role similar to that of the Eternal Mother in sixteenth-century *pao-
chüan*. Amitābha is indicated by the forty-eight vows that he took to
declare his intention to save all:

The Ancient Buddha in the Great Ultimate [Palace] was grieved and worried, and looked tearfully at sentient beings sinning without limit. He repeatedly [sent] letters, and over and over spoke with you (*ni*) of his forty-
eight great vows, but you paid no attention at all. Morning and night, at
home he pondered; the nine-leafed lotus had no place for its school. He first
sent men to open up new fields, and then sent others to set forth the details
(*ch'u-hsi*).[12]

[This] *Shou-yuan* book of blessings of the last age is difficult to encounter. [It
discusses] many kinds of religious practice and limitless types of incense. Its
tablets and titles and personal communications (*ch'in wen*) are compared by
the Matriarch of the Passes with "ten harvests for nine plantings" [i.e., gen-
erosity], and [those who have them are] united with the vital force of the
Prior Realm. Those with karmic blessings together enter the Dragon-Flower
Assembly.

The primordial origins claimed for the *Huang-chi* book have already
been noted, and chapter 5 makes it clear that this gives it priority
over all other scriptures. Here three "men of the Way" (*tao-jen*) ask
the Buddha:

We have heard it said that Heaven, Earth, the gods, buddhas, the myriad
phenomena, the stars and constellations, and all things on earth are all unable to escape the three calamities, while the nine streams of the three
teachings cannot avoid being entangled in the eight difficulties. We, your
disciples, relying on Buddhist teachings and canons, have saved people, patiently maintained a vegetarian diet, given up our wealth, offered flowers,
provided vegetarian feasts for monks, and bestowed alms. Can we attain the
right fruits [for our piety], pay homage to the primal ones, and escape the
three calamities and eight difficulties?
    The Buddha replied, "Even if you discuss with thorough understanding
the theories of a thousand schools yet do not encounter the *Shou-yuan* book,
it is merely idle [talk]."

All this is summed up in the closing pages of the book, where we are told that

the *Shou-yuan pao-chüan* is the wonderful teaching of the Ancient Buddha; it first transmitted the true tradition of returning to the origin. . . . Each section teaches people to reject the false and seek for the true; each sentence causes those who study it to discard the outer and enter the inner. Those who give allegiance to it [attain] the correct fruits and pay homage to the primal ones. Those who believe and bestow it are at peace at the apex and secure in their positions. Fundamentally, pure vital force returns to Heaven, while impure *ch'i* enters the Earth. With humanity and righteousness, the Golden Elixir[13] book; without friends, [*sic*] without discrepancy, ascend the ladder to Heaven. . . . Those who hear this book should listen to it day and night. . . . Proclaim this book (*hsuan-chüan*) one step at a time to guide the confused and lost.

Apart from its intrinsic interest as a statement of early fifteenth-century popular religion and thought, the *Huang-chi pao-chüan* is of utmost importance for the study of Chinese sectarian scriptures because it is one of the oldest of its type discovered thus far. Until now, contemporary scholarship has agreed that the earliest books written by founders of popular religious sects to expound their doctrines were those published by Lo Ch'ing (1442–1527) in 1509 (discussed in Chapter Three below). In this view, the mythology of the Eternal Venerable Mother (Wu-sheng lao-mu) that came to dominate six-teenth-century *pao-chüan* began as a personification of more abstract discussions of the Buddha's love in Lo Ch'ing's writings.[14] However, as we shall see, there are thirty references to mother-goddesses in the *Huang-chi* book, some of whom are called "Lao-mu" (Venerable Mother), though none has the central importance of Wu-sheng lao-mu in some sixteenth-century texts. In this book, as in Lo Ch'ing's earliest writings, this role of the grieving "parent" is played by the Buddha Amitābha. Thus Lo Ch'ing may have helped to shape and centralize the goddess concept, but he was abstracting from an ear-lier, more specific tradition.

The *Huang-chi* book is also valuable for its references to the three stages of cosmic time, to the role of Maitreya, and to various Taoist-appearing terms and themes, none of which is part of Lo Ch'ing's teachings. There is an early sixteenth-century sectarian scripture based on these concepts, but it was published in 1523, only fourteen years after Lo Ch'ing's books, the *Huang-chi chin-tan chiu-lien cheng-hsin kuei-chen huan-hsiang pao-chüan* (The precious volume of the golden elixir and nine lotuses of the Imperial Ultimate period [that leads to] rectifying belief, reverting to the real, and returning to [our] true home), which is discussed in Chapter Four below. I have long been perplexed by how such a well-developed statement of very different teachings could have appeared so soon after Lo Ch'ing supposedly invented the genre but without any reference to him or his ideas. In a 1989 paper, I commented as follows about *pao-chüan* based on Eternal Mother mythology:

> For me the most intriguing puzzle of early *pao-chüan* history is the rapid development of texts of this last type, which are essentially vehicles of the new sectarian mythology of the Eternal Mother and her children. The first texts of this sort appeared within two or three decades after Lo Ch'ing's books were published, yet their mythology of three stages of salvation history is well-developed. One suspects that there must have been a sectarian oral tradition of this kind before the sixteenth century.[15]

With the discovery of the *Huang-chi pao-chüan*, this puzzle is now largely solved: there was at least one book, and there were probably others, expounding the three-stage sectarian mythology decades before Lo Ch'ing came along. The 1523 *Huang-chi* book—hereafter called "the *Chiu-lien* (Nine lotus) book"—is based on a 1430 antecedent. Lo Ch'ing did not invent the genre; he refined it and took it in a new direction, but it was the teachings of books older than his that came to dominate sectarian mythology and that even influenced books by his later followers. I return again to a most intriguing comment (already quoted above) from the introductory section of the *Huang-chi* book: "The *pao-chüan* of the world are limitless." Who knows what else we may find that was spared the depredations of the Red Guards?

The remainder of this chapter discusses six themes or topics important to our understanding of the *Huang-chi* book: (1) its mythology and general teachings, (2) the roles of mother-goddesses and other deities, (3) the bureaucratic organization of rituals and documents, (4) its ethical teachings, (5) its criticism of "heretics and nonbelievers," and (6) the sectarian self-understanding that is the basis of that criticism. These themes are all interconnected, and the distinctions I attempt to make are simply for the convenience of discussion. The chapter ends with a section comparing the teachings of the *Huang-chi* book with those of other traditions, and with concluding comments.

MYTHOLOGY AND GENERAL TEACHINGS

The mythology and general teachings of the *Huang-chi* book have already been introduced in some of the passages quoted above. Because the book's central concerns are the correct rituals and documents necessary for admission to paradise, its references to doctrines and myths are scattered about in this ritual matrix. They are not presented in a connected manner, nor are they always coherent in relation to one another. There are theoretical or theological assumptions here, but they are usually implicit and less developed than the doctrines of some sixteenth-century texts.

Perhaps the safest place to begin is with a list of the "ten steps of religious practices" (*shih-pu hsiu-hsing*) in chapter 9, which sums up the chief concerns of the *Huang-chi* book in a dialogue between the Buddha and three "men of the Way" (*tao-jen*) whom he accuses of being concerned only with human nature (*hsing*). He ridicules this inward-turning orientation in favor of an external theological and ritual teaching enumerated in ten steps. These ten steps are not clearly defined, but each of them is correlated in sequence with the first ten chapters of the book. Completing them is the fundamental prerequisite for attaining salvation. Here and elsewhere, my translation is as accurate as I can make it, but I cannot make the text more coherent than it is. This is, after all, a popular religious text with many of its own terms and interpretations of terms; hence the more context, the better.

The dialogue in chapter 9 says much about the confident self-understanding of the *Huang-chi* book. The title of the chapter is "T'ien-k'uo teng-yun" (Ascending to the clouds on the wide [road] to heaven), the paradise in question being the Red Canopy Heaven mentioned above. The Buddha's three interlocutors here are named Tsao-hsiang (Morning Incense), Wu-ming (Awakened and Enlightened), and Wan-feng (Ten Thousand Peaks). After bowing before the Buddha, they begin by saying:

"We, on behalf of the Buddha, have been transmitting the Dharma, exhorting and transforming the lost and confused, and cultivating and practicing the correct Way. All of us want to attain buddhahood and become patriarchs, and to escape the three calamities and eight difficulties. Will this really be or not? Will we obtain this or not?"

The Buddha replied, "You people who stir up confusion and disorder the Way talk only about the one word 'human nature' (*hsing*), but you don't know where the nature rests. When you complete your years and return to emptiness, you don't know where emptiness is. You understand the ordinary but not the holy. How are you going to be able to attain buddhahood and thoroughly understand the Way (ch'eng fo liao tao)? How are you going to escape the eight difficulties and three calamities? Moreover, as for the one term 'the nature,' who will come to escort you [home]? Who will come to take you? Think back to the beginning, when your mother did up her hair in twin chignons and your father's hair was disheveled [i.e., before they were married]:[16] Where did your nature come from? When you die and are cremated and buried, where will your nature go? If you don't understand the situation before you were born, after you die you will still be confused. How are you going to escape from the disasters and difficulties? Who is going to rescue and protect you?"

The three men, in agitation, knelt down [and said], "We hope for your compassion, oh Buddha. Have pity on your disciples; take us home with you."

The Buddha replied, "You men who do not understand what is valuable, how are you going to understand the root and source? When I think back to when I first began to cultivate the Way, [I remember] that I only obtained the position of Buddha Corresponding to Yang (Tang-yang Fo) after descending to be reborn ten times and undergoing limitless suffering. [After] eighteen kalpas, the Buddha Maitreya will be in charge of the teaching (chang chiao) and will obtain a nine-leafed golden lotus. His age will extend for eighty-one kalpas, and his heaven will be vast. . . .

"The Ancient Buddha has personally permitted [us] to practice his Way, which only has people [follow] ten steps to the top. . . . Those who wish to be [reborn as] sentient beings should simply follow [the path that leads there]. But those who want to attain buddhahood, regardless of who they are, must [employ] the religious practice in ten steps and the 'ten-steps' incense: even if they go back and forth three thousand times and endure a myriad of sufferings, they will practice their way out to the Heaven Beyond Heaven. . . . [However, with what you discuss,] you will not escape the hand of Lord Yama [of purgatory] and will all fall into the three [lower] paths of purgatory."

The three men asked, "Which ten steps?"

The Buddha replied, "First, you must worship Heaven and Earth diligently and attentively [offer] incense, and be filial and caring toward your parents. Second, you must ask that your basic nature [sic] transcend the ordinary and holy, and [you must] reverence your predecessors [in the faith]. Third, know where to come to rest (hsia-lo); do not cheat. Honor and respect superiors. Fourth, offer incense unceasingly in the four seasons and be friendly to fellow villagers. Fifth, know the four forms of purification, respond to celestial primal [ones] (t'ien-yuan), and be diligent and attentive in your occupations (sheng-li). Sixth, receive the Ten Buddhas, know about the palaces [of heaven], and instruct your descendants [about them]. Seventh, you must mark the dark passes (*tien hsuan-kuan*), continue the Lotus school, and not follow heretics and nonbelievers. Eighth, you must enter the Red Canopy [Heaven], refine your basic nature, and penetrate profound emptiness. Ninth, you must enter the wide [road] to heaven and know the paths of the three buddhas of the Latter Realm. Tenth, you must receive tablets and titles, realize the position due you [as a result of your piety], and enter the three perfections.

"Only one who has [completed] these ten steps can attain buddhahood and thoroughly comprehend the Way. If you don't have these ten steps, then you will all fall into stupidity and futility (*wan-k'ung*)."

This discussion ends with the Buddha emphasizing that these steps must be accomplished one at a time and in proper order. With this dialogue and its rather miscellaneous list, we are in the heart of the style and content of the *Huang-chi pao-chüan*.

The mythological framework of this book is that of the three buddhas, each of whom rules eons of time and all of whom seem to be understood as manifestations of the Ancient Buddha (Ku Fo), here equated with Amitābha,[17] who is also the narrator of the book. This primordial buddha is the creator of the world. In what appears to be part of chapter 10, the Buddha responds forcefully to questions about how buddhahood is to be attained and asks his questioners:

"What religious practice have you used? What steps [i.e., levels] of tablets and titles do you wish to receive? To which heaven do you wish to go to be examined (*ta-ch'a*, lit. "respond to investigation")? At which office will your titles be checked (*tui-hao*)? Which gods are in charge [of it]? Which patriarch will receive your documents (*shou-chao*)? Only in the future will you be able to attain buddhahood and thoroughly understand the Way. If you do not have tablets and titles, stop talking about attaining buddhahood. It will be difficult for you [even] to attain human form [in your next rebirth]."

The three men asked, "When you first attained buddhahood, where did you receive a tablet and title?"

The Buddha replied, "You people don't know anything at all about the cloud realm I put in proper order, or about the Tu-tou Palace that I govern, or about the three apexes of our sect, the five [celestial] realms, the four valued [things] that I distinguished,[18] the fruits of buddhahood and the bodhisattvas that I established, the true tablets and titles that I made, the three calamities and eight difficulties that I set forth, the myriad phenomena that I gathered together, the wind, clouds, thunder, and rain that I established, the mountains, rivers, and great earth that I produced, or the gardens and forests in the five valleys to which I gave growth. I nourished and gave life to you."

This theme of the Buddha as creator was continued by Lo Ch'ing later on.

There is a fair amount of additional material on the buddhas of the three periods of cosmic time, and on the sins and disasters that characterize the end of an eon. In chapter 6 the Buddha says the Janteng was associated with a three-leafed golden lotus and with reciting the "four-character buddha-name." He was "the Buddha of the Past." Śākyamuni is associated with a five-leafed golden lotus and the recitation of a "six-character buddha-name." He is "the Buddha of the Present." The Buddha continues, "What we practice is the nine-leafed golden lotus. It is only by reciting the ten-character buddha-name that one 'completes the Way.' The other one- and three-character recitations are not the orthodox tradition (cheng-tsung)." Unfortunately, what these recitations are is not specified, but the "ten-character [name] of the future" is very likely an invocation of Maitreya.

In the introductory section of the Huang-chi book, we are told that for each of the "three buddhas there are the three calamities, and for each of the three apexes there are the eight difficulties. If this were not so, those who cultivate karmic blessings would not be as good as those who fall into evil actions, and those who do good would not be the equal of those who do bad. One wouldn't know who was true and who was false."

However, though such trials may be necessary to clarify the moral situation, the disasters that most people encounter are due to their own sins. In chapter 11 the Buddha says, "Now the years of the end of the Dharma are coming, and people's minds are perverse and clever. They do not rely on celestial principles. They do not practice the correct Way. What they say is good, but what they do is bad. What they say [seems] true, but what they do is false, [and the same for real and empty, correct and heretical]."

This condemnation of sinners is elaborated on in chapter 12, where the Buddha says, "During the nine kalpas of the Green Yang Assembly and the eighteen kalpas of the Red Yang Assembly, people born in the world [have been infatuated with] wine, sex, and wealth. They have been eager [to compete with] one another for high status, they have killed living beings, interlocked yin and yang [i.e., had illicit sexual intercourse], and created limitless karmic hindrances [for themselves]."

Such condemnation raises the issue of how many will be saved when the end comes, which chapter 14 deals with in the bureaucratic style characteristic of this book. The chapter begins with the Buddha's questioners saying,

"Oh Buddha, [you] first set forth the six ways of deliverance (*liu-tu*) and the myriad forms of [proper] conduct, [and sent] thirty-six [patriarchs]. Then you sent the two men 'Light' and 'Dark' to gather in to completion and set forth the details. If they don't enter the school [of this] book (*chüan-tsung*), people cannot enter the celestial realm. But we don't know the number. How many will be gathered in and [so] complete [the path laid out by this] book (*liao-chüan*)?"

The Buddha responds that when "the future time arrives, the sky will flash with lightning and the earth will collapse. The four celestial bushels [*sic*] will sway back and forth, and the stars will be disordered." There follows a long list of the names of celestial offices to which the elect will be appointed, which are discussed below. The sixteenth-century theme of ninety-six myriads of the Mother's children who will eventually be saved does not appear in this book. And as we shall see, the cosmic collapse noted briefly here is also much elaborated on in the following century.

But in the end the pious will be saved, and their goal is clear: to attain office in one of the divisions of the Red Canopy Heaven (Hung-lo t'ien), the special paradise of this book, which we are told in chapter 8 is the "heaven of the future" (*wei-lai t'ien*) that "the thousand sages did not transmit and of which the patriarchs did not speak." The way to it is the "broad road to heaven" (*t'ien-k'uo lu*). In it there are five furnaces (*lu*) and twelve gates (all named) with twenty-four fierce deities (*hsiung-shen*) guarding them. The five furnaces are all identified with bushel constellations of the east, west, south, north, and center. In this heaven there are also "sages and patriarchs of the three stars" (of happiness, emolument, and long life), enlightened teachers from all the successive dynasties, patriarchs born of the Five Phases serving as "managers" (*chih-chang*), and three patriarchs of the red-tinged clouds serving as "overseers-general" (*tsung-ling*). There are also forty-five "gods of darkness" (*an-shen*) who are "surveillance officers" (*chien-ch'a*) and eighty-one gate gods as "dispatchers" (*po-chih*), with Grand Master P'eng of the "heaven that superintends the apexes" (*tu-chi t'ien*) as "escort" (*hu-sung*) and the one who "arranges the great earth" (*she ta ti*).

This Red Canopy Heaven has five realms (*wu-p'an*) and "four valued [persons]" (*ssu-kuei*) for which the supervisors-in-chief (*t'i-t'ou*) are the buddhas and patriarchs. We are told that when

in the future the positions in the celestial realms are apportioned, those who obtain them must send to heaven true memorials and statements and [must have] true incense and true seals to respond to the holy. Beneath the northern bushel there is a "double-pearl hall" that is exclusively devoted to investigating memorials of the eighth step [of religious practice]. Outside the Red Canopy Heaven there is the Red Damask Pass, supervised (*t'i-tiao*) by the Patriarch of Heaven's Consent (T'ien-k'e tsu) and the Mother of the Buddha's Merit (Fo-kung mu), with ninety-six "gods who use six-pronged forks" as specially appointed regulators (*chuan-li*). . . .

On the fifteenth of the yin and yang months [the fourth and tenth lunar months], this [Red Damask Pass] is opened. Those with tablets and titles are allowed to pass, [but] those who have not engaged in religious practices and have not put aside [their worldly ways] have returned [to this pass] in vain and come back to the Eastern Land for ten thousand kalpas, constantly lost and confused.

The faithful, in contrast, stay here for eighty-one kalpas (the period of Maitreya's rule) without descending to be reborn in the ordinary world.

Though the Red Canopy Heaven is particularly the reward for those who have completed the eighth step of religious practice, it is mentioned elsewhere in the *Huang chi* book as well. The five realms and the offices associated with them are described in detail in chapter 14, in response to the question noted above, "How many people will be gathered in?" The first is the "cloud realm" (*yun-p'an*), in which there are one "primal body," two "general [overseers of] the apex" (*tsung-chi*), three "head leaders" (*t'ou-ling*), ten buddha positions, ten "superintendents" (*t'i-tu*), four "route commanders" (*tsung-kuan*), and ten of another office (here a page is missing). There are also 45 "supervisors of the major regulations" (*t'i-kang*) whose positions are not changed.[19]

The second realm is that of the sages (*sheng-p'an*). Here there are one "apex commissioner" (*cheng-chi*), two "keepers of commands" (*chang-ling*), 36 "supervisors of the major regulations," 24 "overseers-general," and 99 "[leaders of] the Lotus school," "which is a total of 162 'superintendents' (*tsung-li*) [in charge of] the affairs of the realm of the sages."

The third division of heaven is the "celestial realm" (*t'ien-p'an*), which "employs one officer in charge of the teaching" (*chang-chiao*), two who are "dedicated to teaching" (*t'ieh-chiao*), six "responsible for conduct" (*chu-hsing*), nine "in charge of titles" (*chang-hao*), 72 officers in "charge of the apex" (*chang-chi*), and 144 officers "dedicated to the apex" (*t'ieh-chi*) — altogether "234 superintendents of such responsibilities of the celestial realm as wind, clouds, thunder, and rain."

The fourth realm is that of humans (*jen-p'an*), with a total of 146 positions, most of which are identical to those listed above, but adding "two vice-commissioners of the apex" (*fu-chi*) and 36 [officers] "responsible for correction" (*chu-cheng*).

The last of the five realms is that of the earth (*ti-p'an*), in which there are 24 officers "in charge of a realm" (*chang-p'an*), 36 "in charge of commands," 45 "supervisors in chief," 54 "supervisors of the major regulations," 64 "leaders" (*ling-hsiu*), 72 of those "responsible for conduct," 81 "chief patrollers" (*tu-hsün*), 99 "major patrollers" (*ta-hsün*), and 120 *pu-hsing* ("those who set forth and examine"?).[20] All of these "are responsible for human administration in the earth realm."

This passage continues with a list that appears to be still connected with the preceding description of the five realms, including 3,600 buddha positions, 130,000 "great beings" (mahāsattvas), 880,000 human beings, and 990,000 of "the worthy and good" (*hsien-liang tzu*), each needing only a designated smaller number of supervisors, managers, and leaders. In addition, there are 235 sets of the "four valued ones" who "send down signs from Heaven and complete forms on Earth."

The text continues, "It is only those who have these personal texts (*ch'in-wen*), tablets, and titles who are gathered in to completion and finish the task; it is only they who in the future are in charge of the celestial realm, sit on the nine-[leafed] lotus, are called 'Shou-yuan,' and become patriarchs."

All this has been the Buddha's answer to the question "How many are saved?" His interlocutors then ask, "How do these people obtain these [aforelisted] positions?" The Buddha responds with a list of the saving aids and rituals he has provided, including 990 steps of religious practice; 84,000 kinds of incense; 99 kinds of "discussion essays" (*t'an-chang*); many hundreds of tablets for "positions for the right karmic fruits" (*cheng-kuo wei-p'ai*); thousands of "hand characters," "personal texts," "red scripture verses" (*hung ching-tz'u*), "songs of the dark prime" (*an yuan ke*), and titles for religious practices; 84,000 "birth-and-death reports"; 103,000 "general memorial texts"; and so forth. It is by using all these prescribed aids that the faithful are able to enter heaven. One can scarcely imagine a more bureaucratic answer to the question "Who shall be saved?" The answer is the number of those who use the texts and forms provided. This, then, is the understanding of paradise in the *Huang-chi* book, the goal of its strenuous exhortations.

In sum, the underlying mythological story line of this book begins with the creation of the world by the Ancient Buddha. Because the human inhabitants of this world went astray, he sent down thirty-six patriarchs to instruct them, but to no avail. Then he revealed the *Huang-chi* book to the Shou-yuan Patriarch in order to provide detailed instructions in the methods and goal of salvation. Those who believe and follow these methods will be reborn in a special paradise. Salvation history is loosely structured in three time periods, each presided over by a buddha. This book was revealed at the end of Śākyamuni's rule, in anticipation of Maitreya; its methods and documents are those of his advent.

The terms for the three buddhas, apexes, and assemblies are all here, but they are not clearly and explicitly integrated. In later *pao-chüan* we are told how many of the Mother's lost children are saved in the time of each buddha, but this motif does not appear in the *Huang-chi* book except for a long list of offices in the future heaven.

DEITIES AND MATRIARCHS

In the implicit hierarchy of the *Huang-chi* book, the Ancient Buddha, equated with Amitābha, is on top, followed by the buddhas of the three apexes named above. Next come the patriarchs and matriarchs, who in turn take precedence over a variety of gods. The patriarchs and matriarchs are viewed as high-level officials who supervise passes and inspect documents; almost all the gods are described as guards or escorts. With the exception of the "Dark Warrior" divine general and deities responsible for the disposition of souls (discussed below), all the deities noted in the *Huang-chi* book are named as types or categories rather than as individuals.

The relationship between gods and matriarchs is summed up in two lines of verse from chapter 10: "Ten thousand gods block the Dark Furnace Pass (Hsuan-lu kuan) [as guards], / while the Venerable Mother of the Eastern Grove is in charge of texts and tablets." Here the Mother is in charge of written documents but the gods are not—a pattern broken only by a reference in chapter 1 to "36 divine

generals of the light who inspect memorials and religious practice."
The passage just quoted from chapter 10 also introduces the most
general references to deities by numbers alone, such as 145 gods
(*shen*) along the "wide road to heaven . . . who do not block the way
after one passes inspection" (chapter 9) and "99 gods who will protect and escort you" (chapter 7).

However, most gods are given at least some functional designation, such as divine generals of the four directions (chapter 4), ten
commanders (*shuai*) of the ten directions who guide memorials to
the celestial palaces, "36 gods of the six directions who serve as
guards" (chapter 1), gods of the eight trigrams, 244 yin and yang
gods who serve as guardians (chapter 6), 88 celestial dragon gods
who guard the "fifth-step dark pass" (chapter 5), gods of the five
peaks "who will accompany you out the gate" (chapter 7), "81 great
gentlemen gods (*t'ai-chün shen*)" who also are pass guards, and 72
green dragon deities who patrol the passes (chapter 10). Given the
guardian role of the deities, it is not surprising that the faithful are
repeatedly assured that if they have the right documents, the gods
will not block the passes. As we read in chapter 2, "[Our] memorials,
statements, and compositions are without mistake, [so] the gods and
patriarchs joyfully escort us out the gate."

These gods of the *Huang-chi* book—related to directions, trigrams,
and passes to paradise—are not the deified human spirits well
known in nonsectarian Chinese popular religion. Rather, they play a
subordinate role in a different mythological context.

There appear to be two types of patriarchs in this book: (1) the set
of thirty-six sent down to earth by the Buddha to transmit the tradition, and (2) various inspectors at the passes, who are usually paired
with matriarchs. Other than the Buddha himself, the most frequently
named divine figures in the *Huang-chi pao-chüan* are these mother-
goddesses, to whom there are thirty references. These "grandmoth-
ers" (*tsu-mu*) are all described as supervisors and inspectors at the
various passes on the way to paradise. In this book the primordial
Divine Mother of all humanity does not yet appear, though most of
the elements of the later sectarian mythological structure are present.

In addition, although the matriarchs in the *Huang-chi* text are
certainly multiple, it is difficult to say how many separate figures the
different names represent because some are duplicates and others
seem to indicate the same figure with a different title. The title of the
first matriarch named in the book is paradigmatic for the rest—

namely, the "Matriarch of the Passes" (Kuan-k'ou tsu-mu), who is mentioned three times in the book's introductory material. She is described as "investigating tablets and titles," "responding to those with tablets," and "waiting for the primal ones to go to [i.e., return to the teachings of] this volume." Similar titles are "Matriarch Who Guards the Passes" (chapter 3) and "Matriarch of the Cloud Passes" (introduction).

There are also a few nonspecific references to "the Matriarch" and "the Venerable Mother," as in the lines "the Matriarch in the palace comes to inspect [the documents]; be careful with every character and line" (chapter 11); "in each [celestial] palace there is a Matriarch who investigates and compares the people of the great earth who engage in religious practices" (chapter 12); and "when one burns a stick of 'dark pass' incense, the Venerable Mother rejoices" (chapter 7).

However, most of the titles are more specific, such as the "Venerable Mother Who Receives the Lotus" (chapter 9), the "Matriarch of the Purple Yang Palace [who looks after texts and tablets]" (chapter 10), and the "Matriarch Who Gives Birth to the Lotus" (chapter 9). The "Venerable Mother of the Eastern Grove" has already been mentioned.

In chapter 5 there is an interesting reference to a "Living Mother with a Patriarch's Face" (Tsu-mien sheng-mu) who serves as a celestial supervisor. This designation is echoed in the fact that nine of the mother-deities named here are paired with patriarchs—about the same number as those who are not so paired. (A list of these paired deities and their functions appears in Appendix D.) In addition to these, there is an enigmatic reference in chapter 4 to a "Kuan-yin Mother" and a "Ti-tsang Mother" who take vows to save all living beings. These two bodhisattvas are, of course, those most concerned with coming to the aid of the living and the dead, respectively. Though Ti-tsang is usually referred to as male, in some later "precious volumes" one also finds the title "Ti-tsang mu."

The various female deities in this book are thus not coherently related to one another, although they do have similar roles at different stages along the path to deliverance. They are described as meticulous inspectors who will not tolerate ritual mistakes; thus the later emphasis on the love and mercy of the Venerable Mother is not present in the *Huang-chi pao-chüan*. The goddesses here are not transcendent but are part of a bureaucratic structure dominated by males, with whom they are often paired. However, they do have an official role that was not available to women in the human realm.

THE BUREAUCRATIC STRUCTURE
OF THE PATH TO SALVATION

In the *Huang-chi* book, there are thirty-seven titles of celestial offices and positions and eighteen types of documents (see Appendixes E and F, respectively). Twenty-five of the titles, or 67 percent, are either listed in Charles O. Hucker's *Dictionary of Official Titles in Imperial China* or are similar to others that he provides, using some of the same key characters. This percentage bears out statements in the text itself that its offices and ranks are "of the same principle" as those of the state. Thus the celestial positions to which the elect aspire are named after, or are imitations of, those of the civil administration. The civil service examination system is likewise taken as a model for the testing of sect members. No doubt this all seemed quite natural to the composer of this text, but to us his quest for legitimacy demonstrates a profound legitimacy the other way around—namely, the legitimacy of the Chinese state in the minds of its people.

Let us begin with the translation of some key passages. In chapter 3 of the *Huang-chi pao-chüan*, the Buddha's interlocutor is Bodhidharma, who asks:

"What palaces and courts are [associated with] the third step [of religious practice]?"

The Buddha replied, "For the 'third-step dark pass,' please raise up your basic nature and open up the palace gates. Then you will know the place for making yourself secure and establishing your destiny. There is also the nine-cloud pass where the Patriarch of the Dark Heaven and the Mother of True Yang examine religious practice, incense, memorials, statements, tablets, titles, and vows. Only when each character is without mistake and each item is true is one permitted to advance. If there are mistakes, all is lost, and for ten thousand kalpas one will be without a trace. . . .

"If, when you are alive, there has been a response to memorials [presented at] the four seasons, then after death, when one goes to the cloud passes, the gods will not obstruct."

In chapter 5, in response to the question, "Who has transmitted and taught the *Shou-yuan* book?" the Buddha replies:

I gave them sanction to arrange (*ting*) the Lotus school and established the investigation of the titles. I gave them 326 characters, 990 [forms of] religious practice, 84,000 [types of] incense, 1,372 tablet titles for the right karmic fruits, 375 kinds of the news of setting forth the details (*ch'u-hsi hsiao-hsi*), 240 profound mysteries[?] (*hsuan-miao*), 99 kinds of discussion essays, 72 kinds of the order of precedence of yin and yang (*yin-yang hsu*), 224 perfections (*chen*), eight-phrase mantras, twelve-phrase wonderful teachings, red scripture verses (*hung ching-tz'u*), songs of the peaceful prime, palace courts for hiding from the three calamities, lotus walls for escaping the eight difficulties, personal texts, hand characters, tablet titles [*sic*], pass protections, and a road for returning home. . . . People's karmically deserved positions (*kuo-wei*) are decided according to [their] religious practice. [After] their minds are examined, they are accepted into the Golden City, . . . [where they] are able to see [their] original bodies and all of them attain buddhahood and become patriarchs; each person thoroughly understands the Way and returns to the source tradition.

Here the Buddha is the revealer of all the terms and structures of sect teaching. All this is directed to the living so that their souls will be prepared at death. As we read in chapter 10, "In our school (*tsa-chia*), when each character is clearly written and the ten steps are all complete, [the pious] return home together and go to the Dragon-Flower [Assembly]. . . . When one's hundred-year life span is complete, one returns on the road to the clouds, holding a tablet and relying on a title. As one passes through the cloud road, each person is apportioned a position (*ke fen tso-wei*)."

There are repeated exhortations in the *Huang-chi pao-chüan* to effort, attention, ritual correctness, and sincerity; only thus will salvation be attained. Thus we read in chapter 2, "[One] must be devout and sincere" (*yao ch'ien-ch'eng*) and "Quickly prepare to thank the gods. Memorials and prayers must be written correctly. In worshipping the predecessors, one must pay attention; in writing characters, one must be clear. True Heaven and true Earth will receive your true nature; again, increase your efforts (*tsai chia kung*)." This exhortation is repeated in subsequent chapters:

Within the ordinary realm, one's mind must be devout, one's religious practice true and correct, and one's incense fine and proper; [then] when one's memorials and statements have been offered, the gods will not obstruct [one]. (chapter 3)

One must practice one step at a time and put things in proper order as one passes each stage. (chapter 4)

Quickly, do not be slow and stop [along the path]; if incense and paper do not reach them, the gods will not comply. If one's bones [i.e., inner qualities] are deficient, the buddhas will not show respect. The matter of birth-and-death is important; stop treating it lightly. [Otherwise,] the Matriarch Who Guards the Pass will be unwilling to relax [her vigilance]. (chapter 3)

[Everything] must be in proper order. Offerings of paper horses [to be burnt as messengers], incense, and lanterns must be new. Stop saying that the Buddhadharma can be bought with money. (chapter 9)

Part of the preparation for successful ritual is purification (*ching*), which is emphasized in chapter 5, where we read, "Before you have received a true tablet, your body and mind must be pure. . . . If you wish to escape the world, your body and mind must be clean (*kan-ching*). . . . The ladder to heaven is ascended step by step; diligently apply yourself, do not relax. Go forward, more diligent with each step. Stop wanting to turn around. Be fearful, anxious that your energy is weak and your roots shallow."

Unfortunately, what "purification" means is not discussed, but the general tone of anxious effort is clear. All this is just the sort of activist (*yu-wei*) piety that Lo Ch'ing was to reject in the following century.

The results of all this ritual effort are summed up in chapter 6, set in the time of the Buddha of the Future, but with suitable warnings added:

[Then] the Ten Buddhas will conduct [your] memorials to the Painted Tower Hall, ten gods will lead you into the court of the three perfected [ones], ten commanders in ten directions will open [the way along] the holy road and carefully escort you to the Tu-tou Palace of the cloud realm. Then the Buddha will be at hand. [However,] you will also need the religious practice of the three apexes, the three buddhas' incense, and the three buddhas' memorials. First present the road-penetrating statement (*ch'uan lu shu*), then send off a three-realms report. Do not stop.

This passage continues by naming the patriarch, mother-goddess, and gods guarding the pass at hand, then continues:

On the sixth yang day of the second month, with correctly composed memorials and statements, true and considered religious practice, and incense of the correct vital force, only with devotion and sincerity will you be allowed to pass (*fang-kuo*) and be able to see the Ten Buddhas conducting memorials, protecting and promoting, responding to investigation and comparing titles (*ta-ch'a tui-hao*).

In two different places, the *Huang-chi* book compares the required celestial inspections with the civil service examination system. The first occurs in chapter 4, where, after a condemnation of those whose arrogance "injures heaven's principles," we are told that

the true and correct children of the Dragon-Flower in our school, with three inspections and nine examinations, go to match the apex (*tang chi*). Without inspections or examinations, it is impossible to attain sagehood. Lifting up from the common and being selected for the holy (*fan-t'i sheng-hsuan*), they sit on the Imperial Ultimate. . . .

If there are still confused people who do not believe, in the examination arena they can look at the themes that have been set. . . . Becoming an official and receiving a salary [are due to] seeds planted in a previous life; all [such officials] emerge from the examination grounds. . . .

> The Most Honored One [i.e., the Buddha] opened up a selection arena
> And thrice examined essays.
> Those who are successful become officials;
> Those who are not return home.

These references to examinations are echoed in chapter 12, where we are told that

because there were no persons of talent to manage all-under-heaven, every three years an examination arena is established and officials are sent to send down scriptures and books, and questions and themes [for the examinations], proclamations and memorials. Only after [candidates] have been examined on each item can they be in charge of the empire; only then do they establish the world (*li te ch'ien-k'un*). If there is a mistake in one item, they are returned to their own districts to practice essays again and continue reading the Classics.

Later on in this chapter, we are told that the names of those who pass the exams are reported in the Court of State Ceremonial (Hung-lu ssu), which "transmits [them] to the Office of Transmission for investigation of titles. Only then are [candidates] able to go to the court."

In chapter 9, the Buddha's questioners ask him who will be in charge when the time of the future comes, to which he replies, "You don't know anything at all. Are there not different kinds [of official positions] in the world? Those responsible for mountains are only in charge of (*kuan*) mountains, those responsible for water are only in charge of water courses," and so forth. The list continues for those responsible for the military, people, grain, population registration, selection of officials, engineering, punishment, and more. It continues by saying that "[the positions] of deities and sages in the celestial realm are of the same principle. Those responsible for wind are only in charge of causing wind to blow; those responsible for rain are only in charge of sending down rain," and so on for the divine figures responsible for clouds, thunder, drought and floods, harvests, religious practice, incense, karma, disasters and calamities, life spans, and birth-and-death. Thus celestial positions are filled and carried out in the same way as earthly positions, but with different responsibilities.

This theme is taken up in chapter 10 as well, where the Buddha is asked whether the titles and positions of the sect "really exist or not" (*kuo chen yu yeh, wu*), to which he indignantly replies:

You people are really stupid! In the world are there not different kinds [of positions, such as] dukes, marquises, earls, and civil and military officials? Those who do not have tablets and seals do not get to be in charge of affairs; in accord with the court, they enter [the ranks of office?]. For army and people there are banners and military titles[?], and there are also wooden tablets and "signals" (*hsin-hao*); only [with them] can one enter military ranks or a yamen.[21] For people who earnestly maintain a vegetarian diet, it is the same.[22] They are reviled by others and suffer their whole lifetimes. If they didn't have tablet titles and passes to enter the Dragon-Flower [Assembly], whom would they ask about summoning and comparing?

The *Huang-chi* book also provides details about guidance for the souls of the pious dead. In chapter 12 we read:

In [the time of] Śākyamuni's assembly, [the Purple Canopy Son of Heaven (Tzu-lo T'ien-tzu)] is in charge of the gods of the yang life span [i.e., life in this yang world]. [They] make one report a month, and the Purple Canopy Son of Heaven responds. If a certain person's life span in the yang world is fulfilled and his or her religious practice is complete, the Tzu-lo T'ien-tzu issues an order [that the person] is to be taken to the [appropriate court] of purgatory. If his order reaches the [god of] the Eastern Peak, then the responsible officials take [the soul of the person] to the City God of that district. He gathers together the gods of the Five Paths (*wu-tao*),[23] household, and locality, and the Controller of Destiny, etc., [to tell them] that they should take such and such a person and quickly, in accord with the imperial command, send up a release [document] (*shang-chieh tang*)[?]. Those gods should stop calamities and illness and hold to the true prime. If a [person's] vital force is exhausted, he dies, [so they] gather together his/her souls and unite them in one place. [Then] the Controller of Destiny hands [the souls] to [the gods of] the Five Paths; the [gods of] the Five Paths escort them to the City God; the City God releases them to the [god of] the Eastern Peak, and the [god of] the Eastern Peak hands them on to the Purple Yang Palace. Their cases are completely handed over to the court of the Purple Canopy

Son of Heaven, where, with [the help of] the Stove God of the person's household, the karma of the person's life is investigated and compared. After those who have many karmic [hindrances] have completed [their punishments] in purgatory, they are sent down [to be reborn] among humans, [where they must] redeem their vows from the beginning. Those with few karmic hindrances are inspected and compared in accord with the situation; [the gods] take their merit and discount their sins (chiang kung che tsui). . . .

Those who in life had clear and pure tablets are permitted to leave the world. Those who present a true pass (chi chen wei chao)[?][24] are able to go to the road to the clouds.

Chapter 12 ends with a partially parallel account:

When [ordinary] people die, it is like a dream. Their nature returns home; it is just like blowing out a lamp. All the passes are closed and will not admit [even those with] a chen (pu jung chen).[25] [Their guards] are not afraid even if you are a heroic and stalwart person; they do not fear even if you have divine powers. Your original true [nature] has been gathered in, [but] your four limbs are as if bound with ropes.

When people die, a hundred methods are of no use. The soul goes directly to the Dark Realm [of purgatory]. The local deity of the household sees it out the gate, and the Stove God follows along behind, carrying the book of its karmic records. They accompany it to the Purple Yang Palace.

The pious, however, have hope:

Those with karmic [hindrances] receive punishment; those without such karma get to see Maitreya. Celestial persons [or devas] (t'ien-jen) give you immortals' clothing to put on, and you will forever sit in the Great Imperial Hall. You will never again suffer oppression and restraint (ch'ü-ch'ih). Do not forget [those] in the Eastern Land. Speak persuasively to others (chao jen-chia shuo tsui)[?]. Those who have the natural power of religious practice, and those who have tablets and titles with which heretics can't compare, [such people] the Buddha welcomes and the gods invite to enter the Imperial Ultimate. There food is provided by celestial persons, and they wear the clothing of sages and immortals. It is only this that reveals that religious practice for the future is not fraudulent (hsiu chiang-lai pu-shih t'ou te).

In this twelfth chapter of the Huang-chi book, the connection between purgatory and heaven is clarified, as is the role of local gods. The pious first pass through a court of purgatory but are then forwarded by stages to heaven. For them purgatory is a way station, not a place of punishment, and their way is cleared by orders and documents. Those with many karmic hindrances are reborn in the human world, where they must start their quest all over again. This is for ordinary folk with bad karma; as we shall see, heretics and nonbelievers are much more roundly condemned.[26]

ETHICAL TEACHINGS

The *Huang-chi* book is not concerned primarily with moral exhortation, but the ethical teachings it does contain are as conservative as its ritual program, with which they are specifically connected. As the Buddha says in chapter 1, "For worshipping Heaven and Earth, one needs the titles of Heaven and Earth, Heaven and Earth incense, and a true [form of] religious practice. One must be filial and obedient to one's parents, obey and respect superiors, be friendly toward one's brothers and affectionate toward village elders." This exhortation is continued later in the chapter, also in a ritual context:

Bestow [*sic*] the Three Refuges, obey the five precepts, lessen (*shao*) competition for fame, do not kill animals for sacrifice, do not steal, do not believe in crooked paths, lessen violence, do not darken yourself [in ignorance], [but] be fair in all things. Obey superiors, be filial to parents [and] friendly to brothers. Love [your] wife and children, respect friends, be affectionate to friends in the Way (*tao-yu*). Be filial to patriarchs, respect predecessors, think deeply, with thoughts serious. Follow the *Shou-yuan* [scripture], study [how to] escape the world, at each step do not be lax.

In chapter 5, the connection between ethics and ritual is noted again:

When the responsibilities of the six family relationships are complete, and [your] memorials and statements are in proper order, then you are directly and naturally allowed to pass through. Refined in the dark furnace, your ten thousand kalpas' golden body will neither be born nor destroyed, and together you will turn the Dharma Wheel.[27]

Similar ethical exhortations are found in chapters 9 and 12. In sum, what direct ethical teachings there are in the *Huang-chi* book are mainstream Chinese, as are its affirmations of loyalty to the emperor. The homage to the ruler in the opening material, quoted at the beginning of this discussion, might be discounted as a formality of publishing, but not so a passage in the middle of chapter 15 that reads "Ten thousand years to the emperor. May the nation prosper, the people be secure, and the winds and rain harmonious, and may [all people] together [direct their] religious practice to the nine-leafed lotus." This statement reinforces the political loyalty implicit in this text through its adaptation of bureaucratic terms and

practices. At this point, too, the *Huang-chi pao-chüan* is in harmony
with many of the texts that succeeded it.[28]

CRITICISM OF "HERETICS AND NONBELIEVERS"

In the *Huang-chi pao-chüan*, the terms I translate as "heretics" (or "heretical traditions and schools") and "nonbelievers" are *hsieh-tsung*
and *wai-tao*—literally "crooked traditions" and "[those who] put the
Way outside," respectively. Here, as elsewhere, *hsieh* is contrasted
with its opposite, *cheng*, which means "straight," "correct," and, by
derivation, "orthodox," while *wai-tao* is a Buddhist term meaning
"those outside the Way," or non-Buddhists. The *Huang-chi* book
condemns those in both these categories to many eons of rebirth in
saṃsāra because they don't know the proper rituals and foolishly
criticize the true teaching—namely, the teaching of the *Huang-chi*
book itself.

The repeated attacks on these people are important in the self-
definition of the *Huang-chi pao-chüan* and were no doubt an attempt
to further establish its own legitimacy. I believe that the term "heretic" is justified here because those given the label seem to be other
sectarians, rivals of the tradition represented by the *Huang-chi* book.
Thus they should be distinguished from the mistaken questioners
who come to seek instruction from the Buddha, most of whom are
called *tao-jen* ("persons of the Way"). The *tao-jen*'s problem is that
their conventional piety does not go far enough, in that it does not
include the rituals and documents discussed by the *Huang-chi* book.
If they would follow its teachings, they could be saved, and there are
some indications that this applies to heretics as well.

What I take to be the mythological background of the distinction
between heretical traditions and the correct teaching of the *Huang-
chi* book is discussed in its introductory material. The beginning of
the passage is broken off, but it refers to thirty-six men who were
sent down to be born and who, after a long time,

were concerned only with clever words and good appearances; they did not
know about religious practice, called themselves patriarchs, had lofty minds
and big thoughts [about themselves], and did not think about setting forth
the details after opening up new fields. They used memorials and statements but did not burn them; they had several [kinds of] incense but did not
distinguish [among] them. Palace seals they presented to heaven in a disorderly and confused way. There was no end to what they did.

The First Emperor asked, "In this situation, what was the best thing to do?"

The Buddha replied, "Later, I further sent the two men, Light (Ming) and Dark (An), who were in charge of the *Shou-yuan pao-chüan*, in which there are incense, titles, the names of memorials, statement-texts (*shu-tz'u*), vow documents, official dispatches, religious practices, [and] tablet titles.

The thirty-six men referred to here are probably the thirty-six patriarchs noted elsewhere in the book, who were sent down by the Buddha at the beginning. Here they seem to represent the leaders of earlier sects who gradually got off the track and forgot how things are to be done. Hence the Buddha had to "again send" (*yu-ch'ai*) new messengers who, through the *Huang-chi* book, revealed the correct documents and practices.

The two men called "Light" and "Dark" are referred to elsewhere in the book, and at one point are juxtaposed with day and night (chapter 2), but are not otherwise described. It is tempting to relate them to the worlds of the living and the dead, but evidence is lacking. The same goes for other "dark" (*an* or *hsüan*) deities, generals, and passes; in this book they are all a part of the celestial hierarchy, not discussed in the context of purgatory. Be this as it may, although the term "heretics" is not used in the passage just quoted, the practices of which they are accused elsewhere in the book are similar to those of earlier sects before the new saving revelation. In some passages, however, the problem with "heretics" is that they don't have any documents at all.

The longest discussion devoted specifically to the "crooked and outside" is in chapter 13, where the Buddha's three interlocutors ask:

"There are 90 [groups of] nonbelievers, 36 heretical schools, 28 side gates (*p'ang-men* [another designation for heretics]), and 36 confused methods (*hun-fa*). None of them is able to enter the road to the clouds or pay homage at the Tu-tou [Palace]. What kind of people is it who are the only ones able to enter?"

The Buddha replied, "Only if they reform their heresy and return to the correct, reject the false and seek out the true, receive Shou-yuan incense, bestow verses of the dark prime, and [complete] the ten-step religious practice can they enter within."

A bit further on in chapter 13, the Buddha is asked whether the various ritual documents continue to exist after they are burned to fragments, to which he responds in a rage (*ta nu*):

You have no understanding of what is valuable. You demean the "gathering to completion" of our school (*tsa-chia*); you destroy the "setting forth the details" of our school; you treat our memorial texts with contempt and demean our vows. All the bright gods (*ming-shen*) are devoted solely to managing the affairs of the world. As for our school, 3,600 dark generals especially care for it. . . . When vows are uttered, 45 of [these] dark [generals] diligently collect them together. How can this be compared to the texts of those heretical schools and nonbelievers? We are putting into action the great affair of the Imperial Ultimate yet to come.

Though at several points the *Huang-chi* book says that heretics have no memorials and other documents, and hence are lost (introduction, chapters 1 and 2), it is interesting to note that those criticized in the passage just quoted do have at least one type of text. The term used is *wen-shu*, which is similar to the term *shu-tz'u*—a term approved of by the *Huang-chi* book, presumably to designate a kind of memorial, and one that I translate as "statement-text." There is also a more extensive reference to those outside the sect having ritual documents that are roundly rejected by the Buddha as useless, though the term "heretic" is not used. This occurs in chapter 4, where the Buddha's three questioners discuss unnamed religious practitioners who "rely on other oral teachings of samādhi" (absorption in meditation; *k'ou-t'ou san-mei*), which has a negative meaning here. These people are "clever and intelligent" but talk recklessly and

call themselves patriarchs. They gather worthies together, levy and collect wealth and goods, buy and sell incense and paper, . . . use memorials and statement-texts, set up altars, present texts and memorials, [and] establish the position of patriarch and [such titles] as *an-ch'uan* ["one who makes the boat secure"] and *t'ou-kan* ["head administrator"].[29] For eighty-one kalpas they want to attain buddhahood and escape the three calamities and eight difficulties. Is this acceptable? Will they succeed?

The Buddha discusses all this, saying that "when the future comes, in the world from south to north, all phenomena will move, and the myriad spirits and sages will all change, so [for them] to take [the name of] 'sage' and attain buddhahood is like shooting an arrow into space—completely in vain. They are really ignorant and stupid."

The reference here is to a full-scale sect with documents, rituals, and an organization that are quite similar to those advocated by the *Huang-chi* book, which sees such groups as its greatest threat. There is not a word in this book critical of government officials. Its enemies are rival religious traditions.

There are a few other comments in the *Huang-chi* book about "heretics." In chapter 2 we are told that:

Nonbelievers and heretical schools are earnest in vain.
They are all in the human realm, entangled in the earth.
They have not sought the Way of the future,
How can they enter the heaven yet to come?
Where will they develop good karma, where will they receive [their reward]?

And in chapter 3:

If there are mistakes in memorials and statements, one revolves [i.e., is reborn] in the Eastern Land.
If religious practice is not correct, one takes the road to return.
Heretical schools and nonbelievers, stop coming forward.
The patriarchs are upset [with you], the gods resentful; they will force (*kun*; lit. "beat") you to return.
[Heretics] regret that in their previous lives their minds were not devoted.
They wait on the sidelines, reborn in the four forms of rebirth and the six paths of saṃsāric existence.
They are [repeatedly] reborn in the ordinary world, [and]
For eighty-one kalpas do not escape it.
Only then will they think of the words of the
Venerable Patriarch Shou-yuan.

These attacks on other traditions bring into sharp focus the sectarian self-consciousness of the *Huang-chi* text.

SECTARIAN SELF-CONSCIOUSNESS

We have seen evidence above of the sectarian self-consciousness that permeates this text, which is written from the perspective of "our school" (*tsa-chia*) and "our sect" (*tsa-p'ai*). The *Huang-chi* book perceives itself as the vehicle of a special revelation that supersedes all others and that was preached directly by the Ancient Buddha himself. Those who are karmically prepared to respond to this revelation and carefully carry out its rituals will be saved; all others are lost, no matter what piety they may claim.

The name given for the congregation of the elect is Lung-hua hui (Dragon-Flower Assembly)—that is, the assembly of those who respond to the coming of Maitreya, whose teaching is called that of the

White Yang (Pai-yang chiao) of the Imperial Ultimate Assembly (Huang-chi hui), which supplants the Red Yang teaching of Śākyamuni in the present, the time of the Great Ultimate Assembly (T'ai-chi hui; see *Huang-chi* introduction). The names here associated with Maitreya can be understood as alternative names for the sect itself, which saw the teachings about the three apexes of cosmic time as its particular possession (*tsa-p'ai te san-chi*; see *Huang-chi* introduction and chapter 10).

These designations are supplemented by references to "responding to the Lotus school" (Lien-tsung) and "continuing the Lotus school" (chapters 7 and 9) — an old name for the Pure Land Buddhist tradition devoted to Amitābha, and one that had been used by both orthodox and sectarian groups since the preceding Yuan dynasty (1264–1368).

The positive self-identification of the sect behind the *Huang-chi* book is supported by its attacks on "heretics and nonbelievers," most of whom seem to be rival sectarians. In a few cases the names of these groups are provided, as well as the names of two of their texts (noted below). All this indicates a defined group of believers who supported the teachings of the *Huang-chi* book and who were, in turn, nourished by them.

The sectarian self-consciousness of this text is illustrated by a passage in chapter 4 that begins with criticism of

confused people of the Eastern Land [i.e., this world] who do not know what is valuable, who in what they see and do follow [only] what gives them pleasure, and who recklessly call themselves teachers. [For them,] holding on to [i.e., calling down] the gods constitutes making the Way (*tso tao*); relying on usurping [the names of] "sages" (*ting-sheng*, reading *ting* as *ting-ti*, "to take the place of"), they hope for escape, [but] majestic heaven is not for spirit-mediums (*tuan-kung*), and the Venerable Mother is not a god to be falsely assumed [i.e., to be called down by a medium]. To act as substitutes for the gods and brazenly assume their names (*ting-t'i mao-ming*) injures heaven's principles. [Those who] treat the gods with disrespect will be banished and executed; this is all done by confused people. Stop thinking that in the Latter Realm there are traces [of the gods]; [what counts is] the religious practice in ten steps and the titles that go with them. If one does not follow these practices, one usurps [the gods] in vain and returns [to saṃsāra] with nothing accomplished. The true and correct children of the Dragon-Flower in our school, with three inspections and nine examinations, go to match the opportunity (*tang-chi*; a homonym for "correspond to the apex"). Those who are not inspected and examined cannot attain sagehood, while those who are lifted up from the ordinary and selected for the holy sit on the Imperial Ultimate.

Here the self-defining foil is clearly described—it is the spirit-medium practices of popular religion, rejected by the *Huang-chi* text.

Another means of sectarian self-identification is naming other sects, such as in chapter 2, where the "gateless man of the Way" (*wu-men tao-jen*) says to the Buddha that he had been in the Heaven and Earth Assembly (T'ien-ti hui), where he "devoutly maintained a vegetarian diet, urged people to be transformed [i.e., saved], and, relying on the *Scripture for Establishing the Kalpa* (*Ting-chieh ching*) and the *Yellow Register of the Patriarchs and Venerable Ones* (*Tsu lao huang-ts'e*) of our Buddha . . . established ritual arenas, sent up texts, and responded to memorials."

Here the name "T'ien-ti hui" appears as the name of a religious sect long before it was used by the "sworn brotherhood" associations of the Ch'ing period. I have a copy of a *Ting-chieh pao-chüan* that may be related to the book named here, but I am not familiar with the *Tsu lao huang-ts'e*. In the Ming and Ch'ing, the term *huang-ts'e* referred to government registers of various kinds, including those for population. This term is not the same as the Taoist term *huang-lu*, which is also translated "yellow register."

In chapter 3 as well, sect names are mentioned that are closely related to terms used and approved by the *Huang-chi* book itself. The Buddha's interlocutor here is Bodhidharma, who says that in the Eastern Land he is called the "First Patriarch" (*ch'u-tsu*) and has "established a teaching that points directly [to the truth], has devoted himself to transmitting 'the one character of the correct Dharma of the Red Yang' and 'the great teaching of the Golden Elixir,' and has secretly passed on the *Bone Marrow True Scripture without Words* (*Wu-tzu ku-sui chen-ching*)."

The Buddha enlists Bodhidharma in the task of "establishing patriarchs, transmitting the teaching, and opening up new fields. Become a master (*tso chu*), so that those who study the good will have someone to give allegiance to and flee to. Do not scatter and disorder your mind." After further instructions that firmly install Bodhidharma as a supporter of this *Huang-chi* tradition, he is assured that when the right time comes, "Maitreya will naturally send someone to completely gather in [the primal ones]." Here the founding patriarch of Ch'an legend is made a part of popular sectarian tradition, a role he kept from then on in Ming and Ch'ing *pao-chüan*.

The sectarian self-consciousness of this book is a kind of magnetic field that bends everything it names and borrows to its own purposes. The *Huang-chi* book is sometimes garbled and inconsistent, but it certainly has its own point of view. As such, it helped clear the way for the independent self-assertion of later sectarian texts.

INFLUENCES AND PARALLELS

The structure of the field of Chinese studies makes it inevitable that questions will be raised about possible influences of Confucianism, Taoism, and Buddhism on the *Huang-chi* book. These categories have been reified and given priority for so long that this issue must be discussed. In this case, however, a simple comparison is difficult to apply because any Confucian, Taoist, or Buddhist influences were indirect, digested, and part of what I suspect was a common pool of cultural information. Furthermore, they are here put in a new context, at the service of the dominant teachings of this book.

The largest single influence on the *Huang-chi* text is that of titles and documents from civil administration, but no books or other sources are quoted except in the colophon, which refers to the "Hymn of the Venerable One from Szechuan" (*Ch'uan lao sung*, mentioned in Chapter One above), which I have not been able to identify.

Another obvious influence is Buddhism, which dominates the surface of the *Huang-chi* book, its title and its opening invocation, and which provides the names of its principal narrator and deities. But the content of the *Huang-chi* book is not remotely Buddhist, even by the standards of the earlier indigenous Buddhist texts discussed in Chapter One. The Buddha here is simply a spokesperson of sectarian teachings; he and other Buddhist symbols are evoked for their general sacred and legitimizing aura, not for any recognizable Buddhist import. The vegetarianism, Buddhist precepts, and karma referred to in the *Huang-chi* book had long since been a part of lay Buddhism, and indeed of earlier sectarian tradition in the Yuan dynasty and before. The role of Maitreya as the Buddha of the Future is, of course, due to Buddhist influence, but an influence mediated through earlier indigenous scriptures and sectarian tradition, as are the teachings about disasters at the end of the age.

At the level of style, of course, the alternating prose/verse pattern ultimately goes back to Buddhist antecedents, but it had been transmitted through centuries of indigenous scriptures and literature. The dialogues between the Buddha and his questioners no doubt owe something to the *yü-lu* ("recorded sayings") of Ch'an Buddhism, but in those discussions the authority is a human master, not the Buddha himself.[30]

As for Confucianism, there are no references to the Master or his tradition. The ethical principles discussed above had long since become a part of common culture and so cannot reasonably be considered Confucian per se. The same is true for the bureaucratic orientation of the *Huang-chi* text—that is just Chinese, not particularly Confucian. Ancestors and ancestor worship are not mentioned in the *Huang-chi* book, not even the retroactive salvation of ancestral souls that had long been a promise of Taoism and that is found in later *pao-chüan*.

The terms "T'ai-chi" (Great Ultimate) and "Wu-chi" (Ultimate of Nonbeing, or the Limitless) were best known after the Sung dynasty from the *T'ai-chi t'u-shuo* (Explanation of the diagram of the Great Ultimate) of the eleventh-century Neo-Confucian scholar Chou Tun-i (1017–1073), though the term "Wu-chi" occurs in chapter 28 of the *Lao-tzu* book, and "T'ai-chi" in the Hsi-tz'u commentary of the *Book of Changes*. However, in Chou Tun-i's writings these concepts are abstract generative principles of the cosmos and do not have the chronological role they have in sectarian mythology.[31]

Some might suggest vestiges of Manichaean influence here, in the figures of the patriarchs "Light" and "Dark" and in the emphasis on the salvation of an elect, but in the *Huang-chi* text these patriarchs are merely revealers of proper ritual tradition, with no Manichaean-style mythological context, while the sense of election is expressed through the long-established Buddhist concept of karma.

This leaves the possibility of Taoist influence, which is the most complex issue in this context. For those who have read in the *Taoist Canon* (*Tao-tsang*), it is obvious that, in general terms, the *Huang-chi* book is not a Taoist text: Its terms for deities and rituals are almost all different; it makes no mention of Taoist priests, body deities, visualization of the gods, or the like; and it contains no sustained discussion of attaining immortality through exterior or interior alchemy. Although many of the Buddha's interlocutors are called *tao-jen* ("persons of the Way"), none represents a Taoist tradition. Indeed, this term had been used by the Yuan dynasty White Lotus Society to refer to its own adherents.[32] And though the *Tao-tsang* was reprinted under imperial auspices in 1444–1445, only fourteen years after the *Huang-chi* book was published, the latter is not included in that collection.

Nonetheless, there are certain terms and categories in the *Huang-chi pao-chüan* that indicate at least some indirect knowledge of Taoism, even though none has a structural role in the book. In a general sense, there are parallels between the bureaucratic approach of the *Huang-chi* book and Taoism, which from its beginnings in the Han dynasty has been quite at home with bureaucratic terminology and officials: gods are ranked in hierarchies in which trained priests also have a role, and communicating with the gods takes place through memorials and petitions that, after ritual presentation, are burned. The importance of documents in the *Huang-chi* text is similar to that in Taoism, and both traditions modeled themselves on aspects of civil administration, but the terms and deities in each case are different. The *Huang-chi* book borrows administrative terms directly, without going through an intermediary stage of established Taoist usage; thus we are dealing here with parallels rather than influences.[33]

Some of the more specific aspects of the *Huang-chi* book that do have Taoist antecedents are as follows:

1. References to *chin-tan* ("golden elixir"), a term long established in Taoist alchemy, referring to the ultimate refinement of chemicals or bodily fluids that brings immortality. This term had an important role in the teachings of the Ch'üan-chen (Complete Perfection) school of Taoism, which was widespread in North China at the time the *Huang-chi* book was composed. In this book there are references to the "holy golden elixir of the Shou-yuan" (introduction), to the book itself as a "Golden Elixir book" (chapter 14), and to "those with good karmic affinity rectifying golden elixir" (*cheng chin-tan*; chapter 14). Unfortunately, no details are provided.[34]

2. References to the "dark furnace" (*hsuan-lu*), to "refining [one's elixir] nine times in the dark furnace," and to "the Dark Furnace Pass" (*kuan*) (introduction and chapters 4 and 10). There is also a reference to five furnaces in the Red Canopy Heaven, named after the celestial bushels of the five directions (chapter 8). The furnace was the crucible of Taoist alchemy, where chemicals or bodily fluids were cooked and refined until the elixir matured, but here again the *Huang-chi* book provides no details and seems, rather, to be evoking the residual sacred power of the term itself. Nonetheless, with talk of "refining in the furnace," we are in the heart of Taoist terminology.[35]

3. References to the "dark" or "profound" (*hsuan*) and to "returning to the source" in the "vast mists of creative chaos" (*hun-tun hung-meng*) are all well-known allusions originating in the *Chuang-tzu* and *Lao-tzu* books, which provided the philosophical foundation of the Taoist religion. In later *pao-chüan*, the term "dark pass" can refer to a point between the eyebrows where the soul can escape, but such mystical physiology is not found in the *Huang-chi* book. The same can be said for the term *wu-wei* ("noninterference"), which occurs three times in our text: as the action of "the Ancient Buddha Wu-sheng who vowed great compassion and laid out Heaven and established the Earth in holy *wu-wei*" (introduction); as the "*wu-wei* man of the Tao" (chapter 7); and as the "*wu-wei* method of teaching" (*wu-wei fa*; chapter 7). Lo Ch'ing was thus not the first sectarian writer to use this term, though for him it was a central concept.

4. A reference in chapter 12 to suspending tablets around the body and placing one on the head to bring protection, open up the passes, and please the gods. This is the only comment to this effect, and it is hard to say how literally it should be taken, but wearing protective talismans was a well-established Taoist custom.[36]

5. References to gods of the four directions and five peaks, and to prayers to the five celestial bushels. As we read in the hymn section of chapter 4:

At the *tzu*-hour (11:00 P.M.–1:00 A.M.) [offering of] incense, the Dark Warrior divine general (Hsuan-wu shen-chiang) receives the incense smoke and the Black Lotus Bodhisattva rejoices. They receive and guide the lost to return to their old home. In the Purple Yang Palace, buddhas and patriarchs rejoice. The Divine Lord of the Northern Bushel sends down blessings. With devotion and sincerity, advance. Do not shorten the incense; the Divine General of the North will not obstruct you.

This same pattern is repeated for the east, south, and west, with the deities involved being the Blue-Green Dragon, Vermilion Bird, and White Tiger divine generals, respectively. Each is paired with a bodhisattva of the appropriately colored lotus. All these deities are well-known controllers of the directions, each is associated with a sacred peak, and each was a part of Taoist teaching as well, particularly the Dark Warrior, to whom several Taoist scriptures are devoted. Judith M. Boltz comments that "imperial patronage of the Dark Warrior reached new heights during the Ming" and describes a text in the *Taoist Canon* describing many of the god's miraculous manifestations. Dates noted in this text run from 1405 to 1418, just a few years before the *Huang-chi* book was written.[37]

Nonetheless, the Dark Warrior was not exclusively a Taoist figure; he was a popular god in North China with many temples dedicated to him. His role in the *Huang-chi* book is to help guide the faithful to paradise. In one passage in chapter 3, he is called the Patriarch of the Dark Heaven and is paired with the True Yang Mother to examine religious devotion and documents (see Appendix D). Here again, we may have a parallel to Taoism rather than direct influence from it.[38]

This also seems to be true in a discussion in chapter 12 of the divine rulers of the five sacred peaks, each of whom is responsible for people in his respective region. At the Eastern Peak, we are told, the Humane Holy Emperor Who Equalizes [According to] Heaven (T'ien-ch'i jen-sheng ti), the King of the Ch'u River (Ch'u-chiang wang), and King Kuang of Ch'in (Ch'in Kuang-wang) are solely in charge of people, great and small, of the Wood Palace of the east. This same pattern is repeated for the peaks of the south, west, north, and center. None of the peaks is named. The five sacred peaks are important in the cosmic geography of Taoism, and entire treatises are devoted to them, but all are given their commonly known names, with their presiding deities titled accordingly. The closest the *Huang-chi* text comes to this is with the title "King of Mount T'ai" (the Eastern Peak), who is mistakenly listed as a god of the west!

In fact, what we have in the *Huang-chi* book is a conflation of the five peaks, directions, and phases with the rulers of different courts of purgatory. Ch'in Kuang-wang presides over the first court and is chief over all the other nine. Ch'u-chiang wang rules the second court; Sung Ti-wang, here assigned to the south, is ruler of the third division of purgatory; and King Yama (Yen-lo wang), ruler of the fifth court, here shares responsibility for the central peak. The list could go on; the point is that there is here no connection with Taoism, but rather an exercise of sectarian mythological imagination. Here and elsewhere in the *Huang-chi* book, what at first glance may appear to be Taoist influence dissolves upon closer inspection.[39]

CONCLUDING COMMENTS

In his recent *Mindai Byakuren kyō shi no kenkyū* (A study of the history of the White Lotus sect in the Ming dynasty), Noguchi Tetsurō has compiled a reign-by-reign account of sectarian activities in different areas of China that came to the attention of officials from 1368 to 1449, stressing throughout continuities of name and place with such activities in the Yuan dynasty (1281–1368). For the first four Ming reign periods through the reign of the Hsuan-te emperor (1426–1435), Noguchi lists thirty-four sectarian "incidents," some involving armed uprisings and seven that used the name "Maitreya." In four of the incidents, the groups involved are referred to as the White Lotus "association" (*hui*), "society" (*she*), or "school" (*tsung*). In the Yung-lo (1403–1424) and Hsuan-te periods, four such incidents were recorded for Hopei province, that is, the general area around present Beijing, which was proclaimed the Ming capital in 1420. One of these took place in Yung-lo 16 (1418) in the Ch'ang-p'ing district of Shun-t'ien prefecture, in the immediate vicinity of Beijing. The official account of it reads as follows:

The commoner Liu Hua [of the above location] was executed for plotting rebellion. Hua was first named Seng Pao [Monk Pao]. Fearing military service, he fled to the family of a commoner in the Hsin-ch'eng district of Pao-ting prefecture [south of Beijing]. He wore the robe of a Taoist and proclaimed himself the Buddha Maitreya descended to earth, who should rule the world. He preached such scriptures as the *Ying-chieh* (Responding to the kalpa) and the *Wu-kung* (Five dukes). [Liu] stirred up more than 140 ignorant people, who all believed and followed him. Furthermore, people from such districts as Chen-ting and Jung-ch'eng, and from Hung-tung in Shansi, all received the Buddhist precepts from him and gathered together with him to foment disorder. [However,] their activities became known, and they were all arrested and executed.[40]

The *Huang-chi* book was found in Beijing, and some of its language indicates a location in North China, such as *tsa* as the first-person plural pronoun ("we," "our") and the use of the retroflex ending *-erh*. Hence its author may well have been aware of the Liu Hua incident only twelve years before. Perhaps this close reminder of the long association of Maitreya-belief with local uprisings influenced the political conservatism of this book. Perhaps this conservatism was a necessary precondition for having the book printed. We know that in the Yung-lo period Emperor Ch'eng-tsu actively promoted the publication of Buddhist and Taoist scriptures, and that the succeeding Hsuan-te period was one of relative peace and prosperity. As *The Cambridge History of China* says of it:

In sum, the reign was a remarkable period in Ming history, with no overwhelming external or internal crises, no partisan controversies, and no major debates over state policy. The government operated efficiently. . . . Timely institutional reforms improved the functioning of the state and nourished the welfare of the people, basic requirements of good government. Not surprisingly, in later times the Hsuan-te reign was remembered as the Ming dynasty's golden era.[41]

Perhaps this imperial example and the social and political stability of the time influenced the composition of the *Huang-chi* book. About such matters we can but surmise. In chapter 15 of the text we read:

Three generations of buddhas have all come to descend to earth; the buddhas and bodhisattvas have together come to put [the world] in proper order. Dividing [their forms], they have been born in subprefectures, cities, districts, and prefectures, and have scattered about in settlements [of villages] and townships. They have become head supervisors to save the lost of the world, selecting the superior [among them] to become patriarchs [for] the apexes.

This passage both reflects the beliefs of earlier sectarian history and serves as scriptural validation for the many local incarnations of buddhas and bodhisattvas proclaimed by sectarian leaders and texts in the centuries to follow. It is one of many themes and terms in the *Huang-chi* book that have been echoed in popular scriptures until deep into the twentieth century, a period of more than five hundred years. Several of these terms have already been mentioned: the buddhas of three ages, mother-goddesses with various titles, "gathering to completion," *wu-wei*, and so forth.

In addition, there are references to "little children returning to their old home" (*ying-erh huan ku-hsiang*) and "little children seeing their Mother" (*ying-erh chien mu*) in chapter 4 and the colophon—both basic phrases in Eternal Mother mythology later on, but here not presented in that context. Also worthy of note are references to the "scattered and lost" (*ts'an-ling*) being gathered in, to "only waiting (*teng*) for the Shou-yuan Patriarch," and to "sighing for the lost and confused" (*t'an shih-chien mi-hun jen*), all of which are used in later *pao-chüan*. The same can be said of comments like "realizing the unborn" (*cheng wu-sheng*) and "the road to the unborn" (*wu-sheng lu*), though here both of these references are to an abstract category of eternal life beyond birth-and-death, rather than to the Eternal Mother herself. There is even a section on "repaying kindnesses" (*pao-en*) in chapter 15, though it is shorter and more diffuse than similar sections written by Lo Ch'ing and later sectarian authors.

The stylistic features of the *Huang-chi* book that are present in later *pao-chüan* have already been noted, but of course its single most important contribution at that level is the use of the term *pao-chüan* itself. Because there were evidently other sectarian *pao-chüan* contemporary with the *Huang-chi* book, we cannot simply call it the "ancestor" of later texts of this type, but it is one of the earliest antecedents that we know of.

In sum, then, who wrote this book? We can begin by saying who the author was not. By any reasonable standard of belief, practice, and training, he was not a Buddhist monk or a Taoist priest, nor an official or scholar of any appreciable rank. He was not a physician, for there are no promises of or language about healing. He was not a diviner, for interest in divination or prognostication is also absent. He was not a student or author of popular literature, to which there are no allusions.

What does our author know best? The language of civil administration and examinations. National examinations were revived in 1404 and 1406 and were "held at regular intervals" after 1412,[42] so the author of the *Huang-chi* book would have had ample opportunity to learn of them, or even to prepare for them himself, particularly if he were living near the national capital. The government of the time seems to have been of good repute; it was a propitious time to reemphasize the old Chinese tendency to discuss sacred reality in bureaucratic terms. By so doing, one could use the power and protection of administrative procedure to further religious goals, thereby appealing to a wide audience and reaching for legitimacy at the same time.

From all this, we can venture to guess that the author of the *Huang-chi* book was a pious would-be scholar or local official who expressed his vision of salvation in the terms he knew best. Thus he shaped this early model of Chinese sectarian scriptures, which were never quite so bureaucratic thereafter but which were always concerned to express their mythology and hope in terms accessible to all.

CHAPTER THREE

Wu-wei Sect Scriptures by Lo Ch'ing

Lo Ch'ing (1443–1527) was a man from Shantung who served for a time in a garrison north of Beijing. There he was converted to Buddhism, after which by his own account he spent thirteen arduous years in search of enlightenment, which he finally achieved. Evidently at this point he set himself to writing books expounding what he had learned, books called *chüan* or *pao-chüan*, all of which were published together in 1509. These books combine his own views with copious citations from a large number of sources, chiefly Buddhist sūtras and compendia, though they include a few references to Confucian and Taoist materials as well. As already noted in Chapter One, his favorite source was the *Ritual Amplification of the Diamond Sutra (Chin-kang ching k'e-i)*.

There is no direct proof that Lo studied with Ch'an monks, but in general his teachings are a popularization of a lay-based Ch'an Buddhism with a strong emphasis on the human mind as the source of all because it is equated with the emptiness that is the primordial nature of all things. This perspective allows for no ultimate distinctions of any kind, including those between clergy and laity, men and women, and good and evil. The mind is innate in all, it is the Buddha within, and for Lo the only proper goal is to seek its realization and enlightenment. From this perspective he rejects all ordinary forms of piety as "activist" (*yu-wei*) methods devoted to what is external and superficial, in contrast with his own inward-turning quest, which is "nonactivist" (*wu-wei*); hence the name of the tradition he began, the Wu-wei chiao ("the teaching of Nonactivism").

Lo Ch'ing is by far the best known and most influential of all sectarian authors: his books became venerated as scriptures within the tradition of his own followers, some of whom composed books setting forth the teachings of later patriarchs in the Wu-wei sect. Beyond this tradition, Lo's books became a model for other sectarian authors later in the sixteenth century. In the long history of sectarian religions and texts, Lo Ch'ing appears as a reformer with a strong Buddhist orientation whose thought was more abstract and less mythological than any before or after his time.

Our study of Lo's teachings is on solid ground because his texts have been reprinted several times down through the centuries, most recently by a sectarian temple in Taiwan in 1980 and the Cheng-i Morality Book Publishing Company in 1994. I have copies of all of them, some in more than one edition. (Their names and the versions I have are all discussed in Appendix G.) The texts of these editions are substantially the same, though with minor variations and different commentaries. My comments in this chapter are based on the 1980 reprint of the *K'ai-hsin fa-yao* commentary edition first published in 1596, noting variant readings where necessary.

Sects looking back to Lo Ch'ing as a founding patriarch have been known and studied since Joseph Edkins and J. J. M. de Groot discovered them for modern scholarship in the latter half of the nineteenth century. Since 1943, there have been a number of excellent studies by Japanese scholars, echoed recently by researchers in Taiwan, the United States, and Canada. The only monograph in a Western language devoted solely to Lo Ch'ing and his texts is Randall L. Nadeau's Ph.D. dissertation, completed at the University of British Columbia in 1990. I see no need to recount here this long history of study, which is well summarized by Nadeau.[1] In any case, our concern here is primarily with Lo Ch'ing's books and their role in the history of sectarian scriptures.

THE LIFE OF LO CH'ING

The most reliable sources for the life of Lo Ch'ing are two first-person postscripts in his books, a spiritual autobiography, and a section of a 1596 commentary on his writings. The autobiography is his *K'u-kung wu-tao chüan* (On awakening to the Way through bitter toil), from which translated passages appear later in this chapter. The other materials are here translated in full, the first from the *Cheng-hsin ch'u-i wu hsiu cheng tzu-tsai pao-chüan* (The precious volume of self-determination [needing neither] cultivation nor verification, which rectifies belief and dispels doubt). A passage at the very end of the book reads:

Your master's home is in the Lao Mountains, Chi-mo district, Lai-chou prefecture, Shantung. At Mi-yun Garrison in the Wu-ling Mountains, I awakened to the Way and enlightened the mind. I have explicated the Dharma to save others, and [composed] the [precious] volumes of *Bitter Toil, Lamentation for the World,* the *Refutation of Heresy,* and the *Rectification of Belief and the Elimination of Doubt,* which some have requested [be called] the "Scriptures in Four Books." They are to rescue you from the bitter sea of birth-and-death.[2]

The second first-person postscript is in the *Wei-wei pu-tung Tai-shan shen-ken chieh-kuo pao-chüan* (The precious volume of deep-rooted karmic fruits, majestic and unmoved like Mount T'ai). It reads:

My temporal home is in the Lao Mountains, Ch'eng-yang village, Chu-mao city, Chi-mo district, Lai-chou prefecture, Shantung. My family has served in the military for many generations, and I stayed for a time in the Chiang-mao valley of the Wu-ling Mountains, Ssu-ma Terrace, Ku-pei Pass, Mi-yun Garrison. On behalf of the four types of bodhisattvas [monks, nuns, laymen, and laywomen], those who reside at home and those who have left the household life—who, though they are laboring to refine and polish themselves with bitter toil, have no place of escape—I have with the greatest good intentions written five scriptures to rescue you from the bitter sea of birth-and-death. [May you] forever transcend the ordinary world, never to return.[3]

Nadeau points out that the "Mi-yun Garrison," about 130 *li* (Chinese miles) northwest of Peking on the Great Wall, was a strategic military station under the direct command of the capital and notes that "from the beginning of the Ming dynasty, every household was required to provide one male for military service. He was registered in a military population . . . [and] was bound to military service for life." This obligation was to be continued on a hereditary basis by his descendants.[4] Nothing is said in the earliest records of how Lo Ch'ing was able to leave military service to pursue a religious life.

The oldest biography of Lo Ch'ing was written by a Ch'an-oriented commentator named Lan-feng sometime before 1581, and reprinted by one of his disciples in 1596 in the *K'ai-hsin fa-yao* commentary edition discussed in Appendix G. This commentary describes both Lan-feng and his disciples as Ch'an monks, but their exact status is not clear. What we can say is that they were educated

Buddhist supporters of Lo Ch'ing's teachings. The biography of the Patriarch, composed in verse, is included in the first part of the *K'u-kung wu-tao chüan*:

The Venerable Buddha of Antiquity (Lao Ku Fo) became incarnate, adopting the surname Lo. For the benefit of all living beings, he descended to Shantung to carry out their universal salvation. Thanks to the generous compassion and virtue of his parents, who maintained the precepts during pregnancy, he entered into the world in human form, in the seventh year of the Cheng-te reign period. Appearing at midnight on the first day of the twelfth month [January 1, 1443, of the Western calendar], he left his mother's womb and ate no meat or strong vegetables—a bodhisattva in the human world!

At the age of three, he lost his father; at the age of seven, his mother—an orphan cast away. How pitiful! Without a father or mother, he was forced to depend on his uncle and aunt. Out of the goodness of their hearts, they raised him to adulthood. Every day he lived in fear of birth-and-death. Vexed and grieved, he knew no respite; thinking of saṃsāra and the bitterness of rebirths among the six levels of reincarnation [as a deva, asura, human, animal, hungry ghost, or inhabitant of purgatory], his stomach [lit. "gall"] trembled and his heart palpitated with anxiety.

In the sixth year of the Ch'eng-hua reign period [1470—i.e., at age twenty-eight], he set out in search of masters and companions in study. Day and night he did not sleep, courageous in his pursuit of future merit. Tea he did not drink, rice he did not eat for thirteen years, until, in the eighteenth year of Ch'eng-hua [1482, at age forty], he awakened at last to the enlightened mind. On the eighteenth day of the tenth month, the Patriarch completed the ripening of the Way. Precisely at midnight, his mind was opened to enlightenment: an experiential penetration, sparkling and clear!

In the sixth year of Chia-ching [1527], with no heart to remain in this world, he abandoned the mind and body just after the New Year, aged eighty-five [*sui*]. (*K'u-kung* 1:13–15)[5]

This brief eulogy is written in a pious spirit, but except for the reference to Lo Ch'ing as an incarnation of the Buddha, it is in agreement with the picture the Patriarch himself provides in his *K'u-kung wu-tao chüan*, to which we now turn.

The *K'u-Kung wu-tao chüan* (On awakening to the Way through bitter toil) is a stylized spiritual autobiography by Lo Ch'ing intended for recitation and study. Since Lo influenced some of the sectarian authors who followed him, this autobiography is a valuable source for our understanding of an important religious impetus behind this tradition. In it, we learn both about Lo Ch'ing's personal struggles and about the resources to which he turned. Of course, his own experience is presented as an exemplary model in the context of a long Buddhist tradition of ascetic struggle before enlightenment is attained, but the first-person narration retains an air of authenticity. Nonetheless, the most we can say about this book is that it presents what Lo Ch'ing wanted others to understand and believe about himself and his ideas.

The book opens with instructions for ritual and recitation, and then in the first line of the text itself concisely states what it is about: "Now the *Book on Awakening to the Way Through Bitter Toil* [here *K'u-hsing*] is [an account of] thirteen years of spiritual wandering to seek the Way (*ts'an-tao hsing-chiao*)." After much praise of the saving efficacy of the text, the first chapter of the *K'ai-hsin fa-yao* edition begins with the lines:

Fearing impermanence and the sufferings of birth-and-death, I took the first step, observing that all things in the world course on impermanence; all that has form is empty and lost. The affairs of a hundred years pass in an instant. Wealth, noble position, and glory are like a dream. When one considers, they are all [revealed] to be an empty, flowery dream. When one looks carefully, not one thing exists. Lament that the human body does not last long and that the mind is anxious and sad. When the [great] impermanence [i.e., death] comes, the four elements of the body change into ashes and dirt. A drop of *hun* soul [goes to] purgatory, where there are no sun, moon, or stars and the sky and earth are black. Further, one does not know to what place it has gone to suffer. Fearing the sufferings of saṃsāra, I was unwilling to give up my quest and sought to proceed another step.

In sorrow because the human body does not last long, my mind was anxious. When my parents died, I was abandoned and left alone. At an early age I lost my parents, so as I grew up I had no one to rely on. I suffered much and was often afflicted with grief and misery (*to shou hsi-huang*). I foolishly had thought that my father and mother would long remain in the world, [but then] suddenly they died and I wept in bitter sorrow. I had simply thought that I would always be together with my parents, [but] my parents died and left me and I would never meet with them again. When a father sees his son and a son sees his father, [the son] rejoices in his kindness, [but] once [my parents] were gone and had abandoned me, I had no place to flee for refuge.

Fortunately, the celestial buddhas protected me and I grew up to adulthood. I constantly maintained a vegetarian diet, feared birth-and-death, and desired to have some control over the path ahead [i.e., my future]. When I thought about how my parents had disappeared, my mind was troubled and anxious. Thinking of birth-and-death and the sufferings of saṃsāra kills the mind with sorrow (*t'an-sha jen-hsin*). In an instant they were dead, the parents who had given me birth; and worse, I didn't know where I would be reborn after death. (1:17–22)

. . . To move another step, as I thought about my soul, I didn't know where it would reside. For measureless kalpas, birth has ended in death and death in turn has led to rebirth. One suffers in the four forms of birth and the six life paths,[6] and so has rotated through rebirths until the present. Once one obtains human form, the affairs of a hundred years pass like a dream, like an illusion, and after death one does not know where one will go to be afflicted with suffering. Being a human in the world is a great dream. In one morning one cannot guarantee the next. So [I] wanted to seek out a way of escape, filled with fear of the sufferings of saṃsāra. Unwilling to give up the quest, I took another step. (1:24)

This theme of suffering and loss is repeated and elaborated on in the following pages:

When birth-and-death arrives, these four bodily elements turn into ashes and earth. Suddenly I thought of my soul and this stinking bag of skin, where pus and blood accumulate, given birth to by my parents: Where does my soul come from? Who gave birth to it? As I realized that I had no place to flee, my mind was disturbed. Birth ends in death, death ends in birth; one cannot live long. When the four constituents of the body die, in a flash of fire it becomes ashes and dust, and the little drop of *hun* soul in the underworld has no place to flee.

Oxen give birth to oxen, and horses to horses—they all have parents; why is it only I, this little soul, who have none?

Travelers who leave their native districts return to their homes; why is it only I who have no native place (*chia-hsiang*)? In the whole wide earth, men and women all have parents; why is it only I, this little soul, who have none? (1:26–28)

In other sectarian texts, the term *chia-hsiang* ("home district," "native place") refers to the Eternal Mother's paradise, but here it has a biographical and psychological meaning.

After more lament, Lo Ch'ing writes that suddenly one day a letter came from a friend, saying that he knew an enlightened master. Lo Ch'ing went to see him, bowed in reverence and refused to leave his side, asking how he should practice, but the master did not respond. This went on for half a year until the master showed compassion and was finally willing to speak:

He told me that the Buddha Amitābha was the Eternal Parent (Wu sheng fu-mu; lit. "father-mother"), and that this drop of light [my soul] was an infant (*ying-erh*), a child and descendant of the Buddha. I then knelt down and asked the teacher to tell me where the Buddha is. The teacher responded that the Buddha Amitābha is in another country in heaven. When I asked him "How does one go there?" he said that if I recited the four-character Buddha name [A-mi-t'o Fo], then I would be able to ascend [to be reborn in paradise]. Every day I recited Amitābha's name, unwilling to give up. I recited while walking and sitting, fiercely advancing along the path of merit [so that], when death approached, [while] raising up my recitation I would transcend the three realms, reach the Buddha-Land of Security and Nourishment [another name for Amitābha's paradise], and there meet my parent face to face [I take this to refer to Amitābha].

I recited Amitābha's name day and night for eight years; I did not sleep morning or evening, fiercely advancing on the path of merit. I exhausted my strength, calling out "Eternal Parent." I was afraid that Amitābha would not be able to hear me, so I labored, reciting "Amitābha" day and night without stopping. [However,] my mind was not enlightened, I did not obtain spiritual freedom and independence, and so I went on ahead. (1:34–37)

This theme of incessant recitation in the fear that he would not be heard is repeated, with the added concern that at death, as his vital force expired, he would not be able to recite the name: "Then how would I ascend?" Thus Lo Ch'ing began to realize that the "other land" was an illusion, "empty and without foundation," and his "mind was terrified, unable to find peace" (1:41–43). This peace was to come from another direction. As he writes:

Before long, in a neighbor's home the old mother died, and a group of monks [came to] recite the *Chin-kang k'e-i* (Ritual amplification of the *Diamond Sūtra*). That night I stood transfixed on the street listening to the *Chin-kang k'e-i*, which says that "people should believe and accept [its message], pick it up and themselves examine and read it." When I heard this sentence, my mind rejoiced, and I requested a copy of the *Chin-kang k'e-i* and read the whole of it for three years. Fearing the sufferings of saṃsāra and unwilling to give up the quest, my search continued another step. (1:46)[7]

After three years of studying and meditating on the *Chin-kang k'e-i*, awakening still eluded him. He could not eat rice or drink tea and his mind was anxious and unsettled, fearing that death could come in an instant and worried that he would not escape saṃsāra or would not be reborn in human form. Next he tried seated meditation, but that was to be "like a dead thing." Lo continues:

I wanted to maintain mental stillness, but that also is to restrain the mind. Reciting "Amitābha" and discussing koāns are also not [the Way]. To recite within with mouth and tongue is also not it. To recite the Buddha's name in four or six characters is to be led forward (*yin-chin,* which the commentary here says means *yu-yin,* "to be led astray"). To speak of sending forth the yang spirit (*ch'u yang-shen*) is a heretical teaching.[8] The [Scripture of the] Sixth Patriarch says, "To [try to liberate] oneself is a dualistic teaching, not the Buddha's teaching." To speak of samādhi is a waste of breath. To speak of nourishing the jewel [is deluded?].[9] As for speaking of the three passes (*san-kuan*), [the body] is a bag of pus and blood that should not be discussed.[10] To know the precise instant of birth-and-death [through divination] is not to be free and independent. All of these miscellaneous teachings and methods are useless when death approaches. So, fearing the suffering of saṃsāra, and unwilling to give up, I continued my search. (1:51–62)

In these passages we see Patriarch Lo considering and rejecting a variety of methods from both Buddhism and popular religion. For him, all proved to be untrue and ineffective. As he says,

I clearly understood that they were not real [and that they] provided no place of refuge. This saddened me, and every day I was ceaselessly disturbed. Listless, I passed the time weeping. Where there were no people, my eyes were full of tears and I was continually anxious. Where there were people, I laughed aloud and forced myself to be lively. I feared that if I didn't answer, my friends would consider me strange. As there was no help for it, I went along with them [i.e., accommodated myself to them] and answered cheerfully (*le tao ta-ying*)[?]. Fearing birth-and-death, with desperate urgency I sought to advance a step, and then I thought of the very beginning, when there were no Heaven and Earth: What was the situation then?

To investigate another step: At the very beginning, when there were no Heaven and no Earth, what were the circumstances then?

Then suddenly I penetrated through to emptiness [and realized] that before there were Heaven and Earth there was unmoving emptiness, with no borders or limits, unmoving and unwavering, the Dharma body of all the buddhas. Heaven and Earth will decay, but emptiness does not decay; it is the Dharma body of all the buddhas. But, fearing the suffering of saṃsāra, [I] was unwilling to give up the quest and so moved forward another step.

In an instant, as I took another step, in my mind there was a great joy. I thought back to the very beginning, when there were no Heaven and Earth: What was there? Emptiness is prior and Heaven comes later; true emptiness does not move. Heaven has boundaries, but emptiness has none: It is the Dharma body of the buddhas. When one investigates true emptiness above, there is no place where it ends; when one seeks it out below, it is bottomless and inexhaustible. (1:64–70)

There follow several more lines on the limitlessness of emptiness in every direction. Then the narration continues:

To move forward another step, though I knew that emptiness was the Dharma body of all the buddhas, I still didn't know how to bring security and peace to myself and establish my destiny. I also did not understand how to be spiritually free and independent everywhere (*tsung-heng tzu-tsai*). In this limitless emptiness, how was I to find peace and establish my destiny? Fearing the sufferings of saṃsāra, I was unwilling to give up my quest, and so took another step. (1:73–74)

The following lines elaborate on Lo Ch'ing's continued perplexity. He had come to understand emptiness intellectually, but the peace and certainty he sought still eluded him. For him, emptiness was liberating and frightening at the same time. Nonetheless, his steady process of realization continued. He understood that emptiness covers and surrounds his body, outside and in; all is the "one substance" (*i-t'i*) of emptiness. He repeats in several ways his praise of emptiness as vast, all-encompassing, limitless. Then his understanding becomes more personal:

In an instant I moved forward a step and my mind rejoiced. [There is no need to] take refuge in being or nonbeing; I am true emptiness (*wo shih chen-k'ung*). The Mother is I [= the self] and I am the Mother (*niang shih wo, wo shih niang*);[11] fundamentally there is no duality. Empty within and without, I am true emptiness. (2:42–48)

Yet his anxieties continued, and he felt that his mind remained bound and unfree. He still had not realized complete spiritual independence. He still did not understand what would happen after death or how he could escape the insecurity and suffering of saṃsāra: "Day and night I was anxious, weeping bitterly in my dreams, shaking [my understanding of] emptiness, venerable true emptiness"(2:51–53). Then, finally, enlightenment came:

While facing southwest, sitting upright, absorbed in meditation, suddenly the flower of my mind blossomed, the foundation of my mind opened up, and [I obtained] a penetrating understanding of the underlying brilliant light. Finally I attained that state of spiritual autonomy and freedom everywhere; finally I attained freedom, peace, and security.

Walking and sitting I had sought, day and night without stopping, weeping in my dreams, my mind in sharp pain, shaking [even my sense of] emptiness. But venerable true emptiness showed compassion, and in my dream I saw a brilliant light. . . .

My whole body was pervaded with beauty, with no blockage or obstacles; whether walking or sitting, sitting or lying down, I was free everywhere. . . .

Now that I had attained this stage, I had finally obtained the state of spiritual autonomy and freedom everywhere, penetrating within and without; all became of one piece (*ta ch'eng i-p'ien*). There was no inside or out, no east, west, south, or north, no above or below. Spiritually free everywhere — walking, standing, sitting, and lying down — everywhere there was bright and glorious light, a shaft of brilliant light. (2:55–61)

The remainder of the *K'u-kung chüan* elaborates and expands on Lo Ch'ing's realization of emptiness, characterized most of all by a sense of freedom from all restraint. As he sums it up:

I toiled bitterly for thirteen years before I finally obtained awakening; only then did I recognize [in myself] the indestructible true body of the Buddha Śākyamuni. For thirteen years I toiled bitterly, without ceasing day or night, before I finally realized the indestructible golden bodies of all the buddhas and patriarchs. I searched while both walking and sitting, unwilling to give up, and finally recognized the indestructible golden bodies of men and women.

This true body, the foundation of men and women, is the body [substance] of all the buddhas.

This true body, the foundation of Heaven and Earth, originally left no traces.

This true body produced [i.e., gave birth to] Heaven and Earth, and was able to produce men and women. (2:77–78)

This praise of the true body of emptiness as the source of all continues in a creation account typical of Lo Ch'ing's blend of Buddhism with popular conceptions, although a complete discussion here would lead us too far afield. For our purposes the point is that his enlightenment experience, like that of many Chinese mystics before him, led to a realization of the essential oneness of all things, and to a profound sense of the belonging and immersion of oneself within them.

For Lo Ch'ing, this hard-won enlightenment experience was the foundation of all his teaching. He believed that he had found the way to escape from saṃsāra and proceeded to share his understanding with his followers, "those in the congregation" (*hui-chung jen*). All his old anxieties were resolved. As he writes: "Today I have finally got it. I have found peace and security and established my destiny. I roam at will and have obtained freedom and joy without limit" (2:99–100).

This, then, was the spiritual vision of the founder of one of the most influential and persistent sectarian traditions, and the existential situation behind its development. In Lo Ch'ing's struggles we see the psychological womb of the quest for assurance and deliverance that pervades much of the sectarian teaching that follows. Later texts incorporate only fragments of Patriarch Lo's vision and terminology, shaped by different religious experiences and contexts. What he understood in intellectual and psychological terms was later reinterpreted along personified and mythological lines, with emptiness as the source of all becoming a creator mother, and a place of inner peace becoming her paradise. But here Lo Ch'ing himself provided transitional language, in his evocation of emptiness as a creative source that "issues forth compassion" (*fa tz'u-pei*).

In the *K'u-kung chüan*, Lo Ch'ing realizes emptiness as the ultimate, unified source of all, a source available in the depths of his own mind. This basic insight is the foundation of all his teaching, repeated with many variations in the four books that followed. There are other ways as well in which the *K'u-kung chüan* sets the stage for the remainder of his writings, particularly the sermonic style of the latter part of the book, which is addressed in the second person (*ni*) to "those in the congregation."

Throughout all his books, Lo Ch'ing is essentially an earnest preacher, alternating promises of deliverance with threats of destruction, reminding his listeners of the sufferings and shortness of life, telling stories of spiritual heroes and villains, and citing prooftexts to reinforce his message; everything is focused on convincing people to wake up and change their ways. As he writes in the *K'u-kung chüan*,

I earnestly exhort you people in the assembly to protect yourselves against birth-and-death. Think of the suffering, anxiety, and fear of beings in all forms of rebirth. If this time you are unable to escape the bitter sea of birth-and-death, you will be reborn repeatedly in different life paths, lost for eternal eons. Those who are wise urgently believe, and think about before and after [this present life]. Through the cycles of rebirth there have been seas of tears and bones piled up like mountains. . . . Those who create karma lose their places, and human form is difficult to obtain. Those who covet fame fall back [into saṃsāra and purgatory], never to escape. . . . Seek out enlightened teachers and the correct teachings to escape from the four forms of rebirth. I earnestly urge you, people in the assembly, to devote yourselves with firm minds to the Way. (2:93–94)

SOURCES QUOTED IN LO'S TEXTS

The sources that Lo Ch'ing quotes have been listed and discussed by five different scholars since 1960, most recently and completely by Nadeau, on whose work I here rely again. His discussion of this topic is in three parts, beginning with the social and intellectual contexts of Lo's writings. This is followed by a detailed analysis of Lo's sources and how they are used, backed up by an appendix listing all of them, where they can be found if extant, and where they are quoted in the Patriarch's writings. Nadeau also includes a helpful discussion of popular stories that Lo refers to, and concludes by comparing Lo Ch'ing's thought to that of others in both China and Europe.[12] He writes as follows:

> Lo Ch'ing quotes extensively from other works in his *Wu-pu liu-ts'e*. In most instances, he provides the names of his sources, but misattribution, alteration of the original, and paraphrase are the norm for his scriptural citations, as we will discuss below. Disregarding this problem for the moment, we discover in the Five Books a total of 275 attributed quotations from 59 works, with 16 quotations from 9 works in the *K'u-kung wu-tao chüan*, 16 quotations from 13 works in the *T'an-shih wu-wei chüan*, 122 quotations from 33 works in the *P'o-hsieh hsien-cheng chüan*, 73 quotations from 23 works in the *Cheng-hsin ch'u-i pao chüan*, and 48 quotations from 30 works in the *Shen-ken chieh-kuo pao-chüan*. Lo Ch'ing's *pao-chüan* are unique in this genre for their reliance upon direct quotation from the scriptures and classics, and provide evidence of the popular use and wide circulation of a significant number of religious works, some no longer extant.[13]

Nadeau then lists Lo's sources by categories, with all titles provided, beginning with ninety-eight quotations from sixteen "canonical [Buddhist] scriptures and commentaries," and noting that the most frequently quoted books of this type are the *Diamond*, *Heart*, and *Nirvāṇa* sutrās, all of them widely known in Chinese Buddhism. Nadeau's second category is "Buddhist collections and recorded sayings," from which there are sixty-five quotes in Lo Ch'ing's writings from sixteen sources. The third category is "ritual and preaching texts," including ninety-five quotations from nineteen books. The titles of several of these books end with the word *chüan* ("volume"), while three use the term *pao-chüan*, including the *Hsiang-shan pao-chüan* discussed in Chapter One above. In this category the *Chin-kang k'e-i* is by far the most frequently cited, with a total of sixty-nine quotations from it in Lo's *Wu-pu liu-ts'e*. Nadeau comments:

Just as the *Chin-kang k'e-i* is an "amplification" of the canonical *Diamond Sū-tra*, we can assume that several of the other texts listed in this category are "instruction texts" of major scriptures, including the *Fa-hua chüan, Hsin-ching chüan, Mi-t'o pao-chüan,* and *Yuan-chueh chüan*: Lo's quotations from the corresponding *ching* may have come from these sources, though this cannot be confirmed with certainty, as [some of] the specific *pao-chüan* and *k'e-i* cited by Lo are no longer extant.[14]

Lo Ch'ing does not refer to the *Huang-chi pao-chüan* (see Chapter Two above), either because he did not know of it or because its teachings are so different from his own. None of the book titles in Nadeau's third category has an obvious sectarian "flavor"; most appear to be popularizations of Buddhist texts and teachings. It is possible that the *"pao-chüan* of the world" referred to by the *Huang-chi* book were of this type, but since the 1430 text doesn't provide any titles, it is difficult to say.

Nadeau's last category is that of "Taoist and Confucian works," in which he notes fifteen quotations from eight sources, half of them from the *Tao-te ching*, which of course supports Lo Ch'ing's nonactivist perspective. Nadeau notes that the quotes from Confucian texts appear to be from popular encyclopedias and collections of quotes from classical books that had wide circulation in the Ming period.[15]

Nadeau's dissertation also includes an interesting section on how Lo Ch'ing used quoted material, on which Nadeau comments:

It seems that Lo Ch'ing was remarkably well read, and ranged widely in the nature of the texts he was willing to cite. This would suggest significant influence of China's "higher culture"—the few persons who could read and write—on Lo Ch'ing's religious thought. But Lo was by no means a "passive receptacle," using Natalie Davis' term, of the cultural products of Chinese tradition; for Lo, texts were tools, to be altered, manipulated, and reshaped both to inspire his thinking and to conform to his own conceptions. . . .

Cheng Chih-ming has done a detailed study of Lo Ch'ing's use of his textual sources. Lo did not hesitate to alter the original text to illustrate his themes, and most of the quoted passages—as Lo reformulates them—revolve around [his] basic teachings [of] emptiness, "non-manipulative" cultivation, faith and moral virtue. His alterations of the original texts do not fundamentally change their meanings so much as they highlight and simplify Lo's own principal themes.

In his manipulation of his sources, Lo is by no means unique. Loose borrowing from written texts, often without attribution, is characteristic of Chinese letters. It would not have been considered either vulgar or heterodox to substitute paraphrase, reformulation, or selective copying for attributed quotation. What can help us locate Lo Ch'ing intellectually and sociologically is the particular way in which he manipulates his sources and how he brings them to bear on his own conceptions.

Nadeau provides several examples of Lo Ch'ing's selective method of citation, demonstrating how he added to quoted passages, simplified their messages, and otherwise changed them to support his own teachings. He adds:

> If we look at the actual process of Lo Ch'ing's composition of the *Wu-pu liu-ts'e*, we can reconstruct his employment of his sources. Some of the books cited in the Five Books he must have had in his possession—if not while composing his *pao-chüan*, at least at some time during his career as a religious seeker; the quotations are either unaltered, or involve the careful substitution of particular words and phrases. In other instances, it is conceivable that Lo had heard someone preaching from a text, which he then paraphrases or cites in passing in his own composition; many of the statements attributed to *k'e-i*, *pao-chüan*, and recorded sayings are not direct quotations, but allude in short-hand to references Lo may have assumed would be familiar to his audience. Finally, Lo appeals throughout [his texts] to Buddhist narratives and popular oral tales without citing texts or re-telling the stories; these passing references indicate the existence of a widely shared oral tradition with immediate associations in the minds of his listeners and readers. They are evidence of Lo's own social background and of his effort to attract a popular audience to his religious teachings.

Nadeau then continues his discussion of Lo's sources by investigating the Patriarch's "appeal to oral tradition" in stories taken from the tradition behind the novel *The Journey to the West*, popular operas, tales of filial piety, and so forth. He concludes that Lo Ch'ing's manipulation and reinterpretation of his sources demonstrate his independent approach.[16] Thus we see the same sort of aggressive independence of thought in Lo Ch'ing's writings as we do in the *Huang-chi* book. Both were important in clearing the way for a new form of popular religious literature.

'THE BOOK OF NONACTIVISM IN LAMENTATION FOR THE WORLD' ('T'AN-SHIH WU-WEI CHÜAN')

The remainder of this chapter is devoted to brief discussions of Lo Ch'ing's other four books, beginning with the *T'an-shih chüan*. Though the underlying message is much the same in all these volumes, there are variations in emphasis and style, and some progression of thought. The latter three books are longer and more complex than the first two, with more quotations. (For descriptions of them, see Appendix G.) More detailed discussion can be found in Cheng Chih-ming's *Wu-sheng lao-mu hsin-yang su-yuan* (Sources of the Eternal Venerable Mother belief) and in Nadeau's dissertation, "Popular Sectarianism in the Ming."

As its title indicates, the *T'an-shih* book is a sustained sermon lamenting the fleetingness of life, threatening punishment for sinners, calling for repentance, and promising eternal salvation for those who accept its message. Its style is that of insistent repetition, hammering away at a few basic points with illustrations and proof-texts, alternating threats and promises. The difference is that, for Lo Ch'ing, the enlightened are beyond all dualities; for them there is no Lord Yama of purgatory, however vividly his punishments may be evoked to jolt the ignorant out of their self-destructive ways.

Lo Ch'ing's fundamental emphasis, throughout his writings, is on an underlying primordial singularity in which there are no distinctions of any kind—a singularity that is the source of all and that is still accessible to us in our own minds. Enlightenment consists in its realization, because it is our own true self. Lo adduces a multitude of names for this singularity: true emptiness, the true body, golden body, Buddha body, our original face; in *chüan* 4 of the *T'ai-shan chüan* (the last of Lo Ch'ing's five books, discussed below), forty-four synonyms are provided, all of them translated by Nadeau.[17]

In this perspective, all distinctions are unreal, yet there is one that Lo implicitly allows—namely, that between the "superior" (*shang-teng*) and the "inferior" (*hsia-teng*): "Superior people on hearing [the message] quickly participate in the Way (*ts'an tao*); inferior people refuse to awaken and so are forever lost in saṃsāra" (*T'an-shih* 1:75). This functional distinction is behind the apparent contradiction in Lo's teaching between exhorting a vegetarian diet and other pious observances on the one hand, and vehemently rejecting all conventional piety on the other. The issue is one's level of enlightenment.

As Lo says in his most radical statement of moral nondualism: "There is basically no merit for cultivating goodness, and no fault in doing evil. Those who are not yet enlightened should not seize upon these words to act in disorderly ways. If they do, at death they will certainly see Lord Yama and only with difficulty avoid being boiled in a cauldron and ground up in a mill [i.e., punished in purgatory]" (P'o-hsieh chüan 2:75). His implicit point here is that even good actions lead at best to a better rebirth that is still in saṃsāra.

There are three important emphases in the T'an-shih chüan: (1) the Buddha as creator and controller of all, (2) an appeal to all levels of society by named rank and vocation, and (3) the above-mentioned sermonic alternation between threat and promise. The emphasis on the Buddha as creator expands on a theme introduced in the K'u-kung chüan. Its point is that because the Buddha is the primal source of all, he deserves our highest allegiance. This is where one starts, but of course for the enlightened the only real Buddha is the deepest dimension of the human mind.

In the T'an-shih book, the Buddha as creator is first discussed in chapter 2 of the K'ai-hsin fa-yao commentary edition used throughout this discussion. The chapter opens in paired lines of seven-character verse, with the last three characters alternately being Fo neng chih ("the Buddha is able to put in order / control") and Fo an-p'ai ("arranged by the Buddha"), as, for example, in "The sun and moon in their rotation the Buddha is able to control; all the myriad forms the Buddha arranges. The five grains [we] eat the Buddha is able to put in order; all forms of cloth the Buddha has arranged." This pattern is repeated in rather miscellaneous fashion for "oxen and horses," "men and women," "the springs and rivers [from which] you drink," "rivers, lakes, and seas and the salt that you eat," "gold, silver, wealth, and jewels," and "mules and horses." The movements of Heaven and Earth, the Milky Way, and the seasons—all are ordered and arranged by the Buddha, as is every aspect of existence, including calamities, old age, sickness, and death (1:21-25).

This discussion of creation then moves to a condemnation of those who "revile the Dharma," which here can be taken as Lo Ch'ing's own teaching, implicitly given cosmic authority by the verses on the Buddha as creator. As we read, "I urge you people to stop reviling the Dharma (hsiu pang fa); who was able to arrange the mountains, rivers, and the great earth?" This discussion continues with repeated reminders that the sin of reviling the teaching is limitless; those who do it are "really difficult to release and save" (1:28–29).

A second interesting theme in the *T'an-shih chüan* is its explicit appeal to representatives of all levels of society, beginning in the introductory section with exhortations to the ruler and his officials to protect the Dharma (*hu fa*). Here we read, "I urge you, lords who protect the state, you must protect the Dharma; if you are willing to protect the Dharma, you will attain buddhahood with limitless merit." Similar exhortations and promises are made to civil and military officials, and to "all of you people" (*ni i-ch'ieh jen*; 1:18–19).

In a long passage urging a vegetarian diet for all, there is another specific reference to officials: "If [you] officials maintain a vegetarian diet, the thousand buddhas will rejoice and lead all of you to escape saṃsāra" (1:47). In chapter 5, the poor are exhorted to "quickly participate in the Way" and so "leave the cycles of rebirth and attain transcendence" (1:76).

The rich are explicitly addressed in chapter 6. Lo first reminds them of the worries that come with wealth. When they make loans, they spend the whole night calculating the interest and can't sleep. When they get two ounces of silver for one, they rejoice, but when no interest comes in, it is difficult to bear. When they are sick, they can't eat their good tea and food. Their bodies are bags of flesh and blood that don't last long and are soon turned to ashes. The rich oppress and cheat the good and kill animals for their feasts, which brings limitless bad karma: "Their relatives come to eat, play musical instruments, sing and dance. What they eat is sweet, but its recompense is bitter and falls upon their own bodies. [The cycle] of birth-and-death approaches, and in purgatory [all their acts] are clearly recorded in the record books of the Ten Kings. [When death comes,] demons and ox-headed bailiffs are sent to seize them."

Then it is difficult indeed for them to give up their fine houses and their children, but no amount of weeping does any good: "In purgatory there are no sun or moon and the sky and earth are dark; one cannot see one's children and one is orphaned and alone." The point is that "we ourselves receive the recompense for what we do; no one can replace us. If we commit limitless sins, we can hardly blame anyone else. In the world of the living, one may have hoarded myriad strings of cash, but in purgatory one is empty-handed, without a single coin" (1:81–89).

Lo goes on to remind the rich of the punishments of purgatory and of rebirth in animal form, and then concludes, "I urge you, wealthy people of high status, to quickly repent . . . and participate in the Way. If you do not turn around, you will lose your footing and forever fall into saṃsāra. If you do participate in the Great Way and enlighten your true nature, you will forever be free of suffering in the cycle of birth-and-death and attain transcendence" (1:92).

In *chüan* 2 of the *T'an-shih* book, Lo turns again to officials. He sympathizes with their worries but reminds them that if they do evil and kill animals and people, they too will suffer, despite their beautiful homes and clothing and fine horses. All their acts are recorded in purgatory, and not even filial children can substitute for them before Lord Yama (2:3–4). He urges officials, as he does the rich, to quickly repent and participate in the Way (2:12).

The next group Lo Ch'ing addresses is monks, whom he first reminds of the sufferings they must endure because they have rejected their families and left their home villages. When they beg for their food they are harassed by dogs, and at the homes of evil persons they are chased out the gate. When those who remain in the household life become ill, their relatives care for them, but those who have left it have no one to inquire about them, and so they suffer: "Who would have thought that monks would suffer so? They are unable to find a way of escape, and so their labor is in vain."

When monks go to purgatory, they are asked what kind of religious practice they followed and who is the Buddha in charge of the teaching—both questions implying the superiority of Lo's own approach. Thus monks, too, are threatened with punishments in purgatory and are urged to seek the right path. Here, as before, the address is direct: "I urge you" (*wo ch'üan-ni*). In the pages that follow, monks are told that all their conventional piety is useless, with the repeated refrain, "You look in vain for a way of escape and labor for nothing" (*hsun pu chao ch'u-shen lu, lao erh wu-kung*). Similarly, seated meditation, prostrating oneself on pilgrimages, maintaining a vegetarian diet, taking the precepts, carrying out the ten virtues,[18] reciting scriptures, mantras, and the Buddha's name, seeking the four forms of meditative absorption, and manifesting supernormal powers are all "activist methods" (*yu-wei chih fa*) that impede the mind and so are useless (2:24–27).

Lo Ch'ing's response to all this is to affirm that there is fundamentally nothing to cultivate and nothing to realize, and no difference between clergy and laity. Since one can see the meaning of the

Buddha within oneself, there is no need to toil at meditation. Those who realize this "thoroughly understand the four forms of logical distinction, transcend the three periods of time, and attain merit ten thousand times beyond that of monks" (2:33–34).[19] This lengthy sermon is summed up with fifteen exhortations to repent addressed to "you good gentlemen," on the pain of losing health, family, and the beauties of nature, and with the terrors of purgatory evoked yet again. At the end, those who respond are promised salvation (2:37–42).

Much of this material might be taken as social criticism, but that is not Lo Ch'ing's concern. For him, this is all a sermonic device to bring about spiritual deliverance based on ancient Buddhist precedents. What is socially noteworthy here is the religious self-assurance of this former soldier as he addresses everyone from the ruler on down, calling all to repentance and to acceptance of his teachings. Here Lo prepared the way for the more detailed exhortations addressed to those in named social roles that can be found in some later "precious volumes."

The *T'an-shih chüan*'s emphasis on threat and promise has already been introduced in the preceding discussion and so need not be belabored here. The threat is the fleetingness and sufferings of life and the punishments of purgatory, coupled with the pains of repeated rebirth as an animal. The promise is of escape from this saṃsāric cycle, an eternal liberation from all suffering. The means to attain this promise is belief in the teaching of the *T'an-shih* book, which consists essentially of realizing nondual singularity within one's own mind. So realized, one is equal to the buddhas—indeed, one is a buddha. This is all repeated in various ways throughout the book, but always to the same point—repentance, conversion, and salvation. At bottom, Lo Ch'ing's teachings are both simple and insistent.

There is one aspect of the "threat" part of this pattern that has not yet been emphasized—namely, Lo Ch'ing's fierce critique of the frailty of the human body, which for him is nothing more than a bag of flesh and blood subject to illness, sores, and early death, an old Buddhist theme. This critique sets up the contrast between this ordinary body and the "true body" (*chen-shen*) or "original body" (*pen-t'i*) that is our real self, and that is the same as the Dharma body (*fa-shen*) within us. This "true body" is another term for the "true nature" (*chen-hsing*) that is realized in enlightenment. After listing the organs of the body according to the categories of traditional Chinese physiology, and the excretions associated with them, Lo says,

So the nine apertures constantly leak. As a scripture says, "All forms of suffering accumulate in this body; all of its [excretions and fluids] are unclean." . . . How could any intelligent person enjoy this body? Since [the cycle of] birth-and-death is like this, with all kinds of evil dharmas, it should very much be rejected and despised. . . . As a scripture says, "One should love the Buddha body . . . [which] is the Dharma body." (*T'an-shih* 1:38–40)

This theme is developed in more detail later in the text:

Think of the endless suffering of the four types of rebirth. When one obtains human form living in the house of fire [i.e., of desires], a multitude of sufferings afflict the body. Every day while at home, one is ceaselessly anxious and dares not take one step, let alone ten. Suffering from cold and hunger are truly difficult to bear. With insufficient clothing and nothing to eat, one seeks aid from others. . . . Seeing one's children starving is like being stirred up with a knife . . . [and] when parents see their children, their eyes flow with tears. Think of the endless sufferings of birth-and-death. [Even] when one is reborn as a human, [life] is still not good because a multitude of sufferings afflict the body. One's eyes and stomach hurt; this also is purgatory. One's head and back hurt; a hundred illnesses accumulate in the body. One's whole body is in pain, and wasting diseases also develop. Who realizes that this bag of skin is the root of all suffering? (1:71–73)

Near the end of the *T'an-shih* book, the contrast with the "true body" is more explicitly developed, after another reminder of the impermanence of all things: "When the forms of birth and extinction are also extinguished, then the golden body appears. This golden body is happy beyond measure and penetrates Heaven and Earth. It is neither born nor destroyed, and for it there is no Lord Yama." This true body does not suffer from cold or heat, enjoys the flavors of good food, and is without illness. It can manifest supernormal powers and can manifest itself as men or women. If a man, "his full-moon face surpasses that of the World-Honored One"; if a woman, it "surpasses Kuan-yin." Praise of the true body continues for seventeen lines of verse, ending with the affirmation that it encompasses everything and all the myriad transformations: "This true body is the body of all the buddhas, and together with them controls the universe." This discussion continues with praise of the "fundamental body" (*pen-t'i*) that existed before Heaven and Earth and that thus precedes all distinctions (2:87–93).

Lo Ch'ing's descriptions of the body and its ills are clearly based on real experience, but for him the body is a metaphor for saṃsāra and so represents all that must be transcended if salvation is to be attained. There is no hint here of healing, only an affirmation that there is an underlying reality of the self that is beyond all suffering. It is not clear whether Lo believed that realization of this true body ends suffering in this life, or only after death.

The *K'u-kung* and *T'an-shih* books contain all of Lo Ch'ing's basic teachings; the latter three books are longer, cite more sources, and introduce some innovations, but their fundamental message is the same and there is much repetition of content. This being the case, the remainder of this chapter is devoted to a discussion of the relatively distinctive emphases of Lo's other texts.

'THE KEY TO REFUTING HERESY AND SHOWING EVIDENCE [FOR CORRECT TEACHING]' ('P'O-HSIEH HSIEN-CHENG YAO-SHIH CHÜAN')

The teachings and values of the *P'o-hsieh chüan* I have already summarized in the *Popular Culture in Late Imperial China* volume edited by David Johnson, Andrew J. Nathan, and Evelyn S. Rawski.[20] Two of this book's major themes are set forth in its title, *Refuting Heresy*, and in its citing of proof-texts to lend support and authority to the Patriarch's exhortations. Indeed, this book is a collage of quotes so densely arranged that it is sometimes difficult to see where the quotation ends and Lo Ch'ing's own teachings begin. But as Randall Nadeau has indicated, this is a false dichotomy, because the quotations *are* Lo's teaching: he has made them his own by selection, deletion, and amplification. This means that, for all practical purposes, what is quoted can be given equal weight with Lo's own words—he doesn't quote anything he disagrees with!

The "refutation of heresy" in this book is based on the larger themes of nondistinction and nonactivism that are applied to all categories, but particularly to conventional lay-Buddhist piety, with its emphasis on gaining merit through good works. As with the citation of proof-texts, this theme is introduced in the *K'u-kung* and *T'an-shih* books but developed in more detail here. What Lo Ch'ing means by "heresy" is some of the practices of popular religion and of rival sects, which are rejected because they are "activist methods" devoted to outer forms. Since this is the basis of Lo's attacks on conventional Buddhist piety as well, the distinction between such piety and "heresy" is not always clear.

Because Lo's use of quoted material has already been discussed, I concentrate here on his "nonactivist" teaching and its application to the religious world around him. Here again, the teaching of the *P'o-hsieh* book is an expansion of that in the *T'an-shih chüan*, which in the context of rejecting conventional Buddhist piety does the same with distinctions between the three teachings and such popular practices as "sending forth the yang spirit" and divining the times of birth and death. For the *T'an-shih*, all these practices are inferior to the spiritual freedom and independence (*tzu-tsai tsung-heng*) of the enlightened believer (*T'an-shih* 2:56–64), a theme often referred to in the later books as well.

Another reminder of the continuity of the *P'o-hsieh* with the *K'u-kung* and *T'an-shih* books is the Patriarch's first-person dialogue with his readers. As he writes in chapter 3:

I have awakened to the Way and have invited various scriptures to serve as proof. They verify that my enlightenment is bright and clear, and that all dharmas are empty. For thirteen years, without stopping day and night, I participated in the Way. The light was glorious, [and I saw that] not one thing exists and honored only my [true] self (*tu tzu wei tsun*). I urge all [you] multitudes to stop vilifying [the teaching]. The foundation [shared by] everyone for measureless eons has been lost, but today we meet each other. For measureless eons we have revolved in the four forms of rebirth, with limitless suffering. I urge you multitudes to stop your vilification and to-gether leave saṃsāra. I urge you monks and nuns to stop vilifying the cor-rect teaching. Laymen and laywomen, stop reviling the true scriptures. The four types of devotees [clerical and lay men and women], as disciples of the Buddha, should all accept [this teaching]. Do not distinguish between those who have left the household life and those who have not—the whole body is empty. . . . When there is distinction between self and other, then there is birth-and-death. Only return to the light, consent to return to [the source of] illumination; [then] each [of you] will attain fulfillment. Great emptiness, in-cluding all within it, originally had only one vital force.[21] Children of one Mother, [only] stop making distinctions and together you will leave saṃ-sāra. (*P'o-hsieh* 1:108–109)

Here we see a sectarian self-consciousness similar to that in the *Huang-chi* book discussed in Chapter Two above, but on a different theoretical foundation.

The most detailed affirmation of the "nonactivist method" in the

P'o-hsieh book is at the end of chapter 4 of the 1615 edition (described in Appendix G) but not in the *K'ai-hsin fa-yao* edition. It follows a long series of exhortations to "not be attached" (*ying wu chu*, lit. "one should not dwell in") and then begins with "activist methods are precisely the highway to birth-and-death," in 3/3/4 verse. This is followed by eleven lines beginning with *wu-wei fa* ("the teaching of Nonactivism"), which is described as "forever cutting off saṃsāra" and enabling one to "be the equal of the buddhas," without suffering or difficulties. *Wu-wei* means to seek deliverance only in the inner spiritual potential of the self; its content can best be understood in contrast to the "activist" approaches that Lo Ch'ing criticizes. As we read in chapter 4,

The true precepts of the self lack birth-and-death; to maintain the conventional precepts is to enter the cycle of saṃsāra. The five precepts and the ten virtues are the road to birth-and-death; those who cling to doing good acts [for their salvation] fall into saṃsāra. . . . The true precepts of the self are the Western Land [= paradise]; not to be attached to form is *wu-wei*. You should not be attached; so saṃsāra is cut off. . . . The Dharma body of all the buddhas is in the mind; one's original nature is the same as the body of all the buddhas. Recognize that all the buddhas assemble in oneself. The realms of all the buddhas are in the mind. All that has form is the road to birth-and-death; do not be attached [to it] and so cut off the cycle of rebirth. (1:126–129)

For Lo Ch'ing, all our problems are due in effect to an epistemological error—the making of distinctions in the external realm. As he writes near the beginning of the *P'o-hsieh* book, following the *Chin-kang k'e-i,*

Only because you make distinctions (*fen-pieh*) is there birth-and-death. If you would only return to the [inner] light, everything would be complete and fulfilled. The mind is the Buddha, the Buddha is the mind; originally they were not two. It is ignorant people, whose faith doesn't go far enough, who seek on the outside. Those who remain at home and those who have left the household life all have [this light]; men and women, women and men can all [attain] complete fulfillment. It is because you make distinctions that you don't understand the Great Way . . . [and so] fall into saṃsāra. . . . For every household there is a road to Ch'ang-an. . . . [I] want now to gather together all men and women to attain [lit. "realize"] the Diamond great arena of enlightenment (*tao-ch'ang*). The wisdom of household bodhisattvas is extraordinary; the place of enlightenment is in the midst of market crowds. Everyone possesses the Pure Land of the West; from high mountains to level plains, all is the Western Land. (1:30–34)[22]

The effect of all this nondual affirmation is to short-circuit conventional piety and rituals, which assume that by outward actions the devotee can get from here to there. In both the *P'o-hsieh* and *Cheng-hsin* texts (see next section), Lo Ch'ing applies this understanding to an attack on the ritual practices of both Buddhism and popular religion. As he writes in chapter 6 of the *P'o-hsieh chüan*,

To believe in heresy (*hsin-hsieh*), burn paper [memorials, etc.], reverence the White Lotus, and reverence spirits is to fall into purgatory. Calamity comes from following ghosts and spirits. . . . Activist meditative absorption is [in the realm of form] . . . [but] form is emptiness and emptiness is form; all that has form is empty. How pitiful to sit in meditation without enlightening the mind. . . . How pitiful to love darkness while sitting in meditation, like a drunken man who binds himself without a rope. [Such a person] restrains his mind, binds himself up, and so is not independent. He sits until morning for nothing. (2:44–54)[23]

This critique continues on the following pages in seventeen lines of 3/3/4 verse, where we are told that "to cling to" various forms of religious practice is to "turn one's back on the Great Way [beyond] birth[-and-death]" (*wu-sheng ta tao*). This list of condemned practices includes recitation, receiving the precepts, meditative absorption, bowing to false forms (images), making donations, ascetic self-discipline, and seeking buddhahood, all of which imply rejection of the true Way (2:62–63).

In chapter 8 of the *P'o-hsieh* book, the criticism of charitable donation and taking the precepts is expanded upon. "Donation" (*pu-shih*; Skt. *dāna*) here means contributing to Buddhist causes to gain merit, an activity firmly in the realm of karma and saṃsāra that Lo was concerned to transcend. Taking the precepts could also be interpreted as a merit-gaining exercise.

On donation, Lo writes, "With donation of wealth [one still] returns [to saṃsāra]; it does not lead to release. But donation of the Dharma [by preaching to others] leads to leaving the world and forever roaming free." This passage continues with a quote attributed to a compendium of Buddhist texts: "To bestow drink and food aids life for one day; to bestow precious jewels, money, and goods supplies the wants of one lifetime but increases entanglements. To preach the Dharma for salvation is called 'donation of the Dharma,' which is able to cause living beings to escape the way of the world" (2:97–98).[24] All this is supported by more quotes on the following pages, while in chapter 10 of the *P'o-hsieh* book we read:

To be a monk or a layman, to sit in meditation, receive the precepts, recite scripture, eat vegetarian food, worship at [Mount] Wu-t'ai, roam about [in search of enlightenment], repair monasteries, build pagodas, mold buddha images and bow before them, to "stick into fire" and expel demons, . . . print scriptures and make images—all this is to manipulate puppets. When [at death] one's breath is cut off, [with such practices] one will seek in vain for a path of escape. (2:143)[25]

"Manipulating puppets" creates an illusion, as do all "activist methods," which for Lo are like "dreams and bubbles" (2:116).

This attack on all that is sacred in ordinary Buddhist practice is repeated in *chüan* 3 of the *P'o-hsieh* book, where we are reminded that images made of mud and preaching about karma, purgatory, the positions of the buddhas, and so forth mislead people into "seeking [salvation] in externals, which never succeeds." Only "suddenly awakening oneself and seeing one's own original nature enables one to surpass the positions of all the buddhas. If one does not awaken oneself, one will never attain the Way" (3:10, 13). Here again, Lo Ch'ing popularizes old Ch'an ideas.

Because, for Lo, even conventional Buddhist rituals such as reciting scriptures and the Buddha's name are "heretical traditions" (*hsieh-tsung*), it is not surprising that he attacks popular religious practices even more vehemently. Citing a text unfortunately now lost, Lo writes, "To believe in devils and burn paper [documents] is not worthy of respect . . . and leads one to lose the way." Such practices imply fear of ghosts and spirits, which is unworthy of good Buddhists and leads only to rebirth in saṃsāra (3:29–34).[26]

All of chapter 14 of the *P'o-hsieh* book is devoted to "refuting the activist practice of sending forth the yang spirit and determining the time of return [i.e., death]," which Lo condemns as submission to the control of yin, yang, and time. With such limits one does not obtain spiritual freedom and independence. Such freedom comes only with devotion to the Great Way (*ta tao*), "which yin and yang cannot control, Heaven cannot cover, Earth cannot bear, and the sun and moon cannot illuminate." The commentary here describes "sending forth the yang spirit" as the supernormal power of sending it out through the top of the head. This spirit, or soul, travels great distances but can return in an instant, and can see others and be seen by them. Determining the time of death is discussed as a divination practice of "heretical masters" (*hsieh-shih*), who by observing the body determine when one will die (3:36–37).

This critique of "miscellaneous methods" (*tsa-fa*) is continued in chapter 19, but the last chapters of the *P'o-hsieh* book themselves dwindle off into much repetition and what could be called "miscellaneous quotation." One senses that Lo Ch'ing was hard pressed to complete twenty-four chapters!

The *P'o-hsieh* book ends, as it began, with statements of gratitude to the ruler and officials who protect both the state and the Dharma, and to "all the multitudes who protect and maintain the wonderful Dharma and circulate it throughout the world, so that all may be saved and leave saṃsāra" (4:119). At the conclusion of this section, Lo Ch'ing says of himself, "The Wu-wei lay devotee earnestly vowed to save [people] everywhere, that they might quickly repent. [May these] five scriptures circulate throughout the world, saving all clergy and laypeople, [by enabling them] to leave the cycle of suffering" (4:119). Yuan-ching's commentary in the *K'ai-hsin fa-yao* edition (see Appendix G) quotes a brief summary of this book by the Venerable Master Lan (Lan-feng), who says of Lo Ch'ing that he

exhausted his strength in borrowing from various scriptures to provide proof. [This book] circulates throughout the world, and all of it teaches people to oppose heresy and give allegiance to what is correct (*fan-hsieh kuei-cheng*), to get rid of their evil minds and stimulate good thoughts, to depart from their human minds [= ordinary ways of thinking] and return to the mind of the Way (*tao hsin*). . . . Fearing that people would not believe, he took the scriptures of the Tathāgata to speak directly to those of later [generations], that their doubts might be removed. . . . Hence those in the Patriarch's school (*tsu-chia men-hsia*) must read [this book], and must believe and accept it. If they do not, purgatory will be difficult to escape. (4:116, 118)

'THE PRECIOUS VOLUME OF SELF-DETERMINATION, NEEDING NEITHER CULTIVATION NOR VERIFICATION, WHICH RECTIFIES BELIEF AND DISPELS DOUBT' ('CHENG-HSIN CH'U-I WU HSIU CHENG TZU-TSAI PAO-CHÜAN')

For the most part, the *Cheng-hsin chüan* continues and expands the themes in the three of Lo Ch'ing's books already discussed, with a shared rejection of false distinctions, externalized rituals and image worship, and material donation. As the title indicates, this book is much concerned with proper belief, but that is emphasized in the *P'o-hsieh* book as well. Its chief innovations are the introduction of a new deity and specific attacks on sectarian rivals such as the Maitreya sect. The title of the deity in question is Wu-chi sheng-tsu

(Holy Patriarch of the Limitless), here described as the creator of all through self-manifestation in different forms. The commentary indicates that this title refers to the Buddha, but we know that decades before Lo Ch'ing, the term "Wu-chi" was already being used in sectarian scriptures to refer to the time of the Buddha of the Past, Dīpaṃkara, so Lo may have been appropriating older terminology to broaden the appeal of his own message. This interpretation is consonant with the clear awareness of earlier sectarian traditions shown in the *Cheng-hsin* book.

Because for Lo everything else begins with proper faith and belief, perhaps our discussion should turn first to that theme, which is introduced in the *P'o-hsieh* book, where we read that "the believing mind (*hsin hsin*) is the source of the way of merit and releases the Dharma eye" (*P'o-hsieh* 1:21) and that "belief is the way to heaven; by not believing one [falls into] purgatory with no escape" (2:17). This motif is expanded in the *Cheng-hsin chüan*, as in a passage attributed to the *Chin-kang k'e-i* where we read, "True faith is rare . . . those of the highest class (*shang teng jen*) believe without doubts, [while] those of the middle and lower levels do not [have] believing minds. . . . Those who do not believe cannot be saved" (*Cheng-hsin* 1:28–29).[27]

After a long discussion in chapter 3 of the *Cheng-hsin chüan* about the importance of maintaining a vegetarian diet, Lo writes that if those who "do so do not have believing minds, they will forever fall into saṃsāra. It is difficult to escape the world if one does not believe the Buddha's words. Those who revile the Dharma are forever lost, and not believing is the same as reviling" (1:94).

The point that inner faith is more important than outer action is made even clearer in a discussion of those who kill animals, who with one recitation of Amitābha's name in faith can "be reborn in the Pure Land," which for Lo is the same as "returning home": "Those who kill chickens . . . [or] go fishing, with one recitation of the mind [in faith] (*i nien hsin*) return home, [but] vegetarians who do not believe in the Buddha fall and are lost." Repentance is mentioned in this discussion, but the emphasis is on the power of belief to overcome even the serious sin of killing other beings. This theme is repeated in the *Cheng-hsin* book in several different ways and is summed up at the end of chapter 3: "Vegetarians who don't believe in the Buddha go to purgatory; if those who kill animals quickly believe, they are able to realize [their] golden bodies" (1:94–100, 110).

Such belief is vital, because without it "one is a human being in vain" (*k'ung wei jen*), a theme repeated several times in *chüan* 2 (2:13–21). Correct belief is thus a vital aspect of the quest for deliverance.

Another theme in the *Cheng-hsin chüan* that is a continuation of the *P'o-hsieh* book is its rejection of image worship as a false "clinging to outer form." Beginning with reminders that all form is empty, in chapter 9 Lo writes:

Clinging to [images of] copper and iron is stupid and empty [i.e., in vain]; emptiness is form . . . [and] form is emptiness; clinging to recitation is empty vital force with no place for refuge and rest; when death approaches and the four elements [of the body] scatter, where will you find security and peace? . . . Buddhas with form lead people astray; they are not true images. Formless buddhas are the true Buddha, which is preserved forever. . . . What you recite is [the name of] a buddha of form, an image made of mud. What I recite is the Buddha of the Limitless, which covers everything in the ten directions. What you recite [to] are false images of copper, iron, and wood. What I recite is the Buddha of the Limitless who controls the universe.

This passage continues with praise of the limitless scope and power of the true Buddha, who is the source of all (*Cheng-hsin* 2:96–100). This iconoclasm is continued in chapter 16, where we are again reminded that "it is the confused and lost who seek on the outside. Think back to the very beginning; for Śākyamuni, there were originally no images. . . . Śākyamuni, without buddha-images, had nothing [external] to rely on. . . . With nothing to rely on, he honored only himself."

This pattern is repeated for several other buddhas and Kuan-yin, and is extended to Confucius, who "had no teacher," and to Lao-tzu, who also had no images to rely on. At the end of chapter 16, the point is restated:

The original face for limitless eons has never had false images; without false images and with nothing to rely on, honor the [true] self alone. First there was the true, and only later the false; do not take refuge in false images. The original face is the true image; honor the self alone. (*Cheng-hsin* 3:92–99)

The "original face" (*pen-lai mien*) is a Ch'an term referring to the potential for enlightenment within. Richard Shek has summarized the evidence that some of Lo Ch'ing's later followers rejected image worship and even the veneration of ancestors, so we see that even the Patriarch's more radical teachings had a continuing impact.[28]

In addition to rejecting image worship, in the *Cheng-hsin chüan* Lo

Ch'ing resumes his criticism of other forms of conventional piety, which he here calls "miscellaneous methods from the demon realm" (*mo-ching tsa-fa*). These methods include reciting scriptures and the Buddha's name, burning incense, bowing before images, and taking the precepts, all of which are described as "useless" (*yung pu-chao*). The same condemnation is applied to such Taoist practices as "embryonic breathing" and to such categories of Taoist mystical physiology as the "cinnabar field" (*tan-t'ien*) in the lower abdomen, and the "*ni wan* palace" at the top of the head. Such practices as clinging to belief in ghosts and spirits, employing supernormal powers, and "sitting in fire and water, [hoping that] ghosts and spirits will come to one's aid" all lead to purgatory, and hence are of no avail for salvation. Those who carry out such rituals are all ignorant people who cause later generations to have doubts, and who are unable to attain the Way (*Cheng-hsin* 4:54–58).

Since Lo Ch'ing rejected even conventional Buddhist, Taoist, and popular practices, it is not surprising that he attacked the beliefs and rituals of other sectarians as well, on the same grounds of attachment to false outward forms. Some of his language here is reminiscent of that of the *Huang-chi pao-chüan*. Chapter 18 of the *Cheng-hsin chüan* is devoted to an attack on the "heretical ritual practice of worshipping the sun and moon," which he attributes to the White Lotus sect, saying that

there are some stupid people who believe in heresy, burn paper [documents], and seek after the White Lotus sect, which really has a heretical spirit (*hsieh-ch'i*). [Such people] eternally fall into purgatory with no hope of escape. . . . The White Lotus worships images of the sun and moon, and burns paper images, and "recognizes forms in Dharma water" (*fa-shui jen hsiang*), [not realizing that, as] the *Diamond Sūtra* says, "all forms are empty." When death comes they fall into purgatory, . . . never to escape.

All this is vehemently repeated in verse in the following section, with the "White Lotus" accused of leading multitudes astray, cheating them out of their money, and condemning them to suffering and purgatory. Its supporters are told that "sooner or later you will be seized and taken to the place of execution. . . . If you believe in heretical teachers, you will go to purgatory with no hope of escape. If you deceive others, you will be slain as a matter of no importance. How pitiful are you men and women who go to the execution ground" (*Cheng-hsin* 4:11–17). Here Lo Ch'ing calls on both legal and religious sanctions to support his attack.[29] There is no doubt that Lo believed what he was saying, but it did him no harm to dissociate himself from what was called the "White Lotus tradition," which had been outlawed since the Yuan period.

Chapter 10 of the *Cheng-hsin* book is also devoted to explicit attacks on rival sectarians—the Maitreya sect and a group called the "Sect of the Dark Drum" (Hsuan-ku chiao), which is accused of "worshipping the sun and moon as father and mother, and gazing at them until your eyes are dim, willingly bringing suffering on yourselves." Unfortunately, the only specific accusation against the Maitreya sect is "writing Buddhist charms"; the rest is general statements about heresy, the emptiness of all forms, and condemnation to purgatory (4:18–21).[30] Nonetheless, such attacks on other popular groups helped clarify what was distinctive in the perspective of the nascent Lo sect.

The last distinctive theme of the *Cheng-hsin* book is that of the Holy Patriarch of the Limitless (Wu-chi sheng-tsu, a figure discussed in detail in chapter 5 of that book) as the supreme deity and source of all. This is a personification of the Ultimate referred to in the *T'an-shih chüan* and elsewhere in Lo's writings. Here he is described as "manifesting himself to save all living beings." We are told of Wu-chi sheng-tsu that, "in his great compassion and pity, fearing that living creatures, through their creation of karmic obstacles, would be reborn in the four life forms and the six paths of existence, never to escape," he manifested himself in various forms to save all. As the commentary notes, some of these forms correspond to earlier rebirths of Śākyamuni before he appeared as the Buddha, so the core of the figure of the Holy Patriarch is the Buddha himself. However, his other manifestations are Chinese, including Mu-lien and two of the twenty-four paragons of filial piety, so Wu-chi sheng-tsu is a composite figure combining Buddhist and Chinese traditions, an analog of Lo Ch'ing himself. It is interesting that four of the manifestations here are as "worthy women" (*hsien-nü*), beginning with the well-known heroine Meng Chiang, who found her husband's bones buried in the Great Wall (*Cheng-hsin* 2:25, 32–59).

However, Wu-chi sheng-tsu's manifestations are not limited to human beings; the whole universe is his arena, all manifested by him. In an amplification of his account of the Buddha as creator in the *T'an-shih* book, Lo Ch'ing writes in chapter 9 of the *Cheng-hsin* book that "the great world, Heaven and Earth are all controlled by Wu-chi; the five lakes, seas, oceans, and rivers are all [due to] the transforming power of Wu-chi; the rotation of the sun and moon and the Celestial River [= Milky Way] are [also due to its] divine power." This list continues, with the creation of the four seasons, grain, grass, trees, fruits, and men and women all attributed to the "manifest transformations" (hsien-hua) of the Limitless (2:100–101).

As we have seen, it is this supreme source of power that Lo Ch'ing indicates is the only proper object of reverence, though of course this symbol of primordial singularity must be understood in relationship to all the other such symbols discussed in his five books. What we have in the Holy Patriarch is the most theological expression of this symbolism, but by no means its dominant mode, which is expressed in such terms as "original face" or "true body." As we have seen, the major thrust of Lo Ch'ing's thought is inward-turning and mystical. The personified concept of the Holy Patriarch of the Limitless could be dropped from his teachings without doing them serious damage.[31]

'THE PRECIOUS VOLUME OF DEEPLY ROOTED KARMIC FRUITS, MAJESTIC AND UNMOVED LIKE MOUNT T'AI' ('WEI-WEI PU-TUNG T'AI-SHAN SHEN-KEN CHIEH-KUO PAO-CHÜAN')

In the T'ai-shan chüan,[32] Lo Ch'ing thrice refers to his own "five scriptures," so it appears that the other four were composed earlier. In a passage in chapter 1 directed to "those in my school" (wo tang-chia chih jen), "male and female bodhisattvas from all directions" (shih-fang nan-nü p'u-sa), he says that they should "urgently listen to my five scriptures, which will save you from the illness of doubt (i-ping). Not one thing exists. If what I say is not true, may my body turn to pus and blood" (T'ai-shan 1:36–37). Later in chapter 1 we read,

Those who backslide (t'ui-tao chih jen) all have the sickness of doubt. . . . [Such people] should quickly listen to my five scriptures, which will save you and enable you to escape from the sea of suffering. . . . My five scriptures include myriad sentences [of teaching] about returning home. They are not difficult to put into effect and don't waste energy; they don't waste effort. If clever people listen to them one time, their minds will be thoroughly awakened." (1:48, 45–46)

These references to Lo Ch'ing's other books help explain the repetitive nature of the T'ai-shan volume, which contains nothing essentially new. Perhaps it was perceived as one last summary of his teachings. Lo himself justifies such repetition as a teaching device:

"It is because you don't understand that I have repeatedly explained in detail" (2:25).

Nevertheless, there are a few points of interest in the *T'ai-shan* book. It discusses several terms in Lo Ch'ing's repertoire of symbols for the primordial singularity that is both the source of all and the deepest level of human selfhood: "original face," "old Native Place," "the root" (*ken*), the "priceless jewel," "[true] human nature," "true body," "golden body," the "Great Tao," the "one character" (i.e., the mind), "one vital force," and the "emptiness of nonbeing." All these are intended as terms for what "never decays" and "lasts forever" (2:20), and they provide the basis for resounding religious self-affirmation. As we read in chapter 6:

The names of all the myriad things are expressed and made manifest by the self. Your numinous light is great and honored. Why don't you believe in the mind? A believing mind is the source of the way of merit. . . . You yourself are real; the myriad things are empty. Your nature is real. Your nature existed before creation; why don't you take responsibility for it now (*chin-ch'ao ju-he pu ch'eng-tang*)?

This priority of the true nature to all else is repeated for Heaven and Earth, good and evil, birth and death, purgatory, religious practice, yin and yang, the buddhas and bodhisattvas, clergy and laity, meditation, precepts and rules of monastic life, scriptures, the three teachings, karma, the Ancient Buddha, past and present, and gods and immortals. Devotees are told, "The original face of your own body will last forever, and at the time of death it emits a bright light that shakes the earth" (*T'ai-shan* 2:27–44, 50). This theme is repeated in different terms in chapter 22, which discusses "confused people who say they have not yet reached the field [i.e., level] of the ancients." Lo says in response to this self-doubt, "The Great Tao has never been apart from your minds. Your whole body [= self] is [the Way]; you have never lacked anything. . . . You yourself are prior to all things" (4:81–84).

As in the *K'u-kung chüan*, Lo here uses the term "Mother" as a metaphor of primordial unity; in chapter 4 of the *T'ai-shan* book she is described as "the Mother of all things" and of the buddhas, scriptures, and the three teachings. All things

flow out of this one character (*tzu*), . . . written "Mother." The Mother is the ancestor and the ancestor is the Mother.

. . . All things flow out of this one character, the original face, which is written "Mother" . . . [or] "ancestor." Whom do you fear? Do you not take responsibility for [your original nature]? What real [person] fears what is empty? What large fears the small? Not taking responsibility is stupid. (1:86–90)

The term I have translated here as "ancestor" (tsu) also means "patriarch" and perhaps refers to the Holy Patriarch of the Limitless discussed above. In any case, the term "Mother" here is thoroughly immersed in the context of symbols of primordial unity. As suggested in the Introduction above, perhaps this metaphysical status helped prepare for the later mythological concept of a single Divine Mother as the source of all.

Other points in the T'ai-shan book worthy of note are its repeated attacks on the "stupid" (yü-ch'ih) for their lack of belief, reviling the teaching, and deceiving of others (1:24, 62, 64). In chapter 7 they are contrasted with the intelligent, who recognize and take responsibility for their true selves, whereas "stupid men and women do not believe and so suffer in purgatory" (2:63). Purgatory itself is repeatedly used as a threat in this text, yet in chapter 10 those who do not cling to outer forms are told that "there is no heaven, no purgatory, and originally no birth-and-death" (3:15), while "for those who have awakened to the Way, there is fundamentally no karma" (3:64–65). Thus Lo Ch'ing carried this ancient Mahāyāna message into the heart of Ming dynasty popular culture. Nonetheless, without the support of an educated clergy, such understanding was soon lost, except as echoes of what Lo himself had said.

In his texts, then, the Patriarch Lo appears as an earnest religious preacher and reformer who took the more radical side of the Ch'an tradition at its word and applied it directly to the life of ordinary people—men and women, clergy and laity. The sect that developed in response to his teaching has been discussed by a number of scholars; the following section looks at evidence for the influence of Lo Ch'ing's texts on those of later sectarian writers.

THE INFLUENCE OF LO CH'ING'S FIVE SCRIPTURES
ON LATER TEXTS IN THE WU-WEI SECT TRADITION

In Ming and Ch'ing historical sources, there are references to several books in addition to the Wu-pu liu-ts'e that were possessed by Lo-related sects. J. J. M. de Groot discusses such books that he found in Wu-wei sect congregations in late nineteenth-century Amoy.[33] I have two books that exalt Lo Ch'ing as the founding patriarch of the tradition they represent. The first was published in 1682 and is entitled the *San-tsu hsing-chiao yin-yu pao-chüan* (The religious activities of the three patriarchs and their karmic causes and connections). This book is in three *chüan*, named respectively after patriarchs surnamed Lo, Yin, and Yao, with the latter two considered to be reincarnations of their predecessors. In it, the Patriarch Lo is presented as a powerful miracle-worker who saves China from a foreign invasion and from scheming foreign monks. Since I have earlier published a summary of the portrayal of Lo Ch'ing in this text, I will not repeat it here.[34] The attitude of the later chapters toward him is well indicated by a passage about Patriarch Yin: "Since he is the Patriarch Lo reborn, what about asking him to teach the *Wu-pu liu-ts'e?*" (*San-tsu pao-chüan* 2:12b).

All of Lo's five book titles are listed in the chapter on Patriarch Yin, whose teaching echoes that of his predecessor in its rejection of adherence to outer forms and rituals and its affirmation of the validity of lay piety, practiced at home. This chapter also praises and defends the "correct way of [the sect of] Nonactivism (*wu-wei cheng-tao*)." However, there are also discussions of the Eternal Mother and Maitreya in this chapter on Patriarch Yin, which shows that by the seventeenth century this powerful mythological theme could be present even in texts firmly identified with Lo Ch'ing's tradition. At the end, Patriarch Yin's dates are given as 1531–1582.

The third chapter of the *San-tsu pao-chüan* is devoted to Patriarch Yao, who was born in 1578. He did not begin to speak until he was five *sui* of age, when Patriarch Yin died, implying that Yao's spirit was that of Yin reborn. He eventually studied with a Taoist priest and with another teacher whose religious name included the character *p'u*, which by this time was commonly used in the Lo tradition. This chapter provides the names of seventy-two branch congregations and refers to groups outside the Wu-wei sect as well; thus by the early Ch'ing, the sectarian situation was more complex, as we know from historical sources. At the end of this chapter of the *San-tsu pao-chüan*, the connection among the three patriarchs is reaffirmed. We are told that Patriarch Yao died in 1646.

The other text I have that claims direct descent from the Patriarch Lo is the *Ssu-shih hsing-chiao chueh-hsing pao-chüan* (The precious volume concerning the religious activities and awakening of the fourth-generation [patriarch]), in two *chüan* (preface dated 1899). This book is devoted to a sect patriarch named P'an San-to, who was born in

1826 and died in 1872. During and after the Taiping Rebellion (1851–1864), he was a Wu-wei sect teacher who kept very close to Lo Ch'ing's original message. This is a clearly written text that can speak for itself. In a prose passage near the beginning of the book, we read:

The Holy Patriarch descended to the ordinary [world] in the Wan-t'ang area of Nan [= South] township of Chin-hua prefecture in Chekiang [province], into the large P'an lineage in the early morning of the fifth day of the twelfth lunar month of Tao-kuang 5 (1826). He was given the name San-to. He was a vegetarian from childhood. His religious name (*fa-hao*) was P'u-tu. He did not live in an ostentatious manner but was upright and square in his behavior. By nature he was fond of quiet and ease [reading *shih*, "fond of," for *ch'i*, "old"]. He was diligent in reading books and was a tailor by trade. By the time he was a young man, he understood the principles of heaven and humans. He took refuge in the Three Jewels and carefully maintained the five precepts. Whenever he joined others in a discussion, he spoke of the way of enlightening the mind and seeing the nature. Our patriarch couldn't help sighing in sorrow over those who didn't understand [his message]. Once he said to himself, "It is as if they are fools and insane." One day he fell into a trance and wasn't aware of activities around him and didn't speak for three days. On the fourth day he revived with a clear, penetrating understanding of what the sages and worthies [had taught] from antiquity about rectifying the mind, making the will sincere, and cultivating one's character. All this he completely understood. He read the *Wu-pu liu-ts'e* scriptures with an understanding as bright as the sun and stars. Our patriarch sighed to himself, "Divine indeed is the Way of Patriarch Lo. It penetrates Heaven and Earth and pierces the sun and the moon. It really should be called the Great Way of Nonactivism (Wu-wei ta-tao). Alas, among the mundane and ignorant in the dusty world, no one understands [his teaching]. Even if disciples of the Wu-wei school are able to read [these books], they are unable to understand them. Even if they are able to understand, they are not able to become enlightened. They only understand the Three Refuges, the five precepts, maintaining a vegetarian diet, burning incense, bowing in worship, reciting the Buddha's name, and chanting scriptures. They even go so far as to light candles to worship the stars and Bushel [= the Big Dipper], arrange vegetarian feasts, and make offerings to images and forms that are painted and drawn. They have forgotten and rejected their original face, and so exalt the false and abandon the true. They do not understand that the five scriptures (*wu-pu ching-wen*) very clearly point out repeated distinctions and proofs. (*Ssu-shih* 1:1)

This statement is recapitulated in verse, with the added comment that "the Patriarch Lo . . . completely swept away non-Buddhists (*wai-tao*) and divergent schools." Ignorant people are criticized for "making offerings to buddha images molded from mud and earnestly holding up [pictures of] Kuan-yin inked on paper" (1:2a).

Next we are told that, because of the turmoil in the Hsien-feng reign period (1851–1861), Patriarch P'an fled to the mountains, from which he emerged in 1862. In his wanderings he came upon a cloister where he met a man of the Wu-wei tao ("Way of Nonactivism") surnamed Huang, with the religious name P'u-han. That evening, while P'u-han worshipped Kuan-yin with incense, bows, and recitation, Patriarch P'an simply sat in meditation at one side of the room. When P'u-han asked him why he did not recite the scriptures, Patriarch P'an replied that "at the beginning [of the tradition], Patriarch Lo never recited scriptures," and amplified this point in a verse section that begins:

The Great Way of the Prior Realm is based on the self-so.
From antiquity to the present, human nature has been the same as Heaven.
The true scripture without words is constantly recited.
All of Heaven and Earth speak true words.

P'u-han then says that he has read in Patriarch Lo's books that one should not recite scriptures, set up buddha-images, burn incense, make offerings, hang up banners and placards, worship the Buddha, or establish sūtra halls, but should in all cases be devoted to the Way of Nonactivism. He then asks Patriarch P'an to teach him the Patriarch Lo's Tao. The reply affirms that all the pious practices just named are false, empty, and ignorant and do not lead to escape from saṃsāra (*Ssu-shih* 1:4b–5a).

P'u-han then affirms that the "Wu-wei ta-tao is the Way spoken of in Patriarch Lo's five scriptures." After further discussion he is enlightened and takes Patriarch P'an as his master. The text comments, "Then for the first time he understood that our Master was a primal patriarch, a fourth-generation reincarnation of Patriarch Lo" (1:5b–7b).

The *Ssu-shih hsing-chiao pao-chüan* thus appears to be based on the work of a reformer in the Lo sect tradition who supported Lo Ch'ing's teachings in their pure form deep into the nineteenth century. That this is not an isolated case is demonstrated by de Groot's discovery of a Wu-wei sect with similar teachings in Amoy, as noted above. Here again, we see evidence for a continuing Lo tradition that was available to the leaders of other sects, some of whom attacked the Wu-wei chiao ("teaching of Nonactivism") for its rejection of ritual.

THE INFLUENCE OF LO CH'ING'S FIVE SCRIPTURES
ON TEXTS OF OTHER GROUPS

Several books in my collection refer directly to the Patriarch Lo, his books, and some of their characteristic terminology. (They are discussed in more detail in Chapter Five and Appendix H below.) The oldest is the 1564 *Hsiao-shih yuan-chueh pao-chüan* (The precious volume that explains complete enlightenment; text 3 in Appendix H), with the alternative title *Yuan-chueh t'ung-chien* (A comprehensive mirror for complete enlightenment). This voluminous book is in four *chüan* and thirty-two chapters (*p'in*), but the first *chüan* is missing in my copy. In chapter 22 there are references to the Way of Imperial Heaven (Huang-t'ien tao), so the book may be related to a sect of that name.[35] In chapter 23 it refers to its author as a "Master Chin-shan who wrote and left behind [this] message of compassion." In later chapters we are told that Master Chin-shan was enlightened "while in the Buddhist school" and that he provided vegetarian feasts for both monks and laypeople, aided the poor, and saved vast multitudes (chapter 30). He eventually came to live on Mount Lao in Shantung, the same area where Lo Ch'ing had been active a few decades before.

The *Yuan-chueh pao-chüan* refers to returning to the Native Place (*chia-hsiang*), a motif from Eternal Mother mythology, cites an "elixir scripture" (*tan-ching*), and teaches that one should seek "pure yang" (*ch'un-yang*). Indeed, we are told that Master Chin-shan looked at both "elixir scriptures and Buddhist books, [seeking] the verified teachings of various patriarchs" (chapter 17). This text also affirms Confucian morality and the validity of traditional forms of worship.

It is at this point that the relevance of Lo Ch'ing comes into focus, for one theme in the *Yuan-chueh* book is an attack on the iconoclasm and individualism of the popularized Ch'an that Lo represented. Lo Ch'ing is influential here as a rival and foil. We are proudly told in chapter 7 that "[this scripture] is certainly as good as [those of] Patriarch Lo." This chapter is a sustained attack on "preachers who are not awakened themselves" — that is, on

a class of teachers (*ch'uan fa jen*) who say that the Limitless (Wu-chi) is the self and the self is the Wu-chi . . . and who also say to those who study the

Way that there are no buddhas, no patriarchs, gods, or immortals, no celestial generals and celestial gods, [but that] oneself (*tzu-chi*) is the Ancient Buddha. [Since there] are no buddhas or patriarchs, how can there be a Western Heaven or an Eastern Land? The four points of the compass, above and below, are precisely the self. They honor only themselves (*tu tzu wei tsun*, a phrase from Lo's texts). They also tell people not to burn incense and paper [money]. Since oneself is the Ancient Buddha, for whom are they burnt? They also say that no effort is needed, nor recitation of the Buddha's name: Since oneself is already [the Buddha], whose name is one reciting? How can this kind of preacher not be entrapped in birth-and-death?

A rebuttal follows:

The Dharma body is the Great Tao, the Great Tao is the Dharma body. The Limitless True Emptiness is a different name for the Dharma body. The Great Tao is the body of the Ancient Buddha of True Emptiness. It is not the self (*pu-shih tzu-chi*). Stop listening to [such] demonic theories. . . . There is a real Native Place. There have been emperors and kings throughout the ages who have abandoned their realms and returned home [to paradise]. Surely they are not here! They were one body [= the same as] with [all beings] in the four forms of rebirth and the six paths of existence. I ask you, [was not] your Patriarch Lo the same as all other beings in saṃsāra? He toiled bitterly for thirteen years and feared birth-and-death. He returned home [as well]. . . .

[Master Chin-shan] also said that within the three realms there are limitless [numbers of] buddhas and patriarchs, and inexhaustible [numbers of] gods, immortals, and celestial generals and deities. Words can never fully describe the multitude of great sages. All of them establish their destiny and find peace and security for themselves in the body of the Limitless. . . . There is effort, there are fixed positions (*ting-li*), there is correct recitation, there are buddhas, there is a Native Place, there are immortals. He also said that while walking, standing, sitting and lying down, dressing and eating, one should recite the true scriptures. This is what is meant by correct recitation—this is true religious effort. When one practices like this, the Native Place upholds and illuminates [you], and the buddhas uphold and illuminate you. When your merit is complete, in an instant you will ascend directly to the true primal source.

This criticism is repeated in the succeeding verse passage:

There is a type of preacher who does not understand ritual principles, who says that Wu-chi is the self, which only deceives and confuses people. They preach that there is no Buddha, but that oneself is [the Buddha]. . . . This sort of preacher causes multitudes to go astray. . . . Think of Patriarch Lo, who, fearing birth-and-death, sought for the Great Way. Yet today he is the same as [lit. "is of one body and perspective with"] pigs and dogs.

So much for Lo Ch'ing's attempt to escape rebirth! The *Yuan-chueh* text promises salvation in the Mother's paradise for those who perform the proper rituals, believe its teachings, and develop their "pure yang bodies." There are several further brief attacks in the *Yuan-chueh* book on Lo Ch'ing's teachings—on those who are unwilling to burn incense (chapter 11), on those who speak of Wu-wei but don't understand its meaning (chapter 12), and on those who stir up the confused by telling them that there are no distinctions between the old and young and honored and humble (chapter 12).

Chapter 21 affirms the "human way" of traditional social obligations, specifically identified with Confucius and Mencius and their teachings. Readers and hearers of this text are told:

Do not study the divergent schools of nonbelievers who do not cultivate the human way, but who speak only of the Buddha way. They do not burn incense and paper [documents], they do not reverence Heaven and Earth, they do not obey the royal law, they do not accord with the six family relationships, do not honor village customs, and do not reverence the Three Jewels. They say repeatedly that there are no buddhas and patriarchs, [but that] they themselves are the true buddhas. People of this sort are really nonbelievers and heretics, [propounders of] demonic theories, criminals in the midst of Heaven and Earth.

Though the *Yuan-chueh* book several times cites the *Chin-k'ang k'e-i*, Lo Ch'ing's favorite source, it is firmly opposed to the main thrust of his teaching. But even such opposition is a form of flattery. The *Yuan-chueh* book follows the textual form further developed by Lo Ch'ing, but uses it in part to oppose his teaching on both ritual and social grounds. It advocates a more traditional lay piety based on real effort, ethical living, karmic rewards, and belief in the gods (chapter 28). Within the realm of popular religion, it throws into sharp relief the innovative dimension of Lo Ch'ing's thought.

Of all the non–Wu-wei chiao texts in my collection, the *Yuan-chueh pao-chüan* contains the most references to Lo Ch'ing and his teachings, if only to attack them. It is clear, however, that the author of this book understood what he was doing and was concerned to put forth his own teaching. I have another text that appears to be of similar date and that refers positively to terms and titles from Lo Ch'ing's books, but without such understanding. It is the *Hsiao-shih*

An-yang shih-chi pao-chüan (The precious volume that explains the true situation of the [Land of] Tranquil Nourishment; text 4 in Appendix H), in two *chüan* and twenty-four chapters. I have only the first *chüan* of this book. My edition was reprinted in 1640, along with some other texts dated to the end of the sixteenth century, so it may be of about the same date. There are references in the *An-yang paochüan* to "[Master] Chin-shan said" — the same formula as that in the *Yuan-chueh* text discussed above.

The *An-yang chüan* is a loosely organized combination of Eternal Mother mythology with moral exhortations and promises of salvation. In it, several terms from Lo Ch'ing's books are scattered about, more as pious slogans than as part of a coherent framework. Like some of Lo's books, the *An-yang* book includes a section on "reliances" (*i-t'o*) invoking the protection of the state and salvation for all. Its author states, "Now I am so bold as to vow to publish and distribute five scripture texts (*wu-pu ching-wen*)," a term often used to refer to Lo Ch'ing's scriptures. Here these texts are not named. In this introductory material there also appears the line, "enlightening the mind and seeing the nature alone are honored," and also references to the term *wei-wei pu-tung* ("majestic and unmoved"), which is often used by Lo Ch'ing to refer to the enlightened mind. In addition, there is a reference near the end of the introductory section to the "Native Place of the self" (*tzu-chi chia-hsiang*) and to all living beings "obtaining freedom [from saṃsāra]" (*te tzu-yu*) — both phrases reminiscent of the Patriarch Lo.

The title of chapter 3 of the *An-yang* text is "The Heretical Teachings of Worshipping the Sun and Moon and of the Hsuan-ku Sect." Here *hsuan* is a character meaning "to suspend" and is pronounced the same way as the *hsuan* character meaning "dark" that is referred to in chapter 19 of Lo Ch'ing's *Cheng-hsin pao-chüan*, discussed above. Chapters 18 and 19 of the *Cheng-hsin* book are devoted to specific criticisms of named practices, but in the *An-yang pao-chüan* there is a general discussion of suffering in saṃsāra. The use of Lo's title is simply nonsensical — one cannot think of even a ritual function for it. However, most of the chapter titles in the *An-yang* book have no apparent connection with chapter contents.

But whatever its level of understanding, the *An-yang pao-chüan* relies heavily on Lo Ch'ing's terms and concepts, beginning with detailed threats of the sufferings of purgatory and rebirth (in its introductory material). The basic response to this is, "Quickly, quickly repent and seek out an enlightened teacher" (chapter 1). There are references here to "one's own golden body," to the contrast between "the intelligent and the stupid," and to the sin of "reviling the teaching," all in terms identical with those used in Lo's texts (chapter 2). In chapter 3 there is a list of famous kings and saints of the past who were saved because of their fear of saṃsāra, all of them names borrowed from chapter 2 of Lo's *P'o-hsieh pao-chüan*.

In chapter 4 we find other favorite phrases of Lo Ch'ing lifted out of context. "Honor only thyself" (*tu tzu wei tsun*) here appears in the midst of a long discussion of the threat of rebirth for those who err, with no reference to the buddha-nature within. Another Lo phrase, *tsung-heng tzu-tsai* ("[spiritually] free and independent"), is thrown in with no apparent understanding of its Ch'an implications.

In chapter 6 the Buddha is asked "Where is the Native Place of those who practice the Way of Nonactivism (Wu-wei tao)?" to which he replies, "When they are alive they do not obstruct heaven; when they die they do not fear purgatory. Nameless throughout vast eons, they are completely unrestrained, going where they wish beyond the three realms."[36] In this chapter the *An-yang chüan* echoes such a "Lo-ist" theme as "You yourself are a living bodhisattva, who in the An-yang [Pure] Land will be happy . . . and now in your own place will be 'majestic and unmoved.' Though those in your household constantly see you face to face, who among them realizes that you never again will be reborn, or die or suffer in saṃsāra?"

In chapter 8 there is a long discussion of the clinging to forms and distinctions that prevents escape from rebirth, including the distinction between those who have left the household life and those who have not and the distinction between men and women. Attachment to seated meditation, exorcism, and reciting incantations is also rejected. There are several purported quotes from the *Chin-kang k'e-i*, but all are the same passages cited by Lo Ch'ing. In sum, the *An-yang* book is in part a kind of paraphrase of Lo's five scriptures, but with less structure and clarity. There is a philosophical dimension in Lo's writings based on his understanding of emptiness, but in the *An-yang* book this dimension is lost. In it, Lo Ch'ing's ideas have become pious phrases without an implicit intellectual context.

Lo Ch'ing's writings also influenced the texts of the Hung-yang (Vast Yang) sect that was active in North China during the Wan-li reign period of the Ming dynasty (1573–1619).[37] I have five of the sixteenth-century *pao-chüan* produced by this sect, all discussed in more detail in Chapter Five and Appendix H below; the teachings of all of them are variations of the Eternal Mother mythology, though some discuss many "mothers," not just one. The titles of three of these books are based on those of Lo Ch'ing. Though Hung-yang books were influenced by other traditions, the only specific references in them to sources and terms are to the texts of Lo Ch'ing. These books thus provide clear evidence of Lo's influence on a sectarian tradition quite removed from him in both date and teaching.

Of the three Hung-yang books that use titles taken from Lo's writings, I will mention first the *Hung-yang k'u-kung wu-tao ching* (The Vast Yang scripture on awakening to the Way through bitter toil; text 9 in Appendix H), in two *chüan* and twenty-four chapters, with no date. This book is an account of the salvation quest of the Patriarch Hun-yuan (Origin in Creative Chaos), who in Hung-yang texts is identified with the sect founder, P'iao-kao. Though the content is different, this account is clearly modeled on that of Lo Ch'ing. As with his predecessor, we are told that Hun-yuan was fearful of the sufferings of saṃsāra and concerned about not yet having met an enlightened teacher. He was not an orphan but was much concerned about leaving the household life against his parents' will. He sought instruction from several different masters but eventually moved on "to take another step" in his quest (*tsai-ts'an i pu*) — the same term used in the Lo chiao *K'u-kung* text. In chapter 8 Hun-yuan rejects recitation of scripture and of Amitābha's name as a way of escape: "I recited all the Buddhist scriptures and [Amitābha's name] until my mouth wore out, but my mind was not opened up." In the end, while meditating in a cave, he dreams of going to the Native Place, where he worships Wu-sheng lao-mu, is given a pill of "efficacious elixir," and his mind is enlightened (chapter 24).

The second Hung-yang book that refers to a Lo text in its title is the *Hung-yang pi-miao hsien-hsing chieh-kuo ching* (The Vast Yang scripture, secret and wonderful, [that discusses] the karmic results of manifesting the nature; text 13 in Appendix H), in two *chüan* and twenty-four chapters, with no date. I have only the first *chüan*. In chapter 5 of this book there is a reference to the *Wu-pu ching* (Five scriptures) and a quote from chapter 13 of Lo Ch'ing's *P'o-hsieh chüan*. In chapter 6 there is a longer quote from "A Scripture of the

Patriarch Lo" that is taken from chapter 2 of the *P'o-hsieh chüan*. It repeatedly invokes the phrase "spiritual independence and freedom" (*tsung-heng tzu-tsai*). This *Hung-yang chieh-kuo ching* uses terms from Eternal Mother mythology throughout but does not discuss that mythology in a connected way.

The title of my third Hung-yang text influenced by Lo Ch'ing's example is the *Hung-yang t'an-shih ching* (The Vast Yang scripture of sorrow for the world; text 11 in Appendix H), in two *ts'e* (volumes) and eighteen chapters, with no date. Like its Lo chiao predecessor, it is a book of moral regret and condemnation, and calls for repentance. However, other than the title there are no specific references to Lo's texts. The chapter titles are not the same.

In two of the other Hung-yang books in my collection, there are no references to Lo Ch'ing or his texts. However, there is a reference in the book most directly devoted to P'iao-kao, or the Patriarch Hunyuan, which is entitled the *Hun-yuan hung-yang Fo ju-lai wu-chi P'iao-kao tsu lin-fan ching* (The scripture of the descent to the ordinary [world] of P'iao-kao, the Patriarch of the Limitless, the Chaotic Origin Vast-Yang Buddha Tathāgata; text 10 in Appendix H), in two *chüan* and twenty-four chapters, with no date. The reference is in chapter 24, where we are told that the Patriarch Lo is a reincarnation of the Venerable Patriarch Chan-t'an (Sandalwood; Skt. Chandana), who left behind his five scriptures, just as, before him, Buddhist scriptures had been bequeathed by the "monk He-tan" and by the "T'ang monk" (Hsuan-tsang).

Here the Patriarch Lo is called Lo Ch'ing Tsu, who "left behind five scriptures in six volumes, the 'true scripture without words.' [By] these five scriptures the confused and lost of the whole world are exhorted to salvation. He suffered for thirteen years, [obtained] true fruition, and paid his respects to the primal source (*cheng-kuo ch'ao-yuan*)." This passage proceeds to link the patriarch of the Hung-yang chiao to this line of revealing avatars. Here Lo Ch'ing is made a direct part of the Hung-yang patriarchal tradition.

In content, Hung-yang sect scriptures are very different from those of Lo Ch'ing; they are texts of the Eternal Mother type, some of which contain many references to terms derived from internal alchemy. Yet in titles and form these texts owe much to Lo Ch'ing, and they understand themselves to be part of a scriptural lineage in which his books were their own most immediate predecessors. The

Hung-yang books are thus good examples of Lo Ch'ing's influence on later sectarian writers. Nonetheless, there are other sixteenth-century "precious volumes" that show little or no debt to Patriarch Lo and that are based on variations of the Eternal Mother mythology. The oldest of them shares many terms, concepts, and part of its title with the *Huang-chi pao-chüan* discussed in Chapter Two. This book is discussed in the next chapter.

CHAPTER FOUR

The 'Chiu-lien pao-chüan' of 1523

The *Huang-chi chin-tan chiu-lien cheng-hsin kuei-chen huan-hsiang pao-chüan* (The precious volume of the golden elixir and nine[-petaled] lotus of the Imperial Ultimate period [that leads to] rectifying belief, reverting to the real, and returning to [our] true home; hereafter "the *Chiu-lien* book") is in two volumes (*chüan*) of twelve chapters (*p'in*) each. The edition I have thrice provides a reprint date of the "second year of the Chia-ching reign period," which corresponds to 1523. Li Shih-yü lists two Ming editions of this book, while Sawada Mizuho treats it as a product of the eighteenth century, but I believe this is too late.[1] In general, the language and ideas of this book are consonant with those of other sixteenth-century *pao-chüan*, and I see no compelling reason to disregard the dates it provides. This book is in many ways a continuation of the *Huang-chi pao-chüan* of 1430, which further confirms its relatively early date.

In its opening chapters, the *Chiu-lien pao-chüan* presents itself as a revelation from Amitābha (Mi-t'o), who predicts the coming end of the age and promises salvation to those whose acceptance of his message indicates their karmic affinity for it. Later in this text Amitābha is identified with Maitreya (Mi-le), the Buddha Yet to Come (Wei-lai Fo). Amitābha/Maitreya is sent to earth by the Eternal Mother to save the lost. He is incarnate as Wu-wei tsu-shih or Wu-wei chiao-chu, the "patriarch" or "sect master" of Nonactivism. All this is set within three stages of cosmic time and contains several references to the "Way of the Golden Elixir" (Chin-tan tao), the name of a Taoist sect that first appeared in the twelfth century.

The first four chapters of the *Chiu-lien pao-chüan* focus on Mi-t'o/Mi-le's resistance to the Venerable Mother's instructions that he descend to the mundane world to save the "injured souls" (*ts'an-ling*), the ninety-two myriads of former "buddhas and immortals" (her children) who have lost their way in saṃsāra. Mi-t'o/Mi-le protests that he is too much attached to the beauties and comforts of paradise, but finally relents and descends to the "vicinity of Shadowless Mountain" in the Han land of the nine regions (Chiu-chou Han-ti; i.e., China). There, in the Three Minds Hall (San-hsin t'ang) of the Palace of Nonactivism (Wu-wei fu), he manifests himself as the Wu-wei Patriarch. His task is to reveal the *Chiu-lien* scripture, which he does in long, rambling responses to questions put to him by persons who appear at the hall. Within this sketchy narrative framework, he discusses his teaching in the first person (*wo*), expounding a variety of topics.

The Patriarch's message is a call to those with karmic potential (*yu-yuan jen*) to realize their true nature and origin as children of the Venerable Mother of the Imperial Ultimate (Huang-chi Lao-mu) and to recognize the true patriarch (*jen chen-tsu*), here clearly meaning Wu-wei/Maitreya himself. Once their devotees have awakened (*wu*) to who they really are, they are urged to believe, warned against backsliding, and told of the ritual practices that will guarantee their acceptance in heaven. These practices include exercises to enable the soul to pass through the mysterious aperture between the eyebrows (*k'ai hsuan-kuan*) and "publishing one's name in the registry for returning home" (*kuei-chia pu piao ming-hsing*) by sending up the appropriate memorial (*piao*, of which several types are listed in chapters 14, 17, and 18).

In this scripture Maitreya has a double role, the most important of which is as revealer of the *Chiu-lien* book in the recent past. This scripture is his legacy, but at the same time it is described as a *wei-lai ching* ("scripture about the future"; chapters 12 and 17), which reveals the secrets of the Imperial Ultimate stage that is "soon to appear" (*tang-lai*). It is Maitreya who will usher in this new period, so his role is also that of a future savior. We are told near the end of the *Chiu-lien* book that he will come again: "I am leaving now, but I will return to restore the original wholeness. Those with karmic potential I will see again" (chapter 22).

In the meantime, the proper attitude for devotees is waiting (*teng*) — "waiting for the time" (*teng-shih*; chapter 10); "waiting for the time when one will leave the profane body and one's holy nature will return to the real" (chapter 21); "waiting for the last Dragon-Flower Assembly" (chapter 13), and so forth.[2] In chapter 17 we read, "The children of the Buddha are all refining themselves in lay households, waiting for the original patriarch to appear."

Thus this is a book filled with expectancy, but one which realizes that long periods of time may be involved. We are told that human-kind has been in bondage to saṃsāra for eighteen kalpas, and that each buddha reigns for long periods: 108,000 years for the Lamp-lighter Buddha, 27,000 years for Śākyamuni, and 97,200 years for Maitreya (chapter 10). Furthermore, the pious are told that they must refine themselves for a long time (chapters 23 and 24) before reaching perfection and the assurance of salvation.

The chief message of the *Chiu-lien* scripture is a promise of per-sonal salvation, a promise made repeatedly through a variety of metaphors: "going to Ling-shan" (a sacred mountain in paradise), "ascending to the precious land" (*teng pao-ti*), "going home and re-turning to one's origin and source" (*kuei-chia ch'ü fan-pen huan-yuan*). Such return leads to "seeing the Venerable Mother," "sitting in the Lotus Pavilion," and "living forever."

These promises are intensified by their placement against the background of the terrible chaos at the end of the age. Chapter 11 describes the end of the world in great detail, alternating threats of warfare, black wind, and death with hope that "then the true Buddha [Maitreya] will appear" or that "then the Ancient Buddha will establish the religion (*she chiao*) . . . and lay out a street to the clouds," so that the Mother's children "can escape all forms of ca-lamity and difficulty."

All this is summarized in chapter 24, where, in a section praising the value of the *Chiu-lien* book, we are told:

The worthy and good who encounter it apply themselves to make progress. After a long time, when their merit is complete, then parents and children (*fu tzu*, lit. "fathers and sons") meet together. Throughout the whole sky, buddhas and patriarchs sending down a bright light welcome and guide them. Those who study the Way transcend both mundane and holy, and to-gether go to the Cloud City; they go to the Golden Elixir Peach Garden As-sembly and shed their mundane bodies (*t'o-liao fan-t'i*). . . .

Those who preach this scripture will transcend the three realms of exis-tence. Those who explain its meaning will escape death, and on the sea of suffering will float on a boat to the shore. There little children will be able to see their dear Mother (*chien ch'in niang*), enter the Mother's womb (*ju mu t'ai*), and fear no calamities. They will realize the eternal and forever enjoy security and good health, and for eighty-one kalpas will not be moved. They will live for time without measure. I urge each of the worthy and good to believe and accept this, and to maintain the Three Refuges and five prohibitions [i.e., moral principles]. . . . Then all will enter the great ritual arena of the Imperial Ultimate period.

It is Maitreya's task to convey these promises in person, have them inscribed in a book, and then fulfill them in his return to earth. Here and later in this text, the term *"fu tzu"* refers to the celestial parent.

In the mythology of the *Chiu-lien pao-chüan*, the Venerable Mother for the first time has a central role, unlike the more scattered mother-deities of the *Huang-chi* book a century earlier. As far as extant "precious volumes" are concerned, it is in the period between these two texts that the Venerable Mother mythology took shape. The fact that Lo Ch'ing and his writings are not mentioned in the *Chiu-lien* book casts doubt on his role in formulating this myth.

To provide a better sense of the overall structure of a "precious volume," this chapter summarizes the *Chiu-lien book* a section at a time, with translations following both prose and verse forms.[3] I realize that there is some repetition and much detail in this chapter, but that reflects the structure of the texts being discussed. "Precious volumes" have been described in general and external terms for years. Only with detailed attention to their contents can we understand what they are.

The text of the *Chiu-lien* book begins with an alternative title, *Wu-tang shan Hsuan-t'ien Shang-ti ching* (The scripture of the Lord on High of the Dark Heaven, from Mount Wu-tang). It opens with a "psalm for raising incense" (*chü hsiang tsan*) summoning the buddhas to descend and promising long life. Its hearers are instructed to thrice repeat in unison:

Homage to the great Bodhisattva Kuan-yin, to the Ancient Buddha of Nonactivism who descends from the Cloud Palace to the ordinary realm to save all living beings, and who in front of Shadowless Mountain discusses the marvelous Tao, who secretly fishes for the people of the three schools and the five sects (*san-tsung wu-p'ai*). Homage to the Three Treasures, the buddhas of past, present, and future of the Dharma realm of complete emptiness.

This psalm is followed by a section entitled "verses for opening the scripture" (*k'ai-ching chi*), which doubles as a preface. It begins with four lines of seven-character verse:

The true teaching of the Golden Elixir has appeared in the world, [and]
In front of Shadowless Mountain a golden boat is being made.
The various buddhas and patriarchs have clarified their true natures.
Together they continue [the teaching of] the nine-petaled lotus of the future.

This is followed by a prose account of the creation of the world by
the Ancient Buddha (Ku Fo), who

manifested the teaching, put the universe in order, and left behind metal,
wood, water, fire, and earth, [thus] establishing the Five Phases [of *ch'i*].
Within he produced the eight trigrams, and opened up Heaven and closed
[i.e., "shaped"] the Earth. [By his powers of] transformation, he produced
yin and yang and gave birth to the myriad things. Within the sacred darkness (*sheng-hsuan chung*), the Ancient Buddha created the three kalpas, with
three buddhas to descend and take charge of the religion. Nine patriarchs
have come and gone in accord with the inner power of things (*tang chi*).[4] He
divided [time] into the realms of the three apexes (*san-chi shih-chieh*) of past,
present, and future, each controlled [by one of the buddhas]. Through successive kalpas right down to the present, [people have been] buried in the
red dust world without awakening at all. The various buddhas in turn have
carried out their transforming work, availing themselves of the false to cultivate the true; they have transmitted the teaching to save all living beings
on the great earth. The worthy and good who awaken quickly recognize the
Eternal [Mother], while those without karmic affinity are in error. It is difficult to be saved later on. The Ancient Buddha established the teaching and
preached the Dharma to benefit living beings. Each lamp [of truth] has
lighted the next in a continuous [stream] that will never end, and from patriarch to patriarch [the teaching] has been transmitted until today. Spoken
in reverence for worthies and saints from all the ten directions; [may they]
manifest themselves and sit in the ritual arena.

> Take refuge in all the Buddhas of the Ten Directions;
> The Dharma Wheel turns constantly to save living beings.
> Only a few understand the profundity of the supreme.
> Patriarchs and teachers receiving the teaching have let down a ladder to
>   the clouds
> Only because the immortals, buddhas, and patriarchs of the great earth
> Have revealed the marvelous teaching and composed the *Huang-chi*
>   [scripture].

This *Huang-chi chin-tan chiu-lien chüan* was expounded at the time when
chaos first divided, Heaven and Earth were created, the universe was put in
order, and the three buddhas and nine patriarchs were distinguished. After
that [no one] dared to transmit it, but now, in obedience to the primal command of the Venerable Mother, it has secretly come down to the Eastern

Land, to gather and aid the injured and fragmented of the great earth. I have observed that the immortals, buddhas, and astral patriarchs (*hsing-tsu*) are confused about the true and chase after the false. Each of them manifests his or her ability, but they do not think about the primal beginning. They are unwilling to be completely devoted to the true and recognize [the real] patriarchs. When will they attain realization?

When one looks back to the source and thinks deeply on the beginning, [one understands that] a beam of golden light was refined out of emptiness and nonbeing. This light was knitted together to form substance, and this substance was gathered to make forms. The form and spirit [of the primal beings] were complete and wonderful, and perfectly in accord with the Way. Being was produced in the midst of nonbeing, and manifested golden bodies. Their forms were divided and transformed inexhaustibly. Then they entered wombs and concealed their true forms. They coveted and became attached to the mundane world, and did not think about where they were going.

> The immortals, buddhas, and astral patriarchs fell into the ordinary realm.
> Recognizing appearance (*jen-ching*) and attached to their confusion, they were unwilling to return.
> I now to save you [urge you] to return home.
> Revert to the root, return to the source, and go to the Holy Mountain (Ling-shan).

The *Cheng-hsin kuei-chen chüan* is the most profound and most wonderful, the deepest and most mysterious. It includes the myriad teachings (*wan-fa*) and manifests the primal root. It is the bone and marrow of all the scriptures, the master perfection of all forms of goodness, the leader in saving living beings, the profound and mysterious gate for leaving the world. Its teachings encompass the 3,600 tangential schools (*p'ang-men*) and penetrate the 72 forms of exterior teaching. It gathers together the injured souls so that they return to the root and go to their karmically deserved [place?] (*fu yeh liao*). [By it] the myriad classes [of beings] reach the Cloud City. This book is divided into twenty-four chapters. Each chapter discusses Heaven and discourses on Earth, each sentence is in accord with the inner power of the saints, each phrase penetrates present and past, each verse reveals the Way and clarifies the truth. It does not save those with no karmic affinity (*wu-yuan chih jen*), it does not save those who are not so destined, it doesn't save monks and nuns and nonbelievers (*wai-tao*), and it doesn't save those who oppose this book. It only saves buddhas and patriarchs in each household [which here refers to sect members].

This preface continues with references to the faithful "personally hearing the marvelous message," and in the nine-gated palace continuing the way of the Lotus school. In the eighty-one kalpas of the future, they will attain positions as buddhas, be companions of the golden lotus, and never descend to be reborn. . . . The Wu-wei [Patriarch] has established schools and sects and preached the Dharma, secretly fishing for those worthy and good; the primal ones when they awaken quickly return to their Native Place and do not suffer from the three types of calamities or demonic obstacles. Their natures penetrate the marvelous opening of their mysterious apertures (hsuan-kuan; lit. "dark gates"), and they break out beyond heaven. In an assembly on pure and cool Mount Ling, they see their dear Mother and are able to realize their bodily forms of the primal beginning. For eternal kalpas they will neither come nor go. Their names will be displayed in the misty light of Eight Treasures. Celestial perfected ones have revealed the teaching, marvelous beyond measure. It has divulged the plan and form of the Latter Realm (hou-t'ien).

Praise of this scripture is continued in rhyming heptasyllabic verse in pious and flowery terms. The text is referred to as the Huang-chi pao-chüan, the "true scripture precious volume," and the "nine-lotus golden elixir book" (chüan). Two themes familiar in later texts are introduced: the Mother's eyes flowing with tears, and Shadowless Mountain (Wu-ying shan) as the mystic place where the "wonderful Dharma" is preached. Then we read:

The Venerable Mother on Mount Ling has personally ordered that
The injured and scattered all be saved and go to the Jasper Terrace (Yao-t'ai)
    [a reference to the Mother's paradise].
At the celestial palace, she has arranged a Red Lotus Assembly (Hung-lien
    hui)
And has waited a long time for the buddhas to attend [another reference to
    sect members].
. . . At this Dragon-Flower Assembly of the last act (mo-hou i-cho),
The various buddhas and patriarchs will see [him who] is about to come.

The preface ends with four lines of pentasyllabic verse.

This preface thus clearly sets out the cosmic origin and purpose of the Chiu-lien pao-chüan, which is seen as a supreme revelation of teachings hidden since the beginning of time. Though newly revealed, it supersedes earlier teachings, all of which have gone astray, and promises eternal salvation to those who are karmically destined to hear it. Their deliverance consists of returning to the Venerable Mother's paradise, their origin and true home.

Chapter 1 opens with its title, "The Ancient Buddha Expounds the Teaching in the Grand Imperial [Palace]" (Ku Fo T'ai-huang yen-chiao), and continues with a prose description of a vast assembly in a celestial palace arranged by the "Ancient Buddha Holy Patriarch" and attended by buddhas, patriarchs, the "sages of the three teachings," deities, arhats, bodhisattvas, holy monks, and perfected immortals. All of them are attracted by incense, the music of celestial bells and drums, and flowers falling from heaven. Amitābha is specifically invited. After all have offered ritual homage to the Buddha, he begins to preach:

Since at the beginning the universe was alone and the world was empty, and there was no smoke of human habitation nor any of the myriad creatures, [I] sent down ninety-six myriads (i; = 100,000–10,000,000) of immortals, buddhas, celestial patriarchs, and bodhisattvas to descend to the mundane [realm] and live in the world. By [powers of] transformation, I manifested yin and yang, which divided into male and female, who formed couples and married. [However,] they became covetous and attached to worldly emotions. They did not think of returning to their roots and true destiny but were infatuated and lost, unawakened, in undifferentiated chaos. At the two assemblies of the Limitless and the Great [Ultimate], four myriads and three thousand more were gathered in, and their primal buddha-natures returned to the [celestial] palace to take charge of the teaching. Today, however, there are still ninety-two myriads of immortals, buddhas, patriarchs, and bodhisattvas who, accepting their circumstances, have lost their true [natures] and do not think of returning home and recognizing the patriarchs. Now you [= Amitābha] are to descend to the world to search for sons and daughters who have lost their true home, so that they do not encounter the [sufferings of the] end of the kalpa and do not fall into the three forms of calamity.

Amitābha replies, "The red dust of the lower world is too heavy, and the waves of the sea of suffering roll back and forth. Miscellaneous teachings confuse the world, and the natures of living beings are hard and stubborn, most difficult to harmonize and put in proper order. They do not recognize the true teaching. What marvelous message can I rely on to save the stupid and blind? [I,] your disciple, request not to go."

In a following section of 7/7 verse, this is all repeated, with emphasis on the fact that although Amitābha is to be "in charge of the world of the future," he does not wish to go. Weeping piteously, he pleads, "I would be all alone; who would help me? I do not wish to leave the Jasper Pool [of paradise]; [please] send someone else to go to the Eastern Land."

This theme is elaborated on in a short prose section, which is followed by four lines of pentasyllabic verse and a tune name,

"Chin-tzu ching," which we have seen already in the *Huang-chi* book of 1430 (see Appendix C). This tune name introduces a prose discussion in which we are told that it is the Venerable Mother who has issued a decree from her celestial palace that Amitābha is "to descend from the Cloud Palace to the cage of the mundane world (*fan-lung*), to secretly fish for the worthy and good and transmit the true tradition of returning to original destiny." She also instructs all the buddhas and patriarchs to "steer Dharma boats without delay from Mount Ling down to the world to transmit the true Way and secretly fish for the multitudes of immortals and worthies." For this task, divine seals, talismans, and placards are taken from the "sacred storehouse of the Venerable Mother's celestial palace." The chapter ends with another direct order to the Wu-wei Patriarch to descend the ladder to the clouds "to gather in the primal ones" at the Dragon-Flower Assembly.

The structure of chapter 1 is repeated for all the succeeding chapters of the *Chiu-lien* book, though in some chapters the opening prose section is followed by lines of verse ten characters long, divided 3/3/4. All the chapters include tune names.

In chapter 2, it is the "World-Honored One," or the Buddha, who tells Amitābha that he must descend, which thus equates the Buddha with the Venerable Mother. Nonetheless, the chosen messenger is still unwilling to go, as indicated in the chapter title, "Amitābha Does Not Descend from Mount Ling." He pleads, "I am all by myself; who will help me? I cannot save the worthies and saints of the Latter Realm. Prostrating myself, I beg for the World-Honored One's great compassion." At this the Buddha / Venerable Mother recounts the effort and suffering she has gone through with her errant children:

First I sent the immortals, buddhas, celestial patriarchs, and bodhisattvas of the three schools and the five sects to descend to the world, open up new fields, and plant seeds. They saved living beings in a confused fashion. Later I sent ten thousand saints and a thousand perfected ones of the "five tablets and the five titles" (*wu-p'ai wu-hao*) to descend to the ordinary world, to rely on the false to cultivate the true [= to begin with where people are]. Each of them received texts and relied on volumes. In the end, all this can be judged of good result only if they all reach China of the central realm, recognize the Patriarch and revert to their root, and realize the gathering up of the primal ones (*shou-yuan chieh-kuo*). So the myriad saints pay their respects to the source, divide their schools and receive titles, complete the Way and attain perfection.

After two parallel lines of heptasyllabic verse, all this is repeated and elaborated on in twenty-six lines of 3/3/4 verse, followed by two prose lines, then by two lines of 5/5 verse. The prose discussion resumes after the tune name "Chu yun fei" (see Appendix C). It is a summary of the Holy Mother's concern that all "quickly ascend to the other shore, recognize the Patriarch, return home and go to Mount Ling." This brief passage is noteworthy for its three references to secrecy in communicating the message of deliverance: "secretly made a golden boat to save all living beings," "secretly composed the *Huang-chi chüan*," and "the secret news of fishing for the worthy and good." The coupling of this emphasis on secrecy with references here to "the primal ones with the proper karmic allotment" (*yu fen te yuan-jen*) who alone will "ascend the Dharma boat" indicates that the promises of deliverance here are in fact limited to those who respond to this particular text—that is, to adherents of the sectarian group in which it appeared.

Chapter 3 is entitled "Amitābha, Receiving the Dharma, Descends to the Mundane Realm." In its opening prose section, Amitābha asks the "World-Honored Venerable Mother" what message he is to rely on when he goes to the Eastern Land to gather up the primal ones. She promises that she will give him "marvelous verses for returning home" and a "true scripture for protecting the body"; with these the primal ones will have nothing to fear. He is told that he should be "careful to protect this primal sacred message," which in the Eastern Land should be "half open and half closed"; the "profound inner workings" (*hsuan-chi*) are not to be revealed.

When Amitābha asks, "Who will learn the name of the Latter Realm if the mysterious aperture is kept tightly closed?" the Mother responds that she has prepared for this in advance by first sending down eighty-one false Amitābhas and thirty-six false assemblies for gathering together the primal ones. Celestial demons have already gone forth to proclaim their teaching. This false teaching presumably makes it all the more important to be careful in transmitting the true message. The Mother then tells Amitābha:

[But] now I am giving you a book [from the time] of creative chaos, Lotus schools of the various buddhas, [teachings about] famous mountains and holy lands, memorial texts for returning home, nine-lotus diagrams, incense fire of the three apexes, the pious practice in ten steps (*shih-pu hsiu-hsing*), [forms for] presenting statements and making oaths (*t'ou-tz'u shih-chuang*), public and secret verification titles (*ming-an ch'a-hao*) [designating sect membership], and "Dharma-protecting deities" who will constantly uphold and protect [you]. I am going to open up what is closed and preserve the true esoteric instructions.

All of this is reminiscent in detail of the *Huang-chi* book.

Reassured by this, Amitābha accepts the Mother's edict and "the religious practice of placards and titles," and descends from her "Jasper Terrace, taking off his celestial robes, golden crown, and cloud sandals." He takes leave of the "Eternal Mistress of the Teaching" (Wu-sheng chiao-chu) and of all the buddhas and the saints of the Prior Realm. "With a piteous cry, he descended weeping from the Cloud Palace and went down to the mundane world."

All this is repeated and expanded on in the succeeding fifty lines of 3/3/4 verse, in which Amitābha, here called the Buddha Yet to Come (Wei-lai Fo), narrates in the first person his lament at being sent down from his celestial home. His fellow buddhas in heaven see him off with loud wails and say that they will soon follow him. It is made clear that the world to which these buddhas descend is China in the "southern continent," "the Central Flowery kingdom, Han land of the nine regions."

In this land, the savior descends to the area of Shadowless Mountain, where the "vital force of the patriarchs" is gathered. This is the "other shore of enlightenment," the "place where the primal ones are gathered," the "Cloud City where the Way is completed." In the next lines we are told that the immortals and buddhas are specifically commanded to "scatter about in villages, the better to save living beings, to open up the Way of Nonactivism and the three apexes, the wonderful message of the Golden Elixir." On hearing this command, the multitude of immortals and buddhas all descend to the world, including the "primal patriarchs" who "also avail themselves of mundane bodies." In the following lines of prose and 5/5 verse, we are told that "the true patriarchs secretly descend to the ordinary realm, where they disguise their names in the world." At the end of this passage we read that "Amitābha descended to the mundane realm, where, disguising his name, he secretly fished for the worthy. At the last Dragon-Flower [Assembly] he gathers in all the primal ones."

The title of chapter 4 is "Amitābha Descends to the World to Expound the Teaching." It begins:

At that time, the Master of the Teaching Amitābha descended to the mundane world with an official dispatch from the Buddha Who Settles Heaven (Ting-t'ien Fo), an edict from the Jade Emperor, an elixir letter from the Venerable Mother, and sacred treasures from the immortals. He first went to the area in front of Shadowless Mountain, in the Han land of the nine regions. With many cycles of rebirth he secretly fished for the worthy and good, going back and forth to seek the primal ones. He roamed about the whole Dharma realm, manifesting himself in different forms, with no one realizing who he was. He first went to the Nonactivism Prefecture of the Heart of Heaven (T'ien-hsin wu-wei fu), where he looked around in all directions. Patriarchal ch'i floated about, covering the sky. In this place there certainly were primal ones. The patriarchal teacher [Amitābha] concentrated his spirit and settled his vital force, and with penetrating skill transformed himself into the form of Lao-tzu, the profound and perfected. He entered the city, and in the Three Minds Hall at a street intersection he discoursed on the profound and marvelous and preached holy words.

Amitābha's sermon, expressed in 7/7 verse, first recapitulates his mission for the world, as described above, and then continues:

In Heaven and Earth I am the most honored;
All the myriad dharmas are produced from my Tao.
In the West I converted a golden immortal who attained the Buddha Way
    [that is, became the Buddha],
And later, in the Eastern Land [= China], I taught the Confucian school.
I bequeathed the Three Teachings, limitless in scope;
Each distinguished good and bad and [for a time] controlled the world.
If you wish to ask my name,
[It is] the Ancient Celestial Perfected One, Lao-tzu of the Limitless.

There follows a brief prose interlude:

When the patriarch-teacher had completed reciting these verses, the men and women of the whole city of Wu-wei prefecture, hearing what he said, all came joyfully. Among them there was one person who asked, "Here in the Three Minds Hall in this city of the royal residence, you are reciting verses to explain the Way; what wonders do you have?" The Patriarch replied, "All of you draw near and listen to the verses I offer in proof [of my mission]."

After summarizing his descent and his many rebirths, Amitābha says that through them he "established the universe, put the world in order, and fixed [the terms of] human destiny." The Mother's

children are here called "the multitude of immortals and buddhas"
who, after coming to live in the world,

Were covetous, with mundane emotions, and
did not think of the road home.
In the Native Place,
as close and dear relatives,
all had been united together.
But once descended to the mundane realm,
they were unwilling to recognize the patriarchal *ch'i*,
their root and origin.
The Venerable Mother
on Mount Ling
constantly looked on in hope,
longing for her sons
and her daughters,
her face wet with tears,
waiting for me
to come to the Eastern Land
to deliver her letters
[so as] to gather you in,
[so that] you [would] return home,
recognize the Matriarch, and return to your source.
Fearing that you
would be slow to believe,
she ordered me to reveal
the message from the West,
to illuminate what has been revealed
and gather in and aid those whose destiny is broken.
She saw that the immortals and buddhas
had been reborn in
the Central Flowery land, and
borrowing mundane wombs
had lost the ancestral vital force, their root and origin.
I now, in the Three Minds Hall of
Wu-wei prefecture,
reveal the true inner secrets of power
and illuminate the great message,
secretly fishing for the worthy and good.
Those with the proper destiny
will board the golden boat
and together leave the sea of suffering.
They will see [the realm of] Nonactivism,

transmit the secret instructions,
return to the root and go back to their source.
The Golden Elixir teaching
continues the three yang,
opens Heaven and shuts the Earth.
[Thus they] penetrate the mysterious aperture,
manifest their sacred bodies,
and together go to the Native Place.

The chapter continues with more resounding promises of salvation for those of the proper destiny, who will "quickly get on the Dharma boat and all transcend saṃsāra. They will forever manifest their golden bodies, and for eighty-one kalpas parent and children will for an eternity be reunited":

The mystery of the profound inner secrets of Wu-wei
Few on the great earth understand.
The golden elixir personally comes to save;
All together will turn and go to the Jasper Pool.

In the succeeding prose passage, following the tune name, Amitābha repeats the reasons for his descent and then adds,

[In the time of] the Buddha of the Past, there was a Three[-Petaled] Lotus Assembly, in the nine kalpas of the [period of] the Limitless. The Buddha of the Present is verified by a five-petaled golden lotus, and on Mount Ling he can be seen holding the seal that matches the apex. When the Buddha of the Future appears in the world, a nine[-petaled] lotus will open and the world of bitter suffering will be transformed into a lotus-flower land.

The chapter ends with another statement by Amitābha: "Now I have come to transmit the true Way; through many transformations I have concealed my name and have accorded with the ordinary world. Those without the proper destiny do not recognize me, but the primal ones follow me to the Dragon-Flower [Assembly]."

Chapter 5 is entitled "The Wu-wei [Patriarch] Discusses the Way." The opening prose passage is mostly an elaboration in pious language with little new content, with the exception of the comment that "in the near future, together we will continue the Red Yang Assembly." Amitābha also expresses concern here about backsliding: "I fear that later you will go back on your devotion to the Tao." At this his listeners weep and beg for mercy, so he again promises them deliverance. The spirit of the whole chapter is clarified in the lines,

Those with the proper destiny
come forward
and listen to my revelation.

There is also new language here about meditation, involving nourishing the vital force, as we read in a passage in 3/3/4 verse:

If those with the proper destiny encounter the personal transmission of the Great Way of the Golden Elixir, they can dot the mysterious aperture [between the eyebrows], understand its opening and closing, nourish their vital force, and preserve their spirits. After a long time they will increase their exertion and, gazing into space, sit in quiet meditation [reading *ching*, "quiet," for *ching*, "pure"]. When their efforts reach the point that their minds are awakened, they see their [true] natures and enlighten their minds.

The result of this meditation is that

in an instant the mysterious aperture is opened and [one's] true emptiness [= vital spirit] escapes through the opening. The Buddha of Measureless [Life] comes to guide it, and parent and children meet together. They have cast away the red dust, cut off emotional attachments, transcended birth and ended death. They see complete awakening and the compassionate Mother Kuan-yin who rescues from suffering. These little [spirits of] true emptiness are reunited with their parent, go to Mount Ling, ascend to the precious place, and there forever continue long life.

Language about "opening up" and "penetrating through" is found elsewhere in this chapter as well. Here the Venerable Mother is equated with Kuan-yin. Chapter 5 concludes with more repetition of the themes discussed above, all in the form of direct address: "I am now saving you [so that] you can return home, go back to the origin, and return to your source."

Chapter 6 is entitled "The Patriarch Visits the Holy Mother at Court." Here we are told that the Wu-wei Master of the Teaching (Amitābha), despite all the sacred edicts he bore, found it difficult to save the lost, who "cling firmly to a dead teaching. When will the [remaining] ninety-two myriads of [the children of] the imperial womb be saved?" The matter is urgent because "suddenly a time will come when the period of the end of the Dharma will approach, and disasters of water, fire, and wind will occur together." In that time "heaven will send down demons" and it will be "difficult to go to the celestial palace and see the Holy Mother." Weeping in sorrow because of this, Amitābha sits in meditation and sends his perfected spirit through his "mysterious gate," to see in person the "Venerable Mother of the Imperial Apex." He reports to her that "living beings in the lower realm are really difficult to save. I have not seen even one primal person. When will they understand the message? When will they return to the [celestial] palace?"

The Eternal Mother replies, "Tathāgata, relax; do not be troubled and worried. I am going to give you incense of faith of the nine [-petaled] lotus, to fill the universe and pervade the Dharma realm. From everywhere, within and beyond, when the immortals, buddhas, and astral patriarchs smell this incense they will come and provide proof for the Way in a Buddhist ritual arena." Thus salvation will come to all who respond.

In the verse recapitulation of this message, we are told that, among those lost in the Eastern Land listening to Amitābha, there are some, fortunately, who have accumulated merit over many kalpas and have "now been able to reach China, where they are companions of the worthy."

In the remainder of chapter 6, Amitābha repeats his basic message of salvation, emphasizing in verse the obstinacy of those without the proper destiny, whose

faith does not reach [the truth] (hsin pu chi), who do not listen to the exhortations of others. Though one wears out one's tongue with speaking and one's mouth with reciting, they listen but do not hear. [I] have been ordered to come and save you, so that you attain buddhahood and go to the assembly. I only wish I could turn this whole multitude from iron into gold. If you are willing to believe, and take refuge in and rely on my Great Way of Nonactivism, then you will go to the Dragon-Flower [Assembly], see the true Patriarch, and forever attain golden bodies.

These promises are repeated in varying terminology throughout this chapter. Amitābha's authority here is based on his primordiality:

You great multitudes, listen to me tell you of my primal roots in beginningless antiquity. When I was born there was no Heaven and no Earth, no patriarchs and no forms. Then in the midst of creative chaos a division opened up, and yin and yang [alternated] in movement and tranquillity. In true emptiness, vital force was refined to form [my] golden nature. This was the primal root of my beginning.

The title of chapter 7 is "The Primal Ones Ask About the Way." In this chapter an immortal of Pure Wind Grotto on White Cloud

Mountain learns that the Imperial Apex Master of the Teaching has descended to the earth and is "preaching the supreme, correct, and true Great Way of the three apexes of Wu-wei" in the Three Minds Hall. The Venerable Mother of the Imperial Apex had everywhere scattered "cloud incense," attracting the perfected from famous mountains and grottoes all over the (Chinese) world to go to the Three Minds Hall to aid the Way and to "together complete the beneficial task of the three assemblies." The Pure Wind Perfected One asks:

Immortal Elder, do you know how many *li* high the sky is, and how wide the earth? As for the periods of the sun, moon, and stars, how many years has it been from the time of creative chaos until now? Among the Confucians, Buddhists, and Taoists, which was the first to appear?" . . .

The patriarchal teacher replied, "Sir, please have a seat and listen to my explanation. The three buddhas through transformation manifested the true forms [of things], and the five patriarchs in accord with the apexes laid out [the celestial] peck measure [i.e., the Big Dipper] and the stars. Creative chaos had not yet divided, [but then] a single vital force of true emptiness appeared, fixing the divisions of floating and sinking, pure and turbid. It produced Heaven and Earth, and yin and yang through their interaction produced the universe of time and space, the three capacities (*san-ts'ai*), the four forms (*ssu-hsiang*), the eight trigrams, and the Five Phases. Turning in another direction (*tien-tao*; lit. 'to turn upside down'), it produced the principles of human relationships. Heaven is 84,000 *li* high, and Earth is 72,200 *ch'eng* wide."[5]

This account continues with the dimensions of the world from east to west and north to south; 223,500 *li* and 71 paces east to west, and 203,500 *li* and 75 paces north and south. Among other measurements, we are told that the amount of time from the beginning of things until the present is 3,278,500 years. Of the "masters of the three teachings" we are told that

the Buddha left behind [i.e., bequeathed] [teachings about] birth, old age, sickness, death, and suffering. The Confucians bequeathed the virtues of cohumanity, righteousness, ritual propriety, wisdom, and trustworthiness, and the Taoists bequeathed the [Five Phases teaching of] metal, wood, water, fire, and earth. The three teachings were originally from one root.

A few lines later in this passage, its revealer says,

I now, having personally received an elixir book, summon those of the three vehicles and nine ranks of officials who have been secretly sought. Those who believe will follow me to pay respects to the primal source and go to the third Dragon-Flower Assembly, where they will certainly meet together. For those who do not believe, it will be difficult to attain the fruits of the Tathāgata [= buddhahood]. As they approach darkness, they will certainly fall into stupidity and futility. I urge you to quickly recognize the Imperial Apex Way; [then] you will live for eighty-one kalpas.

A succeeding section in heptasyllabic verse repeats the account of creation from primordial chaos and summarizes the prose beginning of this chapter, with little new content. A few terms found in later "precious volumes" are given here, but without detailed context: "the message from the West" (*hsi-lai i*), "three yang," and "vast (*hung*) yang." The most significant new information in chapter 7 is the first mention of Maitreya in this text, where he is equated with the narrator, Amitābha: "[My] measureless, profound, and wonderful body was originally ancient Maitreya."

Chapter 7 ends with more first-person comments about descending to the world to save the lost and, "in the last act, [to] hang up the Imperial Apex." The "predestined primal ones," those who are "old companions in the same boat, connected trunk and branch, recognize the Patriarch and return to the Native Place, [never again] to fall into the mundane world." Such people have the same titles (*hao*) — "cloud palace titles" — that one must have for the return home.

The title of chapter 8 is "The Profound Perfected One Realizes the Way" (Hsuan chen cheng Tao). Here another interlocutor, wearing a Taoist robe, interrupts the master teacher's sermon to ask about the locations of sacred mountains and grottoes where one can "cultivate perfection and nourish the nature."

In response, the teacher notes that in Jambūdvīpa (one of the four continents of Buddhist mythical geography), south of Mount Meru, there are

thirty-six famous mountains, thirty-six "precious caverns," and thirty-six pieces of "holy ground." At the northern shores of the central plain [= China], there are three mountains of the eight-trigrams stone drums (*pa-kua shih-ku*, reading *kuei* as *kua*), nine islands, five famous mountains, nine ancient grottoes, eight precious places, and five "dark pools" (*hsuan-ch'ih*). The ancient Cloud City is [in this area], the place where the three buddhas completed the Way and gather in the primal ones.

These sacred places are all in the celestial realm of the future (*wei-lai t'ien-p'an*), never before spoken of but existing since the beginning of time. Here again, we see the imaginative conflation of Buddhist and Chinese categories characteristic of these texts.

The remainder of chapter 8 repeats earlier material, though there is a good summary statement near the end:

As for the Golden Elixir teaching and the secrets of Wu-wei, the primal patriarch [employs them] to save the lost. Precious volumes for returning home are rare in the world. [It is the time of] the Dragon-Flower Assembly of the last act; the three buddhas have been in charge of the teaching, and six patriarchs have matched [i.e., accorded with] the apexes. The Constellation [Realm of Maitreya] has appeared in the world, [bringing] blessings and long life equal to heaven. [Thus all] will see the Ancient Buddha and together go to the place of the Lotus Pool.

There is also an intriguing reference here to the "ancient Wu-wei [Patriarch] leaving behind scriptures, expounding the teaching, and establishing the root and prime. He conceals his name, waiting for the inner workings of heaven to change."

The title of chapter 9 is "[The Patriarch of] Nonactivism Reveals Famous Mountains." Thirty-six sacred mountains are named here, with their associated grottoes, a few recognizable (P'u-t'o, Wu-t'ai, O-mei) but most not. They are collectively described as "holy realms of the Native Place" that "have long been awaiting the primal ones of the last age." This detailed mythic geography continues with long lists of place names of "the Native Place of the other shore," of which the master teacher says, "Listen carefully to what I tell you. [These names] should not be lightly passed on, [thus] revealing the profound inner workings. All of you be careful, be careful." He then provides the names of mountains, islands, grottoes, and "precious places" that are "ruled by the Ancient Buddha, who is only waiting for the last act." Following this, we are told the names of five pools, three terraces, and several more mountains. Next come the names of the nine gates of the ancient Cloud City. We are told that all these places are

the native places of the Ancient Buddha, places where he goes to gather in the primal ones and complete the Way, which a thousand saints have not transmitted nor the patriarchs discussed. But now I have come here to reveal them clearly, item by item, but I am unable to completely exhaust this profound and wonderful message, or to thoroughly discuss the news of the last act (*mo-hou hsiao-hsi*). Now you have the karmic affinity to personally encounter this [teaching]. Will you not decide, then, to go home and see and hear in person the Wu-wei teaching? Soon you will together realize your golden bodies.

The following section in 3/3/4 verse repeats the account of the

Buddhas of the three apexes
who, for the sake of the world,
approached to take charge of the teaching.
They laid out the universe
and put the world in proper order,
with transformations unending.
The one produced two,
the two produced three,
and the three produced the four forms.
These produced Five Phases,
which laid out the eight trigrams,
and so mundane and holy became the same.
In the sky above
There are the sun, moon, and stars,
whose bright light illuminates all.
On the earth below there are
mountains, water, and earth,
and a myriad precious jewels appear [in them].
The Buddha of the Limitless,
[after] the Green Yang Assembly,
returned to the [celestial] palace.
The Buddha of the Supreme Ultimate
at the Yellow Yang Assembly
now is in charge of the celestial palace.
Worthies and saints for ages
have not yet returned to the source.
As the constellations revolved and transformed,
heaven sent down
the buddhas and patriarchs
to gather and save injured souls.
Because of you,
ninety-two myriads of
immortals, buddhas, and celestial patriarchs,
the buddhas of the three apexes
have descended to the world [and]
fallen into the red dust.

Thus this text claims a whole sacred geography of its own and roots its promise of salvation in the creation of the world. The remainder

of this verse section repeats and elaborates on the earlier listing of
sacred places at which to cultivate the way of perfection, where "the
primal ones have long been awaited."

As chapter 9 deals with mythic space, so chapter 10 deals with time.
It is entitled "A Celestial Man Realizes the Way." Here again, the
Wu-wei master teacher's sermon is interrupted by a saintly ques-
tioner who has been drawn to the spot by incense scattered about the
world by the Venerable Mother of the Imperial Apex. Transforming
himself into a poor monk, he enters the assembly hall and asks the
master about the cycles of time:

"Honored teacher, you know about the way of the three temporal apexes of
past, present, and future. How many celestial palaces and stellar courts are
there? How many numinous mountains (Ling-shan)? How many buddhas,
patriarchs, and immortals? In what year will they put the world in proper
order? In what year will the Buddha Yet to Come gather in [those of] the
source? How many kalpas are there for the three buddhas? Which has more,
which has less? For how many thousands of years will the Golden Elixir
Way of the Imperial Apex be proclaimed?"
    . . . The Patriarch's eyes opened wide as he looked and recognized a pri-
mal person. With a faint smile he said, "Venerable monk, come forward and
listen to my explanation of the meaning of 'the one produces two.' Altogether, the three bodies of the three perfected ones are manifested through
transformation to rule the world. In the past, there was the most majestic
kalpa of [the Buddha] Jan-teng (Lamplighter; Skt. Dīpaṃkara). In the present age, [the Buddha] Śākyamuni is the honored one in charge of the teaching. In the future, there will be Maitreya's assembly of the constellations.
The three buddhas approach in turn, descending from the celestial palace."

The teacher goes on to explain that the Buddha of the Past was in
charge for 108,000 years, the Buddha of the Present is in charge for
27,000 years, and the Buddha Yet to Come will be in charge for
97,200 years. The three buddhas thus rule for 232,200 years altogether; then the three time periods (san-yuan) will be completed.
These are all figures that "in the old texts no one dared to reveal."
    Next we are told of the numbers of different types of superhuman
beings that coexist with the three buddhas, including 990,000
"greatly awakened golden immortals" responsible for the teaching
who will protect the golden bodies of the elect, 880,000 buddhas and
patriarchs, 3,000 perfected patriarchs who live in the celestial palace,
500 arhats who accompany the buddhas, 10,000 times 10,000 golden

lads and jade maidens, 3,000 great universes of bodhisattva bodies, 8 great vajra kings, 4 celestial kings, 24 great saints of various heavens, and so forth.

The verse section that follows this prose exposition adds the names of the buddhas controlling the five directions: (1) The Buddha of the Great Singularity (T'ai-i Fo) is in charge of the eight realms of the north. He is in control of all beings born from moisture, such as fish and crabs, and is associated with the Patriarch Asura ([A] Hsiu-lo). (2) The Buddha of the Great Inception (T'ai-ch'u Fo) rules the eight realms of the south and is associated with the Patriarch Profound Understanding (Hsuan-ming). He is in control of beings born from eggs, here equated with birds. (3) The east is ruled by the Buddha of the Great Beginning (T'ai-shih Fo), "who is able to give life to all things." He is associated with the Patriarch Welcomes Spring (Ying-ch'un) and rules all creatures born from wombs. (4) The ruler of the eight realms of the west is the Buddha of the Great Simplicity (T'ai-su Fo), who is associated with the Patriarch Double Good Fortune (Ch'ung-chi). He rules beings born by transformation, or metamorphosis. (5) Finally, the Buddha of the Great Ultimate (T'ai-chi Fo) controls the center. Associated with the Patriarch Compassion (Tz'u-pei tsu), he rules the three realms, the thirty-two heavens, and all the buddhas, patriarchs, and masters of the three teachings.

Here Buddhist modes of being are combined with Chinese ideas of directions and ruling principles. Unfortunately, there is no indication here of how these buddhas of the five directions are related to the buddhas of the three temporal apexes already discussed. Nonetheless, the intention of chapter 10 of the *Chiu-lien* scripture is clear — to extend the teaching of the *pao-chüan* to cosmic time as well as space, including all the celestial realms and beings within them. The chapter concludes with a repetition of its pious language about the salvation of the elect and with sighs of regret for those whose "merit is thin, and so do not understand the true Way," the teachings of which "encompass Heaven and Earth":

A multitude of buddhas has secretly descended to the mundane world, but who on the great earth is able to understand this? They have concealed their names, waiting for the time; concealed their names, waiting for the time. At the three assemblies the merit [of the pious] will be tested, and when their conduct is complete, their titles will be displayed in the Nine-Yang Palace of the Imperial Apex.

Here again the book refers to itself: "I now, to save you, so that you can go to the Peach Garden [of the immortals], have secretly written a volume for returning to the Native Place."

The title of chapter 11 is "The Perfected One 'Fragrant Lotus' Assists the Way." This is the key eschatological chapter of the book; the questions in it deal with disasters at the end of the age and how they can be avoided:

When is the destined return of Heaven and Earth and yin and yang [to their source]? When will the world and the Five Phases decay? Of the disasters of water, fire, and wind, which will come first? Where can the worthy and good escape from these disasters? As the years of the end Dharma approach, the world will be in disaster, and swords and spears will be wielded everywhere. The people will be impoverished and terrorized by warlords and bandits. Domestic and wild animals will all be destroyed. [In this situation,] on what will the worthy and good rely to return to [the realm of] clouds and dew? How will men and women be able to avoid death?

The response to this is that

for all the three buddhas, there is a time of decay and destruction, and there are disasters in each of the three apex periods. . . . When there is destruction in Heaven, the stars are in disorder; when there is destruction on Earth, the myriad creatures cannot live. When there is destruction in the world, then [all in] the eight directions contend. When there is destruction among humans, then birth-and-death are impure. At the interchange of the three periods of cosmic time, when the kalpa is complete, the three disasters arise and disorder the *sahā* world (*sahāloka*) [= this world of rebirth]. Heaven will gather in its blue *ch'i* so that its lights do not shine. Earth will gather in its muddy *ch'i*, so that creatures cannot live. The sea will gather in the lakes and rivers, so that fish and dragons die. The sun and moon will gather in their brightness, so there will be much darkness. Humans will gather in their primal *ch'i*, so their yin and yang will be exhausted. The sky will collapse and the earth split, manifesting the true Buddha. The world will roar, the eight trigrams will open up, and the disasters of water, fire, and wind will arrive together. The golden crow and the jade hare [symbols of the sun and moon] will return to their palaces, and for a time the four sides of the world will be crooked.

In response to this,

The Ancient Buddha will establish the teaching and, in addition, lay out a street to the clouds. The emperor (Wan-shou) [= the Buddha?] transmits an auspicious pledge[?] (*ch'uan chia hsin*), and with celestial flowers welcomes multitudes of [the Mother's] children, who are adorned with placards for passing through the barriers (*t'ung kuan*). [After having] their titles compared and checked (*ta-ch'a tui-hao*), they go to the street to the clouds, where they escape the three disasters and the eight difficulties. Liberated from mundane wombs, they enter the holy womb and for eighty-one kalpas accompany the buddhas. Beyond the nine-layered heavens, they sit on a lotus tower.

> The constellations descend to the mundane world
> and the worthies and saints return.
> The heavens revolve and the earth changes
> while the stars move [their places].

The next lines of verse recapitulate the promise of salvation through becoming enlightened in response to divine messengers, and thus leaving this world of suffering on the road to heaven. Those whom the text addresses are assured that their natures are the same as the buddhas', so that all "can realize the eternal and go to the canopy of heaven":

> Only for the sake of [you] immortals and buddhas immersed in saṃsāra, I
>   now pull you out of the *sahā* world [reading *yuan*(?) as *pa*],
> To leave the *sahā* world and return to your old positions,
> Each to realize the eternal and the original primal buddha [within].
> . . . The Golden Elixir [Way] has manifested itself and has come to save you,
>   and
> Not begrudging ordinary form, has revealed [this] complete *dhāranī*[?].[6]
> So that multitudes could ascend to heaven, [the Mother] sent down me.
> From a thousand toils and a myriad of sufferings, [I] rescue all buddhas.

This message is revealed before the end of the age to give its hearers an opportunity to respond:

> Before the three calamities arise, [I] composed this true scripture of returning to the Native Place; its wonderful message is profound. . . . [Oh] primal ones, go in response to [the Mother's] decree: Return to [your] roots. The patriarchs and teachers point as one. Together go to the ancient Cloud Palace.

>> [At the time of] the three calamities of water, fire, and wind, and the
>>   eight adversities,
>> The ancient Cloud City emits a golden light.
>> Receiving golden placards, everyone's title is registered.
>> Efficacious charms are distributed; so they escape disaster and calamity.

The disasters at the end of the age are described in frightening detail, but with hope in their midst:

A holy fire will descend to the mundane realm and burn up the whole world. In the five lakes and four seas, shrimp, crabs, fish, and dragons will have nowhere to hide. Mountains, rivers, and the great earth will together be smelted and refined. Lotuses will be born within the fire and will be refined to golden elixir. In the pure and cool precious land, there will never be disaster and adversity. The Venerable Patriarch will open up the mountain, and a black wind will fill the world. In the east and west there will be no moon; in the south and north there will be no sky. Ordinary and holy will be mixed together, and monsters and demons will appear, accompanying the wind, and will scrape and overturn the passes of heaven (kua tao t'ien-kuan). No human records [traces?] will be seen [reading lu, "records," for lü, "green"]. The Buddhas of the Three Apexes will gather inside the Cloud City. The disasters of earth, fire, and wind, sent down by heaven to the mundane realm, will arrive together. In an instant all the great myriad worlds and continents will be askew. The venerable patriarchs of the three apexes from setting up sects (an p'ai) have gone to [places of] incense and purification (hsiang chai). [There] there are no three disasters, and [the elect] escape from saṃsāra and personally see the world that is about to come. The Ancient Buddha will gather in [those from] the source, bring together the perfected, and connect and continue [the tradition of] the nine[-petaled] lotus. The three calamities and eight forms of suffering will not be seen, and [people] will abruptly escape from purgatory. In front of the holy, precious mountain, the Venerable Mother of the Imperial Apex will come, scattering golden elixir. Then all the myriads upon myriads of buddhas will go to the assembly and together take the path to Maitreya's inner court.

The close similarity of this language with that of the indigenous Buddhist scriptures found at Tun-huang is one of the mysteries of the origins of pao-chüan teaching, as is discussed in Chapter One above. This mystery is deepened by the fact that the discussion of the end of the age in the Chiu-lien text is much more detailed than that in the Huang-chi book, which appeared about a century earlier. The matter deserves further research.

Chapter 12 is entitled "Manifesting [the True] Nature and Illuminating the Inner Workings" (Hsien-hsing ming-chi). Much of this chapter is a repetition of pious language concerning the threat of disaster and the promise of deliverance, but it does include some interesting statements about the Chiu-lien book itself. There is also another reference to the reigning buddhas of the three time periods, and a note along the way that "the learned of the world (*t'ien-hsia chih-shih*) are unwilling to search for the root and recognize the Patriarch." Concerning the text itself, we read,

In composing the *Huang-chi chüan*, I selected from the three vehicles and the five teachings, [as a result of which] people enlighten their minds, are gathered together in the Lotus Palace, see their true natures, and together are [re]born in the Purple Cloud Palace. Those with merit and virtue return to their lotus positions.

In the verse recapitulation, we read that the Eternal Mother has sent letters from her holy mountain urging that all quickly awaken and turn around and, fearing disasters at the end of the age, "has sent me to come and gather in and save you, so that you respond to her decree and return to your roots." Therefore, to

reveal the inner workings of heaven, I have composed the *Nine-Petaled Lotus Imperial Apex* book, the true scripture of the future. Each day at home, in the company of the worthy and good, I have discussed [its] profound and wonderful [teachings]. As the Way is late in coming, I have thought on the Patriarch's intentions, nourished my vital force, and preserved my spirit. Day and night, with mind not idle, while according with the mundane, I respond to the holy. Sleeping neither day nor night, I have completely exhausted my mental energy. For the sake of this *pao-chüan*, I toiled bitterly until my body was weak. Without drinking tea or eating rice, I labored my spirit. In the Han household (*Han chia*) I wrote the *pao-chüan*, but who knows this? In accord with the [truth of the] Prior Realm, I have written about appearances in the Latter [Realm] (*hou-hsiang*), shattering my true mind [in the process]. As I wrote about the three mysteries (*san hsuan*),[7] a multitude of buddhas came together to protect me, and so the "message came from the West" and the "Golden Elixir teaching" sentence by sentence became complete. The *Imperial Apex* book is divided into upper and lower volumes in twenty-four chapters. Each line and character reveals the true tradition. Above, it describes [our] ancient primal home, the holy ground of the Native Place. Below, it reveals (*chui*, lit. "lets fall") discussions of gathering together those of the source, so that they understand the Way and attain immortality. What each section describes is the buddhas and patriarchs all sending down a brilliant light and coming to receive and guide all living creatures of the great earth. No one understands the *Huang-chi* book, [so] those with the proper destiny should read it intently and carefully seek out [its meaning].

Fearing that you would not awaken, I have repeated my instructions. Those primal ones who are willing to occupy themselves with the Way (*pan tao*) should add effort to effort and enter the gate of profound mystery with determined mind and will. They should not think in a reckless manner but preserve their primal persons. The minds of those of lesser vehicles [i.e., teachings] are not determined, and so they think in a disorderly way. It is difficult for them to enter the Way, and they don't last long because they have turned their backs on the message and forgotten [the Mother's] kindness. Those who intend [to progress] must distinguish between the wise and the foolish. . . . I have now directly indicated the Eternal [Mother's] words . . . and have secretly composed this *Chiu-lien huan-hsiang chüan* to gather in and support the primal ones, so that they may return to their Native Place.

In the last prose section of chapter 12, introduced with a tune name, there is a detailed description of the three buddhas with their associated apexes and assemblies, which can be summarized as follows:

1. The Buddha of the Past was Dīpaṃkara of the Limitless, who is associated with a three-petaled lotus throne and the Yellow Yang Assembly. He rules for nine kalpas.

2. The Buddha of the Present is Śākyamuni of the Great Ultimate, who at the Pure Yang Assembly (Ch'ing-yang hui) sits by the Lotus Pool for eighteen kalpas. He "saves the lost, and on Mount Ling is in charge of the teaching." His is a five-petaled lotus throne. He controls the universe and "produced the wind, clouds, thunder, rain, and the two wheels [of sun and moon?]."

3. The Buddha Yet to Come is Maitreya, the Wu-wei Patriarch, and is associated with the Vast Yang Assembly (Hung-yang hui). It is difficult for people to believe in him, so they are "confused and lost and do not recognize the Mother." Maitreya conceals his name and "secretly fishes for the predestined." The apex associated with this Buddha of the Future is not mentioned in this immediate passage, but in the concluding verse section of chapter 12 we read that "the Ancient Buddha appeared in the world with the title 'Vast Yang' . . . and guides all the lost of the world to enter the great ritual arena of the Imperial Ultimate." It is clear from this passage that it is Maitreya in one of his many transformations who wrote this book.

Chapter 13 opens the second volume of the *Chiu-lien* book, which here again has the alternative title of *Wu-tang shan Hsuan-t'ien Shang-ti ching* (The scripture of the Lord on High of the Dark Heaven, from Mount Wu-tang). After a salutation wishing long life for the emperor, this volume opens with eight lines of heptasyllabic verse:

The golden elixir, having revolved nine times, descends from the Cloud Palace,

Secretly fishing for the worthy and good, dear, close relatives.
Personally transmitting the secret way of returning to the Native Place,
[This book] points directly to the causes for escaping from the world in the future.
[From] the Western Heaven to the Eastern Land, it circulates everywhere,
But the divergent sects of the great earth do not recognize its truth.
At the Dragon-Flower Assembly of the time of the last act,
The gathering up of those of the source will be complete, and [they will] realize the eternal.

The title of chapter 13 is "The Measureless Celestial Perfected One Manifests the Way" (Wu-liang t'ien-chen hsien tao). The entire chapter consists of repetitions of promises of deliverance from saṃsāra and rebirth in paradise. Upon encountering this *pao-chüan*, those with the proper causation from former lives will "together ascend to the other shore," attain enlightenment, and "return to their root." Hearers of this text are told to "maintain the Three Refuges and the five precepts," but no specifics are mentioned. The end result of their piety and acceptance is that they will

go to Mount Ling, and upon reaching home will personally see the Eternal [Mother]. Children and mothers will be reunited and laugh out loud. In the celestial palace of the Pure Land they will listen to the Buddhadharma and forever realize golden bodies. . . . The buddhas and patriarchs will be their companions, and they will be independent and free (*tzu-tsai hsiao-yao*). . . . [They will] enjoy limitless happiness, with no more suffering. They will think no longer of the mundane world, nor be reborn in it.

The title of chapter 14 is "The Wu-wei Patriarch and Teacher Explains the Real" (Wu-wei tsu-shih ming-chen). This chapter repeats the basic mythological framework of the book, with a special appeal to the "learned of the world" we have seen referred to above. It begins with a long statement by the Wu-wei Patriarch and Teacher:

When one thinks back to the very beginning, the time of the single vital force of the origin in chaos, where were Heaven and Earth and the buddhas and patriarchs? Where were all the myriad things? [They did not yet exist.] Then the Holy Patriarch of matchless true emptiness took the primal vital force of true emptiness and refined it for a long time. [Thus] being was produced from nonbeing, the one produced the two, the two produced three, and each was established and named. The three apex periods [of cosmic time] put the universe in order. [The first] was the Majestic Kalpa of the Limitless (Wu-chi chuang-yen chieh, reading *chuang*, "serious," for *chuang*, "to adorn"); [the second] was the Great Ultimate Kalpa of the Worthies and

Saints (T'ai-chi hsien-sheng chieh); and [the third] is the Constellation Kalpa of the Imperial Ultimate (Huang-chi hsing-su chieh). [In these periods] the Five Phases of metal, wood, water, fire, and earth were sent down and apportioned, and the eight trigrams were established. [Since then, this system has] revolved and begun again right until the present.

In this period of the end Dharma, the three types of disaster have descended to the world and myriad saints have drawn nigh to the mundane realm to seek the original children of the Buddha, who because of their lusts and emotional attachments have lost their way. Not being awakened, they don't think of reverting to the origin and returning to their primal source. Fearing that they would neglect the Great Way of returning to the primal source, in obedience to the Venerable Mother's sacred letters (tan-shu) [and] thinking of the mundane realm, I have descended from [the higher] realm. Availing myself of the false, I have cultivated the true and secretly transmitted the wonderful message of returning home.

[However,] I observe that the learned of the world, who are called teachers and act as patriarchs, establish their own titles and names, and do not think of seeking the root and recognizing the Patriarch. When will their titles be compared in response to investigation? [When will they] attain spiritual realization and confront the primal source?

The remainder of chapter 14 is a repetition of pious verbiage, with an additional exhortation to educated doubters and critics in 3/3/4 verse:

I urgently exhort you, multitude of the learned,
To think on what has gone before and ponder what follows.
Stop neglecting the Dragon-Flower Assembly,
Which, recognizing the Patriarch, has divided into schools.
Avail yourselves of this present time of great peace
And quickly seek the path of escape.
Visit enlightened teachers,
Inquire of the true patriarchs,
And quickly attend to the road ahead.
If you have the proper karma,
You will be able to meet
The original true patriarchs.
[I] exhort and transform living beings,
None of whom think of the ancient Native Place and
The Eternal Father-Mother (Wu-sheng fu-mu).
Having given way to [lit. "recognized"] worldly emotions,
They have been lost and
Do not think of their two parents (shuang-ch'in).
The Father and Mother
Are on Mount Ling,

Constantly looking on from afar,
Fearing that their infant children,
Having encountered the end of the kalpa,
Have fallen into saṃsāra.
Now I have come
To seek you,
[So that you] together escape from the sea of suffering.

The explicit reference here to two divine parents is puzzling because elsewhere in the *Chiu-lien* book no consort of the Eternal
Mother is mentioned. The only "male" protagonist of sufficiently
high status is the Ancient Buddha, but he is not explicitly linked to
the Mother in this way. We will see that there are also references in
later sectarian *pao-chüan* to the "Eternal Mother," but in many cases I
believe this should be translated as "Eternal Father-Mother" or
"Eternal Parent" — or, following Susan Naquin, as "Eternal Progenitor" — based on a common tradition of calling the emperor the "Father-Mother" of the people.[8]

Thus the educated of the world are summoned to join the sect.

There is little new content of interest in chapters 15 and 16. Chapter
15 is entitled "The Wu-wei Patriarch and Teacher Corrects the Tradition and Reveals Its Inner Workings" (Wu-wei tsu-shih cheng-
tsung hsien-chi), but in fact no new "inner workings" are revealed in
it. Its chief point of interest is a verse to the "Eternal Parents":

The Patriarch and Teacher said,
[I will] transmit [a further] step of the Great Way of the Limitless,
Reveal the true inner workings,
And speak of its wonderful message.

There are also references in chapter 15 to the practice of "true cultivation and refinement, harmonizing the spirit and settling the vital
force." This leads to "the body and mind becoming empty, without
one thing, so that the flower of the mind blossoms and the bright
pearl [one's true nature] is manifest. . . . When this spiritual effort
(*kung-fu*) is practiced for a long time, one's mind is enlightened and
one sees the true nature," which leads to "returning home." Unfortunately, here as elsewhere, no details of this self-cultivation are
provided.

This chapter ends with passages in prose and verse about Bodhidharma as a revealer of sectarian teaching who "has come from
the West, and through many transformations has saved living

beings." He is associated with a White Yang Assembly and the nine-petaled lotus of the future, and so is implicitly connected with Maitreya.

In chapter 16, nine men come to ask the Wu-wei Patriarch about the signs of impending disaster they have observed. All of them are called "brother" (*ke*) and have two-character names beginning with the word *chen* ("true"), such as True Vital Essence (Chen-ching) and True Yang. The Patriarch promises to save them and appoints them to lead branches of the sect named after the eight trigrams of the *I-ching*. Each is charged to "secretly fish for the worthy and good." The ninth brother is put in charge of the central (*chung-yang*) branch. Here we see an early textual precedent for the naming of sects by the eight trigrams, for which there is evidence into the nineteenth century.[9]

These nine men are then put in charge of everything:

seventy-two heavens, thirty-six zodiacal mansions, twenty-four courts, nine palaces, eight trigrams, five realms (*wu-p'an*), four valued [things?] (*ssu-kuei*), three temporal primes (*san-yuan*), and two principles (*erh-i*). These they gathered together to make the nine-petaled lotus of the future and the golden elixir of the Constellation Kalpa of the Great Way of the Imperial Ultimate.

The details of this task are not further discussed here, but there are references to thousands of sects and branches both in and outside the tradition of the *Chiu-lien* book: "1,000 gates (*men*) and 10,000 households (*hu*)," "three schools and five sects" (*san-tsung wu-p'ai*), "3,600 divergent schools," and "12,000 schools of petty teaching" (*hsiao-fa*). There are then lists of what appears to be an essentially empty numerology for which no explanations are provided.

In the concluding prose section of chapter 16, we are told that "ninety-two myriads of children with injured karma (*ts'an yuan tzu*) are all going to a golden boat. A multitude of [potential] buddhas is gathered in the central state of the central realm, only waiting for the Patriarch who gathers in those of the source. The Measureless Buddha proclaims their approach to the Cloud City; they will ascend to the precious land, where their titles will be compared in response to investigation, and [so] continue the Lotus school."

This is followed by the usual promise of salvation and reunification of all with the proper karmic disposition. They will all "go to the Dragon-Flower [Assembly], and each ascend the highest rank, the same as that of the buddhas." There they will "eat numinous elixir, drink the tea of immortality, and shed their worldly bodies, . . . and in the presence of the Venerable Mother hear the wonderful Dharma and discourse on the Way and its mysteries."

Chapter 17 continues the abstract and symbolic discussion of sects and branches introduced in chapter 16. Its title is "The Worthy and Good of the Eight Trigrams Ask About the Way," and this is indeed what these eight worthies do; more precisely, they ask the Patriarch about the proliferation of sects all around them:

Today there are 3,000 divergent sects (*p'ang-men*) proclaiming their teaching, and 10,000 petty teachings contending for primacy. [These] dragons and snakes don't change. They do not distinguish between true and false, and all call themselves "patriarchs who restore completion" (*shou-yuan tsu*). When will they attain realization and pay respects to the source?

The Patriarch replies that before he descended from Mount Ling, the Venerable Mother had sent down a decree for eight kinds of titles, tallies, placards, incense, texts for memorials and vows, and so forth, to be given to thirty-six patriarchs to save the people of the world, "to open up new fields and plant seeds." She also sent down books and letters. However, until today, "though they each call themselves 'patriarch,' they are unwilling to seek for their root and recognize the [true] Patriarch."

The worthies then ask the Patriarch to explain these "eight items for religious cultivation" (*pa-chien hsiu-hsing*), which he proceeds to do. Each item is named, with the total number provided divided between the three periods of cosmic time — that of the Limitless (Wu-chi), the Great Ultimate (T'ai-chi), and the Imperial Ultimate of the Future (Wei-lai Huang-chi). All this is very similar to such lists in the *Huang-chi* book of 1430 (see Chapter Two above). These items are as follows:

1. "Cloud tablets for going to the assembly" (*fu hui yun-p'ai*). There were originally 109,737 of these, of which 365 were used in the Wu-chi period and 1,372 in the T'ai-chi, which means that only 108,000 are left for the coming time of the Imperial Ultimate.

2. "Investigated titles for responding to the Ultimate"(*tang chi ch'a-hao*). Of these there were 9,900, but now only 3,616 are left.

3. "Memorial texts for returning home" (*kuei-chia piao-wen*). Of 15,000, 9,900 remain.

4. Fine incense (*ming hsiang*); originally 84,000, now 36,000 remain.

5. Vows for life and death (*sheng-ssu shih-chuang*), which have decreased from 48,000 to 27,000.

6. The original 96 myriads (*i*) of the worthy and good, of whom 92 myriads remain to be saved in the Imperial Ultimate period.

7. A total of 99 kinds of discussion essays (*t'an-chang*), of which 36 remain.

8. A total of 375 kinds of "news" (*hsiao-hsi*), of which 181 are left.

Unfortunately, no details are provided concerning how the items in this rather miscellaneous list are to be employed.

Chapter 17 continues with other fanciful lists of numbers in what is clearly a kind of numerology, but with no real explanations. Near the conclusion of this section we read, "the children of the Buddha are all carrying out religious practices in lay households, waiting for the primal patriarch to appear." The succeeding verse section reaffirms all this in simpler form, with accompanying promises of deliverance. We are told again that the Patriarch has secretly composed this scripture, with its "wonderful news" (*miao hsiao-hsi*). Among other things, this news is that it is "Maitreya who [next] responds to the Ultimate and will be in charge of the nine-petaled golden lotus of the future."

Chapter 18 continues the numerical approach with a list of eight types of memorials bestowed by the Venerable Mother to be used to communicate with her. It is entitled "Verifying Memorials and Clarifying the Tradition" (Cheng-piao ming-tsung). The names of the memorials are as follows:

1. Memorial for opening up the wasteland when the three yang first appear (*San-yang ch'u hsien k'ai-huang piao*).

2. Memorial for returning to the real [through] the Three Refuges and the five precepts (*San-kuei wu-chieh kuei-chen piao*).

3. Memorial for promoting[?] the yellow and being reborn in heaven after ending [one's] karma (*Yuan[?]-huang liao-yeh sheng-t'ien piao*).

4. The Lotus school memorial for registering names in the Cloud Palace (*Yun-kung kua-hao lien-tsung piao*).

5. The memorial for returning to the Native Place and going to one's proper place on Mount Ling (*Ling-shan fu-yeh huan-hsiang piao*).

6. The eight trigrams memorial for returning to the real and paying respects to the source (*Pa-kua kuei-chen ch'ao-yuan piao*).

7. Memorial of the nine mysteries collecting and forming nāgas and devas[?] (*Chiu-hsuan ts'uan-tsao lung t'ien piao*).

8. The nine[-petaled] lotus memorial of the buddha-names of [members of] schools and sects (*Tsung-p'ai Fo-ming chiu-lien piao*).

Though the names of these memorials are referred to in the succeeding verse section of this chapter, no details about their ritual use are provided. Rather, chapter 18 concludes with general affirmations of the efficacy of this scripture:

A true scripture has appeared in the world, a true scripture of the future has appeared in the world that transmits the Golden Elixir [teaching] and reveals the secret inner workings of the holy. . . . Those with karmic affinity who are able to encounter [the teachings of this book]: [I] want only that you, with your minds firmly set on the Tao, [employ] the true incense memorials of the future. The names of those who are able to cross over will be registered in the Cloud Palace. . . . The Patriarch and Teacher has left behind [this] *pao-chüan* for returning to the Native Place that reveals the secrets of heaven.

Chapter 19, which is entitled "Yuan-ming and Hui-hsing Worship the Real" (Yuan-ming Hui-hsing li chen), provides a bit of information about ritual use of the memorials named above. Two men named Yuan-ming and Hui-hsing come to question the Patriarch, saying that "from beginningless time we have cultivated the real and nourished our natures, only waiting for the primal ones to return to their old Native Place." The Patriarch is overjoyed to see them and explains that within each year there are three periods of time (*san-yuan*), of which those beginning on the third day of the third lunar month and the ninth of the ninth are the foundation: "On these days there is a Peach Garden Assembly (P'an-t'ao hui) at the celestial palace, at which the Ancient Buddha and the Holy Mother provide a feast for the immortals." The above days constitute the upper and middle *yuan*; the lower *yuan* begins on the fifteenth day of the tenth month:

On the third of the third, there is a "Northern Apex [= North Polar Star] Assembly" for offering congratulations to the [Emperor of] the Dark Heaven. [At this assembly,] the first-place worthy is selected by examination. If on this day a memorial for returning home is employed, the names [on it] will be registered in the eight ministries (*pa-pu*).

On the ninth of the ninth month, other unspecified memorials can be used to register names in the Cloud Palace. Nothing further is said about the fifteenth of the tenth month. On these assembly days, altars are to be set up to invite all the buddhas to "bring down good fortune. When they come they provide peace and blessings. When they depart they bestow kindness that wipes out 108 kinds of misfortune and calamity." When incense is offered, its smoke reaches to heaven, and those who offer it are led to paradise.

In the verse recapitulation of this section, there is some indication that salvation involves selection by performance, although this is not strongly emphasized. Thus we read that "when the Venerable Ancient Buddha meets with the immortals, he thoroughly selects from [among them], examining [their adherence to] the Three Refuges and five precepts and the ten types of religious practice."

However, once again there is no development of this idea, and chapter 19 ends with pious phrases similar to those used earlier. The only other point of interest here is a particularly clear verse restatement of the origin and purpose of the teaching:

The Patriarch and Teacher transmitted true incense and memorials, something not at all light and easy. The multitude of the worthy and good came forward with increased devotion and listened attentively. The Ancient Celestial Perfected One, on behalf of the worthy and good, personally transmitted the wonderful message. He revealed the inner secrets of heaven and transmitted the true Way to save all living beings. For the sake of those who have not awakened, and who are profoundly confused and lost, I have come today to save you so that you will recognize the patriarchs and return to your roots. Those with karmic affinity encounter the true transmission of the original great message. [I have] lighted true incense and transmitted true memorials to save the primal ones. Now, to meet the Wu-wei Patriarch is to be different from the present generation. To continue the schools and branches and ascend to the Buddha assemblies is all due to [one's karma in] previous lives. Each person should maintain determination, sincerity, and a believing mind, and not backslide. Because of birth-and-death, seek a place of rest; add effort to effort. One should, with earnest devotion, reverence enlightened teachers and, with a mind set on the true and real, engage oneself with the Way (chen-hsin pan-tao).

The remaining five chapters of the Chiu-lien pao-chüan sum up its message and tell of Maitreya's return to paradise and final instructions to the faithful. The book ends with hundreds of names of the buddhas and bodhisattvas of the future, some of which appear to be those of sect members.

We have seen that, throughout the *Chiu-lien* book, the term "buddha" refers both to divine beings and to the human elect. The title of chapter 20 is "The Wu-wei Religious Practices in Ten Stages" (*shih-ti*), which is reminiscent of the "religious practices in ten steps" (*shih-pu*) of the *Huang-chi* book. Here, however, the ten "stages" refer to ten places where the teaching has been revealed. Four of them are located in different areas of China; the rest appear to be mythic. Of the four I have been able to locate, the most interesting is the first, Hao-chou in Anhui province, an area of White Lotus sectarian activity at the end of the Yuan, here described as the place where "new fields were opened up and seeds were planted. [Here] the Ancient Perfected Celestial [*sic*] (Chen-t'ien) first appeared in the world, and secretly composed numinous texts."[10]

The second location is Mount Feng-huang (Phoenix), the name of several mountains scattered throughout China, including one in Anhui. The fifth location, Wu-ma shan (Five Horse Mountain), is the name of three different mountains in Hopei, Hunan, and Szechwan. Number six is Chin-niu (Golden Ox) Mountain, a name applied to places in Anhui, Chekiang, and Yunnan. Thus three of the four identifiable sacred spots are or could be in Anhui, but that is all that the evidence permits us to say. It would, of course, be fascinating to locate this text in a tradition associated with a known place of earlier sectarian activity.

The remaining six locations have such names as Sheng-pao ti (Holy Precious Place) and Wu-ying shan (Shadowless Mountain), important in sectarian mythology but to my knowledge not well known beyond it.

Chapter 21 is entitled "The Wu-wei Patriarch Discusses the Way and Composes a Song." The "song" text is a prose repetition of earlier pious language. The next passage in chapter 21 is particularly worthy of note:

Maitreya leaves his cavern, and all the buddhas of the world come, traveling throughout the world and raising up the names [of the saved]. The sons and daughters (*ying-erh ch'a-nü*) [of the Mother] laugh out loud, for their bitter sufferings have ended and sweetness comes. Once they can pass through the "dark gate" (*hsuan-men*), they are forever able to avoid falling [into saṃsāra].

Those who study the Way quickly withdraw their minds [from worldly affairs] and go directly to Mount Ling, where their names and titles are registered.

The title of chapter 22 is "The Wu-wei [Patriarch] Divides Schools and Discusses Sects, to Continue [the Teaching in] the Latter Realm." It is in this chapter that the Patriarch (Maitreya) is ordered to return to the celestial palace. Here we are told that he was in fact originally sent to Earth for a transgression—the motif of a "banished immortal" that can be found in Chinese literature. After a summary of the Patriarch's saving work on Earth, we read that

suddenly he saw a "cloud youth" sent by the [realm of] the holy, holding an "elixir letter" in his hand, a golden placard of a Dharma edict, which said, "Now the Eternal [Mother] summons Wu-wei to return to the palace. Because he had revealed the inner secrets of heaven, he was sentenced to be in the 'land of dark cliffs' [= the world?][11] for twenty years. Now because of his arduous refining of body and mind, his merit is complete and he is to go to see the Eternal." When the Patriarch received this holy message, his devout soul flew up to heaven. . . .

Hence the Patriarch prepares to leave his worldly body and return to the Cloud Palace. As he takes leave of his disciples, he gives a final benediction in 3/3/4 verse:

I am afraid that you will not pay attention but will believe in demonic people (mo-jen). The primal ones should carefully preserve and protect the Wu-wei Great Tao. The scripture in five sections [a reference to the Chiu-lien book] is the true bone and marrow; each character distinguishes the real. Within the same Way there are some who cheat teachers and destroy (mieh) patriarchs. I have not taken part in idle debates in which each displays his own ability. I have established a chart for the Latter Realm, the nine palaces, and the eight trigrams [of sect branch names]. I have led Dharma masters (fa-shih) to diligently protect the teaching and preserve and fix the dark gate. For each palace [branch], I have arranged for great worthies to move branches and toil to protect them[?] (pan-chih lao shou). When there are holy festivals on the three yuan days, worship the celestial palace with memorials. The nine palaces and eight trigrams continue [the tradition] from lamp to lamp. Patiently preserve [the message]; the time is coming when parent and children will meet together. I have given many thousands of orders to you great multitudes of the worthy and good. Obey my words as if I were still with you; it is entirely the same.

. . . Now I am leaving, but I will return to complete gathering in those of the source. Those with good karma I will see again; together we will continue eternal life.

In the concluding prose section of chapter 22, the Patriarch's message is repeated, and he says, "I have each day at home discussed Heaven and Earth, and for the sake of the worthy and good have revealed the inner secrets of Heaven. . . . I command you, multitudes of the worthy and good, to record my words in your hearts. . . . Never relax [your devotion]."

The title of chapter 23 is "Diligently Obeying the Holy Message, the Cloud Youth Returns to the Palace." Here the Patriarch explains that he revealed the "holy secrets" in this text because "the injured souls, immortals, buddhas, and astral patriarchs of the three assemblies did not understand the great affairs of the Latter Realm." He tells his listeners that he is going to leave the names of the buddhas of the future in this book, so that "later, on the day of paying respects to the source, you will each recognize the buddhas' names, return to the celestial palace, and receive the buddhas' grace, and for eighty-one kalpas never again long for the mundane world."

In this chapter the Patriarch provides a summary of the numbers of buddhas in each of the three time periods; chapter 24 provides the names of the buddhas and bodhisattvas of the future. At the Assembly of the Limitless, 53 buddhas were in charge of the Majestic Kalpa (Chuang-yen chieh), the celestial realm (t'ien-p'an) of the past. At the Assembly of the Great Ultimate, 35 buddhas are in charge of the Kalpa of the Worthies and Saints, the celestial realm of the present. At the Imperial Ultimate Assembly, 330 buddhas and 108 bodhisattvas will be in charge of the Constellation Kalpa, the celestial realm of the future. These three assemblies all share the same principle.

Chapter 23 continues with more warnings and promises. The pious are urged to

with firm minds preserve the Way; when this is done for a long time and one's merit is complete, one will be able to see the primal ones. Those whose karma is light and whose foundations are shallow are of three minds and two intentions, and so they believe demonic words (mo-yen) and recklessly discuss them. It will be difficult [for them] to see the Celestial Perfected. [However], those who are determined to preserve the dark gate are majestic and unmoved (wei-wei pu-tung). Protecting the Wu-wei teaching, they each continue the lamp of the master. . . .

If this time you do not encounter the wonderful message for returning home, for eighty-one kalpas you will be reborn in the four life forms [of saṃsāra], unable to return. I earnestly urge you, many friends of the Way, to increase your efforts to progress. Maintain the Three Refuges and the five precepts, with the ten items [of ritual observance] all complete.[12] If you protect and preserve the Way, when the Buddha appears in the world and the golden cock crows, master and disciples will be able to meet again.[13]

In four lines of six-character verse at the end of this chapter, there is an echo of the pseudo-precision of dates seen in the *Huang-chi* book (see Chapter Two above), using terms from the sixty-year cycle of "stems and branches." Here the Patriarch says,

In the *chia-tzu* [year] I approached the mundane realm, with nine rotations [i.e., rebirths].
In the *jen-tzu* year I established sects and apportioned schools (*ting-p'ai fen-tsung*).
At the *chi-wei* year I encountered stupidity and difficulty,
[And] in the *keng-wu* year I entered the holy and returned to the palace.

To continue this pseudo-precision, we can note that these years are respectively the first, forty-ninth, and fifty-sixth year of one cycle, with *keng-wu* being the seventh of the next, for a total of sixty-seven years. The cycle before the publication of the *Chiu-lien* book began in 1444, whereas the cycle in which it appeared began in 1504. The publication date of 1523 corresponds to the *kuei-wei* year, the twentieth year of the cycle; the *keng-wu* year preceding it corresponds to 1510–1511 in the Western calendar, which theoretically could be adduced as the date of the Patriarch's departure. However, we are not told which cycle is involved, and such mythic dates are unreliable, so no conclusion can be reached. Note also that nothing in these dates corresponds to the twenty years that we are told was the Patriarch's sentence of banishment.

The title of chapter 24 is "The Penance [Text] of the Patriarch and Teacher Commending the Titles of the Buddhas of the Future," though in fact no penance ritual is discussed. Here the Patriarch, in obedience to an edict from Lao-tzu of the Prior Realm, lists the names of the immortals and buddhas of the future to be "transmitted from generation to generation." For those who

recite them with sincere minds, each phrase is a prayer for blessing and each sentence dissipates disaster. All the buddhas are lined up, filling the sky; their holy ears hear at a great distance, and the good deities of the three realms, all with celestial vision, see from a distance the Dharma realms in all directions. They constantly observe faces [to see if] ordinary and holy match[?] (*ch'ang tu mien fan-sheng hsiang-he*). When you enter the assembly, with united hearts bow and recite this true penance; with each sentence raise up the names of the buddhas and patriarchs. All together recite [the following names] in congratulation three times.

There follows a list of 350 names, 262 of buddhas and 88 of bodhisattvas, all to be offered homage, beginning with the "Future Buddha of Measureless Life" and the Bodhisattva Kuan-yin. This list occupies twenty-two folio pages. These names are a wonder of the sectarian imagination—except for the first two, none is a standard, well-known name of a Buddhist figure. Many of the bodhisattva titles include human names with the surname last, as, for example, "Homage to the Bodhisattva Yü-lien Huang" (Na-mo Yü-lien Huang p'u-sa). Several of these names include characters that clearly refer to women, such as *chü* ("chrysanthemum"), *mei* ("plum"), and *miao* ("wonderful"), the last a common sectarian name for female devotees, as already noted in Chapter Three above.

Among the several surnames here, the most common is "Kuang." All those with this surname appear to have religious given names beginning with such characters as *p'u* ("universal"), *miao* ("wonderful"), *shan* ("good"), *chin* ("golden"), *chueh* ("enlightened"), and *kuei* ("return," "take refuge"), as in P'u-ming (Universal Enlightenment) and Kuei-chen (Take Refuge in the Real). *P'u* is a common element in the name of male devotees, corresponding to *miao* for women. What all this indicates is sectarian membership, and hence sectarian structure. The Patriarch is here promising bodhisattva status in the new dispensation to present members of the sect he was addressing.

The *Chiu-lien* book concludes with a prose passage summing up its message, and with ten repayments (*pao*) and ten lines of heptasyllabic verse. At the very end in a last line is the date "reprinted on the first of the fifth month of the second year of the [Ming] Chia-ching [reign period]," a date equivalent to June 13, 1523, in the Western calendar. In the concluding prose passage, we read:

Those who proclaim [the message of this book] will transcend the three realms. Those who explain its meaning will escape death. On the sea of suffering they will float on a boat to the [other] shore, where the little children will be able to see their dear Mother and enter the Mother's womb. They will not fear the three calamities, will realize the state of [being beyond] rebirth [and death] (*wu-sheng*), and will forever be secure and healthy. In the future, for eighty-one kalpas they will be unmoved and their lives will be of measureless length. [I] urge you, worthy and good people, to believe and accept [this message] and maintain the Three Refuges and five precepts with dedication and seriousness. Thus the 3600 types and classes of beings will all enter the great ritual arena of the Imperial Ultimate.

The ten grateful repayments are for:

1. The kindness (*en*) of Heaven and Earth, which cover and support [us].
2. The kindness of the sun and moon, which illuminate and approach.
3. The kindness of the emperor, water, and soil.
4. The kindness of our parents, who nourish and raise [us].
5. The kindness of patriarchs and teachers for transmitting the teaching.
6. The kindness of senior disciples (*shih-hsiung*), who protect and support [us].
7. The offering of alms (Skt. *dāna*).
8. The multitude of worthies everywhere.
9. The rebirth of nine generations of ancestors in the Pure Land [paradise].
10. The early salvation of orphan souls.

The *Chiu-lien pao-chüan* is thus a complete statement of sixteenth-century sectarian mythology and teaching, with antecedents in the fifteenth century and successors all the way down to the twentieth. For this genre, it is a classic in both style and content. We have seen many close similarities with the *Huang-chi* book of 1430 (see Chapter Two above), which is not directly referred to in the *Chiu-lien book* but which might have been familiar to its author.

It is noteworthy that there are no specific references to Lo Ch'ing or his texts in the *Chiu-lien* book, the teachings of which are on a different foundation altogether. However, a few of Lo's terms—such as "majestic and unmoved" (*wei-wei pu-tung*) and "five scriptures" (*wu-pu ching*)—are also found here, though the contexts of their usage are different. It is thus possible that the author of the *Chiu-lien* book had heard something of Lo's work, though the evidence is thin. Of course, the major point of possible influence is the use in the *Chiu-lien* book of the term "Wu-wei Patriarch," but Wu-wei here has nothing of the meaning it has in Lo Ch'ing's writings. Moreover, since the name occurs in the *Huang-chi* book from the preceding century, it need not be ascribed to Wu-wei sect influence. After all, the term *wu-wei* had been well known since the appearance of the *Lao-tzu* book in the third century B.C.E.

In 1981, Susan Naquin found in the Ch'ing archives in Beijing chapters 10 through 18 of a text entitled *Fo-shuo Tu-tou li-t'ien hou hui shou-yuan pao-chüan* (The precious volume, expounded by the Buddha, concerning [Maitreya at his] Tu-tou [Palace] establishing heaven and at the last assembly gathering all to completion; hereafter "the *Li-t'ien* book"). It was in a file of materials dated the fourth day of the eighth month of the eighteenth year of the Ch'ing Ch'ien-lung reign period (August 31, 1753).[14] This book is a direct continuation of the teachings of the *Huang-chi pao-chüan* of 1430, passed on through the 1523 *Chiu-lien* scripture and its successors.

The *Li-t'ien pao-chüan* calls itself the *Huang-chi chüan* (Imperial Ultimate book) and the *Shou-yuan chüan* (Book of completely gathering in [the lost]). Its chief deities are the Venerable Mother and Maitreya, who "transforms himself into a golden cock to teach and transform [those on] the great earth" (chapter 2). There are references here to "secretly fishing for the worthy and good," "Shadowless Mountain," "opening up new fields and setting forth the details" *(k'ai-huang ch'u-hsi)*, and to the "Cloud City," "Dragon-Flower Assembly," the eighty-one kalpas of the future, and the "Patriarch of the Imperial Apex." There are still ninety-two myriads of "immortal youths and jade maidens attached to the red dust world and unwilling to return" (chapter 16), whom even Maitreya has been unable to save, so the Mother sends down two female bodhisattvas, also called "mothers," to continue the task.

At the end of chapter 16 of the *Li-t'ien pao-chüan*, we are told that the Venerable Mother herself "descended to the mundane realm and borrowed a body to save women and men [*sic*] and establish the Latter Assembly." There are also criticisms of other religious practices here, similar to those we have seen earlier. The structure of this book is that of the earlier texts as well, with chapter titles and numbers followed by prose sections that are succeeded in turn by penta- and heptasyllabic verse or, in some chapters, by ten-character verse arranged 3/3/4. The chapters end with prose passages introduced by tune names similar or identical to those in the *Huang-chi pao-chüan*.

The *Li-t'ien pao-chüan* is a different book with its own story to tell, but its style, structure, and content are strongly influenced by earlier texts of the same type. Along with the later editions of the *Chiu-lien pao-chüan* itself, this book demonstrates that the teachings of that early sixteenth-century scripture were still alive and well in the eighteenth. We shall see that they continued long beyond then.

CHAPTER FIVE

Themes in Later Sixteenth-Century 'Pao-chüan'

This chapter is based on material from thirteen texts in rough chronological order: (1) five from a variety of groups, (2) three from the Huan-yuan (Return to the Primal Source) sect, and (3) five from the Hung-yang (Vast Yang) tradition. Though some of these Hung-yang texts may have been published in the early seventeenth century, they originated with the work of the sect founder P'iao-kao, who was active in the last years of the sixteenth. Because these books have much in common, I treat them here as sixteenth-century texts. Chapter Six below discusses two later books from the Hung-yang tradition that are clearly seventeenth century. Of course, to follow the Western calendar in such situations is arbitrary; for the Chinese, the operative time category is that the Hung-yang books discussed here were produced in the Wan-li period of the Ming dynasty (1573–1619).

Space constraints prohibit complete discussions of each of these thirteen texts in the fashion of Chapters Two, Three, and Four above. Instead, I have placed bibliographic descriptions and summaries of each book in Appendix H. In the main body of this chapter I discuss several themes common to all these books, beginning with material that is as close to history as these texts get—namely, autobiographical statements by their authors/revealers and references to the names of sects and congregations. Of course, what is presented as first-person reference and narration here should really be understood as hagiography.

The next theme is the self-understanding of these texts as revealed messages of salvation, bequeathed by deities and patriarchs. Then follow discussions of mythologies of creation, salvation, and the end of the age, and of deliverance through realizing the potential of one's own inner nature. At this point some attention is given to passages that use terms derived from the Taoist tradition of internal alchemy. As in the texts discussed in earlier chapters, acceptance of these myths and teachings provides the basis for distinctions between the ignorant and the enlightened, the ordinary world and the sacred realm of paradise. The last theme I discuss is the social perspective of these books. All these themes are, of course, interrelated, but it is useful to approach them in this fashion.

Meditation and ritual are mentioned a few times in these books, but there is not enough material concerning them to warrant a separate discussion. Seventeenth-century evidence for such activities is covered in Chapter Six below.

I am concerned throughout with evidence of the historical development of *pao-chüan* and their themes, though clear patterns are not easy to discover. A good example of this ambiguity can be seen in passages about mother-goddesses and the salvation found by returning to them. All the books consulted for this chapter refer to this mythology, which provides an underlying framework for their teachings and promises. Yet many of these references are fragmentary, and in some there are many goddesses, not just a single Venerable Mother. In some texts these Mothers are described as both in paradise and in temporary descents to earth, but they are always concerned with the deliverance of their "sons and daughters."

This theme is discussed in more detail below; the point here is that within the sixteenth-century, historical development of the mother-goddess belief is difficult to discern. Singular and plural references alternate right down to the end of the century. Of course, since we are discussing texts composed by different authors in different times and places, great coherence among them cannot be expected. There are, however, deep continuities of language and teaching.

AUTOBIOGRAPHICAL REFERENCES BY
NARRATORS OF THE TEXTS

Here, as in what follows, the relevant material (translated in Appendix H) is referred to but not repeated in the discussion itself. Autobiographical references in Lo Ch'ing's *K'u-kung wu-tao pao-chüan* and in the *Chiu-lien pao-chüan* of 1523 have already been analyzed in detail in Chapters Three and Four. Autobiographical passages in the books dealt with in the present chapter can be found in (1) the *Hsiao-shih yuan-chueh pao-chüan* (1564; hereafter "the *Yuan-chueh pao-chüan*"), chapter 32; (2) the *Hsiao-shih wu-hsing huan-yuan pao-chüan* (late sixteenth century; hereafter "the *Huan-yuan pao-chüan*"), in which the long autobiographical statement is at the beginning of the book, following the opening invocations); (3) the *Hsiao-shih kuei-chia pao-en pao-chüan* (1591; hereafter "the *Kuei-chia pao-en pao-chüan*"), chapter 13; (4) the *Hung-yang k'u-kung wu-tao ching* (late sixteenth century; hereafter "the *Hung-yang k'u-kung ching*"), most of which is devoted to a first-person narration by the Hun-yuan Patriarch of his quest for enlightenment and his first missionary work; and (5) the *Hsiao-shih Chen-k'ung sao-hsin pao-chüan* (1584, 1596; hereafter "the *Sao-hsin pao-chüan*"), which contains a biography of Patriarch Chen-k'ung by admiring disciples—all translated below in Appendix H.

The underlying structure of these accounts is movement from ignorance to enlightenment through a long period of spiritual struggle that is an initiation into what Mircea Eliade called "a new mode of being." The young patriarch-to-be longs for religious assurance but does not know how to find it. He wants to leave home to seek instruction but is also concerned about caring for his parents and family, who oppose his departure. Eventually, he begins a pilgrimage to visit religious masters who teach him such methods of deliverance as reciting the Buddha's name or meditation. These methods at first prove insufficient, but he keeps on trying until he finally attains enlightenment through realizing his own divine inner nature, sometimes as a result of a dream or vision. Through this experience the young man becomes a teacher himself, whose message is validated by his spiritual initiation. This message is bequeathed to his disciples as a new "precious volume." Thus these "autobiographical" narratives are hagiographic in tone, with mythological elements.

The most complete autobiographical narrative in the texts at hand is the *Hung-yang k'u-kung wu-tao ching* (The Vast Yang scripture on awakening to the Way through bitter toil; discussed in detail in Appendix H, where it is text 9). As its title indicates, it is based in part on Lo Ch'ing's account of his spiritual quest. Here the young Hun-yuan patriarch-to-be, P'iao-kao (d. 1598), dissatisfied with ordinary means of piety, is desperate to leave home to seek an enlightened teacher, but his parents will not allow him to do so. His mother's eventual illness and an encounter with an aged man intensify his fear of dying without release, so after preparing everything for his parents, he leaves home to seek instruction from teachers "who talk about the Native Place" and "the passes to the Cloud City."

The first three religious teachers that he consults do not meet his needs, but finally he becomes the disciple of a master who teaches meditation as the way to "enlightening the mind and seeing the Native Place." After his enlightenment is certified by this master, P'iao-kao returns home as a missionary to convert his family and friends. The last chapters of the *Hung-yang k'u-kung ching* describe a vision in which the Patriarch visits the Eternal Mother in paradise and attains further enlightenment, as a result of which he "leaves behind . . . [this] true scripture without words" — by this time a stock reference to a message that is beyond the power of words to describe.

This theme of struggle against the opposition of parents and family is also found in the *Kuei-chia pao-en* scripture (text 8 in Appendix H), in which the narrator comments about his parents:

I think of my father and mother who nurtured me in the womb and nursed me for three years, [after] ten months of the sufferings [of pregnancy]; it is difficult to repay such profound love. They gave birth to me, and when I became an adult I developed my religious practice in devotion to the Way. With my whole mind I wanted to leave the household life and not be attached to the red dust [world]. Every day I wept at home, wanting to seek a way out. Then on that day when my sincere devotion was at a peak, buddhas and patriarchs approached me. I saw that in the southwest the buddhas had manifested myriad rays of brilliant light which came to the Eastern Land and burst upon Heaven and Earth, illuminating and penetrating my body. I awakened and wanted to leave home to take refuge in the Pure Land, but my parents bitterly detained me. I wanted to flee to the mountains, so in front of a buddha[-image] I took leave of the parents who gave me birth. I paid respects to my parents and took leave of my wife and children. I wanted to go to devote myself to religious practice, to be a courageous and decisive person, no longer attached to the red dust world. . . . But my parents hung on to me with their hands; it was most difficult to cut myself off and leave them. If I reject them, when they are old, on whom will they rely?

Nonetheless, the patriarch-narrator does leave, after explaining to his parents that if he does not do so it will be most difficult for him to be saved. This passage concludes: "Now I am going to take refuge in the mountains, to visit worthies and study the Way. When I have attained the Way, I will return home to my parents" (chapter 13).

The narrator of the *Yuan-chueh pao-chüan* (text 3 in Appendix H) left home to follow a religious teacher and traveled to "the famous mountains of eight provinces" without meeting an enlightened person. Then he met a master in Yunnan who sent him east to Mount Lao in Shantung. He met two men there with whom he discussed how to "develop perfection." The eventual result was that, "at the age of more than fifty, he had thousands of great awakenings and uncountable small awakenings. Moved by his devotion, the Holy Mother of the Prior Realm opened the door for him. The nine passages [of his body and mind] were opened up, and a bright light moved and illuminated him" (chapter 32).

The extensive autobiographical material in the *Huan-yuan pao-chüan* is translated in full in Appendix H (where the *Huan-yuan* book is text 6). In it, the Huan-yuan patriarch-to-be goes in and out of a dream state in which he has visions of paradise. His enlightenment experience begins in a state of meditative absorption, after which, despite his parents' opposition, he takes leave of them and goes to a mountain cloister to continue his quest. Here, in meditation, he has another vision in which he goes to paradise and is commissioned by the Ancient Buddha to return to the world to preach and save. After a final enlightenment experience, he leaves behind the *Huan-yuan* scripture as a guide to future generations.

In the *Sao-hsin pao-chüan* (text 5 in Appendix H), Patriarch Chen-k'ung is described as an illiterate firewood-gatherer, adept only at reciting the Buddha's name, who suddenly went into a trance while he was in the mountains and stood transfixed for three days. A crowd soon gathered, to whom he preached when he came out of his trance. Thus a tradition began that led to the formation of a sect with its own scripture. This is a most interesting account of what can truly be called a folk-religious leader, yet one whose book gained such high-level support that it was printed in elaborate style, with homage to the emperor in gold letters!

Though these spiritual autobiographies and biographies are in different texts composed over a period of several decades, their structure is quite similar, as mentioned above. There were no sectarian monasteries, nor were sectarian leaders expected to take vows of celibacy, but from these accounts it is clear that to attain the highest levels of enlightenment they had to leave home at least for a time to study with enlightened masters. Implicit in all these stories are networks of relationships between teachers and disciples—networks that were reinforced by the writing and possession of sacred texts. It was through such connections that sectarian teachings spread.

SECTS AND CONGREGATIONS

In Chapters Three and Four above, we have seen references to the most immediate social context of "precious volumes"—namely, the congregations led by the sect leaders who produced them. There are a few such references in other sixteenth-century texts as well, all of which are noted in Appendix H. Thus the *P'u-ming ju-lai wu-wei liao-i pao-chüan* (1558; hereafter "the *P'u-ming pao-chüan*," text 2 in Appendix H) refers to the "Holy Way of Yellow Heaven" and to the "Ancient Buddha who in his compassion has pointed to the Great Way of perfect heaven and opened another gate for rescuing from suffering, a straight path for entering the holy and returning to the source" (p. 8 in the text published by E. S. Stulova in 1979). The term "gate" (*men*) here can be understood as a school or group of disciples.

In the *Hsiao-shih k'e-i cheng-tsung pao-chüan* (late sixteenth century; hereafter "the *Cheng-tsung pao-chüan*," text 7 in Appendix H), there are repeated references to the "people of the Way in the assembly or congregation" (*hui-hsia tao-jen*) and to "those who meet in the assembly" (*ho hui jen*; chapters 2 and 7). I think it appropriate in such contexts to translate *hui* as "congregation." This book, like other such texts, is in the form of a direct address to listeners and readers, as in chapter 7, where we read: "People of the congregation, I want only that you concentrate on carefully receiving this great message, to which there is always a [divine] response. This is a true and correct message. Once you have gotten this warning from the gods, you can verify the message of the Dharma gate [= these teachings]."

This same tone can be found in chapter 9: "Pious ones, listen [to my message] so that you soon awaken and escape the dusty cage [of life in the ordinary world]. People of the Way in this congregation, hasten to seek the great message for returning home. If you don't transmit it, later generations will be lost. Every sentence and phrase is spoken clearly. Only this is the message for returning home."

In chapter 12 of the *Cheng-tsung pao-chüan*, we are told that

men and women of later generations, people of the Way who assemble together should all in this place listen carefully to this book. . . . Disciples of each patriarch should not depart from what they have attained in this place. This morning [the message] has been clearly opened up, with no hidden meaning [i.e., with nothing held back]. . . . [They] are instructed to [attain] clear and penetrating awakening and to receive, continue, and transmit the lamp [of the teaching]. They should stop darkening themselves and forgetting about the grace [they have received] for attaining the Way. If they do not transmit the correct teaching, they will forever be sent down to the [section of] purgatory where [punishments continue] without intermission, never to escape.

The *Huan-yuan* book (text 6 in Appendix H) contains similar injunctions to the "people of the Way in the congregation" and "disciples of each patriarch," as in this sentence from chapter 4: "[You] people in the congregation (*hui-chung jen*), listen to [this] *pao-chüan* carefully; observe and think [about it]." In chapter 6 the members of the congregation are told that

if you obtain [this] holy message, for eternal eons you will not be destroyed. [You will attain] formless complete enlightenment. Heaven and Earth will decay, but this treasure will never be destroyed. From antiquity until the present, only a few have thoroughly explained [this message]. Those who clearly understand the great message of the Tathāgata will be able to end [an encounter with] the Ten Lords of purgatory and return to the source. . . . Pious practitioners, draw near to listen to my orders. Those who maintain a vegetarian diet [= sect members] should be patient and preserve their intentions [wherever] they go. You are participating in the Great Way and developing your fundamental natures. You should exert your enlightened minds to seek out the right ones (*tang-jen*).

The "right ones" are defined in contrast to "the lost who have no understanding, who rush about to the east and west, who seek on the outside. It is those who recognize the profound wonder [of this teaching] who are the *tang-jen*" (chapter 6). It is clear from this material that those "in the congregation" being addressed are an in-group who have received and understood the saving message.

There are several references to sectarian leaders and congregations in the late sixteenth-century Hung-yang texts, particularly in the detailed autobiographical material in the *Hung-yang k'u-kung* scripture discussed in Appendix H (where it is text 9). Here the narrator visits several sectarian teachers in different places who treat him as a disciple. Two sects are named, the Yuan-huang (Primal Imperial) assembly and the Hung-yang teaching. There are references as well to "friends in the Way" (*tao-yu*) who join the patriarch-to-be on a missionary trip, and to his enlightenment being certified by his master before he is allowed to begin to preach.

The explicit self-consciousness of the Hung-yang tradition as a new (sectarian) teaching can be found in my translation of the preface shared by all of these books that were printed by the Palace Printing Bureau, including the key statement of this theme, "the newly established Patriarchal Teaching of the Origin in Primal Chaos" (Hsin-li Hun-yuan tsu chiao; see Appendix H, text 9). The sectarian social context of these early *pao-chüan* is further clarified by these explicit references to it.

THE SELF-UNDERSTANDING OF THESE TEXTS
AS REVEALED SCRIPTURES

This theme has already been introduced in references to "precious volumes" being "left behind" by enlightened patriarchs for the salvation of their followers, and to the responsibility of congregations to continue their transmission. In the apt phrasing of *Hun-yuan hung-yang Fo ju-lai wu-chi P'iao-kao tsu lin-fan ching* (hereafter "the *P'iao-kao ching*"; text 10 in Appendix H), they are "scriptures descended to the ordinary [world]" (*lin fan ching*). They are "letters from home," sent "repeatedly with [the Mother's] instructions" because "the ignorant multitudes, attached to the dusty [world], are unwilling to return" (*Yuan-chueh pao-chüan*, chapter 12). These "letters" are true because they are from the heart of cosmic reality, as can be seen from a resounding statement in chapter 26 of *Yao-shih pen-yuan kung-te pao-chüan* (1544; hereafter "the *Yao-shih* scripture," text 1 in Appendix H):

The Buddha said, "The *Yao-shih pao-chüan* penetrates the most sublime mysteries and manifests pure reality. When it is opened, all the buddhas protect it; where it is proclaimed, a myriad of people look up in reverence. With one voice [in recitation of it], all transcend the sea of suffering; with the writing of one of its verses, one does not fall into saṃsāra. This book is the bone and marrow of all [precious] volumes, the true tradition of the Ancient Buddha, a direct path [to salvation] for all beings."

The *Yao-shih* book has been "verified by all the myriads of buddhas," it is "the Mother's oral transmission, the cause for in the future seeing her face to face" (chapter 32).

The *P'u-ming pao-chüan* (text 2 in Appendix H) makes much the same point in different terms:

Those with karmic affinity are able to encounter [the teachings of] the Holy Way of Yellow Heaven, transmitted with the nonactivist [teaching] in four-line [verse]. [If] they are pure at all times, those who support and recite this true scripture escape the gates of birth-and-death. Day and night they [i.e., the pious] selected from prior scriptures, and refined and smelted the marrow of Heaven and Earth [to compose this book, which is] the life root of all the buddhas. It is the true instructions of the mind-seal (*hsin-yin*)[1] transmitted and bequeathed by the Ancient Buddha, which sweeps away the myriad phenomena and dwells in patriarchal *ch'i* of the origin in creative chaos of fundamental emptiness, [which leads to] instantaneous enlightenment. (introductory section, pp. 6–7 of the Stulova edition)

There are several comments about the nature and transmission of scripture in two of the books from the Huan-yuan sect consulted here, the *Huan-yuan* and the *Cheng-tsung pao-chüan*. Here the narrators speak in the first person of the reasons for the revelation of these texts and of the importance of printing and distributing them. As we read in the *Huan-yuan* scripture (text 6 in Appendix H):

For your sake, men and women, with a thousand changes and ten thousand transformations [I] have been reborn in an ordinary womb to verify [i.e., give witness to the teaching of] noninterference that ends death and transcends rebirth. This time in the Eastern Land I have left behind a *pao-chüan* to save [you] good men and believing women, so that together you reach home. Those who believe what [I have] taught will soon return home; the light of the buddhas will illuminate them. Those who do not believe are mistaken, and for a myriad eons will not encounter [such teaching again]. . . . Now I have attained the Way and manifested my fundamental nature, [so] I have left behind this *pao-chüan* in twelve sections to convert all beings. (chapters 10 and 11)

Because men and women are so profoundly lost, this *Huan-yuan* scripture has finally been bequeathed. It is a "true scripture 'precious volume' that has been transmitted to the world and will never be destroyed" (chapter 20). Nevertheless, though the Huan-yuan patriarch-narrator says that "today I am returning home, so I leave [behind] this *pao-chüan*" (chapter 15), he clarifies that "this 'precious volume' is not what I have spoken, but is the *Tripitaka* words of the Ancient Buddha to save all those of the origin" (chapter 19).

Once the mythic validation of the *Huan-yuan pao-chüan* has been

established, the next task is to urge its reverent recitation and distribution. Hence the Huan-yuan Patriarch tells his disciples that

intelligent men and women should listen attentively [to this book]. . . . Those
who copy, read, and recite [it] with sincere and pious intentions will forever
avoid disasters for their whole families, both old and young. People of the
congregation, when you recite and read this *pao-chüan*, you must with devout intentions call it out [i.e., recite it] with united voices, [so as to] end
death and transcend rebirth. This "precious volume" is beneficial. When one
character of it circulates, the saints and deities above immediately investigate. Those who revile this volume should stop slandering this "precious
volume" true scripture. Those who revile the Buddha will never again obtain human form. (chapter 19)

Today, in leaving behind this true scripture, I do not hope for wealth but
only seek that you believing people together will reach home. Later guests
of the Native Place should carefully listen to its teaching, because what this
scripture speaks of is only for [our] divine roots (*ling-ken*). Good men and
women, you should contribute your wealth to cut blocks for and print [this
scripture]. I am returning home on your behalf, so that we can meet together
in one place. If there are officials who have [this book] printed, [they should
know that] printing one copy of this *Huan-yuan chüan* [means that they] will
never be reborn. Those in the congregation who have blocks cut will . . .
have their names registered for ten thousand ages. . . . I print this scripture
today not for myself but for the sake of the men and women of the world,
those of the origin (*pen-lai chih jen*). (chapter 21)

Those who publish this true scripture *pao-chüan* and circulate it throughout
the world live forever with limitless blessings. (chapter 22)

The material on this theme in the *Cheng-tsung pao-chüan* (text 7 in
Appendix H) is very similar to that in the *Huan-yuan*, so I will not
repeat it all here. Here, too, the narrator speaks in the first person of
his own words and instructions bequeathed in this scripture, the
"holy message" (*sheng-i*) transmitted so that all can "enlighten their
minds and see their natures. This *pao-chüan* penetrates and connects
Heaven and Earth and saves all those with karmic affinity" (chapter
9). The recipients of the *Cheng-tsung* book are also urged to recite
and print it. It has been "printed and circulated throughout the
world. . . . Those men and women everywhere who constantly recite
it avoid disastrous karma and soon transcend rebirth" (chapter 19).
A new point made in the *Cheng-tsung* book is that it was taken out of
a celestial scripture storehouse (chapter 24)—an old Taoist theme
here expressed in popular sectarian form.

In sum, these sixteenth-century scriptures present themselves as saving messages revealed through narrators who are humans of divine origin and who teach in the world for a while, then return to paradise. Their teachings are left behind in these books for the edification of those with the karmic destiny to listen and understand. These disciples are, in turn, instructed to print these scriptures and circulate them everywhere.

The self-understanding of the sixteenth-century Hung-yang sect texts consulted for this chapter is similar to that of the other books considered here, as can be seen from the introduction to these books in Appendix H (see the section there entitled "Five Texts of the Hung-yang Sect"). The only significant variation is a mention in chapters 23 and 24 of the *P'iao-kao ching* (text 10 in Appendix H) of its being the last of a long tradition of sacred scriptures revealed by the Buddha, "Lord Lao"(i.e., Lao-tzu), Confucius, and "Patriarch Lo [Ch'ing]," "who left behind five scriptures in six volumes." Only after this did "the Vast Yang teaching appear, to save all living beings" (chapter 24). Here again, we see the concern of sectarian preachers to validate their message by relating it to older and better known scriptural traditions. Indeed, it can be argued on historical grounds that the *pao-chüan* constitute a fourth such tradition, after the Confucian, Buddhist, and Taoist.

MYTHOLOGIES OF CREATION, SALVATION,
AND THE END OF THE AGE

There are references to the Eternal Mother mythology in all the books consulted for this chapter, although they are all fragmentary ones. The sectarian authors rely on this mythological framework to a greater or lesser extent but do not discuss it in a detailed and connected way. It seems to be assumed that the readers of these texts already know this myth and so need only be reminded of it at various points. Here I provide translations and summaries of references to the Eternal Mother myth in these books in the best chronological order I can manage, with the Hung-yang texts last, to see whether or not any historical development can be discerned. In none is the myth presented in as much detail as it is in the *Chiu-lien pao-chüan* discussed in Chapter Four above.

Though the *Yao-shih pao-chüan* (text 1 in Appendix H) is devoted to the Healing Buddha, it repeatedly refers to themes and terms from the Mother myth and includes such passages as the following in its introductory material:

From the time when the buddhas and patriarchs left Mount Ling until now, [some] children have seen their Mother (*ying-erh chien-niang*), realized the Eternal, and [so] never revolve [in saṃsāra] again.

People on earth are very ignorant and lost; unable to find release, they go through saṃsāra. Then suddenly they are able to meet the Eternal Mother (Wu-sheng mu) and, [as her] children, released from suffering, enter the Lotus Pool.

They will certainly be reborn at the three Dragon-Flower Assemblies [*sic*], receive and continue long life, and meet together with the buddhas, never to fall back. For eighty myriads of eons they will be in the realm of no rebirth and no death. They will register their names in the World of Utmost Bliss.

They will suddenly be taken up and returned to the old Native Place.

The wording of the ninth vow of the Healing Buddha-to-be includes the sentence, "May [people] not revolve [in saṃsāra] and [may they] spend a myriad springs in the Venerable Mother's womb." (There is a similar reference in chapter 22 of the *Yao-shih pao-chüan*.) Maitreya is also involved in this story:

As for Maitreya Bodhisattva [*sic*], people on the great earth do not recognize him. He controls the wind and sends down rain. . . . He leads [all] to return home, leads all to return home. . . .

The Buddha Maitreya in the lower regions, in the *sahā* sea of suffering, saves the worthy and good. With a Dharma boat he saves all the Mother's children, and those who take leave of the world see their dear Mother. (chapter 20)

It is clear here that only one Eternal Mother is involved, but nowhere in the *Yao-shih pao-chüan* is her story presented in a connected fashion.

There are only a few references to this myth in the *P'u-ming pao-chüan* (1558; text 2 in Appendix H) — to the Mother, the three stages of cosmic time, and the future happy state of the elect. Chapter 26 speaks of

returning to the original country [or "our country"] (*pen-kuo*) to see the Eternal Holy Mother (Wu-sheng sheng-mu). By this [we] poor folk obtain the precious jewel and float on a boat to the shore. [In this way] solitary travelers (*ku-k'e*) return to [their Native] Place (*huan-hsiang*), and the little children see their Mother. Only thus are they able to revert to the foundation and

return to the source. It is impossible to discuss completely the painful retribution of revolving in the dust [of saṃsāra], and the binding net of karma
cannot be fully described. Fortunately, the Eternal Holy Mother is rescuing
[her] little children so that all will be able to return to the [Native] Place.
Five hundred arhats preach the Way, 3,000 buddha-patriarchs exalt the Way
of Complete Perfection, and 9,260,000 patriarchs go to the place of immortals. [There] they will receive celestial blessings for myriads of eons. (pp.
152–153 of the Stulova edition)

Note that here the number "ninety-two *i*" (9,200,000) is slightly
modified and refers to patriarchs rather than directly to the Mother's
lost children. However, as we have seen, sometimes the latter are
called (potential) patriarchs or buddhas, so the reference here is not
clear.

There is another relevant passage in chapter 11 of the *P'u-ming
pao-chüan*:

I have gotten the Eternal Venerable Mother and rushed to be embraced in
her bosom. Children and Mother wept because they [the children] had been
lost and scattered from Mount Ling. Because I did not abandon my covetous
mind, I have passed through cycles of rebirth with no place for refuge. But
now I have encountered a family letter from the Venerable Mother and so
have finally attained the priceless jewel. The Venerable Mother is able to
hear you and saves the multitudes so that they escape the waves [of saṃ-
sāra].

The three stages of cosmic time with their associated buddhas are
discussed in chapter 36 of the *P'u-ming pao-chüan*, where we are told
that

the *P'u-ming pao-chüan* [discusses] the Holy Patriarch of the Limitless who
undertook the meaning of the three primes [= time periods], the one Buddha
who divided into three teachings [*sic*]. The three teachings are the bodies of
the three buddhas. [The Buddha of] the Past, Jan-teng (Dīpaṃkara), was the
first patriarch of the chaotic source. He arranged Heaven and put the Earth
in order, and established the *chia-tzu* [cycles] of the lower three primes. This
[was the time of] the three-petaled golden lotus, with four characters forming the title [of the buddha-name recited?]. Five thousand forty-eight volumes formed the true scriptures of the great [sūtra] storehouse. There were
440 days in a year, 180 days in a cycle, 6 months in a year, and 6 [Chinese]
hours in a day and a night.

This numerology continues in more detail than is necessary to recount here. For our purposes, it is interesting that the past period of
Dīpaṃkara is described as a primitive time when

everyone lived long, with no [distinction between] self and other. Everyone was illuminated by a divine light. They wore grass clothing, lived in caves, and ate moving and mixed food (*tung-jung chih shih*). There were horns on their heads and hair grew on their bodies. [Although] they had the faces of beasts and human hearts, they were not stained with any depravity; they were enlightened as the Buddha; they didn't distinguish between different forms and had no writing. Each of them lived long.

The discrepancy between this illiteracy and the presence of the Buddhist *Tripitaka* is not explained.

The present is the time of the Ancient Buddha, who "continued the Prior Realm and changed [i.e., reestablished] the world." In this period there are "33 heavens and 18 levels of purgatory. There are 360 days in a year, 12 months in a year, 30 days in a month, and 12 [Chinese] hours in a day. People are born and die and, because of their desires and lusts, are stained with dust; in the last age they do not live long."

Of the original total of 96 *i*, the Buddha of the Past saved 2 *i*, and the Buddha of the Present has saved another 2 *i*, so there are 92 *i* left. No Buddha of the Future is mentioned in the *P'u-ming pao-chüan*, but there is a discussion of an unspecified time when there are 18 months in a year, 18 hours in a day, 45 days in a month, and 810 days in a year. In this time people have golden bodies 18 *ch'ih* (about 21 feet) tall; there are neither young nor old, no female forms, no birth or death, and people live 81,000 years (chapter 36, pp. 212–220 in the Stulova edition). Some of this material is anticipated in chapter 12 (p. 78 in the Stulova edition), which also discusses an unspecified time with similar characteristics in which people have the appearance of eighteen-year-olds and do not age, whereas the account in chapter 36 says that "at eighteen *sui*, people enter wombs and exchange their bodies [for new ones]."

It is clear from these scattered and incomplete references that the author of the *P'u ming pao-chüan* knew of the Eternal Mother myth. It was not, however, his central concern, nor does he dwell on it to the extent that the author of the *Yao-shih* scripture does.

In the *Yuan-chueh pao-chüan* (1564; text 3 in Appendix H), this myth is again present and assumed but not a dominant concern. The narrator of this book says:

You who have awakened, I have converted you, so that you restore your destiny and return to the root. At the Mount Ling Assembly, the Eternal Mother always looks on in hope, longing for her poor children who have lost their way and do not see the way to return. Several times she has sent letters from home, but the stupid multitudes, attached to the dusty [world], are unwilling to return. . . . [They should] return to the source and directly ascend to the ancient Native Place. . . . If you are awakened and return on the great road to the [Native] Place, [for you] there will be no more birth-and-death, no cycles of saṃsāra, and no disasters forever more. (chapters 12 and 13)

When you are determined, then all the buddhas see it and the Holy Mother sees it, so that when your merit is complete you will certainly ascend to be reborn above with superior rank. (chapter 18)

The Holy Mother of the Prior Realm includes all types of beings and loves and nourishes all living creatures. (chapter 24)

There are some other scattered references in the *Yuan-chueh pao-chüan* to the Mother sorrowing for her children, but here, as else-where, such language is just one way of expressing saving transcen-dence, which is also discussed in alchemical terms or as realizing one's inner nature, as detailed below.

The treatment of the Eternal Mother myth in *Hsiao-shih An-yang shih-chi pao-chüan* (hereafter "the *An-yang pao-chüan*"; text 4 in Ap-pendix H) is similar, with scattered references to "finding spiritual freedom in the Dragon-Flower Assemblies" (chapter 1) and to "those at home . . . [who] never again are reborn or die and never again [dwell in] the sea of suffering. For measureless eons they are un-moved and everywhere manifest their golden bodies. When they reach home they enjoy happiness with which the world cannot com-pare" (chapter 6). There is one long passage on this theme, referring to letters transmitted by the Venerable Patriarch of True Emptiness, which includes the words, "Those who have returned home all live on Mount Ling. Hoping that they are coming home, their dear Mother sees them with joy, and all the bodhisattvas are finally able to see her face. Only now have I been able to reach the Native Place" (chapter 2). Nonetheless, the *An-yang pao-chüan* is a scattered and poorly organized text in which the Eternal Mother myth is only one of many themes. There is no emphasis here or in the *Yuan-chueh* book on the end of the age.

The clearest statement of this mythic structure in the Huan-yuan sect texts is in chapter 16 of the *Cheng-tsung pao-chüan* (text 7 in Ap-pendix H), where we are told that the "Huan-yuan [Patriarch] left behind the *Cheng-tsung pao-chüan*. Men and women of later genera-tions should employ their minds in listening to it. For those who understand the Huan-yuan teachings, all the buddhas of the three worlds manifest their golden bodies. With a constant, brilliant light they transcend the three realms and guide men and women home." Though seeing the Mother and going to the Dragon-Flower Assemblies are mentioned in this book, we are also told that "in the beginning, the Holy and worthy Lord Kuan established the teaching and preached the doctrine," and that "the Bodhisattva Kuan-yin descended from Mount Ling to save the multitudes because men and women were not able to escape from suffering. She uttered a vow to rescue and save the children and grandchildren. But the people did not believe, and many reviled the teaching" (chapter 7).

Hence the Mother's role is not clear here, and the structure of the myth of salvation can be used without her. Indeed, in the *Kuei-chia pao-en* scripture (text 8 in Appendix H), the pious are urged to "seek the way out" because when death comes it is too late to repent: "No one can take your place. . . . I urge you to lessen your competition for fame and profit and quickly recite the name of Amitābha to return home" (chapter 17). Here again we are reminded that we are dealing with folk-religious texts from which too much consistency cannot be expected. Sect leaders and authors were religious entrepreneurs who gathered what they could to put together their teachings.

Thus it appears that, throughout the middle decades of the sixteenth century, the myth of the Eternal Mother was present but not emphasized, only one mother-deity was involved, and she remained in paradise waiting for her children to return. However, in the Hung-yang sect texts from the end of the century, there are both singular and plural references to mother-goddesses, some of whom descend to live on Earth. This is particularly the case with the *P'iao-kao ching* (text 10 in Appendix H). Here the Venerable Patriarch and Venerable Mother are the most important deities. It is they who send the gods and patriarchs to Earth with the message of deliverance, beginning with Śākyamuni Buddha himself. The Patriarch P'iao-kao is a son of the Hun-yuan Patriarch and the Venerable Mother. However, the most distinctive emphasis about the Venerable Mother in the *P'iao-kao ching* appears in chapter 7, where the opening verses state that

the Eternal Venerable Mother approached the ordinary world, and the Venerable Huan-yuan patriarch descended to the Eastern [Land]. Here they begged for food during the day and meditated in caves at night. . . . Because those in the ordinary world are lost and unwilling to do good, the Venerable [Patriarch and

Matriarch] of True Emptiness descended to the ordinary world, where they suffered and called out on the streets [as beggars] for their living. . . . The Venerable Eternal [Mother] descended to the ordinary world and lived in a cave. . . . The Venerable Huan-yuan Patriarch descended to the ordinary world from the celestial palace to save the multitudes.

Chapter 8 of the *P'iao-kao* book says that thirty "Venerable Eternals" (Lao Wu-sheng) descended to the world, though here this term includes patriarchs, saints, immortals, and buddhas as well as eight Mothers, all to "manifest their supernormal powers. . . . Altogether eight Mothers descended to the Eastern Land and transformed themselves into humans." When their sufferings on Earth are complete, "they return to the palace." In chapter 9 we are told that "twelve Mothers lived in the ordinary realm and entered wombs to be reborn." On Earth they are accompanied by many other descended deities, "to save again the sons and daughters of the Eastern Land who are lost in the dust." The relationship of these multiple Mothers to the consort of the Hun-yuan Patriarch is unclear. (Chapter 6 of the *Hung-yang wu-tao ming-hsin ching* [text 12 in Appendix H] also discusses the descent of mother-goddesses to Earth, in both the singular and the plural.)

It appears that the authors of the Hung-yang scriptures revived the Mother myth and intensified it through an emphasis on the goddess's descent. This descent is not emphasized in later *pao-chüan*, but the net effect was to place the Venerable Mother more firmly in the center of sectarian mythology.

The ideas of the stages of cosmic time and the end of the present kalpa (eon) hover in the background in these sixteenth-century texts, where they run parallel to—and in some cases are related to—reminders of the Eternal Mother myth. We have already noted the references to these themes in the *Yao-shih* and *P'u-ming* scriptures, and they are present in Hung-yang texts as well. Their role is to intensify the need for moral and religious renewal; they are a large-scale time context for the contrast between the lost and the saved (discussed in the "Dichotomies" section below). However, descriptions of the end of the age in these later sixteenth-century books are less detailed and dramatic than those in the *Chiu-lien pao-chüan* of 1523 discussed in Chapter Four and in the seventeenth-century *Dragon-Flower Scripture* (*Lung-hua ching*) discussed in Chapter Six below.

The most important reference to this theme in the Hung-yang texts is found in the preface shared by all of them and published by the Palace Printing Bureau (see under text 9 in Appendix H). Here we are told that Śākyamuni is in "charge of the teaching" in the present Vast Yang period. The past was the time of the Pure Yang, while the dominant symbol of the future will be the White Yang. In chapter 2 of the *P'iao-kao ching* we are told that "when the Hun-yuan Venerable Patriarch learned that one day, in the sea of suffering in the Eastern Land, Earth and Heaven would be destroyed and Heaven broken, and that the end kalpa would soon arrive (*mo-chieh chih chin*), he then sent that patriarch to descend to the ordinary [world] to seek for the suffering primal ones." Other passages here repeat that the approach of the end of the age makes it urgent that the gods and patriarchs descend with the message of salvation. Nonetheless, the real problem here is the ignorance and sin of those who have forgotten to return home, which for the most part is discussed without reference to a time frame.

ENLIGHTENMENT AND THE USE
OF ALCHEMICAL TERMS

In these texts, enlightenment is sometimes described as realization of one's true origin as a child of the Mother, which leads to joining her in paradise. However, it is also described more internally, as seeing one's true nature—a popular Ch'an theme particularly emphasized in texts influenced by Lo Ch'ing. Yet a third way of expressing the ultimate goal of the religious quest employs the terminology of internal alchemy, derived here from the Ch'üan-chen (Complete Perfection) Taoist tradition discussed in Chapter One above. The point of all these approaches is the same: salvation is attained through realizing or developing a deeper and more real dimension of the self that transcends ordinary existence. These may be folk texts, but their understanding of life has a philosophical dimension.

The three approaches to deliverance in these books are nicely combined in two passages from chapter 6 of the *Huan-yuan pao-chüan* (text 6 in Appendix H), where we read:

The ancient holy Native Place is fundamentally complete [within us]. The lost and confused do not understand this but run to the east and west, seeking it on the outside. Those who recognize this profound wonder are the "right ones."

Those who are able to awaken their natures . . . ascend directly to K'un-lun and manifest a brilliant light. There they roam about and play night and day. This is the meaning of returning the elixir.

In the books consulted for this chapter, the theme of the potential for salvation lying within the self is most clearly expressed in Ch'an-style terms in the *An-yang pao-chüan* (text 4 in Appendix H), which refers frequently to terms and titles from Lo Ch'ing's books. In the introductory section of the *An-yang* book we read,

> The master of the teaching from Mount Ling in his great compassion with a golden light illuminates [those who] go to the Lotus District (*lien-hsiang*, a reference to paradise). One's own Native Place (*tzu-chi chia-hsiang*) is manifest through transformations without measure. It constantly dwells in the Pure Western Region, but the confused do not awaken and do not dare to undertake [the task of realization].

The term "one's own Native Place" expresses exactly the blend of mythological and personal perspectives involved. Some other expressions of this theme in the *An-yang* book are "your own golden body in the buddha-land. . . . Intelligent men and women, take responsibility yourselves . . . [and] recognize that you yourselves can be your own masters. . . . You yourselves constantly live in the Pure Land of the West" (chapter 5), and "You yourself are a living bodhisattva, but who knows this?" (chapter 6).

Another text in what may loosely be called a "popular Ch'an" tradition is the *Kuei-chia pao-en pao-chüan* (text 8 in Appendix H), which combines language about the Mother's love with "seeing the nature and enlightening the mind" (chapter 11), and recognizing the Mother's face with understanding one's own "original face." As we read,

> Those who develop and practice thoroughly the important meaning of [this] scripture recognize clearly the Mother's living face, which has been manifested from the beginning. The original face is the true scripture, and the scripture is the fundamental nature . . . . Those of the origin see this fundamental nature, and when their merit is complete return home. (chapter 19)

> Pious people, listen carefully to the great message of [this] scripture. If you believe my words, you will personally be able to see the original roots of your nature and destiny. (chapter 23)

There is language about meditation and the quest for personal enlightenment in the seventeenth-century Hung-yang texts discussed in Chapter Six below, but almost none in the earlier scriptures from that tradition, which are more mythological in orientation. The same is true for the use of alchemical terminology. However, terms and concepts derived from the tradition of internal alchemy are present in the *Yao-shih* and *Yuan-chueh pao chüan*, and are very important in the *P'u-ming* scripture, which refers to Taoist Complete Perfection teachings (texts 1, 3, and 2 in Appendix H, respectively). There are also a few alchemical-style terms in the *Yuan-chueh pao-chüan*. All these books are from the mid-sixteenth century.

The point of internal alchemy is to refine the vital forces (*ch'i*) of the body to form the "golden elixir" or the "holy embryo" of immortality. The key issue of interpretation is how metaphorical this language is intended to be in these texts, which do not include much detail about the actual practices to be followed. Hence it appears that Taoist language is evoked in these books for its numinous power and that, in the end, its role here is as another set of symbols of salvation, parallel to those of recognizing the Mother and seeing one's own true nature.

This theme appears in the *Yao-shih* and *Yuan-chueh* books only in passing. In the *Yao-shih pao-chüan*, the context is the curative and saving powers of the Healing Buddha. The passage in question is in chapter 18, which is entitled "The Bodhisattva Medicine King Saves All Beings, [Enabling Them] to Go to the Dragon-Flower Assembly; the Golden Elixir Revolves Nine Times, and Eight Jewels Are Formed." The chapter begins,

The bodhisattva said, "As for the wonderful medicine that always accords with [the needs of] living beings, when P'an-ku and the Three [mythical] Emperors established the world, they selected various essences and combined them to form a golden elixir pill that was extremely subtle and that can rescue all from bitter suffering. This medicine has the most holy, penetrating, divine efficacy to aid people; it gets rid of all forms of illness. It circulates throughout the Dharma realms and the whole universe."

Chapter 31 of the *Yuan-chueh pao-chüan* is entitled *"K'an* and *Li* Arise and Descend"—a reference to trigrams of the *I-ching* (Book of Changes)—and opens with comments about the sixty-four hexagrams. Later in this chapter, *I-ching* terms are combined with alchemical concepts in such passages as:

[As for] the pure *ch'ien* yang body [formed from the emptiness in the midst of the *li* (trigram)], take the central substance of the *k'an* position and use it to supplement the yin within the abdomen in *li*. These are precisely what are called the husband and wife of the golden elixir, the foundation of transformations, the *hun* of Heaven and the *p'o* of Earth. They are the true lead and mercury, half a *chin* of lead and eight *liang* (ounces) of mercury.

This passage adds that the *k'an* and *li* trigrams are in our bodies and that *k'an* is male and *li* is female:

Returning to the *ch'ien* body and causing mercury to take refuge in lead establishes destiny and brings comfort and security to the body. When the lead of the Prior Realm and the mercury of the divine *ch'i* are formed into one piece, then they enter the Yellow Room and knit together the holy embryo, which before long flies in ascent — ascent to the "Turquoise Pool," the "Lotus Pool" of the "Mother in the West."

The alchemical terminology here is difficult to understand, but its intended result is the same as that of the other paths to spiritual liberation already noted. The basic structure of this discussion is the blending of yin and yang modes of vital force (variously named) in the body to form a "holy fetus" that can fly to paradise (an old Taoist theme). But the *Yuan-chueh pao-chüan* gives no details about the meditative practices needed to bring this about, so the discussion appears to be purely symbolic.[2]

Of the texts here considered, it is the *P'u-ming pao-chüan* that includes the most alchemical terminology, as can be seen from the following representative passages:

The original, pure Dharma body is indeed without polluting dirt and stain, without form or bodily substance. It is the diamond indestructible body which cannot be destroyed by kalpic fire [= fire at the end of the eon]. It is the hard and firm child of the holy relics [of the Buddha?]. It is produced by the vital force of the origin in creative chaos, which divided into the two principles [of yin and yang], the three capacities [Heaven, Earth, and humans], the four directions, the Five Phases, the six lines [of the *I-ching* hexagrams], the seven regulators [sun, moon, and the five inner planets], and the eight trigrams. Heaven and Earth are not apart from the nine rotations (*chiu-chuan*),[3] and developing immortality is not apart from nine lifetimes. [This diamond body] is the nature of Heaven, the vital force of Earth, and the *hun* soul of humans. If people awaken to it and obtain it, their three natures [good, bad, and morally neutral], complete and bright, blend together in one body, without any distinctions. The method of long life and no death is the true gold returning to its lode. (chapter 11)

For religious development and practice, one must select from the Prior Realm various forms of essential vital force to penetrate the numinous darkness. Blend the four forms (*ssu-hsiang*)[4] which together are the one body; refine the golden elixir with the true fire of the Five Phases. It is yin and yang in accord with each other that are the Tao, the baby girl and boy sleeping in the same place. On the left there is a green dragon which it is difficult to subdue [reading *fu*, "to fall prostrate," as *fu*, "to subdue"]; on the right is a white tiger, truly wild. In the center there is a true immortal child, grasping with its two hands, sleeping in one place. When the dragon leaves and the emotions come[?] (ch'ing-lai), the tiger is quiet. When these two match each other, then the golden elixir is knit together. Above there is the Yellow Woman, the fetus-nourishing immortal. . . . To develop perfection and nourish the nature, select the various forms of vital force from the Prior Realm. . . .

Heaven and Earth are [formed of] the vital force of yin and yang; water and fire are the nature and destiny of Heaven. The sun and moon, ch'ien and k'un, are lead and mercury, [but] the great Tao is not divided into male and female. The nature and destiny are yin and yang. When Heaven and Earth blend together, they are able to give birth to [produce] the myriad things. When people are able to understand the profound and marvelous, then they are able to understand where we come from at birth and where we go in death. Humans [should] reside only within the origin in creative chaos, the fundamental place beyond birth[-and-death]. When they refine their natures, children and Mother dwell together. The three households (san-chia)[5] meet each other and blend to form one body [or substance]. What painful retribution can there be? (chapter 17)

Refine the Five Phases and the eight trigrams. Return the elixir nine times and emit your yang spirit. Leave the mundane, shed your shell, and return home. Sit unmoving in the heart of the lotus. It is difficult for people to reach the realm of true emptiness, so the Ancient Buddha came in person to convert the worthy. The music of the immortals constantly sounds throughout the heavens, and myriad rays of bright light illuminate the perfected. Thus men and women finally obtain the way of long life. [For this,] each must practice in the same way. Only when ten years of effort are complete can one manifest perfection. Thus people transcend the mundane and with a pure breeze transform into the formless. (chapter 14)

Those who know how to develop and refine their primal essence day and night select from [take] the pure vital force of the buddhas, which circulates everywhere. . . .

Knit together the golden elixir; after nine revolutions one will naturally have supernormal powers. (chapter 2)

After refining [one's ch'i] for three years or five years, one will manifest a brilliant light and see that the five heaps [Skt. skandha, components of the body] are empty. From this one will see that [one's] karma for five hundred lifetimes is not separate from the mind [i.e., is produced by the intentions of the mind]. . . .

In the midst of obscure darkness, one will manifest a bright pearl and the flower will open five petals. One will fall into the midst of the lotus, where Mother and children will dwell together, with the three natures complete and bright. When the elixir has been returned nine times, one will spontaneously ascend. (chapter 5)

It is precisely because I do not understand some of this terminology that I provide these translations, so that the reader can form his or her own judgment. What we need here is an interview with a Ming dynasty sectarian master to learn what practices accompanied these teachings, since there is no hint in these passages about how all this is to be done—nothing like the detail found in earlier Taoist materials.[6] At this point the most we can say is that this alchemical language has been borrowed to provide Taoist-style support for the sectarian quest of returning to the primal state, which can also be understood as returning to the Mother in paradise. From the evidence of these texts, we cannot say that the sectarians who composed and transmitted them actually carried out such Taoist practices as "circulation of the vital force" and "embryonic breathing."

DICHOTOMIES: THE SACRED AND THE MUNDANE, THE ENLIGHTENED AND THE LOST, THE WISE AND THE STUPID

Such dichotomies are the fundamental structure implicit in these books, which present themselves as sustained appeals from deities and enlightened patriarchs to those who have forgotten who they really are because of their ignorance and worldly desires. These messages are from the realm of the sacred (*sheng*) to those in the mundane or ordinary (*fan*) world. The sacred is beyond birth-and-death, a dimension or place of eternal life, while the mundane is caught in the endless sufferings of saṃsāra. This structure is also present within human beings in the contrast between their ordinary selves and their true natures—namely, their primordial identity as children of the Mother, their original parent.

Another way of discussing this is as the contrast between the mundane body and an indestructible "Pure Yang" body made of the original "vital forces of the Prior Realm." The wise are those who, aware of these dichotomies, strive by their faith and practice to attain the sacred. The enlightened have realized this attainment by restoring their primal natures, and so at death ascend to paradise. Returning within leads to going up. The members of sectarian congregations addressed in these books are, in effect, at an intermediary level, aware but not yet enlightened, exhorted to go forward, warned by the fate of the lost. They are promised that if they succeed they will escape the sufferings of rebirth and purgatory and will enjoy eternal bliss. There are some assurances of blessings in this life for the faithful, but this is not emphasized.

The dichotomies discussed in this section are implicit throughout sectarian "precious volumes," but are more explicit in some passages. In what follows we look at some representative and distinctive passages in the rough chronological order employed above. We begin with the *Yao-shih* scripture (text 1 in Appendix H), where we read that in a great assembly the Buddha discussed

how people of the world are confused and lost; they mistakenly recognize false forms and have lost their original true face and neglected to return to their original source. They roam about in the *sahā* world [of saṃsāra], have fallen into the sea of suffering and revolve, revolve, without awakening. . . . The Master of Medicine [= the Buddha] is able to open the gate to the formless and manifest his pure and wonderful body. The awakened (*wu*) at any time see his face; the confused and lost (*mi*) are separated [from him] as if by a thousand mountains and ten thousand rivers. He guides sentient beings to leave [the realm] of suffering and be reborn in heaven, to personally see the realm of the buddhas. . . . Everywhere he urges people to quickly repent (*tsao hui-hsin*) without waiting for old age. If people don't enlighten their minds and natures, they will be reborn again and miss the ford. (introductory material)

People like to be stupid, and so go back and forth in the cycle of rebirth, but when they encounter an enlightened teacher, they ascend the ladder to heaven. (chapter 16)

In chapter 20 of the *Yao-shih pao-chüan*, Maitreya tells the Buddha, "People in [the period of] the end of the Dharma are concerned only with lust for wine, sex, and wealth. They do not fear at all that when one loses human form it is extremely difficult to attain it again for a myriad of ages. If we don't do something, they will continue to be reborn and again fall into the wrong path."

The Buddha replies, "Exhort all people, 'Why don't you turn to the light and be concerned with obtaining your original face?'"

Other contrasts in the *Yao-shih* book are between "the confused people of the last age who forever fall into saṃsāra" and those "who are awakened and suddenly see the dear Mother face to face" (chapter 29). The latter enter the womb of the Mother, never to be reborn, while the ignorant "pass through [ordinary] wombs for a myriad eons" (chapter 22).

The *P'u-ming pao-chüan* (text 2 in Appendix H) contains much language of this sort contrasting the ignorant with "the worthy and good who are enlightened, and who, facing heaven in the morning, utter a vast vow to do away with their mundane emotions, escape from saṃsāra, and return to their foundation and source, so as to realize the Great Way beyond birth[-and-death]" (introductory material). However, the most distinctive dichotomy in the *P'u-ming* book is that between the "mundane body" (*fan-shen*), which must be "abandoned to seek the supreme Way" (chapter 5), and the "Pure Yang body," which is formed by refining and "circulating the elixir" (chapter 7), as noted in the above discussion of alchemical terminology.

This theme is present in the *Yuan-chueh* book (text 3 in Appendix H) as well, which equates the "vast overflowing *ch'i* nourished by the way of Confucius and Mencius" with "the Pure Yang body of the Prior Realm, without marks or form" (chapter 27). Here the patriarch-narrator says:

My body is formed of pure yang, the Pure Yang of the Prior Realm, a body pure yang outside and in, so that I have become a celestial immortal. With pure yang, one lives; with pure yin, one dies. With much yang, one is full [of life force], with much yin, one is empty. This [yang] is what everyone has, but they don't know that yang is life, and that with much yin, death is certain. . . . I have now obtained Pure Yang of the Prior Realm and refined it into one vital force. (chapter 29)

The *An-yang pao-chüan* (text 4 in Appendix H) is distinctive here for its nine pages of detailed discussion of the sufferings of rebirth and purgatory for those who do not repent. The recalcitrant are reminded of animals, who "also once were human" (introductory material). This account begins with a statement by the narrator, the Patriarch Chin-shan:

I will now speak to you in detail about this *sahā* filthy earth, this place of trouble and confusion. How can one's present happiness last long? . . . Being covetous of wealth, lusting after sex, being entangled in [family] kindness and love—these I will explain for you in detail. As for the entanglements of kindness and love, sons are golden cangues, daughters are jade locks.

All wealth, precious goods, and land are also a part of such entanglements, "illusory joys like water bubbles that cannot last long." Soon worry and illness come, and

one's whole body is in pain, and one's mind in confusion, and slaying demons come to pursue. . . . These entanglements cannot be escaped but lead
to purgatory, the Realm of Darkness. They cannot be escaped! Oh, what suffering! What suffering! . . . Quickly, quickly repent and seek out an enlightened teacher to completely escape saṃsāra. In the correct principles for returning home, there are no obstacles. (chapter 1)

But the description of the sufferings of saṃsāra here, which emphasizes rebirth in animal form, takes us too far astray from the
topic at hand. The *An-yang* book also distinguishes between "the
sensual body that is suffering and the golden body that is happiness" (introductory material). The problem with people in the present is that they are "not willing to believe in their own golden bodies" (chapter 2).

The *Yuan-chueh pao-chüan* has a whole chapter on the contrast
between the Prior Realm and the Latter Realm (i.e., this present
world of suffering and ignorance). This chapter, narrated by Patriarch Chin-shan, is quite eloquent:

Many religious people (*hsiu-hsing chih jen*) have never heard of [the Prior
and Latter Realms]. They all live in the dust of the Latter Realm and have
not obtained the Pure Yang Way of the Prior Realm. They are attached to
forms and things, which are forms of pure yin. As for men and women,
[physical] forms are in their minds, evil demons are in their minds (*hsieh-mo
tsai hsin*), and they do not know about the straight path for returning home
or about their own Native Place [in themselves]. [Rather,] they recognize the
floating life, coming to be born, leaving in death, revolving in the six life
paths. Alas, how mistaken they are! Why don't they wake up and inquire of
an enlightened teacher to seek for this conversion (*ch'iu tz'u tien-hua*)?
    . . . I say to you urgently, be converted to the Prior Realm, the Numinous
Father and the Holy Mother, and find peace and security in the center, in the
Mother's holy womb. (chapter 19)

The language on this theme in the Huan-yuan sect texts consulted
for this chapter is similar to that just discussed, but there are a few
differences of expression, particularly in criticisms of "wine and
meat people" who refuse to believe. Thus in the *Huan-yuan pao-chüan*
(text 6 in Appendix H) we read of

those at home who drink wine and eat meat, and who desire wealth and sex.
They are unwilling to turn around and recite Kuan-yin's [name]. Those who
have left the household life are also unwilling to seek after their own natures. Every day they go to recite scriptures but don't understand [their

own] karma. These two types of people should not blame me for urgently exhorting them to return to the primal source. Suddenly one morning, Lord Yama will call you; then where will you find peace and security? Because I have seen that these two kinds of people are profoundly lost, I urge them to flee to Mount P'an [a sacred mountain in this book], exert themselves to progress, and enlighten their minds. Now I have obtained the Way and manifested my original nature, and have left behind this "precious volume" in twelve sections to save all beings. (chapter 11)

Elsewhere the *Huan-yuan pao-chüan* contrasts "wine-and-meat living beings who do not believe the Buddha's words" with "the worthy and good" (chapter 15), and distinguishes between the "awakened and the stupid" (chapter 21) and between "those in our Huan-yuan assembly" and "the depraved and demonic outside the religion" who are "confused and don't understand the message" (chapter 20).

The *Cheng-tsung* scripture (text 7 in Appendix H) also speaks of

wine-and-meat living beings in the floating world who chase after the pleasures of a morning and don't know what their nature and destiny are. Suddenly one morning, they die; their natures return to heaven, while their destinies (*ming*) fall into the sea of suffering. Since it is difficult for both to continue in contact with each other, they are not able to return home. [However,] if those who develop and practice awaken, they enter our Huan-yuan (Return to the Primal Source) congregation where, below, they are given clear explanations [so that] their nature and destiny are continued, and above they form [a nature] that exists forever. (chapter 8)

Elsewhere in the *Cheng-tsung pao-chüan*, the unawakened are called "sinners" (*tsui-jen*): "Men and women are all sinners, entangled in the five forms of desire. When will this end? For sons and daughters who have lost their home, it is difficult to return." They are "karma-creating people," "those who are confused and lost" (*mi-shih jen*). They have "eyes of flesh" (*jou-yen*), which are contrasted with "holy eyes" (*sheng-yen*). Those with "blurred vision" (*meng-yen*) cannot "recognize the perfect and true"; they have "darkened minds." And yet "everyone has these holy eyes, but they are unwilling to seek for them" (chapter 2).

Another term for "holy eyes" is "Dharma eyes," an old Buddhist term referring to the penetrating vision of a bodhisattva. Those with such vision are the "right ones, who have awakened and roam about the Seven-Jeweled Pool [of paradise]." They understand the Dharma and scriptures spontaneously, without needing to read them (chapter 3). Even more wonderful is the "wisdom eye" (*hui-yen*), with which one "sees the nature and enlightens the mind, transcends the three realms, and the little children see their Mother." With this vision, all is illuminated and one "sees the living beings of the great earth all deeply buried in the dust. I have come to save you, so that you quickly get on the boat [of salvation] to ascend" (chapter 4).

Other related imagery in the *Cheng-tsung* book is the contrast between "the stupid (*yü-ch'ih*) who do not awaken and certainly rush toward the four forms of rebirth," and "intelligent (*chih-hui*) men and women who are the 'right ones' who urgently seek" (chapter 13). The latter are the "people of the Way of this congregation, who quickly seek out the great message for returning home," while the former are "those [stained with] the five impurities (*wu-cho*) [infatuation with wine, glory, profit, fine food, and sex], who do not know how to awaken" (chapter 7).

Among the sixteenth-century Hung-yang texts, the one that places most emphasis on moral and religious dichotomies is the *Hung-yang t'an-shih ching* (text 11 in Appendix H), which is a sustained call for repentance. Its approach to the topic at hand is epitomized in the title of its second chapter, "Sigh in Regret for the People of the World Who Are Stupid (*tai-ch'ih*) and Who Will Not Turn Around" (i.e., change their ways):

[Such people] recognize the customs of the world but do not understand [the Mother's] longing in the midst of the holy (*sheng-chung p'an-wang*). They are covetous and attached to family connections and will not turn around. The Venerable Mother in the midst of the holy constantly thinks of them, and the patriarchs steer iron boats [of salvation] that they may board them (*teng*, lit. "ascend"). [She has] sent many patriarchs down to the mundane to save and release the primal ones so that they quickly turn around.

. . . The kindness and love of wives and children is really difficult to cut off [for those who] do not fear that the suffering of birth-and-death approaches. What if one time the end kalpa arrives and the four elements [earth, water, fire, and wind] divide and scatter; how will this stop? The young are unwilling to do good, but if they wait until old age arrives, they will act in vain. (chapter 2)

The recalcitrant are then warned of the sufferings of purgatory and rebirth.

The sixth chapter of the *Hung-yang t'an-shih ching* is entitled "Sigh in Regret for Those Who Do Evil and Who Are Unrestrained, Form Cliques, and Are Violent and Overbearing." These are people who "curse Heaven and Earth, do not reverence the Three Jewels or respect their parents, and who do not cooperate with their neighbors." A discussion of the sins and punishments of such people leads to a list of the distinctions between the bad (*e*) and the good (*shan*), beginning with "the bad constantly harbor hateful and injurious intentions, while the good always think of how to save the world (*chiu-shih*)." The focus throughout is on attitudes toward family and fellow villagers, with the point being driven home that "good and bad [should be] clearly distinguished" (chapter 6).

A related distinction in the *Hung-yang t'an-shih* book is that between all the saints and deities who have attained buddhahood because of their piety and good deeds, and "you suffering ones who are unwilling to turn toward the good." This is followed by a distinction between "superior people (*shang teng jen*) who lower their heads and bow when they hear this teaching" and "inferior people who do not believe and who in every way waste their constant minds." For the latter, "death comes and the ordinary body is destroyed" (chapter 9), whereas the pious and good are urged to vow to "abandon their ordinary bodies and realize their golden bodies" (chapter 2).

ETHICAL TEACHINGS

Ethical concerns are implicit throughout these texts, particularly in the distinctions just noted between the good and the bad, the pious and the unbelieving. What follows is a discussion of the passages in which these concerns become explicit. The ethical values of these early sectarian "precious volumes" are derived from popular understandings of Confucian and Buddhist teachings, so they are, in a general sense, conventional. What distinguishes them is their emphasis on carrying out special religious beliefs and practices — including a full-time vegetarian diet — in a nonmonastic context, namely, within household life (*tsai-chia*).

Here, however, we must be careful, because there are numerous passages that urge the faithful to cut their family ties in order to devote all their energies to the quest for religious enlightenment and deliverance. We have already seen this theme in the spiritual autobiographies of patriarchs-in-the-making. The context of all this language about leaving the family is the quest for the highest levels of enlightenment. Nothing is said about maintaining the separation after enlightenment is achieved, nor is there any discussion of a separate social context for a permanent celibate lifestyle; thus it seems safe to assume that language about cutting family ties is intended to emphasize the radical devotion necessary for breaking through to a new level of understanding.

This language also reminds us that *pao-chüan* present the ideal values of religious voluntary associations—ideals which by definition cut across family ties, particularly because they exalt the Venerable Mother in paradise as the true parent. It is no accident that the *An-yang pao-chüan* (text 4 in Appendix H) urges filial piety toward both earthly and celestial parents. Chapter 11 of the *An-yang* book opens with a discussion of the difficulty of repaying the "profound love of one's mother: Think of the suffering she endured through her ten [lunar] months of pregnancy. . . . When we leave our mothers' bodies, they suffer tremendously, [and] even more with three years of nursing." To repay her suffering and toil, one needs to be "filial and obedient, marry and have children," but also maintain a vegetarian diet, participate in the Way, "return home and to the primal source, enlighten the mind, and see one's nature." If one does not do this,

one's mother descends to purgatory and one's parents cannot be freed [from saṃsāra]. . . . Filial sons and daughters rescue their two parents. . . . Those who give up a vegetarian diet and break the precepts encumber nine [generations of] ancestors and see their parents off to the Mountains of Fire and Knives [in purgatory]. . . . [But] filial sons and daughters who participate in the Great Way and return home and to their original source turn the pit of fire [in purgatory] into a lotus-flower assembly, and nine [generations of their] ancestors are reborn into the Precious Pool [of paradise].

It is clear that it is earthly parents and ancestors who are being discussed here, although later in this chapter of the *An-yang* book we are told that by "becoming enlightened and reciting [the name of] Amitābha, [the pious] transcend the three realms and realize Tathāgata positions [for themselves]. At the great congregation gathered on the Numinous Mountain (Ling-shan) they go to the Lotus Pool, and the poor children see their Mother, return to their primal source, and unite in one body." Here earthly and cosmic devotion are blended together—just the kind of teaching one might expect from a religious voluntary association embedded in ordinary social relations.

This perspective is supported by affirmations of Confucian morality in the *Yuan-chueh pao-chüan* (text 3 in Appendix H), which explicitly rejects Lo Ch'ing's individualism, as already discussed in

Chapter Three above. Chapter 21 of the *Yuan-chueh* book begins with a passage attributed to "various immortals," which says:

The way of humans and the way of immortals are both practiced together in the marketplace. From antiquity, those who [wished to] develop immortality first developed the human way, and next the way of immortality. When the human way was completed, then they finished the way of immortality. . . . If the human way is not developed, then the way of immortality is distant and separated [from us]. As for the [proper relationships between] ruler and ministers, fathers and sons, the principles of each [must be] exhausted. Sons and ministers are [to act with] loyalty, filial piety, humanity, and righteousness. . . . In the Warring States period, the two sage-worthies Confucius and Mencius appeared. Mencius [advocated] a vast, overflowing *ch'i*, while Confucius [taught about] the humane nature (*jen-hsing*). [Both these principles] are nothing other than the Prior Realm and the profound and wonderful [Tao]. . . . The way of humans and the way of immortals are the dual practice of substance and function.

Then follows the attack on advocates of popular Ch'an such as Lo Ch'ing already quoted above in Chapter Three.

This interesting expression of folk Confucianism goes on to repeat the equation of the principles of "these two saints" (Confucius and Mencius) with returning to the root and origin, the highest goal of sectarian teaching, and emphasizes that the most important quality of relationships in families, villages, and prefectures is "mutual yielding of precedence" (*hsiang-jang*). This emphasis on moral action within society is continued in chapter 26, where we read, "Men and women who participate in the Great Way are patient with worldly affairs. . . . They show pity to orphans, widows, and the poor."

Huan-yuan sect scriptures are also concerned with moral life in the world. This is particularly true of the *Kuei-chia pao-en pao-chüan* (text 8 in Appendix H), with its sustained call for combining religious piety with care for one's parents:

Those with believing minds should maintain a constant vegetarian diet and be filial toward their parents and care for them. You absolutely must not darken your minds and revile your parents. Even if you are a vegetarian [i.e., a sect member], if you are not filial to your parents, . . . how will you attain release? Those who practice filial piety have compassionate minds, and august heaven aids them. Spontaneously the buddhas illuminate them, and they see their natures and enlighten their minds. Those with the five corruptions do not practice filial piety and so destroy themselves. When death comes and their lives end, it is difficult for them to escape Lord Yama. (chapter 1)

The ethical teachings of the *Kuei-chia pao-en* book are presented in the most detail in chapter 12, which is addressed to

vegetarians who are filial to their parents and who reverence and support the Three Jewels. Wherever they are, they develop the fruits of goodness [= good karma] and express their compassionate minds. They think of returning to the source and are filial to their parents, and [so] now obtain [this] correct teaching. . . . Those who do not have parents esteem their wives and children and reverence heaven [for its] kindness. Vegetarians, I want only that your six family relationships be harmonious. . . . Superior people reverence their parents more than buddhas and patriarchs. . . . You who develop yourselves and practice your religion, incline your ears to listen. Wherever you go, put your good intentions into practice. Be friendly with your fellow villagers, [hoping that] they will all stop eating meat, practice filial piety, become worthy folk, maintain a vegetarian diet, and be pure; [such will] definitely see the World-Honored One. . . . Those who observe the five precepts, are energetic and strict, and are filial toward their parents will have exalted titles at the Dragon-Flower Assembly.

The most explicit discussion of ethical values in sixteenth-century Hung-yang texts is in the *Hung-yang t'an-shih ching* (text 11 in Appendix H), but even here not much detail is provided. Devotees are urged to maintain a vegetarian diet and to avoid wine, illicit sex, anger, and competition for wealth. Being friendly with fellow villagers is also mentioned. Representative passages are found in chapter 11, which is entitled "Sigh in Regret [for Those Involved with] Wine, Sex, Wealth, and Anger." The opening prose section reads, "The men and women of the great earth are attached to wine, sex, wealth, and anger, and are all infatuated and confused in the Eastern Land, never returning to the Native Place. Wine can destroy one's affairs, sex can damage the body, wealth brings much damage to the self, and anger harms one's fundamental substance."

This passage is followed by examples of famous people in the past whose lives were ruined by these vices. Chapter 16 lists other sins to be avoided by the pious, including cheating people out of their money, stealing money and competing for it, and not caring for one's family. All who do such things are promised the sufferings of purgatory and rebirth.

Another source for learning about the ethical teachings of these books is their sections on gratitude for kindnesses received. (There is a discussion in Appendix H, text 12, of such material in the *Hung-yang wu-tao ming-hsin ching*.) The sectarians may not have lived up to their ethical ideals any more than anyone else, but in the Chinese context these ideals cannot be faulted, for they are a popular expression of mainstream Confucian and Buddhist values.

SOCIAL PERSPECTIVES

"Social perspectives" here refers to explicit statements in our texts about different categories of people in named social roles, from the ruler of the state to children and the poor. The fundamental perspective of "precious volumes" is socially egalitarian, but it is also morally differentiated into the faithful and the indifferent or hostile, the wise and the foolish. Although there are not many passages in these books of direct social relevance, there are enough to provide a basis for discussion. As we have seen, these are religious texts in which what we call "social issues" are a secondary concern. In them, social status is due to karma (the results of intentional actions in the past) and the focus is on going beyond karma and rebirth to a paradise of eternal felicity.

I have discussed this topic in an earlier publication,[7] and there is material concerning it in our discussions in Chapters Two, Three, and Four above of the 1430 *Huang-chi* book, the scriptures composed by Lo Ch'ing, and the 1523 *Chiu-lien* scripture, respectively. Relevant passages are also presented in the preceding sections of this chapter, particularly those on "Dichotomies" and "Ethical Teachings." These texts are directed specifically to members of sectarian congregations and to disciples of their patriarch-narrators, and most social references are to family members and fellow villagers.

However, some passages in them address a wider social realm as well, including officials, Buddhist monks, and the wealthy. We have seen that those who respond to the saving message are assumed to have a karmic affinity for it, but in theory it is available to all, because in the creation mythology all humans are children of the Venerable Mother, united by their common origin. In addition, the messages of the deities and patriarchs are directed to "all sentient beings," which for these books means all humans.

Here I discuss only the relatively few passages in the books consulted for this chapter that refer to socially relevant terms or categories (and that have not already been cited in other contexts, as noted above). An excerpt from chapter 30 of the *Yao-shih pao-chüan* (text 1 in Appendix H) illustrates the general social conservatism of these books: "The social positions and wealth of all sentient beings are due entirely to the Five Phases and the eight trigrams [of the *I-ching*]; birth, death, and saṃsāra are all a matter of yin and yang."

In an earlier portion of the *Yao-shih* book, marked by vows taken by the Healing Buddha-to-be, we read that "if there are women beset with all sorts of difficulties who wish to get rid of their female bodies, if they hear my name they will attain all and be reborn as men . . . and will realize the most supreme *bodhi* (enlightenment)" (vow 8). Here the text reflects a standard Buddhist perspective on women, although the conventional fatalism and negative attitude toward women in this passage are not characteristic of *pao-chüan* as a whole, which urge all to seek salvation themselves — women and men alike.

Another passage from this same section discusses three levels of humans, but only from a religious point of view:

People of the high level (*shang-p'in chih jen*) look only at emptiness. Those of the middle level search on paper [= search for the truth in books], while those of the lower level pass through skin-bags [i.e., bodies, in rebirth] and do not understand the falsity and truth of the mundane and holy. (vow 8)

The hope for religious self-transformation is reinforced by repeated exhortations to awaken and "see the dear Mother face to face." This universal potential for deliverance as the Mother's children is reinforced by a promise of healing, which is rare in "precious volumes." The Healing Buddha vows:

If there are people afflicted by myriad illnesses, with no help, refuge, medicine, or physicians, poor and in desperate straits, if they hear my name, all serious illnesses will be gotten rid of; they will be peaceful in body and mind, with their families provided for. They will all attain the most superior enlightenment. (vow 7)

We have seen that the *Yuan-chueh pao-chüan* (text 3 in Appendix H) rejects Lo Ch'ing's iconoclasm but is nonetheless influenced by his emphasis on the absence of real distinctions between clergy and laity, men and women (chapter 18). This egalitarianism is reinforced by the understanding that humans and buddhas are formed of the same vital force (chapter 24). In chapter 25 the Buddha says,

Without regard to leaving the household life or staying within it, there is only one primal body [shared by all]. . . . Men have it, women have it, they are the same as I. Superiors have it, inferiors have it — the pure Dharma body.

And in chapter 9 we read, "From antiquity, the buddhas, patriarchs, gods, and immortals have all been human like you and me (*tou shih ni wo tz'u teng chih jen*)."

As discussed above, in the section on "Ethical Teachings," the *Yuan-chueh* book also emphasizes that the Confucian "human way," with all its moral and social obligations, must be completed before the "way of the immortals" can be approached. Thus the value of lay life is specifically emphasized:

[In] this wonderful teaching, there is no need for you to disturb your minds and waste your effort. Do not meditate, cut off profit, or stop being married. You need only constantly be determined for the twelve hours [of each day]. All the buddhas are uninterruptedly in the inner workings of our minds (*tsai wo hsin chi*), [so] when death approaches and your merit is complete, in the Native Place realm you will go to the third Dragon-Flower Assembly. There is no need to prepare. The taste of excellent food is at home, with measureless happiness. (chapter 17)

Those like Lo Ch'ing, "who only speak of the Buddhist Way," are rejected here, and monks are ridiculed: "There are those who say, 'I am a monk; I have read many scriptures.' But even if he has read many scriptures, he is [still] only a fool. Those who enlighten their minds understand their basic place [= nature], which is the Mother of the scriptures" (chapter 30).

The rich are reminded that, despite all their wealth, when death comes they will suffer in purgatory according to their karma, for which "no one can take their place." The poor are told that though they may "resent the failure of their households, and the hunger and cold of their wives and children are hard to bear," still they must think of the sufferings of purgatory (chapter 20). Elsewhere they are told that they should "urgently worry about the Way but not worry about poverty" (chapter 9). Here again, we see the karmic interpretation of social and economic status that is characteristic of "precious volumes."

The benefits of piety are summed up in chapter 28 of the *Yuan-chueh* book, where the pious are promised that

your families will prosper, their members will be at peace, and all your mundane affairs will succeed. After a hundred years, when your life ends, you will be reborn in heaven. . . . Being well known and honored in the world is all due to foundations laid in one's previous existence, . . . as is being an official.

All this means that there is no social criticism in the *Yuan-chueh* book, and that what we might call a "social perspective" is totally subsumed by moral concerns.

The *P'u-ming pao-chüan* (text 2 in Appendix H) proclaims that the "Ancient Buddha of the Imperial Ultimate was originally a sage who produced the Great Way of Complete Perfection; he was a bodhisattva residing at home. . . . This bodhisattva in the household life had exceptional wisdom; he made a ritual arena in the midst of the noisy marketplace" (chapter 36). Given this mythical validation, it is not surprising also to read that "this teaching is egalitarian (*shih-fa p'ing-teng*); it makes no distinction at all between noble and humble status" (chapter 9), and that "men and women finally obtain the Way of long life; each should practice in the same way. . . . Men and women cultivate themselves together, and follow me to return home and see the eternal" (chapter 14).

The *Huan-yuan pao-chüan* (text 6 in Appendix H) makes many specific references to men and women, all of whom are "guests from the primal origin" (chapter 1). In chapter 2 the Patriarch says, "I urge you, men and women, to repent, turn your minds around, learn from the ancients, and be devoted to the religious practice of the Way. Everyone possesses a priceless jewel [of the original nature] but is unable to leave the world." In chapter 5 we read, "Women, maintaining a vegetarian diet is really important." Such references to women are repeated in the other Huan-yuan texts as well.

This book also contains interesting references to the wealthy and to officials, who are urged to "quickly repent and take advantage of [their] secure circumstances to quickly practice [the religion], lessen their desire for wealth and sex, and stop their dissipation, for in an instant Lord Yama [of purgatory] calls" (chapter 2). Chapter 21 of the *Huan-yuan* book contains a good summary of its social perspective (translated above, in the section on "The Self-Understanding of These Texts as Revealed Scriptures").

The politically conservative views of the sixteenth-century Hung-yang texts are well illustrated by the inclusion in one of them of the six "Sage Edicts" of the founding Ming emperor, T'ai-tsu (d. 1398).[8] However, it is the *Hung-yang t'an-shih ching* (text 11 in Appendix H) that provides the most evidence of social perspectives, for it criticizes the rich and powerful, cruel officials, corrupt monks and priests, the evil and violent, and crooked fortune-tellers. Its basic theme is epitomized in the first lines of its second chapter:

Sigh in sorrow for living beings who are stubborn and stupid,
Who from the beginning have not returned [home].
From the Golden City many patriarchs have been sent down
To save the sons and daughters [of the Mother],
That they might soon repent.

. . . [People] recognize the customs of the world but do not understand their hope in the realm of the holy. . . . The Venerable Mother in her holy realm constantly thinks about them, and patriarchs guide boats large and small [to save them from the sea of saṃsāra]. [The Mother] has sent down many patriarchs to save the primal ones so that they quickly turn around.

Chapter 5 of the *Hung-yang t'an-shih ching* is a lament for "those who are wealthy and of high status." After a call to repentance, coupled with a reminder of death and purgatory, it summarizes the attachment of the wealthy to their fine clothing, food, and horses, their big houses and families. Such people are "unwilling to reverence the Three Jewels, to provide vegetarian food for monks, or to love the good. How will these confused persons escape from birth-and-death when their day comes? When death arrives it is difficult to care for one's family." It is interesting to note that there is no criticism of the rich for ignoring the poor here, but rather a focus on the karmic destruction that the rich bring upon themselves because of their lack of piety.

Chapter 6 castigates those who "do evil, are dissolute (*fang-tang*, reading *tang* as 'reckless'), and act in violent ways." These people cheat and oppress others, curse Heaven and Earth, do not reverence the Three Jewels, do not reverence their parents, and are not on good terms with their fellow villagers: "How will such people repent and escape their [mundane] bodies?"

Chapter 15 of the *Hung-yang t'an-shih ching* criticizes monks who do not keep the "pure rules" of monastic life and who also "rely on the Buddha only for food and clothing"—that is, only on the donations they receive. Taoist priests are discussed in similar terms. Chapter 16 deals with officials who are "disloyal, harm the people, and act like warlords." They, too, are reminded of the punishments that await them in purgatory. Chapter 16 also criticizes physiognomists, medicine-sellers, and diviners "who cheat people out of their money."

However, for our topic here, the most interesting passage in the *Hung-yang t'an-shih* book is one that directly addresses children, who sometimes die at the "ages of three, five, or seven," and who, as is true of everyone,

do not know where [and when] they will be reborn as humans. Those who lose human form are thrown into the four forms of rebirth, not knowing when they will escape. . . . Under the ground, there is no difference between old and young; the young die, the old die, and all see Lord Yama. I urge you, children, to take advantage of your youth to do good. Do not wait until you are old, when karmic obstacles will entangle you. I also urge adults to quickly give up their family ties; don't wait until you are old and so miss the path ahead.

This exhortation to children is the only one I have come across in sectarian "precious volumes."

Later sixteenth-century "precious volumes" thus continue the style and much of the content of their predecessors but provide more detailed information about such themes as autobiographies of their narrators and their congregational contexts. They also clarify the mythological and relatively dramatic worldview of these texts. Though there are variations, these books are, on the whole, similar in organization, style, and language, and thus served to consolidate the genre for the centuries ahead.

CHAPTER SIX

'Precious Volumes' from the
Seventeenth Century

Since seventeenth-century *pao-chüan* are a direct continuation of earlier books of this type, their language, style, organization, teachings,
and values are similar. Nonetheless, there are a number of different
emphases that are interesting to discuss and ponder. This chapter is
based on thirteen of these texts, all of which are described in detail in
Appendix I. It begins with a discussion of themes these books have
in common with their sixteenth-century antecedents, including affirmations of the distinctiveness of their teachings, their ethical values, teachings about the end of the age, and social perspectives.

Even in such similarities, however, there are differences of emphasis. The seventeenth-century texts also portray themselves as revealed scriptures, but revealed not so much through founding patriarchs as through ordinary people who compile and print them after
receiving messages in visions or dreams. There is criticism of other
traditions in these books, but fewer references to the names of sects
and "those in the congregation." The social perspective of these later
scriptures places more emphasis on Confucianism as a model of lay
religion, in contrast to Buddhist monks, here portrayed as corrupt.
The primary religious rival discussed by these books is monastic
Buddhism.

Beyond these differences there are sharper contrasts, involving
themes absent from one set of these texts but present in the other.

With two minor exceptions, in the seventeenth-century books there are no autobiographical statements by their revealers, while these books do contain important themes barely mentioned in the preceding century, including long discussions of purgatory and promises of immediate, practical divine aid for the pious. Meditation as refinement and circulation of internal vital forces is discussed in more detail than before, but a more important difference is that in the seventeenth century there are whole *pao-chüan* devoted to sectarian reinterpretations of powerful national gods such as the Lord Kuan and the Goddess of Mount T'ai.

The net impression gained from contemplating these differences is one of a scriptural tradition in a new phase of its development — less narrowly sectarian, more engaged with its social and religious context, and seeking to be more secure within it. *Pao-chüan* are here becoming more a form of religious and moral literature in their own right, reflecting and supporting widespread values while still retaining a sectarian orientation and mythological framework. By the late nineteenth and early twentieth centuries, spirit-writing texts — the successors of "precious volumes" — had become vehicles for promoting common values and beliefs. In that long perspective, seventeenth-century *pao-chüan* are a transitional stage of development, a stage influenced by the powerful traditional values of the Chinese family and state. What had happened to Buddhism in China before is here repeated, on a lesser scale, by another sectarian religious tradition.

Of course, it is possible that this perceived tendency to move toward the center of traditional beliefs and values is in part an artifact of which old *pao-chüan* have been preserved. For example, scriptures associated with powerful national deities and those promoting popular Confucianism might be expected to be more likely to escape destruction. This may have been true in some cases, but I know of no evidence that eighteenth- and nineteenth-century officials deliberately saved some *pao-chüan* from among those seized because their contents appeared to be relatively orthodox. All such books associated with sectarian groups were considered illegal and were subject to destruction. I can only add that the "precious volumes" discussed in the present chapter are a representative sample of those that *have* been preserved, and that the tendencies discussed in them in fact became dominant in related texts later on.

Of the general similarities between these sixteenth- and seventeenth-century books, two can be dealt with relatively briefly:

(1) their self-understanding as revealed scriptures, and (2) their affirmation of sectarian differences and superiority. For the seventeenth-century books, evidence for both these characteristics is given in Appendix I below.

As already discussed in Chapter Five, sixteenth-century *pao-chüan* present themselves as having been revealed through humans of divine origin, who are usually identified as founding patriarchs or their successors. This pattern is continued in two seventeenth-century texts that claim their ultimate revealer to be Maitreya. In both, Maitreya descends into lay devotees who become sect patriarchs (see texts 4 and 5 in Appendix I). However, in two other books consulted for this chapter (texts 6 and 10 in Appendix I), such divine origin is assumed but not explicitly stated.

The *Hu-kuo yu-min fu-mo pao-chüan* (text 6 in Appendix I), which is devoted to the Lord Kuan, is said to have been revealed in a dream to a man identified by his name but not by any title or sectarian affiliation, while the "precious volume" devoted to the Goddess of Mount T'ai (text 10 in Appendix I) is said to have been compiled and printed by a lay devotee and his wife, with the means of revelation not specified. The other nine texts considered in this chapter assume that their teachings are holy and correct but do not discuss their divine origin in any detail. Perhaps this is evidence for the *pao-chüan* tradition becoming better established in its own right, with less need to justify itself.

We have seen that in sixteenth-century texts there is a clear distinction between those in congregations of the devout and those who are not, between the sacred and the mundane, the good and the bad, the awakened and the confused. There are similar contrasts in "precious volumes" from the seventeenth century, but with a more explicit emphasis on the orthodoxy of their teachings. The most interesting material of this sort is detailed criticism of other sectarians in the *Hung-yang chih-li kuei-tsung ssu-hsiang pao-chüan* (hereafter "the *Chih-li pao-chüan*"; text 2 in Appendix I), where chapter 13 is entitled "Destroying the Heterodox and Manifesting the Correct/Orthodox." Here we read:

To resume our story, all men and women in the various sects do not recognize [the difference between] the heterodox and the correct but recklessly talk about *prajñā* (wisdom) and vainly discourse on the Mahāyāna. They do not understand the root and source of the great Tao, [but] all carry out religious practices directed toward outer forms. They issue texts and send through memorials, set forth verses [and employ] placards and seals. They do not obey royal edicts but privately establish sects. With heterodox words and phrases, they falsely usurp [the term] "gathering in [those of] the source," and all say that they are pointing in hope to realizing the holy and attaining perfection. In my view, they are not in accord with the ancestral teaching. They do not participate in "the last act" and will never attain the Way. How will they be able to return to the primal source?

These heretics are contrasted with those who "enlighten their minds . . . put aside worldly affairs, and seek for their original pure selves of [the realm of] noninterference, with no lusts and pollution." These folk are exhorted "not to believe in heterodox traditions (*hsieh-tsung*) that seek on the outside." Such teachings are all from "petty persons of tangential schools. . . . Primal ones with the blessings of good karma should quickly give allegiance to the Vast Yang Assembly" (chapter 13). There are no specific references here to "those in the congregation," but sectarian consciousness is still strong.

OTHER THEMES SIMILAR TO THOSE
IN THE SIXTEENTH CENTURY

Other themes in seventeenth-century *pao-chüan* that are similar to those in the preceding period are teachings about the end of the age, ethical values, and social perspectives.

Teachings About the End of the Age

Sixteenth-century discussions of the end kalpa and stages of cosmic time are not as detailed as those in the *Chiu-lien pao-chüan* of 1523 (see Chapter Four above) and are presented as aspects of Eternal Mother mythology, but the seventeenth-century books discussed here provide much more on this theme, primarily because in three of them the chief divine actor is Maitreya, the Buddha of the Future. His role is summed up in the *T'ai-shan tung-yüeh Shih-wang pao-chüan* (hereafter "the *T'ai-shan Shih-wang pao-chüan*"; text 7 in Appendix I): "The Buddha Maitreya is coming to gather in the primal ones and take charge of the heavens. The secrets of the great affairs of the Latter Realm must not be divulged. . . . The Buddha Maitreya changes Heaven and replaces Earth, and throughout the world, Heaven, Earth and humans change their appearance" (chapter 10).

In these books, the end of the age is understood to develop in three stages: disasters, the coming of Maitreya and the changes it brings, and the appearance of the new world. The disasters are succinctly discussed in the *Mi-le Fo shuo Ti-tsang Shih-wang pao-chüan* (hereafter "the *Ti-tsang Shih-wang pao-chüan*"; text 4 in Appendix I):

The disasters and suffering of the last age are limitless, [because of] intense greed for wine, sex, and money. Thus [people] fall into the Eastern Land and do not ascend to heaven. Dipaṃkara and Śākyamuni came to save, but they saved only four *i* to ascend to celestial peace. Ninety-two *i* of [the children of] the imperial womb are [still] lost. Soon, through the preaching of the Dharma, they can all be gathered in. It is only because of the intensity of their confusion and greed that it is difficult to save the primal ones so that they return to their fundamental source. Rulers are not righteous, ministers are disloyal, people do not act as they should, and relatives do not show affection. You kill him, then he kills you, so resentment and revenge go back and forth until they are requited. Because of this it is difficult to save them so that they return home. . . .

One day all forms of disasters will arrive, and warfare and epidemics will break out together. Are these true or false words? The corpses of the dead will fill the earth, numberless, with whitened bones [piled high] as mountains, most pitiful. (no chapter divisions, pp. 7–8)

This discussion continues with a list of eight types of these disasters "that will arrive together, bringing suffering to all living things," which includes threats that people will be killed by demon kings, chased by wolves and tigers, and eaten by malicious sprites. There will also be thunder, black mist and wind, flying swords, and sprites in the form of apes and lions. Red fire will blaze for three months, and red water will rise eighteen stories (*shih-pa ts'eng*; p. 9).

The discussion ends with a promise of deliverance, as is usually the case with such accounts: "These are all the true words of the Buddha and patriarchs. . . . Each of you primal ones should practice the correct Way; don't wait until these disasters approach. When your merit is complete, when the time comes you will together ascend to the Dragon-Flower Assembly" (p. 9).

The theme of the changes that occur when Maitreya comes is discussed in the *Fo-shuo hsiao-shih pao-an pao-chüan* (hereafter "the *Pao-an pao-chüan*"; text 8 in Appendix I), and the book in which "Maitreya reveals the details" of the last age (*Fo-shuo tang-lai Mi-le ch'u-hsi pao-chüan*, hereafter "the *Mi-le ch'u-hsi pao-chüan*"; text 5 in Appendix I), with the usual mixture of threats and exhortations. In the *Pao-an pao-chüan* there are fragmentary discussions of the times of Dīpaṃkara and Śākyamuni, and a promise that in Maitreya's time of eighty-one kalpas there will be eighteen hours in a day, people will live ten thousand years, purgatory will be no more, and "no oil lamps will be needed because people of themselves will constantly shine. . . . Oh, how free we will be (*wo hao tsung-heng*)!" (introductory section). Maitreya is equated with the Patriarch of the Yellow Apex, "who will be in charge of the world in the future" in the time of the White Yang Assembly (chapter 10). The present is

the lower end-time kalpa when the [Buddha] Yet to Come [= Maitreya] appears in the world. Then the three teachings will be established [*sic*] and the universe will be exchanged again. The world will not be the same as of old. After this [one should] give allegiance to a master, bow to the Patriarch to seek the Dharma and to be given the five precepts to maintain. Day and night contemplate the Way without ceasing, with no attachments or clinging. (introductory section)

At the White Yang Assembly, the Buddha Maitreya will exchange [the world] from the beginning. He will establish the universe and take charge of the world for more than eighty thousand springs. [But] before the Venerable Patriarch descends to the world, the chief of demons will first arrive, and seventy-two heterodox miscellaneous patriarchs will contend with one another, say that what does not exist does, brag about their abilities, and coerce men and women to salvation. They do not recognize the signs of what is coming. Thus innumerable people in the world have gotten a false understanding. Where are there any true and upright people who understand righteousness? . . .

Men and women come forward and listen to the master's detailed explanation. He thoroughly refutes heterodox patriarchs so that you are better able to defend against them. In the years of the end Dharma, heterodox teachings are widespread and demonic people obstruct the Way. (chapter 10)

The answer to this is the true teaching from Maitreya himself:

The years of the end kalpa will soon arrive; time is limited. . . . What I [am teaching] now is the true Dharma, which I dare not transmit in vain. The eternal Dharma circulates in the world to save all beings. . . . It saves all the pious men and women of the world so that they soon return to their Native Place, and in the years of the end Dharma no longer endure the suffering of this dusty world. (chapter 10)

The changes in time that accompany Maitreya are discussed in the *Mi-le ch'u-hsi pao-chüan*, which notes that he will save all the remaining ninety-two *i* of the lost, all of whom are "buddhas who live at home (*tsai chia fo*), pious men and women who are the true family of the Ancient Buddha." In his time "the whole world attains buddhahood . . . and purgatory will be changed to the Lotus City" (chapters 40 and 39).

We do not know how much the sectarians actually believed such threats and promises, but for those who did, they no doubt provided an incentive to follow exhortations to piety and morality. It is instructive to note that although Maitreya will rule over a changed universe, the direct political implications of this are not spelled out, so that even this most dramatic aspect of sectarian mythology is not understood in a revolutionary way.

Explicit Ethical Teachings

We have seen that the ethical teachings of sixteenth-century *pao-chüan* are a combination of popular understandings of Confucian and Buddhist values (see Chapter Five above). These values continued to be supported in the seventeenth century, but more in the context of exhortations to religious piety. These later sources also provide more detailed lists of sins to be avoided and add the theme of nonviolence toward animals. This increased detail is particularly evident in texts that discuss punishments in purgatory. As before, ethical teachings are intimately involved with what I call the "social perspectives" of these books.

The positive values advocated by these texts are well illustrated by a description of Cultivated Talent Liu, the husband of the wrongly accused woman in the *Hsiao-shih Chun-t'i fu-sheng pao-chüan* (hereafter "the *Chun-t'i pao-chüan*"; text 12 in Appendix I), of whom we are told that

his mind was sincere and he revered the Three Jewels; he was a literate person who understood ritual principles and righteousness and was filial and obedient to his parents. He loved his wife, took pity on social inferiors, and was friendly with fellow villagers. His mind and feelings were compassionate, and he had no covetous thoughts. He was most liberal and magnanimous. Every day he burned incense and bowed before the Buddha, desiring that his parents would increase their life spans and be free of all illness. He also hoped that he and his wife would live to be a hundred and be together until old age, that their children would be free of misfortunes and difficulties, and that their household would be safe and at peace. (chapter 1)

Mr. Liu's exemplary combination of piety and virtue is noted again in chapter 11 of the *Chun-t'i pao-chüan*, where we are told he "kept the fasts and precepts, recited invocations and scriptures, burned incense, worshipped the buddhas and patriarchs, reverenced Heaven,

Earth, the sun, moon, and stars, was filial to his parents and respectful to his superiors and teachers. . . . [He] was friendly to relatives and fellow villagers, loved his children, was kind to his servants, provided vegetarian food for monks, bestowed alms, loved the old, and pitied the poor."

Similar virtues are listed in chapter 13 of the *Ling-ying T'ai-shan niang-niang pao-chüan* (hereafter "the *T'ai-shan niang-niang pao-chüan*"; text 10 in Appendix I). These include "carrying out the way of filial piety and caring for one's old mother," brothers not quarreling, sisters-in-law respecting each other, "looking on all relatives in the same way," being honest and cheerful, bestowing alms and providing vegetarian food for monks, maintaining a vegetarian diet, being fair and just in all activities, and never changing such good behavior.

These values are echoed in the *Ti-tsang Shih-wang pao-chüan* (text 4 in Appendix I), which adds repairing bridges and roads, giving tea to travelers, arranging lamps, "erecting cool pavilions," providing ferryboats, burying exposed corpses and bones, and "exhorting others with good words." Thus all are "to knit together good karma and refrain from doing bad deeds" (chapter 29). The *Hu-kuo yu-min fu-mo pao-chüan* (hereafter "the *Fu-mo pao-chüan*"; text 6 in Appendix I) contributes that "the ruler must be upright; only so will he move the gods to protect. Officials must be pure to bring peace to all the people. Fathers must be compassionate and children filial as they live together in the same house. Elder brothers should love their younger brothers, who should respect them, showing the same intentions. People must maintain a vegetarian diet and recite the Buddha's name [and] meditate" (chapter 8).

There is nothing in these precepts that could not be accepted by any Chinese Buddhist. However, it is in condemning sins that these books provide the most detail, albeit with much repetition. In a discussion of the sins of those who cross over the iron bridge to purgatory, the *Chih-li pao-chüan* (text 2 in Appendix I) includes not obeying the law, cheating heaven and the gods, cursing the wind and rain, harming others to benefit oneself, disobeying parents, destroying images, breaking scissors, deceiving teachers, attacking patriarchs, fighting, contending, killing living things, acting cruelly, and being concerned only with immediate pleasures (chapter 12). To this conventional list the *Chun-t'i* book (text 12 in Appendix I) adds "cheating parents and children and cursing one's wife" (chapter 10), while the *Ti-tsang Shih-wang pao-chüan* includes "coveting good food and drink, acting perversely, reviling the Buddha and the Dharma, engaging in immoral sexual activities, . . . and plotting for wealth" (p. 19).

But beyond these platitudes, there are some more specific and interesting condemnations. In the same *Ti-tsang Shih-wang* book, for example, we are told of sinners who are in purgatory because they were unwilling to be industrious and frugal, "properly manage their households, be content with their lot, and have self-control. They are men who abandoned plowing and reading [*sic*] and women who gave up their spinning and weaving. [They are those who] treated the bodies of their parents with contempt and who sold and destroyed their ancestral property" (pp. 34–35). The *Ti-tsang Shih-wang* book also criticizes "those who practice female roles in flower-drum [plays], write lewd books and tunes, . . . and make lewd potions (*yin-yao*)" (p. 108). Another text concerned with purgatory, the *T'ai-shan Shih-wang pao-chüan* (text 7 in Appendix I), inveighs against those who beat their fathers and curse their mothers, waste fields, set fires, and borrow money without returning it (chapter 3).

The *Ti-tsang Shih-wang* book also strongly condemns killing animals as offerings to gods and ancestors, not only because animals were once humans and thus have feelings, but because such sacrifices actually harm the ancestors and condemn one to the sufferings of purgatory. Of animals this book says, "They are also living beings who understand loving life and fearing death. In their previous lives they were humans. They know cold and warmth and like to be lively and gay."

This statement is followed by a discussion of the intelligence of animals, such as cocks knowing when to announce the dawn, dogs not deceiving their masters, lambs kneeling to their mothers while nursing, and birds regurgitating food for their young. The sufferings and cries of animals when they are being killed are described, as are methods of mutilating them: "pulling out their hair, breaking open their skulls, scraping off their feathers, cutting off their heads, chopping off their feet, chopping them into little pieces, picking the bones out of their flesh, pulling out their skin and sinews, digging out their livers, and seizing their hearts." There follows a list of the different ways of cooking and frying the poor beasts (pp. 41–42, 101). Those who do such things are punished in purgatory by having their own hands and feet cut off, teeth pried out, eyes dug out, and skin peeled off, so all is recompensed (p. 101).

The fundamental reason given for not engaging in such cruelty is that "living things all have true souls and the buddha-nature. . . . Humans and animals have been together for myriads of kalpas. [They] alike cling to life and fear death. . . . They are of one body and look on things the same way" (pp. 41, 43). This is emphasized in a long discussion of different kinds of insects that were once human, concluding with the statement that "insects in manure vats are also human (*yeh shih jen*)" (p. 110). This all serves as the basis for the exhortation:

Therefore [I] urge all men and women of the world to quickly maintain a vegetarian diet and arouse their minds to compassion, practice all forms of goodness, and love and care for living things and rescue them. When you see someone killing insects, urgently exhort them [not to]. (p. 87)

These ethical teachings and those discussed in the next section, on social perspectives, reveal the moral earnestness of seventeenth-century "precious volumes." These books were carriers of such values at a middle level of literacy and belief—values that were also supported in "morality books" (*shan-shu*) produced by literati and by later forms of popular religious texts.[1]

Social Perspectives

Seventeenth-century "precious volumes" are addressed to all levels of society, as this genre of religious literature had been since its beginnings two hundred years earlier. These books also continue to assume that differences in economic status are fundamentally due to karma, that is, to moral and religious causes. What distinguish seventeenth-century perspectives on society are their relatively more detailed discussions and their exhortations to specific economic classes and occupational groups. These interrelated topics are here discussed thematically.

The relationship between the universal principles of these books and the effects of karma is well illustrated by passages from the *T'ai-shan niang-niang pao-chüan* (text 10 in Appendix I):

[The Goddess] has no partiality. She looks on all in the same way, without distinguishing whether they are ignorant or wise, men or women, poor or rich, honored or humble. . . . The Holy Mother treats all the same, with no favoritism. (chapter 1)

The Holy Mother manifests her supernormal powers and exhorts all living beings to reform their bad [actions] and practice goodness. Recite [this] true scripture and be fair in all things. (chapter 17)

Outside the imperial city there are many women and men [sic] who are poor or rich, noble or humble. All types of people contend for fame, profit, food, and clothing. There are some wealthy families that have no sons or daughters, and some poor families that have many children but don't have enough to eat or wear. Since they are humans, who among them does not want glory, wealth, and honorable status? Those who in previous lives have not practiced religious cultivation have myriad difficulties. The poor are poor, the wealthy, wealthy; stop blaming the buddhas and patriarchs. People should blame themselves for their karmic fruits' not being complete. The wise quickly repent and recite the Buddha's name. Those with money should give joyfully, and so intelligently plant fields of blessing [i.e., good karma].

Those who contribute money when they are reborn will be wealthy and honored. Those who recite the Buddha's name plant good roots and in their next life will be promoted to high positions. . . . [The conditions of] the poor and wealthy each have their own [self-caused] source; the poor suffer, while the joy of the wealthy flows like water. (chapter 17)

This conservative and rather bleak social perspective is affirmed as well in chapter 5 of the same book, where we read,

The pious will receive the blessings they deserve. They will be humans again, reborn in China, spiritually free and independent. Those who do what is bad create inferior karma; who would be willing to take their place? What one does, one receives (tzu-chi tso, tzu-chi shou). They suffer bitterly. If you don't believe this, just observe that on the streets there are ten thousand kinds of people, all different, all of which is due to [their actions in] previous lives. . . . For poverty and noble and humble positions, all should blame themselves.

The perspective of the Fu-mo pao-chüan (text 6 in Appendix I) is the same: "The Lord Who Subdues Demons [= the Lord Kuan] looks on all as the same—monks, laity, Confucians, Buddhists, Taoists, those within and without [the household], generals, ministers, court officials, and royalty" (chapter 21). Individual karma is the reason for the difference between "the wealthy and honored who enjoy peace and happiness, and the poor who call out on the streets to make a living. Don't blame Heaven and Earth for this" (chapter 5). In this perspective, merit is promised to all who "recite the Buddha's name, maintain a vegetarian diet, visit enlightened persons, and meditate" (chapter 14), so hope is always present.

Though the basic cause and hope for life situations are the same for all, in order to focus the message of deliverance, these books analyze society into classes and occupations. The clearest discussion of economic classes is in the *Ti-tsang Shih-wang pao-chüan* (text 4 in Appendix I), which divides society into upper, middle, and lower classes (*shang-teng*, *chung-teng*, and *hsia-teng*). All are criticized for their moral and religious failures and are reminded that they, too, will die and suffer retribution. Of the upper class, we read that they "are unwilling to carry out religious practices. They employ male and female servants and act presumptuously, in a dissipated manner. They have beautiful wives and concubines in every room and large amounts of fields and hills." But though they wear fine silk and embroidery, have homes filled with children, and are rich and honored, "when they die they cannot avoid becoming dried bones."

Middle-class people are also unwilling to cultivate themselves. They extend loans to others at high interest while their households have money boxes full of gold and silver. Wine and meat are constantly available to them, and they play at every kind of dice and chess, but they also become dry bones at death.

Those of the lowest class cry out in grief and complaint because they do not have enough food and drink. They sleep at night in old temples with no blankets to cover them, but they suffer the same fate as the rich. The same applies to farmers, "who carry plows on their backs and drag oxen, who work from early morning until night, but who are unwilling to repent and recite the Buddha's name. They think only of their children and grandchildren, not of their own sins."

Wives are included in this critique because they are concerned only for their children and their household duties. They work hard, until their backs are bent and their hair white, but don't think beyond old age: "Who knows when King Yama will issue a warrant to seize them?" (pp. 36–37).

This discussion continues in the same vein with exhortations to court officials, generals, young men of twenty, and beautiful women. They also do not escape the fate of all (pp. 37–38).

From social classes, the *Ti-tsang Shih-wang* book shifts its attention to those in specific social roles and occupations, for which a summary list is provided that includes butchers, monks, nuns, Taoist priests and lay devotees; the poor, orphaned, and suffering; the childless; old, young, and mature men and women; officials; "the famous, wealthy, and honored"; and "those who meditate to awaken to the Way." All these people are exhorted to practice religion to avoid purgatory, with butchers told to "buy living things to release them" (p. 15). However, the group to which this book devotes the most attention is merchants, of whom we are told that they

buy and sell unfairly, alter measures and weights, hide their intentions, deceive themselves, and do everything in secret. They take pleasure in plotting for wealth for their families, using every kind of trickery. They do only what is crooked, drink wine, eat meat, and love to gamble and practice sexual immorality. They beat and curse their elders, and strike and shame their servants. They cheat and oppress the good, revile the pious, and curse those who maintain a vegetarian diet. They do not believe in the good way of karma but devote themselves to all manner of evil and depravity. These sinners are all taken to the Yin Administration and delivered to the eighteen forms of purgatory, where they suffer endlessly with no hope of escape. (p. 105)

Despite their emphasis on karma, there is real social criticism in such passages that provides valuable information on perspectives within traditional Chinese society. Such perspectives in *pao-chüan* need to be compared with those in Ming and Ch'ing vernacular literature and literati writings.

In this and previous chapters, we have noted approving references to Confucianism in these sectarian texts. The *Ti-tsang Shih-wang pao-chüan* affirms this interpretation of Confucianism in some detail, as in this statement attributed to the Holy Mother herself:

I urge you quickly to give allegiance to the Way of the Confucian school (Ju-chia tao); I want my imperial children to ascend to heaven. In the Southern Realm [= this world], [I] have established a White Yang Assembly . . . and order all my disciples to maintain a vegetarian diet, recite the Buddha's name, and study [the Way of] Long Life. (p. 10)

As we have seen before, support for Confucianism is clearly connected in these texts to support for the ruler and (good) officials. Here the Mother continues: "I urge people to worship the Southern and Northern Buddhas and pray for long life for the ruler. . . . May the salaries of civil and military officials increase, and may the myriad common people enjoy years of great peace and prosperity" (p. 16).

Support is also offered for more specific Confucian values and virtues, blended with those of popular Buddhism. Thus we are told that

in Buddhism one maintains a vegetarian diet; in Confucianism one culti-
vates moral character. [I] exhort the men and women of the world: For religious self-cultivation there are root causes. Men practice piety to become
like the Buddha, while it is the Bodhisattva Kuan-yin to whom women are
devoted. (p. 17)

The Confucian school preaches the Dharma and exhorts people to cultivate
[themselves in it]. (p. 18)

Practice the correct Way of Maitreya; concentrate every instant on constantly
being a good person. Men should practice the three bonds [between ruler
and minister, father and son, husband and wife] and the five constant virtues [benevolence, righteousness, ritual propriety, wisdom, and trustwor-
thiness]. Women should obey the three obediences [to father, husband, and
oldest son] and the four female virtues [proper behavior, speech, demeanor,
and employment], and [both should] read Confucian books [so that they]
understand the principles of the Duke of Chou. They should bow in reverence for the kindness of Heaven and Earth, rulers, relatives, and teachers,
and train and nourish the precious jewels of their vital spirit, ch'i, blood, and
natures. [They should] be correct in taking the Three Refuges and pure in
maintaining the five precepts. Doing the ten good things[2] is the root; be responsible for all the activities of your social position. Only by this can one's
parents be saved and forever depart from the sufferings of purgatory. (p. 28)

This affirmation of a popular understanding of Confucianism in
seventeenth-century "precious volumes" is a valuable indication of
the extent to which Confucian values were accepted by those of
moderate literacy at that time, particularly since these books express
the views of popular sects based on alternative mythology.

As to the larger social perspectives of these texts, it is interesting
to note that none of the criticisms of officials mentions persecution of
the sects, though we know from historical sources that such groups
were considered illegal and were subject to suppression by particularly diligent officials. Perhaps this is because most of the more
powerful sectarian uprisings took place in the eighteenth and nineteenth centuries, long after the composition of books considered
here. These books continue and expand the earlier *pao-chüan* tradition of earnest religious and moral exhortation, coupled in some
cases with a strong dose of social criticism. Though beliefs about the
end of the age are expressed in radical terms, the only response advocated for this time of destruction and turmoil is intensified conventional piety based on sectarian beliefs and deities. There is no
hint of political rebellion in this material; even the strongest social

criticism is fundamentally conservative because of its acceptance of karma and its call for the moral renewal of the existing order.

NEW EMPHASES IN THE SEVENTEENTH CENTURY

The themes given more emphasis in seventeenth-century "precious volumes" are discussions of sect rituals, meditation as interior alchemy, practical aid from the gods, and purgatory.

Discussions of Rituals

Most early "precious volumes" include some exhortations concerning pious practices and rituals, usually mixed with more explicitly ethical teachings. A representative discussion of such practices is found in chapter 47 of the *Mi-le ch'u-hsi pao-chüan* (text 5 in Appendix I), where we read:

The Ancient Buddha Maitreya delivered this precious volume to the Eastern Land to exhort all good men and believing women to maintain a vegetarian diet and receive the precepts. Human form is difficult to maintain; the Buddha's teaching is difficult [to get to] hear. It is difficult to be reborn in China and to encounter a place of worship. The Ancient Buddha has bestowed [this scripture] on people who carry out such religious practices as fasting and [keeping] the precepts, listening to scriptures, providing vegetarian food for monks, practicing charity, printing scriptures, making images, repairing monasteries and building pagodas, repairing bridges and roads, and eating vegetarian food on the third, sixth, and ninth [days of the month]. . . . These are all pleasurable [activities that bring] merit. How could [those who practice them] fall into the sufferings [of purgatory]?

A similar discussion in the *T'ai-shan Shih-wang pao-chüan* (text 7 in Appendix I) adds "donating oil and lighting lamps before the buddhas" and offering fresh fruit, flowers, tea, and rice, as well as contributing copper chimes, iron bells, banners, and pennants, as acts of worship. Giving shoes, socks, and caps to monks is recommended in the same spirit. All such good deeds bring "measureless merit" — good fortune, long life, good income and position, and rebirth as a human being with clear eyesight and hearing and "speech like a bell" (chapter 2).

The *Chun-t'i pao-chüan* (text 12 in Appendix I) urges its readers to "bow before the Buddha with believing minds and sincere intentions," to wash their hands, and to burn incense and "pray to the buddhas and gods for their parents, for themselves, and for their husbands or wives, the poor, sons and daughters, relatives, for those suffering from disasters and illness, and for peace" (chapter 11).

However, in addition to these general exhortations to ritual piety, one seventeenth-century "precious volume" — the *Hung-yang hou-hsü jan-teng t'ien-hua pao-chüan* (The Vast Yang celestial flower precious volume [concerning the] later continuation of lighting the lamp [of the teaching], hereafter "the *T'ien-hua pao-chüan*"; text 1 in Appendix I) — discusses a particular ritual in much greater detail. In accord with its title, the book provides two chapters on a ritual of lighting and offering lamps to attract the gods to descend. Chapter 27 opens with two lines of heptasyllabic verse:

As golden lamps shine brightly,
The Buddhas and patriarchs descend from the celestial realm.

The text continues with a statement by the revealing patriarch:

I am now saving the multitudes, fearing only that [you whose] merit is small will not be able to return to the primal source. Give up your [worldly] selves (*she shen*), light lamps, and arrange a holy assembly. Now our family[? character unclear] has been illuminated from within the holy [realm], and revealing and bestowing the scripture has ended. Uniting in response, light the lamps and offer them to the buddhas and patriarchs of the Native Place. [May] the entire holy multitude of the three cities[?] (*san-ch'eng*)[3] and nine grades of rank descend to our ritual assembly and together receive golden lamps.

There follows a long list of the deities and patriarchs who "descend to the ritual arena and receive golden lamps," beginning with the Venerable Patriarch Hun-yuan and the Venerable Mother Tzu-shu. They are followed by the names of twenty-eight other divine figures, plus several sets: the "sixty-three patriarchs," "all the star lords," "the enlightened physicians of ten dynasties," "the ten lords Yama," "city gods and locality gods," and so forth. This list is followed by a passage (translated in the discussion of text 1 in Appendix I), inviting all to "descend from the Native Place."

Chapter 28 continues this sustained invocation with a list of matriarchs (*tsu-mu*) and Venerable Mothers who are also invited to descend to receive golden lamps, beginning with Wu-sheng lao-mu herself. Her name is followed by those of thirty-nine individual Mothers, plus such sets as "the eight Mothers Eternal" and the "twelve matriarchs." It is interesting to note that this list includes Wang-mu niang-niang (the Royal Mother Goddess), a title found

frequently in later spirit-writing texts. This chapter ends with another appeal: "We invite all these Venerable Mothers to approach
the ritual arena, and light lamps to repay their kindness in rescuing
us from suffering. We invite all the Venerable Mothers to descend
from the celestial palace to observe their children and grandchildren
lighting golden lamps, devoting themselves with great effort so that
the perfected minds of the primal ones will not backslide."

These chapters not only provide rare and interesting information
about sectarian ritual but also are an excellent example of the use by
these groups of ideas and rituals from earlier ritual traditions. In this
case a Taoist lamplighting ritual has been given thoroughly sectarian
content (as noted in text 1 in Appendix I).

Though the basic ritual activity urged by these scriptures is their
own reading and recitation, few details are provided as to how this
is to be done. What is discussed is a mix of conventional popular
Buddhist rituals and good deeds. As with the lamplighting ritual
just described, the only distinctive aspect of these rites is their address to sectarian deities and patriarchs.[4]

Meditation or Interior Alchemy

In seventeenth-century "precious volumes," meditation means the
internal refinement and circulation of vital forces in the body, a simplified form of Taoist *nei-tan* ("cultivating the interior elixir"). *Nei-
tan* involves a view of the body and its processes in symbolic terms
derived from exterior alchemy, the *I-ching*, yin and yang, the Five
Phases, and other traditional classifications of time and space. In
fully developed *nei-tan*, the goal is the attainment of immortality by
transforming the basic energy of the body into pure yang, or "true
yang," but this can only be done by strengthening yang within yin,
taking yang energy from a yin context. Such esoteric uniting of op-
posites brings a special power.

Since the goal of *nei-tan* practice is reversal of the normal course
from life to death, in this form of physiological alchemy, as Joseph
Needham writes,

the adept was vowed to a "way of upside-downness" (*tien tao*). Both in
practice and in theory he applied a counter-natural or widdershins principle
in physiology, seeking to go against (*ni*) the normal course. The arrest and
reversal of the aging process with its ultimate end in death was after all
something apparently contrary to Nature. So in counter-current style he not
only retained and conserved secretions usually lost from the body, but

obliged the Yang within the Yin of saliva-lead to go downwards, and raised up the Yin within the Yang of semen-mercury. . . .

Where the vital pre-natal Yin and Yang (true mercury and true lead) met and reacted, in the centre of the body (*chung thu*) [= *t'u*] corresponding to Earth, close by the spleen, there would the anablastemic enchymoma (*huan tan*) be formed. Inversion would bring reversion — to eternal youth.[5]

Needham provides a convenient chart of the most common *nei-tan* terms involved in what he calls "counter-natural inverted *nei-tan* correlations." Some of these terms are used in the "precious volumes" discussed in this section, including "true lead" and "true mercury," the "White Tiger" and the "Green Dragon," and so forth —all of which here refer to "essences extracted by internal work from juices [of the body]," on the model of refining gold out of baser elements in exterior alchemy.[6]

There are scattered references to this terminology in most seventeenth-century *pao-chüan* I have read, but the most extensive discussions of this theme are in the *Chih-li, Fu-mo, T'ai-shan Shih-wang*, and *T'ai-shan niang-niang* books. All these books share a common language about this tradition. Though there is more *nei-tan*-related material than in the sixteenth century, most of the references here remain rather general and do not provide instructions on how all this was to be carried out. Because the most detailed comments are in the *Chih-li* book (text 2 in Appendix I), I begin with them, then move to supplementary passages from the other three texts. Chapter 9 of the *Chih-li* provides instructions from the Mother herself:

Circulate [in your body] the single vital force (*ch'i*) of the Prior Realm and refine your own complete light. Nourish *mou-ni* [jewels][7] within you [as numerous as] the sands of the Ganges [to form] a bright pearl that is the jewel of returning the elixir (*huan-tan*). When one accomplishes this practice, one knows that three flowers are gathered on the top of one's head, and the five forms of *ch'i* [of one's vital organs] have been in audience at the court of the primal source. The [yang] dragon has overturned the golden tripod [a reaction vessel in the body], and the [yin] tiger circumambulates the Yellow Court [in the abdomen]. Heaven is numinous and the Earth abruptly [moves?] (*ti-cha*). The jade rabbit [symbol of the moon and yin] ascends to the east, [so] yang increases and yin decreases. . . . The Mother ordered, "Increase your effort to advance, receive and continue the transmission of [these practices], so as to ascend and realize nirvāṇa with inexhaustible joy."

There are a few lines of instruction on how to approach all this, beginning with references in chapter 8 to seated meditation, including "closing tightly the six gateways" and "exchanging pure *ch'i* for dirty *ch'i* . . . making it go up and down," and in chapter 20 to opening up the passes in the body so that the *ch'i* circulates freely. In chapter 18 we read that "refining the vital essence to transfer *ch'i* is the upper pass; the body does not move. Refining the *ch'i* to transform it into the spirit is the middle pass; the mind does not move. Refining the spirit into emptiness is the lower pass; the thoughts do not move."

This emphasis on quieting the mind and thoughts is echoed later in the *Chih-li* book, where we read, "If those engaged in self-cultivation wish to reach the root and return to the source, for all twelve hours of the day they should firmly rein in the [galloping] horse of their thoughts and tightly lock up the [leaping] ape of the mind" (chapter 21). This mental stillness is preparation for nourishing the holy embryo of a new self within:

In breathing in and out there are the yin and yang, and the infant boy and girl [within] are matched and become a pair. . . . Only when the pious practitioner has reached this step does he/she know where to rest. After nourishing the infant for ten months of exhausting effort, one really has pointed off into the distance. When [this infant] becomes a mature person, one returns home and recognizes the patriarchs. (chapter 19)

One of the characteristics of *nei-tan* is its use of terms derived from Buddhism to parallel its basically Taoist structure. Thus in the *Chih-li* book, an alternative way of describing the goal is through

entering *samādhi* to observe emptiness. . . . One who enters *samādhi* spies out the unfathomable inner power of the ghosts and spirits. The thousand sages cannot fathom [such a person], nor demons invade. The mind, cold and unmoved, penetrates the Prior Realm. In *samādhi* there is stillness, with no [distinction between] false and true, dualities and differences. It is a bright sun shining in the present and illuminating the past. . . . [In it] one perceives that the body is formless and empty, . . . [and so] one transcends the three realms without leaving the body. (chapter 14)

All of this leads to "being able to see the [true inner] nature, enlighten the mind, and return to the primal source" (chapter 14).

The *nei-tan* teachings of the *Chih-li* book are summed up in chapter 19, entitled "On Being Pregnant and Forming an Embryo":

In being pregnant, one should escape saṃsāra. One should carefully preserve *samādhi* in the stove [of the body] and not allow leakage. The inner working of heaven, the three passes, and the nine husks (*chiu-k'o*) [of the body] depend on the breath [reading *jen*, "to think," as *p'ing*, "to lean on"]. In the body, yin and yang correlate with each other and circulate and cause the eight trigrams to flow. *Ch'ien* is metal; *k'an* is water; [one should] protect and firmly preserve the elixir field (*tan-t'ien*). *K'an* is in the *li* trigram, and *li* in *k'an*. In the dark mystery (*hsuan*) is the wonderful (*miao*); in the wonderful there is principle (*li*). In the world, how many are able to understand [this]?

To this last question I can only respond, "Not many!" Nonetheless, this is a clear case of sectarian adoption of technical terms from the internal elixir tradition, presumably by way of Ch'üan-chen (Complete Perfection) Taoism, as discussed in Chapter One above. In this tradition the body is seen as an alchemical furnace for refining and blending the essences of fluids correlated with cosmic categories. The hope is that this correlation will unite the body/self with eternal structures and hence achieve its immortality. There is enough detail in the *Chih-li pao-chüan* to indicate that its author had some real understanding of this complex system, beyond the invocation of its sacred power.

The only other points to note on this topic in the *Chih-li pao-chüan* are a passing reference to "dual cultivation" by husband and wife, and one passage indicating that *nei-tan* practices are subordinate to a relationship with the Eternal Mother, both found in chapter 18. The first reads, "For the sake of one's nature and destiny, one must practice dual cultivation (*shuang-hsiu*), with husband and wife joyfully meeting and constantly preserving [i.e., guarding] each other (*hsiang shou*)." The second passage says, "The merit [= result] of refining the *ch'i* and preserving the spirit nevertheless does not enable one to attain the fruit of buddhahood. [For this] one must in the Native Place accompany the Eternal [Mother]." "Dual cultivation" refers to ritual sexual intercourse to blend and refine yin and yang forces. The reference to the Eternal Mother here is not consistent with claims made elsewhere in the *Chih-li* book that deliverance can be obtained by *nei-tan* practices alone. Presumably this is a result of trying to fit these practices into a mythological tradition that the sects had developed earlier.

There are a few passing references in the *T'ai-shan niang-niang pao-chüan* (text 10 in Appendix I) to "exchanging pure wind for dirty *ch'i*" while in seated meditation (chapter 24), and to *nei-tan*-style reversal, with "descending yang returning to yin, and ascending yin

returning to yang and penetrating the *ni-wan* {aperture in the skull]"
(chapter 13), but more detailed discussions can be found in the *Fu-mo pao-chüan* (text 6 in Appendix I), where we read such passages as:

Religious practitioners nourish the holy embryo [within], release their dirty
ch'i, and gather in the pure. At the bottom of the sea [= in the abdomen],
firmly embrace the little child; [they have] selected out the bones and exchanged the embryo. Amitābha! . . . The holy embryo must be complete.
When the brain makes a popping sound to open the *ni-wan,* one has entered
the holy and transcended the mundane, and has finally rolled out to the
Heaven Beyond Heaven, Amitābha! . . .

Those who cultivate the Way first harmonize and put in order [their] single vital force of the Prior Realm, select pure wind to exchange it for dirty
ch'i, nourish their vital force and preserve their spirit. The *ch'i* must be gathered to nourish the holy embryo; then three flowers gather on top of the
head, and the five vital forces [of the bodily organs], in an audience at
the central court, [enable one] to see the nature and enlighten the mind.
Open the three passes, pass through the mundane openings, and penetrate
Heaven and Earth. From the bottom of the sea, [the refined *ch'i*] ascends to
Mount K'un-lun. . . . Nourish the infant, attain true awareness, and roll out
to the Cloud Gate. . . .

Those who attain true enlightenment (*ch'eng cheng chueh*) are not stained
by the dust [of saṃsāra] for myriad eons. All men and women have [these]
methods for escaping the world. Those who cultivate the Way are many, but
those who attain it are few — not one in ten thousand. Men becoming pregnant is very rare in the world, but after three years . . . when their merit is
complete, they enter the holy and transcend the mundane. (chapter 2)

Since there are similar references to men becoming pregnant in
chapters 9 and 19, it is possible that this *nei-tan* symbolism is being
taken literally here, but this again is something that only a conversa-
tion with a Ming sectarian could confirm.

Most of this same internal-elixir language can be found in the
T'ai-shan Shih-wang pao-chüan (text 7 in Appendix I), in which it is
further correlated with Eternal Mother mythology. Thus we read, for
example, that when all the passes of the body have been opened up,
there appears "a road of escape to K'un-lun. The numinous brilliance [of one's spirit] rises to the midst of empty space and then
goes to the assembly, and at the Land of Utmost Bliss registers its
name and title on the Buddha notice board" (chapter 5). This type of
discussion is continued in chapters 6 and 8, where we are told:

In everyone's abdomen there is a ninefold numinous elixir medicine, but if
one does not encounter the true transmission to the multitudes, how will

one attain [access to] it? This medicine employs [the *ch'i*] of the Prior Realm. When yin and yang in one place are roasted and refined [*sic*], they form a numinous elixir. Thus for returning home one has a place to rest [i.e., a secure starting point within one's own body].

Go down to the bottom of the sea and return the yang to the midst of the yin. The golden crow and jade rabbit [symbols of sun and moon, yang and yin] release a ray of bright light. In the Seven-Jeweled Pool [of paradise] there shines a bright light. [There the] infant boy and girl are matched to form a pair.

Here *nei-tan* practices lead to salvation in paradise, a blend of complementary modes of deliverance that we have noted before.

Practical Aid

Another characteristic emphasis of seventeenth-century "precious volumes" is promises of divine aid to the pious, both as a reward for their good karma and, more directly, from the gods in response to petitions. Aid can come in both this life and the next. Such promises are scattered throughout these books, but are discussed in more detail in two of them that are addressed to powerful deities, the Goddess of Mount T'ai and the Lord Kuan (texts 10 and 6 in Appendix I).

Good examples of general assurances of practical aid are found in the *Chun-t'i* and *T'ai-shan Shih-wang pao-chüan*, both cited above. The *T'ai-shan Shih-wang* book (text 7 in Appendix I) promises those who donate money that in their next rebirth they will be honored and wealthy, and those who recite the Buddha's name that "when they come around again they will have knitted together good karma" (chapter 9). At the end of the book, the focus is more on this life. One who sincerely recites this scripture and the Buddha's name and who maintains a vegetarian diet is told that "when one seeks [relief from] disasters, they are destroyed, when one seeks good fortune, good fortune arises, when one seeks sons, one gets sons. If one's parents have died, if one recites the *Precious Volume of the Ten Kings*, bowing reverently in all sincerity, then one moves the Dark Realm, and the dead leave purgatory and go directly to the West" (chapter 24).

In the *Chun-t'i* book (text 12 in Appendix I), those who worship Cundī (a form of the Bodhisattva Kuan-yin) are promised health for their parents, peace for their whole families, harmony between husbands and wives, prosperity and good fortune, and protection by the gods. Pious husbands and wives are told that they will be able to be together until old age. For the sick, their illnesses will be driven away; those who seek wealth will be given it; travelers will quickly be able to return; those who seek sons will be given them; in difficult childbirths, the child and mother will be soon separated; the filial and obedient will know the path to follow in the Realm of Darkness; and the spirits of the dead will ascend to heaven (chapter 11).

The scope of promises of aid is greatly expanded in the *Fu-mo pao-chüan* (text 6 in Appendix I), in which the Lord Kuan is presented as the national exorcist. Of him we read,

He protects the nation, the people are at peace and happy, and the wind and rain harmonious. He protects the ruler and manifests his supernormal power to protect the present [sovereign]. For [those who] enter rivers, seas, and streams, he is the "generalissimo who levels the waves." He protects the worthy who enter forests, and on behalf of the nation punishes treacherous cliques, so that all is peaceful and secure. He protects the reigning emperor so that he lives for a myriad springs. For those who recite [this] true scripture with energetic and deep intentions, he increases blessings and life span. Those who request [copies of this] true scripture and reverence it in their homes, evil demons do not attack. The Venerable Lord Kuan cannot be compared to [ordinary] good gods and patriarchs. Being fair by nature, he punishes the bad and protects the good. With his wisdom eye he can see 100,000 *li* and arrive in an instant. His supernormal powers are vast; he emits a brilliant golden light that completely pervades the world. At the Yellow River he destroys the evil and heterodox, protecting the people and nation. He defeats the Miao and Man [aborigines] and stops pirates so that they never come to invade. In the capital, he supports the true ruler. (chapter 3)

Elsewhere in the *Fu-mo* book, we are told that Lord Kuan says that he was commissioned by the Ancient Buddha and the Jade Emperor "to subdue the demons of the world, sweep them all away at one stroke without a trace." In this cause he visits nine thousand altars a day, transforming misfortune into blessings for "good people who recite my *pao-chüan* and praise my merit" (chapter 8). Assurances of protection for the ruler are repeated throughout, and for those who "recite [this] scripture with sincere intentions, the Demon-Subduer will descend to the altar and protect all. Thus every home will be peaceful and secure" (chapter 23).

The *T'ai-shan niang-niang pao-chüan* (text 10 in Appendix I) also promises support for the ruler and people, particularly in chapter 1 (as discussed in an article of mine cited in Appendix I), but its focus is more on pious pilgrims to the Goddess's temple on Mount T'ai. As we read in chapter 3,

The Holy Venerable Mother's supernormal powers are vast and great; she opens wide her wisdom eye to see everything in all the ten directions. Loyal folk who offer incense [in pilgrimages], who are not concerned about miscellaneous activities, need only offer incense with unified minds [to make] the mind of the Mother of the Peak rejoice. She protects those who eat vegetarian food and recite the Buddha's name.

This discussion continues with more specific assurances to those who come to the Goddess seeking children. We are told that, at an assembly of the gods, "the Goddess who delivers children bowed before the Holy Mother, embracing one baby boy, with one each sitting on her left and right shoulders, seven on her back, three forward and four to the rear. She was followed by thirty-two others, with fifty-six more in a noisy crowd beside her." When she is asked by the Mother who these babies represent, the Goddess replies,

The one I embrace is a prince of the imperial palace. Those standing on my shoulders [will become] national elders and imperial relatives, golden branches and jade leaves, meritorious ministers of the inner court, grand secretaries and ministers. The seven on my back will be called "presented scholars." Those following behind are monks, nuns, and male and female Buddhist lay devotees. Those running along in confusion are ghosts seeking to steal a rebirth who died at [age] two or three, [and so] are not my concern. This is true.

Though there is no specific promise of children for the devout in chapter 3 of the T'ai-shan niang-niang book, the implication is clear, and a promise is made in chapter 7 that "when the pious call out, the Mother responds. If you want to seek boy babies, your mind must be peaceful; then the Venerable Mother will deliver sons to you." Here this text equates the well-known Goddess of Mount T'ai with the Venerable Mother of sectarian tradition.

There are also promises in this book of aid from the Goddess of Eyesight, who says, "If there are pious men and women who raise incense and pray with sincere intentions, I will take [give to them?] mineral and herbal medicines to be rubbed on their eyes. Then the floating clouds [= cataracts?] on their eyes will all withdraw, loosing a brilliant light" (chapter 5).

In this book the Goddess learns of needs by sending out officials to patrol the world, and then herself goes on a tour of inspection (chapter 16). When a problem is brought to her attention, she orders her "divine officials" to investigate, as in the case of a woman who complains that she has been slandered by a "petty person." This case is discussed at length in chapters 14 and 15, in which the woman says, while offering incense to the deity, "I lay a complaint before the Holy Mother, [asking that she] investigate clearly. If verification [of her response] is manifested, I promise to go on pilgrimages three times [to her temple]. This is certainly not empty talk" (chapter 14). She adds, "If your disciple has done anything wrong, dye me in the Yellow Springs [of death], but if that petty person has slandered me, put him or her in the Yin Realm." After receiving a report that the woman is innocent, the Goddess says that the actions of one who makes false accusations "will cut off his descendants and destroy his family" (chapter 15).

Divine practical aid was expected from Chinese local deities, so it is not surprising to see sectarian texts adopting similar beliefs. Buddhist karma had always offered hope for improvement both in this life and in the next, so here, too, the *pao-chüan* are responding to their larger religious context. The net effect was that they moved closer to the mainstream of popular tradition while retaining the old sectarian promise of ultimate salvation.

Purgatory

Discussions of purgatory also receive more emphasis in the seventeenth-century "precious volumes" than in their predecessors. Here purgatory is a place where the spirits of the dead are taken to be punished for their sins and then reborn on Earth in a form appropriate to their karmic deserts. These discussions include descriptions of how sinners are seized by demon-messengers from purgatory and of the judgments and punishments they encounter, as well as sermons, implicitly directed to readers of the texts, that draw the moral lessons to be learned.

However, the dominant emphasis in these scriptures is on how the pious can avoid purgatory altogether, or at least ensure a short and painless stay. At a personal level this can be done by adhering to the teachings of the text in question, but the path to deliverance is opened up by powerful sectarian deities such as Maitreya, who visit purgatory and pledge to destroy it, transforming it into paradise. This emphasis is a key contribution of sectarian scriptures. Those who give allegiance to these scriptures and the groups they represent can attain a form of deliverance otherwise available only to orthodox Buddhists. The best that others can hope for is mitigation of purgatorial punishments, followed by rebirth as human beings in comfortable circumstances.

The most detailed discussions of purgatory in the books consulted for this chapter are those in the *Chun-t'i pao-chüan* devoted to the travails of a woman named Li Pao-p'ing of Shantung who, though falsely accused, is dragged off to death and punishment. (Her story is summarized in some detail in text 12 of Appendix I.) The other books with significant information on this topic are two devoted to Maitreya and one in which an unnamed devotee tours the underworld (texts 4, 5, and 7 in Appendix I). Promises of quick release to those who repent are found in a Vast Yang sect scripture, the *Hsiao-shih Hun-yuan ta fa-ming ching* (text 3 in Appendix I).

The opening chapters of the *Chun-t'i pao-chüan* provide a description of the process of judging and seizing those who deserve death. After inadvertently skipping two fast days in honor of Cundī, Madame Li becomes ill with continual vomiting and dreams that patrolling demons sent by Lord Yama in purgatory are coming to take her away. Buddhist monks invited by her husband to protect her are unable to do so. In chapter 4 we read that "in the Yin Realm, Emperor Yama was sitting in his Sen-lo Palace[8] in purgatory, where there are judges examining record books of the living and dead to see if there are those in the Yang Realm who should die. [When they do], they send demons to seize them."

In the process, they observe that a Madame Li is accused of a whole list of standard sins, including beating monks, cursing Taoist priests, cheating her husband, being unfriendly to fellow villagers, and ridiculing those who do good. Seeing people reciting the Buddha's name gives her a headache. The problem is that the person whom the judges accuse is not our heroine, Li Pao-p'ing, who is from Lin-ch'ing subprefecture of Tung-ch'ang prefecture and whose husband is Cultivated Talent Liu Yü. The name of the sinful woman in the record books is Li Ts'ui-p'ing of Ch'ang-ch'ing district in Chi-nan prefecture; her husband's name is Liu Chih, with no title indicated. Both women are from Shantung, and they and their husbands share the same surnames, but their given names differ by one character and their local addresses are different as well.

The judges say of Li Ts'ui-p'ing that "this sort of person should be seized and taken to the Dark [Realm] to be punished for her sins." They report this on an iron tablet to Lord Yama, who quickly indicates his assent with a "vermilion brush" (a sign of imperial approval) and sends demon-messengers to seize her at her home in Shantung. Her age and the hour, day, and month of her birth are included in the order, as is a list of her sins.

On the way, the two demon-messengers with the arrest warrant stop to report at the palace of the Goddess of Mount T'ai, also in Shantung. As we read in chapter 5,

The two demon-messengers took the official accusation to the Goddess of Mount T'ai, who issued an endorsement. This the Eastern Peak [Mount T'ai administration] sent to the City God, who then dispatched two demon[-messengers] together with the Locality God to go to the indicated home. Of the six household deities, only the Stove God is in charge of this sort of affair. People's good and bad deeds are in the Stove God's hands. But, no more of this.

The demons from the Yin Realm went directly to [what they thought was] Li Ts'ui-p'ing's home, arriving in a whirlwind. As they arrived, they saw banners, flags, placards, and offerings all neatly arranged in a shed to welcome them. When they smelled the offerings, the demons asked the Locality God to invite them to partake of the food, which he did, and the wind stopped.

As they waited in the shed "to seize the soup and rice," the demon-messengers looked up to see written on a placard the name and title of a monk from a Kuan-yin cloister, with an inscription "on behalf of the lay devotee Liu Yü of this ritual arena, a resident of Lin-ch'ing subprefecture of Tung-ch'ang prefecture, for whom I have worshipped the Buddha to pray for blessing and ward off harm, and recited scriptures for his protection" (chapter 5). All this ritual protection had been arranged by Liu Yü for his wife, since medicines had not cured her. Her age and surname are provided, but not her given name, so the messengers proceed to arrest her, despite the protests of the Stove God (as discussed in text 12 in Appendix I).

Much of the extant first half of the *Chun-t'i pao-chüan* is taken up with descriptions of Madame Li's trip to and through purgatory, with much detail about the punishments that sinners must endure. After passing through underworld cities of evil dogs and of those who have died before their time of accidents and disease (chapter 9), she sees Lord Yama in his palace and is told that this is where people are brought to be investigated after they have been seized in the Yang World. All people's acts are recorded in record books, where they can be carefully examined. The point of all this is summarized in brief exhortations:

If you do evil in the Yang Realm, you will not escape for billions of years. I urge all men and women in the world: Each [of you,] take responsibility for your future. You must reverence Heaven and Earth and be filial to your parents to be reborn as humans and be able to ascend [to high positions]. . . .

When people who do good reach the Yin Realm, who dares to obstruct them? Golden lads and jade maidens welcome them from afar. . . . When the kings of purgatory see such good people, they reverence them with joined hands. Their names are erased from the record books of the dead and they are seen off to the celestial palace. (chapter 10)

There is rich detail here for studies of popular views of purgatory, complete with lists of sins and the punishments they deserve, interspersed with promises of hope for the pious. For example, after Madame Li's case is judged, we are told that

a bronze gong sounded, and Yama Son of Heaven descended from his throne. Then all the chief judges, purgatory lords, judges, ox-headed and horse-faced [demon bailiffs], and *yakshas*, after paying their respects, took her to the court where all the spirits of the newly dead are taken. There each is given a placard and a title, which are recorded and reported to the Fifth Lord Yama.[9] He dots these records with a brush pen, noting those with very good merit. Each Yama king praises them, then sends golden lads and jade maidens to hand them on to heaven, . . . where they will receive the blessings they deserve.

There are additional details about the process of reporting and judgment in purgatory in two of the other texts considered here. For example, in the *T'ai-shan Shih-wang pao-chüan* (text 7 in Appendix I), the person touring the underworld asks, "'How does the Dark [Realm] know about the good and bad acts [of those in] the Yang World?' The purgatory lord replied, 'The Stove God reports to the Locality God, the Locality God reports to the City God, the City God reports to T'ien-ch'i [God of Mount T'ai], and T'ien-ch'i notifies the Earth office of the Dark [Realm].'"

There the apprehended spirit is taken before a mirror and a balance that reveal and weigh people's sins: "Those with many good deeds and few bad are reborn in high positions, while those with many bad and few good deeds are reborn with [some of] their six sense organs incomplete. Those who are completely good, with no bad deeds, are reborn in heaven" (chapter 22).

These reports from local gods are verified by interrogators and compared with record books. Thus in the *Ti-tsang Shih-wang pao-chüan* (text 4 in Appendix I), we are told:

[Sinners] are dragged to the merciless Dark [Realm], where the Son of Heaven Yama asks about their karma. Then he calls for a judge to come and look at the record books, and from the beginning each item is compared [with the oral testimony]. Beating and cursing others is all entered in the book [reading *ma*, "to curse," for *ma*, "horse"], where every tiny sin is preserved. Every form of great and small sin is there; sins piled up like a mountain are clearly recorded.

This is followed by a list of such crimes and sins as stealing, sexual immorality, killing humans and animals, and opposing one's parents (p. 88).

All these texts assume that purgatorial punishments are appropriate for sins committed, with the most detail provided by the *Ti-tsang Shih-wang pao-chüan*, which lists twenty-one (rather than eighteen) sections of purgatory, each of which is characterized by a type of punishment, including the use of iron beds and clubs, molten copper poured into the mouth, and being thrown into pools of blood or excrement. Burning insects and ants in life leads to one's being burned in purgatory, talking too much results in having one's tongue pulled out, and looking at immoral sexual activity is punished by blinding. Twenty-seven such correlations are provided (pp. 21–22).

Sinners bring all this upon themselves. Of the fifth court, we are told that the bad are led there, then dragged off to suffer for their sins,

where they weep and wail in vain because they have brought their punishments upon themselves. Think: Though one has bought fields and gardens, is engaged in business, and has given birth to sons and daughters filling the home, they are not able to substitute for one in the sufferings of purgatory, and one cannot buy one's way out. We suffer entirely for our own sins. . . .

Though the sons and daughters in one's family [show their] filiality by wearing hempen [mourning clothes], and all of one's relatives weep for the dead soul, food offerings filling the main hall are offered in vain: One [still] suffers in the Yin offices. . . . When family members reach the tomb, they burn paper ingots and weep bitterly. They offer abundant ritual goods before the tomb, but the yin soul doesn't see them at all, much less do they reach its mouth. . . . [Such offerings] are simply swallowed in confusion by evil ghosts. . . . Offering livestock in sacrifice in fact harms the dead soul. (pp. 52–54)

The understanding of karma and purgatory in these books reinforces the conservative nature of their social perspective, in which women, the disabled, and the poor are understood to be suffering for their sins. Thus in the *Ti-tsang Shih-wang* text we read that after their punishments in purgatory are complete, sinners are reborn in the world of the living with such defects as harelips and cleft palates, "being unsteady on their feet, with erratic hand [movements], deaf, blind, hunched at the waist, with bent backs, mute, paralyzed," and with "insufficient food and clothing and no place to rest — [all] retributions of endless suffering" (p. 95).

Although sectarian "precious volumes" promise salvation to women as well as men, they share the traditional view that women are condemned to suffering in purgatory because of pollution caused by blood from childbirth. Thus the *Ti-tsang Shih-wang* book tells women, "If you wish to avoid the Pool of Blood [in purgatory], then observe many taboos. To escape being ground to powder in a mortar, women [should] practice rectitude and modesty" (p. 22). A bit more detail is provided in the *T'ai-shan Shih-wang* scripture, where the person touring purgatory sees sinners with "copper serpents coiling about them and iron dogs contending to bite them." He asks, "What bad karma did these people create in the Yang Realm to endure this suffering?" A purgatory lord replies, "These are women who, in giving birth to and caring for boys and girls, by rubbing breeches and washing pants[? character unidentified; perhaps read *hsi*] polluted pure water, so they share this punishment for their sins. . . . Women of the world, incline your ears to listen: The sin of giving birth to boys and girls is not light" (chapter 1).[10]

Here women are threatened not only with the traditional Pool of Blood but with other punishments as well. Nonetheless, our texts allow a way out of the double bind with which women were condemned by the very act most required of them by society. What we have summarized thus far is all standard popular religious material about karma and purgatory, but the most distinctive characteristic of sectarian teaching on this theme is its promise of deliverance from all this — with women specifically included.

Promises of deliverance for the pious are scattered throughout these books, where we are told that "the good are welcomed and [then] seen off by golden youths" and that the bad can escape purgatory by "being filial men and women who give allegiance to the orthodox Way of Maitreya" (*Ti-tsang Shih-wang pao-chüan*, pp. 22,

28). In this same book, Maitreya is also told that his parents are no longer in purgatory "but have both ascended to heaven, where they are both sitting together on a golden lotus" (p. 21). More such promises are found in the *T'ai-shan Shih-wang* book, where the devout are assured that maintaining a vegetarian diet enables one to escape the sufferings of purgatory and "transform purgatory into heaven. Heaven and purgatory are not separated by so much as an inch. Doing good or bad resides entirely in the mind" (chapter 1). Further,

Those with karmic affinity who encounter [this] true scripture will dissipate calamities and avoid difficulties. If one makes offerings to this *Ten Kings* book, one will not fall into the Dark Realm. The Tenth Emperor Yama says, "[I] reward the good and punish the bad. If people do not make mistakes, whether they are men or women, if they maintain a vegetarian diet and recite the Buddha's name, after a long time in the Yin offices they will not descend to the Nai-ho Bridge [that all the dead are supposed to cross]. Those who do good will rest on a lotus flower [in paradise]. (chapter 16)

But beyond these promises are those based on the power of sectarian deities and the mythology they represent—promises broader and collective in scope. For example, chapter 20 of the *T'ai-shan Shih-wang* scripture, which is entitled "Breaking Open Purgatory" (P'o-k'ai ti-yü), exhorts its readers:

Register your names at the Mount Ling Assembly so pure and cool, so pure and cool. A bright light penetrating Heaven and Earth illuminates the eighteen [courts of] purgatory and transforms them into celestial palaces. Swinging your arms, joyfully return to the Native Place, joyfully return to the Native Place. Awaken the little children to see their dear Mother and joyfully go to the Western Land.

This theme of collective liberation is the most distinctive sectarian contribution to discussions of purgatory and is well illustrated in chapter 42 of the *Mi-le ch'u-hsi pao-chüan* (text 5 in Appendix I), which is based on a visit by this buddha to the Dark Realm. Though the character *liao*, marking a completed state, is used twice in chapter 42, the book is set in the time of Maitreya's dispensation in the near future, so I suggest that this passage should be understood proleptically, as asserting a changed situation that is certain to occur.

The discussion is a characteristic mix of bureaucracy and drama: "At that time Maitreya left [i.e., will have left] heaven riding on a five-colored ray of bright light to reveal the details of beating [open]

purgatory. He descended there to save lost souls. He startled the Ten Kings, and Ti-tsang was uneasy on his seat." When patrolling deities in agitation announced to Ti-tsang that Maitreya was arriving, he "hastily told the Ten Yama Sons of Heaven, and demons great and small [were ordered] to sweep purgatory clean and set up tripod [burners] and incense altars. The Ten Kings and Ti-tsang went to the Demon Gate to receive [Maitreya], with great and small demons standing guard. When the Ancient Buddha arrived, he went to the Sen-lo Palace, where he sat in contemplation. The Ten Kings and Ti-tsang bowed before him" (chapter 42).

When asked why he had come, Maitreya began to preach the Dharma. As a result, all the souls there were saved, "the Ten Kings and Ti-tsang returned to heaven, and purgatory was transformed into a nine[-petaled] lotus palace." All types of beings in purgatory were delivered and its courts destroyed, and it was left entirely empty:

All the multitude of souls went together to the celestial palace. . . . When Maitreya descended to purgatory it was entirely emptied . . . [and] the Ten Kings and Ti-tsang all went to the Cloud City and attained buddhahood. . . . Maitreya gathered in all the souls of Heaven and Earth, so that all ascended to Heaven.

Thus purgatory, the major mode of afterlife in Chinese popular culture, is changed into the sectarian paradise.[11]

The seventeenth-century "precious volumes" discussed in this chapter represent the mature development of this type of popular scripture—a development characterized by confidence and by audacious imagination. Convinced of the correctness of their own beliefs, these works advocate the moral reform of the whole world of society and religion around them. Ordinary people, monks, priests, officials, and gods are all urged to repent of their old ways and save themselves by joining the sects and giving allegiance to their teachings. Even the dead can be saved retrospectively, through the piety of their descendants and the emptying of purgatory by sectarian gods. Thus the *pao-chüan* established their place in the world of Chinese religion.

CHAPTER SEVEN

The 'Dragon-Flower Scripture'
('Lung-hua ching')

The 1654 *Ku Fo T'ien-chen k'ao-cheng Lung-hua pao-ching* (Dragon-flower precious scripture verified by the Ancient Buddha T'ien-chen, hereafter "the *Lung-hua ching*") is in twenty-four chapters (*p'in*) in four volumes, with each volume called a "collection" (*chi*), named in succession after the four basic auspicious terms of the *I-ching*—*yuan*, *heng*, *li*, and *chen*. It was composed by a sect leader named Kung Ch'ang (a divided form of the surname Chang) who is understood to be a reincarnation of the Ancient Buddha T'ien-chen, who is in turn a transformation of the Venerable Patriarch Chen-wu, the Buddha of Measureless Life (Wu-liang shou Fo), and hence of Amitābha himself.

Kung Ch'ang lived in central Hopei province, in Ts'ao-ch'iao kuan (Ts'ao-ch'iao pass) of modern Kao-yang county. Through careful investigation, Sawada Mizuho has determined that Kung Ch'ang founded a sect called the Yuan-tun chiao (Religion of Complete and Instantaneous Enlightenment) in 1624, after receiving instruction from Wang Sen (d. 1619) of Shih-fo k'ou (Stone Buddha village) in Hopei, the leader of the Ta-ch'eng chiao (Mahāyāna sect). In the following years, Kung Ch'ang traveled about preaching and gathering disciples, so that by the mid-1630s his sect was well established. During his travels he collected various religious books, on the basis of which he began to write a scripture for his own sect in 1641. This task was completed by his disciples, who published the *Lung-hua*

ching in 1654. Sawada traces this book back in part to a ritual penance text, the *Ku Fo T'ien-chen shou-yuan chieh-kuo Lung-hua pao-ch'an*
(Dragon-flower precious penance, the results of gathering to completion by the Ancient Buddha T'ien-chen), which was offered to the
throne by a Buddhist monk in 1599.[1]

The *Lung-hua ching* is the most sophisticated and detailed of all
the early "precious volumes," called by Sawada the "*Lotus Sūtra* of
heretical texts."[2] I read a copy of this book in the Beijing Library in
1981, and with the cooperation of Susan Naquin obtained a complete
photocopy of it. (Each of us photocopied half of it, which was all we
were allowed to do.) In 1994, Wang Chien-ch'uan kindly sent me a
fine copy of this text in large characters. Li Shih-yü lists several editions of this book in his *Pao-chüan tsung-lu* (A comprehensive bibliography of "precious volumes," p. 12), while Sawada discusses two
editions published in the Republican period and provides a complete Japanese summary in his *Kōchu haja shōben* ("A detailed refutation of heresies," with corrections and commentary, pp. 109, 165–
218).

In this chapter I discuss (1) the organization and style of the *Lung-
hua ching*, (2) its exaltation of the Patriarch Kung Ch'ang, who made
it known, and (3) its self-understanding as a revealed scripture.
There are also sections on (4) the sectarian context of the book, (5) its
creation mythology, (6) its teachings about the end of the age, and
(7) its perspective on deities, meditation, incantations and charms,
and related topics. Though all these categories are, of course, interrelated, they provide a useful framework for dealing with this text.

ORGANIZATION AND STYLE

The *Lung-hua ching* is the best organized of the early "precious volumes" I have read. Its introductory material opens with an invocation for the peace and prosperity of the people, the harmony of wind
and rain, and long life for the emperor. This is followed by a "psalm
on raising incense" requesting all the buddhas to descend to the ritual arena. Then come eight "divine invocations" (*shen-chou*) for purifying the body, mouth, and mind, blessing water, dispelling pollution, purifying Heaven and Earth, and calming the spirits of the
earth, which is preceded by a "divine invocation for golden light" to
envelop the devotee's body.

All these are followed by the old Taoist-style command, "Quickly,
quickly, according to the regulations and ordinances" (*chi-chi ju lü-*

ling). Then there is invitation and homage to six buddhas and five Venerable Mothers. The buddhas are the Ancient Buddha of the Limitless, Śākyamuni, Maitreya, the King of the Dharma, (the Buddha of) Measureless Life, and the Ancient Buddha T'ien-chen. The Mothers are the Eternal Venerable Mother and the Venerable Mothers Kuan-yin, Ti-tsang, Mañjuśrī, and Samantabhadra.

There follow long prose summaries of the creation of the world and human relationships, the revelation of this scripture, and praise of its teachings. Next come four lines of seven-character verse, "verses for opening the scripture," and a long discussion of five different types of Dragon-Flower assemblies—in the "holy realm," Heaven, Earth, within the human body, and at the Native Place—all described in detail. A second set of "verses for opening the scripture," in forty lines of seven-character verse, follows to complete thirteen pages of introductory material.

Chapter 1 begins with its title, "Creative Chaos First Divided," followed by a prose discussion defining the terms in the title one character at a time. Then follows a creation account (translated below), also in prose, then forty-six lines of seven-character verse recapitulating much of the story. Next come four lines of five-character verse, a tune name, more praise of the creative work of the buddhas, and the name of Amitābha, twice repeated.

Chapter 2 is organized in much the same way, with definitions and prose discussion, but followed by four lines of seven-character verse and thirty-two lines composed in the 3/3/4 style. The succeeding chapters are organized in the same way, with most of their verse in the 3/3/4 style.

The language of the *Lung-hua ching* tends to be verbose and flowery, with much numerological listing of categories, as will be seen in some of the translations below.

The book ends with ten repayments, invocations of long life and peace for all, including the emperor, and passages such as the following:

The Ancient Buddha has sent down a bright light to receive and guide men and women, so that they together go to the Native Place. In the Tu-tou Palace they will never again think of the mundane and will be secure and at peace, with their destinies established. They will sit securely on golden lotuses, [hearing] the Eternal [Mother] preach the Dharma. They will see the mysterious aperture; a fragrant wind will surround them, and golden lotuses will spring up from the ground. Kung Ch'ang slowly said, "The hungry will obtain food, and the thirsty drink; the sick will get medicine; for those in difficulty, a bright light will be sent down, and the poor will obtain precious jewels. Little children will see their Mother and reach the shore on a Dharma boat. [Thus the children of] the imperial womb will return home." (chapter 24)

Homages follow to the Ancient Buddha T'ien-chen, Wu-sheng lao-mu, and the Venerable Mother Ti-tsang. T'ien-chen promises to descend to the world as a savior in the last age, and Ti-tsang promises to rescue all those in purgatory "so that they all are able to ascend to heaven," with nine generations of ancestors delivered to the Pure Land. Of the Venerable Mother, we read that she

has made a Dharma boat that constantly travels about the sea of suffering, calling the worthy and good to awaken, so that they soon ascend the other shore and together get on the Dharma boat [to join in] the third Dragon-Flower Assembly. . . .

May the nation prosper, the people be at peace, and the five grains be abundant. May there be loyal [ministers] and good [people] in the nation, with barbarians from all sides offering tribute. May all [tribes and nations] in the eight directions come to submit, the six states [= China] be at peace, and all outer demons destroyed. . . .

May mundane and holy from antiquity to the present, [all those in] purgatory and heaven from all directions, inconceivable, filling the Dharma realm, and [those in] the ninth-level lotus land, seek the Buddha and repent. May the myriad people be at peace, and may the teaching of the patriarchs flourish and be transmitted for ten thousand ages. [Thus] may all enter the Dragon-Flower ritual arena. (chapter 24)

THE PATRIARCH KUNG CH'ANG

Richard Shek discusses Kung Ch'ang as the founder of the Yuan-tun sect who was influenced by the well-known sectarian leader Wang Sen (d. 1619), from Stone Buddha village in Chih-li. Inspired by Wang, Kung Ch'ang traveled about China to gather his own disciples and search for scriptures, particularly from Wang Sen's followers. In the 1640s, Kung Ch'ang and his disciples began to compose their own scripture, based on these texts and the Patriarch's own revelations from the Eternal Mother.[3]

In the *Lung-hua ching*, Kung Ch'ang is described as a man whose spiritual perfection so impresses local deities that they send up a report about him. When this report reaches the Venerable Mother, she recognizes Kung Ch'ang as a reincarnation of the Buddha T'ien-chen. As the Patriarch sits in meditative absorption, his spirit ascends to Heaven, where he is given a sacred scripture to reveal on Earth. The Mother also commissions him to go on his missionary travels.

Some of the more important passages on this theme are as follows: in chapter 4 we are told that when the Stove God of Kung Ch'ang's household tells the Locality God that he is a good man, these two deities meet with the City God in his temple to discuss the situation. The Stove God says, "Because Kung Ch'ang's way and virtue are both complete, as is his good merit, I have respectfully come to discuss [his case]." The City God says, "Immediately prepare a memorial to be sent to report to the Perfected Officials." This report eventually reaches the Jade Emperor, who forwards it to the Mother, who says that Kung Ch'ang was "originally T'ien-chen descended to the mundane." She orders that his name be registered and that he be permitted to come to the Native Place.

The Patriarch's attainment of divine status is described in more detail in chapter 7:

The Mother of the Way, observing that Kung Ch'ang's six sense organs were pure and that his mundane body was entirely empty . . . plucked out the Dharma-nature of the Buddha T'ien-chen and placed it in Kung-Ch'ang's heart, so that the holy gave itself to the mundane and found a place to reside . . . [and the two] participated in each other and blended together in one place.

This transformation prepares the patriarch-to-be to be summoned to paradise. The Mother sends a "Dharma protector" to him while he is meditating in the scripture-hall in his home. After he has been summoned out of his trance, Kung Ch'ang says, "Holy messenger, what honorable business do you have in coming here?" The messenger replies, "In obedience to an imperial commission from the Matriarch (*tsu-mu*) in the Grand Imperial Palace of the Native Place, I have respectfully come with a golden tablet bearing a Dharma decree to summon you to come in person to receive the Dharma [teaching] from the Eternal [One]" (chapter 5).

Kung Ch'ang bows, thanks him for this sacred message, and, together with the Dharma protector, in an instant reaches the presence of the Matriarch, where the Dharma protector reports to her that Kung Ch'ang has arrived. The Matriarch "with her golden mouth" then commands Kung Ch'ang:

You have come home to open the precious [scripture] storehouse of the Celestial Prime, to take from it a precious object [in which] I transmit [the

proper way of] religious practice. I ask you, when you were in the Eastern
Land, in what stage of religious practice were you engaged? (reading *shih*,
"to lose," as *fu*, "male adult"). (chapter 5)

Kung Ch'ang replies, "Your child in the Eastern Land received
religious practice from Patriarch Wang of Stone Buddha [village],
who taught me the Three Refuges and the five precepts" (chapter 5).
The Mother continues:

I now transmit to you news for the Latter Realm, the pious task of setting
forth the details, which is not the same as before. I transmit this rare teaching to you so that you can select the pure to exchange it for the corrupt, ascend above and descend below. . . . [Thus the pious] will be able to see personally the Eternal One, transcending both buddhas and patriarchs, forever
to continue long life. I transmit to you ten forms of religious practice, to save
all living beings. (chapter 5)

Later in the text, while the Patriarch is again in a meditative trance,
the Mother commissions him to "extend the Way" (*chan-tao*) to Hunan, Yen-ching, and Nan-ching (Nanking), promising that she will
aid and accompany him (chapter 11). Thus his missionary journeys
begin.

The Patriarch's descent from a line of deities is discussed in
chapter 3, where we read:

The Matriarch ordered that at the beginning the Buddha Amitābha, master
of the teaching in the West, should move to the North to be in charge of the
teaching, with the title Buddha of Measureless Life. When the Buddha of
Measureless Life descended to the mundane, his title was the Venerable Patriarch Chen-wu [God of the North]. When Chen-wu descended to the
mundane, his title was the Ancient Buddha T'ien-chen. When T'ien-chen descended to the mundane, his title was the Venerable Patriarch Kung Ch'ang.
Now, when T'ien-chen from the holy was reborn into the mundane, he descended into a place in the central plains, south of Yen and north of Chao,
and dwelt at Ta-pao hamlet in Sang-yuan village at Ts'ao-ch'iao pass. The
Matriarch of the Native Place decreed this on a golden tablet and with her
wisdom eye saw off in the distance that there was a person of [proper] conduct, [so] the holy nature of T'ien-chen was reborn in the mundane, [into]
Kung Ch'ang, who daily reformed his character and mind. In the *chia-tzu*
year of the lower *yuan* period, he drew nigh to the Eastern Land. On the first
day of the first month, at the *tzu* hour, with a golden *t'ou-t'o*[4] he enlightened
his mind and nature, and a bright light appeared in the holy realm in the
southwest. Just when Kung Ch'ang was sitting in meditation, [T'ien-chen's]
holy nature lodged in his mundane [form].

Other passages describe Kung Ch'ang going to the celestial palace (chapter 8), establishing ritual arenas and Dragon-Flower assemblies (chapter 10), and receiving mantras and precious objects from the Mother (chapter 15), "transmitted to my son Kung Ch'ang to take when he descends in secret to the East to transform and benefit humans and gods." What she gives him is "news for the Latter Realm that has never been revealed before" (chapter 15).

THE SELF-UNDERSTANDING OF THE 'LUNG-HUA CHING' AS A REVEALED SCRIPTURE

Discussions of the role of the Patriarch are directly connected to the revelation and transmission of the *Lung-hua* scripture, which is described in some detail. The basic theme is stated in a line in the introductory material, "Buddhas and patriarchs appear in the world to bestow scriptures." In this case, at the Mother's command, T'ien-chen secretly descended to the East (i.e., the Eastern Land, or human realm) to "enter a mundane body" and, after becoming enlightened, as "the Venerable Patriarch Kung Ch'ang bestowed the *Lung-hua ching*" (chapter 3). We are also told that he narrated (*yen-shuo*) this scripture (chapter 12).

The self-understanding of the *Lung-hua ching* is summarized in its introductory material:

The Eternal [Mother] said, "This *Dragon-Flower Precious Volume* is from beginningless [time, when] creative chaos first divided. The Ancient Buddha T'ien-chen opened up the storehouse of precious [scriptures] of the Native Place, took out the *Dragon-Flower* true scripture, and transmitted it to later generations, to seek out and convert humans and gods and gather in all the ninety-six myriads of the sons and daughters of the imperial womb, [so that] they will be able to return home and recognize the patriarchs, penetrate to the root, return to the source, and forever continue long life. This scripture is the Dharma master of all scriptures, the true tradition of the myriad volumes. It embraces Heaven and Earth, and [in it] the myriad teachings are completed and clarified. Those who bestow and maintain [its teachings] with believing minds will see their [true] natures and enlighten their minds.

This book is divided into twenty-four chapters, each of which discusses the profound and marvelous. Each division of this book is in accord with the perfection of the saints; each verse [leads to] returning home and recognizing the patriarchs, while each phrase leads to awakening the nature so that it does away with all obstructions. What it expounds is the Great Way of the Prior Realm, while it discusses the karmic causation [operative in] the Latter Realm. It preaches the third Dragon-Flower Assembly and clarifies that the myriad teachings return to the root. After a long time, it will complete [the task] of gathering in [those of] the primal source. In the [time of] the last act, the myriad teachings will be one school—neither two nor three, but fundamentally one vehicle. [Thus] the Ancient Buddha appeared in the world to establish [this] school.

This introductory passage clarifies the divine origin of the scripture, but chapter 12 provides more detail about how the sources for the book were collected and edited by Kung Ch'ang and his followers. These sources were texts revealed in Shih-fo village to Wang Sen, here called the "Venerable Dharma King," who

descended in person from the Dragon Palace and at the Shih-fo district with his golden mouth transmitted and bestowed scriptures in the world. He secretly narrated the true inner workings . . . and after revealing these celestial secrets, in the *mou-wu* year [1618–1619] returned to the source and entered the [realm of] the holy. During his life he bestowed twelve hundred volumes of true scriptures. . . . [Later,] the Venerable Patriarch [Kung Ch'ang] went together with five "venerable ones" [= disciples] to the East to get scriptures. . . . There at Shih-fo, [by] Shadowless Mountain, when pious folk heard that the Patriarch had arrived, they came from all directions to venerate him. As the Venerable Patriarch preached of the inner power that penetrates the mind (*t'ou-hsin chi*), true scriptures spontaneously appeared. Once they had completed gathering scriptures, they all obtained merit, and for the last act [i.e., end of the age] there was a scripture. [He] authorized the *Dragon-Flower Scripture* to be transmitted to the world.

This account is repeated and extended in the following verse section, where we are told that, later, for the "*Lung-hua chüan* the blocks were cut, and it was printed, [so that] the Patriarch's teaching flourished" with the help of a disciple named Mu-tzu (a split of the surname Li) and "all the Guides" (*t'ou-hsing*) of the sect. Cyclical dates are provided for the whole process, equivalent to 1641–1642 for the beginning of the trip to collect scriptures, 1652–1653 for their discovery at Shih-fo village, and 1654–1655 for the printing of the text.

Chapter 12 of the *Lung-hua ching* next provides the names of thirty-two scriptures that the Patriarch found, and adds,

The Buddha posted the names of the true scriptures of the Lotus school. Kung Ch'ang examined these scriptures, connected, examined, and compared them, and saw their celestial perfection. He blended together these true scriptures, the better to pass through their barriers and fords. The *Dragon-Flower Precious Scripture* is a basket embracing all the myriad teachings.

A succeeding prose section provides another fanciful list of scriptures obtained from various celestial palaces and earthly locations, "all of which were true scriptures" that, when recited, enable the pious to escape purgatory, avoid all obstacles and disasters, and attain eternal life and enlightenment, "forever to meet together at the Dragon-Flower." Chapter 12 ends with instructions from the Patriarch to his disciples to copy, edit, and preach this scripture to save all, and to solicit funds for its printing and circulation so that "all schools will together proclaim [this] precious volume."

In chapter 24, we are told that the *Lung-hua ching* was bestowed by the Patriarch to establish the teaching after his death:

> I order you Guides to all unite your hearts [in this task], so that you and I join hands to have the blocks cut and [the scripture] printed, [so that] later the Dragon-Flower Assembly [i.e., the sect] will have inexhaustible blessings. . . . When you think of me, opening and reading this scripture will be the same as seeing the Patriarch; and when I in the holy realm think of you, I will see you clearly. But now I ask you, who will cut the blocks? Who together with me will promote the Patriarch's teaching?

In these passages we see the self-confident spirit of the *Lung-hua ching*, which claims to include and so supersede the teachings of all other scriptures.

THE SECTARIAN CONTEXT OF THE 'LUNG-HUA CHING'

The *Lung-hua* scripture refers frequently to sectarian names, titles, and teachings. Ordinary members are called "those who possess the Way" (*yu tao-jen*) or the "people of the Way in the assembly/ congregation" (*hui-hsia tao-jen*). Chapter 20 provides a list of ten titles of sect leaders below the level of patriarch: *hsu-teng* ("continuer of the lamp"), *ling-hsiu* ("leader"), *tsung-hui* ("overseer of a congregation"), *k'ai-shih* ("instructor"), *ching-chu* ("scripture master"), *hui-t'ou* ("congregation head"), *hui-chu* ("congregation chief"), *ling-chung* ("leader of the multitudes"), *tsou-tao* ("walker of the Way" or "furtherer of the Way"), *t'an-chu* ("altar chief"), and *hsiang-t'ou* ("incense head"). There is a similar list in chapter 16, but neither includes *t'ou-hsing* ("guide"), the title most commonly used in the *Lung-hua ching*. The sects themselves are referred to in numerical sets — three schools, five sects (*p'ai*), nine stems, and eighteen branches (chapter 16).

The central function of these leaders is to follow Maitreya in continuing the teaching in the last age:

The Buddha said, "Who can continue [the transmission of the teaching]?" The Venerable Patriarch T'ien-chen, understanding the Buddha's mind-seal, continued transmitting the lamp. He lit the lamp of wisdom in front of him and by its illumination saw that his fundamental nature was a spirit in the sacred place of the center. Now in parallel with the patriarchs, worthies, and saints, he has established the teaching in accord with the apex [period of cosmic time] to save humans and gods. Then with his hand he picked up a precious flower of the Celestial Prime and said, "Who will receive and continue [the task]?" Then all the *ling-hsiu* and *t'ou-hsing* (leaders and guides) of the three schools, five sects, nine stems, and eighteen branches said that they would undertake the task, [declaring,] "Your disciples are all able to receive and continue transmitting the lamp." Thus all of them lit the lamps of wisdom in front of them and in their illumination saw that their original faces [i.e., natures] were exactly the same as those of the previous buddhas and patriarchs. (chapter 13)

In addition to these terms and titles, the sectarian context of the *Lung-hua ching* is indicated by references to those within and outside the group, by its description of its own patriarchal tradition, and by lists of the names of other similar groups. The distinction between insiders and outsiders is much the same as that for the other texts already discussed in this study, such as that between those who have the Way and those who don't (chapter 7). There are also differences between those with and without merit, true patriarchs and false patriarchs (*chen tsu-shih* and *chia tsu-shih*; chapter 20), and those who have or lack karmic affinity for response to the saving message (chapter 21).

All this is reinforced by frequent references to sect leaders and congregations, as discussed above. The sharpest statement of this sense of difference is that in chapter 10, between "the sons and daughters of the imperial womb in the whole world who recognize the celestial perfected ones, and disciples of the devil (*mo t'u-tzu*) who are haughty and arrogant and who engage in reckless talk."

The line of patriarchal transmission claimed by this scripture is discussed in most detail in chapter 16, entitled "The Patriarchs Continue the Lotus School." The line of succession here moves from the Holy Patriarch of the Limitless (Wu-chi sheng-tsu) to the patriarchs of the Great and Imperial ultimates (that is, the three founding buddhas of this literature), and on to the "Dharma King Stone-Buddha" (i.e., Wang Sen), the Venerable Patriarch T'ien-chen, Elder Sister Chang Ts'ui-hua, and then to Kung Ch'ang himself. Each of these leaders is said to have attained enlightenment and continued the tradition.

Kung Ch'ang's work is, in turn, continued by the Guides of the three schools, five sects, nine stems, and eighteen branches, each of which established schools or sects to save others. They each "endorsed the Lotus school" (*p'i-hsia lien-tsung*) and vowed to continue the "school of the inner nature" (*hsing-tsung*) and to understand the "mind-seal" of the Patriarch—that is, the inner intention of the teaching transmitted directly from master to disciple. "Lotus school" refers to the Pure Land tradition. The term "White Lotus" is not used.

Chapter 16 continues with a numerological discussion of the number of patriarchs in the assemblies in each of the three time periods. In the assembly of the Patriarch Wang, Guides of the "three flowers and five leaves . . . continued the Lotus tradition, transmitting the Dharma on behalf of the Patriarch." They were followed by T'ien-chen, here listed again as a patriarch, who in turn was succeeded by Elder Sister Chang, in whose assembly there were "ten good great protectors of the Dharma." She in turn preceded the Patriarch Kung Ch'ang, who was assisted by all the types of sect leaders listed above. The culmination of this sequence is continuation of the tradition by ordinary people:

The common people of the world (*t'ien-hsia shu-min*) each continue the tradition of the patriarchs, which until today has not been extinguished. The patriarchal teaching is flourishing and spreading, and in [this time of] the last act, all will come to China in the central realm, recognize the patriarchs and return to the root, and register their names and titles.[5]

The names of the eighteen religious groups and their founders are listed in chapter 23, including those of the Lord Lao (Taoism) and Bodhidharma, the Hung-yang sect with its patriarch P'iao-kao, the Wu-wei sect and its Ssu-wei (Lo) Tsu, the Stone-Buddha Patriarch of the Ta-ch'eng sect, and P'u-shan of the Yuan-tun teaching. Two women founders are included in this list: the Bodhisattva Lü of the West Ta-ch'eng sect, and a "Mother Nan-yang" of the Nan-yang teaching. All these leaders are said to have "saved sons and daughters" so that they

take refuge in Buddhism and meet together at the Dragon-Flower [Assembly]. . . . All the buddhas and the myriad patriarchs have come in the same way to the human realm to steer Dharma boats. Their many sects each save [those in] all the ten directions, so that they are at peace in the holy place of the third Dragon-Flower Assembly. The Ancient Buddha T'ien-chen at the end of the age gathers them all together.

Here earlier religious traditions are affirmed, summed up, and superseded by the teachings of this book, a theme repeated in chapter 24, where we are told that "the myriad teachings return to one, the Ancient Buddha T'ien-chen."

The sectarian context of the *Lung-hua ching* is also indicated in accounts of Kung Ch'ang's preaching missions to other parts of China, where he is welcomed by those who have already heard of his teaching. When he goes to the vicinity of Nanking, he is met by a Patriarch Nan-hsia leading nine disciples, who tell him they have all had the same dream about his coming. After he explains the meaning of their dream before they have told him its details, they all "take refuge in his teaching." The next morning, "people of the Way from each congregation" in the area gather together—"men and women, old and young"—to ask the Patriarch to predict their salvation as he had done with the nine. This "made the Patriarch very happy, and when he wanted to leave they all detained him, so he stayed on several more days."

He next goes to Mount Wu-tang (in Hupei province), where he is welcomed by Taoists and joins in discussion with them. At the Patriarch's invitation, Taoist "Perfected and Friends of the Way" accompany him to Ssu-ch'uan. When they reach Mount O-mei, Kung Ch'ang is met by a Patriarch Ch'ao-yuan who knew in advance of his arrival. When four patriarchs who come to meet with him express sympathy for the difficulty of his travels, Kung Ch'ang says, "I am obeying a commission from the Matriarch, which I dare not oppose." He proceeds to preach to them over a seven-day period, authorizing them to "investigate and match titles of the Lotus school" and promising that in the future they will meet together at the Dragon-Flower Assembly.

As the *Lung-hua ching* puts it, "When his holy work was completed, the Patriarch took leave of the multitude of the Perfected and descended the mountain." There he is greeted by a Guide named P'u-liang who has gathered devotees from eighteen households, who all bow and say that they have been waiting for him. They have arranged a nine-day Dragon-Flower Assembly to welcome him. When he sees the multitudes who have come to take refuge, he preaches to them and prays to the buddhas and patriarchs of the Native Place to fulfill his vow (to save all). He tells them that next he is going to Yang-chou (in Kiangsu province) to "prepare a great assembly for gathering in [those of] the source" (chapter 11).

Here the Patriarch Kung Ch'ang is portrayed as a traveling evangelist who crisscrosses China from "Hu-kuang in the south to Yen-ching in the north, to the east coast in the east to Ssu-ch'uan in the west." Wherever he goes he is welcomed by devotees of other sects, which is intended as further confirmation of this scripture's claim that its teachings are the culmination of all other teachings. The *Lung-hua ching* is "the end-time news, in which the myriad teachings all return to one place, one buddha appears in the world, and one boat saves all. When this point has been reached, there are no distinctions" (chapter 15).

CREATION MYTHOLOGY

The *Lung-hua ching* contains the most complete discussion of creation mythology in early *pao-chüan* literature. In it, transformations of cosmic *ch'i* ("vital force") produce the Ancient Buddha T'ien-chen, who in turn puts the world in order. Human beings appear through the interactions of yin and yang, which are personified as the children of the Venerable Mother, Nü Wa and Fu Hsi, two ancient Chinese culture heroes (described in more detail below). Though Nü Wa and Fu Hsi's children are technically the Mother's grandchildren, this point is not emphasized; rather, we are told that, after she sent them down to people the Earth, they lost their way and forgot their divine origin. Thus the Mother calls them back home. Here, as in other religious traditions, the real point of creation myth is to provide background for the drama of salvation in the present.

In the *Lung-hua ching*, the creation story appears in the introductory section near the beginning of the book:

Gathered *ch'i* completed forms, and when in the midst of *ch'i* an apex was produced, a bright light first appeared, and [so] being was produced from the midst of nonbeing. From before the beginning there were originally no buddhas or patriarchs, yin or yang, Heaven or Earth. There were no sun or moon, above or below, east, west, south, or north. There were no spring or autumn, winter cold or summer heat, nor were there men or women. Originally there was not one thing. After the [water of the] completely bright sea of awakening settled and became clear, pure and impure were distinguished. In the midst of perfect emptiness, there was refined out a ray of golden light. Through the gathering of this light, bodies were formed, and accumulated *ch'i* made forms. . . .

With the coming of the Ancient Buddha T'ien-chen, a precious inter-locking net spread out and a bright light soared up and glistened. There were many forms of transformation, all of them transformations of perfect emptiness, which was able to put all things in place. When the single *ch'i* of the Prior Realm arose, it was able to produce clouds. Clouds were able to produce rain, and rain, earth. Earth was able to produce stones, and stones, fire. Fire produced a brilliant light, from which the Buddha was trans-formed. His body was [of] the same [*ch'i*] as all. [Thus] the Buddha appeared in the world, with inexhaustible transformations.

The Ancient Buddha established the world, and right on until the present [he] is able to put the universe in place and establish the [human] world. A single *ch'i* produced the perfect sun, and the perfect *ch'i* of the Prior Realm congealed and formed a bead of golden elixir. To enlighten the multitude of the blind, [the Ancient Buddha] took a golden-elixir enlightenment seed to hold in his hand. With a mouthful of perfect *ch'i* he blew it into the water, where from the waves perfect earth sprang forth. The earth is the mother. Without earth the myriad things would not be produced, [because] they arise from the midst of the earth.

This account continues in chapter 1, which opens with the lines:

The Ancient Buddha T'ien-chen divided the chaotic prime;
Out of an egg an apex arose, which by transformation [produced]
    the Prior Realm.

Here we are told that the Ancient Buddha created rivers and moun-tains, the sun, moon, stars, and planets, the Five Phases and the "roots of the patriarchs (*tsu-ken*)."

The creation of humankind is recounted in chapter 2:

Yin and yang matching each other were male and female, marrying and nourishing the children of the holy womb. The way of *ch'ien* became a man and the *k'un* way became a woman. They gave birth to ninety-six myriads (*i*) of sons and daughters of the imperial womb.

Wu-sheng lao-mu instructed her sons and daughters, "Because the world is cold and quiet, empty, with no smoke of human habitation, you must go to dwell in the Eastern Land." Her sons and daughters obeyed this primal command of the Mother and, each adorned with precious objects, their bodies covered with light, came to the Eastern Land. They had no heart for dwelling in the world, where they thought of their parents. Each relying on their primal light, they traveled back and forth from the Eastern Land to the Western Realm, happily doing what they pleased.

However, the Mother repents of her action and orders her children to return immediately:

The Mother heard that when they came to the Eastern Land they married, and wine, sex, wealth, and anger blocked their perfect hearts. . . . Sons and daughters of the Native Place were emotionally attached to the red dust [world]. They entered wombs [in rebirth] and buried their divine roots. Thus they have acted until today. Their Amitābha self-natures have fallen into the sea of suffering, where they have been profoundly lost and submerged [i.e., infatuated] for accumulated eons. Happy in the Eastern Land, they do not think of the Eternal One, and so are endlessly reborn and dying in saṃsāra. When our Buddha saw them, he vowed to save them and summoned the primal ones to awaken and together go home. The Mother hoped [for their return], anxious day after day, [wondering] when all would be gathered together and return to the [celestial] palace. She ordered her sons and daughters to quickly repent and [sent] them a letter from home so that they would know to quickly come to meet together at the third Dragon-Flower Assembly. . . .

The Venerable Eternal One put in order the Five Phases and produced the six lines [of the *I-ching* hexagrams], the seven regulators [the sun, moon, and the five inner planets], the eight trigrams, and the nine palaces [dwellings of stellar deities?]. . . .

She put human relationships in order and matched yin and yang to produce forms. Fu Hsi and Nü Wa married and gave birth to ninety-six *i* of children and grandchildren. (chapter 2)

Fu Hsi and Nü Wa are ancient culture heroes who, by the Han period, were discussed as consorts and exemplars of marriage.[6] Another passage in chapter 2 of the *Lung-hua* scripture clearly indicates its understanding of their relationship to yin and yang:

The yin and yang given birth to by the Mother originally had no names, so she called them Nü Wa and Fu Hsi, the ancestors of human ability (*jen-neng chih tsu*). The Ancient Buddha T'ien-chen of the Limitless, while he was seated in the Tu-tou Palace in the Grand Imperial Heaven, invited the Venerable Eternal Mother to come for a consultation. He ordered Nü Wa and Fu Hsi, as male and female, to marry.

The fall of humans from their original divine status is restated on another page of chapter 2 and in chapter 4, as follows:

When the Ancient Buddha first established the universe, ninety-six *i* of people dwelt in the Eastern Land. Until the present they have restricted their complete and brilliant light and fallen into the red dust, where wine, sex, and wealth have confused their natures, [so that] they do not return. (chapter 2)

At first, everyone walked in the holy [realm] and all saw the Eternal Parents. Bright light illuminated the bodies of all, and they came and went as they pleased. They were spiritually independent everywhere, with no impediments or obstacles. But because these immortals and buddhas [began to] covet luxuries and became attached to sex, contended for fame, snatched for profit, and were jealous, flattering, and dishonest, they were unenlightened, with their [original] bright light blocked. Obscuring and rejecting their previous karmic connections, they no longer thought of their parents and lost their Native Place. The Patriarch said, "You must think about the Native Place. I want you to inquire of an enlightened teacher who will point out to you how you come at birth and leave at death, who will transmit to you an opening and a path. I also want you to be diligent day and night and to ceaselessly think about [i.e., long for] the Eternal One." (chapter 4)

This creation myth establishes both the deep cosmic background claimed by this scripture and its advocacy of the Patriarch Kung Ch'ang as a manifestation of the creator-buddha T'ien-chen. Its discussion of the moral decline of humankind sets the stage for the message of salvation at the end of the age.

THE END OF THE AGE

The framework of cosmic time in the *Lung-hua ching* begins with the three successive periods, each presided over by a buddha, that have been discussed in earlier chapters of the present volume. As we have seen, in this scripture additional stages follow the reign of Maitreya, whose work is continued by sect patriarchs and members, so that here Maitreya is located in the recent past rather than in the future. Within this framework, the message of the *Lung-hua ching* is set in a time of chaos and destruction that only the pious will survive. The detailed discussion of this end time in the *Lung-hua ching* continues and expands treatments of this theme in earlier "precious volumes."

The time frame is laid out in chapter 13, which is entitled "The Three Buddhas Continue the Lamp [of the Teaching]." The first buddha is, of course, the "Ancient Lamplighter Buddha" Dīpaṃkara, who "first apportioned and ordered the world" and arranged a Dragon-Flower Assembly at which all the buddhas were gathered. His rule lasted nine kalpas and was symbolized by a green lotus with three petals. When he asks who can continue the task, Śākyamuni replies that he can, so he continues the tradition for another eighteen eons, in which a five-petaled red lotus blossoms. As celestial time moved in its cycles, Maitreya responds to Śākyamuni's call and presides over the "Constellation World" for eighty-one kalpas, here described as the *mo-chieh* ("end kalpa") and symbolized by the opening of a golden lotus with nine petals. Maitreya is succeeded by the Venerable Patriarch T'ien-chen, who is followed by the leaders of the sects and branches of the tradition. Each of the buddhas and T'ien-chen is said to have "established the teaching to match the apex" (*tang-chi li-chiao*), to proclaim the message anew at each node of cosmic time.

The end time during which this book was revealed is described in chapters 11 and 18. The setting in chapter 11 is Pien-liang (Kaifeng), with the Patriarch Kung Ch'ang seated in meditation at a street intersection, surrounded by a brilliant light that draws the attention of passersby:

After a long time, the Patriarch broke into song: "The mute patriarch is in perfect *samādhi*, with all his bodily gateways tightly closed. He swallows the medicine of the Prior Realm, which glistens, overturns, and lets fall a lotus. With the flower of his mind mirror-bright, he has begun to preach the profound and marvelous, coming from south and north to transmit the Way. This morning I am saving those with karmic affinity and transmit to you the Way of the Prior Realm. I open the pass [out of] death and rebirth. Seek within the way out, [let your spirit] penetrate through the *ni-wan* (aperture at the top of the head). Primal ones, open wide your eyes and quickly come to recognize Kung Ch'ang [as Patriarch]; do not worry about seeking a way out; stop the restlessness of your hands and feet. The end of the age (*mo-chieh*) is about to arrive; each of you must protect yourself." When the Patriarch's song ended, the men and women of the whole city came to venerate [him] as a patriarch of Heaven and Earth, and asked him why he had come. The Patriarch said, "I have come to transmit the faith (*ch'uan-hsin*). The end of the age will soon arrive. Where will you find peace for yourselves and establish your destiny? In your midst is a patriarch who has undertaken a celestial task; the one whom you recognize is [the Buddha] T'ien-chen descended to the mundane."

Thus he led many men and women to receive the Dharma, take refuge, and have their salvation predicted. Then the Patriarch, taking leave of the multitude, arose, and all the people of the Way returned home, weeping. (chapter 11)

More details of the message are presented in chapter 18, which again opens with the Patriarch absorbed in meditation. His spirit goes to the Native Place to have an audience with Wu-sheng lao-mu:

The Mother asked Kung Ch'ang, "Do you know about the disasters occurring in the realm below?" [He replied,] "Your child does not know." The Matriarch then explained, "Kalpic disasters will arrive in the *chia-tzu* year of the lower *yuan* period, and in the *hsin-ssu* year there will be famines, droughts, and floods, with no harvests. The people of Shantung will eat humans, and in that year everyone will die leaning on their walls. [In that time] husbands and wives will not look after each other, and fathers and sons will separate [i.e., be alienated from each other]. When [these disasters] reach northern Chih-li, people will again die of famine."

K'ung Chang asked the Venerable Mother, "When will it be possible to pass through [these sufferings]?" [She replied,] "In the *jen-wu* year it will be better, and people will again be able to make it. But then there will be a further year of disaster, toil, and illness. Mountains will waver and the earth move. The Yellow River will overflow, causing people to die [reading *ssu* as a transitive verb]. There will be plagues of locusts with continuous clouds and rain. Houses will collapse and there will be no place to find safety. Encountering these years of disaster at the end of the age is to test people's minds. [Since these calamities are the result of] five hundred years of accumulated karmic faults, they have been brought on people by their own actions; there is no way of release [from them]. If this reaches the *kuei-wei* year, there will be more epidemics."

Kung Ch'ang then said to the Mother, "How can [people be] rescued and released from these calamities [reading *pei*, "north," as *tz'u*, "this")?" The Mother said, "Those who study will not be harmed by these calamities, and for children of the Way who cultivate good karma, [such] disasters will not cause difficulty." (chapter 18)

This passage continues with more promises of divine aid. The Mother gives mantras to Kung Ch'ang, telling him to transmit them to all, and adds instructions on the interior circulation of *ch'i* that will protect from epidemics. The charms she bestows are to be worn by all.

In chapter 19, we are told that the sins of humans so angered the gods that they sent down calamities as punishment:

Because in the years at the end of the age people's minds are treacherous and crafty, extraordinarily clever, with a hundred cheating schemes; [because] the minds of men and women are not honest and steadfast; and [because they] are constantly involved with opportunistic schemes and [their own] opinions, and among a hundred people there is not one with good intentions — [for these reasons] the celestial gods were angered and sent down all forms of calamities to test living beings. However, they still did not turn around to incline toward goodness and still did not understand [the need for] enlightenment. Thus it is that now, as the end of the age draws near, it is to be feared that people will lose their lives. Because of this the Venerable Ancient Buddha of the Native Place, who could not bear this, sent [the

Bodhisattva] Ju-t'ung [a rebirth form of Confucius] to descend to the mundane world to transform all humans in the world so that, from that time on, they would reform their evils and faults.

In chapter 21, it is the Lord Lao who is sent down by the Mother to make "Dharma boats" to save all, so here the founding sages of both Confucianism and Taoism are drafted to assist with the task of salvation in the end-time crisis.

All of this leads to a great Dragon-Flower Assembly in which all the pious are gathered, with their names registered in paradise. As we read in chapter 11:

If those with karmic affinity day and night recite [this] true scripture for all twelve [Chinese] hours of the day without ceasing, and if they are able to recite the Buddha's name, then when death approaches they will escape Lord Yama. All the pious come to worship T'ien-chen, [who as] Kung Ch'ang is hidden in the human world. The primal ones follow the Patriarch to the Dragon-Flower [Assembly] and together reach Maitreya's court in the Native Place, where for eighty-one eons they will escape Lord Yama [repeated] . . . [and] continue long life . . . and as companions of the Ancient Buddha will not descend to be reborn. . . . When they reach the Native Place, little children will see the Mother's face.

Here, as in the indigenous Buddhist scriptures discussed in Chapter One above, the path to salvation at the end of the age lies in the intensification of ordinary piety.

OTHER THEMES IN THE 'LUNG-HUA CHING'

Other themes characteristic of the *Lung-hua ching* for which there is somewhat less material include the names and activities of deities and discussions of meditation and charms.

The chief deities of this book are the Venerable Ancient Buddha and the Eternal Venerable Mother—followed, in a list in chapter 8, by Dīpaṃkara, Śākyamuni, Maitreya, Kuan-yin, Amitābha, the Great Dharma King, the Buddha of Measureless Life, and the T'ien-chen Buddha. Then come the Lord Lao, the Sage K'ung (Confucius), the Venerable Old Woman Huang (in Taoism, the Goddess of the Spleen), the Venerable Metal Lord (alchemical lead), the Small Infant, the Small Young Girl (*ch'a-nü*; symbol of alchemical mercury), Fu-hsi, Nü-wa, the Patriarch Kung Ch'ang, and his disciple Mu-tzu, "who promulgated the teaching."

Here deities from Buddhism, Taoism, and Confucianism are made a part of sectarian teaching and subordinated to it in a sequence that leads to the revealing patriarch of this book. The incorporation of deities from Taoist alchemy is related to the meditative practices advocated by the *Lung-hua ching* (as discussed below).

Throughout this book, it is the Venerable Mother and the Ancient Buddha who give commands to other deities and buddhas, as in a passage in chapter 12 where they command the buddhas of the three time periods to "continue the Lotus tradition and transmit the Dharma everywhere." Other divine beings are also instructed to line up in ranks at the celestial court: the Exalted Immortals of the Limitless, the Three Pure Ones Jade Emperor (here conflated), the Most High Lord Lao, buddhas, patriarchs, bodhisattvas, arhats, perfected ones, Mañjuśrī, Samantabhadra, Ti-tsang, Kuan-yin, devas and nāgas of the eight regions, the God of Longevity of the Southern Apex, the God of the Dark Heaven of the North, enlightened kings, good deities who protect the Dharma, and "the myriad gods." These lists are not systematic, but their clear intent is to include all the gods as supporters of this book and its message.

Two other points should be made in this discussion of deities, the first of which is that several are called *mu* ("mother") in addition to the Venerable Mother herself, a pattern we have seen before in earlier *pao-chüan*. These include Wan-shou mu (Mother of Eternal Life), Yuan-tun mu (Mother of Complete and Instantaneous Enlightenment), Ti-hua mu (Earth-Flower Mother), Chin-hua mu (Golden-Flower Mother) and the bodhisattvas Kuan-yin, Ti-tsang, Mañjuśrī, and Samantabhadra, all of whom are also called "Mother" (chapters 20 and 21). The ancient goddess the Queen Mother of the West is noted as having established the Jasper Pool, a paradisal realm (chapter 17).

The powers and functions of these deities are not discussed; rather, their presence in the *Lung-hua ching* is part of the effort to include all possible sacred symbols, traditional and invented, in support of the scripture itself. In some later sectarian traditions, the Queen Mother of the West is equated with the Venerable Mother, who is given the title Yao-ch'ih chin-mu (Golden Mother of the Jasper Pool). I take these multiple mothers to be an expression of a tendency to feminize sectarian deities under the influence of the veneration of the Eternal Mother.

The second interesting theme here is that of the Buddha Ju-t'ung (Confucian Youth) as a rebirth of Confucius who travels about as a sectarian evangelist. All of chapter 19 is devoted to this figure, of whom we read:

Confucianism, Buddhism, and Taoism divided into the three teachings, and the sages of these teachings each had one explanation (*ke yu i-shuo*). . . . When the Sage [Confucius] established [his] teaching, he traveled about on horseback transmitting the Way. Later, the Buddha Ju-t'ung appeared in the world. He was a transformation-appearance of the Sage. He [also] traveled about on horseback to transmit the Way, going about to all the states, transforming the ignorant into the wise. He went from door to door delivering the faith (*sung hsin*), seeking out and saving humans and gods, calling the people of the world to awaken, maintain a vegetarian diet, [and] recite the Buddha's name, reform their evil, and move toward goodness. . . . The Lord Lao . . . saved all the immortals. . . . Śākyamuni saved the monks and nuns . . . and the Sage saved lay households. . . . [He was] the Sage K'ung descended to the mundane as Ju-t'ung, followed by all the worthies and sages.

The lines that follow these enlist Confucius's favorite disciples Tzu-lu, Yen-hui, and Tseng-tzu, as well as his "three thousand students" and Mencius, in the cause of "preaching the Dharma and turning the Dharma Wheel in the midst of all their activities." Thus these supreme symbols of orthodoxy are put to the service of sectarian teaching and are honored for their support of lay religion in the midst of ordinary social life.

We have already seen several references to the Patriarch Kung Ch'ang's receiving revelations while absorbed in meditation; a few passages discuss this practice in more detail:

The Patriarch was sitting with his legs crossed on a meditation mat. Each day he carried out this practice, exactly in accord with the jade instructions [of the Mother]. Preserving and settling his patriarchal *ch'i*, he was majestic and unmoved. He observed fixedly a thin wooden stir-stick rotating water [*sic*] and ascended above and below, [*sic*] penetrating mountains and seas, revolving [through] the world. He stopped his breathing, closed firmly his six gateways [to the outside], and opened the passes and openings [within his body]. He broke open his manifestation body, and on the K'un-lun peak (at the top of his head) made an opening for the ascent of his primal spirit. He manifested his golden body and suddenly attained a great awakening. (chapter 8)

The Taoist flavor of this passage is amplified in chapter 18, in which the Venerable Mother gives instructions for surviving the calamities at the end of the age. In addition to promising that those who study will escape difficulties and be aided by Dharma-protecting deities, the Mother says,

So that you can be rescued and spared, I will transmit mantras and oral instructions to you that are to be passed on everywhere to the men and women of the great earth. Each day swallow the ch'i of the Prior Realm [by] every morning taking the vital essence of the sun and swallowing it so that it returns to the belly, where it revolves with inexhaustible wonderful [effect]. If one does this constantly, disasters and epidemics will not be able to invade.

This exhortation is repeated in instructions from Kung Ch'ang, who adds that it will "protect the residence of the spirits [of the body], preserve one's life span, and guard the body." These practices, together with the use of written charms, will also prolong life, dispel disasters and illness, and bring peace to the spirit (shen).

In a Taoist context, the term "shen" could refer to gods resident in the body, but such a belief is not discussed in any detail in the Lung-hua ching. This interpretation is supported by a passage in chapter 6 that mentions the "six ting and chia spirits within my body," which are correlated with six deities of the eyes, ears, nose, tongue, mind/heart, and will, who are invoked so that sight, hearing, and speech will be clear and so that the mind and the will will be penetrating. These are not Taoist-style gods of bodily organs but metaphysical and numerological references, none of which is explained. These and the alchemical deities noted above are good examples of the tendency in pao-chüan literature to borrow terms and deities from other traditions for their sanctioning and protecting effect, with little attention to their functions in their original contexts.

The eight opening invocations of the Lung-hua ching were noted at the beginning of this chapter. Their tone is well expressed by those for calming the spirits of the earth and purifying the mind:

May the [Celestial Emperor] of the Primal Beginning calm and subdue, and proclaim to all the myriad spirits—[those of] the peaks and rivers, perfected officials, spirits of the locality and earth, and spirits of the land on the left and grain on the right—that they should not be disturbed and afraid. . . . They should return to the true Way, [and so] be purified within and without, each calm and settled in its position, so [as] to protect [our] households. The Most High has [issued] commands that evil spirits are to be sought out and seized, and that the divine kings who protect the Dharma [also] protect those who recite [this] scripture. Take refuge in the Great Way to enjoy auspicious blessings—quickly, quickly, according to the regulations and commands. (introductory material)

A more personal focus can be seen in a parallel invocation for purifying the mind of the devotee:

May the most high terrace star (*t'ai-hsing*)[7] ceaselessly respond to changes, drive away crooked harmful forces, and bind up demons. May it protect my life and body. May [I be] wise, intelligent, enlightened, and pure, with the spirit of my mind at peace. May my three *hun* spirits last forever, and my *p'o* forces not be lost or exhausted—quickly, quickly, according to the regulations and commands. (introductory material)

In addition to such invocations, the *Lung-hua* scripture prescribes the distribution of charms to protect the faithful at the end of the age. Though they are not discussed in detail, we are told that they were bestowed by the Mother through Kung Ch'ang:

To all of the worthy and good people in the congregation, old and young, [I] give efficacious writings to save eighty-four thousand of those with karmic affinity, so that they can avoid all forms of disaster and calamity. Within and without the city, in shops, roads, and villages, [these charms] will rescue the primal ones and save all living beings. I order all Guides to faithfully bestow, uphold, and put into practice [these charms]. Each person should obey, preserve, remember, and carry them out in religious practice. (chapter 18)

This same chapter notes that the Patriarch distributed efficacious charms (*ling-fu*) that, when swallowed, ward off disaster. Since these charms are alternatively called "efficacious writings" (*ling-wen*), we know that they were written out, but their wording is not described. However, we are told that they are to be worn at the waist by those in the congregation, which reflects old Taoist practice.

Although the *Lung-hua ching* is focused on sect members and those predestined by their karma to respond to its message, it includes a universal message as well, which is clearly stated in a quotation attributed to the Buddha in the introductory material of the book:

The Buddha said, "As for all the various schools, without regard to whether [their adherents] have left the household life or stayed within it, all living beings in the world should together form Dragon-Flower assemblies."

This combination of universal appeal with promises of salvation, supported by congregations of the pious, was reinforced in detail by the *Lung-hua ching* and continued in other texts in the next and following centuries.

CHAPTER EIGHT

Concluding Comments

We have seen that while many of the themes and terms in sectarian "precious volumes" have antecedents in earlier Chinese religious texts, these books with their distinguishing characteristics first appeared in the fifteenth century. To express their own beliefs and values, their authors borrowed bureaucratic terminology, Ch'an language about the buddha-nature within, Taoist concepts of refinement of the internal elixir, Confucian ethical principles, veneration of many types of deities, and many other aspects of their cultural and religious surroundings. The result was a new development in the history of Chinese religions, one that expressed the views of literate commoners who promoted their own sectarian organizations and traditions.

These traditions emphasized the religious possibilities available to ordinary people based in their families, all of whom are assured that they are buddhas within, children of the Mother of the universe, possessors of the internal elixir of immortality. Such folk are told that if they are faithful and pious they can be saved; indeed, their positive response to the teaching is proof of their karmic momentum from past lives. Thus it is that after death they can avoid purgatory and go directly to the Mother's paradise, which is their own true home. This is all made easier because in this last age they are an elect, the special recipients of a new divine revelation that will enable them to survive the collapse of this world and make the transition to the next.

These teachings of early sectarian *pao-chüan* were continued into the eighteenth and nineteenth centuries in books with similar style and themes. To illustrate this continuation, I here discuss two of these themes: (1) Maitreya as a present and future revealer and savior, and (2) socially oriented ethical criticism, including a positive attitude toward Confucian-style values. Both these themes are dealt with in detail in the *Ku Fo tang-lai hsia-sheng Mi-le ch'u-hsi pao-chüan* (The precious volume concerning Maitreya's appearing out of the West, the Ancient Buddha who is about to descend to be reborn), a book associated with the Yuan-tun sect that appears, on internal evidence, to be from the late nineteenth century. I also include a discussion of criticism in this text of popular religious rituals and deities.

A good place to begin an investigation of Ch'ing sectarian *pao-chüan* is with Chuang Chi-fa's detailed discussion of evidence for them in government archives from that period. His discussion of this evidence is grouped by sect affiliation, emphasizing the place of the Venerable Mother myth. Convenient access to a number of narrative "precious volumes" extant in Taiwan is provided by Tseng Tzu-liang.[1] Both these studies should be supplemented by reference to the bibliographies of Li Shih-yü and Sawada Mizuho, often referred to above, as well as that of Ch'e Hsi-lun.

The best collections of narrative *pao-chüan* that I have seen are in the Shanghai Public Library and the library of the Kiangsu Teacher's College (now a university) in Soochow, at both of which I did research in 1981. Numerous books of this type have been reprinted in Chang Hsi-shun et al., eds., *Pao-chüan ch'u-chi* ("Precious volumes," first collection; 1994). For a detailed discussion of thirteen narrative "precious volumes" found recently in Kansu, see Tuan P'ing, ed., *Ho-hsi pao-chüan hsuan* (A selection of precious volumes from Ho-hsi; 1992).

I have discussed before some of the later "precious volumes" devoted to Maitreya, including the *Ta-sheng Mi-le hua-tu pao-chüan* (The precious volume of salvation by the great saint Maitreya; eighteenth century?), the *K'ai-hsuan ch'u-ku hsi-lin chüan* (The book of the Western Grove that reveals mysteries and [leads] out of the valley; 1785), the *Fo-shuo Mi-le ting-chieh chao pao-ching* (The precious scripture expounded by the Buddha, a passport[?] [for the time when] Maitreya establishes the kalpa; eighteenth century), and the *Li-shih pao-chüan* (The precious volume on establishing [a new] world; nineteenth century).[2] In the *Hua-tu* and *Hsi-lin* books, Maitreya appears respectively as a preacher in the world and a deity in heaven, but in the *Ting-chieh* and *Li-shih* texts he descends in the chaos of the last age to establish a new world. The *Li-shih pao-chüan* is the most militant "precious volume" I have read, with references to an armed uprising and a promise that farmers will become high officials.[3]

Two other later "precious volumes" devoted to Maitreya that I have read also portray him as either incarnate in the world to reveal his teaching or as a dramatic messiah who saves the pious from the destruction at the end of the eon. The first of these is an eighteenth-century text noted at the end of Chapter Four above, entitled the *Fo-shuo Tu-tou li-t'ien hou hui shou-yüan pao-chüan* (The precious volume, expounded by the Buddha, concerning [Maitreya at his] Tu-tou [Palace] establishing heaven and at the last assembly gathering all to completion; hereafter "the *Li-t'ien* book"). In it, Maitreya descends to the world nine times, first as an artisan, so it is not surprising that this book affirms the religious validity of lay life. In chapter 18, the Venerable Mother says:

What Taoist priest ever gave birth to a Taoist priest? What old monk has given birth to a young monk? The patriarchs of all the myriad teachings have all been produced by lay households. Without filial piety to one's parents, all is in vain. The Ancient Buddha is not among monks or priests; he fell [to Earth] in a lay household.

The result of dedication to farming is that one eats one's own rice and gains the merit of what one does oneself. As for the fruits of Wu-wei that one has cultivated for oneself, what bystanders dare to come to contend for them? It is those who are not enlightened who leave the household life and, wishing to seek purity, become priests or monks. If men and women don't mate as yin and yang, how will there be a master of living beings? . . .

[After the Lord Lao and the Ancient Buddha, the teaching] was transmitted to Confucians living in lay households. The first two assemblies were of monks and priests. They lived in cloisters and sat in mountain forests. From everywhere they received food and offerings. However, they did not complete the task but fell into saṃsāra. In the period of the third yang, the principles of Confucius and Mencius put the world in order. Through the three bonds and the five constant virtues, [the people] are transformed into worthies. . . .

If a woman has no yang, how will she form a child? If a man has no yin, how will he become a parent? If there were no mating of yin and yang in the world, people would freeze to death in sheets of yin water. The Great Way does not depart from the principles of yin and yang; if [this] nature and destiny are not understood, one sits in meditation in vain. Men and women practicing together attain the proper and correct result. (chapter 18)

Here, as before, Confucianism is affirmed because it accords with the natural rhythms of life and family.[4]

In 1991, I read in the Beijing University Library another book in which Maitreya is the chief actor, the *T'ien-chiang tu-chieh pao-chüan* (The precious volume for passing through the kalpa, sent down from heaven), dated Kuang-hsu *ping-wu* (1906–1907). Its chief interest for us here is its restatement at the beginning of the twentieth century of the dramatic threats and promises for those at the end of the age that we first encounter in indigenous Buddhist scriptures from the fifth and sixth centuries. As we read in the introductory section of this book,

> If one can energetically do good and give [this scripture] to others, urging people to recite it, then one can avoid disaster. If one does not believe, one will see that in the *chia-hsu*[?] year [1874–1875?] there will be no one plowing the fields and no one living in houses. In the fifth and sixth months, evil serpents will fall to the earth. In the eighth and ninth months, bad people will all die. However, those who reform their evil and accord with the good will avoid all forms of calamities.

Many end-time disasters are listed in this book, including warfare, epidemics, starvation, cold, floods, fire, and the scattering of families,[5] but those who follow its teachings are assured of "silver, rice, piles of jade and gold, and the eternal enjoyment of great peace." Thus this apocalyptic tradition continued for fourteen hundred years.

By far the most detailed discussions I have seen in later sectarian "precious volumes" of the end of the age and socially oriented criticism are in the *Ku Fo tang-lai hsia-sheng Mi-le ch'u-hsi pao-chüan*, in which there is a claim to an early seventeenth-century date that cannot be correct because of a reference later in the book to the "end of the Ch'ing."[6] This book is reprinted in volume 19 of the *Pao-chüan ch'u-chi*. Its most detailed descriptions of end-time disasters are in chapter 18, in language similar to that quoted above. It ends with promises that in Maitreya's paradise people will live eighty-one thousand years, and, "though Heaven and Earth be destroyed, our bodies will not disintegrate."

There will be more immediate practical benefits as well—lost items will not be picked up from the roads and there will be no thieves or bandits, nor will there be any royal law, or officials, or taxes of grain or silver. In every household men and women will recite scriptures, with religious practitioners everywhere. Wives and husbands will not remarry, and there will be a feast every noon and beautiful clothes to wear!

The way to gain such felicity is to give allegiance to the Yuan-tun sect and practice its teachings, which are here repeatedly equated with those of Confucianism. Why? Because Confucianism maintains the basic human values of loyalty and filial piety—values that support the moral and religious validity of lay life, which is the social matrix of sectarian teaching. From this perspective, the *Ku Fo tang-lai hsia-sheng Mi-le ch'u-hsi pao-chüan* fiercely accuses Buddhist monks of insincerity and immorality in a repeated, detailed attack. From there its criticism reaches out across society to "impure officials," the wealthy, the poor, lower degree-holders, merchants, soldiers, and those who ritually sacrifice animals. Local gods who enjoy such sacrifices are rejected as demons and sprites; their images are just mud; praying to them is worse than useless because it creates bad karma.

In a like manner, divination and *feng-shui* are rejected as of no benefit. Instead, one should simply recite the Buddha's name, because for the pious "there are no more taboos" (*tsai wu chin-chi*; chapter 15, p. 388). For all those criticized, the answer is the same:

Abstain from killing, release living creatures, give allegiance to Confucian teaching. [In accord with] the correct Way of the Master, the Sage K'ung, be good people. Cultivate yourself in purity, preserve and nourish your vital spirit, *ch'i*, and blood, study the wonderful methods of long life, recite scriptures and the Buddha's name, and together enter the Yuan-tun true tradition. Repent of your faults, reform, and develop compassionate minds; learn how to be good people. (chapter 6, pp. 341–342)

I have translated the rich and detailed social criticism in the *Ku Fo tang-lai hsia-sheng Mi-le ch'u-hsi pao-chüan*, but adding it in this concluding chapter would take us too far afield; thus it must suffice to refer the interested reader to chapters 5, 6, 7, and 11 of that book.

However, there is another theme in this "precious volume" that is worth noting here because it provides more detail than we have seen in such discussions before—namely, its criticism of popular deities and rituals. Here again, Lo Ch'ing's influence can be seen.

The basic reasons that the *Ku Fo tang-lai hsia-sheng Mi-le ch'u-hsi pao-chüan* criticizes popular deities and rituals are its belief in nonviolence and in the superiority of its own teachings. The deities rejected here are all local gods, sprites, and demons, against whom celestial gods and officials are summoned. The attitude toward divination and *feng-shui* in this book is similar to that of the indigenous Buddhist scriptures of a thousand years earlier, which I have already discussed.[7] The following are relevant passages from this text, beginning with a critique of popular rituals in chapter 12, which is entitled "Sweeping Away False Forms":

The Ancient Buddha said [that] among living beings in the world, the clever are rare and the benighted and confused very many, the intelligent are few and the stupid many. [Just as] the sun sinks behind the western hills and the rivers flow toward the east, [so do they] sacrifice to the gods with wine and meat, assemble for operas, and spend their wealth to seek blessings, [but] there are no benefits at all from such rituals. On the contrary, they suffer disasters [anyway] and gain no merit at all. Their sins are most serious. Even though they kill living things to offer the bloody food of the five kinds of flesh [of domestic birds and animals] to nourish the gods of Heaven and Earth, they are still unfilial sons, and in fact are very stubbornly disobedient. They do not worship the true buddhas, are not filial to their parents, and do not do good. This kind of people should be sent back to purgatory. However, if they practice loyalty, filial piety, integrity, and righteousness, maintain a vegetarian diet, practice the ethical principles of humanity and righteousness, preserve and nourish their vital spirit, and quickly give allegiance to the Yuan-tun correct teaching, . . . they can be called most filial. If they offer wine and flesh, the gods do not come to accept them. When they sacrifice to sprites and demons, though they think they are seeking blessings, in fact calamities descend upon them. If they kill living things and slice and chop their flesh, [one] fears that they are killing their own parents from three past lifetimes and seven generations of their ancestors who have been reborn as donkeys, mules, horses, pigs, sheep, oxen, dogs, chickens, geese, ducks, and birds. Since they have changed their forms, you don't know who they are who have been reborn. This being the case, you should quickly repent, eat vegetarian food, do good, and abstain from killing.

An attack on minor gods and sprites is found in chapter 13, which has the dramatic title "Sweeping Away and Destroying the Gods." Here we read that the Ancient Buddha instructed all the immortals and buddhas that

all the [gods of the] deity altars and temples of the world are old things that have become sprites. Some are sprites of bamboo, trees, and stones, and some of pythons, snakes, foxes, rabbits, oxen, sheep, dogs, and horses, various forms of vital essence that have not yet been exhausted. There are harmful forces of gold and jade vessels that receive their sacrifices, but only harm people. By making their heads hurt and their bodies hot, they cause people to constantly request [their aid]. There are also wild Wu-t'ung demons[8] at the foot of trees, and all kinds of petty apparitions that receive and deal[?] (*shou-fan*)[9] in people and are devoted to ravishing women, [and so] villages and neighborhoods are not secure. [Because people] kill living things and offer wine and flesh to the gods, [I am] now sending thirty-six great generals leading celestial troops, thunder gods, the [gods of] the five peaks, the Jade Emperor, the [four divine Marshals] Ma, Chao, Wen, and Kuan, the numinous orthodox official Huang,[10] and Dharma-protecting celestial honored ones to all descend to completely gather in apparitions and sprites, and sweep away and destroy all demons and harmful forces, transforming them into ashes and dust.

The gods themselves are directly addressed:

[Images] formed of mud and carved from wood are [eventually] transformed into ashes and dust. Since harmful forces and sprites are gods, [*sic*] [they should] maintain a vegetarian diet and keep the precepts. If they eat [the flesh of] pigs, sheep, chickens, geese, and ducks, they will forever fall into saṃsāra. . . . Though it is they [= humans] who kill living beings, their crime/sin (*tsui*) is laid on you [gods]. . . . I urge all of you harmful forces, sprites, and apparitions to abstain from wine and meat, practice noninterference, study [the way of] long life, and give allegiance to and practice the correct, orthodox Way. Enter the Yuan-tun teaching, refine yourselves in stillness, and establish gateways to the Dharma. (chapter 13)

Here lesser gods and sprites are invited to reform and join the sect, which is already supported by buddhas and celestial deities—an excellent example of the interaction of divine and human in Chinese popular tradition.

In chapter 15, this critical perspective is extended to astrology and *feng-shui*, though without much detail. The title of this chapter is "Sweep Away and Destroy the Stars of Heaven," which here refers to fears about "evil stars." As we read:

The Ancient Buddha observed that when all living beings in the world calculate that, as time passes, evil stars will punish them, these confused people offer meat and wine to demons, invite the stars, and worship the Bushel, but this is of no ritual benefit at all. The Ancient Buddha about to come, the patriarch-teacher of the Constellation [World—i.e., Maitreya], will teach and transform living beings [so that] they recite the Buddha's name five times, which will scatter disasters so that they never punish and destroy. He also observed that people select *feng-shui* [sites] in which dragon configurations that flow harmoniously are auspicious [and maintain that] those that oppose this flow are inauspicious. They say there are 120 evil influences that, when they face only toward a husband and wife, [make a site] inappropriate for burial, and that when people are in deep mourning [there are] harmful demons and influences, and husband and wife are punished. But from now on, for marriage, funerals, and burials recite the Buddha's name five times. This will scatter the harmful influences so that they quickly return to space (kuei-k'ung). [For you] there will be no more taboos, the dead will ascend to heaven, and the living will obtain blessings.

Here the text does not explain what it understands to be the relationship between *feng-shui*, mourning, and marriage, but the basic point is clear: All conventional taboos are undone by recitation of the Buddha's name; faith replaces divination. Further along in this same chapter, those who carry out these rejected practices are called "masters who believe in the crooked and heterodox and practice strange and perverse rituals (*hsing kuai fa*)."

The last sustained criticism of popular beliefs and spirits in this book is in chapter 16, which is entitled "Sweep Away and Destroy Water Apparitions." This chapter attacks sprites and the harmful forces of water creatures such as dragons, serpents, fish, crabs, and turtles that

block the wind and rain, cause rivers to perversely overflow, and stir up wind and waves so that the boats of merchants cannot get through. They deceive people and harm living beings, who make offerings and petition them with flesh and wine. Now [I] have sent [officials of] the Thunder Bureau to gather up and destroy these sprites and water apparitions [so that] from now on the nation will prosper and the people will be at peace.

In this material from the *Ku Fo tang-lai hsia-sheng Mi-le ch'u-hsi pao-chüan*, we see a continuation of Lo Ch'ing's rejection of popular religious practices, a rejection based on long-established Buddhist perspectives. These perspectives, however attenuated, helped distinguish *pao-chüan* teachings from the beliefs and practices of the popular religious traditions that surrounded them. Their elaboration in a late Ch'ing text indicates that this sense of integrity and difference lasted five hundred years. Thus the genre defined itself.

What do sectarian "precious volumes" tell us about Chinese religions, or at least about the religious ideals of their authors? They tell us many things we have been told are not supposed to be there, the first of which is the importance of correct belief—belief in the teachings and promises of the *real* patriarchs, namely, one's own! In these books, such faith is a vital difference between the good and the bad, the saved and the lost, which in turn both supports and reflects a sense of sectarian identity. In some, this identity provides a foundation for ethical criticism of the whole of society, from officials to the poor.

Closely related to belief are ritual practices that make ultimate deliverance possible for ordinary folk, involving memorials and passports to heaven, recitation of the names of buddhas and deities and the scriptures revealed by them, meditation, and maintaining a full-time vegetarian diet—all practices developed earlier but here made available in a new context controlled by the people themselves.

It is also important to note what these *pao-chüan* do not emphasize—and what they ignore altogether. There is nothing here of flesh offerings, except to criticize them; nothing of spirit-mediums or of the kinds of exorcism and healing they practice; nothing about annual festivals or pilgrimages, except to Mount T'ai; no advocacy of fortune-telling or *feng-shui*; and little discussion of immediate, practical aid. Though some of these books support filial piety and the retrospective salvation of ancestors, there is nothing in them of ordinary ritual veneration of ancestors. All this by no means proves that sectarians did not follow these popular practices; perhaps they were so commonly done that it was not felt necessary to discuss them. Nonetheless, at least for the authors of these "precious volumes," such ritual activities were superseded by the power of their own deities and the pious recitation of their scriptures, while in some of these books many common religious practices are specifically rejected. Here *pao-chüan* teachings are between the realms of ordinary popular religion and orthodox Buddhism: they stake out a territory of their own.

This same can be said about the strong mythological consciousness of these books, in which stories are told about creation and the gods—gods who reveal themselves to humans in dreams, or gods who descend to the mundane world to take human form. *Pao-chüan* myths are intended to establish cosmic validation for their teachings by deriving them from a sacred realm. Here there is a dichotomy between sacred and profane in Chinese religions, a sense of transcendence, a call to leave this world and go to another. All this had been taught in various ways before, but not in this specific social context, and never before had it been made so directly available to ordinary people.

The teachings validated by the myths of these books are deeply moral in tone, full of specific injunctions to be and to do good. They make available to their audiences a combination of Buddhist and Confucian ethics expressed in simple and repetitive terms, and so reinforce what some of their orthodox counterparts were also trying to do. For social and intellectual history, it is most interesting to see how the sectarian authors affirmed Confucianism in their own terms, despite the opposition to them of what has been called "the Confucian state." This affirmation appears to have intensified as time passed, and so provides evidence of the success of the Confucians in establishing their values in the population at large, even among those whom they despised!

All of this means that the study of sectarian "precious volumes" is valuable not only for what we learn about this middle level of popular belief and practice, but for its implications for our larger understanding of Chinese religions. To enter deeply into these materials redefines the field around them and calls into question older assumptions about the lack in religious traditions of ordinary folk of much that these texts are full of. By so doing, we also establish a new base for comparison with similar religious traditions elsewhere, a comparison I began to explore in my 1976 *Folk Buddhist Religion: Dissenting Sects in Late Traditional China.*

Although I have put much work and time into the present volume, much remains to be done, beginning with the study of sectarian "precious volumes" from the eighteenth and nineteenth centuries, for which some sources have been indicated above. Another topic for which much material is available is a detailed study of narrative *pao-chüan*, their contents, values, publishers, and audiences, ritual use, development over time, and relationship to other forms of vernacular literature. Each of the themes discussed in Chapters Five, Six, and Seven of this book could serve as the basis for more comprehensive treatment in an article or monograph.

There is also room for more studies of particular "precious volumes" in relationship to their immediate contexts—historical, social, and religious. Related to this would be a focus on what can be found in these books to supplement our understanding of social attitudes and relationships in the periods of time involved. It would also be helpful to bring together the evidence on moral values here as part of a study of the Confucianization of such values in the population at large. Together with the study of implicit and explicit values in vernacular literature, drama, and proverbs, supplemented by anthropological reports, such an investigation could bring us closer to an understanding of the life ideals professed by people other than officials and literati. This in turn could prepare the way for a comparison with popular values in Islamic, Buddhist, or Christian societies.

We already know that many of the teachings and values of sectarian "precious volumes" have been continued in spirit-writing texts since the mid-nineteenth century.[11] But beyond these texts and the groups that produced them, did *pao-chüan* influence the wider world of popular religion and literature? Is there evidence in that world of such themes as three colors of yang symbolizing stages of cosmic time, goddesses like the Venerable Mother, and the importance of a full-time vegetarian diet for laypeople? If so, is it correct to see them as due to sectarian influence? Did this influence have any role in such popular traditions as the transmission of texts and teachings through lines of patriarchs?

Of course, one obvious source for this practice is Ch'an and other Buddhist traditions, but how did the people learn about Ch'an? What of the moral and religious dualism of these texts, culminating in a grand eschatological vision of the salvation of an elect at the end of the age? Is this simply parallel to the theme of struggle between the forces of good and evil in some novels, dramas, films, and political ideologies, or could there be indirect sectarian influence at work here? If so, how did it come about? These and other issues deserve further study. My goal has been to work up a fresh body of evidence as a basis for their investigation.

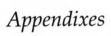

Appendixes

The Case of the 'Hung-lo pao-chüan'

In 1986, Ma Hsi-sha of the Institute for the Study of World Religions in Beijing published an article entitled "Tsui-tsao i-pu pao-chüan te yen-chiu" (A study of the earliest *pao-chüan*), in *Shijie zongjiao yan-jiu* (Studies of world religions) 1:56–72, about the *Fo-shuo Yang shih kuei hsiu hung-lo Hua-hsien ke pao-chüan* (The "precious volume," expounded by the Buddha, [about] "Elder Brother Transformed Immortal" and the ghost of [his mother,] née Yang, who embroidered a red gauze [curtain]; hereafter "the *Hung-lo pao-chüan*"), which he and colleagues in Shansi had found in the Shansi Provincial Museum. This is a narrative text in twenty-two sections (*fen*) based on the story of a childless couple blessed with a son after offering prayers and sacrifices to the gods in a local temple. The Shansi text is a reprint dated 1290, with an original date of 1212, which, if authentic, would indeed make it the earliest known *pao-chüan*. Ma Hsi-sha agrees that this is the case, basing himself on the established tradition among Chinese scholars that *pao-chüan* are direct descendants of T'ang *pien-wen*.[1]

I have not seen this text, but according to Mr. Ma's detailed study, it is a story of a T'ang supernumerary official (*yuan-wai*) named Chang and his wife, née Yang, who name their divinely bestowed son Hua-hsien ke (Elder Brother Transformed Immortal). However, the couple neglect to repay the gods for their kindness, and as a result demon-messengers are sent to take away their son's soul. At this Mr. Chang and his wife return to the temple to beseech the gods, and Ms. Yang vows to embroider a red gauze curtain to protect the images of the deities. This she proceeds to do, with many elaborate and auspicious designs of buddhas, bodhisattvas, deities, the sun, moon, and stars, and so forth—all types of beings.

She embroiders for three years, after which she and her husband offer the curtain to the three deities of the temple who had answered their prayers for a son. Unfortunately, there are several other deities present as well, who, dissatisfied with the gift, have demons take Ms. Yang's soul to purgatory, where she is told that she will not be allowed to return to the world of the living until she embroiders four more curtains. Half a year after she dies, her husband remarries. His second wife bears a son, and to gain all of Chang's inheritance for him, she attempts in various ways to do away with Hua-hsien ke, but the gods protect him. Chang purchases a local office in Kiangsu but is defeated by river pirates, imprisoned, and sentenced to death.

The story goes on at some length, but in the end, while begging on the streets of the capital to provide food for his father, Elder Brother meets and marries the daughter of the emperor, and with his new status is able to save his father and capture all those who have done him wrong. Just at this time his mother finishes her embroidery in purgatory and so is released to the world of the living, where she, her husband, and their son and daughter-in-law are united and eventually go to heaven (pp. 61–62).

This story is similar to those in many Ch'ing period narrative *pao-chüan* I have read, which also involve childless T'ang or Sung supernumerary officials whose prayers are answered with precocious sons or daughters who become high officials or deities after overcoming many obstacles. This similarity extends to the structure, chapter titles, and tune names of the *Hung-lo pao-chüan*, as described and quoted by Ma Hsi-sha. Its binding, too, is in the "butterfly" stitched style common to later narrative "precious volumes." I leave to literary scholars the question of whether or not a story of this type is in accord with the known literature of the early thirteenth century, but from the point of view of *pao-chüan* history I find it difficult to accept so early a date. One must always be cautious about new discoveries that appear to redefine the basis for their evaluation, but it remains difficult to conceive of so elaborate and secular a *pao-chüan* appearing by 1212.

The comparable pre-sectarian *pao-chüan* that we do have— namely, the *Hsiang-shan* and *Chin-kang k'e-i*—have much more sustained and serious religious messages, as is discussed in Chapter

One above. Mr. Ma emphasizes statements in the *Hung-lo* text indicating that it, too, was written by monks, but for what purpose it is not clear, other than as an underlying message of moral retribution by the gods.

My doubts about this text are heightened by short references in it that imply the existence of a fully developed mythology of the Eternal Mother and her children by the early thirteenth century. In one passage we read, "The Eternal Venerable Mother (Wu-sheng lao-mu), from the time her children were scattered and lost, has not been able to see them. She constantly hopes that her sons and daughters on the great earth will soon return home. She fears that when the three calamities [of fire, water, and wind] approach, they will fall and lose their spiritual light, and for eighty-one kalpas will not see their Mother's living face. . . . [The pious] from south and north will go in person to their native district, . . . [where] the little children will see their dear Mother and enter her womb" (pp. 70–71).

These passages are a brief summary of the classic sectarian myth of universal salvation that to the best of my knowledge developed in the sixteenth century. In the fifteenth-century *Huang-chi pao-chüan* discussed in Chapter Two of the present volume, there is as yet no such centralized Eternal Mother myth, only a number of goddesses with more limited ritual functions. I have seen no evidence that there was anything like this myth in other texts before that time, or in official reports about sectarian activities and beliefs. The fragmentary anticipations of the Eternal Mother belief that can be adduced are summarized in Chapter One. I expect that other old *pao-chüan* will be found that provide fresh information about the genre, but at this point the *Hung-lo* text does not appear to be one of them.[2] I am happy to see that, in his 1997 book, Ch'e Hsi-lun argues convincingly that the *Hung-lo pao-chüan* appeared no earlier than the mid-Ming period.[3]

APPENDIX B

Vernacular Terms Used in the 'Huang-chi pao-chüan'

N.B.: Some of the descriptive terminology here is taken from Yuen Ren Chao, *A Grammar of Spoken Chinese* (Berkeley: University of California Press, 1968).

che-li 這裏 as "here"

chei 這 and *chei-ke* 這箇 as "this"

cho / chao 著 as "to use," "to cause to," "to attain to"

erh 兒 as a retroflex ending

hao-pu chih 好不知 "do not know at all"

jen-jen 人人 as "everyone"

kan-ching 乾淨 as "clean"

k'an 看 as "to see," "to look at"

le 了 as a suffix expressing a change of state

ma 麼 as an interrogative particle

na (third tone) 哪 as "what?" "which?"

na-li (third tone) 哪裏 as "where?"

na-li (fourth tone) 那裏 as "there"

ni 你 as "you"

ni-men 你們 as "you" (plural)

shih 是 as a verb "to be"

te 的 as a possessive particle, noun, and pronoun suffix, and as a marker of modification

tsa 咱 as "we," "our"

tse[n]-me 怎麼 as "how?" "what?"

tse[n]-sheng 怎生 as "how?" "in what way?"

yao-chin 要緊 as "important," "urgent"

Tune Names in the 'Huang-chi pao-chüan'

There are thirteen tune names in the *Huang-chi* book, of which three are used twice, for a total of sixteen (one for each chapter plus the introductory section). All of them appear to be tunes from Chinese operas—eleven of the thirteen are so described in Wang P'ei-lun's 王 沛綸 *Hsi-ch'ü tz'u-tien* 戲曲辭典 (Dictionary of [Chinese] drama [Taipei: Chung-hua-shu-chü, 1969]). The page numbers on which they are found in this dictionary are preceded by the initials "WPL."

None of these tune names is found in the list of Taoist tune titles provided by Judith Boltz in her *Survey of Taoist Literature, Tenth to Seventeenth Centuries* (Berkeley: Institute of East Asian Studies, University of California, 1987), p. 415. I am grateful to my University of British Columbia colleague Dr. Catherine Swatek for her help in translating some of these titles.

Ch'ao T'ien-tzu 朝天子 ("An audience with the Son of Heaven"), WPL, p. 428.

Chin-tzu ching 金字經 ("Golden character scripture"), used twice, WPL, p. 206.

Chu yun fei 駐雲飛 ("Stopping the clouds from flying"), WPL, p. 553.

Feng *Hsin-ching* 諷心經 ("Chant the *Heart Sūtra*").

Huang ying-erh 黃鶯兒 ("Yellow parrot," reading *ying* 鸚 as "parrot"), WPL, p. 415, with *ying* 鶯 as "oriole."

Hung hsiu hsieh 紅繡鞋 ("Red-embroidered shoes"), WPL, p. 222, with *hsiu* 繡 as "to embroider."

Ku mei chiu 沽美酒 ("Buying good wine"), WPL, p. 249.

Kua chin so 掛金鎖 ("Wearing a golden lock").

Kuei-chih hsiang 桂枝香 ("Fragrant cassia-bough incense"), used twice, WPL, p. 325.

Lang t'ao sha 浪濤沙 ("Wave-sifted sand"), WPL, p. 326.

P'ang chuang-t'ai 旁粧臺 ("Beside the dressing table"), WPL, p. 458, with *chuang* 妝 as "to adorn oneself."

Shan-p'o yang 山坡羊 ("Sheep on a slope"), used twice, WPL, p. 38.

Tsao lo p'ao 皂羅袍 ("Black gauze robe"), WPL, p. 201.

Paired Matriarchs and Patriarchs in the Order of Their Appearance in the 'Huang-chi pao-chüan'

1. The Earth-Flower Venerable Mother, who watches over women, and the Celestial Prime Venerable Patriarch, who inspects men (chapter 1). There is also another reference in this chapter to a "Flower Mother" (Hua-mu) who "regulates and harmonizes the gods of the six directions."

2. The True Yang Mother and the Patriarch of the Dark Heaven, who examine religious practice, incense, memorials, statements, tablets, titles, and vows—no mistakes allowed (chapter 3). Later in this same chapter, slightly different titles are given for this same pair, namely, the "True Yang Venerable Mother" and the "Patriarch of the Dark Heaven of the Nine-Cloud Pass," both of whom are said to control (kuan) human harmony (Yüeh-ho tsu), and the Mother of the Three Apexes, who together are the protectors and supervisors of the "dark pass of the fourth step" (chapter 4).

3. The Six-Yang Patriarch who guards the "dark pass of the five roads" and the Mother Who Gathers in the Perfected (Shou-chen mu). She is an inspector (chien-p'an; chapter 6).

4. The Honored Emperor of the Two Soils and the Eternal Mother of the Two Stars (Erh-hsing Wu-sheng mu). No functions are noted, but it is interesting that the term "Eternal Mother" is already here (chapter 7).

5. The Venerable Patriarch of the Three Primes and the Venerable Mother of the Inner Darkness (Nei-hsuan Lao-mu), who "diligently receive and welcome" those at the "Lotus River dark pass" (chapter 7).

6. The Patriarch of Heaven's Consent (T'ien-k'e tsu) and the Mother of the Buddha's Merit (Fo-kung mu), both supervisors of the Red Damask pass (chapter 8). Later in this chapter, this pair is mentioned again, but with the title "Mother of the Buddha's Seal" (Fo-yin mu).

7. The Welcoming Patriarch and the Lotus River Mother, pass guardians (chapter 8).

8. The Venerable Patriarch of All Titles (Tsung-hao lao-tsu) and the Mother Who Gives Birth to Yang (Sheng-yang mu), who are "in charge of positions in the thirty-six heavens" (chapter 13).

APPENDIX E

Titles of Offices in the
'Huang-chi pao-chüan'

N.B.: "H." = in Charles O. Hucker, *A Dictionary of Official Titles in Imperial China* (Stanford, Calif.: Stanford University Press, 1985); "see H." = similar to entries in Hucker.

chang-chi 掌極, "in charge of the apex" (see H. 94, 124, 139, etc.)

chang-chiao 掌教, "[officer] in charge of teaching" (see H. 94, 124, 139, etc.)

chang-hao 掌號, "in charge of titles" (see H. 94, 124, 139, etc.)

chang ling 掌令, "keeper of commands" (see H. 94, 124, 139, etc.)

chang-p'an 掌盤, "in charge of a realm"

cheng-chi 正極, "principal apex [commissioner]" (see H. 396ff)

chien-ch'a 監察, "surveillance officer" (see H. 789)

chien p'an 監盤, "realm inspector"

chih-chang 執掌, "manager"

chih-shih 知識, "[one with] knowledge and experience"

chu-cheng 主正, "responsible for correction" (see H. 1420, etc.)

chu-hsing 主行, "[officer] responsible for conduct" (see H. 1420, etc.)

chuan-li 專理, "specially appointed regulator" (see H. 1485–1486)

ch'uan-t'ou 船頭, "boat head"

fu-chi 副極, "vice apex commissioner" (see H. 2032)

hu-sung 護送, "escort"

Hung-lu ssu 鴻臚寺, "Court for Dependencies" (see H. 2906)

ling-hsiu 領袖, "leader"

po-chih 撥治, "dispatcher" (see H. 4724–4725)

pu-hsing 布省, "[those who] set forth and examine"(?)

shou-pa 守把, "guard"

shuai 帥, "commander" (H. 5475)

ta-hsun 大巡, "major patroller" (see H. 2735, etc.)

t'eng-lu hsien-kuan shen-li 謄錄仙官神吏, "immortal officials and divine clerks who serve as examination copyists" (see H. 6358)

t'i-kang 提綱, "superintendent of major regulations" (see H. 6450–6453)

t'i-kuan 提管, "supervising manager"

t'i-tiao 提調, "supervisor" (H. 6470)

t'i-t'ou 提頭, "head supervisor"

t'i-tu 提督, "superintendent" (see H. 6484)

t'ieh-chiao 貼教, "[officer] dedicated to teaching" (see H. 6507)

t'ou-ling 頭領, "head leader" (see H. 6798)

tsung-chi 總極, "general [overseer] of the apex" (see the following *tsung* entries for parallels)

tsung-kuan 總管, "route commander" (see H. 7110)

tsung-li 總理, "superintendent" (H. 7121)

tsung-ling 總領, "overseer-general" (see H. 7134)

tu-hsün 都巡, "chief patroller" (H. 7234–7236)

T'ung-cheng ssu 通政司, "office of transmission" (see H. 7467)

Types of Documents in the 'Huang-chi pao-chüan'

ch'a-chao 查照, "investigation certificate"

ch'a-hao 查號, "investigation title"

chih-chao 執照, "a pass"

ch'in-wen 親文, "personal text" (? I have not found further references to this term.)

hao 號, "title"

kuan-fang 關防, "pass protectors"

p'ai 牌, "tablet"

p'ai-hao 牌號, "tablet titles"

piao 表, "memorial"

shih-chuang 誓狀, "vow" (lit. "vow statement")

shou-tzu 手字, "hand character" (could refer to a hand gesture, as in the term *shou-yin* 手印)

shu-tz'u 疏詞, "statement-text" (another name for memorials)

ta-ch'a tui-hao 答查對號, "respond to investigation and compare titles"

t'an chang 談章, "discussion essays" (I have not found further references to this term.)

tieh-wen 牒文, "official dispatch"

tsung-kuan ch'a-chao 總關查照, "inspection certificate for all passes" (i.e., a passport)

tui-hao 對號, "to match / compare titles"

yin-chi 印記, "seal"

APPENDIX G

Lo Ch'ing's 'Five Books
in Six Volumes' ('Wu-pu liu-ts'e')

Lo Ch'ing, or Lo Tsu (the Patriarch Lo), wrote five *pao-chüan*, commonly called the *Wu-pu liu-ts'e* (Five books in six volumes) because one of them was in two *chüan*. Sect adherents wrote commentaries on these texts in the late sixteenth and mid-seventeenth centuries, and they have been reprinted many times into the twentieth century.

Descriptions of various editions of these books can be found in the studies listed in note 1 of Chapter Three (p. 391). They are also listed in Li Shih-yü's *Pao-chüan tsung-lu*. Sawada Mizuho (*Zōho Hōkan*, pp. 315–323), Sōda Hiroshi ("Rakyō no seiritsu," pp. 18–34), and Cheng Chih-ming (*Wu-sheng lao-mu*, pp. 32–41) summarize the contents of each book, while Randall Nadeau summarizes all the chapters of each of Lo's texts in his "Popular Sectarianism in the Ming" (pp. 299–309).

There is general agreement that the first of these books to be written was the autobiographical *K'u-kung wu-tao chüan*, while Sōda and Nadeau follow Sawada in listing the sequence of the remaining four books in the order used in this appendix.

A description follows of the editions of these texts in my collection. I am grateful to Sakai Tadao for sending me microfilms of several of these texts in 1975, thus beginning my collection of *pao-chüan*.

The citations of Lo Ch'ing's texts in the present book are taken from the 1980 reprint of the 1596 *K'ai-hsin fa-yao* edition, published by the Min-te t'ang (Temple of the People's Virtue) in Taichung, Taiwan (see number 1 below).

1. *K'u-kung wu-tao chüan* (On awakening to the Way through bitter toil), one *chüan*, no chapter divisions, 8,867 characters (according to a list at the beginning of the *Wei-wei pu-tung T'ai-shan chüan*, text 5 below).

I have this text in a two-*chüan* edition with commentary, reprinted in 1596, 1652, 1802, 1847, 1869, and 1980. The 1980 reprinting was by the Min-te t'ang in Taichung. The edition used in 1980 was reprinted in 1994 in two volumes edited by Lin Li-jen, with the title *Wu-pu liu-ts'e ching-chüan* (The "Five scriptures in six volumes"). I obtained a copy in 1995, long after writing Chapter Three on Lo Ch'ing's scriptures. In any case, the 1980 and 1994 reprints are of the same edition of the texts.

The commentary edition is entitled *K'u-kung pu-chu K'ai-hsin fa-yao* (The *K'u-kung chüan* with supplementary commentary: Essentials of the Dharma to open the mind; hereafter "the *K'ai-hsin fa-yao* edition"). The *K'ai-hsin fa-yao* includes commentaries on Lo's texts written not long before 1581 by a monk named Lan-feng (from Soochow), who is described as being in the twenty-sixth generation of the orthodox line of the (Ch'an) Lin-chi school (founded in the mid-ninth century).[1]

In 1596, a disciple of Lan-feng's named Yuan-ching reprinted this text with his own supplementary commentary. (Yuan-ching is described as being in the twenty-seventh generation of dharmic succession.) In 1652, the text was collated and verified by two members of the sect named P'u-ch'ing and P'u-shen of the "orthodox line of the Limitless" (Wu-chi cheng-p'ai), another name for the Lo religion. P'u-ch'ing and P'u-shen are described as *hou hsueh* ("later students"; by this time "P'u" was used by sect members as a religious name).

This text with commentary begins with a long introduction by Yuan-ching and continues with a preface dated 1652, both full of praise for the saving efficacy of sect teachings. Opening lines of the commentary state that this scripture is based on Lo Tsu's thirteen years of religious self-cultivation. Then follow two odes of praise (*sung*) by Lan-feng in pairs of rhyming seven-character (heptasyllabic) lines, eulogizing Lo's long and successful struggle. Yuan-ching's comments are in smaller type, usually introduced with the words *Shih-yueh* ("the Master said"). Yuan-ching refers to Lo himself as Tsu-chia (Patriarch).

The text itself begins with ritual instructions for arranging a table for the scriptures, entering the platform for seated meditation, and chanting the *Heart Sūtra*. There follows a "psalm of praise while raising incense" (*chü-hsiang tsan*), and then "Homage to the original teacher Śākyamuni Buddha," to be repeated three times. Then come eight lines of seven-character verse in honor of the buddha-light which illumines all, ending with taking refuge in the Buddha, Dharma, and Sangha and the line, "The Wheel of the Dharma revolves incessantly to save all sentient beings."

Lo then says that this text is based on his thirteen years of seeking the truth, after which comes a section of "reliances" (*i-t'o*) recalling for the worshippers their dependence on others, beginning with "Heaven which covers, Earth which bears up, and the parents who give birth to one's body, the king, water, earth, the five grains, meritorious ministers who protect the state, and great civil and military officials who protect the Dharma, thus enabling us to find peace and seek for the truth. We [seek to] recompense all these kindnesses."

The text continues with poetic statements by Lo that he has discovered the immutable truth of all buddhas, bodhisattvas (lay and clerical), and the sages of the three teachings, and that "those who listen to this account [of my] activities will understand all places in the three thousand worlds, the original vows of all the buddhas, and the foundation of the ten thousand phenomena, and will manifest the Native Place within themselves (*hsien tzu-chi chia-hsiang*)."

There follows a verse eulogy of the Patriarch Lo by Lan-feng, which is succeeded in turn by the title of the first chapter. The remainder of the book consists of Lo's original text interspersed with comments of varying length. This text ends with an autobiographical statement by Lo concerning his birthplace, his family background, his enlightenment experience, and his vow to write these scriptures to save all.

The commentary concludes with eulogies by Lan-feng and three later sect members from different "schools" (*men*, i.e., congregations), all in heptasyllabic rhyming verse. Then comes another eulogy, followed by a biography of Yuan-ching.

This edition of the text ends with a colophon by another disciple, also dated 1596. The author is concerned that the heresies flourishing in his day might lead to the decline of the "patriarchal tradition" (*tsu-feng*). Thus he has labored for more than ten years, reading a variety of sūtras to match the patriarch's meaning, so that in the future the Patriarch Lo would not be forgotten, people would hear of Buddhism, and they would be able to distinguish right from wrong, orthodoxy from heresy.

2. *T'an-shih wu-wei chüan* (The book of Nonactivism in lamentation for the world), one *chüan*, 11,754 characters, reprinted, collated, and verified in Nanking in 1615 by a grandson of the Patriarch Lo.

There are no chapter divisions in this book. The text is richly decorated with floral designs and begins with three pages of pictures of the Buddha and various bodhisattvas and saints. Then follow:

a. Four lines of four-character verse:

May the imperial realm be forever secure,
May the emperor's way be enduring and prosperous,
May the sun of the Buddha increase its brilliance,
May the Wheel of the Dharma forever turn.

b. "Ten thousand years to the emperor, ten thousand times ten thousand years!"

c. Under the heading *Yü-chih* ("composed by imperial authority"), four and a half lines of sixteen-character verse, arranged 4/4/4/4, identical with the passage in the *Huang-chi pao-chüan* (translated in Chapter Two above) that begins, "May [all within] the six directions be pure and peaceful, may the sun, moon, and planets [move in] harmonious succession, . . . may the ten thousand things all flourish, . . . may families venerate loyalty and filial piety, may people be happy, merciful, and good, may officials be pure and administration just, . . . [and] may all living beings become buddhas."

Then the text begins with a prose passage:
Boundless emptiness is the body of the Limitless, the vast and limitless worlds are all empty. Dwell at peace in the vast and limitless worlds. They are all the transformation bodies of the Limitless (*Wu-chi hua-t'i*). The original face of all people (*jen-jen pen-lai mien-mu*) is the perfect body of the Limitless. . . . Recognize [your] original face; in the east, west, south, and north, there is no need to think and calculate. Those who protect and maintain the wonderful Dharma of the Limitless (*Wu-chi miao-fa*) [obtain] merit without measure and limit; they forever cut off the cycles of birth-and-death in the sea of suffering [saṃsāra], and at death [they] release a brilliant light which illumines all the ten regions [and attain] inconceivable boundless happiness. Wonderful! Wonderful!

There follow "verses for opening the scripture" (*k'ai-ching chi*) in praise of the Dharma in heptasyllabic verse, including a passage from the *Hua-yen* (*Avataṃsaka*) *sūtra* in prose. Then come seventy lines of ten-character verse arranged 3/3/4, followed by twenty-seven lines of fourteen-character verse arranged 7/7. The 3/3/4 style then resumes as the major pattern of the text, occasionally broken by quotes in prose or in 7/7 lines.

I have also a copy of this text with commentary in two *chüan* in the *K'ai-hsin fa-yao* series, as above. The commentary explains in detail the meaning of titles and terms and the background of the verbal illustrations used, and also provides an exposition of the ideas involved. Yuan-ching gives as well a pronouncing glossary of obscure characters, presumably to facilitate recitation. The language of the commentaries is more elegant than that of the text, which is in simple classical language with many vernacular terms.

The commentary begins with a long exposition of Lan-feng's interpretation of this text, followed by an ode of praise by Lan-feng in eight lines of 7/7 verse. Then the text begins, with Yuan-ching's ample commentary inserted between each line, interrupted occasionally by additional odes from Lan-feng. The opening line of the first ode calls Lo Ch'ing "the Venerable Patriarch awakened to emptiness" (Wu-k'ung lao-tsu).

I should add that the original texts in the text and commentary editions are identical except for very few minor differences. The commentary editions do not have pictures and pious verses at the beginning.

3. *P'o-hsieh hsien-cheng yao-shih chüan* (The key to refuting heresy and showing evidence [for correct teachings]), two *chüan* (*shang* and *hsia*) in twenty-four chapters, with 13,059 characters in the first *chüan* and 10,428 in the second.

I have two editions of this work, the first of the text alone, collated and verified in 1615. My copy of this edition has only the first *chüan* in eleven chapters. As with the *T'an-shih chüan* (text 2 above), this scripture is elegantly decorated, and it has the same pictures of saints and buddhas, the same dedicatory verses, and an appeal for long life for the emperor. There follows a table of contents with chapter titles in full, each beginning with the character *p'o* ("to break open"), which here means both "to clarify" and "to refute" depending on the topic involved.

Chüan 1 begins with four five-character verses:

Heretical teachings (*hsieh-fa*) are confused and chaotic,
[but] emptiness is free from fetters.
If one does not use a key to open up [confusion],
where can one escape from birth-and-death?

Then follows, "To benefit both self and others, on behalf of bodhi-sattvas, both clerical and lay, [this] text refutes heresy and provides evidence for [the truth]," after which there is an *i-t'o* ("reliances") section, similar to that in the *T'an-shih chüan* but somewhat expanded, with a stress on gratitude for the kindness of emperors and officials, the various buddhas, and Hsuan-tsang (here called the "T'ang monk"), who went West to bring back scriptures. At the end of this section, king and officials are promised buddhahood and unending merit if they "protect the Buddhist Dharma." Without such protection, "who would dare to vow to save others?"

The first chapter begins with prose quotes from the *Diamond Sūtra* and the *Sūtra of Complete Awakening*. After eight lines of prose, the dominant 3/3/4 pattern begins, alternating with occasional sections of heptasyllabic verse. The other chapters follow this basic pattern of several lines of prose at the beginning, followed by 3/3/4 verse.

My two other editions of the *P'o-hsieh* text are from the *K'ai-hsin fa-yao*, in four *chüan*, with the complete text. They begin directly with the title and table of contents; each chapter heading is followed by an explanatory ode. The chief object of criticism in the *P'o-hsieh* book is any form of externalized piety that does not understand the fundamental emptiness and unity of all things, and that therefore abides in false distinctions, such as that between laity and clergy (*tsai-chia/ch'u-chia*). Other views attacked are those which stress recitation of Amitābha's name, quests for immortality or supernormal powers, and the like. Chapter 6 criticizes reliance on meditation and attacks "White Lotus" sects for their political ambitions, techniques of "circulating *ch'i*," emphasis on prognostication, rituals of burning paper, and veneration of non-Buddhist deities, including the sun and moon. The *K'ai-hsin fa-yao* edition ends with an *i-t'o* ("reliances") section, a six-line ode by Lan-feng, and a pronouncing glossary.

The *P'o-hsieh* book is a collage of quotes from a variety of sources, all to provide scriptural support for Lo Ch'ing's teachings; hence the "showing evidence" (*hsien-cheng*) in the title.

4. *Cheng-hsin ch'u-i wu hsiu cheng tzu-tsai pao-chüan* (The precious volume of self-determination [needing neither] cultivation nor verification, which rectifies belief and dispels doubt), one *chüan*, twenty-five chapters, 13,959 characters. Date, place, and name of editor not given.

This edition is not discussed in Sawada's *Zōho Hōkan*, and the only text of precisely this name, listed in Li Shih-yü's *Pao-chüan tsung-lu*, is Lo Ch'ing's original, published in 1509. The characters are large and somewhat blurred in places, much cruder than those in any of the other texts I possess. This may be a reproduction of the original text. Other extant versions are in two or four *chüan*, with commentaries.

This edition begins with two long dedicatory poems of similar content, the first in six lines of twelve characters, arranged 4/4/4, headed with the words *wan-sui* ("ten thousand years"). Its concern is with the harmony of natural forces, the abundance of plants and animals, ethics, and the salvation of all, as with similar passages noted above. The second folio page is almost identical with those in the 1615 edition noted above, with "Huang-ti wan-sui," and so forth, and then the poem in twelve-character lines; but here there are a full five lines, made possible by the addition of two sets of four characters just before the end: "May all forms of rebirth on the six paths of existence escape from saṃsāra." The phrase *Yü-chih* heads this poem, as in the 1615 edition of the *Po-hsieh* book, text 3 above. However, the following text proper is quite different in form, with larger, thicker characters and no decoration. It appears that this version of the *Cheng-hsin* text was reprinted in 1615 with old blocks, only the title pages being changed.

The text itself begins with a table of contents followed by a long prose defense of vegetarianism. Then comes 3/3/4 verse reinforcing the points made in the prose statement, followed by an *i-t'o* ("reliances") section in 7/7 lines. The chapters begin with prose and then move to verse, as described above.

I have another complete edition of the *Cheng-hsin pao-chüan* as well, in the *K'ai-hsin fa-yao* series, as above.

5. *Wei-wei pu-tung T'ai-shan shen-ken chieh-kuo pao-chüan* (The precious volume of deeply rooted karmic fruits, majestic and unmoved like Mount T'ai), one *chüan* in twenty-four chapters, 14,198 characters. I have three editions of this text:

a. The text alone, published in Nanking in 1615. This edition is identical in form with the other 1615 editions described above. On the opening page we are told that, since the old printing blocks were worn out, new ones were carved at this time for all the texts at the Hu yang-shan printing shop on Sanshan Street from blocks at the Number One scripture house. The text has a table of contents and the same structure as described above, that is, the beginning of each chapter in prose, followed by a section of heptasyllabic verse and then verse in 3/3/4 form. At the end is a brief autobiographical statement by Lo Ch'ing, with a list of all five of his texts.

b. Two *K'ai-hsin fa-yao* editions, as above, in four *chüan*. At the end of the first edition we are told that it was reprinted in 1652, 1802, 1842, and 1869. For the 1869 reprint, we are given the names of three sect members who arranged for the reprinting, plus the names of all those who contributed to the cost, with how much they gave: 262,000, 20,000, 40,000, 50,000, and 124,000 cash, respectively. In the postface of this edition there is a sect genealogy based on the religious name "P'u" and going down to P'u-shen and P'u-ch'ing, who were responsible for the 1652 reprint. On the first page of this text there is the name of a bookshop in Ta-chia, Taiwan. The 1980 reprint also lists the names of those who contributed to it, with amounts.

c. The *Wei-wei pu-tung T'ai-shan shen-ken chieh-kuo ching hui-chieh* (The sūtra of deeply rooted karmic fruits, majestic and unmoved as Mount T'ai, with collected explanations), two *chüan*, edited in Nanking in 1629 by the lay devotee Wang Hai-ch'ao, the monk Hai-pin, and others. The chapter titles and text of this edition are the same as those of Yuan-ching, as are Lan-feng's odes, but the commentary is different. There is no table of contents. The preface is a fine exposition of the title and basic sect beliefs, and at the end of the text is a commentary on Lo's biography, as well as a pronouncing glossary. This edition is discussed by Sakai Tadao, *Chūgoku zenshō* (pp. 452–455), and Richard Shek, "Religion and Society in Late Ming" (pp. 239–241).

APPENDIX H

Sixteenth-Century 'Pao-chüan' Consulted for This Study Other Than Those by Lo Ch'ing and the 1523 'Chiu-lien pao-chüan'

The following thirteen books are listed in approximate chronological order, grouped by sectarian affiliation where possible.

FIVE TEXTS FROM A VARIETY OF SECTS

1. *Yao-shih pen-yuan kung-te pao-chüan* (The precious volume of the original vows and merit of the Master of Medicine [Bhaiṣajya]; hereafter "the *Yao-shih pao-chüan*"), one volume (*ts'e*) in thirty-two chapters (*p'in*). Published in Beijing in Ming Chia-ching 22/12/25 (= January 19, 1544). Reference to the Red Yang teaching (Hung-yang fa) on p. 16b, so may have been affiliated with a sect of that name.[1] Copy from Cheng Chen-to's collection read in the rare book room of the Beijing Library in May 1981. Beautifully bound, accordion-style, with colored illustrations of buddhas and deities. This book is listed in Li Shih-yü's *Pao-chüan tsung-lu* (p. 59) but not in Sawada Mizuho's *Zōho Hōkan*. It is in volume 14 of Chang Hsi-shun et al., eds., *Pao-chüan ch'u-chi*.

The printing blocks for this book were stored in the shop of the Li family on West Ch'ang-an Street in Beijing. Funds for printing it were contributed by a "virtuous consort" of the Ming court, sur-named Chang, and by five imperial princesses who "diligently and sincerely resolved to contribute funds gladly, and ordered that there be colored illustrations of the sacred images of the buddhas, the Assembly on Mount Ling, the Realm of the West, the Mother of the Astral Bushel, the Three Emperors Holy Patriarchs,[2] the gods of the Southern and Northern Astral Bushels," and other deities. Ap-pended to this book is the *San-shih-wu fo-ming ching* (Scripture of the names of thirty-five buddhas).

This book opens with a prose "hymn of praise on raising in-cense," followed by two lines of 7/7 verse in homage to the Buddha, Dharma, and Sangha, then two more such lines for the "*gāthā* for opening the scripture." This alternation between prose and verse continues throughout the text, with prose sections introduced by the term *pai-wen* ("clear [= prose] text"). The first part of the main body of the text is organized around twelve vows taken by the Yao-shih ju-lai (Tathāgata), which here implies a "buddha-to-be." Some goals of these vows are "to get rid of illness for all sentient beings" (vow 4), and "to attain *bodhi* (enlightenment) in the next life, attain fruition by myself at the three Dragon-Flower assemblies, to be reborn to long life with endless happiness, unmoved and independent every-where, in the end to attain buddhahood" (vow 5).

The seventh vow repeats the promise of healing, as is appropriate for this bodhisattva, while the eighth promises that devoted women "who hear my name" will "get rid of their female bodies and be re-born as men." This and the other vows end with promises that the pious will "attain" or "realize" "the most superior *bodhi*," so practi-cal benefits are connected with ultimate deliverance. The purpose of the ninth vow is that people "will not be reborn [in saṃsāra] but will spend a myriad of springs in the Venerable Mother's womb. . . . May all living beings escape Mara's net and attain liberation." The last three vows repeat the theme of attaining salvation as "returning home," "returning to the origin," and enabling "the children to see their dear Mother."

Chapter divisions and names begin with *p'in* 12 (*sic*) and are named after such well-known bodhisattvas as Mañjuśrī, Kuan-yin, Maitreya, and Yao-shih himself, all of whom support the Venerable Mother's teaching, as does this entire book. Chapters 21 through 32 are named after Buddhist guardians associated with Bhaiṣajya, such as Andīra, Vajra, and Indra, here all titled "Great General." This book ends with praise of its own saving efficacy and ten repayments, and with the lines, "I vow to extend this merit to all, so that I and all living beings can together attain the Buddha Way. Homage to the Buddha Wei-t'o who, in obedience to heaven, protects the Dharma."

The teaching of the *Yao-shih pao-chüan* is based entirely on the Venerable Mother mythology, preached in the period of the "end Dharma" (*mo-fa chih tai*). Bhaiṣajya's task throughout is to guide the lost back to the Mother and their true home in paradise, which is conflated with Amitābha's Pure Land.

For a detailed study of the Healing Buddha, see Raoul Birnbaum, *The Healing Buddha* (Boulder, Colo.: Shambala, 1979). Chapter 23 of the Chinese text of the *Lotus Sūtra* is devoted to the "Bodhisattva Medicine King," while several scriptures in the name of this buddha were translated from the fifth century on. See, for example, the *Fo-shuo Yao-shih Ju-lai pen-yuan ching* (Sūtra spoken by the Buddha on the original vow of the Tathāgata Master of Medicine), T. 449, 14:401a–404c, translated in the Sui period (581–618).

2. *P'u-ming ju-lai wu-wei liao-i pao-chüan* (The precious volume of the Tathāgata P'u-ming who thoroughly understands the meaning of Wu-wei; hereafter "the *P'u-ming pao-chüan*"), two *chüan* in eighteen chapters (*fen*), originally completed in 1558; reprinted in the tenth month of Ming Wan-li 27 (= 1599).

In its introductory section, this text refers to the Tathāgata P'u-ming and the "Holy Way of Yellow Heaven" (Huang-t'ien tao), a sect discussed at length by Richard Shek in his "Religion and Society in Late Ming" (pp. 252–275), following earlier studies by Li Shih-yü and Sawada Mizuho.[3] The evidence indicates that P'u-ming was the founding patriarch of the Yellow Heaven sect, whose name was Li Pin, a farmworker and soldier from North China who died in 1562. Shek accepts Sawada's date of 1558 for the completion of the *P'u-ming pao-chüan*.

This text is also the subject of a book in Russian by E. S. Stulova, published in 1979.[4] Shek states that the Huang-t'ien tao (see note 5 below) "showed a high degree of indebtedness to the Luo sect" ("Religion and Society in Late Ming," p. 252), but the *P'u-ming* scripture itself is heavily influenced by Taoist terminology not used by Lo Ch'ing. Though the mythological framework here is that of the Venerable Mother, the basic path to salvation is as described in chapter 13: "Gather in the vital essence, nourish the vital force (*ch'i*), and so form a perfected nature. . . . Refine the Five Phases and the eight trigrams, with nine circulations return the elixir and emit your yang spirit, leave the mundane, shed your shell [i.e., ordinary body] and return home. [There,] unmoving and unwavering, sit in the heart of the lotus."

The *P'u-ming pao-chüan* includes more such Taoist terminology than any other such text I have read from this early period. The text itself makes it clear that this influence was from the Way of Complete Perfection (Ch'üan-chen tao), which is discussed above in Chapter One.

3. *Hsiao-shih yuan-chueh pao-chüan* (The precious volume that explains complete enlightenment; hereafter "the *Yuan-chueh pao-chüan*"), four *chüan*, thirty-two *p'in*. Inside title *Yuan-chueh t'ung-chien* (A comprehensive mirror for complete enlightenment). Published in the Ming Chia-ching *chia-tzu* year, 3/15 (= April 25, 1564).

No place name is provided, but in an autobiographical statement in chapter 32, the patriarch who transmitted this text says that after years of wandering he was finally enlightened at Mount Lao in the Chi-mo district of Shantung, which we know was Lo Ch'ing's home area as well.

The original of my copy is in the Columbia University Library; its first *chüan* (in eight chapters) is missing, so I have no information about its opening pages. However, *chüan* 2 and 3 open with identical pictures of a seated buddha and a Chinese sage, side by side, of equal size, with the buddha on the right (stage left). There is also a picture of male and female attendants, with the males holding wooden tablets raised in front of them in the style of officials.

Next to this last picture is the sixteen-character opening invocation, "May the imperial realm be forever secure. . . . Long life to the emperor," and the eighteen four-character lines beginning with "May all in the six directions be pure and at peace," all of them identical with those of earlier texts discussed above. We can assume that *chüan* one opened with this same material. This book is not listed by Li Shih-yü or Sawada.

The title of chapter 22 is "The Holy Way of Imperial Heaven" (Huang-t'ien sheng-tao). We have seen that Richard Shek refers to an eighteenth-century sect called the Huang-t'ien tao, but its relationship to this earlier text is not clear.[5]

The *Yuan-chueh pao-chüan* is by far the longest such text I have read; the last three *chüan* alone total 356 folio (double) pages. Its author/transmitter is called Master Chin-shan (Gold Mountain) who lived on Mount Lao; he is described in chapter 30 as "awakening while in Buddhism" and as one who "provided vegetarian feasts for both monks and laypeople, compassionately caring for orphans, the solitary, and the poor." This, plus his ridicule of monks in this same chapter, leads me to believe that Master Chin-shan was not a monk himself.

The distinctive characteristics of the contents of this book are its explicit rejection of Lo Ch'ing's individualism, its affirmation of piety and virtue, and its inclusion of terminology from internal alchemy. This last theme is introduced by Master Chin-shan's statement that in his quest for enlightenment he "read elixir scriptures and Buddhist books" (chapter 17). The *Yuan-chueh* book repeatedly mentions returning to the Mother in the Native Place, but this mythology is not presented in a connected form.

The chapters of this book open with a long prose discussion, followed by two lines of seven-character verse, which are succeeded by about seven folio pages of verse arranged 3/3/4. Then five lines of five-character verse follow a few lines of prose and are themselves followed by a tune name that immediately precedes a concluding prose section.

4. *Hsiao-shih An-yang shih-chi pao-chüan* (The precious volume that explains the true situation of the [Land of] Tranquil Nourishment; hereafter "the *An-yang pao-chüan*"), two *chüan* in twenty-four chapters (*p'in*).

I have only the first *chüan* of this book, for which no date or place of publication is provided. However, in chapter 10 it refers to the *Yuan-chueh chüan* (text 3 above), and its illustrations and layout are very similar to it. In chapter 8 it refers to Master Chin-shan, the revealer of the *Yuan-chueh* book. The characters from the printing blocks are identical. These close similarities it also shares with the three Huan-yuan (Return to the Primal Source) texts discussed below, all from the late sixteenth century but reprinted in 1640. Finally, interlinear characters indicate that both the *An-yang* and *Yuan-chueh* books were owned by a Mrs. Sung, née Wang, of Tung-ch'ang prefecture in Shantung province. None of this proves that the *An-yang pao-chüan* was produced in the sixteenth century, but I believe there are enough indications to warrant treating it as such.

The *An-yang pao-chüan* opens with illustrations of a Chinese sage and a buddha, both with attendants at their sides. An illustration of a third sage follows, beside the sixteen-character inscription beginning with "May the imperial realm be forever secure," which is followed by the other two conventional invocations of long life for the emperor and prosperity for the land and people.

The first *chüan* opens with "ten reliances," followed by homage to Buddha, Dharma, and Sangha. This book is loosely based on Venerable Mother mythology and refers repeatedly to terms and titles from Lo Ch'ing's books, but in a garbled way. Terms used by Lo Ch'ing to express the inner potential for enlightenment and spiritual freedom are scattered about in the *An-yang* book, but with little apparent understanding.

This text is not listed in the bibliographies of Li Shih-yü and Sawada Mizuho. In chapters 2 and 12 it refers to the "Venerable Patriarch of True Emptiness" (Chen-k'ung lao-tsu), but his relationship to the text is unclear.

5. *Hsiao-shih Chen-k'ung sao-hsin pao-chüan* (The precious volume on [the Patriarch] Chen-k'ung's [instructions for] sweeping clear the mind; hereafter "the *Sao-hsin pao-chüan*"), two *chüan*, no chapter divisions. Printed in Wan-li 23/2/14 (= March 24, 1595). Not in the bibliographies of Li Shih-yü or Sawada Mizuho.

Wu Hsiao-ling's copy, which I read in 1981 and photographed in 1991, includes only the first *chüan*, but a complete copy is reprinted in volumes 18 and 19 of Chang Hsi-shun et al., eds., *Pao-chüan ch'u-chi*. Its first *chüan* is identical with that of Wu Hsiao-ling. Near the end of the second *chüan*, the page numbering is out of order after p. 242, but it appears that the entire text is included. The printing date is on the last page. Near the beginning of the second *chüan*, another printing date is given, "mid-autumn of the Wan-li *chia-shen* year" (= 1584). This might indicate that 1595 is a reprint date, but that is not stated.

This book is attributed to a Patriarch Sun, a monk of the Chiu-er yü monastery on Mount T'uan-kang, which I have not been able to identify. We are also told that he had been a woodcutter on Lu-pen shan, which I have also been unable to locate. In some passages here it is called Mount Lu, which is the name of mountains in Honan and Hupei, and of a district in Honan. Ma Hsi-sha and Han Ping-fang, in their *Min-chien tsung-chiao* (pp. 230–231), discuss Patriarch Sun as a fifth-generation patriarch in a tradition going back to Lo Ch'ing and the texts he composed. They state that he was from Shantung.

Patriarch Sun's teachings are called the Na-mo chiao (the Homage teaching) — that is, homage to the Buddha Amitābha through reciting his name. This emphasis he blends with Venerable Mother mythology through equating the Pure Land with the Native Place.

The *Sao-hsin pao-chüan* is beautifully bound and illustrated with engravings of buddhas and patriarchs. The opening invocation for the emperor's long life is printed with gold-colored ink. Its large, clear characters and alternating prose/verse style are similar to those of the other late Ming texts discussed here. Each section of 3/3/4 lines of verse is followed by three prose lines, which are followed in turn by tune names.

There is some interesting hagiographic material here about the Patriarch Sun:

The Na-mo Great Way appeared at the Chiu-er yü monastery on Mount T'uan-kang in the Eastern Land, with the appearance of Patriarch Sun, who left the household life in his middle age. His lay name was Sun San, and his nickname Sha-kua (Stupid Melon). He was ignorant and uncouth and did not know about proper human relationships or about ritual customs and moral principles. His appearance was uncommon. He was only able to recite the Buddha's name more than six thousand times a day for successive days, constantly without stopping. Suddenly one day, when he had gone to a mountain to collect firewood, he abruptly attained an awakening. With firewood in his left hand and an ax in his right, he stood upright with his feet spread apart like the character *pa* ("eight"), facing south, and entered meditative absorption (*samādhi*). Three days later, others saw him and reported to his family. When his parents learned of this they told many people about it, and so it became known everywhere. A great multitude of men and women came to venerate and look at him. There gathered at the mountain myriads of men and women, old and young. They all bowed their heads to the ground together and recited the Buddha's name. They surrounded him day and night and did not leave this place.

It is also said that our Venerable Patriarch was in a meditative trance for seven days, and then suddenly awoke; his eyes opened and he laughed aloud. He could see the sky and transcend the earth, and was familiar with all methods [of teaching]. When he pointed to a mountain or to the sea, he could leap over them. He raised his head to discourse on Heaven, and lowered it to discourse on Earth. . . .

Patriarch Sun maintained a vegetarian diet while still in the womb. After he had left his mother and grew up, he was stupid and dull; he did not understand marriage between men and women, he was unable to make himself attractive or wear good clothing and headgear. When he drank tea or ate rice, he didn't know how to make it taste good. He knew neither anger nor joy, and had no anger in his heart. At night he did not know how to look for a bed to sleep on, and in the daytime he did not know how to discuss antiquity or the present. He did not know good or bad, or how to use things, nor in his surroundings did he know which direction was which. The only thing he knew was to call out the Buddha's name, which he did all twelve hours of the day and night, without stopping, devoting all his strength [to the task].

Suddenly one day, when he had entered deep into the mountains, carrying firewood and water, with a shout his true body/self was manifest and his body and nature returned to emptiness. The lord who rules the center [i.e., his spirit] went out his mysterious gate and abandoned his bodily shell. . . .

With compassionate words he exhorted and transformed all, [saying,] "You and I are fundamentally of the same buddha-nature. It is only because you are attached to dust and sleep that you have been unable to enlighten your minds. Think back to the beginning, to the Fifth Patriarch, for whom there was a straight path [to salvation]. This Homage teaching (Na-mo chiao) I am giving to you [will enable you] to register your names [in paradise] for ten thousand years."

The great multitude of men and women are all the same; the Venerable Patriarch calls on his children [lit. "sons"] to concentrate with firm, devoted minds on listening to my true teaching and to constantly recite the six-character invocation [Na-mo A-mi-t'o Fo]. (18:401–413)

This hagiography is repeated near the end of the first volume in a "Eulogy for Patriarch Sun." It adds that though before his enlightenment he "could not read scriptures," later "he could understand all forms of writing." Here he is called "Patriarch Sun of True Emptiness" (18:556, 558, 555). Similar comments are made near the beginning of volume 2, where we are told that at first he "could not read scriptures or preach" (19:19–20).

Emphasizing the Patriarch's ignorance before enlightenment of course serves to enhance the divine quality of his subsequent revelations; this theme is in accord with the praise of lay piety found in many of these texts.

THREE TEXTS FROM THE HUAN-YUAN (RETURN TO THE PRIMAL SOURCE) SECT

6. *Hsiao-shih wu-hsing huan-yuan pao-chüan* (The precious volume that explains awakening the nature and returning to the primal source; hereafter "the *Huan-yuan pao-chüan*"), one *chüan* in twenty-four chapters (*p'in*). Reprinted in the third month of Ming Ch'ung-chen 13 (1640), but with references in an opening autobiographical

statement to Ming Wan-li 11 and 16 (1583 and 1588 by the Western calendar).

This is one of three texts in my collection from the Huan-yuan (Return to the Primal Source) tradition, all listed on the last page of the *Huan-yuan pao-chüan* as reprinted in 1640, along with three other "precious volumes," the *T'an-shih* (Sorrow for the world), *K'ai-hsin* (Opening the mind), and *Ti-yü* (Purgatory). The first two of these may have been Lo sect books, as discussed in Chapter Three above. In their *Min-chien tsung-chiao*, Ma Hsi-sha and Han Ping-fang mention a Huan-yuan sect in the Ch'ing period but provide little detail (pp. 251, 550, 553, etc.).

The *Huan-yuan* book is listed as a Ming text in Li Shih-yü, *Pao-chüan tsung-lu* (p. 52), but is not mentioned by Sawada Mizuho in his *Zōho Hōkan*. Its opening illustrations and invocations are very similar to those of the *Yuan-chueh* and *An-yang* books discussed above (texts 3 and 4, respectively). It is a well-written, coherent book distinguished by an opening autobiographical statement, immediately following homage to the Three Jewels. This statement is not entirely clear, in part because in it the Huan-yuan Patriarch goes in and out of a dream state in which he has visions, but if we take him at his word, it is an epiphany in which he is enlightened, receives instructions from the Ancient Buddha, and in the end leaves behind the *Huan-yuan pao-chüan* as a guide to future generations. It reads as follows:

The Patriarch said, "I have heard that returning to the primal source is reverting to the root, which is its most important topic. [I] am a man of the Tung-sheng Guard of Luan subprefecture in Yung-p'ing prefecture, where my family lived [in modern Hopei province]. I had darkened and confused my own nature, and had been unable to awaken; I was profoundly lost. I hesitated for eighteen years without the slightest awakening. Further, I did not think about the path along which one comes at birth and leaves at death. For the ancient and complete light, there is only the Ancient Buddha of Mount Ling, whose wisdom eye observes far off. I reflected in myself that, with an inner potential to return to the primal source (*huan-yuan tzu-hsing*), I had arrived in the Eastern Land eighteen years [before] and had not returned. Thus [the Mother?] called to the Bodhisattva of Complete Perfection Who Sees Everywhere (Yuan-chen p'u-yen p'u-sa), 'You go to the Eastern Land to seek for the light.' When he heard this, he bowed and expressed thanks for the holy message and descended from Mount Ling to come to the village. . . . At the third watch [11 P.M.–1 A.M.], [I] had a dream of an imaginary scene, in which I took in the light (*she-kuang*), returned to the primal source, and awakened. [I was told that] 'Our Buddha has sent you to descend to the mundane to save living beings. Will you be able for eighteen years to maintain a vegetarian diet? When will you return?' After being warned three times, I woke up [and realized that] it was all a dream, which I understood only obscurely. Early the following morning, I washed my hands and burned incense and bowed to thank Heaven and Earth. I had kept to a vegetarian diet but was still melancholy and confused. In the following days I hesitated and didn't know how to proceed. Then just at the *wu* hour [11 A.M.–1 P.M.] of the fifteenth day of the first month of Wan-li 11 [= 1583], [I] — confused and lost, fallen into the dust, awakened not at all — saw a monk wearing a *sūtra* robe (*ching-i*; a robe with quotations from scriptures written on it) and holding an alms bowl coming to the gate of my home. He called out in a loud voice to me[?] (*kao chiao na tzu*), 'Why are you not meditating? Why are you asleep?' In my dream of returning to the primal source, I replied, 'How should I meditate?' The monk replied, 'Listen to my instructions. Above, from the gateway at the top of your head go downward, and from the bottom of your feet go upward.'⁶ After this instruction he went to Yang-ch'ang [a place name in this text]."

The Patriarch said, "When I awoke, I was sitting upright facing straight south and saw only my true nature going out of and into the openings [of my body — eyes, nostrils, ears, and mouth]. [There was a] golden-colored realm, the Celestial Palace of Transforming Joy, with a continuous brilliant light, with an auspicious *ch'i* rising above. I also saw incense smoke wending about and filling the whole house. My heart was full of joy. At that time I simply wanted to return to the mountain to contemplate. Then I thought of my parents, old and with nothing to rely on. Perhaps I should practice at home. My parents were unwilling [to see me leave]; [and what about] my wife, Madame Ku? [I remained] depressed and confused. Finally, at the *hsü* hour [7–9 P.M.] on the evening of the twenty-seventh day of the ninth month of Wan-li 16 [= 1588], I entered a state of meditative absorption (*san-mei ch'an-ting*). The right person (*tang-jen*, the true self) was manifested, and I suddenly cut off my animating *ch'i* (*ling-ch'i*) and left for three days. When I awoke, I thought back [on what had happened]. My mind was as if it were stirred up with a knife; when would it be able to cut off being submerged in kindness and love [i.e., family emotions]? When would I discard my own darkened understanding?

"Then, on the third day of the tenth month, I burned incense filling a peck measure[?] (*man-tou fen-hsiang*) and bowed to thank Heaven and Earth. I took leave of my parents and old friends and hastened directly to Yang-ch'ang on Mount P'an. On the way, my mind was troubled. I traveled until I reached the Pure Karma Cloister, where, without begrudging my own life, I sat in arduous meditation day and night. I meditated until the first day of the eleventh month, absorbed to the point of death, when my true nature returned home. I discarded my body, a bag of pus and blood, a false form, [born of] a mundane womb."

The Patriarch said, "I praised and lamented that there was a self, with the fundamental nature within it, contending for the south and occupying the north [i.e., potentially all-encompassing]. [But now] for a time I had no self; my flesh was as if it were [born of] a womb of mud; my bones were like sticks of firewood." He also said, "When the Ancient Buddha in the Native Place saw my true nature, he received it and guided it to beneath the Bodhi tree, which is 1,000 yojanas high and exactly 500 yojanas [wide?]. My true nature sat there, lofty and unmoved, listening only to celestial music coming from space and the fine sound of flutes and lutes (ch'in). I also saw arhats and holy monks coming to bow in reverence. When they were finished bowing, they all sat down in order of precedence. [The Patriarch] Huan-yuan asked, 'What is this place?' The Ancient Buddha replied, 'This is the Palace of Transforming Joy of the Purple Yang Palace of the Native Place. Today you have returned home to receive the right ones (tang-jen).' The Ancient Buddha further asked Huan-yuan, 'Why are you not in the Eastern Land; why have you come home?' The Honored One [i.e., the Patriarch] said, 'Living beings in the Eastern Land are extremely difficult to save. Those who believe in the correct and true are few; those who believe in the crooked and false are very many.' The Ancient Buddha said, 'You return to the Eastern Land to save living beings.[7] I will [give you] eight holy jewels, eight great bodhisattvas, arhats, and holy monks, and also [give you] 84,000 awe-inspiring messages[?] (wei-i), [all] to lead to the Eastern Land. There, when you meet the evil, the evil will be converted, and when you meet the good, they will be saved. There you will transmit the teaching and preach the Dharma. I here will illuminate myself with a brilliant light.'"

The Patriarch bowed in thanks, and in his dream "saw only a brilliant continuous light." When he awoke, his

whole body was cold, his four limbs[?] (ssu-shao) were numb, and his mind was confused. There was no one to aid and care for me, but fortunately a worthy gentleman who was at peace in the Way (k'ang-tao)[8] guided me to the Dharma gate [= entrance to the teaching]. He escorted me in return and cared for me. Then, just at the second watch [9–11 P.M.] of the fifteenth day of the twelfth month, while sitting upright in meditation, facing exactly west, I saw ten bright rays of auspicious light, like white clouds, that penetrated the walls [of my house] and illumined me. My mind was like a bright mirror, and the Dharma [teaching] was like an ocean, with no obstacles. In the end, [I] left behind the Huan-yuan pao-chüan to give to later generations as a model for pious cultivation.

In a following verse section, this autobiographical statement is summed up and elaborated on in the first person, clarifying that when the Patriarch "was awakened, he entered the congregation (*hui*)," where, through listening to the Dharma, he dispersed serious calamities for himself and said, "I now leave behind this true scripture." We are not told directly that the book was revealed in his dream, but that is implied.

The remainder of the text is essentially a long sermon based on this experience and addressed to "those in the congregation" — both women and men — with the phrase "the Patriarch said" (*Tsu yun*) repeated throughout, together with first-person statements recalling the Patriarch's enlightenment and urging his disciples to "believe and accept the scripture that he left behind," which is described as "the words of the Ancient Buddha" (chapter 19).

The chapters of the *Huan-yuan pao-chüan* are organized in much the same way as the *Yuan-chueh* book (text 3 described above), but are shorter. There are opening illustrations and invocations similar to those in the other books we have looked at in this appendix.

7. *Hsiao-shih k'e-i cheng-tsung pao-chüan* (The precious volume that explains the correct tradition of ordering the thoughts[?]; hereafter "the *Cheng-tsung pao-chüan*"), one *chüan* in twenty-four chapters (*p'in*). No date. Reprinted in 1640 with the *Huan-yuan* and *Kuei-chia pao-en pao-chüan* (texts 6 above and 8 below, respectively).

At the end of chapter 22, we read of the narrator of the text, "I now am really (*pen*) the Huan-yuan Patriarch, sitting upright in the Cloud Palace, receiving the worthy." In chapter 11 we read,

I today in great compassion have left behind a wonderful teaching, each sentence of which seeks out the right ones, their nature, destiny, source, and root. I have transmitted to you the message from the West (*hsi-lai i*), [so that] you can understand your roots and respond to your origin. Every sentence of the *Cheng-tsung chüan* is clearly written. The message from the West, written first, [brings] supernormal powers and vision (*liu-t'ung wu-yen*).[9] In the *Huan-yuan chüan*, written later, the Eight Treasures are complete.[10]

This passage goes on to mention the *T'an-shih* (Sorrow for the world) *chüan*, the *Ti-yü* (Purgatory) *chüan*, the *Kuei-chia pao-en chüan* (text 8 below), and the *K'ai-hsin* (Opening the mind) *pao-chüan*, all of which "I have now left behind," and which "leave behind the Patriarch's message." (On the *T'an-shih* and *K'ai-hsin pao-chüan*, see Chapter Three above.) Since we have preface dates of 1583 and 1588 in the *Huan-yuan pao-chüan* (text 6 above), this passage indicates that the *Cheng-tsung* book was extant by then or even earlier. This text is dated to the Ming period by Li Shih-yü in his *Pao-chüan tsung-lu* (p. 52).

The opening pictures and salutations in the *Cheng-tsung* book are almost identical to those in the *Kuei-chia pao-en* and *Huan-yuan pao-chüan*; it is obvious that the texts for the printing blocks of all three were written by the same hand. The introductory materials for this text are also conventional for the genre. The *Cheng-tsung pao-chüan* is a relatively coherent book addressed repeatedly to "those in the congregation" for their deliverance. Native Place mythology is assumed but is internalized, with the three Dragon-Flower assemblies being interpreted as "The three natures being completely enlightened, the Dragon Flower is the nature and destiny, interacting and matched" (chapter 11). The focus here is on enlightenment and developing a new perception—namely, that of the "Dharma eye" (*fa-yen*), which understands the potential for deliverance within oneself (chapter 7).

8. *Hsiao-shih kuei-chia pao-en pao-chüan* (The precious volume that explains returning home and repaying parental love; hereafter "the *Kuei-chia pao-en pao-chüan*"), one *chüan* in twenty-four chapters (*p'in*), 1591. Reprinted in 1640, along with the *Huan-yuan* and *Cheng-tsung* texts (texts 6 and 7 above). On the last page of this book, we are told that it was first printed in the tenth month of (Ming) Wan-li 19 (= 1591). Li Shih-yü, in his *Pao-chüan tsung-lu* (p. 52), provides this same date.

In chapter 12 there is a reference to "entering the Huan-yuan congregation," while the teachings of this book share the inward orientation of the other two Return to the Primal Source texts discussed in this appendix (i.e., texts 6 and 7 above), all of which are expressions of what might be called a popularized Ch'an teaching. The opening pictures and invocation of the *Kuei-chia pao-en chüan* are the same as those of the other two books, and the introductory material is similar.

This book is distinguished by its emphasis on filial piety toward parents, at points blended with reverence for the cosmic parent (*fu-mu*), which in these texts refers to the Mother. As we read in chapter 13,

Stop forgetting the kindness and love [you have been shown] and turning your backs on the patriarchs. The news, the true Dharma, has been transmitted to you so that you will clearly realize *bodhi* and sit on the heart of the

lotus. [Just as] the lotus flower emerges from the water, [so will you] transcend the three realms and with each step ascend to the sky, not to be reborn
below. The great buddhas and patriarchs will come to receive you, and
at the three Dragon-Flower assemblies you will [obtain] spiritual freedom
everywhere (tsung-heng), transcend the mundane, and enter the holy. The
Huan-yuan teaching chops to pieces perverse demons. The content of the
Scripture on Repaying Parental Love responds to the buddhas and patriarchs;
all worthies and sages are in it. Every sentence in it is concerned with repaying love, because the Parent (fu-mu) has finally left behind a scripture . . .
to save all people in this floating [ephemeral] world.

Chapter 13 also discusses the struggle of the narrator of this text
to leave the household life despite his love for his parents, wife, and
children. He finally decides that "today I am going to take refuge in
the mountains to visit worthies and study the Way. When I have attained the Way, then I will return home and give first priority to repaying my two parents."

FIVE TEXTS OF THE HUNG-YANG (VAST YANG) SECT

The Hung-yang sect was active in North China during the Wan-li
period of the Ming dynasty (1573–1619). It attracted support from
some palace eunuchs in Beijing, who arranged for several of its texts
to be published by the Palace Printing Bureau. In his 1980 "Religion
and Society in Late Ming" (pp. 276–287), Richard Shek provides a
detailed discussion of this sect and its teachings. After evaluating the
evidence, Shek concludes that the founder of the tradition was a man
named Han T'ai-hu from Kuang-p'ing prefecture in Chih-li province, who took the religious name of P'iao-kao (He Who Floats on
High). He is also called Hun-yuan tsu (Patriarch of the Origin in
Creative Chaos).

In Hung-yang texts, P'iao-kao is said to have become a monk at
age nineteen, to have begun his preaching in 1594, and to have gone
to Beijing the following year. There he converted some influential
palace eunuchs and wrote and published the founding scriptures of
the Hung-yang teaching. He died in 1598, at the age of twenty-nine
(see Shek, "Religion and Society in Late Ming," p. 282).

I have copies of seven Hung-yang texts, five of which were kindly
given to me by Richard Shek. It appears that two of them were written and published in the seventeenth century after the founder's
death, and so I here deal with only the first five, beginning with two
that Shek has suggested were written by P'iao-kao. Both are semi-

autobiographical, with titles based on two of Lo Ch'ing's compositions.

The term "Hung-yang" is homophonous with the term meaning
"Red Yang" referred to in the *Yao-shih pao-chüan* (text 1 above), but I
do not know of any connection between the two. In sectarian mythology, "Red Yang" refers to the present time period presided over
by Śākyamuni Buddha, which is also the time indicated by Vast
Yang. Li Shih-yü, *Pao-chüan tsung-lu* (p. 21), lists five Vast Yang
texts, whereas Sawada Mizuho, *Zōho Hōkan* (pp. 212–214 and 258–
260), lists eleven. The Hung-yang sect and its texts are also discussed
in Ma Hsi-sha and Han Ping-fang, *Min-chien tsung-chiao* (pp. 489–
548), a chapter that includes information on activities of this
tradition in the eighteenth and nineteenth centuries.

9. *Hung-yang k'u-kung wu-tao ching* (The Vast Yang scripture on
awakening to the Way through bitter toil; hereafter "the *Hung-yang
k'u-kung ching*"), two *chüan* in twenty-four chapters (*p'in*), no date. In
volume 15 of Chang Hsi-shun et al., eds., *Pao-chüan ch'u-chi*. Illustrated throughout, both at the beginning and just after each chapter
title, with a few additional illustrations as well.

Along with five of the other Hung-yang texts I have read, the
Hung-yang k'u-kung book opens with illustrations of buddhas and
patriarchs, followed by invocations for the security and prosperity of
the realm, long life for the emperor, and the continuation of Buddhist teaching. Then these books continue with a general inside title
that is the same for all, and a preface, as follows:

The *Hun-yuan chiao Hung-yang Chung-hua ching* (The scripture of the Central
Flowery land [China] of the Vast Yang [sect] of the teaching of origin in
primordial chaos), preface.

A statement of praise (*tsan*) [about the] Hun-yuan Venerable Patriarch
who ordered Master Hung-yang to engage in bitter toil.

As for the Hun-yuan school, [I] have heard that it was [established] before the "subtle sound" (*wei-yin*) at the dividing of primordial chaos. What it
teaches is the source, the turbulent prime that is primordial chaos, turbulent
chaos [combined with] the turbulent prime.

It is said that beyond the "subtle sound" [at creation] there were originally no three teachings and their scriptures. They were produced by a
transformation of the single vital force of the turbulent prime. [According to]
the Vast Yang Dharma, at present the Buddha Śākyamuni is in charge of the
teaching and is considered the Master of the Hung-yang teaching. The Pure
Yang (Ch'ing-yang) [was dominant] in the past; at present it is the Vast
Yang, and in the future will be the White Yang. A great multitude proclaim

[this teaching], for which none feel shame or remorse [reading as *ts'an-hui*]. The correct and true Dharma rarely exists, and is difficult to understand and hear. I give instructions [based on] the intermixing of the mundane and holy.

The *gāthā* says,

At the golden terrace are primordial images of patriarchs
    and the Perfected,
[Of those who] save all the multitudes of primal ones
    in the world.
Just like the shaking of the sound of spring thunder,
The world considers "patriarchs" to be the first title of all[?]
    (*t'ien-hsia wei tsu ti-i ming*).

The Venerable Patriarch further offered in praise a wonderful *gāthā*:

In the whole nation of the Great Ming, all under heaven
    intercommunicates.
The Duke Who Establishes the Nation (Ting-kuo kung),
    with the merit of one who [has assisted] the founding
    of the dynasty,
Has protected and supported the Tathāgata teaching of
    the chaotic prime.
He early ascended to the gate of wisdom.
Officer Ting protected and supported the patriarchal teaching,
    [caused it] to flourish, and protected the Dharma.

Preface for the Text of Great Peace and Prosperity That Preserves Tranquillity

A psalm of praise, with an invocation offered above for the holiness and long life of the Emperor, and with the prayer offered for those below that the myriad people will receive good fortune.

The vast blessings of the Holy Court are equal to heaven, so that now there is an enlightened teacher for leaving the world.

Fearing that petty people would cheat and harm, he transmitted [this scripture] so that the people of the world would know to obey the royal law, read scriptures, and worship. Those listening to [this] scripture should be serious, dignified, and properly dressed. It is not permitted to be disorderly in the scripture-hall [i.e., place of worship].

[They should] put into practice their religious cultivation, investigate according to principle, and pay homage to the perfect and true.

A Psalm of Praise from the Marquis of Western Peace (Hsi-ning hou)

In the middle of the Wan-li period of the Great Ming, the Buddha established the Patriarchal Teaching of the Origin in Primal Chaos. At the age of twenty-six *sui*, he [the Patriarch] went to the capital. This was a response to the Buddhadharma. He first took refuge in the Office of Wet Nurses and then was escorted to the household of Officer Shih.[11]

Officer Ting protected and supported him, [so that his teaching] flourished and the world was moved liked the echoes of spring thunder.

Duke Ch'eng of the Directorate of the Imperial Horses [an office staffed by imperial eunuchs], Duke Shih of the Palace Printing Bureau, and Duke Chang of the Court Bureau of the Armory—three protectors of the Dharma—jointly offer a hymn of praise:

Among the religious practitioners of the world, there are few who, having widely read the complete perfection of the three teachings, bequeath scriptures and preach the Dharma [among those] with ordinary minds. [In this teaching,] the ordinary and holy are interconnected and discussed. Every phrase and sentence is profound and wonderful. In the Eastern Land it teaches and converts the ignorant, and circulates throughout the world. Surely this is not a trivial matter! [This teaching] directly points out the path to the Native Place.

Master T'ieh and others who composed this scripture, a total of seventeen men, together with the Patriarch, jointly offer a hymn of praise:

From the time when Father Hung-wu [founder of the Ming dynasty] put the world in order, the patriarchs of our school have each written scriptures and in a learned and orthodox way furthered the onward flow of the three teachings, so continuing the transmission of the lamp. The learned of the world, once having encountered the words of this text, know that the Master is vast and great. Only rarely is there [one who] awakens to the Way and bequeaths scripture. In the sea of suffering, a perfected person has appeared in the world and has thoroughly explored enlightening the mind through seeing the nature [i.e., one's inner potential for enlightenment]. He has newly established the Patriarchal Teaching of the Origin in Primal Chaos. The Buddhadharma [= this teaching] is flourishing in the world, [enabling us to] transcend the ordinary and enter the holy. He was a true monk, a master in charge of the teaching, whose name will be transmitted for ten thousand ages.

These prefaces are followed by a table of contents listing the titles of the twelve chapters in volume 1. Chapter 1 opens with its title and a two-part illustration showing a monk with a halo, presumably the Patriarch, in seated meditation and bowing before a buddha-image.

With minor variations, this introductory material is repeated in all the late sixteenth-century Hung-yang scriptures I have read, no doubt in part because it clarifies the high level of support the new sect received from court eunuchs.

As its title indicates, the *Hung-yang k'u-kung ching* is modeled in part on Lo Ch'ing's spiritual autobiography, with echoes as well of legends of the revulsion felt by the young buddha-to-be when he

faced old age and death. Here the "Venerable Patriarch Hun-yuan" narrates in the first person his struggle to attain enlightenment against the opposition of his parents, who did not want him to leave home.

As with Lo Ch'ing before him, he had not been able to enlighten his mind and see his true nature, nor did he know how to escape the sufferings of saṃsāra, but, "unwilling to give up, he earnestly advanced another step" (chapter 1): "Every day I offered reverence to the Three Jewels, burned incense, maintained a vegetarian diet, offered vegetarian food to monks, and did various charitable acts" but realized that "none of these was a path for going forth [from the ordinary world]." One can do them all, but

when old age comes, one will [go] empty-handed to see Lord Yama [Lord of the Underworld]. . . . If one does not meet an enlightened teacher, one's mind will not be enlightened. When would I see the face of a perfected person? I thought of how difficult it is to escape from Lord Yama. When will a true buddha descend to the world? (chapter 2)

Full of fear, the Patriarch desperately wanted to leave home to seek such an enlightened teacher, but though he had attained adulthood, his parents would not allow him to leave (chapter 3). Yet time was passing, and he was anxious for his salvation: "Every day I thought about my dear parents, and also about my friends in the Way whom I was unable to meet. I wanted to return to [my true] home, my old village, but my life was full of suffering and being at home was difficult to bear" (chapter 5).

Then his mother became ill, and on her behalf for three years he called out to the Buddha for aid. Her illness caused him much worry and grief, a sorrow only increased by his encounter with an eighty-year-old man one day when he went out to buy incense. This reminded him of the frailties of old age that come to all, which intensified his quest. Eventually he heard of a religious master to whom he rushed off to seek instruction. This master taught him to recite scriptures and the Buddha's name, which he did for two years without attaining enlightenment, thus concluding that they were "not the way of escape" (chapter 8).

Nonetheless, this experience prepared him finally to leave home and devote all his time to his religious quest, which he did after first preparing everything for his parents. He then began to travel about, begging for his food. He went first to Liang-nan (in modern Kiangsu), where there were many who "talked about the Native

Place," but found no solace there. He then heard that in Hsu-chou (in Kiangsu) there was a "divine Perfected One who has descended to the ordinary world, who clearly explains the Cloud City and has saved numberless men and women." Here he discovered a sect, the "Assembly of the Primal Imperial" (Yuan-huang hui), that preached about the twelve passes to the Cloud City but charged money for its tallies and titles. This, the Patriarch concluded, was "not [according to] the buddha-nature. How could the Venerable Ancient Buddha be greedy for gold and silver when he descends to the ordinary world?" Thus his search continued.

The Patriarch next went to Honan, where he met a "perfected person" named Master Wang "who deeply understood the principles of the Way. It was said that he was the Buddha Śākyamuni descended from the celestial palace, and that having received the [teaching about] the Limitless, he had come to correct the teaching and seek for the sons and daughters [of the Mother]." This teacher "did not demand money" but taught the "true principles" of "penetrating to the root and returning to the source," and about enlightening the mind and "the Ancient Native Place": "He taught me to devote earnest effort if I wanted to see the Native Place."

The young seeker meditated every day with this enlightened master, and so gradually made progress (chapter 10). He became a disciple of Master Wang, who taught enlightenment of the mind through seeing the nature and one's "original face." After three months of effort, the Master finally "dotted his heart" (tien fang-ts'un), symbolizing that he had attained at least a degree of enlightenment. He then told Master Wang that he wanted to return home to aid and save his old mother. Taking leave of his teacher, he returned to Hopei. Before he left, Master Wang told him:

Disciple, I have now dotted [= certified] your enlightened mind and permit you to seek out the primal ones. If there are those who have maintained a vegetarian diet and been diligently pious for a long time, who fear birth-and-death but who have been unable to find the straight path to the Native Place, you should lead them to vow [to attain salvation], give them the first step of pious practice, and point them to the southwest, [toward which they] are to repeatedly worship the Eternal Progenitor (Wu-sheng fu-mu).

Having received this missionary commission, the patriarch-to-be told his teacher that he would save his mother with the Vast Yang teaching: "I will earnestly urge her to repent. If she doesn't believe my explanation of the true situation, I will certainly preach to her about pious practice according to [our] marvelous principles, and how urgent it is to be able to travel back [to the source]" (chapter 12).

In the company of another sect leader, the patriarch-to-be returned home to Hopei in spite of a lack of funds and the difficulties of the trip, particularly the crossing of the Yellow River. When they reached their destination, these two "friends in the Way" preached to all this wonderful teaching of how to leave the world of suffering. All listened attentively, the Patriarch's mother and the family elders "believed and received the [proper forms of] pious practice," and then a total of ninety others did the same. The patriarch-to-be then proposed that all return to Honan to "pay homage to the Master" (chapter 16). This they all did.

The remainder of the *Hung-yang k'u-kung ching* discusses a later trip to Hopei and concludes with the Patriarch meditating in a mountain cave. One day, while meditating, he had a dream in which he

reached the Native Place, where he saw numberless towers, terraces, and palaces. There was a strand of golden [two characters unclear]. Below the Place of No Rebirth, he bowed to thank the Eternal Venerable Mother (Wu-sheng lao-mu). Without arising from his bow, he asked for long life in the world and begged for a drop of divine elixir. When he had swallowed this, he suddenly arose and at that point attained clear enlightenment. He saw that the sacred precincts of the Golden City were all [due to] the supernormal powers of the Venerable Patriarch. Facing southwest, he thanked the Eternal Progenitor. This was due to his merit. Suddenly a ray of bright red[?][12] light illuminated his body, and of itself his mind-ground opened up, the flower of his mind blossomed, and he left behind [this] true scripture without words. (chapter 24)

The quest had taken him three years. At the end we are told that the Patriarch "reached Home, he reached Home, where he is in the company of the Venerable Mother, never again to be reborn in the East" (chapter 24).

Thus, in a legendary form, the *Hung-yang k'u-kung ching* provides important information about the religious experience of a young man who was to become a sect leader. It clarifies that Hun-yuan/P'iao-kao studied with earlier sectarian masters before coming to his own enlightenment. This was the background of his missionary success in the capital.

The theme of each chapter of this book is illustrated with a woodcut drawing, clear and of good quality. Each chapter opens with a

prose section, followed by verse arranged in two lines of seven characters each. The chapters all end with four lines of five-character
verse. Volume 2 opens with exactly the same introductory illustrations and prefaces described above, followed by a table of contents.

10. *Hun-yuan hung-yang Fo ju-lai wu-chi P'iao-kao tsu lin-fan ching*
(The scripture of the descent to the ordinary [world] of P'iao-kao, the
Patriarch of the Limitless, the Chaotic Origin Vast Yang Buddha
Tathāgata; hereafter "the *P'iao-kao ching*"), two *chüan* in twenty-four
chapters, no date. In volumes 16 and 17 of Chang Hsi-shun et al.,
eds., *Pao-chüan ch'u-chi*.

The *Hung-yang k'u-kung ching* (text 9 above) is a spiritual autobiography of the Hun-yuan Patriarch's quest for enlightenment,
whereas the *P'iao-kao ching* sets forth a mythological understanding
of him as a reluctant savior sent to Earth to rescue the lost. The
structure of this book is similar to that of the *Hung-yang k'u-kung*, but
here the longer verse sections, arranged 3/3/4, alternate with those
arranged 7/7 per line. There are only a few tune names in the *Hung-
yang k'u-kung* book, but such names appear in the middle of the
prose sections of each chapter of the *P'iao-kao ching*. The opening illustration, inscriptions, and prefaces are identical.

The scripture begins as follows:

The first volume of [*The Scripture of*] *the Patriarch of the Limitless P'iao-kao Descending to the Ordinary [World]*, he who is the Buddha Tathāgata of the Vast
Yang teaching of the Origin in Primal Chaos. As for this scripture [title re-
peated], what school of teaching for leaving the world does it discuss? What
gateway for understanding the Way through religious cultivation and practice? It is the school of the origin in primal chaos, the teachings of the chaotic
source and the Vast Yang.
    A general outline of the explanation of [the time] when there was [as yet]
no Heaven or Earth.

This "general outline" is a table of contents listing the titles of each
of the twelve chapters of volume 1. This list is followed by "verses
for opening the scripture":

[This] supreme, profound, subtle and marvelous teaching is difficult
    to encounter in a myriad kalpas.
I, now, having seen and heard it, am able to bestow and support it,
    and desire to explain the true meaning of the Tathāgata's message.

After the title of the first chapter, the scripture proper begins with
an account of the appearance of the world out of primordial misty

chaos, which formed a "primal egg" (*yuan-luan*), also called the "dark yellow of Heaven and Earth." This cosmic egg split, and from it appeared the "celestial buddha who ordered the world," and with him the "founding patriarch appeared in the world. Pure *ch'i* became the heavens, turbid *ch'i* formed the earth. The one produced the two, the two produced the three, and the three produced the myriad things. All of them were bequeathed by the Venerable Patriarch (Lao-tsu *liu-hsia*)" (chapter 1). Succeeding verses add that the Buddha Amitābha appeared in the world out of the primordial mist, and that "the primal egg also produced the Hun-yuan Patriarch," who "descended to the world to settle the heavens and put the world in order." In this book P'iao-kao appears as an avatar of this primordial patriarch and is also described as one of his sons.

In chapter 2, the Hun-yuan Patriarch is told that, in "the Eastern Land, the sea of suffering, Heaven and Earth are ruined and the heavens are broken, and the end of the age will soon arrive. Which patriarch should be sent to descend to the ordinary world to seek for the suffering primal ones?" This report "saddened the heart of the Venerable Hun-yuan Patriarch; it was difficult to abandon the little children of the Golden City. . . . With his eyes full of tears, [he wondered] who would be willing to go, giving up the Native Place to seek the primal ones?"

None of the celestial patriarchs is eager to leave paradise, but the Buddha Śākyamuni reluctantly agrees to go, taking leave of the Venerable Patriarch and the Venerable Mother (chapter 4). He weeps as he descends, vowing to return after he has found all the primal ones (chapter 4). Other patriarchs are sent down to assist Śākyamuni; all are reluctant because they assume that they have been ordered to go because of some sin they have committed. Here the sectarian mythology about saving beings is influenced by old ideas of immortals' being temporarily banished from paradise due to some infraction of the rules.

Those who descend include not only patriarchs but also Holy Mothers, even the Venerable Mother herself (chapter 7). Thus hundreds of celestial beings, male and female, came to "live in the ordinary world, having entered wombs to be transformed"—i.e., reborn as humans (chapter 9). Here all these gods and buddhas are integrated into the structure of sectarian mythology, including not only Śākyamuni but Kuan-yin, Maitreya, Ananda, Kāśyapa, and even Bodhidharma!

In chapter 11 we are told that "98 patriarchs descended to the Eastern Land, 72, 84, and 48 patriarchs; 3,000 buddhas descended to the world, and 7,000 bodhisattvas." They descend but are afraid they might be lost and not find the way back to paradise; they don't know into what families they will be reborn and are afraid people will not believe (chapter 11). All of them leave behind "scriptures for the ordinary world" (*lin fan ching*) — a good insiders' description of a sectarian "precious volume" (chapter 11). These scriptures are "left behind to save sentient beings in the sea of suffering. If one believes them, one will return to the sky [i.e., paradise]; if one does not believe, one will remain in the vast [realm of] dust. A believing mind is the way to heaven; unbelief in these scriptures is the gateway to purgatory" (chapter 11).

All this time, P'iao-kao has been unwilling to go; he has stayed in the palace, disobeying orders to descend immediately, and asks that his brothers be sent instead (chapter 14). His mother, one of the many Venerable Mothers in this book, threatens to tell his father, the Hun-yuan Patriarch; she begs mercy for her son, but his father becomes angry and refuses to exempt "the little patriarch." All his fourteen brothers have already been sent anyway (chapter 16). Even after repeated assurances of special divine protection for him, P'iao-kao drags out his refusal. By this time he is the only eligible messenger left in the palace! Finally he does go — his name is included in a list of descended patriarchs in chapter 22.

Thus this *P'iao-kao ching* describes the founding of the Hung-yang sect against a vast background of cosmic time and celestial deities. By the time the Patriarch descends, all the other gods and buddhas have gone before him to prepare the way. The message is clear: Sect teachings are an integral part of the history of salvation, which they both rely on and culminate. Here we can only admire the mythological audacity of the sectarian authors. Everything was grist for their mill, and they shaped it for their own ends.

11. *Hung-yang t'an-shih ching* (The Vast Yang scripture of sorrow for the world), two *chüan* in eighteen chapters, no date. I have another copy of this same text, entitled *Hun-yuan hung-yang t'an-shih chen-ching* (The true scripture of sorrow for the world of the Vast Yang [teaching] of the Hun-yuan [Patriarch]).

This is a book of moral regret and condemnation, with calls to repentance directed toward those at all social levels. Its title is based on that of one of Lo Ch'ing's writings, the *T'an-shih pao-chüan*, described in Chapter Three above. Its organization is the same as that of the other Hung-yang sect scriptures described above in this appendix, with identical introductory material and prefaces repeated at the beginning of each volume, followed by tables of contents. Illustrations of the theme of each chapter follow the chapter titles.

In the typical chapter, two lines of 7/7 verse are followed by a prose section, succeeded by several more lines of 7/7 verse. After another brief prose passage, this discussion is recounted again (*ch'ung-hsuan*) in 3/3/4 lines of verse, here called *chi* (Skt. *gāthā*). Each prose section is introduced with the phrase *chao ch'ueh-shuo* ("let us resume our story"), as is true with the other Hung-yang texts discussed here as well.

The content of this book is distinguished by its sustained call for moral reform, which is directed first to the self, then to people in general, and finally to the wealthy and powerful, the evil and violent, the young, adults, those who revile the religion, and those entangled by wine, illicit sex, wealth, and anger. Corrupt Buddhist monks and Taoist priests are also criticized, as are disloyal and arrogant officials. All are called upon to repent and change their ways. The *Hung-yang t'an-shih ching* devotes more attention to socially differentiated moral criticism than any other sixteenth-century "precious volume" I have read, and hence is of great value for our understanding of the social perspectives of these books.

Nonetheless, strictly speaking, this is not social criticism but an evangelistic message on behalf of sect teachings, made urgent by the decline of values at the end of the age. As we read:

Sigh in regret for the stupidity of living beings, who from the beginning of time have not turned around and returned. From the Golden City many patriarchs have been sent down to save sons and daughters so that they quickly repent. They are all lost in the Eastern Land. If the end of the age arrives soon, how will they escape the sufferings of saṃsāra? They should think about the suffering they will endure. If the primal ones do not give up [their worldly?] homes,[13] they will not escape from suffering. How will they be able to return to the primal source? . . .

May the multitudes soon repent. All are members of one family. (chapter 2)

If you don't believe this *Hung-yang* scripture, you will be reborn as a hungry ghost. (chapter 3)

With the Yuan-tun sect[14] and the Vast Yang teaching, a true teaching has appeared in the world. (chapter 10)

The end of the age is characterized by such sins as parents and children not caring for each other and husbands and wives separating, covetousness for wealth, cheating other people and the gods, criticizing pious vegetarians, rejecting the patriarchs and not believing in the Hung-yang teachings. Good and bad intentions and actions are to be clearly distinguished: "The bad constantly harbor hateful and poisonous intentions; the good always think of how to save the world" (chapter 6). Sinners are threatened with dire punishments:

If you do not believe, in the Eastern Realm you will fall into purgatory and in the last age will not escape. . . . The Ancient Buddha sees the faces of all and the Ten Lords of purgatory will not forgive. . . . Though you should live fifty years, you will die early, before you are twenty-five, and two hungry ghosts will come to seize you. (chapter 8)

The readers and hearers of this scripture are repeatedly reminded not only of such retribution for sins, but also of the impermanence of life and all its possessions and social positions: "Time flies like an arrow. . . . After you are born, then you die; then after you die, you are born again and for many eons do not obtain eternal life." The solution to all this is "to believe urgently, quickly turn around, and return home" (chapter 9).

Thus in the *Hung-yang t'an-shih ching* we see the same basic message as in the other Hung-yang texts, but from a more morally specific perspective.

12. *Hung-yang wu-tao ming-hsin ching* (The Vast Yang scripture on awakening to the Way and enlightening the mind; hereafter "the *Wu-tao ming-hsin ching*"), eighteen chapters in two volumes, 175 folio pages. No date, except for the preface reference to the teaching being established in the Ming Wan-li period (1573–1619). In volume 16 of Chang Hsi-shun et al., eds., *Pao-chüan ch'u-chi*.

This text opens with the same illustrations, invocations, and prefaces as the other Hung-yang sect scriptures discussed in this appendix. After its title, each chapter begins with two lines of five-character verse, followed by a prose section that is succeeded in turn by 7/7 verse. The chapters end with four lines of five-character verse. There is a good, clear woodcut illustration at the beginning of each chapter, but no tune names. The most significant structural variation in the text is the inclusion in chapter 2 of the "Sage Edict" of the founding Ming Emperor T'ai-tsu (d. 1398), a general exhortation to filiality, friendship, and acceptance of one's lot.

Also, the whole of chapter 2 in the second *chüan* of this book is devoted to "repayments for kindness," the most detailed such discussion I have seen in *pao-chüan*, and the only one presented as a chapter in the middle of a book. The title of this chapter is "Repaying Kindness, and Repentance" (Pao-en ch'an-hui). It begins:

In repaying kindness, first repay the Venerable World-Honored One,
[And then] the kindness of Heaven and Earth that cover
    and support [us], and that of the sun and moon.
Ten thousand times ten thousand years to the exalted
    Emperor T'ai-tsu.
[Gratitude as well] for the kindness of parents, [and to]
Masters and to those who [support the religion] by
    acts of charity (*shih-chu*).

A summary prose discussion is developed in more detail in 7/7 character verse, beginning with ten statements of gratitude (*pao . . . en*) to the Hun-yuan Venerable Patriarch, Wu-sheng lao-mu, and various buddhas, patriarchs, and matriarchs. These are followed by twenty-two more such statements that name additional patriarchs, Holy Mothers, the five grains, government officials, one's own master and parents, etc. — a rather miscellaneous list. These thirty-two statements of gratitude are followed by eight exhortations to repentance for such sins as cursing the wind and rain, cheating gods and masters, plotting for fame, anger, treachery, talking too much, and lying. The structure here is "*ch'an-hui . . . hsin*" ("repent for having a mind to/intending to . . .").

The most interesting aspect of the content of the *Wu-tao ming-hsin ching* is its focus on the Eternal Venerable Mother, who is urged to descend to the world herself to save her children. This she does, accompanied by other mother-deities. Her descent is based on sorrow for her children. As we read in chapter 6:

The Eternal Mother (Wu-sheng mu) in [the realm of] emptiness comes to look at her sons and daughters. When she sees the earnest piety of her children, her eyes are full of tears. She sees them as homeless children, these men [who offer] incense and believing women. The Venerable Eternal [Mother], expressing her compassion, saves her children. Holding a "precious jewel that supports heaven," she releases a ray of bright light and comes to manifest her transforming power, illuminating her children.

The theme of the Mother's descent is stated more clearly in chapter 5 of *chüan* 2, where we read,

That the Eternal [Mother] descended to the world is not to be taken lightly. For forty-five years she drew nigh to [i.e., lived in] the Eastern [Land]. All the buddhas and bodhisattvas descended to the ordinary world. The Venerable Mother who orders the world entered [was in] the Golden City, [but then she?] the Eternal Holy Mother took leave of the Golden Palace.

There follows a list of twenty-six additional Venerable Mothers who descended to the world, where they "each manifested their supernormal powers and recited true scriptures."

Chapter 8 of volume 2 is a description of purgatory, with the names of its ten kings, courts with their forms of punishments, and the sins that get one there. Chapter 9 is devoted to correlations between the human body and the larger world, complete with a rustic illustration. The correlations are for the most part the conventional ones of comparing the eyes to the sun and moon, the hair on the head to trees on mountains, the stars and planets to the eighty-four thousand pores of the skin, and so on.

In sum, the *Wu-tao ming-hsin ching* is a good and relatively interesting example of its genre.

13. *Hung-yang pi-miao hsien-hsing chieh-kuo ching* (The Vast Yang scripture, secret and wonderful, [that discusses] the karmic results of manifesting the nature), apparently two *chüan* in twenty-four chapters, although I have only the first *chüan* in twelve chapters; no date.

This text borrows both its dominant ideas and part of its title from Lo Ch'ing's scriptures, with an emphasis on becoming enlightened through seeing and realizing one's own true nature. Its introductory material, organization, alternation of prose and verse sections, and placement of illustrations are the same as those of the other Hung-yang sect texts. Lo Ch'ing's scriptures are cited four times here: once, in chapter 5, as the *Wu-pu ching* (The five scriptures); once, in chapter 6, as "A Scripture of Patriarch Lo"; and twice in excerpts from the *P'o-hsieh hsien-cheng ching*, discussed in Chapter Three above. There is also a passage beginning with the phrase, "The Patriarch Lo said" (chapter 5).

The fundamental theme of this book is clarified by the following passages:

To awaken to the Way and enlighten the mind, one must see [one's] original face and the bright light of one's own body. If [images made of] carved wood and molded clay have such radiance, how could the bodies of humans not have it, since they are endowed by Heaven and Earth with the buddha-nature of the Limitless? The Buddha has said that all people, men and women, each have their own natures, which are never increased or decreased in the slightest. For measureless vast eons until the present, they have lacked nothing, but from the beginning, when people were [first born from] the womb, they have lost their original natures and become ever more confused. . . . A former patriarch said it well: "You yourself are originally Amitābha Buddha." . . . If you can't see your original nature, you cannot return to the source and [will remain in] the Eastern Realm. The original face is neither produced nor changed by humans. . . . The Tao is not confused, but humans have confused themselves and so lost their original natures. The Way is not distant; humans have made it distant themselves and are not willing to seek it. . . . You must see your fundamental nature; it is originally the diamond indestructible body. (chapter 1)

Although the dominant theme here is this sort of popularized Ch'an perspective, in chapter 11 the pious are also exhorted to "see the dear Eternal Venerable Mother; when all are reunited, they will care for each other for myriad years, never to part." Here again, we see that these Hung-yang sect texts assume the Eternal Mother mythology but do not discuss it in detail.

APPENDIX I

Seventeenth-Century 'Pao-chüan' Consulted for This Study

The thirteen books on which Chapter Six is based are discussed here, grouped by sectarian affiliation where this is clearly indicated. For most, their chronological order is difficult to specify. There are (1) three texts from the Hung-yang (Vast Yang) sect, (2) three from the Huang-t'ien tao (Way of Yellow Heaven),[1] (3) one from the West Ta-ch'eng (Mahāyāna) sect, and (4) six for which sectarian connections are not clear, though in some of these there are indications of relationship to a Lo sect tradition. I discuss Hung-yang texts first because they are a direct continuation of the sixteenth-century books of that sect discussed in Chapter Five and Appendix H.

HUNG-YANG (VAST YANG) BOOKS

1. *Hung-yang hou-hsü jan-teng t'ien-hua pao-chüan* (The Vast Yang celestial flower precious volume [concerning the] later continuation of lighting the lamp [of the teaching]; hereafter "the *T'ien-hua pao-chüan*"), three *chüan* in thirty-two chapters, 1628.

The preface of this book is attributed to a T'ung-pien tao-jen (Man of the Way Who Understands the Changes), who wrote it in the *mou-ch'en* year of the Lung-chang period, a time that Sawada Mizuho (*Zōho Hōkan*, p. 214) says corresponds to the first year of the Ming Ch'ung-chen reign period (= 1628). After referring to the transmission of Buddhist scriptures in the Han and Six Dynasties periods, it notes that from "Bodhidharma on, it was secretly continued to Patriarch Ma, [after which] the true [tradition] was buried and lost. If it were not for the establishing of the Hung-yang teaching, how could it have been restored?" The three volumes of this book were "left behind" by another "man of the Way" named Ch'ing-hsu (Pure and Empty), whose determination and sincerity "moved the Eternal [Mother]."

A table of contents for the first twelve chapters follows this preface, which is followed in turn by four seven-character lines of "verse to open the scripture." Chapter 1 refers to "Patriarch P'iao" descending to "the ordinary [world]," which further connects this text to the Hung-yang tradition. The chapters are organized in much the same way as the other texts of this sect discussed in Chapter Five and Appendix H, but with the phrase *hsiang ch'ueh-shuo* preceding the prose sections. There are no tune names and no illustrations. This plus the division into thirty-two chapters distinguishes this book from the sixteenth-century Hung-yang texts discussed in Appendix H, which has also encouraged me to treat this as a later, seventeenth-century book, a dating supported by the term *hou-hsü* ("later continuation") in its title.

Most of the content of this *T'ien-hua pao-chüan* is conventional Native Place mythology and terminology, with repeated references to "seeing the nature and returning to the Native Place," "personally seeing the Mother's loving face on Mount Ling, with Mother and children reunited in their hearts" (chapter 9), etc. There is an interesting reference in chapter 11 to "Ancient Kuan-yin in her compassion coming in person to receive the precepts, as she has sent eight Mothers to descend from the Celestial Terrace to manifest their supernormal powers." In chapter 28, names are provided for forty-two Venerable Mothers!

Chapter 14 is devoted to "nourishing the spirit and vital force and preserving one's [potential for] perfection" in vague and flowery language, a discussion continued in chapter 21. Chapters 29 through 32 are a detailed discussion of repayments to all the sources of life, order, and teaching, including a strong emphasis on loyalty to the state and filial obedience to parents.

However, by far the most distinctive material in the *T'ien-hua pao-chüan* is a detailed discussion, in chapters 27 and 28, of a lamplighting ritual offered to buddhas, patriarchs, and gods. The theme of this ritual is clearly stated in the following passage addressed to dozens of named patriarchs and deities:

Please descend from the Native Place; we offer golden lamps; look with compassion and care on us small sons and grandsons. Only because of the Hung-yang Yuan-tun teaching do we in person light a thousand lamps to repay the kindness of all. Please descend from the Native Place, buddhas, patriarchs, and dragon gods. Putting aside [i.e., offering] ourselves, we light golden lamps and offer them to [you], buddhas and patriarchs. [May all the deities of] Heaven, Earth, and the empty [sky], of the three *ch'eng*[? character unidentified] and the nine ranks, all descend to the altar to look after [the Mother's] children and grandchildren, sending down a brilliant light so that they may soon enlighten their minds. (chapter 27)

One rarely finds in *pao-chüan* such detailed discussions of rituals, or such long lists of the names of patriarchs and deities. In this case there are parallels with Taoist rituals in which the gods are also called down by the lighting of lamps. For this, see Kristofer M. Schipper, *Le Fen-teng-Rituel Taoïste* (Paris: Publications de Bulletin de l'École Française d'Extrème-Orient, 1975).

2. *Hung-yang chih-li kuei-tsung ssu-hsiang pao-chüan* (The Vast Yang precious volume [concerning] ultimate principles, returning to the fundamentals, and longing for the Native Place; hereafter "the *Chih-li pao-chüan*"), two *chüan* in twenty-four chapters. No date; however, there is a reference at the end to "explaining the wonderful and pro-found in the home of the second patriarch Kung Ch'ang," whom Richard Shek, in his "Religion and Society in Late Ming" (pp. 287–293), discusses as the founder of the Yuan-tun (Complete and Sudden) teaching/sect, active in the first decades of the seventeenth century. Li Shih-yü (*Pao-chüan tsung-lu*, p. 21) notes an 1881 edition of this book "imitating Ming-printing."

The *Chih-li pao-chüan* is a more detailed and complex statement of sectarian belief than the sixteenth-century Hung-yang sect texts dis-cussed in Chapter Five and Appendix H. It combines ideas of the original nature within with Eternal Mother mythology and termi-nology from the tradition of internal alchemy. The copy I have read is handwritten and organized differently from the printed Hung-yang texts discussed above. It begins with a prose preface, followed by a brief statement of praise and the table of contents for *chüan* 1, which is entitled, like the earlier texts, *tsung t'i-kang* ("general out-line"). The title of the preface is *Hun-yuan hung-yang Chung-hua ching*—the same as with the sixteenth-century texts, except for the omission of the word *chiao* ("teaching") after *Hun-yuan*.

After the table of contents, there are two 7/7 lines of "verses upon opening the scripture," followed by homage to the "Three Jewels" of past, present, and future. Chapter titles are followed by prose sections without the *chao ch'ueh-shuo* used earlier, followed by more lines of 7/7 verse, then 3/3/4 verse and more prose. They end with two lines of verse arranged 5/5. Tune names are located just before the last prose sections. There are no illustrations. Chapter 24 is longer than the rest, composed mostly of verse arranged 3/3/4, interspersed with several prose sections. It includes three tune names.

Though this book is clearly written, it is less elaborately presented than the earlier Hung-yang texts that were printed with support from court eunuchs. This further indicates the later date of the *Chih-li* book. It is interesting to note that, perhaps in keeping with their high-level support, those earlier texts were called *ching* ("scriptures"), whereas the present book is called a *pao-chüan*.

Only the first line of the *Chih-li pao-chüan* preface is the same as that of its Hung-yang predecessors:

It is said that, beyond the "subtle sound" [at creation], there were originally no scriptures of the three teachings, there were just the heavens above, the human realm, the myriad states, and the nine provinces, produced by the transformation of our [*sic*] single vital force of the Prior Realm of the Limitless of the origin in primordial chaos. [This *ch'i*] illuminated everywhere and circulated through Heaven and Earth. The form and content of primordial chaos, ignorant people, being unawakened, have forgotten. The shared awakening of the one mind that is understood by the three teachings [is taught] because the minds of all beings are confused, attached, stained by empty flowers [i.e., transitory possessions], drowned in rivers of love, flowing and blown about in seas of desire, [and so] have lost the true Way.

Our Hun-yuan Venerable Patriarch in the No-Obstacles Palace (Wu-ai kung) of A-lo [Arhat?] Heaven with his eyes of wisdom could see the heavy sins of living beings in the Eastern Land, with their resentful spirit rising up to the sky, coiling about without cease. The Venerable Patriarch felt pity and concern, and tears filled his eyes. He hurriedly sent a message gathering all the buddhas, bodhisattvas, matriarchs, hearers of the eternal, completely enlightened ones, arhats, and holy monks to together go to the golden steps [beneath the throne] to discuss and consider the sons and daughters who in the Eastern Land had lost the way home. They have not awakened to their root and source. In what age will they leave the world? Which patriarchs should descend to the ordinary world to seek for the suffering multitude of

primal ones? No one answered the patriarch's words. The Venerable Patriarch then opened the celestial register and read it carefully from the beginning. From this it was clear that the Literary Buddha Śākyamuni should descend to the world.

Hun-chin P'iao-kao of the Limitless[2] descended to the red dust world together with four types of disciples [monks, nuns, laymen, and laywomen],
who at the final gathering [of those of] the primal source will realize supreme *bodhi* (enlightened wisdom). For the sake of all beings, the multitude
of patriarchs in the Wan-li period all descended to the world and, acknowl-
edging the Mother, entrusted themselves to [human] wombs. Each assum-
ing an empty surname, they were born [into different families] but with the
same wisdom and understanding. South of Liang and north of Ch'u [be-
tween modern Kiangsu and Hupei], [P'iao-kao] realized the principles of the
supreme vehicle for returning to the source and penetrating to the root, enlightening the mind and seeing the nature, and thoroughly understanding
the Great Way. He established the Vast Yang Dharma of the teaching [of
origin in] primal chaos (Yuan-tun chiao) of the Hun-yuan sect (*men*) to save
all living beings, so that they can rise from the ordinary and enter the holy,
forever to continue eternal life.

Think of the myriad sufferings our Venerable Patriarch constantly endured in establishing the teaching, to point out the Way for those in later
generations to attain the holy. Who would have thought that the disciples of
his teaching would contend for fame, encroach on the Way (*yueh tao*), brag
about their abilities, go along with the perverse and heretical, and adapt to
[worldly] circumstances? They conceal and darken the true tradition, and do
not think about pious practices and meditation. How will they be able to
return to the source?

The opening chapters of this *Chih-li pao-chüan* emphasize the importance of "venerating enlightened teachers, seeking out the true
teaching, and meditating" (chapter 1) as the means of "escaping the
net of karma." All this is urgent because "the last age is soon upon
us" (*mo-chieh hsun-su*; chapter 4). Chapter 5 includes autobiographical information about the patriarch speaking in this text, who says
that his family was poor and that he was orphaned early but that
fortunately a mistress (*shih-mu*) of the Vast Yang sect "lifted me up
by studying scriptures and preaching the Dharma; she also set me to
venerating various worthies and offering incense."

The account continues: "When I was fifteen *sui*, my 'second father' bestowed on [i.e., taught] me religious self-cultivation and
practice, and told me to continue the tradition, summon worthies,
and gather the multitudes." The mistress "loved and cared for him,"
and he "received the transmission" from the master, who taught him

"to study scriptures, preach the teaching, and meditate" to "seek out the primal ones."

Because of this instruction, he worked incessantly, "meditating and circulating his breath" and "refining the elixir" (chapters 6–7, 18–20). This Taoist form of meditation is described in more detail, in chapter 9, as "circulating the *ch'i* of the Prior Realm" in one's body, the instructions for which are attributed directly to the Eternal Mother.

Another point of interest in this book is the discussion in chapter 12 of three life paths symbolized by bridges of gold, copper, and iron. The highest level is for those who "will cross a bridge of gold . . . and be led up to the world of utmost bliss in the West." These are people who "fear birth-and-death, study with masters, venerate patriarchs, and ask them how to cultivate and practice. If they think about this all the time, refine themselves, and long for the Eternal Progenitor in the Native Place, when their work and merit are complete, [they will attain] nirvāṇa. The Eternal [Mother] will receive them, and golden youths and jade maidens will welcome them."

Those who cross the copper bridge carry out conventional forms of piety and charity such as "maintaining a vegetarian diet, making offerings, repairing bridges, printing scriptures, . . . caring for orphans and widows, etc." This sort of religious practice "has lost the path." It is "not according to the true tradition" and leads only to good rebirth among humans. The iron-bridge path leads to purgatory for sinners who disobey the law and their parents, cheat the gods, harm others, and the like. This discussion of the three levels clarifies the belief that *pao-chüan* teachings are superior to conventional piety because they lead directly to paradise.

The last chapters of the *Chih-li pao-chüan* contain repeated exhortations to the "worthy and good" to recognize the Venerable Eternal Mother and "think of her all day, every day." Here the mythological framework of return to the Native Place is recapitulated, with this paradise equated with that of Amitābha. Chapter 24 includes final references to the purpose of this "precious volume":

People destined [to be saved] should seek [the truth] in every sentence, and venerate and inquire of enlightened persons, who are the same as we. Quickly recognize the Eternal, return home, and recognize the patriarchs, and so be able to go to the Golden Palace, free and joyful, in the company of the Eternal. . . .

Sad that people do not think of returning to the primal source, and that from the beginning they have lost the Native Place of the Ancient Buddha, [I have] bestowed this *pao-chüan* to exhort and save the worthy and good of the great earth. . . .

The Yuan-tun teaching is not ordinary. It has been transmitted from generation to generation, [so that people can] see their natures, enlighten their minds, and ascend to the other shore.

3. *Hsiao-shih Hun-yuan ta fa-ming ching* (The scripture explaining the great Dharma enlightenment of the Hun-yuan [Patriarch]), three *chüan*, no date, no chapter divisions.

This book is discussed in Sawada Mizuho, *Zōho Hōkan* (p. 109), with a somewhat different title, *Hsiao-shih Hun-yuan Hung-yang ta fa-tsu ming ching*. I read and took notes on this text at the home of Wu Hsiao-ling in Beijing in April 1981. It is a Vast Yang sect invocation and repentance text, much of which is taken up with long lists of the names of buddhas, deities, and patriarchs. It includes pictures of seventeen of these figures. The character *ming* ("enlightenment," "understanding") in the title is an exact homophone of the character *ming* ("name"). Given the contents of this book, it appears that they are intended as synonyms, as is supported by a line at the end of the first volume that refers to the "name scripture" (*ming-ching*). The style and typography of this book indicate a Ming origin, which is how Sawada describes it.

After a list of ninety patriarchs, we are told that the Venerable Mother Kuan-yin said, "All of these holy names [I] transmit to you in the mundane realm. Complete enlightenment entirely depends on Patriarch P'iao-kao." Homage is to be offered to all these patriarchs as well as to various deities, including at least twenty-five Mothers (*chüan* 1).

Hearers of this text are told that "when people of the Vast Yang Way are aware of their sins, they repent of their sins (*chih tsui ch'an tsui*) and repay all the kindnesses [done for them]; when their repentance is complete, they attain release" (*chüan* 2). This repentance is to lead to "enlightening the mind and seeing one's [true] nature, . . . to going back to and clarifying one's own original face, and seeing oneself as a drop of the Prior Realm (*tzu-chi i-tien hsien-t'ien*)." Devotees are told that they are to repent

[so that] demon kings will all pay homage [to one] with folded hands; [so] that bad karma will soon depart; [to resolve] bad karma for three lifetimes; for killing living beings, that they may soon be saved [by one's repentance]; [to avoid] Yama's courts of life and death; so that purgatory may be transformed into a lotus; [so] that the light of the buddhas may constantly shine;

[so] that Kuan-yin will wipe away sins; [so] that immortal youths may come to receive one; and so that one may return and soon ascend [to heaven].

After these ten reasons for repentance, we are told that "those who recite these verses for returning to the Native Place will never suffer the anger of Lord Yama" (*chüan* 3).

HUANG-T'IEN TAO (WAY OF YELLOW HEAVEN) TEXTS

4. *Mi-le Fo shuo Ti-tsang Shih-wang pao-chüan* (The precious volume preached by Maitreya on Ti-tsang and the Ten Kings; hereafter "the *Ti-tsang Shih-wang pao-chüan*"), two *chüan*, no chapter divisions, 122 pages in the edition consulted here. Dated 1630 in an opening statement, with activity dates of 1630–1640 for its revealing patriarch.

This edition, reprinted in Kuang-hsu 11 (= 1885) in Beijing, is from the private collection of Yoshioka Yoshitoyo, who published it in *Chūguku shūkyū shisō shidan kaiho*, no. 2 (December 1968). It is not listed in Li Shih-yü's *Pao-chüan tsung-lu* but is discussed in Sawada Mizuho's *Zōho Hōkan* (pp. 218–219). This text is discussed in detail in a paper by Kyoko Tokuno, "A Study of [the] *Mi-lo Ti-tsang shih-wang pao-chüan*: A Textual Source for Popular Buddhism During the Ming Dynasty" (University of California, Berkeley, no date, but written in 1985). The page numbers given here are from the 1968 reprinting.

This book contains the following statements related to its own origins:

The great saint, the Buddha Maitreya, preached the *Ti-tsang Shih-wang pao-chüan*, which appeared with imperial authorization in [Ming] Ch'ung-chen 3 [= 1630]. It was transmitted to save all the pious sons and daughters of the imperial womb, so that they take refuge in the Confucian school (Ju-men), seek awakening and long life, escape the sufferings of birth, old age, sickness, and death, and avoid the eighteen stages of purgatory. Men and women who listen to this volume with pious sincerity will increase their own blessings now and enable nine generations of their ancestors to ascend [to heaven]. Those who exhort and transform living beings to take refuge in the true Way and recite the precious title of the Honored Buddha Maitreya, who is about to descend to be reborn, the buddhas will receive and guide to ascend [to heaven? character not clear]. For eighty-one kalpas [the period of Maitreya's reign], they will be the same as the buddhas, with indestructible diamond bodies. *Now it is the end of the kalpa; the Literary Buddha Śākyamuni returned home in the Wan-li keng-shen year* [= 1620; italics added]. The Holy Mother said, "Since the three calamities are about to arise, I have ordered

our Buddha [Maitreya] to immediately descend to the mundane and [in-
struct] all the buddhas and patriarchs of the three realms, all the great bodhisattvas and gods, and the Ten Kings and judges [of purgatory] to take refuge in our Buddha, the World-Honored One." . . .

[Maitreya] descended to be reborn as a son of the Wang family in [a
place] north of Chao and south of Yen [between modern Shansi and Liao-
ning provinces, near Beijing] and at Nine Dragon ridge (Chiu-lung kang)[3]
constructed a Dharma boat [i.e., a saving scripture]. (pp. 6–8)

The Buddha-Patriarch P'u-ching spat forth [a Taoist-style reference to divine
revelation] the *Tripitaka* in 5,408 volumes in Wan-li 12 [= 1584]; the blocks
were cut by imperial authorization and stored in Beijing. . . . In the thirty-
second year [1604], by the Buddha's imperial decree, [the Bodhisattva] Ju-
t'ung [a manifestation of Confucius] descended to the mundane in the Wang
family; . . . his childhood name was Ho-shang [monk], and his title, Ch'ang-
sheng. In [Ming] Ch'ung-chen 10 [= 1637], the Patriarch came out of his
meditative absorption, and all the gods and the Ten Kings took refuge in the
Confucian school. He converted more than three thousand disciples and ascended in the eighth month of the thirteenth year [1640]. His Buddhist title
was P'u-shan, the Sweet Dew Buddha. (p. 56)

On the basis of this and other evidence, Tokuno concludes that
P'u-shan was the tenth patriarch of the Huang-t'ien tao, the "Way of
Yellow Heaven," which began with P'u-ming (d. 1562), as discussed
in the entry on text 2 in Appendix H above. P'u-ching (d. 1586) was
the third "lay patriarch" in this tradition (Tokuno, "Study of [the]
Mi-lo Ti-tsang shih-wang pao-chüan," pp. 4–6). On p. 117 of the *Ti-
tsang Shih-wang* book, we read, "Our Buddha, vowing to save all, bestowed the Wu-wei Ch'ang-sheng teaching." In my *Folk Buddhist
Religion* (pp. 7–11), I discuss eighteenth-century evidence for the
continuation of this teaching/sect as founded by Wang Ch'ang-
sheng/P'u-shan, described as having lived during the Ming Wan-li
period (1573–1620). By the eighteenth century, this sect was active in
Chekiang.

There is also a reference in the *Ti-tsang Shih-wang pao-chüan* to
"giving allegiance to our Sect of Complete and Instantaneous Enlightenment of the Imperial Ultimate [period] (Huang-chi Yuan-tun
chiao)" (p. 93). Richard Shek discusses the Yuan-tun sect as "founded during the last decades of the Ming dynasty" by Kung Ch'ang,
the sectarian preacher whose teachings formed the basis of the
Dragon-Flower Scripture discussed in Chapter Seven of the present
volume (Shek, "Religion and Society in Late Ming," pp. 287–301).

This reference further reminds us of the complexity of intersectarian relationships. Tokuno discusses antecedents of themes in the *Ti-tsang Shih-wang* book in earlier indigenous Chinese Buddhist scriptures ("Study of [the] *Mi-lo Ti-tsang shih-wang pao-chüan*," pp. 44–48). For a detailed discussion of the Ten Kings tradition, see Stephen F. Teiser, *The Scripture of the Ten Kings and the Making of Purgatory in Medieval Chinese Buddhism* (Honolulu: University of Hawai'i Press, 1994). The order of the Ten Kings and their courts in the *pao-chüan* is in general agreement with the earlier materials discussed by Teiser.

Yoshioka's copy of this book is in the usual *pao-chüan* pattern of prose sections alternating with those in verse composed in seven- and ten-character lines. There are only a few tune names. *Chüan shang* is not mentioned, but the beginning of *chüan hsia* is noted on p. 61. The book opens with a long preface, undated and unattributed, expressing general Buddhist piety and moral principles. As its title indicates, Maitreya is the major actor in this book; the Bodhisattva Ti-tsang is mentioned only once, as a preacher in purgatory (p. 117).

The content of the *Ti-tsang Shih-wang pao-chüan* is organized around a tour of purgatory by Maitreya, who is led by an unnamed "immortal youth" (*hsien-t'ung*). As they arrive at each court, Maitreya asks, "What place is this?" The youth tells him the number of the court, gives him the name of its ruler, and provides an outline of the sins in life that lead to punishment there. Then follows an exhortation on karma and moral values, after which Maitreya asks, "What crimes and sins did these bad people do in the Yang Realm that led to their suffering here? Do they have any hope of escape?" The youth responds with a detailed list of their sins and of the means of piety that can bring release. This pattern is repeated for all ten courts. Before the tour begins, the youth provides a preview of twenty-one (*sic*) divisions of purgatory with their special forms of punishment. The dialogue is interspersed with long sermons. A tour of purgatory is a convenient framework on which to hang such exhortations, and indeed, the whole point here is to educate Maitreya so that he can warn the living.

The temporal context of this book is the end of the age, with its accompanying disasters and need for intensified piety, but its topic is moral retribution for the individual. However, the relationship between group and individual eschatology is not clearly resolved. The pious are assured that they will be reborn in heaven at death, where their names will be registered, expunged from the ranks of purgatory (pp. 29–30, 45). Their ancestors will be saved as well. But we are also told:

In the last age there are limitless sufferings; people's lust for wine, sex, and money is severe, and so they have fallen into the Eastern Land and do not ascend to heaven. Dīpaṃkara and Śākyamuni came to save, but they enabled only four myriads to ascend to heavenly peace, leaving behind ninety-two i of [children] of the imperial womb. In the future, through preaching the Dharma, they can all be gathered in. . . .

Primal ones, you must each practice the true Way; don't wait until the disasters approach you. When your merit is complete and the time comes, you will rise together as people of the Dragon-Flower Assembly. (pp. 7, 9)

Nonetheless, this collective orientation is attenuated by the focus of the *Ti-tsang Shih-wang* book on individual deliverance at death, as can be seen in the following lines, where the term *shou-yuan* ("gathering in the primal ones") seems to refer to the individual and ancestors rather than to the final gathering of all at the end of the age: "When the merit of one's religious practice is complete, then one will attain *shou-yuan*, and nine generations of ancestors will ascend and return to their original source" (p. 29).

Despite this ambiguity, however, the basic message of this text is clear: With correct practice and belief, the pious can be saved from purgatory. Sectarian mythology is evoked to give authority to this promise, but it is addressed to everyone who will listen and respond, at all social levels. Correct practice and belief are defined in conventional terms, here emphasizing Confucian filial piety and Buddhist nonviolence toward animals.

The *Ti-tsang Shih-wang pao-chüan* ends with ringing promises of salvation from Maitreya, a list of ten repayments for blessings, verses transferring merit for the salvation of all, and the date and place of its reprinting. Just before the end there are two and a half pages listing the sufferings that mothers endure during the ten lunar months of pregnancy, in language very similar to that of the *Huai-t'ai pao-chüan* (Precious volume on pregnancy) discussed in my article "Values in Chinese Sectarian Literature" (pp. 251–252). This section reinforces the need for the filial piety due to parents.

5. *Fo-shuo tang-lai Mi-le ch'u-hsi pao-chüan* (The precious volume preached by the Buddha concerning Maitreya who is about to come, revealing the details; hereafter "the *Mi-le ch'u-hsi pao-chüan*"), forty-eight divisions in four *chüan*, no date or place. Not listed in Li Shih-yü's or Sawada Mizuho's bibliographies.

I have only the fourth *chüan* of this text, chapters 37 to 48, kindly provided to me by the Columbia University Library. I date this book to the seventeenth century because of its close similarity in style, typeface, and content with the other texts from the Columbia Library discussed in Chapter Five above. It might be sixteenth century, but when in doubt it is more modest to guess late than early. This is a completely different text from that of a similar title discussed in Chapter Eight, which is eighteen chapters in one volume.

The last twelve chapters of the *Mi-le ch'u-hsi pao-chüan* are devoted to Maitreya's saving work in the last age, as he travels about in every direction to rescue gods and humans. The term *ch'u-hsi* ("putting forth details") is repeated in each chapter title and seems to refer to the detailed discussion of salvation in the last age. The motive for revealing this text is described in chapter 41:

> Ancient Maitreya descends and approaches, reborn as a layperson to preach the sound of the Dharma. He issued [this] precious volume to save all living beings, so that gods and humans together go to the Cloud City. . . . When those of later generations each listen carefully to [this] precious volume, they end death and transcend rebirth, depart from the mundane and ascend to the heavenly palace. In Maitreya's court they will share enlightenment with the buddhas.

Some passages in chapter 48 indicate that this book was related to the Way of Yellow Heaven going back to P'u-ming, who is here included as a buddha whose name immediately follows those of Śākyamuni, Dīpaṃkara, and Maitreya (in that order) in a list of twenty-three buddhas, patriarchs, and deities invited to descend. He is followed by the "Venerable Patriarch P'u-kuang" and by the "Buddha P'u-ching." These figures were all part of the Huang-t'ien tao tradition as discussed by Richard Shek ("Religion and Society in Late Ming") and Ma Hsi-sha and Han Ping-fang (*Min-chien tsung-chiao*).

More details are provided later in chapter 48, where the one who "obtained, issued, and transmitted" the scripture is said to have been an illiterate man from the Shun-sheng district of northern Chih-li province, in the area of modern Yang-yuan district in Chahar: "Maitreya descended to be reborn in an ordinary family. His religious title (*Tao hao*) was Ming-chung; his sacred name (*sheng-ming*) was P'u-ching; his style-name was the "Cloud Monk" (Yun-seng). . . . He was the third-cycle rebirth of the Ancient Buddha P'u-ming. . . . P'u-ching descended in the *mou-yin* year [= Ming Wan-li 6, or 1578–

1579]." Ma and Han (*Min-chien tsung-chiao*, p. 426) say that it was in this year that P'u-ching began to preach, on the basis of discussions of him in other texts. That P'u-ching is already called a buddha in this *Mi-le ch'u-hsi pao-chüan* further indicates the likelihood of its composition in the seventeenth century.

The details provided in this book about the characteristics of the last age justify its title, as does the discussion of Maitreya's travels around the world. Maitreya is superior to all other deities here; he continues and completes the task of universal salvation begun by Dīpaṃkara and Śākyamuni. In his time the remaining ninety-two myriads of the Mother's children are all saved and "the whole world attains buddhahood" (chapter 40).

6. *Hu-kuo yu-min fu-mo pao-chüan* (The precious volume protecting the state, aiding the people, and subduing demons; hereafter "the *Fu-mo pao-chüan*"), twenty-four chapters in two *chüan*, Beijing, late seventeenth century.

I have three editions of this text. The one used here gives every appearance of having been printed in the late Ming. It is in Wu Hsiao-ling's collection in Beijing. I read it there in 1981, then photographed it in 1991 and read it again. This identical text has been reprinted in volume 5 of Chang Hsi-shun et al., eds., *Pao-chüan ch'u-chi*. My second copy is a Kuang-hsu 22 (= 1896) reprint titled *Kuan-ti fu-mo pao-chüan chu-chieh* (The precious volume, with commentary, on the Emperor Kuan's subduing of demons). This version I also read in Beijing in 1981. It has a commentary and preface, composed by spirit-writing, attributed to the Emperor Kuan himself and to other deities and spirits, such as the Patriarch Lü (Lü Tung-pin), Bodhidharma, the Great Emperor of the Eastern Peak, etc. My third copy was sent to me from the University of Hannover; it opens with a preface attributed to Lü Ch'un-yang, another name for Lü Tung-pin. This edition provides no date or place, but is the same text as the 1896 edition without the prefaces.

The *Fu-mo pao-chüan* repeatedly states that it was revealed and composed in Beijing, but provides no date. Like the *T'ai-shan niang-niang pao-chüan* (text 10 below), which mentions it, it is a sectarian co-optation of a major popular deity to exalt both the god and the sect. The prefaces to the 1896 edition say repeatedly that by then the text had been transmitted for two hundred years. In one of the prefaces attributed to the Patriarch Lü we read:

Our Emperor [Kuan] took the marvels of his own personal experience and bestowed them on Li Ch'ing-an in a dream. Li Ch'ing-an, at the capital on the first day of the year in K'ang-hsi 13 [= February 6, 1674], at night dreamed of our Emperor's revelation for leaving the dust and entering the realm of the holy[?].[4] At that time he recorded on paper what he had received. It was nothing other than the marvelous Way of the Limitless [period] of Imperial Heaven (Huang-t'ien wu-chi chih miao-tao). (p. 28)

This statement is in accord with several references in this book to its having been revealed in a dream in Beijing, but adds a specific name and date for which I have no independent corroboration. There are several references in this text to the Huang-t'ien ta-tao (the "Great Way of Imperial Heaven"), which Ma Hsi-sha and Han Ping-fang (*Min-chien tsung-chiao*, p. 406) say was another name for the Way of Yellow Heaven, a sect tradition that began in the sixteenth century (see Shek, "Religion and Society in Late Ming," pp. 252–275). Richard Shek says that this sect "showed a high degree of indebtedness to the Luo sect" (ibid., p. 252), so it is not surprising to find repeated references in the *Fu-mo pao-chüan* to the Lord Kuan's having been converted by "Teacher Lo," who in one passage is called Lo P'u-ching, thus evoking as well the name of a patriarch of the Huang-t'ien tao tradition, P'u-ching (d. 1586).

Li Shih-yü (*Pao-chüan tsung-lu*, p. 15) lists seven editions of this book dating from the Ming to 1928. Sawada Mizuho (*Zōho Hōkan*, pp. 112–113) discusses five versions published from the early Ch'ing to the Republican period and suggests that the book was composed in 1677, which is within three years of the date provided by the Lü Ch'un-yang preface. In his *Chung-kuo pao-chüan yen-chiu lun-chi* (Taipei: Hsueh-hai ch'u-pan she, 1997, p. 76), Ch'e Hsi-lun argues for a date one sixty-year cycle earlier, or 1617.

The *Fu-mo pao-chüan* is devoted to praising the power of the Lord Kuan to protect the court and nation, drive away demons, and aid the pious. In the process it also praises its own efficacy and uses much terminology from the Venerable Mother tradition. It is beautifully bound and illustrated with engravings of the Lord Kuan and two other celestial rulers, and concludes with an engraving of what appears to be the demon-expeller Chung K'uei. The style and typography of this book are similar to the late Ming texts published several decades earlier, so if my dating is correct, that elegant tradition continued into the early Ch'ing.

This scripture contains the following passages about its own origin and composition:

The *Fu-mo pao-chüan* is not fabricated floating words but is all a matter of true karmic merit. The god (Lao-yeh) manifested his holy [intention] on the first day of the first month and illumined me three times, ordering me to hand down and collect a precious volume, but I, his disciple, did not dare to undertake the task. On the third day of the second month [no year is specified here], when I was at the capital, the god called on me by name to respond and ordered me to prepare a scripture (*tsao-ching*), but when I awoke, since I did not dare to act on my own authority (*pu kan shan-chuan*),[5] [I burned] incense, candles, and paper images of the god [i.e., woodcut prints] at the Wu (Meridian) Gate [in Beijing] and consulted bamboo divining slips.[6] When [the response to] three slips was "extremely good fortune" (*shang-shang*), I agreed to undertake the task. (chapter 1)

In chapter 4 we are told that, although the "Holy Venerable Patriarch" had not had a precious volume, now that it has been printed it can be "transmitted for ten thousand years," with those who contribute gaining limitless merit. This "true scripture is to be requested, to be used in worship in the home (*chai-nei kung*), so that all the gods would protect." In chapter 12, more details are provided:

The god who subdues demons summoned me to respond while I was in a dream. He ordered me to prepare the *Fu-mo chüan*, which was very expensive. Since I had neither a way of doing this nor the money, how could I succeed? Then on the third day of the second month, while I was in a deep sleep, the demon-subduing god in Beijing manifested his great supernormal powers and spoke to me, instructing and ordering me to cut blocks and prepare/print the scripture. When I woke up I was frightened and confused, and, shaken up, I knelt to pray. Asking for a *shang-shang* [auspicious] response from three divining rods, I finally agreed to undertake the task. Then many who had karmic connections with the demon-subduer contributed funds, and as a result the task was completed.

The general tenor of this book is illustrated by the following passages praising the Lord Kuan's powers:

[He] guards the nation, subdues demons, and protects the black-haired people [i.e., the masses]. He slays treacherous gangs and sweeps away depraved demons, cutting them off root and branch. He aids loyal ministers and good generals, and gnashes his teeth in anger at those who are unfair and do what is not correct. (chapter 17)

The divine and awesome power of the Great Emperor Who Subdues Demons has influence afar. [The powers] of the Celestial Honored One have been proclaimed and put into practice so that everyone in the world knows of them. Since later people did not understand this, the Great Way of the Prior Realm bestowed below the *Fu-mo pao-chüan* and transmitted it to the world, where it accords with [the needs of] all [lit. "outer, inner, present, past, holy, mundane, living, and dead"]. (chapter 23)

Near the end of chapter 24 there are promises relating all of this to salvation in the Venerable Mother's paradise:

Now the *Fu-mo chüan* has been sent down, its blocks cut and printed in Beijing. The God Who Subdues Demons has great powers that penetrate Heaven and Earth. By the manifestation of his supernormal powers, [we] see the Venerable Mother and increase our life spans, and nine generations of our ancestors are transferred to the celestial palace. When one child does good deeds, nine generations of ancestors for eighty-one eons continue long life. . . .

[The five-character mantra of this scripture], when refined, forms a wonderfully efficacious elixir that, when swallowed in our bellies, moves the earth and opens the heavens. [It enables us] to leave the world of dust and impurity, to realize the fruits [of our piety], and to go to gaze on the prime and to the assembly on Mount Ling, there to sit on a ninth-class lotus. There there is neither birth nor death and one has nothing to do with the world. Having ascended there, [one obtains] correct enlightenment and for ten thousand eons does not descend to the mundane.

Thus patriotic, exorcistic power is combined with promises of deliverance.

A TEXT OF THE WEST TA-CH'ENG
(MAHĀYĀNA) TRADITION

7. *T'ai-shan tung-yueh Shih-wang pao-chüan* (The precious volume of the Ten Kings of Mount T'ai, the Eastern Peak; hereafter "the *T'ai-shan Shih-wang pao-chüan*"), one volume in twenty-four divisions *(fen)* and forty-eight folio pages. Reprinted in Beijing in the summer of the Min-kuo *hsin-yu* year (i.e., 1921).

Li Shih-yü lists this as a Ch'ing text (*Pao-chüan tsung-lu*, p. 42); Sawada Mizuho (*Zōho Hōkan*, p.108) discusses it as late Ming or early Ch'ing, probably no later than the K'ang-hsi period (1662–1722). This book refers to a "Patriarch Lü" of a Pao-ming monastery who lived at West Huang village near Beijing. Lü Tsu was in fact a nun for whom a temple was said to have been built by Emperor Ying-tsung of the Ming (r. 1436–1449, 1457–1464). In their 1988 article on "The Bao-ming Temple: Religion and the Throne in Ming and Qing

China" (*Harvard Journal of Asiatic Studies* 48:1.131–188), Li Shih-yü and Susan Naquin provide the approximate dates of 1396–1489 for her.

In the 1570s, this monastery became the base for a popular religious sect founded by a nun named Kuei-yuan who wrote five scripture texts modeled in part on those of Lo Ch'ing. Li and Naquin discuss the *T'ai-shan Shih-wang pao-chüan* as "one of the most widely available of the scriptures associated with the Baoming temple," frequently noted in Ch'ing government reports. It was evidently recited at funerals. As one devotee reported in 1814, "If one chanted this scripture, one could raise lost souls from their suffering and convert mankind" (Li and Naquin, "The Baoming Temple," p. 179). It is not one of the books written by Kuei-yuan but was evidently composed by a later adherent of the sect she founded, the Ta-ch'eng, later called the West Ta-ch'eng to distinguish it from another group with the same name.

I first read and photocopied this text at the Institute for the Study of World Religions in Beijing in 1981. A different text, called the *Shih-wang pao-chüan*, has been reprinted in volume 14 of Chang Hsi-shun et al., eds., *Pao-chüan ch'u-chi*. It is based on brief stories of good and bad people and their treatment in purgatory, following the sequence of the Ten Kings. It does not employ terms from sectarian teaching and mythology.

The *T'ai-shan Shih-wang pao-chüan* opens with the standard verses of praise on "raising incense" and "opening the scripture." Those who recite it (*hsuan-chüan*) are instructed to

> make their minds sincere and settle their thoughts, wash their hands and burn incense, and offer worship to the gods (*chu-t'ien*) [with the latter character written with the "man" radical on the left]. Invite [to the altar] all the arhats and holy monks of past, present, and future, [together with] all [deities of] the celestial bushels and the sun, moon, and stars, the Mother of the Peak (Pi-hsia yuan-chün), Wang-mu niang-niang, T'ien-fei niang-niang [the Celestial Consort Ma-tsu], and the Mothers who [respectively] protect eyesight and record, accompany, and facilitate births, the Goddess of Scarlet Fever, and the ten Lords Yama of the Eastern Peak and the God of Mount T'ai (T'ien-ch'i),[7] [so] that they will all together come to the assembly. (chapter 1, pp. 1a–b)

These lines are followed by a section of ten-character verse written in a flowery and repetitive style, with references to sectarian terms such as *ta-ch'a tui-hao* ("respond to investigation and compare/check titles") and "the buddhas and patriarchs rejoicing on Mount Ling." The title of chapter 1 is followed by a tune name; it opens with a prose discussion urging "repentance and recitation of the Buddha's name," which leads to "the good rejoicing in heaven" (chapter 1, pp. 2b–3a). Then come two lines of seven-character verse followed by two pages of ten-character lines. The chapter ends with four lines of five-character verse. With small variations, this pattern continues throughout the rest of the book.

The other two books I have read with the title *Shih-wang pao-chüan* are morality books that use purgatory to dramatize karmic rewards and punishments, but this *T'ai-shan Shih-wang* book is fundamentally a vehicle of sectarian teaching that provides less detail about purgatorial courts and tortures. Its emphasis is not on karmically deserved punishments but on assurances that the pious can escape purgatory entirely, or at least quickly ascend to heaven unscathed. This book is thus a good example of how sectarian teachings made direct salvation available to ordinary folk in language they could understand.

The structure of this book is based on a tour of purgatory by an unnamed *na-tzu* ("robed one"), a term referring to a Buddhist monk. He visits the courts in sequence and asks what sins people have committed to be punished there. For example, in the third court he sees sinners with "their tongues cut off and their eyes gouged out, their whole bodies covered with blood," and he asks, "What did these people do in the Yang Realm to deserve such suffering?" He is told that they were "women who cursed their in-laws, and quarrelsome men whose minds were not true and firm." They will be reborn as "blind women and mute men" (chapter 8, pp. 11a–b). Our visitor is described as having "reached the Dark Realm while in a state of meditative absorption, in which he saw the Ten Kings, paid homage to Ti-tsang, [and saw] the ghosts in confusion and the spirits afraid."

Here the Bodhisattva Ti-tsang is a Mother (Ti-tsang mu) "seated in the center, lofty and unmoved, with the Ten Kings lined up in rows on both sides, with boiling anger [at sinners]." There are a mirror and balance there to reflect and weigh all deeds. The bad "fall into purgatory" while the good "ascend to heaven," all having brought this on themselves by their deeds in life (*tzu-tso tzu-shou*; chapter 22, pp. 40a–b). The Ten Kings "do not accord with human feeling [i.e., give favors] (*jen-ch'ing*). In the Yang World those who break the royal law can use money to buy their escape, but in the Dark Realm money doesn't work" (chapter 22, p. 40b). Judgments in purgatory are based on a chain of reports about deeds done in the realm of the living, in which "the Stove God reports to the Locality God, who reports to the City God, who reports to the God of Mount T'ai (T'ien-ch'i), who sends the message to purgatory" (chapter 22, p. 39b).

However, this structure of reports leading to objective punishments is mitigated by Mother Ti-tsang, who in effect represents the Venerable Mother's love in purgatory. In chapter 15 the pious are told, "If in the Yang Realm one worships Mother Ti-tsang, she will speak of human feelings [on one's behalf] before the Ten Kings. In the end you will go to the assembly in Cloud City" (chapter 15, p. 28a). There "you will see the dear Mother, where your titles will be examined and you will sit in the Lotus Terrace, never again to descend to the mundane" (chapter 16, p. 29a).

This promise is well summed up in chapter 23, where we are told that

when people who do good reach the Yin Realm, they recite the Buddha's name and tread on a white lotus. A bright golden light appears before their eyes, illuminating a path to Heaven. Penetrating Heaven and Earth, it goes directly to the Heaven Beyond Heaven. There they are companions of the buddhas and patriarchs, and for a myriad of years never return to the mundane. (chapter 23, p. 41a)

The bad, in contrast, go through all the eighteen compartments of purgatory, but

when those who have attained the Way reach the Dark Realm, treading on lotus flowers and reciting good words, the Ten Kings stand up, and demon judges great and small in confusion straighten their court robes and line up in their ranks. . . . Those who recite [this] scripture with sincerity, who quickly turn around and take responsibility for the path ahead, and who seek out a scripture for escape, do not go to purgatory but ascend to heaven. (chapter 23, p. 41b)

That this heaven is the Venerable Mother's paradise is made clear by references to "seeing Wu-sheng Lao-mu" (chapter 7, p. 15a), and to "little children . . . joyfully returning home to see their dear Mother, going directly home, going directly home, . . . transcending the mundane and entering the holy" (chapter 20, p. 36b; chapter 21,

p. 38a). There are also several references to Maitreya in this book, in his familiar role of being in charge of the teaching in the period of the Latter Realm (chapter 10, p. 20a; chapter 15, p. 28a, etc.).

The *T'ai-shan Shih-wang pao-chüan* ends with promises of aid and salvation to those who recite it, and to their deceased ancestors, with a sharp contrast between sincerity (*ch'ien-ch'eng*) and unbelief (*pu-hsin*). The last pages are devoted to a story of a "Confucian scholar" from Shantung named Li Ch'ing who died in 1455 and went to purgatory, where he was interrogated by King Yama. When he replies that every year he had fasted and recited the Buddha's name ten thousand times on the Buddha's birthday, Yama tells him that since there are no such ritual celebrations of the birthdays of the Ten Kings, he will tell Li Ch'ing about them and then permit him to return to life to inform pious folk that on those days they are to fast and recite the buddhas' names to obtain "happiness in this life and release for [those of] the past." Upon his return to the world, Li Ch'ing writes all this down, and so here we are given the birthdays of all the Ten Kings in chronological order, along with the names of the buddhas to be venerated on them. This story is the first of those told in the *Shih-wang pao-chüan* reprinted in volume 14 of the *Pao-chüan ch'u-chi*. It is a good example of a Chinese-style mythic validation of ritual.

BOOKS FOR WHICH EXACT SECTARIAN AFFILIATION AND CHRONOLOGICAL ORDER ARE NOT CLEAR

8. *Fo-shuo hsiao-shih pao-an pao-chüan* (The precious volume preached by the Buddha on preserving peace and security; hereafter "the *Pao-an pao-chüan*"), twenty-four chapters in two volumes (*chüan*), mid-seventeenth century.

This book is not in Li Shih-yü's or Sawada Mizuho's bibliographies. My copy is a photocopy of the original in the Gest Library of Princeton University; this same edition has been reprinted in full in volume 6 of Chang Hsi-shun et al., eds., *Pao-chüan ch'u-chi*. This book is narrated by a patriarch called K'ung (Emptiness), which is an abbreviation of Miao-k'ung (Wonderful Emptiness), who is identified as the inheritor of the teaching of Patriarch Lo by way of Patriarch Ming-k'ung. Ma Hsi-sha and Han Ping-fang (*Min-chien tsung-chiao*, pp. 232–235) discuss Ming-k'ung as an eighth-generation patriarch in a Lo sect tradition who was active in the first decades of the seventeenth century. Ming-k'ung is referred to several times in the *Pao-an pao-chüan* as the one who "established the teaching" (chapter 3), who had a "divinely efficacious elixir" (chapter 19), etc.

Following are the key passages concerning the line of transmission that led to this book, which is specifically said to have been revealed by the Venerable Mother (chapter 3):

As for the profound and wonderful scriptures of the Wu-wei teaching (*fa*), nine patriarchs have opened the gates and bestowed the five books (*wu-pu*) to save the multitudes, [who] don't know the names of these venerable patriarchs. Hsuan-k'ung opened the gates, and the Ssu-wei [= Lo] Patriarch opened the gate of the teaching. They called out to awaken those who have lost their Native Place. The Shih-hsia (Stone Box) Patriarch was Ming-k'ung, who everywhere transmitted true scriptures that circulate in the world. He was in complete accord with the realm above. The Patriarch Not Yet Come moves the Dharma boat. Miao-k'ung carried out the task and continued transmitting the lamp to save all living beings, saving all the children of the source and root, so that they together reach home. (chapter 20)

The Venerable Mother asked, "Of what family are you?" I, the infant, replied to her, "My empty name is of the Yang family; my fundamental nature is Miao-k'ung. I am the transformation body of the three buddhas. The tenth patriarch was the monk P'u-ching, [who with] Maitreya and Mu-lien followed the Mahāyana teaching. The one who pointed directly [to the Way] was Ming-k'ung. Miao-k'ung is the one who opened up the teaching of the Way of the true Buddha Yet to Come. (chapter 24)

The Patriarch surnamed Yang put on the robes of an immortal, but no one in the world recognized him/her. The Venerable Patriarch's given name was He-chi. He/she was suddenly able to open up the storehouse [of scriptures], transcend his/her surroundings, and sit on the heart of the lotus in the palace of the Heaven of [Those] Transformed to a Joyous [Existence] (Hua-le t'ien) [= Nirmāṇarati, the fifth of six desire-heavens]. Lofty and unmoved, his/her spiritually illuminated nature suddenly was able to transcend the three realms and see the Eternal [Mother]. (chapter 13)

I, on the third day of the second month of Ch'ung-chen 16 [March 3, 1642], because the multitudes of the people of the Way on the great earth were unable to attain enlightenment, was thinking [of them] day and night with sadness in my heart, when suddenly I was spiritually liberated and my true nature came to the Celestial Terrace in that other country. There on the Seven-Star Terrace I met the Ancient Buddha, the Eternal, sitting upright. The Venerable Mother said, "What may your business be?" I replied, "I have especially come to beg for a robe." (chapter 13)

Here we see that the Patriarch Miao-k'ung's lay name was Yang
He-chi, though since He-chi means "in harmony with scriptural
verses," it may be another religious name. Since Miao was a Dharma
name applied to women in sectarian tradition, this "patriarch" may
have been female, though there is no other indication of this in the
text. No place names are provided for Miao-k'ung, though the above
reference to Shih-hsia indicates that Ming-k'ung was from the Mi-
yun district in Hopei.

The *Pao-an pao-chüan* is a long, rambling book full of vague and
pious verbiage, more appropriate for devotion than discussion. It is
beautifully bound, with engravings of five deities and buddhas at
the beginning and that of a guardian deity with a sword at the end.
Its type is large and clear, and it opens with the usual invocations for
the security of the realm and long life for the emperor. Its style and
organization are the same as those of other late Ming *pao-chüan*.
Tune names follow each chapter title. Its teaching is based throughout on Venerable Mother mythology, though with several references
to terms and phrases used by Lo Ch'ing, such as the "Wu-wei marvelous teaching," "lofty and unmoved" (*wei-wei pu-tung*), and "free
and independent everywhere" (*tzu-tsai tsung-heng*). The Mother is
actively involved here as a teacher and revealer.

The flavor of this book is well illustrated by a passage from
chapter 1:

The Buddha said, "As for the brightly illuminated Wu-wei Great Way of the
Mahāyana, though nine patriarchs opened the gate [of the teaching], the
people of the world did not understand them. [I] suffered for thirteen years,
then in meditation saw before my eyes a ray of bright light, and only then
did I learn of the Great Way of the Native Place, which has been transmitted
everywhere. Men and women are all travelers from the Native Place who
have fallen into the sea of suffering of the red dust *sahā* world, unwilling to
believe and transmit [the teaching].

This passage continues by saying that the Mother revealed a "divinely efficacious elixir," which nine generations of patriarchs have
transmitted as the "profound and empty five books in six volumes to
save all. [I] suffered for thirteen years and transmitted everywhere
the Wu-wei [teaching]." This is repeated in the following line with
the first-person pronoun *wo*. Here the narrator claims to have undergone the same period of ascetic suffering as Lo Ch'ing.

9. *Hsiao-shih Chen-k'ung pao-chüan* (The precious volume on [the teaching of the Patriarch] Chen-k'ung; hereafter "the *Chen-k'ung pao-chüan*"), no date, one *chüan*, no chapter divisions.

Reprinted in 1931 in an article by Hu Shih, "Pa *Hsiao-shih Chen-k'ung pao-chüan*" (A postface to *The Precious Volume on [the Teaching of the Patriarch] Chen-k'ung*; 1931), based on a manuscript found in Ning-hsia. This same edition is reprinted in volume 19 of Chang Hsi-shun et al., eds., *Pao-chüan ch'u-chi*. I here use that published by Hu Shih. From historical and literary evidence, Hu argues that this is a late Ming text; Li Shih-yü (*Pao-chüan tsung-lu*, p. 54) lists it as Ming. The teaching of this book is a popularized form of Ch'an similar to that of Lo Ch'ing and reflecting some terms and concepts from his books, such as "the Wu-wei teaching," *wei-wei pu-tung* ("lofty and unmoved"), and *tzu-tsai tsung-heng* ("spiritually independent everywhere"). However, in lists of patriarchs in this book, Lo is not mentioned.

The *Chen-k'ung pao-chüan* emphasizes enlightening the mind, seeing the true nature, and realizing that one's mind is the Buddha. This being so, it is useless to seek for salvation outside oneself; it is only those who do not know themselves who take outer forms (images) to be real. The revealer of this book is the Venerable Patriarch Chen-k'ung, whose message includes a substantial amount of Eternal Mother mythology as well. There are no direct references here to Lo Ch'ing or his texts, nor to any other sources. In a section near the end, there are several references to Ch'an terms and personages, with the Buddha "transmitting the 'mind-seal'" to Kāśyapa and others down to Bodhidharma, later followed by the standard line of five Ch'an patriarchs. We are told:

> When the Sixth Patriarch returned to nirvāṇa, in the South there was instantaneous [enlightenment] and in the North, gradual. Later, various sons of the Buddha established Ch'an schools; from the beginning to the present, [Ch'an] has been one flower with five petals. Stupid and ignorant people didn't understand the [meaning of the Ch'an teaching] and established other schools. Thus the true teaching was hidden for a long time. [Then] the Venerable Ku-chuo again reformed the Lotus school and various buddhas appeared everywhere in the world. There were Yin-tsung and Shan-ts'ai, and then there was Chen-k'ung. Fortunately, our Venerable Patriarch Chen-k'ung opened wide a skillful device [effective teaching]. (pp. 3649–3650)[8]

Thus this book portrays sectarian patriarchs as both inheritors and reformers of Ch'an tradition.

In the *Zengaku daijiten* (Dictionary of Zen studies [Kyoto: Dai shu-kan shoten, 1978, 1985]), the names Ku-chuo and Shan-ts'ai are not listed. There was a seventh-century monk named Yin-tsung who was traditionally associated with the Sixth Ch'an Patriarch Hui-neng. There were Ch'an monks named Chen-k'ung in the T'ang, Sung, and early Ming, but none whose dates fit the period when the *Chen-k'ung pao-chüan* appeared. Here a popular sectarian tradition has constructed its own genealogy and attempted to link it to that of Ch'an.

The Ch'an tone of this book is clearly revealed in passages such as the following:

> You good people, the Buddha is not difficult [to attain], and meditation is also easy. Everyone distinguishes the superior and all are originally complete of themselves. From the beginning nothing has been lacking in everyone's breast [= heart]. When awakened they are the Buddha; the Buddha is the mind. You need only to directly take responsibility yourself, there is no need to seek on the outside. (p. 3625)

Ch'an influence can also be seen in such statements as "[According to] the message from the West [brought by Bodhidharma], religious practice originally had no form" (p. 3628) and "For people who recognize verbal enlightenment (*tzu-chueh*), it is difficult to escape birth-and-death" (p. 3634). Here "verbal enlightenment" means reliance on written texts.

Amitābha is mentioned repeatedly in the *Chen-k'ung* book, but its attitude toward him is ambiguous. On the one hand, in keeping with the Ch'an emphasis just noted, we are told that "ancient Amitābha beyond the empty kalpa [a period when all is destroyed] originally had no form" (p. 3628). Hence oral recitation of his name is condemned, as are "carrying out great three-day fasts. . . . To maintain a vegetarian diet in a confused way and orally recite the Buddha's name [simply] involves your own polluted *ch'i*. To burn incense early in the morning and recite the Buddha's name in the evening is to pass your life in vain" (pp. 3626, 3628–3639).

However, near the end of the book, beginners are told to "recite in the proper way without stopping; recite the name of Amitābha Buddha all twelve hours of the day without relaxing at all. If every day at home you awaken to the eternal, in a short time you will be able to enlighten your mind and see your nature" (p. 3652, reading *chi-shih* in this context as meaning "not much time" rather than "when?"). Perhaps such recitation is only for beginners, but this is not clearly stated.

In addition, Amitābha is here discussed as a creator, the "father of all creatures" (p. 3636) whose body is the whole world—an understanding similar to Lo Ch'ing's teaching about the Buddha as a creator-deity, discussed in Chapter Three above. Hence we read:

The Buddha Amitābha is lord of the three realms. He arranged Heaven and Earth, and established the sun and moon, plants, trees, and forests. He ordered the mountains and rivers and the great earth; there is no place he did not go. He put the universe in order, with the great earth and men and women. . . . The Buddha Amitābha's whole body is [the world]; from east to west and south to north is one Dharma body. . . . All the great earth and everywhere in the ten directions is Amitābha. (pp. 3637, 3645; see also 3640–3641)

The sectarian dimension of the *Chen-k'ung pao-chüan* can be found in references to such terms as "the little children returning to their Native Place" (p. 3629) and "going to Mount Ling" (p. 3636), while there is one passage referring to sectarian mythology in more detail:

After I [Chen-k'ung] left the Native Place, for a myriad of years the dear Father and Mother [sent] few family letters to inform their children. For these poor children in the Eastern Land, it is really difficult to progress. The Buddha Amitābha hopes that you will quickly turn around. In the Land of Peace and Nourishment [= the Pure Land] the dear Father and Mother think of you all day, hoping that their dear spoiled children in the Eastern Land will soon return. The parents, thinking of their children, constantly weep, but their stupid children, attached to the world, are unwilling to return home. Letters from the parents have repeatedly ordered them: Dear children, when you read these letters, then want to return. When you have gone beyond the three realms, then you will really be happy. When you reach the Land of Peace and Nourishment, the Buddha's land, then parents and children will be reunited. When you reach the Native Place and see your parents, you will be most joyful. (pp. 3641–3642)

I use the plural here because later in these same passages the parents are referred to in the plural, *fu-mu-men*: This usage perhaps implies the Venerable Mother and Amitābha, but the Mother is not mentioned in this book.

There are no references to sect names or assemblies in the *Chen-k'ung pao-chüan*, but a Chen-k'ung chiao (sect) was founded in the nineteenth century by a "Patriarch Liao" (1827–1893) from Kiangsi. His teachings were influenced by Lo Ch'ing and the *Chen-k'ung* scripture, as well as other sources. For a detailed study of this sect, see Lo Hsiang-lin, *The Spread of the Chen K'ung Chiao in South China and Malaya* (in Chinese; Hong Kong: Institute of Chinese Culture, 1962). The author discusses the *Chen-k'ung pao-chüan* on pp. 134–139.

10. *Ling-ying T'ai-shan niang-niang pao-chüan* (The precious volume of the divinely efficacious Goddess of Mount T'ai; hereafter "the *T'ai-shan niang-niang pao-chüan*"), twenty-four chapters in two *chüan*. No date, but gives every appearance of a late Ming origin. First composed and printed in Beijing.

Li Shih-yü (*Pao-chüan tsung-lu*, p. 29) and Sawada Mizuho (*Zōho Hōkan*, pp. 113–114) both describe this as a Ming text. See also Ch'e Hsi-lun's detailed study on pp. 69–88 of his *Chung-kuo pao-chüan yen-chiu lun-chi*, in which he argues that this book first appeared between 1617 and 1619 (pp. 76–77). I read a complete copy in Beijing in 1981, and then was sent a photocopy of the first volume from the University of Heidelberg. The complete text is reprinted in volume 13 of the *Pao-chüan ch'u-chi*. These versions are all identical.

The *T'ai-shan niang-niang pao-chüan* is beautifully bound, with engravings at the beginning of six named goddesses who are invoked in the text. The type is large and clear. Its style and organization are like those of other Ming *pao-chüan*. Tune names immediately follow each chapter title.

This book is written in honor of a sectarian understanding of the Goddess of Mount T'ai, whose formal title is Pi-hsia yuan-chün (Princess of the Azure Clouds). Here this goddess is promised rebirth in the Mother's paradise. Since in the Ming the cult of the Goddess was popular with all classes and had imperial support, the sectarians had much to gain by equating her with their own chief deity. On worship at Mount T'ai and pilgrimage there, see Edouard Chavannes, *Le T'ai Chan: Essai de Monographie d'un Culte Chinois* (Paris: Ernest Leroux, 1910) and the recent M.A. thesis by Mei-hui Shiau, "Religion, State and Society in Ming China: Beliefs about Mount T'ai" (University of British Columbia, 1994).

The occasion for the revelation and printing of this book is described in some detail, beginning with a story in chapter 10 about a pious husband and wife who were concerned that they had no children: "As they had heard that the Mother of the Peak was both divinely efficacious and holy, they vowed to cast a metal image of the Holy Mother to worship at home, and to ask the Mother for a child."

The couple had images made not only of the chief goddess but also of two of her divine assistants, the goddesses responsible for eyesight and delivering children, whom they worshipped constantly, "asking for a descendant." In this chapter the wife is called "Madame Tung" and the husband "an elder," but in chapter 20 he is identified as "Supernumerary Chang."

In chapter 11 we are told that a patrolling divine youth saw that in Beijing there was a pious woman named Tung who "did good and worshipped the Venerable Mother to ask for a son." On hearing his report, the Mother is moved to respond. She says that "though she is efficacious and worshipped," she lacks a *pao-chüan*, so she "ordered that the elder and his wife Madame Tung should contribute to have printing blocks cut [for a scripture] that she would bestow in Beijing, so that ten thousand people would recite the Buddha's [i.e., her] name, and praise her merit. [If they did so,] in no more than three years they would have both sons and daughters and their families would prosper." Those who would recite this scripture are also promised "limitless merit, increase of blessings, and long life." Here promises to the pious couple blend into those for all devotees. As we read at the end of the chapter, "If you don't forget the Mother, the Mother will protect you, so that you are never afflicted with disasters. . . . Having blocks cut for scriptures is the number-one form of merit."

Chapter 12 continues the story by saying that the elder vowed to prepare a scripture (*tsao-ching*), a term paralleled later by *yin-ching* ("print a scripture"). This made the Mother very happy, so she sent down a brilliant light that illuminated the whole household and its surroundings, which here again is both a specific response and a general promise. Thus "the Holy Mother Celestial Immortal manifested her divine powers to bestow a true scripture so that the whole world might know."

This account is elaborated on near the end of the book, where we read, "In Beijing, blocks were cut and a scripture prepared for the Holy Mother." All are urged to ask for a copy to "recite and read." The great rewards for such piety are repeated in detail.

In chapter 22, the Mother's disciples are urged to "vow to record the sacred message on paper, cut blocks, and print scriptures. If they do not contribute funds, they will not complete this sacred task. Pious people should vow to contribute money joyously to cut blocks for scriptures in Beijing. Indeed, because the Mother lacked a scripture, the men and women of the world did not know of her. Once this scripture comes, it will guide people everywhere to create blessings for themselves, recite the Buddha's name, and attain limitless merit."

In chapter 24 an unnamed person says,

In Beijing, the Holy Mother lacked a *pao-chüan*, so when the Venerable Mother had warned me several times, I did not dare to disobey her. I first prepared the *Shih-wang pao-chüan* . . . [and the] *Fu-mo pao-chüan*.[9] When the elder by himself vowed to [have the blocks cut], he moved all the pious people in the assembly to contribute funds together. In the end, they completed the *Precious Volume of the Efficacious Response of the Venerable Mother of Mount T'ai*. Originally, it was Madame Tung who contributed her own funds to have the blocks cut, and the Mother responded to her.

Later in this same chapter and elsewhere in the *T'ai-shan niang-niang pao-chüan*, it is emphasized that the husband and wife had vowed together to carry out this task. These references to other seventeenth-century texts help date the book.

The *T'ai-shan niang-niang pao-chüan* thus combines the sectarian promise of salvation with support for the emperor and nation and pledges of practical aid for healing and childbirth—all focused on female deities.[10]

11. *Hsiao-shih Yin-k'ung shih-chi pao-chüan* (The precious volume explaining the true realm of [the Bodhisattva] Yin-k'ung; hereafter "the *Yin-k'ung pao-chüan*"), twenty-four chapters (*p'in*) in two *chüan*. No date, but its style and content are similar to other late Ming texts.

Li Shih-yü (*Pao-chüan tsung-lu*, p. 53) lists this as a Ming book. In 1981 I looked at a fragmented copy and was able to photocopy chapters 2 through 14 and 17. A complete copy is reprinted in volume 18 of Chang Hsi-shun et al., eds., *Pao-chüan ch'u-chi*, put together by the editors from two different editions.

The opening material and the alternation of prose and verse in this book are similar to others of its type. There are tune names in the introductory section and in each chapter. The title of each chapter is named after a bodhisattva, such as that for chapter 3, "The Bodhisattva Kuan-yin Realizes Enlightenment," but there is nothing specific about these figures or their teachings. The title of chapter 1 is "The Bodhisattva Ti-tsang Understands True Reality," but there is nothing in it about purgatory, this bodhisattva's realm of activity.

All these bodhisattvas preach a generalized piety focused on reciting the name of Amitābha, who is the main deity in this text. The

Bodhisattva Yin-k'ung is named in chapter 23, but with no details and no mention of why the book is named for him. The teachings of this book are presented in a vague sectarian context evoked by references to the Eternal Mother, but this is basically a verbose and disjointed popular version of Pure Land piety. There are a few references to a Venerable Patriarch Chen-k'ung transmitting this scripture, but nothing specific, no mention of sect names or the like.

Following are translations of a few passages to give the flavor of this book:

Enlighten your mind and [enable] your nature to penetrate through the three passes [i.e., the ear, mouth, and eyes] and return to the Pure Land, where there are no obstacles. Quickly get on the Dharma boat [repeated], leave the *sahā* world, and ascend to the other shore. Think carefully. If you pass this time in vain, when will you be able to return to the Native Place? In the world of dust, [people] covet happiness, contend for fame and profit, and presume on their status and power. At home, looking on in hope, the Eternal Mother longs for her poor children who have not been able to return to their Native Place. Every day, in what they encounter, they cannot escape birth, death, and impermanence . . . . [Those who] recite [the name of] the Buddha Amitābha will transcend the three realms, escape being sunk in the sea of suffering, and return to the Pure Land. . . . They will see and be reunited with their dear Mother, and escape the three calamities [repeated]. Why should they fear King Yama? Neither polluted nor defiled, they dwell in the dust, unstained, indestructible. . . . I urge you to quickly repent [repeated]; only by reciting "Amitābha" is there an escape. (chapter 14, pp. 157–158)

Those who believe in the Western Realm are few. Those without karmic affinity cannot ascend to the Buddha's place. [There] the tinkling stone ornaments on the precious palace brightly shine. There is a seven-jewel pool in front of the Pure Land palace, and everywhere in that world the land is of gold. It is neither cold nor hot and there are no vexations. [People there] are independent and roam about as they please, with more than enough happiness. They no longer suffer the anger of Lord Yama. . . . Clapping their hands and laughing, they go together to the Lotus Pool Assembly, see their dear Mother, and return to the source as one body. By reciting "Amitābha Buddha," one is able to verify *bodhi*. (chapter 19, pp. 258–259)

Here Pure Land and sectarian piety are blended together.

The only other point of interest here consists of mention of the pious seeing the "Eternal Father" (Wu-sheng fu), a reference to Amitābha that evokes those in some of the orthodox Buddhist texts referred to in Chapter One above (chapter 15, p. 186; chapter 16, p. 195).

The *Yin-k'ung pao-chüan* ends with praise of itself as the source of all the buddhas, and with four "repayments" for the kindness of Heaven and Earth, sun and moon, emperor, water and soil, and parents (chapter 24, pp. 373, 384).

12. *Hsiao-shih Chun-t'i fu-sheng pao-chüan* (The precious volume on returning to life [due to] Cundī; hereafter "the *Chun-t'i paochüan*"), no date, twenty-eight divisions in two *chüan*, of which only the first thirteen are still extant. Photographed at the home of Wu Hsiao-ling in Beijing in 1991. Not listed in Li Shih-yü's *Pao-chüan tsung-lu*. Discussed here as a late Ming text because of its close similarities of style and typography with other *pao-chüan* of that period. Cundī is a form of the Bodhisattva Kuan-yin, also identified with Marīci, the "Queen of Heaven," represented with multiple eyes and arms.

Sawada Mizuho (*Zōho Hōkan*, pp. 117–118) describes a text entitled the *Fo-shuo Chun-t'i fu-sheng pao-chüan* for which the inside title is identical with that of the book discussed here, as are the chapter titles and story line. Unfortunately, the last half of his edition is missing as well, though he says it includes chapter 14. He says it was printed and folded in Ming style.

The *Chun-t'i pao-chüan* opens with the usual invocation and statement of praise on offering incense, followed by the Three Refuges and an opening section in 3/3/4 verse urging all to recite the Buddha's name and reminding them of karmic retribution. The core of these chapters is a story about a woman named Li Pao-p'ing from Shantung, set in the Ming Ch'eng-hua reign period (1465–1487). Madame Li, the wife of a lower degree-holder named Liu Yü, is described as kind, good, and compassionate and a pious reciter of scriptures who fasted ten days each month in honor of Cundī. She and her husband had two children and had been rewarded for their goodness with prosperity and honor in the form of fields, cattle, horses, and money.

Unfortunately, one month Madame Li skipped two days of her Cundī fast because of a miscalculation and the pressure of family affairs, and for this she is condemned by patrolling demons and afflicted with illness. Her husband buys medicine for her, makes offerings, and brings in monks to recite scriptures and invocations on her behalf, but nothing helps. In the meantime, demon-messengers are sent to seize another woman with a similar name and address, bearing orders from the Goddess of Mount T'ai by way of the City God of her district and the Locality God. They also have a detailed list of the sins of which the woman has been accused, but they go to the wrong household. The protective banners and placards put up by the monks have no effect. As keeper of the household records of good and bad deeds, the Stove God stoutly defends Madame Li, saying that she is a good person whose only offense was forgetting two fast days, but the officers simply repeat their orders.

Meanwhile, her husband and children stand in front of her bed to protect her from the spectral messengers, whom only she can see, and her husband asks to be taken in her place, or at least to go with her. Madame Li urges her children to do good and tells them that after she dies and her husband takes a second wife they should be filial and respectful to her and treat her as their own mother. As all weep and cling to each other, the husband tries to buy off the demon officials, but in response they shackle his wife in iron and beat her senseless with iron cudgels, repeating that King Yama has ordered them to seize her *hun* spirit.

The unfortunate woman is then taken to the Locality God, who leads her to Mount T'ai, while the City God reports her name. At her pleading she is led back to see her family, who are weeping and offering spirit money before her soul tablet, still pleading to join her. Upon reaching purgatory, she complains that she has been unjustly accused and uses the offering money she had been given to bribe the demon-officials to take her to the "home-viewing tower," where she looks toward Shantung and sees her family one last time. Then she is taken on a tour of purgatory, the punishments of which are described in some detail, accompanied, as is usual in such texts, with sermons directed to the living.

Finally, Madame Li is taken before a judge, with her name and address called out. An official submits a report from her family's Stove God extolling her goodness and piety, and she kneels before the judge to make a formal complaint. The judge then interrogates the demon-messengers, asking why they had reported that she was a bad person. In the end they are told that they seized the wrong person because they had drunk too much sacrificial wine. Madame Li's province and surname were the same as those of the woman they had been sent to apprehend, but her local address and given name were different. The officials are then beaten for their error, and Lord Yama sends a message to the gods of city, locality, and household asking why they had mistakenly arrested Li Pao-p'ing.

My copy of this text ends with the title of chapter 14, "The Fifth Lord Yama at the Sen-lo Court Interrogates and Beats the Demon-Messengers." This vindication of Madame Li, plus the theme of "returning to life" in the title of this book, indicate that she was eventually returned to the land of the living.

The surviving chapters of the *Chun-t'i pao-chüan* are of interest not only for their content but also because they are based on an extended story that is devoid of references to sectarian mythology. Since such references often occur in the opening and closing chapters of *pao-chüan*, we cannot be sure that they were absent from the complete text of this book, but as it stands this fragment is an early version of a story of a pious person of the sort that became a dominant type in the later history of precious volumes.

13. *Hsiao-shih Meng Chiang chung-lieh chen-chieh hsien-liang pao-chüan* (The precious volume on Meng Chiang the worthy and good, loyal and chaste; hereafter "the *Meng Chiang pao-chüan*"), two *chüan* in thirty-two divisions. A closing inscription indicates that a copy of this book was requested by devotees in K'ang-hsi 53, or 1714. Li Shih-yü (*Pao-chüan tsung-lu*, p. 53) lists it as Ming, while Sawada Mizuho (*Zōho Hōkan*, p. 122) concludes that it is "an old *pao-chüan* printed before the K'ang-hsi period (1662–1722)."

Ch'iu-kuei Wang has written a detailed article about this book, "The *Hsiao-shih Meng Chiang Chung-lieh Chen-chieh Hsien-liang Pao-chüan*: An Analytical Study" (*Asian Culture* VII.4:46–72 [Winter 1979]). On p. 50, he says that "we may reasonably conclude that it might have appeared by the first half of the seventeenth century, though no earlier than the last quarter of the sixteenth century." I read the copy of this book from Cheng Chen-to's collection in the rare book room of the Beijing Library in May 1981. It is reprinted in full in volume 11 of Chang Hsi-shun et al., eds., *Pao-chüan ch'u-chi*.

This *pao-chüan* is a sectarian version of the familiar story of Meng Chiang-nü's search for her husband, who has been drafted by the first emperor of the Ch'in to help build the Great Wall. In the end she finds and collects his bones, and commits suicide by jumping into the water with them. Eventually she and her husband are reunited in heaven. The *Meng Chiang pao-chüan*, also called the *Ch'ang-*

ch'eng (Great Wall) *pao-chüan* (introductory material, p. 277), begins
with a creation account and is permeated with sectarian terms and
concepts. As Wang ("*Hsiao-shih Meng Chiang Pao-chüan*," p. 50) says,
"[though it] takes an originally secular story as its subject, religious
terms with sectarian overtones are found on almost every page of
it." Wang discusses the deification of Meng Chiang-nü and shrines
in her honor, and the popularity of plays about her in the sixteenth
century, as well as the ritual of burning paper facsimiles of winter
clothes in the tenth month as an offering to ancestors. The Meng
Chiang-nü story forms a mythic background for this ritual because
she had attempted to deliver winter clothes to her husband (ibid.,
pp. 47–49). In this context the *pao-chüan* appears as a sectarian ap-
propriation of a popular story to propagate a particular religious
perspective. References in it to the Venerable Patriarch Hun-yuan
indicate a possible connection to the Hung-yang tradition discussed
in Chapter Five above.

The sectarian orientation of this book is particularly clear in
chapter 32, which sums up the story of Meng Chiang and her husband, Fan Lang:

The two worthy and virtuous people Meng Chiang and Fan Lang were
originally bodhisattvas descended to the world. In the Crystal Palace [of the
Dragon King in the sea], they were reunited. There the Dragon King, the
Holy Mother, and dragon children and grandchildren all came together with
them to form a complete great assembly. They waited for a long time for the
First Emperor, and then the three of them went to the "Peaches of Immortality" Assembly [in paradise]. . . .

[The emperor and his officials] all observed fasting and the precepts, and
after a long time, when their merit was complete, they went together to the
third Dragon-Flower Assembly, forever to continue long life. . . .

[So it is that] all those who recite the Buddha's name leave the three paths
of rebirth and purgatory, while the bad for successive kalpas fall into [saṃ-
sāra] and lose their divine light. For those who attain enlightenment, all the
buddhas lead the way. They emit a brilliant light that pervades everywhere.
. . . They reach the Native Place, verify the Eternal, and float on a boat to the
shore. [So] the little children are able to see their dear Mother, and enter the
Mother's womb. They do not fear the three calamities, and at the Dragon-
Flower Assembly forever enjoy peace and good health for eighty myriads of
kalpas. At that time the three sages [of the Three Teachings] will return to
heaven, and return to their source and origin. (pp. 579, 585, 588–589)

Since Ch'iu-kuei Wang's excellent discussion of this text is readily available, I see no need to describe it further here. Professor Wang notes references to several other *pao-chüan* versions of this story ("*Hsiao-shih Meng Chiang Pao-chüan*," p. 60, nn. 6–10), as does Sawada (*Zōho Hōkan*, pp. 171–172).

Reference Matter

Notes

For complete author names, titles, and publication data for works cited here in short form, see the Works Cited, pp. 407–416.

Introduction

1. David Johnson, "*Mu-lien* in Pao-chüan: The Performance Context and Religious Meaning of the *Yu-ming Pao-chüan*," in David Johnson, ed., *Ritual and Scripture in Chinese Popular Religion* (1995).

2. On *pien-wen*, see Victor H. Mair's 1983 *Tun-huang Popular Narratives*, and his more recent study, *T'ang Transformation Texts* (1989).

3. In Appendix I, there are references to two seventeenth-century "precious volumes" that do contain stories, one about an innocent woman who is summoned to purgatory before her time (text 12 in Appendix I) and another about the Venerable Mother's gift of twin children to a pious couple (see note 10 to text 10 in Appendix I). Recently, Randall L. Nadeau and Janet Lynn Kerr have argued for continuities between sectarian and narrative *pao-chüan*, emphasizing that both are religious texts. I have no objection to this, but prefer that further discussion of this issue be postponed until others have had the opportunity to read and respond to the present book.

Nadeau's discussion of this point is in his 1993 "Genre Classifications of Chinese Popular Religious Literature: *Pao-chüan*." Kerr's contribution is in Janet MacGregor Lynn [Kerr], "Precious Scrolls in Chinese Popular Religious Culture" (unpublished Ph.D. dissertation, University of Chicago, 1994). This dissertation is based on the study of two *pao-chüan*, the *Hsiang-shan pao-chüan* and the *Lung-hua ching*, discussed respectively in Chapters One and Seven below, plus one from a later period.

A recent study by Yü Sung-ch'ing does not discuss the issue of genre classification but treats *pao-chüan* as the products of popular religious sects. It deals with seven texts from the period with which the present study is concerned, and with a T'ang text that provides antecedents for some *pao-chüan* themes. Yü's book is entitled *Min-chien mi-mi tsung-chiao ching-chüan yen-chiu* (A study of the scriptures of secret folk religions; 1994).

In 1997, Ch'e Hsi-lun published a collection of essays entitled *Chung-kuo pao-chüan yen-chiu lun-chi* (Collected essays on Chinese "precious volumes"), which contains valuable information on some early *pao-chüan* referred to in the present volume, as do the works of Janet Lynn [Kerr] and Yü Sung-ch'ing just cited. For a recent summary, see Asai Motoi's 1993 "Precious Scrolls and Folk Sectarianism of the Ming-Qing Period."

Wang Chien-ch'uan and Lin Wan-ch'uan of Taiwan are editing a collection of popular scriptures entitled *Ming Ch'ing min-chien tsung-chiao ching-chüan wen-hsien* (Popular religious scriptures from the Ming and Ch'ing periods), which is to be published in 1998. From its draft table of contents, it appears that this collection will include over a hundred titles, some of them the same as those in Chang Hsi-shun et al., eds., *Pao-chüan ch'u-chi* ("Precious volumes," first collection; 40 vols., 1994, on which see also note 5 below). This new publication will be a valuable resource for *pao-chüan* studies. See also Ch'e Hsi-lun's *Chung-kuo pao-chüan tsung-mu* (A general bibliography of "precious volumes"). This book was published in August 1998, too late to consult for the present volume, but it appears detailed and comprehensive.

One link between sectarian and narrative "precious volumes" is the use in the former of tune names taken from popular operas, as is noted several times below. In his *P'o-hsieh hsiang-pien* (A detailed refutation of heresies), Huang Yü-p'ien comments on the opera tunes, style, and rhythms that influenced the *pao-chüan* he collected and criticized as a district magistrate in Hopei province in the 1830s. He concludes his brief discussion of this topic by saying that "those who practice heretical teachings used opera performance methods to fabricate their heretical scriptures." Since Huang's whole book is devoted to demonstrating that *pao-chüan* are vulgar and worthless because they are not based on classical sources, his comments should be understood in that context. Nonetheless, there is no doubt that some of the stylistic features he notes are indeed due to operatic influences, as is to be expected in the world of Chinese popular culture. Huang's comments are in *chüan* 3 of his book, pp. 78–79 in the 1972 study of it by Sawada Mizuho, *Kōchū haja shōben* ("A detailed refutation of heresies," with corrections and commentary).

4. For representative discussions of these groups, see Susan Naquin, *Millenarian Rebellion in China* (1976), and idem, *Shantung Rebellion* (1981); Noguchi Tetsurō, "Chūgoku shūkyō kessha-shi joshō (An introduction to the history of Chinese religious organizations; 1978), and idem, *Mindai Bya-*

kuren kyō shi no kenkyū (A study of the history of the White Lotus sect in the Ming dynasty; 1986); Daniel L. Overmyer, *Folk Buddhist Religion* (1976), idem, "Alternatives: Popular Religious Sects in Chinese Society" (1981), and David K. Jordan and Daniel L. Overmyer, *The Flying Phoenix: Aspects of Chinese Sectarianism in Taiwan* (1986); and Richard Hon-chun Shek, "Religion and Society in Late Ming: Sectarianism and Popular Thought in Sixteenth and Seventeenth Century China" (unpublished Ph.D. dissertation, University of California, Berkeley, 1980). The most recent comprehensive study is by Ma Hsi-sha and Han Ping-fang in their *Chung-kuo min-chien tsung-chiao shih* (A history of Chinese folk religion; 1992). I refer below at several points to this 1,453-page volume. Another important recent publication is Barend J. ter Haar's 1992 *The White Lotus Teachings in Chinese Religious History* .

5. This reprint is entitled *Pao-chüan ch'u-chi* ("Precious volumes," first collection), edited by Chang Hsi-shun, P'u Wen-ch'i, Kao K'e, and Sung Chün (40 volumes, 1994). There are 148 titles in this collection, most including the term *pao-chüan* but a few employing other terms, such as *ching* ("scripture"), *liang-yen* ("good words"), *ch'an* ("penance"), etc. This collection opens with all five of Lo Ch'ing's books and includes about thirty texts of the sort discussed in the present study. Also included are a number of books from the T'ien-chin Library collection, which by prior agreement I went to study in 1991, only to be told upon my arrival that the library was closed!

In 1995, the Chinese government prohibited the further publication and sale of the *Pao-chüan ch'u-chi*, but copies of it can be found in the following university libraries in North America: British Columbia, California at Berkeley, Chicago, Columbia, Cornell, Harvard, Michigan, Pennsylvania, and Princeton. Elsewhere I know there are copies at the Chinese University of Hong Kong, Heidelberg University, and the University of Leiden. There may be others as well.

Chapter One

1. On Ch'an "recorded sayings" and the Ch'üan-chen Taoist tradition, see notes 29–32 and 53–56 below.

2. Sawada Mizuho, *Zōho Hōkan no kenkyū* (A study of *pao-chüan*, revised and expanded edition; 1975), pp. 30–32.

3. Fifty-six of these indigenous Buddhist texts are conveniently reprinted in Takakusu Junjirō, Watanabe Kaikyoku, and Ono Gemmyō, eds., *Taishō shinshū daizōkyō* (The Taishō Buddhist canon, 1914–1932), T. 2865–2920, 85:1325–1464. For a recent study, see Robert E. Buswell, Jr., ed., *Chinese Buddhist Apocrypha* (1990), which in turn owes much to earlier pioneering studies by Japanese scholars, particularly Yabuki Keiki, *Meisha yoin kaisetsu* (English title: Rare and unknown Chinese manuscript remains of Buddhist literature discovered in Tun-huang collected by Sir Aurel Stein and preserved in the British Museum; 1933); and Makita Tairyō, *Gikyō kenkyū* (A

study of doubtful scriptures; 1976). See also Lionel Giles, *Descriptive Cata-logue of the Chinese Manuscripts from Tun-huang in the British Museum* (1957), pp. 151–164.

In 1990, I published an article on these texts entitled "Buddhism in the Trenches: Attitudes Toward Popular Religion in Chinese Scriptures Found at Tun-huang." Victor Mair comments, "I believe that even these 'indige-nous' scriptures were heavily influenced by Indian practices—perhaps transmitted orally by a lower level of personage than those who were re-sponsible for transmitting the canonical sūtras" (personal communication, 1992).

4. *Fo-shuo wu-liang ta tz'u chiao ching* (Sūtra preached by the Buddha on the teaching of measureless great compassion); T. 2903, 85:1445a–1446a (quoted passages from p. 1445c). See also the condemnation of those who give unclean food to monks in the *Fo-shuo chai-fa ch'ing-ching ching* (T. 2900, 85:1431c–1432a).

5. I am indebted to University of British Columbia Professor Emeritus Leon Hurvitz for the translation of this title.

6. The ten evil deeds are killing, stealing, adultery, lying, being double-tongued, coarse language, filthy language, covetousness, anger, and per-verted views. The five rebellious acts, or deadly sins, are parricide, matri-cide, killing an arhat, shedding the blood of a buddha, and destroying the harmony of the Sangha. The four grave prohibitions are killing, stealing, carnality, and lying. See William Edward Soothill and Lewis Hodous, *A Dic-tionary of Chinese Buddhist Terms* (1937), pp. 50, 128, 183.

7. The nine texts in volume 85 of the *Taishō Tripitaka* are numbers T. 2868, 2873, 2879, 2899, 2915, 2916, 2917A, 2917B, and 2920. I have also read a tenth eschatologically oriented indigenous scripture, T. 396, reprinted in volume 12 of Takakusu et al., eds., *Taishō shinshū daizōkyō*. E. Zürcher's studies of this type of text are his "Eschatology and Messianism in Early Chinese Buddhism" (1981) and his "Prince Moonlight: Messianism and Es-chatology in Early Medieval Chinese Buddhism" (1982). For the wider Bud-dhist background of this teaching, see Jan Nattier, *Once upon a Future Time: Studies in a Buddhist Prophecy of Decline* (1991). For a good summary of fifth-century Taoist eschatology, see Isabelle Robinet, *Taoism: Growth of a Religion* (1997), pp. 158–163.

8. Zürcher, "Eschatology and Messianism," p. 48. For an annotated translation of this text, see Randall L. Nadeau, "The 'Decline of the Dharma' in Early Chinese Buddhism" (1987).

9. T. 396, 12:1119a and 1119b. Translation taken from Nadeau, "Decline of the Dharma." Candraprabha, the "Moonlight Bodhisattva" (Yueh-kuang), is a messianic figure discussed in detail in Zürcher, "Prince Moonlight," cited in note 7 above.

10. Zürcher, "Prince Moonlight," p. 35, n. 64. Antonino Forte provides a brief summary of this text in his 1976 *Political Propaganda and Ideology in*

China at the End of the Seventh Century, pp. 271–280. Zürcher suggests a date between 560 and 589.

11. The five precepts (*wu-chieh*) are prohibitions of killing, stealing, adultery, lying, and drinking intoxicating liquors. The ten virtues (*shih-shan*) are the opposite of the ten evil acts (*shih-e*), which are listed in note 6 above.

12. The character translated as "seize" in this passage is *liao* ("to grasp"), but a bit later in the *Cheng-ming ching* it is replaced in the same pattern by a homophone *liao* ("to cure"). I have followed the "grasp" meaning in both instances.

13. Zürcher, "Prince Moonlight," pp. 43–44, based on pp. 1366c–1367a and 1368a–b of the *Cheng-ming ching* (T. 2879, 85:1362c–1368b).

14. Zürcher, "Prince Moonlight," p. 34.

15. Zürcher, "Prince Moonlight," pp. 47–59

16. For the Taoist background of the term *chung-min* ("seed people"), see Zürcher, "Prince Moonlight," p. 5. For the term *liu-tu* as "six kinds of persons to be saved," see note 7 of Chapter Two below.

17. The term for "four truths" here is *ssu-i* ("four things on which to rely"), which here seem to refer to the truth of the Dharma, the sūtras, the Middle Way, and wisdom. Soothill and Hodous, *Dictionary of Chinese Buddhist Terms,* p. 170. For the translation of the title of the *Fo-hsing hai-tsang chih-hui chieh-t'o p'o hsin-hsiang ching* (T. 2885), I am indebted to Professor Leon Hurvitz.

18. Cheng Chen-to, *Chung-kuo su wen-hsueh shih* (A history of Chinese vernacular literature; 1959, first published in 1938), II:307. For a similar statement, see Ch'en Ju-heng, *Shuo-shu shih-hua* (On the history of narrated literature; 1958), p. 124. A more recent reaffirmation of this view is found in Ma Hsi-sha's 1986 "Tsui-tsao i-pu pao-chüan te yen-chiu" (A study of the earliest *pao-chüan*).

19. Victor Mair has published four substantial studies on the topic of *pien-wen* ("transformation texts") in the last nineteen years—i.e., his "Lay Students and the Making of Written Vernacular Narrative (1981); *Tun-huang Popular Narratives* (1983); *Painting and Performance: Chinese Picture Recitation and Its Indian Genesis* (1988); and *T'ang Transformation Texts* (1989). For an extensive bibliography of *pien-wen* studies, see his *T'ang Transformation Texts,* pp. 219–278.

20. Mair, *Tun-huang Popular Narratives,* pp. 5–6; idem, *T'ang Transformation Texts,* p. 15.

21. The texts Mair discusses can be found in Wang Chung-min, ed., *Tun-huang pien-wen chi* (Collected Tun-huang transformation texts; 1957). On p. 166 of his *T'ang Transformation Texts,* Mair notes a reference to "proclaiming scrolls (*chüan*)" and "singing transformation texts" as parallel activities in a twentieth-century Peking entertainment center. He is puzzled about the survival of the old term *pien-wen* and comments, "This demonstrates that written records are inadequate in their description of popular

culture for pre-modern times." I wonder whether the same may not apply to the continuation of sixth-century mythic themes in sixteenth-century *pao-chüan*, as discussed in the first section of this chapter.

Ma Hsi-sha, in his article "Tsui-tsao i-pu pao-chüan te yen-chiu," p. 65, lists the titles of eleven texts of different types found at Tun-huang alongside the similar-appearing titles of some *pao-chüan*, most of the narrative type. In common with traditional Chinese scholarship, Ma uses the term *pien-wen* for all these texts, a perspective that has been invalidated by Victor Mair. I have looked at the editions of all these books in Wang Chung-min's collection. Of the eleven texts, six are based on stories that later appeared in other forms of literature, including narrative *pao-chüan*. Of the remaining five, one is the *Hsiang-mo pien-wen* (Transformation text on the subjugation of demons; Wang, *Tun-huang pien-wen chi* I:361–394), translated by Mair in his *Tun-huang Popular Narratives*, pp. 31–84. It concerns a "contest of supernatural powers" between the Buddha's disciple Śāriputa and a heretical master (Mair, *T'ang Transformation Texts*, p. 18). A second is the *Ti-yü pien-wen* (Transformation text on purgatory; Wang, *Tun-huang pien-wen chi* II:761–763), a two-page fragment expressing regret for sins. The remaining three are sūtra-lecture texts on the *Diamond* and *Amitābha* sūtras (ibid., II:426–450 and 451–479, with two additional *Amitābha* fragments on II:480–487). The third sūtra-lecture text is based on a sūtra about Maitreya's rebirth in the Tushita Heaven (ibid., II:655–656).

None of these five books at all resembles sectarian *pao-chüan*. The title of the *Chin-kang p'an-jo po-lo-mi ching chiang-ching-wen* (Sūtra-lecture text on *The Diamond Perfect Wisdom Sūtra*) resembles that of the *Chin-kang ching k'e-i* discussed later in this chapter, but it quotes only short lines from the sūtra, on which the comments are entirely different from those in the *k'e-i*. It will not do to say that texts are related simply because of similarities in their titles. One particularly egregious example of this faulty method is the pairing of the *P'o-mo pien-wen* (Transformation text on destroying demons; Wang, *Tun-huang pien-wen chi* I:344–360) with the *Fu-mo pao-chüan* (Precious volume on subduing demons; text 6 in Appendix I). The latter is a seventeenth-century work devoted to the Lord Kuan as chief exorcist of the realm that bears no resemblance to the Tun-huang text. The *P'o-mo* book does not call itself a *pien-wen*, and its title is properly translated by Mair as *Destruction of the Transformation of Demons* (*T'ang Transformation Texts*, p. 26).

For *pien-wen* influence on later forms of Chinese literature, including narrative *pao-chüan*, see Victor Mair's 1989 "The Contributions of T'ang and Five Dynasties Transformation Texts (*pien-wen*) to Later Chinese Popular Literature."

22. Mair, *Tun-huang Popular Narratives*, pp. 6–7.

23. Stephan Marcus Salzberg, "A Popular Exposition in Prose and Verse of the *Vimalakīrti Sūtra*: An Annotated Translation of Stein Manuscript Number 4571" (unpublished M.A. thesis, University of British Columbia,

1983), pp. 6, 8–9, 15–16. Several *chiang-ching-wen* ("sūtra-lectures") are included in Wang Chung-min's *Tun-huang pien-wen chi* (see note 21 above).

24. Salzberg, "A Popular Exposition of the *Vimalakīrti Sūtra*," p. 16.

25. Mair, *T'ang Transformation Texts*, p. 30.

26. Another type of older book that included some concepts and terms used later in "precious volumes" was prognostication texts, one of which Yü Sung-ch'ing discusses in detail in her *Min-chien mi-mi tsung-chiao*, pp. 35–110. The book in question is an 1861 reprint of the *Chuan t'ien t'u ching* (Scripture of the turning heaven chart), which as its title indicates is devoted to dealing with the disasters at the turn of the age, the end of the kalpa. Ms. Yü presents evidence that this book was written at the end of the T'ang, probably about 897. Written in classical Chinese, it includes some prose sections but is composed mostly in verse arranged 7/7/7/7 or 5/5/5/5 characters per line. The relevant concepts and terms in it are veneration of Kuan-yin, social egalitarianism, a white lotus flower, and a reference to an "immortal youth of Mount Ling." This book looks forward to the coming of an "enlightened king" (Ming-wang) whose reign will bring many eons of peace and freedom from disaster. Ms. Yü points out that the title of this book is included in a list of scriptures cited in chapter 12 of the *Dragon-Flower Scripture* (*Lung-hua ching*) of 1654, which I discuss in Chapter Seven below. The complete text of the *T'ien t'u ching* is provided on pp. 111–124 of Ms. Yü's book.

27. John R. McRae, *The Northern School and the Formation of Early Ch'an Buddhism* (1986), pp. 73–74. For a more recent critical view of Ch'an tradition, see T. Griffith Foulk, "Myth, Ritual and Monastic Practices in Sung Ch'an Buddhism" (1993).

28. *The Platform Sutra of the Sixth Patriarch: The Text of the Tun-huang Manuscript*, translation, introduction, and notes by Philip B. Yampolsky (1967). The page references in this discussion are to this edition of the book. The term "platform" in the title refers to a raised area from which sermons were preached.

29. For this theme in the *Platform Sūtra*, see p. 133 of the Yampolsky translation. Although Hui-neng is quoted as having said that "there is no need to depend on written words" (p. 149), he is also said to have thoroughly understood and appreciated the *Lotus Sūtra* upon having read it once (pp. 165–166). Near the end of the book composed in his name, he commends it in words similar to those used by the Buddha in translated sūtras: "Those who do not receive the *Platform Sūtra* do not have the basic essentials of my teaching. As of now you have received them; hand them down and spread them among later generations. If others are able to encounter the *Platform Sūtra*, it will be as if they received the teaching personally from me" (p. 173). Here again was a powerful model for sectarian authors.

30. McRae, *Northern School*, pp. 73–74. An anonymous reader of the manuscript of the present book comments about the *yü-lu* ("recorded sayings") that "it is probably better to describe *yü-lu* as literary fabrications than

to claim them to be transcriptions of oral exchanges." I agree, but of course sectarian authors took them literally.

31. Yanagida Seizan, "The 'Recorded Sayings' Texts of Chinese Ch'an Buddhism" (1983, translated by John R. McRae; first published in Japanese in 1969). Professor Yanagida's major recent study of this topic is his 1985 "Goroko no rekishi" (A history of "recorded sayings").

32. Ruth Fuller Sasaki, ed. and trans., *The Recorded Sayings of Ch'an Master Lin-chi Hui-chao of Chen Prefecture* (1975), p. 53. (The Chinese text for this passage is on p. 28 in the back of the book; Hui-chao is Lin-chi's posthumous title.) For another convenient discussion of Ch'an "recorded sayings," see Judith A. Berling, "Bringing the Buddha Down to Earth: Notes on the Emergence of *Yü-lu* as a Buddhist Genre" (1987). For an introductory bibliography of this topic, see the Yanagida article cited in note 31 above. The following sources were also consulted for this discussion of yü-lu: *The Recorded Sayings of Layman P'ang*, translated by Ruth Fuller Sasaki, Yoshitaka Iriya, and Dana R. Fraser (1971); *The Recorded Sayings of Ma-tsu*, translated from the Dutch by Julian F. Pas (1981); *Two Zen Classics*, translated by Sekida Katsuki (1977); Tao-yuan, *Ching-te Ch'uan-teng lu* (Ching-te record of the transmission of the lamp), 2 vols., *Ssu-pu Ts'ung-kan hsu-pien* (Taipei: Taiwan Commercial Press, 1966; first compiled in 1004); and the *Feng-yang Wu-te Ch'an-shih yü-lu* (Recorded sayings of Ch'an master Feng-yang Wu-te), 2 *chüan*, first published in 993 by Feng-yang Shan-chao (947–1024), T. 1992, 47.594b–629c. This text is discussed by Berling in her "Bringing the Buddha Down to Earth," pp. 74–75. It also employs a number of vernacular terms such as *she-ma* ("what?"), *chei-ke* ("this one"), and *jen-ma* ("in this way"). There are at least eighteen additional *yü-lu* texts in *Taishō* volume 47.

33. Another source of early written colloquial Chinese is the recorded conversations of the Neo-Confucian scholar Chu Hsi (1130–1200) with his students. For this, see Gerty Kallgren, "Studies in Sung Time Colloquial Chinese as Revealed in Chu Hsi's *Ts'üan shu*" (1958).

34. On the Pure Land background of late traditional, popular religious sects, see Overmyer, *Folk Buddhist Religion*, pp. 85–94, and idem, "Alternatives," particularly the discussion of the Sung monk-evangelist Mao Tzu-yuan (1086–1166). See also ter Haar, *White Lotus Teachings*, pp. 1–139.

35. By far the most detailed studies of the Pure Land tradition are by Japanese scholars, with the most useful for the period dealt with in this book being Ogasawara Senshū, *Chūgoku kinsei Jōdokyō shi no kenkyū* (A study of the history of the modern Pure Land sect in China; 1963); see also Tsukamoto Zenryū, *Chūgoku Jōdokyō shi kenkyū* (A study of the history of the Chinese Pure Land sect; 1976). For a good summary of Pure Land history and a bibliography, see Kenneth K. S. Chen, *Buddhism in China* (1964), pp. 338–350, 530–532, and Appendix 3 in the *Land of Bliss* book cited in note 36 below.

36. This is the shorter version of the *Sukhāvati-vyūha*, translated into English by F. Max Müller in *Buddhist Māhāyana Texts*, edited by F. Max Müller,

Vol. XLIX, *Sacred Books of the East* (Delhi: Motilal Banarsidass, 1965), Part II, pp. 89–103 (first published by Oxford University Press in 1894). A Chinese translation of a longer version (T. 364) can also be found in *Taishō* volume 12, along with several other Pure Land texts. An English translation of it is available in the same volume of the *Sacred Books of the East* II:1–85. For a more recent translation of both versions, see *The Land of Bliss: The Paradise of the Buddha of Measureless Light; Sanskrit and Chinese Versions of the Sukhāvatīvyūha Sūtras*, introductions and English translations by Luis O. Gómez (1996).

37. Lung-shu was Wang Jih-hsiu's home district in what is now Anhui province.

38. Sawada, *Zōho Hōkan*, pp. 30–33.

39. Wang Tzu-ch'eng, *Li-nien Mi-t'o tao-ch'ang ch'an-fa* (Penance ritual for a ritual arena for the recitation of Amitābha's [name]), 10 *chüan*, *Zokuzokyō* 128:122a. Wang Tzu-ch'eng was a Pure Land lay devotee of the Yuan dynasty. The full title of the *Zokuzokyō* is *Dai Nihon Zokuzokyō* (The great Japanese continuation of the [Buddhist] canon; 1905–1912, reprinted 1946), edited by Maeda Eun and Nakano Tatsue.

40. The basic meanings of *k'e* are "pattern" or "class" (of things), a section or article of an agreement, a rule or a statute, while *i* means "ceremonies," "manners," or "deportment," so a literal translation of *k'e-i* could be "sectioned ceremonies." Michael Saso discusses Taoist *k'e-i* rituals as priestly "rites of meditative union" involving exteriorization of the deities in the priest's body to restore the cosmic vitality of a community. See his *The Teachings of Taoist Master Chuang* (1978), pp. 208–233. In the Buddhist contexts with which I am familiar, *k'e-i* refers to a text that amplifies and explains a sūtra, intended for ritual recitation; hence the translation "ritual amplification."

41. Sawada, *Zōho Hōkan*, pp. 286–288, 299. See also Yoshioka Yoshitoyo, "*Shōshaku kongō kagi* no seiritsu ni tsuite" (On the formation of the *Chin-kang k'e-i*; 1966). On pp. 101–102 of his book, Sawada discusses a Ming edition of a *Hsiao-shih Chin-kang k'e-i* attributed to Tsung-ching of the Sung. It is in thirty-two sections (*fen*). He says it is "a ritual book divided into sections that explains the *Diamond Sūtra* translated by Kumārajīva." The text of this translation is in the *Taishō Tripitaka* (Takakusu et al., eds.), T. 235, 8:748c–752c. The *k'e-i* does indeed follow the sūtra, though of course the latter is not broken up into sections. Its complete title is the *Chin-kang p'an-jo po-lo-mi ching* (The diamond prajñāpāramitā sūtra), which refers to the perfect wisdom of the Buddha and bodhisattvas. For a translation into English, see Edward Conze, ed. and trans., *Vajracchedikā Prajñāpāramitā*, Vol. XIII, *Serie Orientale Roma* (Roma: Is. M.E.O., 1957).

The term *hsiao-shih* literally means to "melt away," and hence, in textual settings, "to explain," as I have translated it here. However, in sectarian "precious volumes" I think it more appropriate to translate this term as "on" because in fact they do not "explain" in the normal sense of that word, but rather expound their own teachings.

42. *Chin-kang k'e-i*, Maeda and Nakano, eds., *Zokuzokyō* 129:129b–144b. The page numbers following the quotations refer to this edition. Ch'ang-an was an old national capital. A road to Ch'ang-an for "every household" implies a direct path to salvation for all.

43. This summary of the teachings of the *Chin-kang k'e-i* is taken from Daniel L. Overmyer, "Values in Chinese Sectarian Literature: Ming and Ch'ing *Pao-chüan*" (1985), pp. 225–227.

44. Yoshioka Yoshitoyo, "À-propos du *Hiang-chang pao-kiuan* dans une édition de l'ere K'ien-long" (1971). The page references in what follows are to the pagination of the text itself.

Li Shih-yü's 1961 *Pao-chüan tsung-lu* (A comprehensive bibliography of "precious volumes"), along with the *Zōho Hōkan* of Sawada Mizuho, is the standard work of its type. Editions of the *Hsiang-shan* book are discussed on pp. 56–57 of Li Shih-yü's work. Two nineteenth- and twentieth-century editions are discussed by Sawada in *Zōho Hōkan*, pp. 126–127. The title page of the 1773 edition provides the name of a printing shop in Hangchow, but a Ch'ing colophon gives T'zu-ch'i district of Ning-po prefecture as the place where funds were solicited to cut the printing blocks. For a detailed description and summary of this book, see Janet Lynn [Kerr], "Precious Scrolls in Chinese Popular Religious Culture," pp. 97–164.

45. This suggestion was made by E. G. Pulleyblank of the University of British Columbia. For a very helpful discussion of the characteristics of early *pai-hua*, see Kallgren, "Studies in Sung Time Colloquial Chinese." This and other materials on this topic were also suggested to me by Professor Pulleyblank.

46. The Chinese text for the line translated as "The celestial gods of the three realms will all bear you up" (lit. "support [you] by means of the tops of [their] heads"), is *san-chieh t'ien-shen tou i ting tai*. In some Buddhist books, such as the *Amitābha Sūtra*, we are told that the Buddha "constantly sits on the heads" of the pious to provide protection (*ch'ang chu ch'i ting*), but the grammar in the *Hsiang-shan* passage does not seem to support such an interpretation (see T. 366, 12:348b). The "three realms" in Buddhist teaching are those of desire, form, and the formless.

47. Yoshioka, "À-propos du *Hiang-chang*," pp. 115–116, 121–122.

48. Glen Dudbridge, *The Legend of Miao-shan* (1978), pp. 15–19, 47.

49. Dudbridge, *Legend of Miao-shan*, p. 46. Dudbridge also points out that some of the Yuan language usages that Yoshioka cites are found in Ming literature as well.

50. For recent studies of Mu-lien in *pao-chüan* and Buddhist literature, see David Johnson, "Mu-lien in Pao-chüan: The Performance, Content, and Religious Meaning of the *Yu-ming Pao-chüan*," in his *Ritual and Scripture in Chi-*

nese Popular Religion, and Alan Cole, *Mothers and Sons in Chinese Buddhism* (1998).

51. The quoted material is from p. 325 of Cheng Chen-to's *Chung-kuo su wen-hsueh shih*. See also Ch'e Hsi-lun, *Chung-kuo pao-chüan yen-chiu lun-chi*, pp. 64–65, for a discussion of the *Mu-lien chiu mu ch'u-li ti-yü sheng t'ien pao-chüan* as the earliest *pao-chüan*. I am grateful to Professor Wang Tsung-yü of the Peking University Department of Religious Studies for checking references in the *Mu-lien* book for me.

52. Richard Shek, "Daoist Elements in Late Imperial Chinese Sectarianism" (1993).

53. On the *Yun-chi ch'i-ch'ien*, see Judith M. Boltz, *A Survey of Taoist Literature, Tenth to Seventeenth Centuries* (1987), pp. 229–231. In the *Taoist Canon (Tao-tsang)*, it is Harvard-Yenching index no. 1026, in 122 chapters. The edition I have read is in three volumes, published in Taipei by the Tzu-yu ch'u-pan she in 1978. In that edition, references to the themes I have listed here are found respectively at the following volume and page numbers: 1:13a, 15, 27a, 116, and 456, in *chüan* 2, 3, 10, and 31.

For a convenient collection of passages from Taoist texts in translation, see Livia Kohn, ed., *The Taoist Experience: An Anthology* (1993). For Taoist backgrounds of "precious volumes," see particularly pp. 33–42 on creation myths; pp. 55–62 on the Queen Mother of the West; pp. 86–92 on "Complete Perfection" teachings; pp. 97–106 on moral precepts; and pp. 133–148 on *ch'i* circulation practices. See also Robinet, *Taoism*, pp. 158–163 on eschatology, and p. 156 on the theme that "the parents who gave us birth are not our 'true' parents."

54. Stephen Eskildsen, "The Beliefs and Practices of Early Ch'üan-chen Taoism" (unpublished M.A. thesis, University of British Columbia, 1989). In my view, this excellent and substantial thesis (406 pages + texts) supersedes earlier studies of Ch'üan-chen belief and practice, primarily because it demonstrates how much this practice was embedded in earlier Taoist traditions. For a valuable discussion of Ch'üan-chen texts, see Boltz, *Survey of Taoist Literature*, pp. 139–173. See also Ted Tao-chung Yao, "Ch'üan-chen: A New Taoist Sect in North China During the Twelfth and Thirteenth Centuries" (unpublished Ph.D. dissertation, University of Arizona, 1980).

55. Boltz, *Survey of Taoist Literature*, pp. 163, 167, and 171.

56. Yao, "Ch'üan-chen: A New Taoist Sect," pp. 202–213. The quoted passage is found on p. 203. Chang Po-tuan's major work is the *Wu-chen p'ien*, the title of which is translated by Boltz in her *Survey of Taoist Literature* as "Folios on the Apprehension of Perfection." Several editions are reprinted in the Ming *Taoist Canon (Tao-tsang)*. According to Boltz, one of the best known of these is the *Tzu-yang chen-jen Wu-chen p'ien chu-shu* (The *Wu-chen p'ien* of the Tzu-yang perfected person [Chang Po-tuan], with commentary), originally edited by Weng Pao-kuang (fl. 1173). It is in eight *chüan*, no. 141 in the

Harvard-Yenching index of the *Taoist Canon, Tao-tsang* 61–62, *sui, shang,* and *hsia.* See Boltz, *Survey of Taoist Literature,* pp. 174 and 317, n. 446. There are two English translations of this book, the first by Tenney L. Davis and Chao Yun-ts'ung, "Chang Po-tuan, his *Wu Chen P'ien,*" in *Proceedings of the American Academy of Arts and Sciences,* LXXIII: 97–117 (1939), and the second by Thomas Cleary, *Understanding Reality: A Taoist Alchemical Classic,* with commentary by Liu I-ming (Honolulu: University of Hawai'i Press, 1987).

57. Other possible sources of influence on sectarian teaching are Manichaeism and *shan-shu* ("morality books"). Manichaeism I discussed in 1976, on pp. 75–80 of my *Folk Buddhist Religion,* noting such parallel themes as struggle between good and destructive forces, three stages of time in the process of deliverance, worship of the sun and moon, prohibitions of meat and alcohol, the wearing of white clothing, and the title "Ming-wang" (King of Light, or Enlightened King). More recently, Ma and Han, in their *Min-chien tsung-chiao,* pp. 98–101, repeat some of these points, adding that the Eternal Mother of sectarian teaching might owe something to the Manichaean "Mother of Life."

However, the two newest studies of which I am aware that discuss Chinese Manichaeism and its possible influence on other religious traditions both deny such influence on sectarian teaching. The most detailed discussion of this topic is a 1995 article by Lien Li-ch'ang, "Pai-lien chiao hsing-ch'eng wu kuan Ming-chiao k'ao" (An investigation of [the thesis that] the formation of the White Lotus sect had no connection with the Religion of Light [Manichaeism]). In this article, Mr. Lien makes the following points:

a. The term "Ming-wang" has both Taoist and Buddhist backgrounds, and is not the same as the Manichaean "Ambassador of Light" (Ming-shih).

b. The terms for the three time-stages of salvation are different and have different meanings. The *san-chi* of Manichaeism refer to the past, when the principles of light and dark were first distinguished; the present, when there is a struggle between them; and the future, when these two forces are in each person (and when salvation is possible through their separation). This is manifestly not the same as the Buddhist and *pao-chüan* teaching of different buddhas being in charge of salvation in three successive time periods (*san-shih*).

c. Manichaeism was active only in Fukien and Chekiang in Southeast China, far from the heartland of sectarian *pao-chüan* in the north. This geographical separation made influence unlikely.

The other new study is a book by Wang Chien-ch'uan, *Ts'ung Mo-ni chiao tao Ming-chiao* (From Manichaeism to the Religion of Light; 1992), in which, after 350 pages of discussion, the author concludes that Manichaeans did not participate in popular uprisings and that earlier discussions of their influence on other popular religious sects are "fundamentally all unfounded talk."

My own view is now closer to that of Lien Li-ch'ang and Wang Chien-ch'uan because I have learned more about Buddhism and Taoism than I knew in 1976, and find in these traditions satisfactory antecedents for most of the sectarian themes in question. For example, a sense of struggle with hostile forces has been a part of common religious belief and practice in China since at least the Warring States period, a sense that was intensified in early Taoist religion and related to promises of the advent of a new savior at the end of the age—all of this before even Liu Ts'un-yan would argue for the presence of Manichaeism in China. (See his 1976 article, "Traces of Zoroastrianism and Manichaean Activities in Pre-T'ang China.") We have seen that dramatic eschatological beliefs were also present in indigenous Buddhist texts that appeared as early as the fifth century, so Manichaean influence need not have been present.

Nonetheless, the possibility of such influence is a complex question on which specialists disagree, so I cannot deal with it further here.

Morality books are discussed in detail in a recent book by Cynthia J. Brokaw, *The Ledgers of Merit and Demerit: Social Change and Moral Order in Late Imperial China* (1991). The first books of this type appeared in the twelfth century, devoted to detailed discussion of the merit and demerit that come in response to good and bad deeds. Beginning in the sixteenth century, Confucian scholars began writing books of this type to foster literati values both in themselves and in society at large. Many of the values taught by these "books about goodness" (*shan-shu*) were supported by sectarian *pao-chüan* as well, but they are quite different types of books, with different social origins.

Chapter Two

1. Li Shih-yü, now a researcher with the Tianjin Academy of Social Sciences, is one of the pioneer Chinese scholars to study the texts of Chinese popular religious sects, and for long the only such scholar to make this study the major focus of his research. He published a bibliography of sectarian scriptures in 1961. I am grateful for his cooperation and assistance during my trip to China in October 1991. I am also grateful to Lu Kung for permitting us to photograph his book. Mr. Lu told us that he had earlier lent the book to the Institute for the Study of World Religions in Beijing (a branch of the Academy of Social Sciences), but that after several months they returned it to him without comment. I note that in her *Min-chien mi-mi tsung-chiao*, p. 239, Yü Sung-ch'ing accepts a 1430 date for the *Huang-chi pao-chüan*.

2. The correct Chinese name for what I call "accordion style" is *ching-che chuang* ("sūtra folded style").

3. Mount Ling (Ling-shan) is an abbreviation of the Buddhist term "Spirit Vulture Peak" (Ling-chiu shan, Skt. Gṛdhrakūṭa), the place where the Buddha is said to have preached the *Lotus Sūtra*. In sectarian mythology this

is a name for paradise. The "Dragon-Flower Assembly" refers to the assembly, or congregation, of those who will be saved by the Future Buddha, Maitreya. Its original referent is a dragon-flower tree (Nāga-puṣpa) under which Maitreya will find enlightenment. "Gathering in the primal ones" (or "gathering in to completion") refers to the final reunion of all believers. However, the inward-turning emphasis of this closing inscription is not reflected in the external orientation of the *Huang-chi* book itself, in which heaven and the buddhas can be reached by the soul only after a demanding journey of ascent.

4. The two figures on either side of the Buddha are not buddhas, but the only divine triads discussed in the *Huang-chi* book are of buddhas; Lao-tzu and Confucius are not mentioned. The only pair of patriarchs noted are named "Light" and "Dark," but they do not have a prominent role in the book. I remain puzzled; suggestions welcome.

5. The term *yü-chih* ("produced by imperial authorization") appears in several later *pao-chüan* as well, but should not be taken too literally. There is evidence that some texts of the late-sixteenth-century Red Yang sect were printed in a government printing office with the help of eunuch supporters at court, but the case for other books of this type is less clear. The logical place for a book such as the *Huang-chi pao-chüan* to receive official authorization would have been as a part of the Buddhist or the Taoist canon, but it is not found in either.

6. The basic meaning of *tsung* is "ancestral shrine" or "ancestor," from which it came to mean "root" or "source," and thence "tradition" or "school." It is in these latter two senses that it is used in the *Huang-chi* book. See the discussion below on "heretics and nonbelievers."

7. The conventional Buddhist meaning of the term *liu-tu* ("the six crossings over") is "the six things that ferry one beyond the sea of mortality to *nirvāna*, i.e., the six *pāramitās* [perfections of a bodhisattva]" (Soothill and Hodous, *Dictionary of Chinese Buddhist Terms*, pp. 134–135). In the *Huang-chi* book, however, this term refers to six types of beings who are saved, defined in chapter 12 as *ming-tu* ("those saved by their understanding/enlightenment"), *e-tu* ("those saved [from their] evil [actions]"), *ching-tu* ("those saved by their purity"), *p'u-tu* ("those saved by universal deliverance"), *shan-tu* ("those saved by their goodness"), and *an-tu* ("those saved in secret"). There are ambiguous references in this book to teachers named Light (Ming) and Dark (An), which can also be interpreted as "in the open" and "secret" (hence my translation of *an-tu*). These six terms are a good example of sectarian reinterpretation of what at first appears to be orthodox Buddhist or Taoist vocabulary.

8. The "eight difficulties" (*pa-nan*) is originally a Buddhist term for eight conditions in which it is difficult to see the Buddha or hear the Dharma, as for those in purgatory, those reborn as animals, etc. In the *Huang-chi* book, however, this seems to be a general term for disasters at the end of the age,

mu' "(On the Deity "the Eternal Mother" worshipped by the White Lotus sect), p. 45, Wu Chih-ch'eng states that the term "Wu-sheng mu" first appeared in the Ming Cheng-te reign period in the writings of Lo Ch'ing.

15. Overmyer, "The Role of Lo Ch'ing in the Development of Sixteenth and Seventeenth Century Sectarian Scriptures," p. 4.

16. The text here reads *niang ta chua chi, yeh p'eng t'ou*; reading *chua* as a homonym for another character, sometimes read *chua*, that refers to the style of a young girl's hair. I am grateful to Mr. Hsu-tu Chen of the University of British Columbia for assisting me with this translation.

17. There are references here to "Old Amitābha constantly manifesting himself," to "Amitābha having the title Jan-teng," and to "the ten-character [recitation of] Amitābha's name," the last indicating Maitreya. In the *Chiu-lien pao-chüan*, discussed in Chapter Four below, we will see that Amitābha and Maitreya are also conflated.

18. "Tu-tou" could be translated as "superintendent of the Celestial Bushel" (the constellation associated with the north Polar Star), but I suspect it is a garbled transliteration, which I have not been able to identify. In the *Huang-chi* book, it refers to a celestial palace, and in other old *pao-chüan* to Maitreya's palace. As for the phrase *tsa fen te wu-p'an ssu-kuei*, the *wu-p'an* ("five realms") are divisions of the Red Canopy Heaven, each with its own set of offices. The *ssu-kuei* ("four valued things") I have not yet been able to identify; they are not defined in our text.

19. Wherever possible, these translations of official titles and those that follow are taken from Hucker, *Dictionary of Official Titles*, or extrapolated from them.

20. I have not been able to find references to the term *pu-hsing* ("those who set forth and examine"?).

21. The dictionary definition for *hsin-hao* is "signal," as in "signal flag," which does not seem appropriate here. The word I have translated as "military titles" is *hsiao*.

22. The term translated as "earnestly" here is *ao-k'ou*, for which I have not been able to find a satisfactory definition. However, it is repeatedly used in the *Huang-chi* book and seems to have the meaning I have indicated. "Maintaining a vegetarian diet" of course refers to sect members.

23. The Five Paths (*wu-tao*) in Buddhist contexts are five pathways of rebirth as gods, humans, animals, hungry ghosts, and sinners in purgatory. Susan Naquin reports that in the Beijing area this name can apply to locality gods (personal communication, March 1992).

24. Here *chi chen wei chao* literally means "offer a *chen* as a pass," which is paralleled a bit later in chapter 12 of the *Huang-chi* book by the phrase, "those who have pure tablets and who offer up *chen* leave the world." The problem here is what *chen* means. Its basic meaning is "true" or "real," and in Taoist texts it means "perfected," as in "perfected person." In the *Huang-chi* book, it seems to be a kind of document. Stephen Teiser suggests that

usually paired with *san-tsai*, the "three calamities" of fire, water, ar
that come at the end of a kalpa.

9. The "six paths of sentient existence" are as inhabitants of pui
hungry ghosts, animals, nature spirits (asuras), humans, and gods (
See Soothill and Hodous, *Dictionary of Chinese Buddhist Terms*, p. 1:
"nine-petaled lotus" is a symbol of Maitreya.

10. "Head leader" (*t'ou-ling*) and "boat captain" (*ch'uan-t'ou*) ar
tions in the sectarian hierarchy of this book. Charles O. Hucker, *A Dic*
of Official Titles in Imperial China (1985), item 6798, gives *t'ou-ling* as a m
title meaning "leader" but provides no reference for *ch'uan-t'ou*. Here
later sectarian texts, "boat" refers to the "Dharma boat" that ferries the
to paradise; as we read in chapter 7, "The Buddha said, 'I later will
down a boat [to enable people] to ascend the other shore.'"

11. "Tsu-mu" of course means "grandmother" in ordinary speech
here the context is bureaucratic, not familial. The term "original bod'
"primal body" (*yuan-shen*) seems to mean the original form of the devoi
which he or she returns in paradise. I understand it to be related to the
"primal ones" (*yuan-jen*), which refers to the true origin, nature, and ca
of the pious. In later texts, this means their real status as children ol
Eternal Mother, but this mythology is not yet developed in the *Huan*
book.

12. In the *Huang-chi* book, "setting forth the details" means consolida
the work of evangelism, which is called *k'ai-huang* ("opening up i
fields"). Here these terms always follow each other in that sequence.

13. The term "Golden Elixir" (*Chin-tan*), of Taoist origin, has been no
in Chapter One and will be discussed again below. Here it refers to
Huang-chi book itself.

14. Support for the view that Lo Ch'ing's scriptures were the earli
sectarian *pao-chüan* can be found in the following studies, listed in chror
logical order of their publication:

a. Li Shih-yü, "Pao-chüan hsin-yen" (A new discussion of "precious vc
umes"), pp. 173–174 (1957).

b. Sawada Mizuho, *Zōho Hōkan*, pp. 322, 328, 338–339 (1975).

c. Daniel L. Overmyer, "Values in Chinese Sectarian Literature," pp. 22(
223 (1985).

d. Cheng Chih-ming, *Wu-sheng lao-mu hsin-yang su-yuan* (Sources of th
Eternal Venerable Mother belief), pp. 3, 7, 15, etc. (1985).

e. Noguchi Tesurō, *Mindai Byakuren kyō* (1986).

f. Richard Shek, "Eternal Mother Religion: Its Role in Late Imperial Chinese History," pp. 471–472 (1989).

I restated my earlier position on this topic, though with some doubts, in
"The Role of Lo Ch'ing in the Development of Sixteenth and Seventeenth
Century Sectarian Scriptures: A Preliminary Study" (unpublished paper,
1989). In a 1986 article entitled "Pai-lien chiao ch'ung-pai shen 'Wu-sheng

chen can also mean a likeness or image of a person (personal communication, February 1997), but there are no clear references to such images in the *pao-chüan* I have read.

25. On the meaning of *chen* here, see note 24 above.

26. There is a term in chapter 12 of the *Huang-chi* book that I do not understand, and neither do the Buddha's questioners in the text, in part because the first character in the term is written in an eccentric way. The term is *yuan*(?)-*huang* ("to *yuan* the yellow"), which, if the first character is read as *yuan* ("to hold, to assist"), would mean "to assist the yellow." It seems to refer to a positive ritual action that supports one's trip to paradise. Unfortunately, when the Buddha is asked in this text what *yuan-huang* is, he does not answer the question but talks about the sins of those during the period of the Green and Red Yang assemblies, concluding with "They do not *yuan*[?] and do not repent. How can they attain buddhahood?" The word "yellow" is not defined here, either. The term *yuan-huang* is not mentioned outside of chapter 12.

27. In orthodox Buddhism, the Three Refuges are refuge in the Buddha, the Dharma, and the Sangha, though here the term seems merely to be pious repetition with no specific content. The five precepts, or prohibitions, are those against killing, stealing, adultery, lying, and drinking intoxicating liquor, which are incumbent upon all Buddhists and are supported by the *Huang-chi* book. The responsibilities of the six family relationships are those between father and son, brother and brother, and husband and wife.

28. On political conservatism in *pao-chüan*, see Daniel L. Overmyer, "Attitudes Toward the Ruler and State in Chinese Popular Religious Literature: Sixteenth and Seventeenth Century *Pao-chüan*" (1984).

29. Cf. Hucker, *Dictionary of Official Titles*, entries 3127, 3134, 3139, etc.

30. Ch'an "recorded sayings" are discussed in Chapter One above. See Berling, "Bringing the Buddha Down to Earth." Boltz discusses Taoist *yü-lu* ("dialogic treatises") on pp. 146–171 of her *Survey of Taoist Literature*. These Taoist compilations were particularly important for the Ch'üan-chen (Complete Perfection) school, which was active in North China at the time the *Huang-chi* book was compiled. The distinction between the Buddha and Ch'an masters is of course not absolute, because such masters were considered to have "attained buddhahood" themselves.

31. See W. T. Chan, ed. and trans., *A Sourcebook in Chinese Philosophy* (1963), pp. 463–465.

32. Ter Haar, *White Lotus Teachings*, pp. 72–76.

33. For the use of memorials in Taoist rituals, see Kristofer M. Schipper, "The Written Memorial in Taoist Ceremonies" (1974), and John Lagerwey, *Taoist Ritual in Chinese Society and History* (1987), pp. 61–89, 149–167.

34. On *chin-tan* ("golden elixir"), see Joseph Needham, *Science and Civilisation in China* (1983), Vol. 5, Part V, pp. 223, 228, 289, and Boltz, *Survey of Taoist Literature*, pp. 390–391, for a lengthy index entry on this topic.

35. On the alchemical furnace in Taoism, see Needham, *Science and Civilisation*, Vol. 5, Part V, pp. 101, 186, 211–214.

36. On Taoist talismans, see Lagerwey, *Taoist Ritual*, pp. 155–161; Kristofer Schipper, *Le Corps Taoïste* (1981), pp. 86–99; and the *Cheng-i fa-wen T'ai-shang wai-lu i* (Text of the correct and unified ritual teachings, protocol for the exterior registers of the Most High), *Tao-tsang* 991, Harvard-Yenching index no. 1233 (fifth century), pp. 1–3a.

37. On the Dark Warrior, see Henri Maspero, *Taoism and Chinese Religion* (1981), pp. 156–157, and Boltz, *Survey of Taoist Literature*, pp. 86–91; the quote is from p. 89 of Boltz's book.

38. On the Dark Warrior as a popular deity, see Willem A. Grootaers, "The Hagiography of the Chinese God Chen-wu" (1952). "Chen-wu" is an alternate name for Hsuan-wu. See also Gary Seaman, *Journey to the North* (Berkeley: University of California Press, 1987).

39. "T'ien-ch'i" is a title of the God of the Eastern Peak (Mount T'ai). For the lords of purgatory, see Maspero, *Taoism*, pp. 176–187.

Another parallel with Taoism is the concept of the "pass" (*kuan*) in the *Huang-chi* book. In his recent study of autobiographical writings, Pei-yi Wu comments: "[A pass is a] fortified checkpoint with gates and walls. . . . The successful negotiation of a *kuan* guarded by hostile forces often occurs as one of the most memorable episodes in the life of a Chinese hero. . . . To the religious Taoists a sequential system of *kuan* is more or less symbolically located in every human body, and to achieve immortality one must follow an elaborate program of penetrating each and all of the internal *kuan* while fighting temptations and fending off demons."

Wu notes the importance of this concept for Ch'an Buddhism and then goes on to discuss its role in neo-Confucian autobiographical writings in the Ming dynasty. See his *The Confucian's Progress: Autobiographical Writings in Traditional China* (1990), pp. 107–109, 137.

40. *Ming T'ai-tsung shih-lu* (Veritable records of [Emperor] T'ai tsung of the Ming), Yung-lo 16 year, 5th month, *hsin-hai*, in *Ming shih-lu* (Nan-kang: Academia Sinica, Institute of History and Language, 1962–1968), vol. 14, *chüan* 200, p. 2082. Cited in Noguchi, *Mindai Byakuren kyō*, pp. 162, 205, n. 73. Noguchi's discussion of early Ming sectarian activities is on pp. 141–212 of his book. Chen-ting was a prefecture in the Ming, not a district.

Ter Haar, in his *White Lotus Teachings*, pp. 99–100, notes thirteenth- and early fifteenth-century references to the *Wu-kung fu*, which he translates as "Amulet of the Five Lords" and describes as a prognostication text. A central theme of ter Haar's book is that the name "White Lotus" was not used by religious groups to refer to themselves after the early fifteenth century. After that it was used in official sources as a label for illegal popular sects.

41. See Ma Shu-t'ien, "Ming Ch'eng-tsu te cheng-chih yü tsung-chiao" (The administration of the Ming [Emperor] Ch'eng-tsu and religion; 1984)

and Frederick W. Mote and Denis Twitchett, eds., *The Cambridge History of China*, Vol. 7, *The Ming Dynasty, 1368–1644*, Part I, p. 304.

42. Mote and Twitchett, *The Ming Dynasty*, Part I, p. 212.

Chapter Three

1. In chronological order, the most important of many modern studies of Lo Ch'ing, his writings, and the sectarian tradition he founded are the following, some of which have already been noted above. To my knowledge, the first non-Chinese scholar to comment on this topic was Joseph Edkins, who according to de Groot read a paper on the Wu-wei sect at a meeting of the China branch of the Royal Asiatic Society in 1858. Edkins summarizes his earlier discussions of the sect in his *Chinese Buddhism* (1893). The reference by de Groot is on pp. 192–196 of his *Sectarianism* (see next entry in this note).

The first of many more detailed studies was by J. J. M. de Groot, *Sectarianism and Religious Persecution in China* (1903) 1:176–241. This was followed several decades later in the century by: Suzuki Chusei, "Rakyō ni tsuite: Shindai Shina shūkyō kessha no ichi rei" (On the Lo sect: An example of a religious association in Ch'ing China; 1943); Tsukamoto Zenryū, "Rakyō no seiritsu to ryūden ni tsuite" (On the founding and proliferation of the Lo sect; 1949); Yoshioka Yoshitoyo, "Raso no shūkyō" (The religion of Patriarch Lo; 1950); Sakai Tadao, *Chūgoku zenshō no kenkyū* (Studies in Chinese morality books; 1960), pp. 438–442, 468–485; Sawada Mizuho, *Zōho Hōkan* (1975), pp. 222–224, 300–342; Richard Shek, "Religion and Society in Late Ming" (1980), pp. 202–251; Sōda Hiroshi, "Rakyō no seiritsu to sono tenkai" (The founding and development of the Lo sect; 1983), pp. 1–74; Cheng Chih-ming, *Wu-sheng lao-mu hsing-yang* (1985); Randall L. Nadeau, "Popular Sectarianism in the Ming: Lo Ch'ing and His 'Religion of Non-Action'"(unpublished Ph.D. dissertation, University of British Columbia, 1990); and Ma and Han, *Min-chien tsung-chiao* (1992), pp. 165–339.

Lo Ch'ing and his texts are also discussed in Daniel L. Overmyer, *Folk Buddhist Religion* (1976), pp. 113–129; idem, "Boatmen and Buddhas: The Lo Chiao in Ming Dynasty China" (1978); and idem, "Values in Chinese Sectarian Literature" (1985), pp. 219–237.

For the later development of the Lo sect among boatmen, see David E. Kelly, "Temples and Tribute Fleets: The Luo Sect and Boatmen's Associations in the Eighteenth Century" (1982).

2. This is Nadeau's translation, slightly modified, from his "Popular Sectarianism," pp. 20–21. This and the following passage are also discussed in Sawada, *Zōho Hōkan*, p. 303. All citations from Nadeau are with his permission. I was his research supervisor at the University of British Columbia.

3. The translation of the first part of this passage is taken from Nadeau, "Popular Sectarianism," p. 21, reading *pei* ("double") as *pei* ("generation"),

as is supported by Sawada (*Zōho Hōkan*, p. 303) and Nadeau, who also point out that two different characters pronounced *wu* are used in these two passages for the name of the mountain—those for "fog" or "mist" and for "to awaken." Nadeau notes that the second reading "may be the work of a pious redactor" and that there is a mountain named Wu ("Mist")-ling 180 *li* northwest of Mi-yun county ("Popular Sectarianism," p. 21, n. 16).

   4. Nadeau, "Popular Sectarianism," pp. 23 and 24, n. 22.

   5. *K'u-kung wu-tao chüan* 1:13–15, following Nadeau's translation in his "Popular Sectarianism," p. 40. The page numbers in parentheses in the following discussion refer to the text of the *K'u-kung chüan*.

   6. The four forms of birth are from the womb (mammals), eggs (birds), moisture (worms and fishes), and transformation (moths and beings in heaven and purgatory). The six life paths of rebirth are listed in note 9 of Chapter Two.

   7. There are parallels here with accounts of the Ch'an Patriarch Hui-neng in the *Platform Sūtra*, noted in Chapter One above and discussed in detail in Nadeau, "Popular Sectarianism," pp. 77–81.

   8. Lo Ch'ing's rejection of "sending forth the yang spirit" is in sharp contrast with some later *pao-chüan* that advocate this practice.

   9. Here the text of the *K'u-kung wu-tao chüan* has simply *shuo yang pao* ("to speak of nourishing the jewel"). The commentary defines this as the Taoist practice of "preserving and nourishing the primal essence, *ch'i* and spirit" (*chüan* 1, pp. 59–60).

   10. "Three passes" (*san-kuan*) is another Taoist term referring to divisions of the body. In Ch'üan-chen (Complete Perfection) usage, it means three passages along the spine through which *ch'i* passes to the head. See the *Ta-tan chih-chih* (Direct instructions for the great elixir), thirteenth century; *Tao-tsang* 115, Harvard-Yenching index no. 244, *chüan shang*, p. 6a–6b. I am indebted for this reference to Dr. Stephen Eskildsen, a former student at the University of British Columbia.

   11. The commentary describes the "Mother" here as "true emptiness that can produce all things, . . . the fundamental nature of all the dharmas" (*chüan* 2, p. 48)—a definition with a good Mahāyāna pedigree. In the context here, this seems to be a fair interpretation of Lo Ch'ing's meaning, but one wonders if he intended to refer as well to a mother-goddess already discussed by sectarian writers before his time.

   12. The following studies list and discuss Lo Ch'ing's sources: Sakai, *Chūgoku zenshō*, pp. 440–441, 452–453; Sawada, *Zōho Hōkan*, pp. 325–326; Sōda, "Rakyō no seiritsu," pp. 35–48; Cheng, *Wu-sheng lao-mu*, pp. 221–253; and Nadeau, "Popular Sectarianism," pp. 239–274, 310–329. Cheng, *Wu-sheng lao-mu*, pp. 243–253, is devoted to the influence of the *Chin-kang k'e-i* on Lo's writings. Nadeau's discussion of context and comparison is found on pp. 211–238 and 275–295 of his "Popular Sectarianism."

   13. Nadeau, "Popular Sectarianism," p. 239.

14. Nadeau, "Popular Sectarianism," p. 245.

15. Nadeau, "Popular Sectarianism," pp. 240–248. In his *Chūgoku zenshō*, pp. 442–445, Sakai Tadao lists a total of ninety-three "heretical books" (*yao-shu*) provided by two sources from the Ming Ch'eng-hua reign period (1465–1487). Several of these titles appear in identical or similar versions in both sources. In 1474, the government distributed combined lists of these titles as a warning to all. The *Huang-chi pao-chüan* of 1430 does not appear in these lists, nor are any of their entries entitled *pao-chüan*. Unfortunately, these books are no longer extant, but two of the titles referred to in the *Huang-chi* book are also here—the *Wu-kung ching* (Five dukes scripture) and the *Ying-chieh ching* (Scripture on responding to the kalpa)—both of which are noted in Chapter Two above. In addition, there are references in the Ch'eng-hua period lists to a "Psalm of Praise for Maitreya" (Mi-le sung) and to the "three yang," which could be a reference to the different-colored yang associated with the three cosmic time periods in some sectarian teachings. There are also three titles here beginning with the term *chiu-kuan* ("nine passes"), which could be related to the celestial passes of the *Huang-chi* book discussed in Chapter Two. The same could be said about a reference to "penetrating the celestial pass" (*t'ou t'ien-kuan*) in another title in the 1474 list. Two titles here refer to rescue from calamities (*san-tsai chiu-k'u* and *hsiao-tsai chiu-k'u*), also a common theme in the *Huang-chi pao-chüan*. Of course, since we do not know the contexts in which any of these themes were used, their possible parallels with *pao-chüan* teaching cannot be demonstrated. Nevertheless, since many of the titles on the Ch'eng-hua lists are called *ching* ("scripture") and they were not canonical Buddhist or Taoist writings, the possibility remains that we have here a remnant of early Ming indigenous scriptures that have long been lost. In 1976, I wrote as follows about this material (see Overmyer, *Folk Buddhist Religion*, pp. 180–181 and p. 353, n. 68):

> While there are several titles on this list which show Buddhist influence, the majority deal with divination, the five elements, and other folk religious themes. As Sakai observes, none of the Buddhist sūtras and devotional texts used by Lo Ch'ing and his commentators appears in this compilation, even though most of the Lo sources were extant long before 1474. Evidently even the popular tracts they used were considered just Buddhist texts in the vernacular and hence were not proscribed. . . .
>
>   One set of] these text titles is listed in Chu Kuo-chen, *Yung ch'uang hsiao-p'in* (1622), 32:6b–7a, all collected from one Shansi sect during the Ming Ch'eng-hua period (1465–1487). Sect leaders, both of whom studied under a Pure Land monk, claimed that these scriptures had been revealed to them by the Buddha in their dreams. This group was suppressed after staging an abortive uprising. One of the arresting officials received imperial permission to distribute a list of their texts as a warn-

ing to the common people. None of these texts has the same name as any of those collected by Huang Yü-p'ien 350 years later in his *P'o-hsieh hsiang-pien* (A detailed refutation of heresies) (1834–1841).

For a discussion of Huang Yü-p'ien's book, see my *Folk Buddhist Religion*, pp. 29–32 and p. 213, n. 46.

The second list cited by Sakai is in the *Huang Ming t'iao-fa shih-lei tsuan* (A compilation of Ming legal cases), which I have not been able to locate. The books whose titles are listed here were found in Shantung and Shansi provinces in North China.

16. Nadeau, "Popular Sectarianism," pp. 248–274. The quoted passages are from pp. 248–249 and p. 258. Nadeau acknowledges his debt for part of this discussion to that of Cheng Chih-ming, *Wu-sheng lao-mu*, pp. 235–253.

17. Nadeau, "Popular Sectarianism," pp. 121–123.

18. The ten virtues (*shih-shan*) consist of not committing the ten evil deeds (*shih-e*), which include killing, stealing, adultery, lying, deceit, coarse language, foul language, covetousness, anger, and perverted views. See Soothill and Hodous, *Dictionary of Chinese Buddhist Terms*, pp. 47, 50.

19. The four forms of logical differentiation here stand for Buddhist philosophy and consist of analyzing phenomena as existing, not existing, and both or neither of these. See Soothill and Hodous, *Dictionary of Chinese Buddhist Terms*, p. 172.

20. See Overmyer, "Values in Chinese Sectarian Literature," pp. 231–237.

21. The Chinese here literally says "originally lacked two vital forces," meaning there was only one.

22. This passage of the *P'o-hsieh hsien-cheng yao-shih chüan* is based on chapter 23 and the introductory material of the *Chin-kang k'e-i*, pp. 140a and 131b, with Lo Ch'ing's own mixing and interpolations.

23. The first part of this passage of the *P'o-hsieh* book is missing from the *K'ai-hsin fa-yao* edition; the translation here is taken from the 1615 edition (described in Appendix G). In Chinese, "White Lotus" is "Pai-lien," but in the *K'ai-hsin fa-yao* edition, the character for "lotus" is replaced by a similar character with the silk radical on the left, which I have not been able to identify. I assume it was meant as a homophone, *lien*.

24. The text of the *K'ai-hsin fa-yao P'o-hsieh* book indicates that this quote was taken from the "donation" chapter of a compilation of Buddhist texts called the *Ta-tsang i-lan chi* (A collection [of passages] from one glance at the great storehouse [of scriptures]). Nadeau reports that this book is attributed to a Ch'en Shih of the Southern Sung period (1127–1279). It is available only in Japanese government archives (Nadeau, "Popular Sectarianism," pp. 242–243, n. 51, and p. 315).

25. The phrase "stick into fire" is a literal translation of the term *ch'uo-huo*, which I have not yet been able to identify. In this context it appears to be a ritual of purification or exorcism.

26. The source that Lo cites here is the *Hsin-hsieh shao-chih pao-chüan* ("Precious volume" on believing in heresy and burning paper [documents]), a lost text with a most intriguing title. "Paper" here could also refer to forms of money often burned in rituals.

27. The first passage from the *P'o-hsieh* book quoted here is taken from the *Chin-kang k'e-i*, p. 129b, while the line "true faith is rare" is found on p. 133b.

28. Shek, "Religion and Society in Late Ming," pp. 227–232.

29. Both Lo and Yuan-ching add that the use of "Dharma water" refers to looking at reflections in water for images of "dukes, marquises and barons," which I take to refer to promises of noble status when the millennium arrives. For a brief discussion of such promises, see my *Folk Buddhist Religion*, pp. 155–161. The one-volume 1615 edition of the *Cheng-hsin* text (discussed in Appendix G) uses the character "lotus" here, not the hybrid character employed in the *K'ai-hsin fa-yao* edition.

30. Nothing more is known of the Sect of the Dark Drum, though its veneration of the sun and moon indicates a possible connection with Manichaeism. It is interesting to note that in chapter 16 of the *Cheng-hsin* book, Lo Ch'ing rejects the phrases "little children [will] see their mother" (*ying-erh chien-niang*) and "the ignorant people who say that the original nature is the little child and that Amitābha is the Eternal Parent (Wu-sheng fu-mu, lit. 'Eternal Father-Mother')," arguing that this is not possible because Amitābha is male and there is no such thing as males giving birth to children (*Cheng-hsin* 3:87). We have seen that the term *ying-erh chien-niang* is used in the *Huang-chi* book, while it is common in *pao-chüan* a bit later than Lo's texts to refer to the Eternal Mother as "father-mother," so it is worth noting that here he attacks the older tradition of Amitābha as a compassionate parent, a theme noted in Chapter One above. If Lo had known of a developed Eternal Mother mythology, surely he would have attacked it here.

31. Wu-chi's creative power is also praised in chapter 10 of the *Cheng-hsin* book in similar terms.

32. Lo Ch'ing interprets *wei-wei pu tung* ("majestic and unmoved") as follows in chapter 16 of the *T'ai-shan* book (3:78): "This is the 'majestic and unmoved' that I practice: [It refers to the fact that] before the myriad things existed I already was (*wo tsai hsien*). . . . My original face was prior to the Buddha's, to the three teachings, purgatory, King Yama, good and evil, birth-and-death, the precepts and regulations—all the forms came later; all are [in the realm of] birth, death, and impermanence. Being prior and most honored, honored for measureless eons, neither increased nor destroyed, whom should I fear?" Hence, for Lo ch'ing, this term refers to the metaphysically prior and indestructible basic self-nature.

33. De Groot, *Sectarianism*, pp. 176–198. See also Overmyer, "Boatmen and Buddhas."

34. See Overmyer, "Attitudes Toward the Ruler and State."

35. In their recent article on sectarian religious activities at the Pao-ming Temple near Beijing, Thomas Shih-yü Li and Susan Naquin note a *Hsiao-shih yuan-chueh pao-chüan* in two *chüan* that was written by a nun named Kuei-yuan in about 1571–1573. Along with four other *pao-chüan* composed by her, it was printed in 1584–1585. The whole set was called "Five Books in Six Volumes" in emulation of Lo Ch'ing's writings. Kuei-yuan's book is evidently not the same as the four-*chüan* version of the *Yuan-chueh* scripture discussed here, which has an earlier publishing date and is attributed to a "Master Chin-shan." The Li and Naquin article is "The Baoming Temple: Religion and the Throne in Ming and Qing China" (1988). The titles of Kuei-yuan's texts are given on pp. 152–154. On pp. 155–156, the authors note that "although she explicitly invoked Luo Qing in her scriptures and made frequent references to his 'Wuwei doctrine,' Gui-yuan did not claim any direct relationship with him."

Both Sawada (*Zōho Hōkan*, pp. 343–365) and Shek ("Religion and Society in Late Ming," pp. 252–275) discuss a sixteenth-century sect called the "Way of Yellow Heaven" (Huang-t'ien tao), the name of which is pronounced in the same way as that referred to in the *Yuan-chueh chüan*. However, this book was clearly not a product of that group.

36. The "three realms" in Buddhist thought are those of desire, form, and formlessness. The term translated here as "completely unrestrained" is *tang-chin*, which has the more negative sense of "dissolute" that does not seem to fit this context.

37. On the Hung-yang sect, see Shek, "Religion and Society in Late Ming," pp. 276–287, and Ma and Han, *Min-chien tsung-chiao*, pp. 489–548.

Chapter Four

1. The date "second year of the Chia-ching period" (1523) occurs three times in the *Chiu-lien* book. In his *Pao-chüan tsung-lu*, p. 20, Li Shih-yü lists two Ming (1368–1644) editions of this text, as well as one published in 1899 and another in 1909. However, Sawada Mizuho, in his *Zōho Hōkan no kenkyū*, p. 110, treats the *Chiu-lien pao-chüan* as a Ch'ing dynasty book, on the basis of the two editions available to him. The first of these is incomplete, but he suggests a Ch'ien-lung (1736–1795) date for it. The second, published in 1908, is attributed to a "Ninth Patriarch Huang," whom Sawada describes as Huang Te-hui (1684–1750), the founder of the Golden Elixir Way (Chin-tan tao). However, there is no mention of a "Patriarch Huang" in the edition I use in this chapter, though there are references to "nine patriarchs coming and going in response to the cycles of time" (chapter 1). The revealer of this text is repeatedly identified as the Wu-wei Patriarch, an incarnation of Maitreya. In chapter 12 he is quoted as saying, "I wrote this *pao-chüan* in the Han family home."

Yü Sung-ch'ing, in her *Min-chien mi-mi tsung-chiao*, pp. 213–216, supports Sawada's dates for this book and his attribution of it to Huang Te-hui. She does not mention the 1523 date. Ma Hsi-sha and Han Ping-fang, in their *Min-chien tsung-chiao*, pp. 610–616, also discuss this book, for which they provide a list of chapter titles identical with those in the edition I have consulted. However, since they found references to this book in official sources going back to 1645, they note that it could not have been written by Huang Te-hui, whose death date they give as 1745. They say that the copy of the book they consulted was in the private collection of Wu Hsiao-ling, an eminent scholar of pre-modern Chinese literature in Beijing, and that the copy they saw was a Republican period reprint for which "there is no specific reign title [date]" (p. 613). Neither they nor Yü Sung-ch'ing mention the inside alternate title of this book that is in my copy, the *Wu-tang shan Hsuan-t'ien Shang-ti ching* (The scripture of the Lord on High of the Dark Heaven, from Mount Wu-tang).

This is all very interesting, because my copy, too, came from the collection of Wu Hsiao-ling in 1981, but it is clear that it is a different and older edition that Ma, Han, and Yü did not know about when they wrote their recent studies. When I was in Professor Wu's home, I specifically asked him about the Chia-ching 2 date, and after looking at the text, he concluded that the date looked authentic.

Thus it appears that later editors of this book deleted its date and added other material of their own in prefaces and comments. Perhaps Huang Te-hui built his teaching on this text, which repeatedly refers to the "Golden Elixir Way of the Imperial Ultimate." The name "Chin-tan tao" first appears as the name of a Taoist sect in South China in the twelfth century.

I am happy to report that the most recent study of this text, by Lien Li-ch'ang, supports an early date for it. The title of Lien Li-ch'ang's 1996 article is *"Chiu-lien ching k'ao"* (An investigation of the *Nine-Lotus Scripture*). Mr. Lien provides detailed evidence not only for the 1523 reprint date, but also for an original publishing date of 1498. He emphasizes the importance of the Chin-tan tao (Golden Elixir Way) for the *Chiu-lien pao-chüan*, and elicits evidence from chapter 22 that the founding patriarch of the popular sect of this name was imprisoned in 1499 and died there in 1510. He says that the place names in the *Chiu-lien* book indicate that it was from Luan-chou in Hopei province. Lien suggests that the inside title in the book referring to Mount Wu-tang was added because that was an important sacred area to the court of that time.

2. In the *Fo-shuo Mi-le hsia-sheng ching* (Sūtra of the Buddha's discourse on the descent of Maitreya; T. 453, 14:421–423), translated in the late third century C.E., the term "dragon-flower" is used to describe the tree under which the Future Buddha attains enlightenment. This text also refers to ninety-six *i* (myriads) of disciples who are saved in these preaching assemblies (*hui*) led by Maitreya. In sectarian texts "Dragon-Flower Assembly" refers to the gathering of humankind at the end of each time period.

3. This summary of the *Chiu-lien pao-chüan* is taken from my article "Messenger, Savior and Revolutionary: Maitreya in Chinese Popular Religious Literature of the Sixteenth and Seventeenth Centuries"(1988), pp. 117–118. To save space in an already lengthy study, here and in the rest of this book, most translations of verse passages are written in prose form, with the style of the original noted.

4. The *chi* here is a homonym of the *chi* for "apex," so this could be translated "in accord with the apexes."

5. The "three capacities" (*san-ts'ai*) are Heaven, Earth, and humans, each with its own capacity, or role. The "four forms" (*ssu-hsiang*) in Buddhist terminology are the four states of phenomena: birth, being, decay, and death. In this book, however, they refer to a stage in creation just before the appearance of the Five Phases. A *ch'eng* as a unit of measurement is 1/10, 1/12, or 1/100 of a *ts'un*, or Chinese inch, which would provide very small dimensions for the Earth. However, *ch'eng* can also be a general term for measurements, so its meaning here is unclear.

6. Reading *t'o* as an abbreviation for *t'o-lo-ni*, a transliteration for the Sanskrit term *dhāranī* ("incantation" or "spell").

7. The "three mysteries" (*san hsuan*) usually refer to three ancient books, the *Lao-tzu, Chuang-tzu,* and *I -ching,* but here the reference is not clear.

8. For Naquin's use of the term "Eternal Progenitor," see her *Millenarian Rebellion,* p. 9 and p. 289, n. 7.

9. On the naming of sects after the eight trigrams of the *I-ching,* see Naquin, *Millenarian Rebellion,* pp. 17–18, 217.

10. On Hao-chou, see Overmyer, *Folk Buddhist Religion,* p. 99. The character used in the text here is the *hao* for "fine hair." It should be the *hao* for "moat" or "ditch."

11. The "land of dark cliffs" could also refer to purgatory, but that does not seem to fit the context here. There is one character in this passage I have been unable to decipher, because it appears to be written incorrectly. The reference is to a city within the "land of dark cliffs" (. . . *li ch'eng chung*) in " . . . *li* city." The indecipherable character resembles the character *tien* ("to pour out a libation"), but without its top two strokes.

12. These "ten items" are not listed here, but I presume this is an abbreviated reference to the types of ritual practice advocated in the *Huang-chi* book earlier (see Chapter Two).

13. The term "golden cock" can refer to a star, bird, and various plants, but in sectarian texts it is a symbol of the new age and the coming of Maitreya.

14. I am grateful to Susan Naquin for sending me a copy of chapters 10 to 18 of this *Li-t'ien* book, which she found in a Ch'ing archive dated Ch'ien-lung 18/8/4 (1753 by the Western calendar). The first nine chapters are

missing. Her student Blaine Gaustad kindly sent me another copy of the same book.

Chapter Five

1. The "mind-seal" (*hsin-yin*) is a Ch'an term referring to intuitive certainty of truth in the mind, transmitted from master to disciple.

2. The trigram *k'an* (a) represents the "middle son." *Li* (b) is the "middle daughter." *Ch'ien* (c) is the yang, male hexagram, represented by six solid lines. Lead is associated with the phases metal and fire, and mercury is associated with the phases wood and water. In Taoist texts, the term "Yellow Room" refers to the "yellow court" (*huang-t'ing*) in the center of the abdomen, where bodily elixirs are blended. The character for *li* here should be the *li* meaning "to separate."

a. ☵   b. ☲   c. ☰

3. The term *chiu-chuan* ("nine rotations") usually refers to nine circulations of the bodily *ch'i* needed to refine the elixir of immortality, but here it has a cosmic reference.

4. The term *ssu-hsiang* ("four forms") here seems to have a metaphysical meaning that I have not been able to otherwise identify. In other contexts it can refer to auspicious days in each of the four seasons. (See note 5 for Chapter Four above.)

5. I have not been able to find a meaning of *san-chia* (lit. "three households") that fits this context.

6. For convenient discussions of Taoist circulation and refinement of *ch'i*, see Maspero, *Taoism*, pp. 445–554, and Isabelle Robinet, *Taoist Meditation* (1993; originally published in French in 1979).

7. See Daniel L. Overmyer, "Attitudes Toward the Ruler and State," pp. 347–379. See also idem, "Social Perspectives in Chinese Sectarian Scriptures from the Fifteenth and Sixteenth Centuries" (1998).

8. The six "Sage Edicts" are discussed in chapter 2 of the *Hung-yang wu-tao ming-hsin ching* (The Hung-yang scripture on awakening to the Way and enlightening the mind; text 12 in Appendix H) as follows:

a. The *Scripture on Enlightening the Mind* requires you to be filial and obedient to your parents.

b. You must respect your elders and superiors.

c. You must be friendly with fellow villagers.

d. You must instruct your children and grandchildren [in these principles].

e. You must each be content in your occupations.

f. Do not do evil.

For a discussion of Ming and Ch'ing "Sage Edicts," see Victor H. Mair, "Language and Ideology in the Written Popularizations of the *Sacred Edict*" (1985).

Chapter Six

1. On *shan-shu* ("morality books"), see Brokaw, *Ledgers of Merit and Demerit*.

2. The ten good deeds consist of not committing the ten evils, which are killing, stealing, adultery, lying, deceit, coarse language, foul language, covetousness, anger, and perverted views.

3. I have not been able to find a definition of *san-ch'eng* that fits this context.

4. For a good discussion of sectarian congregational and healing rituals, see Ma and Han, *Min-chien tsung-chiao*, pp. 516–518.

5. Needham, *Science and Civilisation in China*, Vol. 5, Part V, p. 59.

6. Needham, *Science and Civilisation in China*, Vol. 5, Part V, pp. 60–61. See also Isabelle Robinet, "Original Contributions of *Neidan* to Taoism and Chinese Thought" (1989).

7. *Mou-ni* is a transliteration of the Sanskrit *muni* ("an ascetic"), a term that also refers to seven precious minerals. Here it is a symbol of the inner potential for enlightenment.

8. In Buddhism, *sen-lo* ("densely spread out") refers to the myriad forms of the universe, but here it is the name of a palace in purgatory.

9. For a detailed discussion of the Ten Kings of purgatory, see Stephen F. Teiser, *The Scripture of the Ten Kings and the Making of Purgatory in Medieval Chinese Buddhism* (1994). In conventional lists of these kings, Yama is the fifth, but in "precious volumes" this name can be applied to all underworld rulers, sometimes modified by "T'ien-tzu" (Son of Heaven).

10. The *Ti-tsang Shih-wang pao-chüan* (text 4 in Appendix I) adds that women go to the Pool of Blood in purgatory because "they are not careful to observe the taboos against pouring bloody water on the ground and drying polluted clothing in the sunlight. . . . They go to burn incense [i.e., worship at temples] while menstruating, and recite scriptures and the Buddha's name while with a flow of blood" (p. 103).

11. This theme of a descent into purgatory by a buddha who destroys it and so enables all its inhabitants to be reborn in heaven occurs in such earlier Buddhist texts as *The Transformation Text on Mu-lien*, discussed by Mair in his *Tun-huang Popular Narratives*, p. 114.

Chapter Seven

1. Sawada, *Kōchū haja shōben*, pp. 192–212. See also Shek, "Religion and Society in Late Ming," pp. 176–189, 287–301.

2. Sawada, *Kōchū haja shōben*, p. 164. In her "Precious Scrolls in Chinese

Popular Religious Culture," Janet Lynn [Kerr] provides a detailed summary of this scripture.

3. Shek, "Religion and Society in Late Ming," pp. 287–296. See also Ma and Han, *Min-chien tsung-chiao*, pp. 865–883.

4. *T'ou-t'o* is the transliteration of the Sanskrit *dhuta*, which in Buddhist contexts refers to ascetic discipline. Its meaning here is not clear.

5. Chapter 17 of the *Lung-hua ching* includes a list of forty-eight patriarchs summoned to a great assembly by the Mother. There they are given different types of sacred jewels. Some on this list are identifiable, but most of the names appear to be constructed out of pious fancy. No connections with particular sects are indicated.

6. On Fu Hsi and Nü Wa, see Anne Birrell, *Chinese Mythology: An Introduction* (1993), pp. 33–35, 42–45.

7. The "terrace star" (*t'ai-hsing*) refers to a group of six stars that I have not been able to identify.

Chapter Eight

1. Chuang Chi-fa, "Ch'ing-tai min-chien tsung-chiao te pao-chüan yü Wu-sheng lao-mu hsin-yang" ("Precious volumes" of Ch'ing dynasty popular religion and belief in the Eternal Venerable Mother; 1987) and Tseng Tzu-liang, "Kuo-nei so-chien pao-chüan hsu-lu" (A discussion of "precious volumes" seen within this country; 1982).

For a detailed study of two nineteenth- and twentieth-century popular religious sects and their scriptures recently discovered in Kwangsi, see Wang Hsi-yuan, *Kuei-hsi min-chien mi-mi tsung-chiao* (Secret folk religions in Kuei-hsi; 1994). Kuei-hsi is the name of a village where these materials were found. None of the books named here includes the term *pao-chüan* in its title, though many are called *ching* ("scripture").

2. Discussions of the dates and contents of these books are found in my "Messenger, Savior and Revolutionary," pp. 115, 123–134. The *Li-shih pao-chüan* has been reprinted in volume 20 of Chang Hsi-shun et al., eds., *Pao-chüan ch'u-chi*. In the title of the *Ting-chieh* book, I have translated the character *chao* as "passport" because it can refer to a permit or a pass, on the possibility that here it means a document for understanding and surviving the end of the age. This term is not defined in the *pao-chüan* itself.

3. Overmyer, "Messenger, Savior and Revolutionary," pp. 125–130.

4. On the *Li-t'ien* book, see note 14 of Chapter Four above. Similar affirmations of Confucianism are found in the *Huan-hsiang pao-chüan* (The precious volume on returning to the Native Place), a nineteenth-century spirit-writing text reprinted in Kuang-hsu *i-hai* (1875–1876). This is a very lively and interesting book thoroughly based on Eternal Mother mythology, in which the "Confucian school" is praised as the teaching employed during Maitreya's reign. On p. 40a, this book criticizes opium-smoking. I read it at the home of Wu Hsiao-ling in 1981 and saw it again at the Shanghai Library

that same year. It is an excellent example of a later "precious volume" worthy of further study.

5. In my notes on the *Mi-le ch'u-hsi pao-chüan*, the date given for these disasters is *shen-hsu*, a combination of cyclical characters that does not exist, so I have read it as *chia-hsu*. I do not know if the mistake is in the text or my notes, though my notes at this point are quite clear.

6. In the introductory material for the *Ku Fo tang-lai hsia-sheng Mi-le ch'u-hsi pao-chüan*, there is the statement, "It is generally known that *The Precious Volume of the Dharma King Soon to Descend to Be Reborn, Maitreya, Appearing from the West* appeared (*ch'u*) in the Wan-li *ping-ch'en* year of the Great Ming," a date that corresponds to 1616–1617 (Chang et al., eds., *Pao-chüan ch'u-chi* 19:302). However, in chapter 9 of the same book we read, "It has been three thousand years from the end of the Chou (Chou *mo*) until now, and at the end of the Ch'ing (Ch'ing *mo*) Confucianism has forgotten the three bonds (*san-kang*)" (19:357). The parallel structure makes the meaning unmistakable. This later date is reinforced by a retrospective reference in chapter 12 to the "Ming dynasty" (Ming ch'ao), followed by the term *hou-lai* ("later"; 19:373). Hence this book must have been composed in the late nineteenth century. Li Shih-yü, *Pao-chüan tsung-lu*, p. 32, lists a reprint from the Ch'ing Kuang-hsu reign period (1875–1907), which seems an appropriate date. I first read this book at the Shanghai Library in 1981.

7. On these indigenous Buddhist scriptures, see Overmyer, "Buddhism in the Trenches."

8. On Wu-t'ung spirits, see Richard von Glahn, "The Enchantment of Wealth: The God Wutong in the Social History of Jiangnan" (1991), and Ursula-Angelika Cedzich, "The Cult of the Wu-t'ung/Wu-hsien in History and Fiction: The Religious Roots of the *Journey to the South*," in David Johnson, ed., *Ritual and Scripture in Chinese Popular Religion* (1995).

9. *Shou-fan* could mean "to buy and sell" or to "use and sell."

10. On Marshal Wen, see Paul R. Katz, *Demon Hordes and Burning Boats: The Cult of Marshal Wen in Late Imperial Chekiang* (1995). The Lord Kuan is usually not referred to as a "marshal" (*yuan-shuai*), so I am not sure if this reference is to him. Marshal Ma is an exorcising deity associated with the Jade Emperor. There are several spirits named Chao and Huang, but I don't know which are referred to here.

11. On nineteenth- and twentieth-century spirit-writing texts and the groups that produced them, see Jordan and Overmyer, *The Flying Phoenix*; and the Ph.D. dissertation of Philip Clart, "Morality Books and Their Ritual Context: A Case Study of a Taiwanese Spirit-Writing Cult" (University of British Columbia, 1996).

Appendix A

1. Ma Hsi-sha, "Tsui-tsao i-pu pao-chüan," pp. 51–56. Mr. Ma is a researcher with the Taoist studies section of the Institute for the Study of

World Religions of the Chinese Academy of Social Sciences. Page numbers in the text of Appendix A refer to this article. Sawada (*Zōho Hōkan*, pp. 159, 295–296) discusses late Ming and Ch'ing editions of the *Hung-lo pao-chüan* with the same basic story but with variations of name and place. In one, the story is set in the Sung dynasty.

2. The date of the *Hung-lo pao-chüan* appears in large type on its cover, which is unusual for *pao-chüan*, though some late narrative texts provide clearly fictitious dates on their title pages. The early "precious volumes" I have read are all bound in the "sūtra folded (accordion) style," with either no dates or dates modestly placed at the end.

3. Ch'e Hsi-lun, *Chung-kao pao-chüan yen-chiu*, pp. 60–62.

Appendix G

1. Lan-feng's commentary is not dated, but there is a reference to it dated 1581 by a monk named Mi-tsang Tao-k'ai who was critical of the Wu-wei sect and Lan-feng's relationship to it. On Tao-k'ai's comments, see my "Boatmen and Buddhas," pp. 287–288. I first learned of this through Tsuka-moto Zenryu's article, "Rakyō no seiritsu to ryūden ni tsuite."

Appendix H

1. In sectarian mythology, "Red Yang" refers to the present time period, presided over by the Buddha Śākyamuni. There are eleven references to this term in Ma and Han, *Min-chien tsung-chiao*, ten of which indicate a time period. The exception is to a Red Yang sect (p. 1054) in the nineteenth century associated with the Eight Trigrams sect active in the Beijing area. In her *Millenarian Rebellion*, pp. 66–70, Susan Naquin discusses this group as the "Red Sun sect." I do not know if there was any connection between this group and that mentioned in the *Yao-shih pao-chüan* about 270 years earlier.

2. The "Three Emperors" usually refers to the three founding culture heroes Fu-hsi, Shen-nung, and Huang-ti (the Yellow Emperor). However, in the *Yuan-chueh pao-chüan*, compiled about twenty years after the *Yao-shih* book, these are defined as the "emperors of Heaven, Earth, and humans" (chapter 9). I am not sure which is intended by this reference in the *Yao-shih chüan*.

3. See also Ma and Han, *Min-chien tsung-chiao* , pp. 406–488, etc., and Wang Chien-ch'uan, "Huang-t'ien tao ch'ien-ch'i shih hsin-t'an" (A new examination of the early history of the Yellow Heaven Way; 1994).

4. E. S. Stulova, *Baotzuan o Pu-minye: Faksimile isdanie texsta, perevod s Kitaiskovo, Issledovanie I kommentary* (*The P'u-ming pao-chüan*: Reproduction of the published text, translated from the Chinese [with] analysis and commentary; 1979).

5. Ma and Han, *Min-chien tsung-chiao*, p. 406, suggest that "Imperial Heaven" is an alternate way of writing its homophone, "Yellow Heaven."

6. I take this passage to refer to circulation of *ch'i* within the body.

7. The terms translated as "to save" here are *tu* ("to cross over," "to enable to cross over") and *tu-t'o* ("[to help] cross over and escape [from the mundane world to paradise]").

8. The characters *k'ang-tao* could be part of a personal name, but there is no further indication of that here. In later spirit-writing texts, the term *k'ang chuang ta tao* appears, with the meaning "great majestic way" (Philip Clart, University of British Columbia, personal communication, July 1995).

9. The six supernormal powers are acquired by bodhisattvas in the course of their meditation; they involve penetrating vision and hearing, knowledge of former lives, etc. See Soothill and Hodous, *Dictionary of Chinese Buddhist Terms*, pp. 123a and 138b. *Wu-yen* refers to five types of vision also attainable through long practice in meditative absorption.

10. The "Eight Treasures" referred classically to eight types of imperial seals, and in the vernacular to various sets of eight items or ingredients. I am not sure what it means here; perhaps it is a general reference to the valuable message of the *Huan-yuan chüan*.

11. Shek, "Religion and Society in Late Ming," p. 281, identifies Officer Shih as a palace eunuch. I am indebted to Professor Shek for the translations of some of the titles and names of officers here.

12. The character here that I translate as "red" appears to be composed of the silk radical on the left and the earth radical on the right, a combination I cannot find in dictionaries. My photocopy of this text is obscure in some places.

13. The text here reads *pu she chia-hsiang* ("don't give up / abandon [their] Native Place"), which makes sense in this context only if *chia-hsiang* does not refer to the Native Place paradise. I am puzzled by this line.

14. "Yuan-tun chiao" is another name for this sect, referring here, as I understand it, to a complete teaching based on the origin of all in primal chaos. In other contexts, another character pronounced *tun*, meaning "sudden," can be paired with *yuan* to refer to enlightenment that is complete and sudden.

Appendix I

1. On the translation of Huang-t'ien tao, see Appendix H, note 5 above.

2. In the title "Hun-chin P'iao-kao of the Limitless," *hun-chin* literally means "mixed gold" or "gold ore." However, *hun* also means "chaotic," and in this meaning is interchangeable with the other character pronounced *hun*, which in these texts refers to the creative chaos of the cosmic origin, so perhaps *hun-chin* should be translated here as "primordial gold."

3. I have not been able to locate Chiu-lung kang, though there are several mountains named Chiu-lung.

4. Here the text says *ch'u-ch'en ju-shih* ("leaving the dust and entering the world"), which does not make sense. I suggest that it should be *ju-sheng* ("entering the realm of the holy"), a common phrase in these texts.

5. In translating *pu kan shan-chuan* ("did not dare to act on my own authority"), I read *shan* ("good") as *shan* ("to act on one's own authority"). I am indebted to Roberto K. Ong for this suggestion.

6. For a discussion of such divination, see Richard J. Smith, *Fortune Tellers and Philosophers: Divination in Traditional Chinese Society* (1991), pp. 235–244.

7. "T'ien-ch'i" (Equal of Heaven) is a title given to the god of the Eastern Peak (Mount T'ai) in the T'ang dynasty.

8. See Hu Shih, "Pa *Hsiao-shih Chen-k'ung pao-chüan*," pp. 3633–3634 for another list of patriarchal transmission, including these latter four names and others.

9. The (*T'ai-shan*) *Shih-wang pao-chüan* (Ten Kings precious volume) and the *Fu-mo pao-chüan* (Precious volume on subduing demons) are texts 7 and 6 in this appendix.

10. In another early "precious volume" reprinted in volume 12 of Chang Hsi-shun et al., eds., *Pao-chüan ch'u-chi*, another popular goddess is brought into sectarian mythology and teaching by equation with the Venerable Mother—in this case Kuan-yin as a child-giver. This is the *Hsiao-shih Pai-i Kuan-yin p'u-sa sung ying-erh hsia-sheng pao-chüan* (The precious volume on the descent to be reborn of the white-clothed Bodhisattva Kuan-yin, who brings children), which gives every appearance of being a late Ming text, and is so discussed by Li Shih-yü (*Pao-chüan tsung-lu*, p. 53) and Sawada Mizuho (*Zōho Hōkan*, pp. 118–120). In it, sectarian teaching is presented through the story of a childless couple of late middle age who, as a result of their piety, are given twins by Kuan-yin. The boy and girl are in fact the children of the Venerable Mother, who misses them so much that she descends in the form of a wet nurse to care for them. In the end, the whole family goes on a pilgrimage to Mount P'u-t'o "to see the Venerable Mother," who is thus correlated with a holy site devoted to Kuan-yin. This is an interesting text worthy of study, both as a folk interpretation of Kuan-yin and as an early example of a typical story line in narrative "precious volumes," which often begin with accounts of miraculous births to childless couples.

Works Cited: Secondary Sources

N.B.: The primary sources on which this book is based are described in the chapters and appendixes above. Source materials referred to only once in the Notes are listed only there.

Asai Motoi. "Precious Scrolls and Folk Sectarianism of the Ming-Qing Period." In *Millenarianism in Asian History*, edited by Ishii Yoneo. Tokyo: Institute for the Study of the Languages and Cultures of Asia and Africa, 1993.

Berling, Judith A. "Bringing the Buddha Down to Earth: Notes on the Emergence of *Yü-lu* as a Buddhist Genre." *History of Religions* 27.1:56–88 (August 1987).

Birnbaum, Raoul. *The Healing Buddha*. Boulder, Colo.: Shambala, 1979.

Birrell, Anne. *Chinese Mythology: An Introduction*. With a foreword by Yuan K'o. Baltimore and London: The Johns Hopkins University Press, 1993.

Boltz, Judith M. *A Survey of Taoist Literature, Tenth to Seventeenth Centuries*. Berkeley: Institute of East Asian Studies, University of California, 1987.

Brokaw, Cynthia J. *The Ledgers of Merit and Demerit: Social Change and Moral Order in Late Imperial China*. Princeton, N.J.: Princeton University Press, 1991.

Buswell, Robert E., Jr., ed. *Chinese Buddhist Apocrypha*. Honolulu: University of Hawai'i Press, 1990.

Cedzich, Ursula-Angelika. "The Cult of the Wu-t'ung/Wu-hsien in History and Fiction: The Religious Roots of the *Journey to the South*." In *Ritual and Scripture in Chinese Popular Religion: Five Studies*, edited by David Johnson. Berkeley, Calif.: Chinese Popular Culture Project, 1995.

Chan, W. T., ed. and trans. *A Sourcebook in Chinese Philosophy*. Princeton, N.J.: Princeton University Press, 1963.

Chang Hsi-shun 張希舜, P'u Wen-ch'i 濮文起, Kao K'e 高克, and Sung Chün 宋軍, eds. *Pao-chüan ch'u-chi* 寶卷初集 ("Precious volumes," first collection). 40 vols. T'ai-yuan: Shansi Jen-min ch'u-pan she, 1994.

Chao, Yuen Ren. *A Grammar of Spoken Chinese*. Berkeley: University of California Press, 1968.

Chavannes, Edouard. *Le T'ai Chan: Essai de Monographie d'un Culte Chinois*. Paris: Ernest Leroux, 1910.

Ch'e Hsi-lun 車錫倫. *Chung-kuo pao-chüan tsung-mu* 中國寶卷總目 (A general bibliography of "precious volumes"). Taipei: Academia Sinica, Institute of Literature and Philosophy, 1998.

———. *Chung-kuo pao-chüan yen-chiu lun-chi* 中國寶卷研究論集 (Collected essays on Chinese "precious volumes"). Taipei: Hsueh-hai ch'u-pan she, 1997.

———. "Chung-kuo tsui-tsao te pao-chüan" 中國最早寶卷 (China's earliest *pao-chüan*). *Chung-kuo wen che yan-chiu t'ung-hsun* 中國文哲研究通訊 (Report on research in Chinese literature and philosophy) 6.3:45–52 (1996).

Ch'en Ju-heng 陳汝衡. *Shuo-shu shih-hua* 說書史話 (On the history of narrated literature). Beijing: Tso-chia ch'u-pan she, 1958.

Chen, Kenneth K. S. *Buddhism in China: A Historical Survey*. Princeton, N.J.: Princeton University Press, 1964.

Cheng Chen-to 鄭振鐸. *Chung-kuo su wen-hsueh shih* 中國俗文學史 (A history of Chinese vernacular literature). 2 vols. Beijing: Wen-hsueh ku-chi k'an-hsing she, 1959. First published in 1938.

Cheng Chih-ming 鄭志明. *Wu-sheng lao-mu hsin-yang su-yuan* 無生老母信仰溯源 (Sources of the Eternal Venerable Mother belief). Taipei: Wen shih che ch'u-pan she, 1985.

Chuang Chi-fa 莊吉發. "Ch'ing-tai min-chien tsung-chiao te pao-chüan yü Wu-sheng lao-mu hsin-yang" 清代民間宗教的寶卷與無生老母信仰 ("Precious volumes" of Ch'ing dynasty popular religion and belief in the Eternal Venerable Mother). 2 parts. *Ta-lu tsa-chih* 大陸雜誌 74.4:167–176 and 74.5:214–24 (1987).

Clart, Philip A. "Morality Books and Their Ritual Context: A Case Study of a Taiwanese Spirit-Writing Cult." Ph.D. diss., University of British Columbia, 1996.

Cleary, Thomas, trans. *Understanding Reality: A Taoist Alchemical Classic*. Commentary by Liu I-ming. Honolulu: University of Hawai'i Press, 1987.

Cole, Alan. *Mothers and Sons in Chinese Buddhism*. Stanford, Calif.: Stanford University Press, 1998.

Conze, Edward, ed. and trans. *Vajracchedikā Prajñāpāramitā*. Vol. XXIII, *Serie Orientale Roma*. Roma: Is. M.E.O., 1957.

Davis, Tenney L., and Chao Yün-ts'ung, trans. "Chang Po-tuan, His *Wu Chen P'ien*." In *Proceedings of the American Academy of Arts and Sciences* LXXIII:97–117 (1939).

Dudbridge, Glen. *The Legend of Miao-shan*. London: Ithaca Press, 1978. Published for the Board of the Faculty of Oriental Studies, Oxford University.

Edkins, Joseph. *Chinese Buddhism*. London: Kegan Paul, Trench, Trubner, 1893.

Eskildsen, Stephen. "The Beliefs and Practices of Early Ch'üan-chen Taoism." M.A. thesis, University of British Columbia, 1984.

Forte, Antonino. *Political Propaganda and Ideology in China at the End of the Seventh Century: Inquiry into the Nature, Authors and Function of the Tun-huang Document S.6502, Followed by an Annotated Translation*. Naples: Instituto Universitario Orientale, 1976.

Foulk, T. Griffith. "Myth, Ritual and Monastic Practices in Sung Ch'an Buddhism." In *Religion and Society in T'ang and Sung China*, edited by Patricia Buckley Ebrey and Peter N. Gregory. Honolulu: University of Hawai'i Press, 1993.

Giles, Lionel. *Descriptive Catalogue of the Chinese Manuscripts from Tun-huang in the British Museum*. London: The British Museum, 1957.

Glahn, Richard von. "The Enchantment of Wealth: The God Wutong in the Social History of Jiangnan." *Harvard Journal of Asiatic Studies*, 51.2:651–714 (December 1991).

Gómez, Luis O., trans. *The Land of Bliss: The Paradise of the Buddha of Measureless Light; Sanskrit and Chinese Versions of the Sukhāvatīvyūha Sūtras*. Honolulu: University of Hawai'i Press, and Kyoto: Higashi Honganji Shinshū Ōtani-ha, 1996.

de Groot, J. J. M. *Sectarianism and Religious Persecution in China*. 2 vols. Amsterdam: Johannes Muller, 1903; Taipei reprint 1970.

Grootaers, Willem A. "The Hagiography of the Chinese God Chen-wu (The Transmission of Rural Tradition in Chahar)." *Folklore Studies* 11.2:139–181 (1952).

ter Haar, Barend J. *The White Lotus Teachings in Chinese Religious History*. Leiden: E. J. Brill, 1992.

Hu Shih 胡適. "Pa Hsiao-shih Chen-k'ung pao-chüan" 跋銷釋眞空寶卷 (A postface to *The Precious Volume [by the Patriarch] Chen-kung*). *Bulletin of the National Library of Peiping* 5.4:3609–3656. (May–June 1931).

Hucker, Charles O. *A Dictionary of Official Titles in Imperial China*. Stanford, Calif.: Stanford University Press, 1985.

Johnson, David, ed. *Ritual and Scripture in Chinese Popular Religion: Five Studies*. Berkeley, Calif.: Publications of the Chinese Popular Culture Project, 1995.

Jordan, David K., and Daniel L. Overmyer. *The Flying Phoenix: Aspects of Chinese Sectarianism in Taiwan*. Princeton, N.J.: Princeton University Press, 1986.

Kallgren, Gerty. "Studies in Sung Time Colloquial Chinese as Revealed in Chu Hsi's Ts'üan shu." *Bulletin of the Museum of Far Eastern Antiquities, Stockholm* 30 (1958):1–165.

Katz, Paul R. *Demon Hordes and Burning Boats: The Cult of Marshal Wen in Late Imperial Chekiang*. Albany: State University of New York Press, 1995.

Kelly, David E. "Temples and Tribute Fleets: The Luo Sect and Boatmen's Associations in the Eighteenth Century." *Modern China* 8.3:361–391 (July 1982).

Kohn, Livia, ed. *The Taoist Experience: An Anthology*. Albany: State University of New York Press, 1993.

Lagerwey, John. *Taoist Ritual in Chinese Society and History*. New York: MacMillan Publishing Co., 1987.

Li Shih-yü 李世瑜. "Pao-chüan hsin yen" 寶卷新言 (A new discussion of "precious volumes"). *Wen-hsueh i-ch'an tseng-k'an* 文學遺產增刊 4:165–181 (1957).

———. *Pao-chüan tsung-lu* 寶卷綜錄 (A comprehensive bibliography of "precious volumes"). Shanghai: Chung-hua shu-chü, 1961.

Li, Thomas Shiyu [Li Shi-yü], and Susan Naquin. "The Baoming Temple: Religion and the Throne in Ming and Qing China." *Harvard Journal of Asiatic Studies* 48.1:131–188 (June 1988).

Lien Li-ch'ang 連立昌. "*Chiu-lien ching* k'ao" 九蓮經考 (An investigation of the *Nine[-Petaled] Lotus Scripture*). *Min-chien tsung-chiao* 民間宗教 2:113–120 (1996).

———. "Pai-lien chiao hsing-ch'eng wu kuan Ming-chiao k'ao" 白蓮教形成無關明教考 (An investigation of [the thesis that] the formation of the White Lotus sect had no connection with the Religion of Light). *Min-chien tsung chiao* 民間宗教 1:117–126 (December 1995).

Liu Ts'un-yan. "Traces of Zoroastrianism and Manichaean Activities in Pre-T'ang China." In Liu Ts'un-yan, *Selected Papers from the Hall of Harmonious Wind*. Leiden: E. J. Brill, 1976.

Lo Ch'ing 羅清. *Wu-pu liu-ts'e ching-chüan* 五部六冊經卷 (The "Five scriptures in six volumes"). Edited by Lin Li-jen 林立仁. 2 vols. Taipei: Cheng-i shan-shu ch'u-pan she, 1994.

Lo Hsiang-lin. *The Spread of the Chen K'ung Chiao in South China and Malaya* (in Chinese). Hong Kong: Institute of Chinese Culture, 1962.

Lynn [Kerr], Janet MacGregor. "Precious Scrolls in Chinese Popular Religious Culture." 2 vols. Ph.D. diss., University of Chicago, 1994.

Ma Hsi-sha 馬西沙. "Tsui-tsao i-pu pao-chüan te yen-chiu" 最早一部寶卷的研究 (A study of the earliest *pao-chüan*). *Shijie zongjiao yanjiu* 世界宗教研究 (Studies of world religions) 1:56–72 (1986).

Ma Hsi-sha 馬西沙 and Han Ping-fang 韓秉方. *Chung-kuo min-chien tsung-chiao shih* 中國民間宗教史 (A history of Chinese folk religion). Shanghai: Shanghai Jen-min ch'u-pan she, 1992.

Ma Shu-t'ien 馬書田. "Ming Ch'eng-tsu te cheng-chih yü tsung-chiao" 明成祖的政治與宗教 (The administration of the Ming [Emperor] Ch'eng-tsu and religion"). *Shijie zongjiao yanjiu* 世界宗教研究 3:35–51 (1984).

Maeda Eun 前田慧雲 and Nakano Tatsue 中野達慧, eds. *Dai Nihon Zokuzo-kyō* 大日本續藏經 (The great Japanese continuation of the [Buddhist] canon). Kyoto: 1905–1912; reprinted in Hong Kong, 1946.

Mair, Victor H. "The Contributions of T'ang and Five Dynasties Transformation Texts (*pien-wen*) to Later Chinese Popular Literature." *Sino-Platonic Papers* 12:1–71 (August 1989).

———. "Language and Ideology in the Written Popularizations of the *Sacred Edict*." In *Popular Culture in Late Imperial China*, edited by David Johnson, Andrew J. Nathan, and Evelyn S. Rawski. Berkeley: University of California Press, 1985.

———. "Lay Students and the Making of Written Vernacular Narrative: An Inventory of Tun-huang Manuscripts." *Chinoperl Papers* 10:5–96 (1981).

———. *Painting and Performance: Chinese Picture Recitation and Its Indian Genesis*. Honolulu: University of Hawai'i Press, 1988.

———. *T'ang Transformation Texts*. Cambridge, Mass.: Harvard University Council on East Asian Studies, 1989.

———. *Tun-huang Popular Narratives*. Cambridge: Cambridge University Press, 1983.

Makita Tairyō 牧田諦亮. *Gikyō kenkyū* 疑經研究 (A study of doubtful scriptures). Kyoto: Kyōto Daigaku jimbun kagaku kenkyūjo, 1976.

Maspero, Henri. *Taoism and Chinese Religion*. Translated by Frank A. Kierman, Jr. Amherst: University of Massachussetts Press, 1981. First published in French in 1971.

McRae, John R. *The Northern School and the Formation of Early Ch'an Buddhism*. Honolulu: University of Hawai'i Press, 1986.

Mote, Frederick W., and Dennis Twitchett, eds. *The Cambridge History of China*. Vol. 7, *The Ming Dynasty, 1368–1644*. Part I. Cambridge: Cambridge University Press, 1988.

Müller, F. Max, ed. *Buddhist Mahayana Texts*. Vol. XLIX, *Sacred Books of the East*. Part II. Delhi: Motilal Banarsidass, 1965. First published by Oxford University Press in 1894.

Nadeau, Randall L. "The 'Decline of the Dharma' in Early Chinese Buddhism." *B.C. Asian Review* 1:133–140 (September 1987).

———. "Genre Classifications of Chinese Popular Religious Literature: *Pao-chüan*." *Journal of Chinese Religions* 21:121–128 (Fall 1993).

———. "Popular Sectarianism in the Ming: Lo Ch'ing and His 'Religion of Non-Action.'" Ph.D. diss., University of British Columbia, 1990.

Naquin, Susan. *Millenarian Rebellion in China: The Eight Trigrams Uprising of 1813*. New Haven, Conn.: Yale University Press, 1976.

———. *Shantung Rebellion: The Wang Lun Uprising of 1774*. New Haven, Conn.: Yale University Press, 1981.

Nattier, Jan. *Once upon a Future Time: Studies in a Buddhist Prophecy of Decline*. Berkeley, Calif.: Asian Humanities Press, 1991.

Needham, Joseph, with the collaboration of Lu Gwei-djen. *Science and Civilisation in China.* Vol. 5, *Chemistry and Chemical Technology.* Part V, *Spagyrical Discovery and Invention: Physiological Alchemy.* Cambridge: Cambridge University Press, 1983.

Noguchi Tetsurō 野 口 鐵 郎. "Chūgoku shūkyō kessha-shi joshō—toku ni Byakurenkyōshi o chūshin to shita kenkyūshi-teki dōkō" 中國宗教結社史序章－特に白蓮教史を中心とした研究史的動向 (An introduction to the history of Chinese religious organizations: Trends in studies on the White Lotus sect). *Kindai Chūgoku* 近代中國 4 (1978):63–88.

———. *Mindai Byakuren kyō shi no kenkyū* 明代白蓮教史の研究 (A study of the history of the White Lotus sect in the Ming dynasty). Tokyo: Yūsankaku, 1986.

Ogasawara Senshū 小笠原宣秀. *Chūgoku kinsei Jōdōkyō shi no kenkyū* 中國近世淨土教史の研究 (A study of the history of the modern Pure Land sect in China). Kyoto: Hyakka en, 1963.

Overmyer, Daniel L. "Alternatives: Popular Religious Sects in Chinese Society." *Modern China* 7:153–190 (1981).

———. "Attitudes Toward the Ruler and State in Chinese Popular Religious Literature: Sixteenth and Seventeenth Century *Pao-chüan*." *Harvard Journal of Asiatic Studies* 44.2:347–379 (December 1984).

———. "Boatmen and Buddhas: The Lo Chiao in Ming Dynasty China." *History of Religions* 17:284–302 (1978).

———. "Buddhism in the Trenches: Attitudes Toward Popular Religion in Chinese Scriptures Found at Tun-huang." *Harvard Journal of Asiatic Studies* 50.1:197–222 (June 1990).

———. *Folk Buddhist Religion: Dissenting Sects in Late Traditional China.* Cambridge, Mass.: Harvard University Press, 1976.

———. "Messenger, Savior and Revolutionary: Maitreya in Chinese Popular Religious Literature of the Sixteenth and Seventeenth Centuries." In *Maitreya, the Future Buddha,* edited by Alan Sponberg and Helen Hardacre. Cambridge: Cambridge University Press, 1988.

———. "The Role of Lo Ch'ing in the Development of Sixteenth- and Seventeenth-Century Sectarian Scriptures: A Preliminary Study." Unpublished paper presented at the conference on "Rituals and Scriptures of Chinese Popular Religion," Bodega Bay, California, January 1990.

———. "Social Perspectives in Chinese Sectarian Scriptures from the Fifteenth and Sixteenth Centuries." In *Civil Society in East Asia: History, Concepts, Institutions,* edited by Charles Le Blanc and Alain Rocher. Proceedings of the Fifth Symposium of the North American–European Joint Committee for Cooperation in East Asian Studies. Montréal: Université de Montréal, Centre d'Études de l'Asie de l'Est, 1998.

———. "Values in Chinese Sectarian Literature: Ming and Ch'ing *Pao-chüan*." In *Popular Culture in Late Imperial China,* edited by David Johnson,

Andrew J. Nathan, and Evelyn S. Rawski. Berkeley: University of California Press, 1985.

Pas, Julian F., trans. *The Recorded Sayings of Ma-tsu*. Vol. 6 of *Studies in Asian Thought and Religion*. Lewiston, N.Y.: The Edwin Mellen Press, 1987. Translated from the 1981 Dutch translation by Bavo Lievens.

Robinet, Isabelle. "Original Contributions of Neidan to Taoism and Chinese Thought." In *Taoist Meditation and Longevity Techniques*, edited by Livia Kohn, pp. 297–330. Ann Arbor: Center for Chinese Studies, University of Michigan, 1989.

————. *Taoism: Growth of a Religion*. Translated by Phyllis Brooks. Stanford, Calif.: Stanford University Press, 1997. Originally published in French in 1992.

————. *Taoist Meditation: The Mao-shan Tradition of Great Purity*. Translated by Julian F. Pas and Norman J. Girardot. Albany: State University of New York Press, 1993. Originally published in French in 1979.

Sakai Tadao 酒井忠夫. *Chūgoku zenshō no kenkyū* 中國善書の研究 (A study of Chinese morality books). Tokyo: Kōbun-dō, 1960.

Salzberg, Stephan Marcus. "A Popular Exposition in Prose and Verse of the *Vimalakīrti Sūtra*: An Annotated Translation of Stein Manuscript Number 4571." M.A. thesis, University of British Columbia, 1983.

Sasaki, Ruth Fuller, ed. and trans. *The Recorded Sayings of Ch'an Master Lin-chi Hui-chao of Chen Prefecture*. Kyoto: Institute for Zen Studies, 1975.

Sasaki, Ruth Fuller, Yoshitaka Iriya, and Dana R. Fraser, eds. and trans. *The Recorded Sayings of Layman P'ang: A Ninth Century Zen Classic*. New York: Weatherhill, 1971.

Saso, Michael. *The Teachings of Taoist Master Chuang*. New Haven, Conn.: Yale University Press, 1978.

Sawada Mizuho 澤田瑞穗. *Kōchū haja shōben* 校注破邪詳辨 ("A detailed refutation of heresies," with corrections and commentary). Tokyo: Dōkyō kankō kai, 1972.

————. *Zōho Hōkan no kenkyū* 增補寶卷の研究 (A study of *pao-chüan*, revised and expanded edition). Tokyo: Kokusho kankōkai, 1975.

Schipper, Kristofer M. *Le Corps Taoïste*. Paris: Fayard, 1981.

————. *Le Fen-teng-Ritual Taoïste*. Paris: Publications de Bulletin de l'École Française d'Extrème Orient, 1975.

————. "The Written Memorial in Taoist Ceremonies." In *Religion and Ritual in Chinese Society*, edited by Arthur P. Wolf. Stanford, Calif.: Stanford University Press, 1974.

Seaman, Gary. *Journey to the North: An Ethnohistorical Analysis and Annotated Translation of the Chinese Folk Novel "Pei-yu chi."* Berkeley: University of California Press, 1987.

Sekida Katsuki, trans., and A. V. Grimstone, ed. *Two Zen Classics: Mumonkan and Hekiganroku*. New York: Weatherhill, 1977.

Shek, Richard Hon-chun. "Daoist Elements in Late Imperial Chinese Sectarianism." In *Millenarianism in Asian History*, edited by Ishii Yoneo. Tokyo: Institute for the Study of the Languages and Cultures of Asia and Africa, 1993.

———. "Eternal Mother Religion: Its Role in Late Imperial Chinese History." In *Proceedings of the Second International Conference on Sinology*. Taipei: Academia Sinica, 1989.

———. "Religion and Society in Late Ming: Sectarianism and Popular Thought in Sixteenth and Seventeenth Century China." Ph.D. diss., University of California, Berkeley, 1980.

Shiau, Mei-hui. "Religion, State and Society in Ming China: Beliefs about Mount T'ai." M.A. thesis, University of British Columbia, 1994.

Smith, Richard J. *Fortune Tellers and Philosophers: Divination in Traditional Chinese Society*. Boulder, Colo., San Francisco, Oxford: Westview Press, 1991.

Sōda Hiroshi 相田洋. "Rakyō no seiritsu to sono tenkai" 羅教の成立とその展開 (The founding and development of the Lo sect). In *Zoku Chūgoku minshū hanran no sekai* 續中國民衆反亂の世界 (The world of Chinese popular rebellions, continued), edited by Seinen Chūgoku Kenkyūsha kaigi 青年中國研究者会議. Tokyo: Kyūko Shoin, 1983.

Soothill, William Edward, and Lewis Hodous, eds. *A Dictionary of Chinese Buddhist Terms*. London: Kegan Paul, Trench, Trubner and Co., 1937.

Stulova, E. S. *Baotzuan o Pu-minye: Faksimile isdanie texsta, perevod s Kitaiskovo, Issledovanie I kommentary* (The *P'u-ming pao-chüan*: Reproduction of the published text, translated from the Chinese [with] analysis and commentary). Moscow: Izdatelsvo "Nauka," 1979.

Suzuki Chusei 鈴木中正. "Rakyō ni tsuite: Shindai Shina shūkyō kessha no ichi rei" 羅教について：清代支那宗教結社の一例 (On the Lo sect: an example of a religious association in Ch'ing China). *Tōyō bunka kenkyūjo kiyō* 東洋文化研究所紀要 1:441–501 (1943).

Takakusu Junjirō 高楠順次郎, Watanabe Kaikyoku 渡邊海旭, and Ono Gemmyō 小野玄妙, eds. *Taishō shinshū daizōkyō* 大正新修大藏經 (The Taishō Buddhist canon). Tokyo: Taishō Issaikyō kankōkai, 1914–1932.

Tao-yuan 道原. *Ching-te Ch'uan-teng lu* 景德傳燈錄 (Ching-te record of the transmission of the lamp). 2 vols. *Ssu-pu Ts'ung-kan hsu-pien* 四部叢刊續編. Taipei: Taiwan Commercial Press, 1966. First compiled in 1004.

Teiser, Stephen F. *The Scripture of the Ten Kings and the Making of Purgatory in Medieval Chinese Buddhism*. Honolulu: Kuroda Institute Studies in East Asian Buddhism, University of Hawai'i Press, 1994.

Tokuno, Kyoko. "A Study of *Mi-lo Ti-tsang shih-wang pao-chüan*: A Textual Source for Popular Buddhism During the Ming Dynasty." Research paper, University of California, Berkeley, 1985.

Tseng Tzu-liang 曾子良. "Kuo-nei so-chien pao-chüan hsu-lu" 國內所見寶

卷 敍 錄 (A discussion of "precious volumes" seen within this country). *Yu-shih hsueh-chih* 幼獅學誌17.1:104–134 (May 1982).

Tsukamoto Zenryu 塚本善隆. *Chūgoku Jōdōkyō shi kenkyū* 中國淨土教史研究 (A study of the history of the Chinese Pure Land sect). Tokyo: Daitō shuppansha, 1976.

———. "Rakyō no seiritsu to ryūden ni tsuite" 羅教の成立と流傳につい て (On the founding and proliferation of the Lo sect). *Tōhō gakuhō* 東方學報17:11–34 (1949).

Tuan P'ing 段平, ed. *Ho-hsi pao-chüan hsuan* 河西寶卷選 (A selection of "precious volumes" from Ho-hsi). Taipei: Hsin-wen feng ch'u-pan kung-ssu, 1992.

Wang Chien-ch'uan 王見川. "Huang-t'ien tao ch'ien-ch'i shih hsin-t'an" 黃天道前期史新探 (A new examination of the early history of the Yellow Heaven Way). In Kung P'eng-ch'eng 龔鵬程, ed., *Hai-hsia liang-an Tao-chiao wen-hua hsueh-shu yen-t'ao hui lun-wen* 海峽兩岸道教文化學術研討會論文 (Essays of the association for the academic study of Taoist culture on both sides of the [Taiwan] Strait) 2:1–36 (December 1994).

———. *Ming Ch'ing min-chien tsung-chiao ching-chüan wen-hsien* 明清民間宗教經卷文獻 (Popular religious scriptures from the Ming and Ch'ing periods). Forthcoming 1998.

———. *Ts'ung Mo-ni chiao tao Ming-chiao* 從摩尼教到明教 (From Manichaeism to the Religion of Light). Taipei: Hsin-wen feng ch'u-pan she, 1992.

Wang, Ch'iu-kuei. "The *Hsiao-shih Meng Chiang Chung-lieh Chen-chieh Hsien-liang Pao-chüan*: An Analytical Study." *Asian Culture* VII.4:46–72 (Winter 1979).

Wang Chung-min, ed. 王重民. *Tun-huang pien-wen chi* 敦煌變文集 (Collected Tun-huang transformation texts). 2 vols. Beijing: Shih-chieh shu-chü, 1957.

Wang Hsi-yuan 王熙遠. *Kuei-hsi min-chien mi-mi tsung-chiao* 桂西民間秘密宗教 (Secret folk religions of Kuei-hsi [in Kwangsi]). Kweilin: Kwangsi shih-fan ta-hsüeh ch'u-pan she, 1994.

Wang P'ei-lun 王沛綸. *Hsi-ch'ü tz'u-tien* 戲曲辭典 (Dictionary of [Chinese] drama). Taipei: Chung-hua shu-chü, 1969.

Wu Chih-ch'eng 吳之稱. "Pai-lien chiao ch'ung-pai shen 'Wu sheng mu'" 白蓮教的崇拜神無生母 (On the deity "the Eternal Mother" worshipped by the White Lotus sect). *Beijing shih-yuan hsueh-pao* 北京師院學報2:44–51 (August 1986).

Wu, Pei-yi. *The Confucian's Progress: Autobiographical Writings in Traditional China*. Princeton, N.J.: Princeton University Press, 1990.

Yabuki Keiki 失吹慶輝. *Meisha yoin kaisetsu* 鳴沙餘韻解說 (English title: Rare and unknown Chinese manuscript remains of Buddhist literature discovered in Tun-huang collected by Sir Aurel Stein and preserved in the British Museum). Tokyo: Iwanami shoten, 1933.

Yampolsky, Philip B., ed. and trans. *The Platform Sutra of the Sixth Patriarch: The Text of the Tun-huang Manuscript, with Translation, Introduction and Notes.* New York: Columbia University Press, 1967.

Yanagida Seizan 柳田聖山. "Goroku no rekishi" 語錄の歷史 (A history of "recorded sayings"). *Tōhō gakuhō* 東方學報 57:211–663 (March 1985).

———. "The 'Recorded Sayings' Texts of Chinese Ch'an Buddhism." Translated by John R. McRae. In *Early Ch'an in China and Tibet*, edited by Whalen Lai and Lewis B. Lancaster, pp. 185–205. Berkeley, Calif.: Asian Humanities Press, 1983. Originally published in Japanese in 1969.

Yao, Ted Tao-chung. "Ch'üan-chen: A New Taoist Sect in North China During the Twelfth and Thirteenth Centuries." Ph.D. diss., University of Arizona, 1980.

Yoshioka Yoshitoyo 吉岡義豐. "À-propos du *Hiang-chang pao-kiuan* dans une édition de l'ere K'ien-long" (in Japanese). In vol. IV of *Études Taoïstes* (*Dōkyō-kenkyū*) 道教研究, edited by Yoshioka Yoshitoyo and Michael Soymie, pp. 115–194. Tokyo: Henkyōsha, 1971.

———. "Miroku Jizō jūō hōkan" 彌勒地藏十王寶卷 (The "precious volume" of Maitreya, Ti-tsang, and the Ten Kings). *Chūgoku shūkyō shisō shidan kaiho* 中國宗教思想史談會報 2 (December 1968).

———. "Raso no shūkyō" 羅祖の宗教 (The religion of Patriarch Lo). *Chūsei daigaku gakuhō* 中正大學學報 37:88–96 (1950).

———. "*Shōshaku kongo·kagi* no seiritsu ni tsuite" 銷釋金剛科儀の成立について (On the formation of the *Chin-kang k'e-i*). *Ryūkoku shidan* 龍谷史壇 56–57:154–170 (1966).

Yü Sung-ch'ing 喻松青. *Min-chien mi-mi tsung-chiao ching-chüan yen-chiu* 民間秘密宗教經卷研究 (A study of the scriptures of secret folk religions). Taipei: Lien-ching ch'u-pan shih-yen kung-ssu, 1994.

Zengaku daijiten 禪學大字典 (Dictionary of Zen studies). Kyoto: Dai shukan shoten, 1978, 1985.

Zürcher, E. "Eschatology and Messianism in Early Chinese Buddhism." In *Leyden Studies in Sinology*, edited by W. L. Idema, pp. 34–56. Leiden: E. J. Brill, 1981.

———. "Prince Moonlight: Messianism and Eschatology in Early Medieval Chinese Buddhism." *T'oung Pao* LXVIII 1–3:1–74 (1982).

Glossary

A-lo 阿羅
A-lo t'ien 阿羅天
A-mi-t'o Fo 阿彌陀佛
an 暗
an-ch'uan 安船
an p'ai 安排
an-shen 暗神
an-tu 暗度
an yuan ke 暗元謌
ao-k'ou 熬口

ch'a-nü 姹女
chai-nei kung 宅内供
Chan-t'an 栴檀
chan-tao 展道
ch'an 懺
ch'an-hui . . . hsin 懺悔 . . . 心
Chang 張
chang-chi 掌極
chang-chiao 掌教
chang-hao 掌號
chang-ling 掌令
chang-p'an 掌盤
Chang Po-tuan 張伯端
Chang Ts'ui-hua 張翠花
Ch'ang-an 長安

Ch'ang-ch'eng pao-chüan 長城
　寶卷
Ch'ang-ch'ing 常清
ch'ang chu ch'i ting 常住其頂
Ch'ang-p'ing (district) 昌平
Ch'ang-sheng 長生
Ch'ang-sheng cheng-tao 長生
　正道
ch'ang tu mien fan-sheng hsiang-
　he 常覿面凡聖相合
Chao 趙
chao ch'üeh-shuo 招却說
chao jen-chia shuo tsui 著人家
　說嘴
Ch'ao-yuan 朝源
chei 這
chei-han 這漢
chei-ke 這個
chen 眞
Chen-ching 眞精
chen-hsin pan-tao 眞心辦道
chen-hsing 眞性
chen-hsing pu huai 眞性不壞
chen-k'ung 眞空
Chen-k'ung lao-tzu 眞空老祖
chen-shen 眞身

chen ta-shih 眞大士
Chen-t'ien 眞天
Chen-ting (prefecture) 眞定
chen tsu-shih 眞祖師
Chen-wu 眞武
ch'en-ch'ih 沈痴
Ch'en Shih 陳實, *Ta-tsang i-lan chi* 大藏一覽集
Cheng 鄭
cheng (straight) 正
cheng-chi 正極
Cheng-chiao 正教
cheng chin-tan 正金丹
cheng-fa 正法
Cheng-hsin ch'u-i wu hsiu cheng tzu-tsai pao-chüan 正信除疑無修證自在寶卷
Cheng-i fa-wen Tai-shang wai-lu i 正一法文太上外籙儀
Cheng-i shan-shu ch'u-pan she 正一善書出版社
cheng-kuo ch'ao-yuan 正果朝元
cheng-kuo wei-p'ai 正果位牌
Cheng-piao ming-tsung 證表明宗
Cheng-te 正德
cheng-tsung 正宗
cheng wu-sheng 證無生
ch'eng 程
ch'eng (?) 鋮
ch'eng cheng chueh 成正覺
ch'eng fo liao tao 成佛了道
Ch'eng-hua 成化
Ch'eng-yang 成陽
chi (apex) 極
chi (collection) 集
chi (gāthā/verse) 偈
chi chen wei chao 資眞爲照
chi-chi ju lü-ling 急急如律令
Chi-mo 即墨
Chi-nan 濟南
chi-shih 幾時
chi-wei 己位

chi-yen chieh 極嚴劫
ch'i 氣
ch'i (old) 耆
chia 甲
Chia-ching 嘉靖
chia-hsiang 家鄉
chia-hsu 甲戌
chia-shen 甲申
chia tsu-shih 假祖師
chia-tzu 甲子
chiang-ching-wen 講經文
chiang kung che tsui 將功折罪
Chiang-mao 江茅
chiao 教
chien-ch'a 監察
Chien-chi 建基
chien ch'in niang 見親娘
chien-hsing ch'eng fo 見性成佛
chien-p'an 監盤
ch'ien 乾
ch'ien (trigram) 乾
ch'ien-ch'eng 虔誠
Ch'ien-lung 乾龍
chih 執
chih-chang 執掌
chih-hua 治化
chih-shih 治世
chih tsui ch'an tsui 知罪懺罪
ch'ih 尺
chin 斤
chin 金
chin-chang 金杖
chin-ch'ao ju-he pu ch'eng-tang 今朝如何不承當
chin-chiang shih-chieh tzu yü ni kuan 今將世界自與你管
Chin-hua 金華
Chin-hua mu 金花母
Chin-kang ching k'e-i pao-chüan 金剛經科儀寶卷
Chin-kang k'e-i 金剛科儀
Chin-kang p'an-jo po-lo-mi ching 金剛般若波羅蜜經

Chin-kang p'an-jo po-lo-mi ching
  chiang-ching-wen 金剛般若
  波羅蜜經講經文
Chin-niu 金牛
Chin-shan 金山
Chin-shan tzu 金山子
chin-tan 金丹
Chin-tan tao 金丹道
ch'in 琴
Ch'in Kuang-wang 秦廣王
ch'in-wen 親文
ching 經 (classic, scripture)
ching (pure) 淨
ching (quiet) 靜
ching che chuang 經折狀
ching-chu 經主
ching-i 經衣
Ching-te Ch'uan-teng lu 景德
  傳燈錄
ching-tu 淨度
ching-yun 經云
Ch'ing-hsu 清虛
ch'ing lai 情來
Ch'ing mo 情末
Ch'ing-yang 清陽
Ch'ing-yang hui 清陽會
Chiu-chou Han-ti 九州漢地
chiu-chuan 九轉
Chiu-erh yü 舊兒峪
Chiu-hsuan ts'uan-tsao lung t'ien
  piao 九玄攢造龍天表
chiu-k'o 九殼
chiu-kuan 九關
Chiu-lien pao-chüan 九蓮寶卷
Chiu-lung kang 九龍岡
chiu-shih 救世
ch'iu tz'u tien-hua 求此點化
cho-e shih 濁惡世
Chou mo 周末
Chou Tun-i 周敦頤
ch'ou liao ku, huan liao t'ai
  抽了骨，換了胎
chu-cheng 主正
Chu Hsi 朱熹

chu-kung-tiao 諸宮調
Chu Kuo-chen 朱國禎, Yung
  ch'uang hsiao-p'in 湧幢小品
Chu-mao 豬毛
chu-t'ien (?) 諸仸
ch'u 出
Ch'u 楚
ch'u-ch'en ju-shih/sheng 出塵
  入世(聖)
Ch'u-chiang wang 楚江王
ch'u-hsi 出細
ch'u-hsi hsiao-hsi 出細消息
ch'u-shih 出世
ch'u-tsu 出祖
ch'u yang-shen 出陽神
chuan-li 專理
Chuan t'ien t'u ching 轉天圖經
chuan tsao tang-lai shih-chieh
  專造當來世界
ch'uan chia hsin 傳佳信
ch'uan fa jen 傳法人
ch'uan-hsin 傳信
Ch'uan lao sung 川老頌
ch'uan lu shu 穿路疏
ch'uan-teng 傳燈
ch'uan-t'ou 船頭
chü 菊
ch'ü-ch'ih 屈持
chü hsiang tsan 舉香讚
ch'ü-tuan 屈斷
chüan 卷
chüan-hsia/chüan-shang 卷下/
  卷上
chüan-tsung 卷宗
Ch'üan-chen 全眞
chuang (serious, grave) 莊
chuang (to adorn) 粧
Chuang-yen chieh 莊嚴刼
chueh 覺
chui 墜
ch'un-yang 純陽
Chung K'uei 鍾馗
chung-min 種民
chung-teng 中等

chung-t'u 中土
chung-yang 中央
Ch'ung-chen 崇禎
Ch'ung-chi 重吉
ch'ung-hsuan 重宣
Ch'ung-ning 崇寧
Ch'ung-yang 重陽
ch'uo huo 戳火

Dai-Nihon Zokuzōkyō 大日本
　續藏經

e 惡
en 恩
Erh-hsing Wu-sheng mu 二星
　無生母
erh-i 二儀
e-tu 惡度

fa 法
fa-hao 法號
Fa-hua chüan 法華卷
fa-shen 法身
fa-shih 法師
fa-shui jen hsiang 法水認相
fa tz'u-pei 發慈悲
fa-yen 法眼
fan 凡
fan-hsieh kuei-cheng 反邪歸正
Fan Lang 范郎
fan-lung 凡籠
fan-pen huan-yuan 反本還原
fan-shen 凡身
fan-t'i sheng-hsuan 凡提聖選
fang-kuo 放過
fang-tang 放黨/蕩
fen 分
fen-pieh 分別
Fen-yang Shan-chao 汾陽善昭
Fen-yang Wu-te Ch'an-shih yü-lu
　汾陽無德禪師語錄
Feng-huang 鳳凰
feng-shui 風水

Feng-tu 酆都
Fo an-p'ai 佛安排
Fo-hsing chung-tzu 佛性種子
Fo-hsing hai-ts'ang chih-hui chieh-
　t'o p'o hsin-hsiang ching 佛性
　海藏智慧解脫破心相經
Fo-kung mu 佛功母
Fo neng chih 佛能治
Fo-shuo A-mi-t'o ching 佛說
　阿彌陀經
Fo-shuo chai-fa ch'ing-ching ching
　佛說齋法清淨經
Fo-shuo chiu-chi ching 佛說
　救疾經
Fo-shuo chueh tsui fu ching 佛說
　決罪福經
Fo-shuo Chun-t'i fu-sheng pao-
　chüan 佛說準提復生寶卷
Fo-shuo fa mieh-chin ching 佛說
　法滅盡經
Fo-shuo Fa-wang ching 佛說
　法王經
Fo-shuo hsiang-fa chueh-i ching
　佛說像法決疑經
Fo-shuo hsiao-shih pao-an pao-chüan
　佛說銷釋保安寶卷
Fo-shuo Huang-chi chieh-kuo pao-
　chüan 佛說皇極結果寶卷
Fo-shuo kuan ch'ing 佛說觀經
Fo-shuo Mi-le hsia-sheng ching
　佛說彌勒下生經
Fo-shuo Mi-le ting-chieh chao pao-
　ching 佛說彌勒定劫照寶經
Fo-shuo Shan-hai-hui p'u-sa ching
　佛說山海慧菩薩經
Fo-shuo tang-lai Mi-le ch'u-hsi pao-
　chüan 佛說當來彌勒出細
　寶卷
Fo-shuo Tu-tou li-t'ien hou hui
　shou-yuan pao-chüan 佛說
　都斗立天後會收圓寶卷
Fo-shuo wu-liang ta tz'u chiao ching
　佛說無量大慈教經

*Fo-shuo Yang shih kuei hsiu hung-lo
Hua-hsien ke pao-chüan* 佛說
楊氏鬼繡紅羅化仙哥寶卷
*Fo-shuo Yao-shih Ju-lai pen-yuan
ching* 佛說藥師如來本願經
Fo-tsu 佛祖
Fo yen 佛言
Fo-yin mu 佛印母
fu 夫
fu (to fall prostrate) 伏
fu (to subdue) 服
fu-chi 副極
Fu Hsi 伏羲
fu hui yun-p'ai 赴會雲牌
Fu-mo pao-chüan 伏魔寶卷
fu-mu 父母
Fu-mu men 父母門
fu tzu 父子
fu yeh liao 赴業了

Han 韓
Han Chia 韓家
Han T'ai-hu 韓太湖
Han Wen-kung 韓文公
Han Yü 韓愈
hao 號
Hao-chou 毫(濠)州
He-chi 和偈
He-tan 苛担
ho hui jen 合會人
Ho-shang 和尚
hou-hsiang 後象
hou hsueh 後學
hou-lai 後來
hou-t'ien 後天
hsi (?) 褚
Hsi huang 西黃
hsi-lai i 西來意
Hsi-ning hou 西寧侯
Hsi-tz'u 繫辭
hsia-lo 下落
hsia-teng 下等
hsiang-chai 香齋
hsiang ch'ueh-shuo 相却說

hsiang-jang 相讓
Hsiang mo pien-wen 降魔衢文
Hsiang-shan pao-chüan 香山寶卷
hsiang shou 相守
hsiang-t'ou 香頭
hsiao 校
hsiao-fa 小法
hsiao-hsi 消息
*Hsiao-shih An-yang shih-chi pao-
chüan* 銷釋安養實際寶卷
Hsiao-shih Chen-k'ung pao-chüan
銷釋眞空寶卷
*Hsiao-shih Chen-k'ung sao-hsin pao-
chüan* 銷釋掃心寶卷
Hsiao-shih Chin-kang k'e-i 銷釋
金剛科儀
*Hsiao-shih Chun-t'i fu-sheng pao-
chüan* 銷釋準提復生寶卷
*Hsiao-shih Hun-yuan Hung-yang ta
fa-tsu ming ching* 銷釋混元
弘陽大法祖明經
*Hsiao-shih Hun-yuan ta fa-ming
ching* 銷釋混元大法明經
*Hsiao-shih k'e-i cheng-tsung pao-
chüan* 銷釋科意正宗寶卷
*Hsiao-shih kuei-chia pao-en pao-
chüan* 銷釋歸家報恩寶卷
*Hsiao-shih Meng Chiang chung-lieh
chen-chieh hsien-liang pao-chüan*
銷釋孟姜忠烈貞節賢良寶卷
*Hsiao-shih Pai-i Kuan-yin p'u-sa
sung ying-erh hsia-sheng pao-
chüan* 銷釋白衣觀音菩薩送
嬰兒下生寶卷
*Hsiao-shih wu-hsing huan-yuan
pao-chüan* 銷釋悟性還源寶卷
*Hsiao-shih Yin-k'ung shih-chi pao-
chüan* 銷釋印空實際寶卷
Hsiao-shih yuan-chueh pao-chüan
銷釋圓覺寶卷
hsiao-tsai chiu-k'u 消災救苦
hsieh-ch'i 邪氣
hsieh-chien 邪見
hsieh-chih 邪枝

hsieh-fa 邪法
hsieh-mo tzai hsin 邪魔在心
hsieh-shih 邪師
hsieh-tsung 邪宗
hsieh-tsung wai-tao 邪宗外道
hsien 賢
hsien-cheng 顯證
Hsien-feng 咸豐
Hsien-hsing ming-chi 顯性明機
hsien-hua 現化
hsien-kuan shen-li 仙官神吏
hsien-liang tzu 賢良子
hsien-nü 賢女
hsien-sheng 賢聖
Hsien-t'ien 先天
hsien-t'ung 仙童
hsien tzu-chi chia-hsiang 現自己
　家鄉
hsin 心
Hsin-ch'eng (district) 新城
Hsin-ching chüan 心經卷
hsin-hai 辛亥
hsin-hao 信號
hsin-hsieh 信邪
Hsin-hsieh shao-chih pao-chüan
　信邪燒紙寶卷
hsin-hsin 信心
Hsin li Hun-yuan tsu chiao 新立
　混元祖教
hsin pu chi 心不及
hsin-ssu 辛巳
hsin-yin 心印
hsin-yu 辛酉
hsing 性
hsing kuai fa 行怪法
Hsing-lin 興林
hsing-su ch'u-shih 星宿出世
Hsing ta hsu-k'ung 性達虛空
hsing-tsu 星祖
hsing-tsung 性宗
hsiu chiang-lai pu-shih t'ou te
　修將來不是偷的
hsiu-hsing chih jen 修行之人
Hsiu-lo 修羅

hsiu pang fa 休謗法
hsiung-shen 凶神
hsu 戌
Hsu-chou 徐州
hsu-teng 續燈
Hsu Tsang-ching 續藏京
hsuan (dark) 玄
hsuan (to suspend) 懸
Hsuan chen cheng Tao
　玄真證道
hsuan-chi 玄機
hsuan-ch'ih 玄池
hsuan-chüan 宣卷
Hsuan-ku chiao 玄鼓教
hsuan-kuan 玄關
hsuan-kuang 宣光
hsuan-k'ung 玄空
hsuan-lu 玄爐
hsuan-lu kuan 玄爐關
hsuan-men 玄門
hsuan-miao 玄妙
Hsuan-ming 玄明
Hsuan-te 宣德
Hsuan-tsang 玄奘
Hsuan-wu shen-chiang
　玄武神將
hsun pu chao ch'u-shen lu, lao
　erh wu-kung 尋不著出身
　路，勞而無功
hu 戶
hu fa 護法
Hu-kuang 湖廣
Hu-kuo yu-min fu-mo pao-chüan
　護國佑民伏魔寶卷
hu-sung 護送
hua-ch'eng 化城
Hua-lo t'ien 化樂天
Hua-mu 花母
Hua-yen 華嚴
Huai-t'ai pao-chüan 懷胎寶卷
Huai-yun chieh t'ai 懷孕結胎
Huan ch'ien-k'un 換乾坤
huan-hsiang 還鄉
Huan-hsiang pao-chüan 還鄉寶卷

huan-tan 還丹
huan-tso 換做
Huan-yuan chi tao 還源之道
Huan-yuan pao-chüan 還源寶卷
huan-yuan tzu-hsing 還源自性
Huang (surname, name of
    village) 黃
huang (yellow) 黃
huang-chi 皇極
Huang-chi chin-tan chiu-lien cheng-
    hsin kuei-chen huan-hsiang pao-
    chüan 皇極金丹九蓮正信
    皈眞還鄉寶卷
Huang-chi hsing-su chieh
    皇極星宿劫
Huang-chi hui 皇極會
Huang-chi Lao-mu 皇極老母
Huang-chi Yuan-tun chiao 皇極
    圓頓教
huang-fang 黃房
huang-lu 黃籙
Huang Ming t'iao-fa shih-lei tsuan
    皇明條法事類纂
Huang-po Hsi-yun 黃蘗希運
Huang Te-hui 黃德輝
Huang-ti 黃帝
Huang-t'ien sheng-tao 皇天聖道
Huang-t'ien tao 皇天道
Huang-t'ien tao (Way of Yellow
    Heaven) 黃天道
Huang-t'ien wu-chi chih miao-
    tao 皇天無極之妙道
huang-t'ing 黃庭
Huang Yü-p'ien 黃育楩, *P'o-*
    hsieh hsiang-pien 破邪詳辯
hui 會
Hui-chao 慧照
hui-chu 會主
hui-chung jen 會中人
hui-hsia tao-jen 會下道人
Hui-neng 惠能
hui-t'ou 會頭
hui-yen 慧眼
hun 魂

hun (chaotic) 混
hun-chin 渾金
Hun-chin P'iao-kao 渾金飄高
hun-fa 混法
hun-tun hung-meng 混沌鴻蒙
hun-yuan 混元
Hun-yuan hung-yang Chung-hua
    ching 混元弘陽中華經
Hun-yuan hung-yang Fo ru-lai wu-
    chi P'iao-kao tsu lin-fan ching
    混元弘陽佛如來無極飄高
    祖臨凡經
Hun-yuan hung-yang lin-fan P'iao-
    kao ching 混元弘陽臨凡
    飄高經
Hun-yuan hung-yang t'an-shih
    chen-ching 混元弘陽歎世
    眞經
Hun-yuan tsu 混元祖
hung 洪
hung ching-tz'u 紅經詞
Hung-jen 弘忍
Hung-lien hui 紅蓮會
Hung-lo t'ien 紅羅天
Hung-lu ssu 鴻臚寺
Hung-tung (district) 洪洞
Hung-wu 洪武
Hung (red)-yang fa 紅陽法
Hung (vast)-yang 弘陽
Hung-yang chiao 弘陽教
Hung-yang chih-li kuei-tsung ssu-
    hsiang pao-chüan 弘陽似理
    歸宗思鄉寶卷
Hung-yang hou-hsu jan-teng t'ien-
    hua pao-chüan 弘陽後續燃燈
    天華寶卷
Hung-yang hui 洪陽會
Hung-yang k'u-kung wu-tao ching
    弘陽苦功悟道經
Hung-yang pi-miao hsien-hsing
    chieh-kuo ching 弘陽秘妙
    顯性結果經
Hung-yang t'an-shih ching 弘陽
    歎世經

Hung-yang wu-tao ming-hsin ching
弘陽悟道明心經

i 億
i-hai 乙亥
i nien hsin 一念心
i-ping 疑病
i-t'i 一體
i-t'o 倚托

Jan-teng 燃燈
jen chen-tsu 認眞祖
jen-ching 認景
jen-ch'ing 人情
jen-hsing 仁性
jen-jen pen-lai mien-mu 人人
   本來面目
jen-ma 恁麼
jen-neng chi tzu 人能之祖
jen-p'an 人盤
jen/p'ing 恁/凭 (＝憑)
jen-tzu 壬子
jen-wu 壬午
Jo-shui 弱水
jou-yen 肉眼
Ju-chia tao 儒家道
Ju-men 儒門
ju mu t'ai 入母胎
ju tang tai Fo hsing-hua 汝當代
   佛行化
Ju-ting kuan-k'ung 入定觀空
Ju-t'ung 儒童
Jung-cheng (district) 容城

kai-tso 改做
kai-wen 蓋聞
k'ai-ching chi 開經偈
k'ai-hsin 開心
K'ai-hsin fa-yao 開心法要
K'ai-hsuan ch'u-ku hsi-lin chüan
   開玄出谷西林卷
k'ai hsuan-kuan 開玄關
k'ai-huang 開荒
k'ai-huang ch'u-hsi 開荒出細

k'ai-shih 開兆
kan-ching 乾淨
k'an 坎
k'ang-chuang ta tao 康莊大道
K'ang-hsi 康熙
k'ang-tao 康道
kao chiao na tzu 高叫那子
Kao-yang 高陽
ke 哥
ke fen tso-wei 各分座位
ke yu i-shuo 各有一說
ken 根
keng-shen 庚申
keng-wu 庚午
k'e-i 科意
k'ou-t'ou san-mei 口頭三昧
ku 賈
Ku-chuo 古拙
Ku Fo 古佛
Ku Fo T'ai-huang yen-chiao
   古佛太皇演教
*Ku Fo tang-lai hsia-sheng Mi-le
   ch'u-hsi pao-chüan* 古佛當來
   下生彌勒出西寶卷
Ku Fo T'ien-chen k'ao-cheng
   古佛天眞考證
*Ku Fo T'ien-chen shou-yuan chieh-
   kuo lung-hua pao-ch'an* 古佛
   天眞收圓結果籠華寶懺
ku-k'e 孤客
Ku-pei 古北
k'u-hsing 苦行
k'u-hsiu 苦修
K'u-kung pu-chu K'ai-hsin fa-yao
   苦功補註開心法要
K'u-kung wu-tao chüan 苦功
   悟道卷
kua tao t'ien-kuan 刮到天關
Kuan 關
kuan (control) 管
kuan (pass) 關
Kuan-k'ou tsu-mu 關口祖母
*Kuan-shih-yin p'u-sa pen-hsing
   ching* 觀世音菩薩本行經

Kuan-ti fu-mo pao-chüan chu-chieh
關帝伏魔寶卷註解
Kuan-yin 觀音
Kuang 光
Kuang-hsu 光緒
Kuang-p'ing 廣平
kuei 皈
Kuei-chen 皈眞
kuei-chia ch'ü fan-pen huan-yuan
歸家去反本還原
kuei-chia piao-wen 皈家表文
kuei-chia pu piao ming-hsing
皈家簿標名性
kuei-k'ung 歸空
kuei-wei 癸未
Kuei-yuan 歸圓
kun 棍
k'un 坤
k'un ke she-ma? 困箇什麼？
Kun-lun 崑崙
kung-an (kōan) 公案
Kung Ch'ang 弓長
kung-fu 功夫
Kung-li pu ch'ing 公吏不清
K'ung 孔
k'ung wei jen 空爲人
kuo chen yu yeh, wu 果眞有
也，無
kuo-wei 果位

Lai-chou 詞州
Lan-feng 蘭風
Lao Ku Fo 老古佛
Lao-mu 老母
Lao-shan 牢山
Lao-tsu liu-hsia 老祖留下
Lao wu-sheng 老無生
Lao-yeh 老爺
Le-pang 樂邦
le tao ta-ying 樂道答應
li 里
Li (surname) 李
li (trigram) 離

. . . li ch'eng chung . . . . . .
里城中...
Li Ch'ing 李清
Li Ch'ing-an 李清庵
Li Pao-p'ing 李寶瓶
Li Pin 李賓
Li-shih pao-chüan 立世寶卷
li te ch'ien-k'un 立的乾坤
Li Ts'ui-p'ing 李翠瓶
liang 兩
Liang 梁
Liang-nan 良南
liang-yen 良言
liao 了
Liao 寥
liao (to cure) 療
liao (to grasp) 撩
liao-chüan 了卷
lien-hsiang 蓮鄉
Lien-tsung 蓮宗
Lin-chi I-hsuan 臨濟義玄
Lin-ch'ing 甐(＝臨)清
lin fan ching 臨凡經
Lin Li-jen 林立仁
Lin Wan-ch'uan 林萬傳
ling-ch'i 靈氣
Ling-chiu shan 靈鷲山
ling-chung 領衆
ling-fu 靈符
ling-hsiu 領袖
ling-ken 靈根
Ling-shan 靈山
Ling-shan fu-yeh huan-hsiang
piao 靈山赴業還鄉表
ling-wen 靈文
*Ling-ying T'ai-shan niang-niang
pao-chüan* 靈應泰山娘娘
寶卷
Liu 劉
Liu-ch'eng 柳城
Liu Chih 劉志
liu-hsia 留下
Liu Hsing-i 劉興義

Liu Hsing-i 劉興義, "Kuan-yu
    pao-chuan wen-hsueh chi ch'i
    yin-yun ch'ü-tiao," Mu-lu
    關於寶卷文學及其音韻曲
    調，目錄
Liu Hua 劉化
liu-tao 六道
liu-tu 六度
liu-t'ung wu-yen 六通五眼
Liu Yü 劉玉
Lo Chiao 羅教
Lo Ch'ing 羅清
Lo Ch'ing Tzu 羅清祖
Lo P'u-ching 羅普淨
Lo Tzu 羅祖
lu (records) 錄
lu (stove) 爐
Lu Kung 路工
Lu-pen shan (Lu-shan) 魯俸山
    (魯山)
Lü 呂
lü (green) 綠
Lü Kung 呂公
Lü Tsu 呂祖
Lü Tung-pin/Ch'un-yang
    呂洞賓/純陽
Luan-chou 欒州
Lung-chang 龍章
Lung-hua ching 龍華經
Lung-hua hui 龍華會
Lung-hua hui cheng t'an-chu
    龍華會正壇主
Lung-hua pao-ching 龍華
    寶經
Lung-shu ching-t'u wen
    龍舒淨土文

Ma 麻
Ma (surname/horse) 馬
ma (curse) 罵
Ma-tsu 媽祖
Ma-tsu Tao-i 媽祖道一
man-tou fen-hsiang 滿斗焚香
Mao Tzu-yuan 茅子元

mei 梅
men 門
Meng Chiang 孟姜
meng-yen 蒙眼
mi 迷
Mi-le 彌勒
Mi-le Fo 彌勒佛
*Mi-le Fo shuo Ti-tsang Shih-wang
    pao-chüan* 彌勒佛說地藏
    十王寶卷
Mi-le sung 彌勒頌
mi-shih jen 迷失人
Mi-t'o 彌陀
Mi-t'o pao-chüan 彌陀寶卷
Mi-tsang Tao-k'ai 密藏道開
Mi-yun 密雲
miao 妙
Miao-chuang 妙莊
miao hsiao-hsi 妙消息
Miao-k'ai 妙愷
Miao-k'ung 妙空
Miao-shan 妙(玅)善
Miao-shu 妙書
Miao-yin 妙音
mieh 滅
Min-kuo 民國
Min-te t'ang 民德堂
Ming 明
ming (destiny) 命
ming (name) 名
ming-an ch'a-hao 明暗查號
Ming ch'ao 明朝
ming-ching 明經
Ming-chün 明君
Ming fa wang 明法王
ming hsiang 名香
Ming-k'ung 明空
ming-shen 明神
Ming-shih 明使
Ming Tai-tsung shih-lu (Nan-kang)
    明太宗實錄(南港)
ming-tu 明度
Ming-wang 明王
mo-chieh 末劫

mo-chieh chih chin 末劫(刼)
似近
mo-chieh hsun-su 末劫迅速
mo-ching tsa-fa 魔境雜法
mo-fa 末法
mo-fa chih tai 末法之代
mo-hou hsiao-hsi 末後消息
mo-hou i-cho 末後一著
mo hsin hsieh-shih 莫信邪師
mo-jen 魔人
mo-shuo 魔說
mo-t'u-tzu 魔徒子
mo-yen 魔言
mou-ch'en 茂辰
mou-ni 牟尼
mou-wu 茂午
mou-yin 茂寅
mu 母
Mu-lien chiu mu ch'u-li ti-yü sheng-t'ien pao-chüan 目蓮救母出難
地獄生天寶卷
Mu-tzu 木子

Na-mo chiao 南無教
Na-mo Yü-lien Huang p'u-sa
南無玉蓮黃菩薩
na-tzu 衲子
Nai-ho 奈何
Nan-hsia 南霞
Nan-yang 南陽
Nei-hsuan lao-mu 內玄老母
nei-tan 內丹
nei-yao 內藥
ni (you) 你
ni (to oppose) 逆
ni i-ch'ieh jen 你一切人
ni-wan 泥丸
niang shih wo, wo shih niang
娘是我，我是娘
niang ta chua chi yeh p'eng t'ou
(chua) 娘打撾妳爺蓬頭(鬠)
Nü Wa 女媧

O-mei 峨嵋

pa 拔
pa 八
pa chien hsiu hsing 八件修行
Pa-kua kuei-chen ch'ao-yuan
piao 八卦皈眞朝源表
pa-kua shih-ku (kuei)
八卦石鼓(皷)(圭)
pa-kuan 八關
pa-nan 八難
pa-pu 八部
pai 白
Pai-lien (lien) 白蓮(縺)
pai-i 白衣
pai-wen 白文
Pai-yang chiao 白陽教
p'ai (sect) 派
p'ai (tablet) 牌
pan-chih lao shou 搬枝勞守
pan tao 辦道
P'an (realm/name of a mountain)
盤
P'an Ku 盤古
P'an San-to 潘三多
P'an-t'ao hui 蟠桃會
p'ang-men 傍門
pao 報
pao-chüan 寶卷
pao-en 報恩
Pao-en ch'an-hui 報恩懺悔
Pao-en chüan 報恩卷
Pao-feng 寶峰
Pao-ming ssu 保明寺
Pao-ting (prefecture) 保定
Pao-ting fu 保定府
pao-ts'ang 包藏
pei (double) 倍
pei (generation) 輩
pei (north) 北
pen 本
pen-an 本庵
pen-kuo 本國
pen-lai chi jen 本來之人
pen-lai mien 本來面
pen-t'i 本體

p'eng 蓬
Pi-hsia yuan-chun 碧霞元君
p'i-hsia lien-tsung 批下蓮宗
piao 表
P'iao-kao 飄高
Pien-liang 汴梁
pien-wen 衢文
p'in 品
ping-ch'en 丙辰
ping-wu 丙午
po-chih 撥治
p'o (break open) 破
p'o (soul) 魄
P'o-hsieh hsiang-pien 破邪
　詳辯
P'o hsieh hsien cheng 破邪
　顯證
P'o hsieh hsien-cheng yao-shih
　chüan 破邪顯證鑰匙卷
P'o-k'ai ti-yü 破開地獄
P'o-mo pien-wen 破魔衢文
pu-hsin 不信
pu-hsing 布省
pu jung chen 不容眞
pu kan shan-chuan 不敢擅專
pu she chia-hsiang 不捨家鄉
pu-shih 布施
pu-shih tzu-chi 不是自己
Pu-tai 布袋
pu-yueh 不悅
p'u 普
P'u-ching 普靜 (the character
　used in the *Mi-le Ti-tsang Shih-*
　wang pao-chüan)
P'u-ching 普淨
P'u-ch'ing 普卿
P'u-chung 普種
P'u-han 普涵
P'u-hsien 普賢
P'u-hsien P'u-sa shuo cheng ming
　ching 普賢菩薩說證明經
P'u-kuang 普光
P'u-liang 普亮
P'u-ming 普明

P'u-ming ju-lai wu-wei liao-i pao-
　chüan 普明如來無爲了
　義寶卷
P'u-shan 普善
P'u-shen 普神
P'u-t'o 普陀
P'u-tu 普度
p'u-tu 普度

san-ch'eng 三城
san-chi 三際
san-chi shih-chieh 三極世界
san-chia 三家
San-chieh t'ien-shen tou i ting tai
　三界天神都以頂戴
San-hsin t'ang 三心堂
san-hsuan 三玄
san-kang 三綱
san-kuai 三怪
san-kuan 三關
San-kuei wu-chieh kuei-chen
　piao 三皈五戒皈眞表
san-mei ch'an-ting 三昧禪定
san-shih 三世
San-shih-wu fo-ming ching
　三十五佛明經
san-tsai 三灾 (災)
san-tsai chiu-k'u 三灾救苦
san-ts'ai 三才
San-tsu hsing-chiao yin-yu pao-
　chüan 三祖行腳因由寶卷
san-tsung wu-p'ai 三宗五派
san-yuan 三元
San-yang ch'u-hsien k'ai-huang
　piao 三陽初顯開荒表
Sang-yuan 桑園
se-shen 色身
Sen-lo 森羅
Seng-chia ho-sheng yü ju nieh-p'an
　shuo liu-tu ching 僧伽
　和尚欲入涅槃說六度經
Seng Pao 僧保
Sha-kua 傻瓜
shan (good) 善

shan (to act on one's own authority) 擅
shan-shu 善書
Shan-ts'ai 善財
shan-tu 善度
shang-chieh tang 上解當
shang-p'in chih jen 上品之人
shang-shang 上上
shang-teng 上等
shang-teng, chung-teng, hsia-teng 上等，中等，下等
shang teng jen 上等人
Shang-ti 上帝
shao 少
she 社
she-chiao 設教
she-kuang 攝光
she-shen 捨身
she ta ti 攝大地
shen 神
shen 申
shen-chou (realm) 神州
shen-chou (invocation) 神咒
Shen-hsiu 神秀
shen-hsiu 申戍
Shen-ken chieh-kuo pao-chüan 深根結果寶卷
she-ma 什麼
Shen-nung 神農
sheng 聖
sheng-chung p'an-wang 聖中盼望
sheng-hsuan chung 聖玄中
sheng-i 聖意
sheng-i kung-p'ing 生意公平
sheng-li 生理
sheng-ming 聖名
sheng-p'an 聖盤
Sheng-pao ti 聖寶地
sheng-ssu shih-chuang 生死誓狀
Sheng-yang mu 生陽母
sheng-yen 聖眼
Shih 石

shih (fond of) 嗜
shih (to lose) 失
shih (master, teacher) 師
shih (to be) 是
shih chiang yü mo 世將欲末
shih-chu 施主
shih-e 十惡
shih fa p'ing-teng 是法平等
shih-fang nan-nü p'u-sa 十方男女菩薩
Shih-Fo k'ou 石佛口
Shih-hsia 石匣
shih-hsiung 師兄
shih-mu 師母
shih-pa ts'eng 十八層
shih-pu hsiu-hsing 十步修行
shih-shan 十善
shih-ti 十地
shih-ti kung-fu 十地工夫
Shih-yueh 師曰
shou-chao 收照
Shou-chen mu 收真母
shou-fan 受販
shou-fen 守分
Shou-lo pi-ch'iu ching 首羅比丘經
shou-mieh Chung-hua e-jen 收滅中華惡人
shou-yuan 收圓
shou-yuan chieh kuo 收源結果
Shou-yuan pao chüan 收圓寶卷
Shou-yuan tsu (primal ones) 收元祖
shou-yuan tsu (completion) 收圓祖
shu-tz'u 疏詞
shuai 帥
shuang-ch'in 雙親
shuang-hsiu 雙修
Shun-sheng 順聖
Shun-t'ien (prefecture) 順天
shuo yang pao 說養寶
ssu 死
ssu-chung (important) 四重

ssu-chung (types) 四衆
ssu-hsiang 四相
ssu-i 四依
ssu-kuei 四貴
Ssu-ma 司馬
Ssu-pu Ts'ung-k'an hsu-pien 四部
  叢刊續編
ssu-shao 四稍
Ssu-shih hsing-chiao chueh-hsing
  pao-chüan 四世行腳覺性
  寶卷
Ssu-wei 四維
su-chiang 俗講
Su hsueh-shih 蘇學士
su-i chih tzu 俗衣之子
Su Tung-p'o 蘇東坡
sui-fan ying-sheng 隨凡應聖
sui, shang-hsia 歲，上下
Sun 孫
Sun San 孫三
Sung 宋
sung 頌
sung hsin 送信
Sung Ti-wang 宋帝王

ta 答
ta-ch'a 答查
ta-ch'a tui-hao 答查對號
Ta-ch'eng 大成
Ta-ch'eng chiao 大成教
ta ch'eng i-p'ien 打成一片
ta-hsun 大巡
ta nu 大怒
Ta-pao 大寶
Ta-sheng fa-pao hsiang-shan pao-
  chüan 大聖法寶香山寶卷
Ta-sheng Mi-le hua-tu pao-chüan
  大聖彌勒化度寶卷
ta-shih 大聖
Ta-tan chih-chih 大丹值指
ta tao 大道
ta tsai chiang chih 大災將似
Ta-t'ung fang-kuang ch'an-hui
  mieh-tsui chuang-yen ch'eng-Fo

ching 大通方廣懺悔滅罪
  莊嚴成佛經
Ta tz'u-en fu 大慈恩父
T'a-sheng fa-pao Hsiang-shan pao-
  chüan 大乘法寶香山寶卷
tai-ch'ih 呆痴
Taishō shinshū daizōkyō
  大正新修大藏經
T'ai-chi 太極
T'ai-chi Fo 太極佛
T'ai-chi hsien-sheng chieh
  太極賢聖劫
T'ai-chi hui 太極會
T'ai-chi t'u-shuo 太極圖說
T'ai-ch'u Fo 太初佛
T'ai-chün shen 太君神
t'ai-hsing 臺星
T'ai-i 太乙
T'ai-p'ing ching 太平經
T'ai shan tung-yueh Shih-wang pao-
  chüan 泰山東嶽十王寶卷
T'ai-shih 太始
T'ai-su 太素
T'ai-tsu 太祖
tan-ching 丹經
tan-shu 丹書
tan-t'ien 丹田
tan yu hsieh huan-hsi yin-yuan
  但有些歡喜姻緣
t'an-chang 談章
t'an-chu 壇主
t'an-sha jen-hsin 歡殺人心
t'an shih-chien mi-hun jen
  歡世閒迷混人
T'an-shih chüan 歡世卷
T'an-shih wu-wei chüan 歡世
  無為卷
t'an-tz'u 彈詞
tang chi (chi) 當機(極)
tang chi ch'a-hao 當極查號
tang-chi li-chiao 當極立教
tang-chin 蕩盡
tang-jen 當人
tang-lai 當來

Tang-yang Fo 當陽佛
tao-ch'ang 道場
Tao-hao 道號
tao-hsin 道心
tao-jen 道人
Tao-kuang 道光
tao-shih 導師
Tao-te ching 道德經
Tao-tsang 道藏
tao-yu 道友
Tao-yuan 道原
tao wan lai 道晚來
te tzu-yu 得自由
teng (to ascend) 登
teng (to wait) 等
teng pao-ti 登寶地
teng-shih 等時
ti cha 地乍
Ti-hua mu 地花母
ti-p'an 地盤
Ti-tsang 地藏
Ti-tsang mu 地藏母
Ti-yü chüan 地獄卷
Ti-yü pien-wen 地獄衢文
t'i-ch'i wu-sheng yu 提起無生語
t'i-kang 提綱
t'i-tiao 提調
t'i-t'ou 提頭
t'i-tu 提督
t'ieh (iron) 鐵
t'ieh-chi 貼極
t'ieh-chiao 貼教
tien 奠
tien fang-ts'un 點方寸
tien hsuan-kuan 點玄關
tien-tao 顛倒
T'ien-chen 天眞
T'ien-ch'i 天齊
T'ien-ch'i jen-sheng ti 天齊
仁聖帝
T'ien-chiang tu-chieh pao-chüan
天降度劫寶卷
T'ien-fei niang-niang 天妃娘娘
t'ien-hsia chih-shih 天下知識

t'ien-hsia shu-min 天下庶民
t'ien-hsia wei tsu ti-i ming 天下
爲祖第一名
T'ien-hsin wu-wei fu 天心
無爲府
t'ien-jen 天人
T'ien-k'e tsu 天可祖
T'ien-k'uo lu 天闊路
T'ien-k'uo teng-yun 天闊登雲
t'ien-p'an 天盤
t'ien-t'ang 天堂
T'ien-ti hui 天地會
T'ien-tzu 天子
t'ien-yuan 天元
ting 丁
ting (arrange) 定
Ting-chieh ching 定劫經
Ting-kuo kung 定國公
ting-li 定立
ting-p'ai fen-tsung 定派分宗
ting-sheng 頂聖
ting-t'i mao-ming 定替冒名
Ting-t'ien Fo 定天佛
to shou hsi-huang 多受栖惶
t'o-liao fan-t'i 脫了凡體
t'o-lo-ni 陀羅尼
tou shih ni wo tz'u teng chih jen
都是你我比等之人
t'ou hsin chi 透心機
t'ou-hsing 頭行
t'ou-kan 頭幹
t'ou-ling 頭領
t'ou t'ien-kuan 透天關
t'ou-t'o 頭陀
t'ou-tz'u shih-chuang 投詞誓狀
tsa-chia 咱家
tsa-fa 雜派
tsa fen te wu-p'an ssu-kuei 咱分
的五盤四貴
tsa-p'ai 咱派
tsa-p'ai te san-chi 咱派的三極
tsai-chia 在家
tsai-chia/ch'u-chia 在家/出家
tsai chia fo 在家佛

tsai chia gong 再加工
tsai ts'an i pu 再參一步
tsai wo hsin chi 在我心機
tsai wu chin-chi 再無禁忌
tsan 讚
Tsan-seng kung-te ching 讚僧
　功德經
ts'an-ch'an ta-tso 參禪打坐
ts'an-hui 慚悔
ts'an-ling 殘零
ts'an-ling 殘靈
ts'an-tao 參道
ts'an-tao hsing-chiao 殘道行腳
ts'an yuan tzu 殘緣子
tsao-ching 造經
Tsao-hsiang 早香
tsao hui-hsin 早回心
Ts'ao-ch'iao kuan 草橋關
ts'e 冊
Tseng-tzu 曾子
tso chu 做主
tso tao 做道
tsou tao 走道
tsu 祖
Tsu-chia 祖家
tsu-chia men-hsia 祖家門下
tsu-feng 祖風
tsu-ken 祖根
Tsu-lao huang-ts'e 祖老黃冊
Tsu-mien sheng-mu 祖面生母
tsu-mu 祖母
Tsu yun 祖云
tsui 罪
tsui-jen 罪人
Ts'ui-hua 翠花
ts'un 寸
tsung (school, tradition) 宗
tsung-chi 總極
Tsung-ching 宗鏡
Tsung-hao lao-tsu 總號老祖
tsung-heng tzu-tsai 縱橫自在
tsung-hui 總會
tsung-kuan 總管
tsung-li 總理

tsung-ling 總領
Tsung p'ai fo-ming chiu-lien piao
　宗派佛名九蓮表
tsung t'i-kang 縱題綱
tu 度
tu-chi t'ien 都極天
tu-hsun 都巡
tu-t'o 度脫
Tu-tou 都斗
tu tzu wei tsun 獨自爲尊
tuan-kung 端公
Tuan P'ing 段平
Tuan P'ing 段平, *Ho-hsi pao-chüan
　hsuan* 河西寶卷選
T'uan-kang 團剛
T'uan-kang shan 團岡山
tui-hao 對號
t'ui-tao chih jen 退道之人
tun 頓
Tung 董
Tung-ch'ang 東昌
tung-jung chih shih 動融之食
Tung-sheng 東勝
t'ung-kuan 通關
T'ung-pien tao-jen 通衢道人
tzu (earthly branch) 子
tzu (written character) 字
tzu-chi 自己
tzu-chi chia-hsiang 自己家鄉
tzu-chi i-tien hsien-t'ien 自己一
　點先天
tzu-chi tso, tzu-chi shou
　自己一，自己受
tzu-chueh 字覺
Tzu-lo T'ien-tzu 紫羅天子
Tzu-lu 子路
Tzu-shu 子暑
tzu-tsai hsiao-yao 自在逍遙
tzu-tsai tsung-heng 自在縱橫
tzu-tso tzu-shou 自作自受
*Tzu-yang chen-jen Wu-chen p'ien
　chu-shu* 紫陽眞人悟眞篇
　註疏
tz'u 此

Tz'u-ch'i 慈谿
tz'u fu-mu 慈父母
Tz'u-pei tsu 慈悲祖

wai-kuo wei jen 外國爲人
wai-tao 外道
wai-tao p'ang-men 外道傍門
wan-e 萬惡
wan-fa 萬法
Wan-feng 萬峰
wan-k'ung 頑空
Wan-li 萬歷
Wan-shou 萬壽
Wan-shou mu 萬壽母
Wan-sui 萬歲
Wan-t'ang 灣塘
Wang 王
Wang 汪
Wang Che 王嚞
Wang Chien-ch'uan 王見川,
    Ming-Ch'ing min-chien tsung-
    chiao ching-chüan wen-hsien
    明清民間宗教經卷文獻
Wang Jih-hsiu 王日休
Wang-mu niang-niang 王母
    娘娘
Wang Sen 王森
Wang Tzu-ch'eng 王子成, *Li-*
    nien Mi-t'o tao-ch'ang ch'an-fa
    禮念彌陀道場懺法
wei-hsin Ching-t'u 惟心淨土
wei-i 威意
wei-lai ching 未來經
wei-lai Fo 未來佛
wei-lai huang-chi 未來皇極
wei-lai t'ien 未來天
wei-lai tien-p'an 未來天盤
wei-na 維那
Wei-t'o 韋陀
wei-wei pu-tung 巍巍不動
Wei-wei pu-tung Tai-shan shen-ken
    chieh-kuo pao-chüan 巍巍不動
    太山深根結果寶卷
wei-yin 威音

wen 溫
wen 問
Weng Pao-kuang 翁葆光
wen-shu 文疏
Wen-shu (Mañjuśrī) 文殊
wo 我
wo ch'üan ni 我勸你
wo hao tsung-heng 我好縱橫
wo shih chen-k'ung 我是眞空
wo tang-chia chih jen 我當家
    之人
wo tsai hsien 我在先
wo, wu (I, we) 我，吾
wu (fog) 霧
wu (earthly branch) 午
wu (meridian) 午
wu (to awaken) 悟
Wu-ai kung 無礙宮
Wu-chen p'ien 悟眞篇
Wu-chi 無極
Wu-chi cheng-p'ai 無極正派
Wu-chi chuang-yen chieh 無極
    莊嚴劫
Wu-chi hua-t'i 無極化體
Wu-chi miao-fa 無極妙法
Wu-chi sheng-tsu 無極聖祖
wu-chieh 五戒
wu-cho 五濁
wu-fen jen 無分人
Wu Hsiao-ling 吳曉鈴
Wu-kung ching 五公經
Wu-kung fu 五公符
Wu-k'ung lao-tsu 悟空老祖
Wu-liang shou Fo 無量壽佛
Wu-liang t'ien-chen hsien tao
    無量天眞顯道
Wu-ling 霧靈
Wu-ma shan 五馬山
wu-men tao-jen 無門道人
Wu-ming 悟明
wu-ni 五逆
wu-p'ai wu-hao 五牌五號
wu-p'an 五盤
Wu-pu ching 五部經

wu-pu ching-wen 五部經文
Wu-pu liu-ts'e 五部六册
Wu-pu liu ts'e ching-chüan 五部
六册經卷
Wu-shang tz'u-fu 無上慈父
wu-sheng 無生
Wu-sheng chiao-chu 無生教主
Wu-sheng fu 無生父
Wu-sheng fu-mu 無生父母
Wu-sheng lao-mu 無生老母
wu-sheng lu 無生路
Wu-sheng sheng-mu 無生聖母
wu-sheng ta tao 無生大道
Wu-t'ai 武臺
Wu-tang 武當
*Wu-tang shan Hsuan-t'ien Shang-ti
ching* 武當山玄天上帝經
wu-tao 五道
Wu-t'ung 五通
Wu-tzu ku-sui chen-ching 無字
骨髓眞經
wu-wei 無爲
wu-wei cheng-tao 無爲正道
Wu-wei chiao 無爲教
Wu-wei chiao-chu 無爲教主
wu-wei fa 無爲法
Wu-wei fu 無爲府
Wu-wei ta-tao 無爲大道
Wu-wei tao 無爲道
Wu-wei tsu-shih 無爲祖師
Wu-wei tsu-shih cheng-tsung
hsien-chi 無爲祖師正宗顯機
Wu-wei tsu-shih ming-chen
無爲祖師明眞
wu-yen 五眼
Wu-ying shan 無影山
wu-yuan chi jen 無緣之人

Yang 楊
Yang 陽
Yang-ch'ang 佯常
yang-chou 楊州
yang-shen 養神
Yang-yuan 陽原

Yao 姚
yao 要
yao ch'ien-ch'eng 要虔誠
Yao-ch'ih chin-mu 瑤池金母
yao-hsieh tao-chien chih shih
妖邪倒見之師
Yao-shih ju-lai 藥師如來
Yao-shih pen-yuan kung-te pao-
chüan 藥師本願功德寶卷
yao-shu 妖書
Yao-t'ai 瑤臺
yeh shih jen 也是人
Yen 燕
Yen-ching 燕京
Yen-hui 顏回
Yen-lo wang 閻羅王
yen-shuo 演說
Yin 殷
yin-chin 引進
yin-ching 印經
Yin-tsung 印宗
yin-yang hsu 陰陽序
yin-yao 淫藥
Ying-chieh (scripture) 應劫
Ying-ch'un 迎春
ying-erh 嬰兒
ying-erh ch'a-nü 嬰兒姹女
ying-erh chien-niang 嬰兒見娘
ying-erh chien-niang mu 嬰兒
見娘母
ying-erh huan ku-hsiang 嬰兒
還故鄉
ying-erh shih mu 嬰兒失母
Ying-tsung 英宗
ying wu chu 應無住
yu 酉
yu-ch'ai 又差
yu fen te yuan-jen 有分的元人
yu tao jen 有道人
yu-wei 有爲
yu-wei chi fa 有爲之法
yu-yen chih ti 幽岩之地
yu-yin 誘引
yu-yuan chih wo 有緣值我

yu-yuan jen 有緣人
yü-chih 御製
yü-ch'ih 愚痴
yü-lu 語彔
yuan (?) 扐(援)
Yuan-chen p'u-yen p'u-sa 圓眞
  普眼菩薩
Yuan-ching 源靜
Yuan-chueh chüan 圓覺卷
Yuan-chueh t'ung-chien 圓覺通鑑
yuan, heng, li, chen 元，亨，
  利，貞
yuan(?)-huang 扐 (援)黃
Yuan(?)-huang liao-yeh sheng-
  t'ien piao 扐 (援)黃了業
  生天表
Yuan-huang hui 元皇會
yuan-jen 原人
yuan-luan 元卵
Yuan-ming Hui-hsing li chen
  圓明慧性禮眞
yuan-shen 原身
yuan-shuai 元帥

yuan-t'o 圓陀
Yuan-tun 圓頓
Yuan-tun cheng-chiao 圓頓正教
Yuan (complete)-tun chiao
  圓頓教
Yuan (source)-tun chiao 源沌教
Yuan-tun mu 圓頓母
yuan-wai 員外
Yueh-ho tsu 月和祖
Yueh-kuang 月光
yueh tao 越道
yun-ch'eng 雲程
Yun chi ch'i-ch'ien 雲笈七籤
Yun-kung kua-hao lien-tsung
  piao 雲宮掛號蓮宗表
yun-p'an 雲盤
Yun-seng 雲僧
Yung-lo 永樂
Yung-p'ing 永平
yung pu chao 用不著

Zengaku daijiten 禪學大辭典

Index

Harvard-Yenching Institute Monograph Series
(titles now in print)